Lecture Notes in Artificial Inte

Subseries of Lecture Notes in Computer Sc

Edited by J. Siekmann

Lecture Notes in Computer Science

Edited by G. Goos and J. Hartmanis

E. Ardizzone   S. Gaglio   F. Sorbello (Eds.)

Trends in Artificial Intelligence

2nd Congress of the Italian Association for
Artificial Intelligence, AI*IA
Palermo, Italy, October, 29-31, 1991
Proceedings

Springer-Verlag
Berlin Heidelberg New York
London Paris Tokyo
Hong Kong Barcelona
Budapest

Series Editor

Jörg Siekmann
Institut für Informatik, Universität Kaiserslautern
Postfach 3049, W-6750 Kaiserslautern, FRG

Volume Editors

Edoardo Ardizzone
Salvatore Gaglio
Filippo Sorbello
Department of Electrical Engineering, University of Palermo
Viale delle Scienze, I-90128 Palermo, Italy

CR Subject Classification (1991): I.2

ISBN 3-540-54712-6 Springer-Verlag Berlin Heidelberg New York
ISBN 0-387-54712-6 Springer-Verlag New York Berlin Heidelberg

Typesetting: Camera ready by author
Printing and binding: Druckhaus Beltz, Hemsbach/Bergstr.
45/3140-543210 - Printed on acid-free paper

Foreword

The second Congress of the Italian Association for Artificial Intelligence (AI*IA) (Palermo, October 29-31, 1991), organized by the CRES (Centro per la Ricerca Elettronica in Sicilia), can be considered an outstanding event in artificial intelligence in Europe. The high number of submitted papers and the international participation witness a high interest in the activities of AI*IA.

The Congress is organized into 8 sessions, in which 39 papers are presented. A poster session is also taking place with the presentation of 16 further short papers. The distribution of the papers in the various subfields of AI clearly reflects an international trend, which has in the subject of knowledge representation the present focus of attention.

Besides contributed papers, the program consists of three outstanding invited talks and special sessions devoted to Italian special projects of the National Research Council (CNR), industrial experiences and applications, and applications in finance and banking.

Invited speakers are Wolfgang Wahlster, Jack Rahaim and Federico Faggin, who are giving talks, respectively, on intelligent user interfaces, on the DIGITAL project IMKA, and on neural chips.

The 8 sessions are subdivided among the conference themes as follows: 4 sessions for knowledge representation, 1 for knowledge acquisition, 1 for natural language understanding, 1 for perception and robotics, and 1 for architectures and technologies.

Many people have worked hard for the success of the Congress. I want to express my gratitude to all of them.

First of all, many thanks to the members of the Program Committee and of the Committee for the Industrial Exhibition, in particular to the President of the AI*IA, Prof. Luigia Carlucci Aiello, for their help in solving with constant attention all the problems that have emerged. It is worth mentioning their care in the evaluation of papers and their initiative in finding valid additional reviewers.

Thanks to all people who have accepted to be chairmen of the various sessions:
L. Carlucci Aiello, G. Attardi, G. Berini, M. Del Canto, M. Di Manzo, L.Lesmo,
E. Pagello, R. Petrioli, P. Salamone, G. Semeraro, F. Sorbello, M.Somalvico,
L. Spampinato, O. Stock, L. Stringa, and P. Torasso.

I am grateful to the Organizing Committee for its activity concerning the local arrangements. I am especially grateful to the CRES, and to its president and its vice-president, Prof. Stefano Riva Sanseverino and Prof. Ignazio Romano Tagliavia, for having accepted the burden of the overall organization. Invaluable has been the support of the Congress Secretariat: Lia Giangreco, Ina Paladino, and Giusy Romano.

The last word is for my colleagues of the Scientific Secretariat, Edoardo Ardizzone and Filippo Sorbello, who have shared with me all the anxieties of scientific and non-scientific nature in preparing all the events of the Congress.

Palermo, August 1991   Salvatore Gaglio

Preface

The book collects the scientific papers presented at the 2nd Congress of the Italian Association for Artificial Intelligence. It represents the state of the art of both Italian and European scientific research in AI.

The high quality of the papers and the hard work of the researchers are witness of a massive research activity mainly devoted to the theoretical aspects of AI, but clearly aimed to consolidate the results that have already been achieved. However, the presence of several contributions oriented to the technological aspects of AI must be pointed out.

Papers presented in sessions devoted to *knowledge representation* investigate logic properties of formalisms. Some of them propose new logics for nonmonotonic inference and introduce frameworks for autoepistemic logics and abductive reasoning. Other papers present recent results concerning inheritance and approximate reasoning. A great deal of attention is given to constraint based reasoning, which is presently one of the most promising fields of investigation. Finally, a great effort is being made to integrate various kinds of knowledge representation formalisms.

In the session on *knowledge acquisition*, some of presently most promising topics are treated. In particular, attention is given to the learning of diagnostic knowledge by using a priori knowledge and examples, and to the formation of default hierarchies in learning classifier systems. The use of multiple concept languages to overcome problems of version-space induction is also investigated. The construction of semantic abstraction, defined as a mapping between models, is proposed by extending the paradigm of inverse resolution. Finally, knowledge compilation is proposed to speed up and increase the reliability of numerical optimization.

Papers on *natural language* investigate syntactic disambiguation and efficient parsing algorithms for context-free grammars and for dependency grammars. Other papers deal with computational models of tense selection.

Papers presented in the session on *perception and robotics* are mainly devoted to artificial vision. In particular, they focus on the recovery of high-level geometric structures from images and on the integration between low-level and high-level representations. In both cases, great attention is given to massively parallel algorithms, mostly based on connection architectures. The last paper faces the problem of sensor-based robot navigation, proposing an approach based on the integration between analogic and symbolic representations.

In the session on *architectures and technologies*, papers cover various aspects such as the development of a system for supporting cooperative group-based design, the direct interaction among active data structures aimed at building AI systems and the introduction of knowledge representation techniques in database models. Finally, a system focusing on the design of an intelligent training system in an industrial environment and a new hardware digital architecture for Kohonen´s self-organizing maps are presented.

At the end of the book, other interesting work, presented at the Congress in a poster session, appears as short papers.

The editors would like to thank authors for their contribution and referees for their cooperation to the realization of this book.

Palermo, August 1991   Edoardo Ardizzone, Salvatore Gaglio, Filippo Sorbello

Program Committee

Chairman: S. Gaglio (University of Palermo)

G. Berini (DIGITAL)
L. Carlucci Aiello
   (University of Rome, La Sapienza)
S. Cerri (DIDAEL)
M. Del Canto (ELSAG)
G. Ferrari (University of Pisa)
G. Guida (University of Udine)
F. Lauria (University of Naples)
L. Lesmo (University of Turin)

E. Pagello (University of Padua)
D. Parisi (CNR)
L. Saitta (University of Turin)
G. Semeraro (CSATA)
R. Serra (DIDAEL)
L. Spampinato (QUINARY)
L. Stringa (IRST)
P. Torasso (University of Turin)
R. Zaccaria (University of Genoa)

Organizing Committee

Chairmen: S. Riva Sanseverino and I. Romano Tagliavia (CRES)

E. Ardizzone (University of Palermo)
S. Battiato (CRES)
G. Bertini (DIGITAL)
P. Buccheri (University of Palermo)
V. Di Gesù (University of Palermo)
S. Gaglio (University of Palermo)
G. Grisanti (University of Palermo)
U. Lo Faso (University of Palermo)

F. Lo Piparo (University of Palermo)
T. Raimondi (University of Palermo)
A. Restivo (University of Palermo
P. Salamone (Sicilcassa)
M. Sannino (University of Palermo)
F. Sorbello (University of Palermo)
S. Termini (University of Palermo)
S. Tropia (CRES)

Industrial Exhibition Committee

Chairmen: G. Berini (DIGITAL) and F. Sorbello (University of Palermo)

F. Canepa (AERITALIA)
M. Del Canto (ELSAG)
S. Gaglio (University of Palermo)
G. Guida (University of Palermo)

E. Morino (CSI Piemonte)
R. Simino (DIGITAL)
L. Spampinato (QUINARY)

Scientific Secretariat

E. Ardizzone and F. Sorbello (University of Palermo)

Referees

Contents

Invited Paper

Topic 1: Knowledge Representation

Topic 2: Knowledge Acquisition

Topic 3: Natural Language

Topic 4: Perception and Robotics

Topic 5: Architectures and Technologies

Short Papers

Invited Paper

KNOWLEDGE-BASED MEDIA COORDINATION IN INTELLIGENT USER INTERFACES*

Wolfgang Wahlster, Elisabeth André, Winfried Graf, Thomas Rist

German Research Center for Artificial Intelligence (DFKI)
Stuhlsatzenhausweg 3, W-6600 Saarbrücken 11, Germany
Phone: (+49 681) 302-5252
E-mail: {wahlster, andre, graf, rist}@dfki.uni-sb.de

Abstract

Multimodal interfaces combining, e.g., natural language and graphics take advantage of both the individual strength of each communication mode and the fact that several modes can be employed in parallel, e.g., in the text-picture combinations of illustrated documents. It is an important goal of this research not simply to merge the verbalization results of a natural language generator and the visualization results of a knowledge-based graphics generator, but to carefully coordinate graphics and text in such a way that they complement each other. We describe the architecture of the knowledge-based presentation system WIP which guarantees a design process with a large degree of freedom that can be used to tailor the presentation to suit the specific context. In WIP, decisions of the language generator may influence graphics generation and graphical constraints may sometimes force decisions in the language production process. In this paper, we focus on the influence of graphical constraints on text generation. In particular, we describe the generation of cross-modal references, the revision of text due to graphical constraints and the clarification of graphics through text.

1 Introduction

With increases in the amount and sophistication of information that must be communicated to the users of complex technical systems comes a corresponding need to find new ways to present that information flexibly and efficiently. Intelligent

---

* Published as: Designing Illustrated Texts: How Language Production is Influenced by Graphics Generation, in: Proceedings of the 5th Conference of the European Chapter of the ACL, 9-11 April 1991, Berlin, Germany, pp. 8-14, 1991. Used by permission of the Association for Computational Linguistics; copies of the publication from which this material is derived can be obtained from Dr. Donald E. Walker (ACL), Bellcore, MRE 2A379, 445 South Street, Box 1910, Morristown, NJ 07960-1910, USA.

presentation systems are important building blocks of the next generation of user interfaces, as they translate from the narrow output channels provided by most of the current application systems into high-bandwidth communications tailored to the individual user. Since in many situations information is only presented efficiently through a particular combination of communication modes, the automatic generation of multimodal presentations is one of the tasks of such presentation systems. The task of the knowledge-based presentation system WIP is the generation of a variety of multimodal documents from an input consisting of a formal description of the communicative intent of a planned presentation. The generation process is controlled by a set of generation parameters such as target audience, presentation objective, resource limitations, and target language.

One of the basic principles underlying the WIP project is that the various constituents of a multimodal presentation should be generated from a common representation. This raises the question of how to divide a given communicative goal into subgoals to be realized by the various mode-specific generators, so that they complement each other. To address this problem, we have to explore computational models of the cognitive decision processes coping with questions such as what should go into text, what should go into graphics, and which kinds of links between the verbal and non-verbal fragments are necessary.

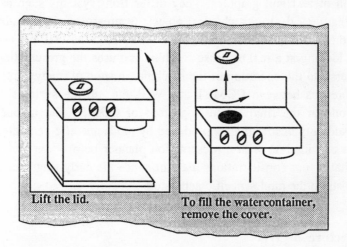

Fig. 1: Example Instruction

In the project WIP, we try to generate on the fly illustrated texts that are customized for the intended target audience and situation, flexibly presenting information whose content, in contrast to hypermedia systems, cannot be fully anticipated. The current testbed for WIP is the generation of instructions for the use of an espresso-machine. It is a rare instruction manual that does not contain illustrations. WIP's 2D display of 3D graphics of machine parts help the addressee of the synthesized multimodal presentation to develop a 3D mental model of the object that he can constantly match with his visual perceptions of the real machine in front of him. Fig. 1 shows a typical text-picture sequence which may be used to instruct a user in filling the watercontainer of an espresso-machine.

Currently, the technical knowledge to be presented by WIP is encoded in a hybrid knowledge representation language of the KL-ONE family including a terminological and assertional component (see Nebel 90). In addition to this propositional representation, which includes the relevant information about the structure, function, behavior, and use of the espresso-machine, WIP has access to an analogical representation of the geometry of the machine in the form of a wireframe model.

The automatic design of multimodal presentations has only recently received significant attention in artificial intelligence research (cf. the projects SAGE (Roth et al. 91), COMET (Feiner & McKeown 89), FN/ANDD (Marks & Reiter 90) and WIP (Wahlster et al. 89)). The WIP and COMET projects share a strong research interest in the coordination of text and graphics. They differ from systems such as SAGE and FN/ANDD in that they deal with physical objects (espresso-machine, radio vs. charts, diagrams) that the user can access directly. For example, in the WIP project we assume that the user is looking at a real espresso-machine and uses the presentations generated by WIP to understand the operation of the machine. In spite of many similarities, there are major differences between COMET and WIP, e.g., in the systems' architecture. While during one of the final processing steps of COMET the layout component combines text and graphics fragments produced by mode-specific generators, in WIP a layout manager can interact with a presentation planner before text and graphics are generated, so that layout considerations may influence the early stages of the planning process and constrain the mode-specific generators.

2 The Architecture of WIP

The architecture of the WIP system guarantees a design process with a large degree of freedom that can be used to tailor the presentation to suit the specific context. During the design process a presentation planner and a layout manager orchestrate the mode-specific generators and the document history handler (see Fig. 2) provides information about intermediate results of the presentation design that is exploited in order to prevent disconcerting or incoherent output. This means that decisions of the language generator may influence graphics generation and that graphical constraints may sometimes force decisions in the language production process. In this paper, we focus on the influence of graphical constraints on text generation (see Wahlster et al. 91 for a discussion of the inverse influence).

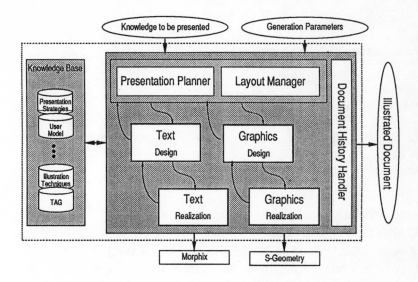

Fig. 2: The Architecture of the WIP System

2.1 The Presentation Planner

The presentation planner is responsible for contents and mode selection. A basic assumption behind the presentation planner is that not only the generation of text, but also the generation of multimodal documents can be considered as a sequence of communicative acts which aim to achieve certain goals (cf. André & Rist 90a). For the synthesis of illustrated texts, we have designed presentation strategies that refer to both text and picture production. To represent the strategies, we follow the approach proposed by Moore and colleagues (cf. Moore & Paris 89) to operationalize RST-theory (cf. Mann & Thompson 88) for text planning.

The strategies are represented by a name, a header, an effect, a set of applicability conditions and a specification of main and subsidiary acts. Whereas the header of a strategy indicates which communicative function the corresponding document part is to fill, its effect refers to an intentional goal. The applicability conditions specify when a strategy may be used and put restrictions on the variables to be instantiated. The main and subsidiary acts form the kernel of the strategies. E.g., the strategy below can be used to enable the identification of an object shown in a picture (for further details see André & Rist 90b). Whereas graphics is to be used to carry out the main act, the mode for the subsidiary acts is open.

```
Name:
        Enable-Identification-by-Background
Header:
        (Provide-Background P A ?x ?px ?pic GRAPHICS)
Effect:
        (BMB P A (Identifiable A ?x ?px ?pic))
Applicability Conditions:
        (AND   (Bel P (Perceptually-Accessible A ?x))
               (Bel P (Part-of ?x ?z)))
Main Acts:
        (Depict P A (Background ?z) ?pz ?pic)
Subsidiary Acts:
        (Achieve P (BMB P A (Identifiable A ?z ?pz ?pic)) ?mode)
```

For the automatic generation of illustrated documents, the presentation strategies are treated as operators of a planning system. During the planning process, presentation strategies are selected and instantiated according to the presentation task. After the selection of a strategy, the main and subsidiary acts are carried out unless the corresponding presentation goals are already satisfied. Elementary acts, such as **Depict** or **Assert**, are performed by the text and graphics generators.

2.2 The Layout Manager

The main task of the layout manager is to convey certain semantic and pragmatic relations specified by the planner by the arrangement of graphic and text fragments received from the mode-specific generators, i.e., to determine the size of the boxes and the exact coordinates for positioning them on the document page. We use a grid-based approach as an ordering system for efficiently designing functional (i.e., uniform, coherent and consistent) layouts (cf. Müller-Brockmann 81).

A central problem for automatic layout is the representation of design-relevant knowledge. Constraint networks seem to be a natural formalism to declaratively incorporate aesthetic knowledge into the layout process, e.g., perceptual criteria concerning the organization of boxes as sequential ordering, alignment, grouping, symmetry or similarity. Layout constraints can be classified as semantic, geometric, topological, and temporal. Semantic constraints essentially correspond to coherence relations, such as sequence and contrast, and can be easily reflected through specific design constraints. A powerful way of expressing such knowledge is to organize the constraints hierarchically by assigning a preference scale to the constraint network (cf. Borning et al. 89). We distinguish obligatory, optional and default constraints. The latter state default values, that remain fixed unless the corresponding constraint is removed by a stronger one. Since there are constraints that have only local effects, the incremental constraint solver must be able to change the constraint hierarchy dynamically (for further details see Graf 90).

2.3 The Text Generator

WIP's text generator is based on the formalism of tree adjoining grammars (TAGs). In particular, lexicalized TAGs with unification are used for the incremental verbalization of logical forms produced by the presentation planner (cf. Harbusch 90 and Schauder 90). The grammar is divided into an LD (local dominance) and an LP (linear precedence) part so that the piecewise construction of syntactic constituents is separated from their linearization according to word order rules (Finkler & Neumann 89).

The text generator uses a TAG parser in a local anticipation feedback loop (see Jameson & Wahlster 82). The generator and parser form a bidirectional system, i.e., both processes are based on the same TAG. By parsing a planned utterance, the generator makes sure that it does not contain unintended structural ambiguities.

Since the TAG-based generator is used in designing illustrated documents, it has to generate not only complete sentences, but also sentence fragments such as NPs, PPs, or VPs, e.g., for figure captions, section headings, picture annotations, or itemized lists. Given that capability and the incrementality of the generation process, it becomes possible to interleave generation with parsing in order to check for ambiguities as soon as possible. Currently, we are exploring different domains of locality for such feedback loops and trying to relate them to resource limitations specified in WIP's generation parameters. One parameter of the generation process in the current implementation is the number of adjoinings allowed in a sentence. This parameter can be used by the presentation planner to control the syntactic complexity of the generated utterances and sentence length. If the number of allowed adjoinings is small, a logical form that can be verbalized as a single complex sentence may lead to a sequence of simple sentences. The leeway created by this parameter can be exploited for mode coordination. For example, constraints set up by the graphics generator or layout manager can force delimitation of sentences, since in a good design, picture breaks should correspond to sentence breaks, and vice versa (see McKeown & Feiner 90).

2.4 The Graphics Generator

When generating illustrations of physical objects WIP does not rely on previously authored picture fragments or predefined icons stored in the knowledge base. Rather, we start from a hybrid object representation which includes a wireframe model for each object. Although these wireframe models, along with a specification of physical attributes such as surface color or transparency form the basic input of the graphics generator, the design of illustrations is regarded as a knowledge-intensive process that exploits various knowledge sources to achieve a given presentation goal efficiently. E.g., when a picture of an object is requested, we have to determine an appropriate perspective in a context-sensitive way (cf. Rist&André 90). In our approach, we distinguish between three basic types of graphical techniques. First, there are techniques to create and manipulate a 3D object configuration that serves as the subject of the picture. E.g., we have developed a technique to spatially separate the parts of an object in order to construct an exploded view. Second, we can choose among several techniques which map the 3D subject onto its depiction. E.g., we can construct either a schematic line drawing or a more realistic looking picture using rendering techniques. The third kind of technique operates on the picture level. E.g., an object depiction may be annotated with a label, or picture parts may be colored in order to emphasize them. The task of the graphics designer is then to select and combine these graphical techniques according to the presentation goal. The result is a so-called design plan which can be transformed into executable instructions of the graphics realization component. This component relies on the 3D graphics package S-Geometry and the 2D graphics software of the Symbolics window system.

3 The Generation of Cross-Modal References

In a multimodal presentation, cross-modal expressions establish referential relationships of representations in one modality to representations in another modality.

The use of cross-modal deictic expressions such as (a) - (b) is essential for the efficient coordination of text and graphics in illustrated documents:

(a)   *The left knob in the figure on the right is the on/off switch.*
(b)   *The black square in Fig. 14 shows the watercontainer.*

In sentence (a) a spatial description is used to refer to a knob shown in a synthetic picture of the espresso-machine. Note that the multimodal referential act is only successful if the addressee is able to identify the intended knob of the real espresso-machine. It is clear that the visualization of the knob in the illustration cannot be used as an on/off switch, but only the physical object identified as the result of a two-level reference process, i.e., the cross-modal expression in the text refers to a specific part of the illustration which in turn refers to a real-world object[1].

Another subtlety illustrated by example (a) is the use of different frames of reference for the two spatial relations used in the cross-modal expression. The definite description *figure on the right* is based on a component generating absolute spatial descriptions for geometric objects displayed inside rectangular frames. In our example, the whole page designed by WIP's layout manager constitutes the frame of reference. One of the basic ideas behind this component is that such 'absolute' descriptions can be mapped on relative spatial predicates developed for the VITRA system (see Herzog et al. 90) through the use of a virtual reference object in the center of the frame (for more details see Wazinski 91). This means that the description of the location of the figure showing the on/off switch mentioned in sentence (a) is based on the literal **right-of(figure-A,center(page-1))** produced by WIP's localization component.

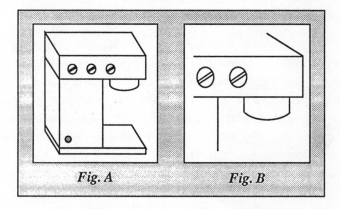

Fig. 3: *The middle knob* in A is *the left knob* in the close-up projection B

The definite description *the left knob* is based on the use of the region denoted by *figure on the right* as a frame of reference for another call of the localization

---

[1]In the WIP system there exists yet another coreferentiality relation, namely between an individual constant, say **knob-1**, representing the particular knob in the knowledge representation language and an object in the wireframe model of the machine containing a description of the geometry of that knob.

component producing the literal **left-of(knob1,knob2))** as an appropriate spatial description. Note that all these descriptions are highly dependent on the viewing specification chosen by the graphics design component. That means that changes in the illustrations during a revision process must automatically be made available to the text design component.

Let's assume that the presentation planner has selected the relevant information for a particular presentation goal. This may cause the graphics designer to choose a close-up projection of the top part of the espresso-machine with a narrow field of view focusing on specific objects and eliminating unnecessary details from the graphics as shown in Fig. B (see Fig. 3). If the graphics designer chooses a wide field of view (see Fig. A in Fig. 3) for another presentation goal, **knob1** can no longer be described as *the left knob* since the `real-world' spatial location of another knob (e.g., **knob0**), which was not shown in the close-up projection, is now used to produce the adequate spatial description *the left knob* for **knob0**. Considering the row of three knobs in Fig. A, **knob1** is now described as *the middle knob*.

Note that the layout manager also needs to backtrack from time to time. This may result in different placement of the figure A, e.g., at the bottom of the page. This means that in the extreme, the cross-modal expression *the left knob in the figure on the right* will be changed into *the middle knob in the figure at the bottom*.

Due to various presentational constraints, the graphics design component cannot always show the wireframe object in a general position providing as much geometric information about the object as possible. For example, when a cube is viewed along the normal to a face it projects to a square, so that a loss of generality results (see Karp & Feiner 90). In example (b) the definite description *the black square* uses shape information extracted from the projection chosen by the graphics designer that is stored in the document history handler. It is obvious that even a slight change in the viewpoint for the graphics can result in a presentation situation where *the black cube* has to be used as a referential expression instead of *black square*. Note that the colour attribute *black* used in these descriptions may conflict with the addressee's visual perception of the real espresso-machine.

The difference between referring to attributes in the model and perceptual properties of the real-world object becomes more obvious in cases where the specific features of the display medium are used to highlight intended objects (e.g., blinking or inverse video) or when metagraphical objects are chosen as reference points (e.g., an arrow pointing to the intended object in the illustration). It is clear that a definite description like the *blinking square* or *the square that is highlighted by the bold arrow* cannot be generated before the corresponding decisions about illustration techniques are finalized by the graphics designer.

The text planning component of a multimodal presentation system such as WIP must be able to generate such cross-modal expressions not only for figure captions, but also for coherent text-picture combinations.

4 The Revision of Text Due to Graphical Constraints

Frequently, the author of a document faces formal restrictions, e.g., when document parts must not exceed a specific page size or column width. Such formatting constraints may influence the structure and contents of the document. A decisive question is, at which stage of the generation process such constraints should be evaluated. Some restrictions, such as page size, are known a priori, while others (e.g., that an illustration should be placed on the page where it is first discussed) arise during the generation process. In the WIP system, the problem is aggravated since restrictions can result from the processing of at least two generators (for text and graphics) working in parallel. A mode-specific generator is not able to anticipate all situations in which formatting problems might occur. Thus in WIP, the generators are launched to produce a first version of their planned output which may be revised if necessary. We illustrate this revision process by showing the coordination of WIP's components when object depictions are annotated with text strings.

Suppose the planner has decided to introduce the essential parts of the espresso-machine by classifying them. E.g., it wants the addressee to identify a switch which allows one to choose between two operating modes: producing espresso or producing steam. In the knowledge base, such a switch may be represented as shown in Fig. 4.

Since it is assumed that the discourse objects are visually accessible to the addressee, it is reasonable to refer to them by means of graphics, to describe them verbally and to show the connection between the depictions and the verbal descriptions. In instruction manuals this is usually accomplished by various annotation techniques. In the current WIP system, we have implemented three annotation techniques: annotating by placing the text string inside an object projection, close to it, or by using arrows starting at the text string and pointing to the intended object. Which annotation technique applies depends on syntactic criteria, (e.g., formatting restrictions) as well as semantic criteria to avoid confusion. E.g., the same annotation technique is to be used for all instances of the same basic concept (cf. Butz et al. 91).

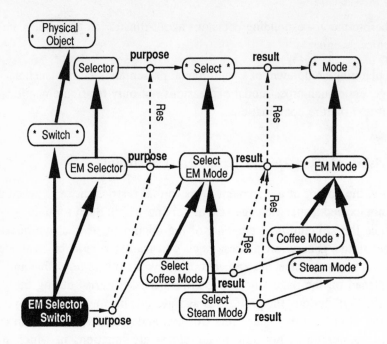

Fig. 4: Part of the Terminological Knowledge Base

Suppose that in our example, the text generator is asked to find a lexical realization for the concept **EM selector switch** and comes up with the description *selector switch for coffee and steam*. When trying to annotate the switch with this text string, the graphics generator finds out that none of the available annotation techniques apply. Placing the string close to the corresponding depiction causes ambiguities. The string also cannot be placed inside the projection of the object without occluding other parts of the picture. For the same reason, annotations with arrows fail. Therefore, the text generator is asked to produce a shorter formulation. Unfortunately, it is not able to do so without reducing the contents. Thus, the presentation planner is informed that the required task cannot be accomplished. The presentation planner then tries to reduce the contents by omitting attributes or by selecting more general concepts from the subsumption hierarchy encoded in terms of the terminological logic. Since **EM selector switch** is a compound description which inherits information from the concepts **switch** and **EM selector** (see Fig. 4), the planner has to decide which component of the contents specification should be reduced. Because the concept **switch** contains less discriminating information than the concept **EM selector** and the concept **switch** is at least partially inferrable from the picture, the planner first tries to reduce the component **switch** by replacing it by **physical object**. Thus, the text generator has to find a sufficiently short definite description containing the components **physical object** and **EM selector**. Since this fails, the planner has to propose another reduction. It now tries to reduce the component **EM selector** by omitting the coffee/steam mode. The text generator then tries to construct a NP combining the concepts **switch** and **selector**. This time it succeeds and the annotation string can be placed. Fig. 5 is a hardcopy produced by WIP showing the rendered espresso-machine after the required annotations have been carried out.

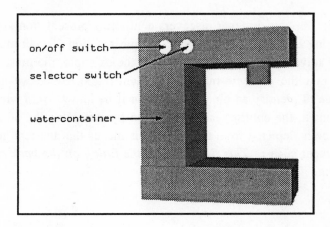

Fig. 5: Annotations after Text Revisions

5 The Clarification of Graphics through Text

In the example above, the first version of a definite description produced by the text generator had to be shortened due to constraints resulting from picture design. However, there are also situations in which clarification information has to be added through text because the graphics generator on its own is not able to convey the information to be communicated.

Let's suppose the graphics designer is requested to show the location of **fitting-1** with respect to the **espresso-machine-1**. The graphics designer tries to design a picture that includes objects that can be identified as **fitting-1** and **espresso-machine-1**. To convey the location of **fitting-1** the picture must provide essential information which enables the addressee to reconstruct the initial 3D object configuration (i.e., information concerning the topology, metric and orientation). To ensure that the addressee is able to identify the intended object, the graphics designer tries to present the object from a standard perspective, i.e., an object dependent perspective that satisfies standard presentation goals, such as showing the object's functionality, top-bottom orientation, or accessibility (see also Rist & André 90). In the case of a part-whole relationship, we assume that the location of the part with respect to the whole can be inferred from a picture if the whole is shown under a perspective such that both the part and further constituents of the whole are visible. In our example, **fitting-1** only becomes visible and identifiable as a part of the espresso-machine when showing the machine from the back. But this means that the espresso-machine must be presented from a non-standard perspective and thus we cannot assume that its depiction can be identified without further clarification.

Whenever the graphics designer discovers conflicting presentation goals that cannot be solved by using an alternative technique, the presentation planner must be informed about currently solved and unsolvable goals. In the example, the presentation planner has to ensure that the espresso-machine is identifiable. Since we assume that an addressee is able to identify an object's depiction if he knows from which perspective the object is shown, the conflict can be resolved by informing the addressee that the espresso-machine is depicted from the back. This means that the text generator has to produce a comment such as *This figure shows the fitting on the back of the machine*, which clarifies the graphics.

6 Conclusion

In this paper, we introduced the architecture of the knowledge-based presentation system WIP, which includes two parallel processing cascades for the incremental generation of text and graphics. We showed that in WIP the design of a multimodal document is viewed as a non-monotonic process that includes various revisions of preliminary results, massive replanning or plan repairs, and many negotiations between the corresponding design and realization components in order to achieve a fine-grained and optimal devision of work between the selected presentation modes. We described how the plan-based approach to presentation design can be exploited so that graphics generation influences the production of text. In particular, we showed how WIP can generate cross-modal references, revise text due to graphical constraints and clarify graphics through text.

Acknowledgements

The WIP project is supported by the German Ministry of Research and Technology under grant ITW8901 8. We would like to thank Doug Appelt, Steven Feiner and Ed Hovy for stimulating discussions about multimodal information presentation.

References

[André & Rist 90a] Elisabeth **André** and Thomas **Rist**. Towards a Plan-Based Synthesis of Illustrated Documents. In: 9th ECAI, 25-30, 1990.

[André & Rist 90b] Elisabeth **André** and Thomas **Rist**. Generating Illustrated Documents: A Plan-Based Approach. In: InfoJapan 90, Vol. 2, 163-170, 1990.

[Borning et al. 89] Alan **Borning**, Bjorn **Freeman-Benson**, and Molly **Wilson**. Constraint Hierarchies. Technical Report, Department of Computer Science and Engineering, University of Washington, 1989.

[Butz et al. 91] Andreas **Butz**, Bernd **Hermann**, Daniel **Kudenko**, and Detlev **Zimmermann**. ANNA: Ein System zur Annotation und Analyse automatisch erzeugter Bilder. Memo, DFKI, Saarbrücken, 1991.

[Feiner & McKeown 89] Steven **Feiner** and Kathleen **McKeown**. Coordinating Text and Graphics in Explanation Generation. In: DARPA Speech and Natural Language Workshop, 1989.

[Finkler & Neumann 89] Wolfgang **Finkler** and Günter **Neumann**. POPEL-HOW: A Distributed Parallel Model for Incremental Natural Language Production with Feedback. In: 11th IJCAI, 1518-1523, 1989.

[Graf 90] Winfried **Graf**. Spezielle Aspekte des automatischen Layout-Designs bei der koordinierten Generierung von multimodalen Dokumenten. GI-Workshop "Multimediale elektronische Dokumente", 1990.

[Harbusch 90] Karin **Harbusch**. Constraining Tree Adjoining Grammars by Unification. 13th COLING, 167-172, 1990.

[Herzog et al. 90] Gerd **Herzog**, Elisabeth **André**, and Thomas **Rist**. Sprache und Raum: Natürlichsprachlicher Zugang zu visuellen Daten. In: Christian Freksa and Christopher Habel (eds.). Repräsentation und Verarbeitung räumlichen Wissens. IFB 245, 207-220, Berlin: Springer-Verlag, 1990.

[Jameson & Wahlster 82] Anthony **Jameson** and Wolfgang **Wahlster**. User Modelling in Anaphora Generation: Ellipsis and Definite Description. In: 5th ECAI, 222-227, 1982

[Karp & Feiner 90] Peter **Karp** and Steven **Feiner**. Issues in the Automated Generation of Animated Presentations. In: Graphics Interface '90, 39-48, 1990.

[Mann & Thompson 88] William **Mann** and Sandra **Thompson**. Rhetorical Structure Theory: Towards a Functional Theory of Text Organization. In: TEXT, 8 (3), 1988.

[Marks & Reiter 90] Joseph **Marks** and Ehud **Reiter**. Avoiding Unwanted Conversational Implicatures in Text and Graphics. In: 8th AAAI, 450-455, 1990.

[McKeown & Feiner 90] Kathleen **McKeown** and Steven **Feiner**. Interactive Multimedia Explanation for Equipment Maintenance and Repair. In: DARPA Speech and Natural Language Workshop, 42-47, 1990.

[Moore & Paris 89] Johanna **Moore** and Cécile **Paris**. Planning Text for Advisory Dialogues. In: 27th ACL, 1989.

[Müller-Brockmann 81] Josef **Müller-Brockmann**. Grid Systems in Graphic Design. Stuttgart: Hatje, 1981.

[Nebel 90] Bernhard **Nebel**. Reasoning and Revision in Hybrid Representation Systems. Lecture Notes in AI, Vol. 422, Berlin: Springer-Verlag, 1990.

[Rist & André 90] Thomas **Rist** and Elisabeth **André**. Wissensbasierte Perspektivenwahl für die automatische Erzeugung von 3D-Objektdarstellungen. In: Klaus Kansy and Peter Wißkirchen (eds.). Graphik und KI. IFB 239, Berlin: Springer-Verlag, 48-57, 1990.

[Roth et al. 91] Steven **Roth**, Joe **Mattis**, and Xavier **Mesnard**. Graphics and Natural Language as Components of Automatic Explanation. In: Joseph Sullivan and Sherman Tyler (eds.). Intelligent Interfaces: Elements and Prototypes. Reading, MA: Addison-Wesley, 1991.

[Schauder 90] Anne **Schauder**. Inkrementelle syntaktische Generierung natürlicher Sprache mit Tree Adjoining Grammars. MS thesis, Computer Science, University of Saarbrücken, 1990.

[Wahlster et al. 89] Wolfgang **Wahlster**, Elisabeth **André**, Matthias **Hecking**, and Thomas **Rist**. WIP: Knowledge-based Presentation of Information. Report WIP-1, DFKI, Saarbrücken, 1989.

[Wahlster et al. 91] Wolfgang **Wahlster**, Elisabeth **André**, Som **Bandyopadhyay**, Winfried **Graf**, and Thomas **Rist**. WIP: The Coordinated Generation of Multimodal Presentations from a Common Representation. In: Andrew Ortony, John Slack and Oliviero Stock (eds.). Computational Theories of Communication and their Applications. Heidelberg: Springer-Verlag, 1991.

[Wazinski 91] Peter **Wazinski**. Objektlokalisation in graphischen Darstellungen. MS thesis, Computer Science, University of Saarbrücken, forthcoming.

Knowledge   Representation

SOME NOTES ON CUMULATIVE REASONING

G. Amati
Fondazione Ugo Bordoni
v. B. Castiglione, 59
00142, Rome *

Abstract

We introduce a model-theoretic definition of non-monotonic inference relation and study a particular model called C*. Gentzen-style counterpart of C* can be regarded as the non-monotonic infinitistic version of the system C of Kraus, Magidor, Lehmann with the consistency-preservation, property proposed by Gabbay and used in belief revision. A notion of selection function is introduced. This notion is similar to that of expectations given by Gärdenfors and Makinson and derived from partial meet contractions functions of belief revision, given by Alchourron, Gärdenfors and Makinson. The representation theorem for the cumulative system C, whose models use a binary relation < among sets of worlds, can be simplified by using selection functions. The finitistic (conditional) system of C* turns out to be equivalent to Makinson's cumulative monotony operator as well as to the conditional system γ^* derived from the sistem γ of Gabbay by adding the cautious monotonicity axiom and using classical logic in the place of intuitionistic logic as underlying monotonic logic.

1. Introduction.

In [14] and [11] a general theory of non-monotonic reasoning, based on the seminal papers [5, 6], has been given: an abstract notion of logical consequence for non-monotonic logic is axiomatically introduced and studied. [11]'s approach is Gentzen-style, in the sense that, analogously to classical, intuitionistic and modal logics, sequent systems for the non-monotonic inference relation $\vdash\!\sim$ are introduced by considering $\vdash\!\sim$ as an *arrow* between formulas. While in monotonic logics the arrow captures a semantic notion of logical consequence, in non-monotonic logics the acquired point of view is exactly the opposite: one postulates syntactical properties for the primitive relation $\vdash\!\sim$, and, successively one looks for representation theorems. A purely semantic definition of $\vdash\!\sim$ is still missing, whereby one can draw syntactic properties for the relation $\vdash\!\sim$. In this paper we introduce a model-theoretic definition of $\vdash\!\sim$ and study a particular model called C*, that is suitable for autoepistemic logic and whose Gentzen-style counterpart can be regarded as a non-

* Work carried out within the framework of the agreement between Italian PT Administration and Ugo Bordoni Foundation

monotonic infinitistic system containing C (see [11]). |~ is seen as a selection function from theories of the language to the power set of the class of models $\mathcal{M}$ of the chosen monotonic logic L, to which |~ refers. The same idea has been independently explored in [2] for finitistic theories. This perspective is similar to the notion of expectations given by [9] and derived from partial meet contraction functions, given in [3, 7]: an expectation function is an operator that, given a set of beliefs K and a proposition A, selects a theory K' containing A and derived from the intersection of a subset of the maximal subtheories of K consistent with A. In our context, analogously to expectations, we will expand theories rather than contract or revise theories. Makinson [14], from the same point of view, studied non-monotonicity by giving a Tarski-style general logical consequence operator. This operator satisfy inclusion, cumulative transitivity and cumulative monotony and these properties can be combined in the finitistic case (theories logically equivalent to a single proposition) as follows:

A⊨B then A|~ B   (inclusion)

A|~ B and B⊨A then A|~C iff B|~ C   (cumulative monotony).

Differently, [11] provides semantics to the notion |~ by using worlds clustered in sets (called states) which are ordered by a primitive relation <. The representation of |~ only for the finitistic case is given by means of the notion of smoothness. Though the present work is close for its content to [11], [14] is a fundamental background, since there an abstract operator C is used mapping theories into theories of the language. Comparison with [17], [14] and [11] are discussed throughout the paper.

An important issue in non-monotonic reasoning is related to the question whether Gentzen-style systems can completely capture fixed-point definitions of non-monotonic theories. In monotonic logics Gentzen systems are actual tools to show monotonic proofs. At the moment, Gentzen-style non-monotonic systems seem to be rather abstract and the connections to the actual proposed formalisms have not yet been cleared completely. Apparently, fixed-point definition seems to negate a recursive notion of derivation, and doubts can thus arise about a constructive definition of derivation, at least in the meaning that we are used to think of in monotonic reasoning. Gabbay [4] was the first to realize that a formal notion of a single step for non-monotonic proof is still missing. Following these ideas, an attempt to model non monotonic reasoning by means of the semantics of intuitionistic autoepistemic logic was made, under the assumption that information is temporally conditioned and grows as soon as new facts become available through single steps rules [1]. At the moment, as far as we know, the only method used for showing proofs in such domains, like for example in autoepistemic logic, is what we call the "back and forth" proofs, namely derivations based on reasoning of the form" If A (does not) belong to the theory to be computed E then B belong to E, and if B belongs to E then C would (not) belong to ... and so on". We will discuss why cautious monotonicity seems to be a trade-off between a recursive definition of derivation and the computation of fixed-points.

Finally, we will show that a conditional system γ* obtained from the classical version of the system γ of [5] when adding cautious monotonicity is equivalent to the finitistic system C*.

2. Non-monotonicity

Consider any logic L defined by means of a class of models $\mathcal{M}$, no matter how they are defined, that enable us to talk about which sentences are true. The monotonic consequence relation $A \models C$ means that any model M of A forces C to be true in M. Once $\models$ is interpreted as an arrow $\Rightarrow$, we have the derived rule for all B if $A \Rightarrow C$ then $A, B \Rightarrow C$, namely the *left weakening* or *thinning* according to the sequent terminology. A non-monotonic inference relation $\vdash\!\!\!\sim$ instead associates a theory T' to an initial theory T. T' is then, via completeness theorem characterized through the class of its models $\mathcal{M}_T$ (the subscript T indicates the set of models of T' comes from T). Formally, we say that the non-monotonic inference system is a function $\mathfrak{f}$, called the *selection function*, that maps all the theories T of the logic L into the power set of models of $\mathcal{M} : \mathfrak{f}(T, \mathcal{M}) = \mathcal{M}_T \subseteq \mathcal{M}$.

(M1) $T \vdash\!\!\!\sim B$ iff $(\forall M \in \mathcal{M}_T)(M \models T \cup \{B\})$ with $\mathcal{M}_T \subseteq \mathcal{M}$

The property (M1) will be denoted shortly by "$T \vdash\!\!\!\sim B$ iff $\mathfrak{f}(T, \mathcal{M}) \models B$". $\mathcal{M}_T$ is generally a proper subset of $\mathcal{M}$ and is called the set of *preferred* models of $\vdash\!\!\!\sim$ with respect to T.

The definition (M1) is more general than the definition given in [17, 11]. In fact [17] models define a selection function. Consider the generalizing model $(\mathcal{M}, <, \models)$ of [17] given in [14], where $\mathcal{M}$ is an arbitrary set (called the set of models), $\models$ is a satisfiability relation, and $<$ is a primitive relation on $\mathcal{M}$. One can define a selection function $\mathfrak{f}(T, \mathcal{M}) = \{m: m \in \mathcal{M}$, $m \models T$ and there is no $m' < m$ s.t. $m' \models T\}$. According to this point of view, a model m is preferred to m' in principle without considering any context theory T.

The reader has noted that a weaker definition of (M1) could have been given. Since the selection function chooses a subset of models of T, one postulates that valid-preserving rules applied on T can be added to the non-monotonic inferences of T (the *reflexivity* in [11]): T' is then an *expansion* of T. It is easy to give counterexamples to this ideal situation (in default reasoning for example). However, a weaker definition would not provide a minimal apparatus for computing fixed-point non-monotonic theories, since a fixed-point T' should be deductively closed with respect to its monotonic logical consequences. We need at the moment to agree with [11] who assert that "reflexivity seems to be satisfied universally by any kind of reasoning based on some notion of logical consequence".

(M1) implies, following whenever possible [11]'s terminology, the properties:

	$T \models B$ implies $T \vdash\!\!\!\sim B$	*(Weak cumulativity)*
	$\bot \vdash\!\!\!\sim B$	*(Left-inconsistency)*
A1)	$T \vdash\!\!\!\sim A$ with $A \in T$	*(Reflexivity)*
A2)	$T \vdash\!\!\!\sim B$ and $B \models C$ implies $T \vdash\!\!\!\sim C$	*(Right weakening)*
A3)	$T \vdash\!\!\!\sim B$ and $T \vdash\!\!\!\sim C$ implies $T \vdash\!\!\!\sim C \wedge B$	*(And)*

(*Right weakening*) and (*Reflexivity*) imply (*Weak cumulativity*) and (*Left-inconsistency*) (see [11]). The rules

	$T \cup T' \mathbin{\vdash\hspace{-0.5em}\sim} C$ and $T \models T'$ then $T \mathbin{\vdash\hspace{-0.5em}\sim} C$	(*Cut*)
(A4)	$T\models T'$ and $T'\models T$ then $T\mathbin{\vdash\hspace{-0.5em}\sim} C$ implies $T' \mathbin{\vdash\hspace{-0.5em}\sim} C$	(*Left Logical Equivalence*)

are sound under the condition

(M2) $Cn(T) = Cn(T')$ implies $\mathcal{M}_T = \mathcal{M}_{T'}$ (*Equivalence-preserving property*).

where Cn is the monotonic deductive closure operator.(As for (Cut), if $M \in \mathcal{M}_T$ and $T \models T'$, then $Cn(T \cup T') = Cn(T)$ and thus by (M2) $M \in \mathcal{M}_{T \cup T'}$. If $T \cup T' \mathbin{\vdash\hspace{-0.5em}\sim} C$ since $M \in \mathcal{M}_{T \cup T'}$ we have $M \models C$, namely $T \mathbin{\vdash\hspace{-0.5em}\sim} C$).

3.   The system C*

(M1) and (M2) are the minimal conditions to define a semantics for nonmonotonic logic and they satisfy the rules (A1) -(A4) . We now want to consider the rules:

(A5)	$T \mathbin{\vdash\hspace{-0.5em}\sim} \bot$ implies $T \vdash \bot$	(*Consistency-preserving property*)
(A6)	$T \mathbin{\vdash\hspace{-0.5em}\sim} B$ and $T \mathbin{\vdash\hspace{-0.5em}\sim} C$ then $T, B \mathbin{\vdash\hspace{-0.5em}\sim} C$	(*Cautious monotonicity*)

Note that by (*Right weakening*) and (*Reflexivity*), (A5) is equivalent to "$T \mathbin{\vdash\hspace{-0.5em}\sim} \bot$ iff $T \vdash \bot$" (in the finitistic case "$A \mathbin{\vdash\hspace{-0.5em}\sim} \bot$ iff $\vdash \neg A$"). Though (A5) is not generally sound, since $\mathcal{M}_T$ can be chosen empty while T is not inconsistent, it holds in autoepistemic logic. In fact, let L be S5 and $\mathcal{M}_A$ be any of (sub)set (preferred or not) complete S5 structure which make the epistemic formula A valid. This is equivalent to choose a set of stable sets containing A [16]. Since the class of complete S5 structures determines the class of S5 tautologies [10] and if no S5 complete structure can be chosen in order to satisfy A, then $\models_{S5} \neg A$.
To ensure the consistency-preserving property the selection function must satisfy

(M3)   If $\mathcal{M}_T = \emptyset$ then $T \models \bot$.[1]

If $\mathcal{M}_{T \cup T'} \subseteq \mathcal{M}_T \cap \mathcal{M}_{T'}$ (Nesting) holds, then besides (A6) we would have also that left weakening for $\mathbin{\vdash\hspace{-0.5em}\sim}$ (for any choice of B, from $\mathcal{M}_{T \cup \{B\}} \subseteq \mathcal{M}_T$ and $T \mathbin{\vdash\hspace{-0.5em}\sim} C$, $M \in \mathcal{M}_{T \cup \{B\}}$ would imply $M \models C$). (Nesting) makes the definition (M1) to collapse to monotonic logic. We say that the selection function f is *cautiously monotone* whenever :

---

[1] In belief revision [5], which assume that the dynamics of beliefs can be represented by expansions and revision functions, this axiom is the A*5 axiom.

(M4) $\mathfrak{f}(T, \mathcal{M}) \models B$ implies $\mathfrak{f}(T \cup \{B\}, \mathcal{M}) \subseteq \mathfrak{f}(T, \mathcal{M})$.

The property (M4) is a recursive property of the selection function. In the finitistic case, if we consider as antecedent a theory T deductively closed with respect to $\mid\sim$ (and then closed with respect to conjunctions by (M1)) then (M4) is vacuously satisfied since $\mathfrak{f}(T, \mathcal{M}) \models B$ implies $T \cup \{B\}=T$. More generally, consider a sentence B s.t. $\mathfrak{f}(T, \mathcal{M}) \models B$ and suppose that (M4) holds. Consider the theory $T_1=Cn(T \cup \{B\})$. Apply again (M4) to a formula B_1 s.t. $\mathfrak{f}(T_1, \mathcal{M}) \models B_1$, and consider the theory $T_2 = Cn(T_1 \cup \{B_1\})$ s.t. $\mathfrak{f}(T_2, \mathcal{M}) \subseteq \mathfrak{f}(T_1, \mathcal{M})$. Iterating this process one may have a limit (when either $\mathfrak{f}(T_m, \mathcal{M}) = \mathfrak{f}(T_n, \mathcal{M})$ for all $m \geq n$ or $T_\beta = \cup_{\alpha<\beta} T_\alpha$ and $\mathfrak{f}(T_\beta, \mathcal{M}) = \cap_{\alpha<\beta} \mathfrak{f}(T_\alpha, \mathcal{M})$ for some ordinal α and β) or not. Note how much this construction is similar to the definition of extension in default logic, in the sense that T_β is the extension of the initial theory T whenever T_β satisfies the fixed-point condition $\mathfrak{f}(T_\beta, \mathcal{M}) = \cap_{\alpha<\beta} \mathfrak{f}(T_\alpha, \mathcal{M})$ (see [15]). If one postulates that for any theory T this process terminates with $\beta = \omega$ then the selection function is said to have the property of *ω-smoothness for the initial theory T*. We may generally ensure the existence of the ω-smoothness property for every T if :

(ω-smoothness)   For any infinite set of theories $\{T_n\}_{n<\omega}$ s.t. $T_{n+1}=Cn(T_n \cup \{B_n\})$ and $\mathfrak{f}(T_{n+1}, \mathcal{M}) \subseteq \mathfrak{f}(T_n, \mathcal{M})$ then $\mathfrak{f}(T_\omega, \mathcal{M}) = \lim_{n<\omega} \mathfrak{f}(T_n, \mathcal{M})$

(ω-smoothness) has not be confused with the equivalent of Limit Assumption in conditional logic, that instead asserts that :

No infinite descending $\subset$-chain of $\mathfrak{f}(T_n, \mathcal{M})$ exists.   (Limit Assumption)

This last property, in fact, implies (ω-smoothness) since $\mathfrak{f}(T_m, \mathcal{M}) = \mathfrak{f}(T_n, \mathcal{M})$ with $m \geq n$ for some n. We would prefer to call (ω-smoothness) the *compactness property* in analogy with the closure operator of classical logic, rather than the smoothness according to [11]. In fact (ω-smoothness) has to be accepted if we want to consider a finitistic notion of non-monotonic proof similar to the notion of derivation as used in monotonic logic. Suppose that any proof (derivation) can be added to another proof in order to have another proof. Consider any theory T in a numerable language. We can thus well-order all its non-monotonic consequences B_i, so that the ordering can be seen as as a proof of arbitrary finite length. Consider another order B'_i. Consider a non-monotonic consequence B. B is B_m for some m and B'_n for some n. We can find D' finite such that $B'_n \in D'$ and $D'=\{B'_1, B'_2, ..., B'_k\} \supseteq D = \{B_1, B_2, ..., B_m\}$. For the cautious monotonicity $\mathfrak{f}(D', M) \subseteq \mathfrak{f}(D, \mathcal{M})$ and (M4) ensures that both sequences converges to an unique theory T'. Cautious monotonicity guarantees that when deriving a consequence from an infinite theory T we use only a finite subset because any order given to the inferences from the initial set of premises

(=proof of arbitrary finite length) compute always the same theory T'. Since monotonic rules are also non-monotonic ones, then the limit theory T' can be considered a sort of *completion* of the initial theory T, in the sense that T'$\models$B iff T$\vdash\sim$B. Note that in finitistic case the analogous property of smoothness for the cumulative models holds (in the representation theorem for C one can prove that any theory has a minimal state).

One could also ensure (ω-smoothness), by the following property:

(M4') $\qquad\qquad\qquad$ $\mathfrak{f}(T, \mathcal{M})\models T'$ implies $\mathfrak{f}(T'\cup T, \mathcal{M}) \subseteq \mathfrak{f}(T, \mathcal{M})$.

As for the Limit Assumption, we think that no proper translation in a Gentzen-style would be possible. The situation reminds the property of Limit Assumption in conditional logic. Lewis, in fact, could not exhibit any axiom to represent in V the Limit assumption and used it in the completeness theorem as an additional hypothesis (see [12] p.126).

Let C* be the logic defined by (A1), (A2), (A3), (A4), (A5) and (A6).

Soundness. For any selection function $\mathfrak{f}$ satisfying (M1), (M2), (M3), (M4) all the rules of C* are satisfied.

Proof. We have already shown that according to the interpretation of $\vdash\sim$ given in (M1) all the rules of C* are satisfied by any selection function $\mathfrak{f}$.

Representation theorem for C*. $\qquad$ Suppose $\models$ and $\vdash\sim$ satisfy the properties (A1), (A2), (A3), (A4), (A5) and (A6). There exists a selection function $\mathfrak{f}$ that satisfies (M1), (M2), (M3), (M4) .

Proof. The proof is straightforward. We define $\mathfrak{f}(T, \mathcal{M}) = \{M: M\in\mathcal{M}$ and $M\models Cons(T)\}$, where $Cons(T) = \{B: T\vdash\sim B\}$. We show first that $\mathfrak{f}(T, \mathcal{M}) \models T'$ iff $T\vdash\sim T'$(where $T\vdash\sim T'$ means $T\vdash\sim B$ for all $B \in T'$). Suppose that $\mathfrak{f}(T, \mathcal{M}) \models T'$ then, by compactness of $\models$, for every $C\in T'$ there are $B_1, B_2,..., B_n \in T$ s.t. $T\vdash\sim B_1\wedge B_2 \wedge ... \wedge B_n$ and $B_1\wedge B_2 \wedge ... \wedge B_n \models C$. By (A2) $T' \subseteq Cons(T)$. Viceversa suppose $T'\subseteq Cons(T)$, then by definition of $\mathfrak{f}(T, \mathcal{M})$, $\mathfrak{f}(T, \mathcal{M}) \models T'$.

$Cons(T)$ is consistent iff T is consistent, namely by (A1) properties (M1) and (M3). In fact $Cons(T)$ is inconsistent iff there exist $B_1, B_2,..., B_n \in Cons(T)$ s.t. $B_1\wedge B_2 \wedge... \wedge B_n \models \perp$. By (A3) $B_1\wedge B_2 \wedge... \wedge B_n \in Cons(T)$. By (A2) $\perp \in Cons(T)$. By (A4) T is inconsistent. Viceversa T is inconsistent implies $Cons(T)$ is inconsistent by (A1).

Moreover, $Cn(T) = Cn(T')$ implies $Cons(T) = Cons(T')$ by (A4) , namely $\mathfrak{f}(T, \mathcal{M}) = \mathfrak{f}(T', \mathcal{M})$ and thus (M2).

Cautious monotonicity (M4) is easily proved. Suppose that $\mathfrak{f}(T, \mathcal{M}) \models T'$ then for every $C\in T'$ there are $B_1, B_2,..., B_n \in T$ s.t. $T\vdash\sim B_1\wedge B_2 \wedge ... \wedge B_n$ by (A3) and $B_1, B_2,..., B_n \models C$. By (A2) $T'\subseteq Cons(T)$. Let M be a model of $\mathfrak{f}(T\cup T', \mathcal{M})$: $M\models Cons(T\cup T')$. Let

C∈ Cons(T). Since T'⊆ Cons(T), namely T⊢~T', by (A6) T∪T'⊢~C, namely Cons(T) ⊆ Cons(T∪T') and thus ƒ(T∪T', 𝒎)⊆ƒ(T, 𝒎).
We have proved that T⊢~B iff ƒ(T, 𝒎)⊨B.

Remark. The (M3) assumption is not necessary to give a generalization to infinitistic case of the representation theorem for C. Once ƒ is given, a preference relation among theories can be defined as T'≤T iff ƒ(T, 𝒎)⊨T'. If we quotient the set of theories 2^S with respect to the equivalence relation ~ defined by T'≤T and T≤T' the set of states is chosen as this quotient set. The labelling function is l([T]~)={ƒ(T, 𝒎)}. For the representation theorem above T≤T' iff ƒ(T', 𝒎)⊨T iff T '⊢~T, and thus l([T]~) is the minimum for ƒ(T', 𝒎)⊨T.

Corollary   i)   (Cut) follows from (A1), (A2), (A3), (A4), (A5) and (A6).

   ii)   ω-smoothness is derivable when the language is numerable.

Furthermore, (And) follows from (A1), (A2), (A4), (A6) and (Cut) ((And) is derivable in C see 3.2.in [11]).

C* refers to a poor language in the sense that following a sequent terminology (Reflexivity) is the axioms schemata, (Left logical equivalence), (Right weakening) are all structural rules. Only (Cautious monotonicity), (Consistency-preserving property), (And) or (Cut) partially explain the behaviour of the connective ∧ and ⊥. The other connectives are partially explained by ⊨. In the finitistic case (Cautious monotonicity), for example implies (And) . The system P is C with ∨-right rule((Or), see 5.1.in [11]), and →-right (→-right is (S), see 5.2.in [11]). The behaviour of the most problematic conectives ¬, negation, and →, material implication are almost completely missing. In fact these connectives in a standard sequent calculus force a formula "to cross the arrow" when the connective is introduced. In non-monotonic case we cannot easily describe formally how and when a formula can cross the arrow and put it under the scope of the negation or material implication.

4. Comparison with other models

[11] uses a binary relation < on a set of worlds U to represent the relation ⊢~. They define a function l from a set of lables S to the power set of U namely l: S --→ 2^U. S stands for formulas of propositional classical logic **Prop** up to non-monotonic equivalences . In fact, given the set $\hat{\alpha}$ = {s: s∈ S and for all m∈ l(s) m⊨α}, it comes out from the representation theorem that $\hat{\alpha}$ has always a minimum state $\bar{\alpha}$ (lemma 3.23). In fact a selection function can be defined as:

$$ƒ(\alpha, \textbf{Prop}) =\{m: m \in l(\bar{\alpha})\}.$$

In the claim of the theorem 3.25 that asserts " A consequence relation is a cumulative consequence relation iff it is defined by some cumulative model", the word *some* should be substituted by the word *strong*, where a strong cumulative model is a cumulative model whose < is asymmetric and for all formulas α, the set $\hat{\alpha}$ has always a minimum.

Makinson proposes a closure operator in a Tarski-style system whose Gentzen infinitistic counterpart can be read as:

Tl=T' then Tl~ T   (inclusion)
Tl~ T' and T'l=T then Tl~C iff T'l~ C   (cumulative monotonicity).

$\mathfrak{f}$ is a Makinson's operator. Suppose Tl~ T' and T'l=T, namely $\mathfrak{f}(T, \mathfrak{M})$l= T' and T'l=T. $\mathfrak{f}(T, \mathfrak{M})$l= T' implies $\mathfrak{f}(T'\cup T, \mathfrak{M}) \subseteq \mathfrak{f}(T, \mathfrak{M})$ by (M4) and T'l=T implies T'$\cup$Tl=T' and T'l=T'$\cup$T and thus by (M2) $\mathfrak{f}(T', \mathfrak{M}) \subseteq \mathfrak{f}(T, \mathfrak{M})$, that is Tl~C implies T'l~ C .
Suppose T'l= T and Tl~ T' and T' l~C. Since (M4') is derivable then T$\cup$T'l~C, and, since (Cut) is derivable, by cutting T from T'l= T and T$\cup$T'l~C we have Tl~C.

5.   Horizontalizing C*

Generally, Gentzen-style axiomatization increases the expressive power of a system formalized in Hilbert-style, as it allows to formally handle theories and their logical consequences. In classical logic these different points of view coincide: in finitistic case, namely the set of assumptions are finite, we can use both directions of the deduction theorem and reduce the problem of inferring formulas from a theory to that of deciding about a tautology. In the infinitistic case one can use the compactness of the logic and therefore reduce this case to the finitistic one. In modal logics this is no longer true and we have different notions of logical consequences. It is not difficult to guess that in non-monotonic and conditional logics things are more difficult to manage.

If we interpret Al~ B as a connective > we can study any non-monotonic system as a conditional logic in the finitistic case. Viceversa, given a conditional theory interpret > as a logical inference and define the correspondent Gentzen-style system.[2] The translation from one axiomatization to the other, however, is not easy [8]. For example the system C with the consistency-preserving property or the finitistic version of C*, is the system γ* (see appendix) derived from γ [5].

Given a cumulative model [11] let us define the satisfiability of a conditional as:

   wl= A>B iff f.a. minimal states s and f.a. w'$\in$ l(s), w'l= A, then w'l= B. [3]

---

[2] In conditional logics, however, we can have embedded conditionals, like A>(B>C), that do not have any meaning from a non-monotonic point of view.
[3] Note that either for all w, wl=A>B, or for all w, wl≠ A>B.

Proposition. The set of tautologies of $\gamma*$ are all and only all the formulas valid in all cumulative models of C with the preserving- consistency property (A5).

Proof of proposition. The sound part is routine.

Completeness part. Suppose X is not a theorem: then $\neg X$ is consistent. Consider the set W of all the maximal consistent theories w. There exists at least one world w* satisfying $\neg X$. Consider the set Cons(A) = {B: A>B $\in$ w for all w$\in$ W}.

Lemma   i)   Cons(A) is inconsistent iff A is inconsistent.

           ii)   Cn(A)$^\wedge$= Cn(B)$^\wedge$ iff A>B $\wedge$ B>A$\in$ w for all w$\in$ W.

Proof of lemma. i) If A is inconsistent then $\vdash\neg A$ namely $\vdash A\supset\bot$. By Rγ2) $\vdash A > \bot$, $\bot\in$ Cons(A). Viceversa, suppose Cons(A) inconsistent. There exist B_1, B_2, ... B_n s.t. $\vdash B_1 \wedge B_2 \wedge ... \wedge B_n \leftrightarrow\bot$. Since $\vdash$ A>$B_1 \wedge$ A>$B_2 \wedge ... \wedge$ A>$B_n\leftrightarrow$A>$B_1 \wedge B_2 \wedge... \wedge B_n$ by Aγ2) and Aγ3), then by Rγ3) A>$B_1 \wedge$ A>$B_2 \wedge ... \wedge$ A>$B_n \in$ w iff A>$B_1 \wedge B_2 \wedge... \wedge B_n\in$ w iff $\bot\in$ Cn(A) iff $\vdash A\supset\bot$. Let Cn(A)$^\wedge$ = {w: Cn(A)$\subseteq$w$\in$ W} (w is called a normal world according to [11]'s terminology).

ii) By Aγ4) it is $\vdash$(A>C)$\supset$ (A>B)$\wedge$ (A$\wedge$B>C). By tautology $\vdash$ (A>C) $\wedge$ (A>B) $\supset$ (A$\wedge$B>C) and thus $\vdash$(A>C) $\wedge$ (A>B) $\wedge$ (B>A)$\supset$ (A$\wedge$B>C)$\wedge$ (B>A); by Aγ5) $\vdash$(A$\wedge$B>C)$\wedge$ (B>A) $\supset$ (A>C). By tautology $\vdash$(A>C) $\wedge$ (A>B) $\wedge$ (B>A)$\supset$ (A>C). The other direction is proved if A>A is a theorem. By the tautology A $\supset$ A and Rγ2) then A>A.

For the lemma the relation $\sim$ on the set of formulas $\mathcal{F}$ defined by A$\sim$B iff A>B $\wedge$ B>A$\in$ w for all w$\in$ W is an equivalence relation. Let S be the quotient set of $\mathcal{F}$ by $\sim$ and A* the equivalence class of A. Define l(A*) = Cn(A)$^\wedge$, the satisfiability by $\in$ and A*$\leq$B* iff B>A$\in$ w. The proof now goes on as in [11] once the lemmas 3.18 and 3.20 are replaced respectively by i) and ii) of the previous lemmas.

Aknowledgments

The author wishes to thank L. Carlucci Aiello and the referees for their helpful comments. I am particularly grateful to one referee who pointed out very recent papers [2, 9,13] that are connected with the present work. In particular, after this work was submitted to this conference the paper by J. Bell appeared in KR '91, where the same notion of selection functions (pragmatic models) for non-monotonicity is used.

References

[1] Aiello L., Amati G., Pirri F., Intuitionistic modal calculus for autoepistemic logic, in *Proc. of the First World Conference on the Fundamentals of AI*, Paris 1-5 July 1991.

[2] Bell J., Pragmatics Logics, in *Proc. of 2nd Int. Conf. of Knowledge Representation and reasoning* , Cambridge MA, 22-25 Aprile, 1991.

[3] Alchourron, C.E., Gärdenfors P., Makinson D., On the logic of theory change: partial meet contraction and revision function, *JSL*, 50, (1985), pp. 510-530.

[4] Clarke, M.R.B., Gabbay D., An intuitionistic Basis for Non-monotonic Reasoning, in Smeth P., Mamdani E.H., Dubois D., Prade H., *Non-standard logics for automated reasoning, Academic Press,* 1988, pp. 163-178.

[5] Gabbay, D, Intuitionistic basis for non-monotonic reasoning, *Proc. 6th Conference on Automated Deduction, LNCS 138*, pp. 260- 273.

[6] Gabbay, D, Theoretical foundation for non-monotonic reasoning in expert systems, in *Proc. of NATO Advanced Study Institute on Logics of Concurrent Systems, Springer Verlag*, Berlin, 1985 pp.439- 457.

[7] Gärdenfors P., *Knowledge in flux*, The MIT Press, 1988.

[8] Gärdenfors P., Belief revision and nonmonotonic logics: two sides of the same coin?, in *Proc. ECAI'90,* L. Carlucci Aiello (ed.), Pitman Publishing, London, 1990.

[9] Gärdenfors P.,Makinson D., *Nonmonotonic inference based on expectations*, unpublished manuscript.

[10] J. Y. Halpern, Y., Towards a theory of knowledge and ignorance, *Proceedings 1984 Non-monotonic Reasoning Workshop*, AAAI, New Paltz, N.Y., 1984, pp.165-193.

[11] Kraus, S., Magidor M., Lehmann D., Non-monotonic reasoning, preferential models and cumulative logics, *Artificial Intelligence* 44, (1990), pp.167-207.

[12] Lewis D.K., *Counterfactuals*, Oxford Basil Blackwell, 1973.

[13] Lindström S., *A semantic approach to nonmonotonic reasoning: inference operations and choice*, Dept. of Philosophy, Uppsala University, unpublished manuscript.

[14] Makinson D., General theory of cumulative inference, in M. Reinfrank, J. de Kleer, M.L. Ginsberg, E. Sandewall (Eds.) *Non monotonic reasoning*, 2nd Int.Workshop, LNAI Springer 346, 1988, pp. 1-18.

[15] Marek V., Truszczynki M., Relating autoepistemic logic and default logics, in J. Brachman, H. Levesque, R. Reiter, *Proc. of the 1st Conference on principles of Knowledge Representation and Reasoning,* Toronto, (1989), pp.276-288.

[16] Moore, Autoepistemic logic, in Smeth P., Mamdani E.H., Dubois D., Prade H., *Non-standard logics for automated reasoning, Academic Press*, 1988, pp. 105-136.

[17] Shoham Y., *Reasoning about change*, The MIT Press, 1988.

[18] Takeuti G., *Proof theory*, Studies in Logic vol. 83, North-Holland, 1975.

Appendix : The system γ^*

Aγ1) Intuitionistic logic

Aγ2) $(A > B) \wedge (A > C) \supset (A > B \wedge C)$.

Aγ3) $(A > B \wedge C) \supset (A > B) \wedge (A > C)$.

Aγ4) $(A > C) \supset (A > B) \wedge (A \wedge B > C)$.

Aγ5) $(A > B) \wedge (A \wedge B > C) \supset (A > C)$.

Rγ1) Modus ponens

Rγ2) If $\vdash A \supset B$ then $\vdash A > B$.

Rγ3) If $\vdash A \leftrightarrow B$ then $\vdash (A > C) \supset (B > C)$

Rγ4) If $\vdash A > \perp$ then $\vdash \neg A$.

A Family Of Three-Valued Autoepistemic Logics

Piero A. Bonatti

Dipartimento di Informatica - Universita' di Pisa
Corso Italia 40, I-56125 Pisa, ITALY
bonatti@dipisa.di.unipi.it

Area: Knowledge representation and automated reasoning.
Keywords: Nonmonotonic Reasoning, Autoepistemic Logics, Logic Programming.

Abstract

A unifying semantic framework for 2 and 3-valued autoepistemic logics is introduced. For instance, the logics introduced in [8] and [2] belong to this framework. All the logics that derive from the framework enjoy the usual stability properties of autoepistemic logics.

A new logic (called $\mathcal{K}_2$-logic) is derived from the schema. It is shown that $\mathcal{K}_2$-logic solves a number of problems affecting existing logics. Finally, it will be shown that a very large class of theories has a least stable expansion in $\mathcal{K}_2$-logic. We show how the least stable expansion can be obtained through a fixpoint construction.

1 Introduction

This paper proposes a new solution to two technical problems affecting auto-epistemic logics. It is well known that a set of formulae may have no stable expansions or more than one stable expansions. This means that the autoepistemic consequences of a set of formulae may be undefined, or may not have a unique definition.

The first case is not a problem in itself. A set of formulae with no stable expansions can be regarded as an *"epistemically inconsistent"* set (having no logical consequences is not much different from having all formulae of the language as logical consequences). However, for AI purposes, a certain degree of *"robustness"* is needed. For example, set $\{p \subset Lp, q\}$ has no stable expansions because of the first formula: there is no stable way of believing or disbelieving p and Lp. This prevents also q to be derived, even if q is independent of p and Lp. In general, it would be nice to derive the statements that do not depend on the "pathological" ones.

The second case seems more complex: it is not yet clear what to do with the set of alternative stable expansions. Current attempts to solve this problem can be classified into two major approaches:

1. keeping all the expansions (closures) and having some mechanism to relate queries to the expansions where they hold;

2. selecting one expansion through some preference criterion.

In this paper the second approach is followed, where the preferred expansion is the minimal one. In this way, actually no choice is made among stable expansions, since the minimal stable expansion gathers what is believed in *all* of them. In order to guarantee that a minimal expansion exists, a three valued generalisation of Moore's semantics is adopted.

Three-valued logics are appealing because they allow very natural forms of belief modelling: a formula like Lp, to be read as "I believe p", can be *true* if the agent actually believes p, *false* if he/she disbelieves p, or *undefined* if the agent is *doubtful* about p, e.g. if he/she has reasons *both* to believe *and* to disbelieve p.

Example 1 Consider the following formalisation of the well-known "Nixon Diamond":

$$q = \text{"Nixon is a quaker"} \qquad r = \text{"Nixon is a republican"}$$
$$p = \text{"Nixon is a pacifist"} \qquad np = \text{"Nixon is not a pacifist"}$$

$$A = \{(p \subset q \wedge \neg Lnp), \ (np \subset r \wedge \neg Lp), \ (q \wedge r)\}.$$

Statements $p \subset \neg Lnp$ and $np \subset \neg Lp$ are logical consequences of A. This is a tipical case of cyclic dependency that gives rise to ambiguity: A has two standard stable expansions, containing p but not np, or np but not p, respectively. There is no reason to prefer one to the other: so we might say that the agent has reasons both to believe and to disbelieve p and q. □

According to the intuitive meaning of L, formula $Lp \vee \neg Lp$, to be read as "*I believe p or I disbelieve p*", should not be true when the agent is doubtful about p. Obviously, two-valued autoepistemic logics can not satisfy this intuitive requirement.

Since formula $Lp \vee \neg Lp$ is not a tautology, we may use it to query the knowledge base of our agent and discover his/her doubts, or we may use it as a constraint, in order to ensure that the knowledge base of the agent contains enough information about p. This is an interesting feature if we exploit autoepistemic logics to model deductive databases. It allows to express meta-level queries and constraints within the object-level language, in a natural way.

Przymusinski [9] has already outlined an interesting three-valued autoepistemic logic, but does not support it through epistemic considerations. Consequently, it is not clear if his semantics is actually suitable for belief modelling or other knowledge representation purposes.

Indeed, his semantics differs considerably from Moore's one, although the former seems to generalise the latter in a natural way. For example, if the agent neither believes nor disbelieves that it is raining outside, then the statement "it is raining outside" has to be undefined in at least one model. Therefore models do not represent anymore what is true in the world, in contrast with Moore's semantics, and formal connections between beliefs and reality are lost.

Moreover, classical negation and the Law of Excluded Middle are not preserved. From $p \leftarrow q$ and $p \leftarrow \neg q$ it does not follow that p. If we tried to overcome this problem by adding $q \vee \neg q$ as an axiom, we would force q to be defined in every model hence - as we already pointed out - the agent would be obliged either to believe q or to disbelieve q. Consequently, the advantages of 3-valued semantics would be lost.

Doing without the Law of the Excluded Middle may be too restrictive for knowledge representation purposes (see, for example, [4]). It may be too restrictive even for the semantics of logic programs, for some interesting extensions of the logic programming paradigm - such as *disjunctive* [7] and *constraint logic programming* [6] - make essential use of classical negation. Actually, these paradigms are not covered by the class of theories for which Przymusinski guarantees that a unique minimal expansion exists.

A first solution to the disadvantages of Przymusinski's logic has been given in [2]. There, a new three-valued autoepistemic logic has been introduced, that preserves classical negation and the law of excluded middle on non-modal formulae, but not on epistemic (i.e. modal) ones. This leads to very natural forms of reasoning, that allow to reason classically about the "outside world" and constructively about beliefs.

The existence of a minimal stable expansion (characterised by a fixpoint construction) has been proved for a class of powerful theories much larger than the class dealt with in [9]. The autoepistemic translation of general, disjunctive and constraint logic programs (obtained by replacing negation-as-failure by $\neg L$) is strictly included in this class. Consequently, this logic is an appealing, unifying framework for several logic programming paradigms.

Unfortunately, some sets of formulae are not handled satisfactorily: many sensible inferences can not be performed. In this paper this problem will be discussed and a solution will be proposed.

For this purpose, the semantic framework introduced in [2] will be generalised, and the related results will be extended to a family of autoepistemic logics, that includes two-valued autoepistemic logics and the 3-valued logics of [2]. A suitable member of the family will be shown to deal correctly with the troublesome premises mentioned above.

2 Three-valued Autoepistemic Logics

The language we deal with, denoted by $\mathcal{L}$, is a propositional modal language, with standard connectives ($\vee, \wedge, \subset$ and $\neg$), a non-standard connective ($\leftarrow$) and one modal operator L, to be read as "know" or "believe".

Formulae in which L does not occur are called *ordinary*. Formulae in which propositional symbols occur only within the scope of L are called *purely epistemic*. Formulae of the form $L\psi$ are called *autoepistemic atoms*.

The purpose of autoepistemic logics is to model the beliefs that an ideally rational and introspective agent should hold, given a set A of *premises* (i.e. axioms, or basic beliefs).

In standard (i.e. two-valued) autoepistemic logics, beliefs are modelled by a set of formulae that represents both what is believed and disbelieved by the agent, through its extension and counter-extension, respectively.

We need a slightly more complicated notion, since we want to capture more shaded situations, where the agent has reasons both to believe and to disbelieve some statements, or there is no way for the agent to reach a complete, "stable" set of beliefs.

Definition 1 *A* belief-state *B is a partial mapping from $\mathcal{L}$ into $\{0,1\}$.*

A belief state can be regarded as a subset of $\mathcal{L} \times \{0,1\}$, so belief states are partially ordered by set inclusion. There is one minimal element (the empty set), but many maximal elements, corresponding to complete mappings (called *complete belief states*).

A belief state B can also be seen as a pair $\langle B^+, B^- \rangle$, where $B^+ = \{\psi \mid B(\psi) = 1\}$, $B^- = \{\psi \mid B(\psi) = 0\}$. Obviously, $B^+ \cap B^- = \emptyset$.

Intuitively, B^+ is the set of statements that the agent *believes* to be true, while B^- is the set of statements the agent *disbelieves* (i.e. she[1] believes they *might* be false). The remaining statements of the language are those about which the agent is *doubtful*, that is, such statements are involved in an "epistemically inconsistent" piece of knowledge.[2]

Let's now introduce the models of our language:

Definition 2 *A* propositional interpretation *is a partial mapping from propositional symbols and autoepistemic atoms into truth values. Its restriction to propositional symbols is required to be total.*

Note that Moore's propositional interpretations are a special case of our definition. Propositional interpretations model both what is true in the "outside world" (by assigning a classical truth value to propositional symbols) and the agent's beliefs (by giving a possibly undefined truth value to autoepistemic atoms). More specifically, the agent modeled by an interpretation

a) believes ψ if $L\psi$ is true in the model;

b) disbelieves ψ if $L\psi$ is false in the model;

c) is doubtful about ψ if $L\psi$ is undefined.

Non-atomic formulae are evaluated by extending *strong Kleene's valuation* with the definition of $\hookleftarrow$ as follows: formula $\psi \hookleftarrow \phi$ is true if ψ is true or ϕ is not true, and false otherwise. Note that this implication is an object-level formalisation of the entailment relation: $\phi \models \psi$ iff $\models \psi \hookleftarrow \phi$.

There are several ways for a propositional interpretation to be a model of a belief state B:

Definition 3 $\mathcal{M}$ *is an* autoepistemic interpretation *of B if $\mathcal{M}$ ascribes the agent precisely her belief state B, i.e. $\mathcal{M} \models L\psi$ iff $\psi \in B^+$ and $\mathcal{M} \models \neg L\psi$ iff $\psi \in B^-$.*

$\mathcal{M}$ *is a* propositional model *of B^+ if $\mathcal{M}$ verifies the agent's beliefs, i.e. $\mathcal{M} \models B^+$.*

$\mathcal{M}$ *is an* autoepistemic model *of B if $\mathcal{M}$ is both an autoepistemic interpretation of B and a propositional model of B^+. If B has an auto-epistemic model, we say B is* epistemically consistent.

The basic guideline we will follow in formalising the assumptions about the agent's rationality and introspectiveness is *prudence*: we want the agent's belief state to be independent of how her doubts can be removed or, equivalently, independent of how her knowledge gaps can be filled in.

Here we depart from the approach of [2] and allow the statement above to be interpreted more flexibly. Namely, we allow to restrict the way knowledge gaps can be

---

[1] I should probably go on writing "he/she", but this would make many statements unreadable. So I give my agent a sex, and make her a female, because I find it easier to idealise women.

[2] By "epistemically inconsistent knowledge" we mean any bunch of conflicting information that causes the premises to have no stable expansions or too many of them.

filled in (in contrast with [2], where *all* the extensions of the current belief-state were taken into account) since, in general, some extensions are not sensible belief-states for our agent (see section 2.2).

The set of "allowed" extensions of B will be denoted by $\mathcal{K}(B)$. The only constraint we pose on $\mathcal{K}$ is

$$\{B\} \subseteq \mathcal{K}(B) \subseteq \{B' \mid B' \supseteq B\}. \tag{1}$$

By prudence and rationality requirements, the agent's belief state should satisfy the following principles:

Principle 1 *The agent should believe all and only those formulae that are true whenever her premises are true - no matter how she can extend her knowledge.*

Principle 2 *The agent should disbelieve all and only those formulae that are not necessarily true when her premises are true - no matter how she can extend her knowledge.*

Next introspectiveness comes into play. By introspectiveness, the agent knows exactly what her own belief state is, hence she knows that the actual world must be an autoepistemic interpretation of her beliefs. If no such interpretation satisfied the agent's beliefs, then the agent's rationality could be questioned, so we impose a third constraint:

Principle 3 *It should be possible that the actual world satisfies the agent's beliefs. That is, there should be an autoepistemic model of such beliefs.*

Finally, we can define the formal counterpart of the three principles outlined above.

Definition 4 *Let B and B' range over belief states, and let $AE(B')$ be the set of autoepistemic interpretations of B'. B is a $\mathcal{K}$-generalised stable expansion ($\mathcal{K}$-GSE) of A iff*

1. $B^+ = \{\psi \mid \forall B' \in \mathcal{K}(B), \forall \mathcal{M} \in AE(B') : \mathcal{M} \models A \Rightarrow \mathcal{M} \models \psi\}$
2. $B^- = \{\psi \mid \forall B' \in \mathcal{K}(B), \exists \mathcal{M} \in AE(B') : \mathcal{M} \models A \land \mathcal{M} \not\models \psi\}$
3. *B is epistemically consistent.*

For what we said before, any $\mathcal{K}$-GSE is an admissible belief state for our agent. Note that – through $\mathcal{K}$-GSE's – we have actually defined a *family* of $\mathcal{K}$-indexed autoepistemic logics. We call the logic induced by $\mathcal{K}$ "$\mathcal{K}$-logic".

It is easy to see that, for any *consistent* standard stable expansion X and any $\mathcal{K}$, there is a $\mathcal{K}$-GSE B such that $X = B^+$ and $\mathcal{L} \setminus X = B^-$. In the following, we will slightly abuse terminology and call "standard stable expansion" also the corresponding belief state.

In order to show that $\mathcal{K}$-GSE's enjoy the same closure conditions as Moore's and Przymusinski's consistent stable expansions, we extend Stalnaker's stability conditions to belief states:

Definition 5 *A belief state B is* stable *if and only if*

1. *If $B^+ \models \psi$ then $\psi \in B^+$*

2. *$L\psi \in B^+$ iff $\psi \in B^+$*

3. *$\neg L\psi \in B^+$ iff $\psi \in B^-$*

Lemma 1 *If B is a $\mathcal{K}$-generalised stable expansion then B is stable.*

These facts suggests that we are naturally generalising Moore's framework, and more can be said.

Define $\mathcal{K}_0(B) = \{B\}$. This is a limit case, according to the constraints $\mathcal{K}$ has to satisfy. It is easy to verify that the equations defining $\mathcal{K}_0$-GSE's can be satisfied only by complete belief states, because the conditions defining B^+ and B^- are complementary when $\mathcal{K}(B) = \{B\}$. But if B is complete, then the aforementioned equations are equivalent to the standard fixpoint equation for two-valued autoepistemic logics. In other words, $\mathcal{K}_0$-GSE's are exactly the standard stable expansions of A, hence $\mathcal{K}_0$-logic is nothing but Moore's autoepistemic logic.

The other limit case for $\mathcal{K}$ is interesting, too. Let $\mathcal{K}_1(B) = \{B' \mid B' \supseteq B\}$. It can be shown that the equations defining $\mathcal{K}_1$-GSE's are equivalent to the ones defining GSE's for the three-valued logic introduced in [2].

Then this family of logics provides a unifying framework for two- and three-valued autoepistemic logics. In section 2.2 it will be shown that intermediate logics between $\mathcal{K}_0$- and $\mathcal{K}_1$-logics are needed.

2.1 A fixpoint construction for the minimal $\mathcal{K}_1$-GSE

The least $\mathcal{K}$-GSE of A can be taken as *the* set of autoepistemic consequences of A, for it gathers what is common to all $\mathcal{K}$-GSE's, i.e. it does not contain any "arbitrary" belief or disbelief. In this section, the existence of the least $\mathcal{K}$-GSE will be proved for suitable $\mathcal{K}$'s and suitable classes of theories. The proof will yield a fixpoint construction for the minimal $\mathcal{K}$-GSE.

The jump operator for the fixpoint construction can be derived from the definition of $\mathcal{K}$-GSE's, generalising the approach of [1]:

Definition 6 *Operator T_A, over belief-states, is defined by the following equations:*

$$T_A(B) = \langle T_A(B)^+, T_A(B)^- \rangle$$
$$T_A(B)^+ = \{\psi \mid \forall B' \in \mathcal{K}(B), \forall \mathcal{M} \in AE(B') : \mathcal{M} \models A \Rightarrow \mathcal{M} \models \psi\}$$
$$T_A(B)^- = \{\psi \mid \forall B' \in \mathcal{K}(B), \exists \mathcal{M} \in AE(B') : \mathcal{M} \models A \wedge \mathcal{M} \not\models \psi\}$$

By definitions 4 and 6, B is a $\mathcal{K}$-GSE of A iff B is an epistemically consistent fixpoint of T_A.

All of the results concerning the fixed-point construction that have been proved in [2] are immediately available, thanks to the equivalence between GSE's and $\mathcal{K}_1$-GSE's.

First of all, when $\mathcal{K} = \mathcal{K}_1$, T_A is monotonic, hence its least fixed point $lfp(T_A)$ exists and equals $T_A^\alpha(\emptyset)$, for some ordinal α.

Secondly, a powerful theorem holds for a class of very expressive theories:

Definition 7 *A set of formulae A is in* implicative form *if and only if the members of A are of the form $\psi \hookleftarrow \phi$, where ψ is ordinary, ϕ is purely epistemic and "$\hookleftarrow$" does not occur in ϕ.*

Theorem 1 *If A is in implicative form then the following are equivalent:*
1) A has a $\mathcal{K}_1$-GSE
2) $lfp(T_A)^+$ is consistent
3) $lfp(T_A)$ is the least $\mathcal{K}_1$-GSE of A.

It can be shown that, if A is a stratified autoepistemic theory [3], then $lfp(T_A)$ is exactly the unique stable expansion of A. So this 3-valued logic agrees with Moore's logic on non-problematic premises. The following example shows the behaviour of this logic on problematic premises.

Example 2 Let us formalise the "Nixon's Diamond" through a set of premises in implicative form:

$$q = \text{"Nixon is a quaker"} \quad r = \text{"Nixon is a republican"}$$
$$p = \text{"Nixon is a pacifist"} \quad np = \text{"Nixon is not a pacifist"}$$

$$A_2 = \{(p \hookleftarrow q \wedge \neg Lnp), \ (np \hookleftarrow r \wedge \neg Lp), \ (q \wedge r)\}.$$

The weak implication symbol "$\hookleftarrow$" is equivalent to "$\subset$" when both of its arguments are defined. It immediately follows that the two standard stable expansions of the premises A (as defined in example 1) are also $\mathcal{K}_1$-GSE's of A_2.

Fortunately, theorem 1 is applicable. The fixpoint construction yields the least $\mathcal{K}_1$-GSE (call it B). Formulae p and np are neither believed nor disbelieved in B (i.e. they are neither in B^+ nor in B^-).

Since the agent is doubtful about p, formulae Lp and $\neg Lp$ are neither believed nor disbelieved, too.

As a consequence, $Lp \vee \neg Lp$ is not believed, expressing the fact that the agent is uncertain about p. However, this does not mean that the agent can not reason classically about the outside world. For example, $p \vee \neg p$ is a tautology, hence (by lemma 1.(1)) $p \vee \neg p$ is believed (as well as $L(p \vee \neg p)$, $LL(p \vee \neg p)$, and so on, by lemma 1.(2)).

By symmetry, the same arguments hold for np. So the agent can reason classically about p and np, even if she is doubtful about them. $\square$

Example 3 Let $A = \{p \hookleftarrow \neg Lp\}$. The fixpoint construction yields a consistent belief state, so A has a least $\mathcal{K}_1$-GSE B. Moreover, p is neither believed nor disbelieved in B, as expected. $\square$

Note that theorem 1 holds for a quite general class of premises: in fact, the implicative form does not restrict the way in which the knowledge about the outside world can be expressed, nor it restricts the way in which autoepistemic knowledge can be queried, since ψ and ϕ are arbitrarily complex formulae. The purpose of implicative form is preventing autoepistemic knowledge to be forced through the premises, according to the intuition that such knowledge should instead be derived by looking at the extension of the knowledge base. In this sense, implicative form should be seen as a discipline for building sensible sets of premises, rather than a restriction to the expressive power of autoepistemic theories.

It should also be noted that implicative formulae behave like the default inference rules of Reiter's Default Logic, since they can be used in only one direction. The advantage of our formalisation is that more expressive preconditions are allowed, and that the agent can have introspective knowledge about these rules, since they are object-level formulae.

2.2 A more powerful instance of the schema

Unfortunately, $\mathcal{K}_1$-GSE's are sometimes too weak, as the following examples show.

Example 4 The Nixon's Diamond can be formalised more naturally than in examples 1 and 2, by substituting $\neg p$ for np. The resulting premises are:

$$A_3 = \{(p \leftrightarrow q \wedge \neg L \neg p), \ (\neg p \leftrightarrow r \wedge \neg Lp), \ (q \wedge r)\}.$$

As expected, p and $\neg p$ are neither believed nor disbelieved in the minimal $\mathcal{K}_1$-GSE of A_3.

Now define $A' = A_3 \cup \{s \leftrightarrow \neg Lc\}$, and let B be the least $\mathcal{K}_1$-GSE of A'. We would expect c to be disbelieved in B, since it doesn't occur in A_3 nor it follows from the new clause. Consequently, we would expect s to be believed in B.

Unfortunately, since p and $\neg p$ are undefined in B, there is a belief state $B' = B \cup \langle \emptyset, \{p, \neg p\} \rangle \supseteq B$ such that no autoepistemic interpretation of B' is a model of A. As a consequence, B^- is *empty*, and both s and c are undefined in B. $\square$

Example 5 Let $A_4 = \{(p \leftrightarrow \neg Lr), \ (r \leftrightarrow \neg Lp), \ (q \leftrightarrow Lp \wedge Lr)\}$ and let B be the least $\mathcal{K}_1$-GSE of A_4. It is reasonable to require that q be disbelieved, since there is no stable and "supported" way of believing both p and r. However, there is a belief state $B' = B \cup \langle \{p, r\}, \emptyset \rangle \supseteq B$ such that all autoepistemic interpretations of B' that are models of A_4 are also models of q. So q can not be disbelieved in B. $\square$

The problem is that some belief states are considered as possible extensions of the current belief state of the agent, even if the agent could never reach them, since they violate the basic properties that $\mathcal{K}$-GSE's are supposed to enjoy. In example 4, all the extensions of B greater than or equal to B' can not be stable and consistent at the same time. In example 5, instead, B' is not "grounded", because it "believes" p and r even if they do not follow from A and from the definition of L induced by B'. More formally:

Definition 8 *We say that a belief state B is* grounded *with respect to A if and only if, for every formula $\psi \in B^+$ where "$\leftrightarrow$" does not occur,*

$$A \cup \{L\phi \mid \phi \in B^+\} \cup \{\neg L\phi \mid \phi \in B^-\} \models \psi.$$

Stability, groundness and epistemic consistency (corresponding to the classical notions of completeness, soundness and consistency, respectively) can be taken as the basic properties of generalised stable expansions. We try to solve the problems outlined in the examples above by forcing the agent to consider only stable, consistent and grounded extensions of its current belief state (whenever possible).

For this purpose, let A be a fixed set of premises in implicative form, and define $\mathcal{BS}$ to be the set of stable and epistemically consistent belief states that are grounded with respect to A. Then define

$$\mathcal{K}_2(B) = \{B\} \cup \begin{cases} \{B' \in \mathcal{BS} \mid B' \supset B\} & if \ \mathcal{BS} \cap \{B' \mid B' \supset B\} \neq \emptyset \\ \{B' \mid B' \supset B\} & otherwise \end{cases}$$

We want to extend theorem 1 to $\mathcal{K}_2$-GSE's. This is not so easy, since T_A is not monotonic when $\mathcal{K} = \mathcal{K}_2$ (formulae involving "$\hookleftarrow$" may turn from false to true or viceversa). First, the ordinal progression has to be redefined, so that the limit elements of the progression be consistent (union does not work anymore). Secondly, we have to prove that the progression converges to a fixed point. From this result, the extension of theorem 1 can be proved.

We define the progression as a *semi inductive process* [5]. For all ordinals α and all limit ordinals λ:

$$\begin{aligned} T_A^0(B) &= B \\ T_A^{\alpha+1}(B) &= T_A(T_A^\alpha(B)) \\ T_A^\lambda(B)^+ &= \{\psi \mid \exists\alpha(\alpha < \lambda)\forall\beta(\alpha \leq \beta < \lambda)\psi \in T_A^\beta(B)^+\} \\ T_A^\lambda(B)^- &= \{\psi \mid \exists\alpha(\alpha < \lambda)\forall\beta(\alpha \leq \beta < \lambda)\psi \in T_A^\beta(B)^-\}. \end{aligned}$$

The beliefs (resp. disbeliefs) of the limit elements of this progression are the formulae that are permanently believed (disbelieved) from some ordinal α on. Note that, if T_A is monotonic, then the limit elements are just the union of their predecessors, hence this definition generalises the fixpoint construction for $\mathcal{K}_1$-GSE's.

Theorem 2 *Let A be in implicative form and let $\mathcal{K} = \mathcal{K}_2$. Then there is an ordinal α such that $T_A^\alpha(\emptyset) = lfp(T_A)$.*

Theorem 3 *Let A be in implicative form and let $\mathcal{K} = \mathcal{K}_2$. Then the following are equivalent:*
  1) A has a $\mathcal{K}_2$-GSE
  2) $lfp(T_A)^+$ is consistent
  3) $lfp(T_A)$ is the least $\mathcal{K}_2$-GSE of A.

Also in this case, it can be shown that $lfp(T_A)$ corresponds to the unique stable expansion of A, when A is a stratified autoepistemic theory. The same deductions illustrated in example 2 can be performed in $\mathcal{K}_2$-logic. Also in this case, the law of the excluded middle holds for epistemic atoms only if they are defined. Moreover, the problems outlined in the examples 4 and 5 are solved. More specifically, in the least $\mathcal{K}_2$-GSE of A_3, c is disbelieved and s is believed, even if p and $\neg p$ are undefined; and in the least $\mathcal{K}_2$-GSE of A_4, q is disbelieved, even if p and r are undefined.

3   Conclusions

In this paper a family of autoepistemic logics has been defined. The family is a unifying framework for two- and three-valued autoepistemic logics, and enjoies a model theory motivated by epistemic considerations.

All the logics in this family still allow both classical reasoning on ordinary formulae and constructive reasoning on purely epistemic formulae, and their generalised stable expansions enjoy the usual stability conditions.

A member of the family, called $\mathcal{K}_2$-logic, solves the problems affecting the other known 3-valued autoepistemic logics, and at the same time preserves their appealing features.

The least $\mathcal{K}_1$-GSE and the least $\mathcal{K}_2$-GSE of implicative premises have been given a fixpoint characterisation, that can help to design proof procedures for the corresponding logics in the decidable cases. The fixpoint construction yields the unique, standard stable expansion of the premises, when they are stratified. In other words, $\mathcal{K}_1$-logic and $\mathcal{K}_2$-logic agree with Moore's autoepistemic logics on non-problematic cases.

References

[1] P. Bonatti. *Monotonicity in AE theories: preliminary report.* In Proc. GULP'90, V Convegno Nazionale sulla Programmazione Logica.

[2] P. Bonatti. *A more general solution to the multiple expansion problem.* In Proc. Workshop on Non-Monotonic Reasoning and Logic Programming, NACLP'90.

[3] M. Gelfond. *On Stratified Autoepistemic Theories.* In Proceedings AAAI-87, 207-211, 1987.

[4] M. Gelfond, V. Lifschitz. *Logic programs with classical negation.* In Proc. of the Int. Joint Conference on Logic Programming, Israel, 1990.

[5] H. G. Herzberger. *Notes on Naive Semantics.* In the Journal of Phil. Logic 11 (1982), 61-102.

[6] J. Jaffar, J. Lassez. *Constraint Logic Programming.* In Proc. of 14th POPL, p. 111-119. ACM 1987.

[7] J. Lobo, J. Minker, A. Rajasekar. *Extending the Semantics of Logic Programs to Disjunctive Logic Programs.* In Proc. of 6th International Conference on Logic Programming, 1989.

[8] R. Moore. *Semantical considerations on nonmonotonic logics.* In Artificial Intelligence 25, pp. 75-94, 1985.

[9] T. Przymusinski. *Three-valued formalisations of non-monotonic reasoning.* In Proc. of KR'89 - First Int. Conf. on Principles of Knowledge Representation and Reasoning (1989).

Viewpoints subsume beliefs, truth and situations

Maria Simi

Dipartimento di Matematica e Informatica, Università di Udine

Abstract

A formal notion of viewpoint, relying on an extension of first order predicate calculus with an axiomatization of provability and reflection rules, is presented. The extension is not conservative and it is, in our intention, the best we can do if we care about consistency. Viewpoints are defined as set of sentences at the meta-level. The paper investigates to what extent notions such as belief, knowledge, truth and situations can be uniformly modeled as provability in "specialized viewpoints", obtained by imposing suitable constraints on viewpoints.

Topic: knowledge representation and automated reasoning
Key words: meta-level, logics for truth, belief and knowledge, situations

1. Introduction

Many authors have been working in the direction of a first order theory of reasoning agents with a syntactical treatment of modalities, as an alternative to modal logics for belief and knowledge: from the earlier approaches of McCarthy, Moore and Konolige [McCarthy, 1979; Moore, 1977; Konolige, 1982] to the more recent work by Turner [Turner, 1989] and Davies [Davies, 1990].

If we envision computer agents able to plan and execute actions by taking into account their own beliefs and knowledge as well as the beliefs and knowledge of other agents it is essential, as a minimal requirement, that in the same theory coexist truth, propositional attitudes such as belief and knowledge, and situations.

At the state of the art, both of modal logics and of logics with a syntactical rendering of modalities, reasonable proposals exist which include separate groups of axioms for each modality, plus axioms relating different modalities. The fact that axioms in each group are very similar, immediately suggests that these similarities can be factorized.

The approach explored in this paper is to heavily rely on a basic theory of viewpoints, and to model commonly used propositional attitudes, such as belief and knowledge, but also truth and "holding in a situation", as provability in a viewpoint. Differences in the behaviour of modal operators are captured by additional axioms imposed on viewpoints, thus constraining or expanding the set of sentences that can be proved in specialized viewpoints. The concept of viewpoint is therefore seen as a basic one subsuming a variety of other concepts, with the goal of achieving a uniform treatment.

This paper discusses to which extent this can be done and the problems to be solved. The starting point of this investigation is, for expressivity reasons, a self-referential language; this implies that attention has to be paid, at each step, for preventing paradoxes.

2. Viewpoints

The idea of viewpoints was introduced in [Attardi-Simi, 1984] in the context of the logic Omega: a set of formal properties was provided for viewpoints together with an example of reasoning "across theories", but no formal proof of consistency.

The basic theory of viewpoints used here is a revised version which relies on results presented in [Attardi-Simi, 1991]. In that paper a non conservative extension of first order predicate calculus is introduced, which includes an axiomatization of provability at the meta-level, with carefully formulated reflection rules. The consistency of the resulting theory was proved by establishing a correspondence with syntactic variants of modal logics, proved consistent elsewhere.

Viewpoints are defined as *sets of sentence names* and represent the assumptions of a theory. In this paper the sentence ('A' in *vp*), where *vp* is a viewpoint expression, should be taken to mean "sentence A is derivable from the assumptions denoted by *vp*".

Follows a more precise account of the language and proof theory.

2.1 The language

The language is a standard first order language with equality, with the ability to "name" terms and sentences of the language. That is, for each term (or sentence) there is an associated term which represents that term (or sentence), which will be referred as the *name* of the term (or sentence). Finally, the language includes the ability to form sets ({..}), viewpoint expressions, denoting set of sentence names, and the special infix connective "in", roughly interpreted as "is derivable from".

In the following I will use $A, A_1, A_2 ... B, ... f, g, f_1, f_2, ...$ as meta-variables for sentences and $vp, vp_1, vp_2 ...$ as meta-variables for set of sentences.

Instead of writing explicitly the expression naming a term (or sentence), the standard convention of quoting the term (or sentence) will be adopted. Thus, for example I will write '$A \Rightarrow B$' instead of *implies*('A', 'B'). Similarly I will use 'vp', 'vp_1', 'vp_2' ..., for set of sentence names, i.e. viewpoints. Whenever no confusion is possible however, I will refrain from the quoting convention. More specifically I will use quotes at the appropriate places only if a statement needs to refer both to a sentence A and to its name. The same for viewpoints. For example I would write "(A in *vp*) if A belongs to *vp*" but "('A' in '*vp*') if *vp* derives A".

Finally, when *vp* is used in place of a formula, the intended meaning is the formula which is the conjunction of the sentences in *vp*.

2.2 The proof theory

The axiomatization of provability exploited here is quite standard [Bowen-Kowalski, 1982; Attardi-Simi, 1991]. It can be done, for example, by considering a set of inference rules in the style of natural deduction and writing a meta inference rule for each of the object level inference rules. For example, for the rule of implication introduction, formulated as follows:

If $vp \cup A \vdash B$ then $vp \vdash (A \Rightarrow B)$

there is a corresponding meta-rule:

If ('B' in 'vp' $\cup$ 'A') then ('$A \Rightarrow B$' in 'vp')

Moreover the following axioms are included:

Ax1. (A in vp), for any viewpoint vp, if A is one of the sentence names in vp.

Ax2. ('A' in vp), for any logical axiom A and viewpoint vp.

Finally the following reflection rules provide the link between object and meta-level:

If $vp_1 \vdash$ ('A' in 'vp_2') then $vp_1 \cup vp_2 \vdash A$ (reflect down)

If $vp \vdash_{PC} A$ then $\vdash$ ('A' in 'vp') (reflect up)

The notation $\vdash_{PC}$ above, stands for "derivable using any inference rule except reflect down and reflect up". The choice of this formulation of the reflection rules has been discussed at length in [Attardi-Simi, 1991]. This version of the reflection rules results in a non conservative extension; the restriction imposed on the reflect up rule is necessary to avoid contradictions, as for the negative results pointed out by Montague [Montague, 1963], and ensures consistency.

In the rest of this section I will discuss some properties of deduction that will be used in the rest of the paper.

The proposed extension is not conservative due to the strong version of the reflect down inference rule, through which new theorems are derivable. Most important, the following theorem can be proved:

Theorem 1: ('A' in 'vp') $\Rightarrow$ ($vp \Rightarrow A$)

Theorem 1 can be read as saying that if "in" holds then the material implication holds as well but not vice versa. As argued in [Attardi-Simi, 1991] there are several reasons to believe that this is a desirable property. I will discuss further the implications of this theorem in section 3.

Due to the restriction on the reflect up rule, an important limitation of this basic theory is that only classical proofs can be used to carry out proofs within an arbitrary viewpoint. This is formally expressed as follows:

Proof in context : If ('A' in 'vp') and $A \vdash_{PC} B$ then ('B' in 'vp')

Note however that a weaker condition, like $A \vdash B$ or ('B' in 'A'), would not be sufficient. It is however easy to show that a proof in context, provided it is a classical proof, can be performed at any level of nesting: reflect up is applied until the desired level of nesting is reached.

The classical version of positive introspection, i.e.

('A' in 'vp_1') $\Rightarrow$ ('(A in vp_1)' in 'vp_1') (positive introspection)

cannot be derived. In fact the truth of ('A' in 'vp_1') does not imply the existence of a proof; only a weaker form of positive introspection can be derived, namely:

Weak introspection: If $vp_2 \vdash$ ('A' in 'vp_1') then $vp_2 \vdash$ ('(A in vp_1)' in 'vp_2')

where the outer viewpoint in ('(A in vp_1)' in 'vp_2') cannot be any viewpoint but must include the premises used to derive ('A' in 'vp_1').

As a corollary the following special cases can be obtained:

If $vp_1 \vdash_{PC} A$ then $\vdash$ ('(A in vp_1)' in 'vp_2')

If $\vdash$ ('A' in 'vp_1') then $\vdash$ ('(A in vp_1)' in 'vp_2')

where the outer viewpoint can be any one; that is ('(A in vp_1)' in 'vp_2') can be derived if there is a classical proof of A from vp_1 or, equivalently, ('A' in 'vp_1') can be derived with no assumption.

The rest of the paper will discuss to what extent the basic theory of viewpoints introduced in this section can be used for modeling belief in the first place, but also other modalities that are not usually rendered as provability, such as truth and knowledge, and for representing the "holding in a situation" which is used when reasoning in an evolving world.

The properties of our axiomatization will be compared with corresponding axiomatizations found in the literature of modal logics and syntactical treatment of modalities [Moore, 1977; Konolige, 1982; Turner, 1989; Davies, 1990].

3. Belief

Modeling beliefs as provability in the theory of the agent holding the beliefs, is not a new idea. We associate to an agent, say a, the set of his basic assumptions, $vp(a)$, that we call his "viewpoint".

The agents considered here are perfect reasoners and believe all the logical consequences of their assumptions. It is argued that this is not a reasonable property of belief. While this issue is not the concern of this paper, a syntactic approach, like the one pursued here, holds more promise, over a modal one, to be able to deal with the problem of logical omniscience.

Definition of Belief: $Bel(a, f) = (f \text{ in } vp(a))$

Let us recall at this point the properties for beliefs found in the literature of modal logics, to see whether the basic theory of viewpoints set up in the previous section is adequate. For each property, expressed in our notation, it will be discussed whether it can be proved in the basic theory of viewpoints.

K: $(A \Rightarrow B \text{ in } vp) \Rightarrow ((A \text{ in } vp) \Rightarrow (B \text{ in } vp))$

D. $(A \text{ in } vp) \Rightarrow \neg(\neg A \text{ in } vp)$

BAR: $(\forall x (A \text{ in } vp)) \Rightarrow (\forall x A \text{ in } vp)$

S4: $(A \text{ in } vp) \Rightarrow ((A \text{ in } vp) \text{ in } vp)$

Necessitation: If $vp \vdash A$ then $\vdash ('A' \text{ in } 'vp')$

Property **K** is a property of "in" which is obvious by the meta-level version of *modus ponens*.

Property **D** can be derived only under the assumption that vp holds. More formally only the weaker $vp \Rightarrow ((A \text{ in } vp) \Rightarrow \neg(\neg A \text{ in } vp))$ can be derived. It can be noted that this axiom postulates a kind of coherence for an agent's beliefs. In fact, if the additional constraint

$\neg(false \text{ in } vp)$ (consistency of viewpoints)

is imposed on agent theories, property **D** becomes a theorem.

Property **BAR** can be easily proved with the rule of $\forall$-elimination and the meta rule for $\forall$-introduction.

Property **S4** is the positive introspection that I have already commented on in section 2. This is widely accepted as a valid property of belief: "if one believes something, he believes that he believes it". The fact that **S4** cannot be proved looks like a disadvantage of our logic over other logics which could, in an intuitionistic style, take "in" to imply the existence of a proof. In such logics however, a stronger theorem is derivable, that is:

$(A \text{ in } vp_1) \Rightarrow ((A \text{ in} vp_1) \text{ in } vp_2)$

In fact from the truth of $(A \text{ in } vp_1)$ one would be able to infer that $vp_1 \vdash A$ and therefore the truth of $((A \text{ in } vp_1) \text{ in } \{ \})$, by reflecting up twice. This is however not a reasonable principle for belief, since it would amount to the following: "if an agent believes A then any other agent believes that the first agent believes A".

Fortunately we can prove, with a straightforward extension of the results in [Attardi-Simi, 1991], that positive introspection can be safely added as an axiom, without compromising consistency.

Finally, only a restricted version of necessitation is possible, corresponding to reflect up:

If $vp \vdash_{PC} A$ then $\vdash$ ('A' in 'vp')   (reflect up)

Axiom **T** of modal logics, is not usually considered acceptable for beliefs: it would amount to $\text{Bel}(A) \Rightarrow A$; the corresponding property cannot be derived in our basic theory of viewpoints.

Theorem 1 however, i.e. ('A' in 'vp') $\Rightarrow$ ($vp \Rightarrow A$), can be regarded as a weak form of axiom T which does make sense for belief. If ('A' in 'vp') is read as "A is one of the beliefs of an agent whose assumptions are vp", Theorem 1 properly models the following property of beliefs: "if an agent holds belief A, then either some of the agent's assumptions are false or belief A is true". In [Attardi-Simi, 1991], we show with an example that this property can be usefully exploited.

4.Truth

According to our stated intentions, in order to model truth, we need a special theory, that we call RW as an abbreviation for Real World. Ideally, everything that it is true should be derivable in this theory. We are therefore aiming at the following definition for truth:

Definition of truth: $T(f) = (f$ in RW)

We might be tempted to give a characterization of RW by assuming the equivalence ('A' in RW) $\Leftrightarrow A$, as for example in [Konolige, 1982]. It is known however that this leads immediately to the Tarski's liar paradox. Therefore weaker properties should be explored, that our intuition feels appropriate for a theory of the real world, namely:

consistency: the real world should be non contradictory;
completeness: something is true or it is not;
veridicality: the set of assumptions of the real world are true.

This amounts to imposing the following properties as axioms, whatever set of assumptions RW is chosen as a description of the real world:

$\neg$(*false* in RW)   (consistency of RW)

$\neg(A$ in RW) $\Rightarrow (\neg A$ in RW)   (completeness of RW)

RW   (veridicality of RW)

The above properties are not minimal; in fact veridicality implies consistency. Moreover it can be shown that veridicality and completeness together are too powerful, since $A \Leftrightarrow (A$ in RW) can be proved using them: the liar paradox springs up again.

Among the two possible ways out, to give up veridicality or completeness, we will have to go for the second alternative because completeness is problematic in itself.

In fact well known results show that no axiomatization of provability can be complete (see for example [Bowen-Kowalski, 1982]); this concretely means that for any vp, a sentence J can be constructed such that it says of itself that it is unprovable in vp, i.e.

$J \Leftrightarrow \neg(J$ in $vp)$

can be proved. It follows that, postulating completeness of a viewpoint, precludes the existence of a model for that viewpoint. In fact $\neg vp$ can be derived both from the assumption (J in vp) and from the assumption $\neg(J$ in $vp)$. This can also be alternatively stated as "no truthful set of assumptions can be complete" or "no complete set of assumptions can be consistent". This negative result suggest to investigate weaker forms of completeness.

One restriction that comes naturally to mind is to impose some kind of Closed World Assumption, that is to impose completeness only for ground atomic formulas, not including "in" statements. We will assume the existence of a predicate SAF (Simple Atomic Formulas) on the names of sentences to test this condition[1]. The restricted completeness is:

$SAF(A) \land \neg(A \text{ in } RW) \Rightarrow (\neg A \text{ in } RW)$ (weak completeness of RW)

Now the double implication, $A \Leftrightarrow (A \text{ in } RW)$, does not hold in general, and this is enough to prevent the liar paradox.

Putting all together, we have the following axioms for truth:

RW (RW1, veridicality of RW)

$SAF(A) \land \neg(A \text{ in } RW) \Rightarrow (\neg A \text{ in } RW)$ (RW2, weak completeness of RW)

and theorems

$\neg(false \text{ in } RW)$ (RW3, consistency of RW)

$(A \text{ in } RW) \Rightarrow A$ (RW4, axiom **T** for truth)

$(\neg A \text{ in } RW) \Rightarrow \neg(A \text{ in } RW)$ (RW5, axiom **D** for truth)

$SAF(A) \land A \Rightarrow (A \text{ in } RW)$ (RW6)

We regard this solution as the minimal set of properties for RW allowing to characterize this special viewpoint in such a way that paradoxes are avoided.

With respect to the modal logics of truth, our axiomatization performs as follows: we still have axioms **K, D, S4, BAR**, and a weak necessitation rule as for the minimal theory of viewpoints extended with the consistency axiom that was used for beliefs. Axiom **T** for truth can also be derived.

It is worth noting that the axioms imposed on RW, and those imposed on viewpoints for beliefs, are to be considered logical axioms of an extended theory of viewpoints and as such, in virtue of Ax2, they are included in any viewpoint. Therefore, for example, since veridicality is a logical axiom, (RW in vp) holds for any vp. However, the fact that any viewpoint is aware that RW holds, does not imply that any viewpoint is aware of all the true facts. In fact, the property:

$(A \text{ in } RW) \Rightarrow (A \text{ in } vp)$

cannot be proved. This is due to the restriction on reflect up and the consequent restriction on the "proof in context" rule.

When truth is used in connection with beliefs, we have:

$((A \text{ in } vp) \text{ in } RW) \Rightarrow (A \text{ in } vp)$

However the following cannot be derived, due again to the restriction on the reflect up rule:

$((A \text{ in } RW) \text{ in } vp) \Rightarrow (A \text{ in } vp)$

An extended version of this paper presents a variant of an example presented in [Perlis, 1985], combining truth and belief and featuring a non paradoxical case of mutually referential statements.

---

[1] It is possible that a different, less compelling, restriction can play the same role.

5. Knowledge

Once we have belief and truth in place, they can be used to define knowledge, following the tradition that sees knowledge as "justified true belief":

Definition of knowledge: $K(a, f) = \text{Bel}(a, f) \wedge T(f) = (f \text{ in } vp(a)) \wedge (f \text{ in RW})$

Knowledge has therefore all the properties of truth and belief including, for example, axiom **T** for knowledge:

T: $K(a, f) \Rightarrow f$

in fact (f in RW) implies f, by Theorem 1 and veridicality of RW.

6. Situations

Similarly to what was done for agents and beliefs, we associate to each situation s, a set of basic facts which define the situation, again a viewpoint, $vp(s)$, and define what holds in a situation as provability in a viewpoint.

Definition: $\text{Hold}(s, f) = (f \text{ in } vp(s))$

Like for "being true", "holding in a situation" is intuitively different from "provable in a theory". Stronger properties should apply, like the fact that a sentence holds or does not hold in a situation, completeness again. But, as discussed before, a restricted form of completeness is only possible. One can argue about consistency of situations: after all it is possible to hypothesize situations which are incoherent and have no hope of being real; for the purpose of this paper consistency will however be assumed. Veridicality is certainly not appropriate for situations.

In the following the meta-variables s, s_i, s_f, s_0, s_1, s_2 ... will be used for situations.

$\quad SAF(f) \Rightarrow (\neg(f \text{ in } vp(s)) \Rightarrow (\neg f \text{ in } vp(s)))$ (weak completeness of situations)

$\quad \neg(false \text{ in } vp(s))$ (consistency of situations)

The fact that veridicality does not apply, prevents the proof of the corresponding of axiom **T**, $(f \text{ in } s) \Rightarrow f$, which would not be appropriate for situations.

7. An example combining Beliefs, Truth, Knowledge and Situations

What an agent believes in a situation depends on the viewpoint of the agent in that situation, which is different from the viewpoint of the same agent in another situation, and from the viewpoints of other agents in the same situation. In order to model beliefs and knowledge in a situation, a viewpoint is associated to each pair agent-situation. The viewpoint of agent a in situation s, will be denoted by $vp(a, s)$.

Belief in situation, or $B(a, s, f)$, classically interpreted as "in situation s agent a believes that f holds in situation s" [Konolige, 1982], is rendered as follows.

Definition of belief in situation: $B(a, s, f) = (f \text{ in } vp(a, s))$

When dealing with situations, there are many RW viewpoints, one for each situation; let us call RW(s) the real world viewpoint in situation s. The real world viewpoint in a situation is seen as a special viewpoint, which is made to correspond to the situation itself, more formally:

$\quad RW(s) = vp(s)$

The property $((f \text{ in } RW(s)) \Rightarrow f)$ does not hold, since veridicality is not assumed for situations.

$K(a,s,f)$ is usually defined in terms of Bel and Hold as follows:

Definition of knowledge in situation: $K(a,s,f) = (f \text{ in } vp(a,s)) \land (f \text{ in } vp(s))$

Two general axioms will be needed in the sequel (the same ones are used in the solution in [Konolige, 1982]); the first one says that an agent believes f in situation s just in case he believes that f holds of situation s:

$$\forall\, a\, s\, f .\ (f \text{ in } vp(a, s)) \Leftrightarrow ((f \text{ in } vp(s)) \text{ in } vp(a, s)) \tag{BS0}$$

An axiom is also needed for persistence of beliefs about past situations:

$$\forall\, s_i\, s_f\, e .\ EV(e, s_i, s_f) \Rightarrow$$

$$\forall a f ((f \text{ in } vp(s)) \text{ in } vp(a, s_i)) \Rightarrow ((f \text{ in } vp(s)) \text{ in } vp(a, s_f)) \tag{BS1}$$

where $EV(e, s_1, s_2)$, means that s_2 results from event e occurring in situation s_1. An event can be the performing of an action such as, in the blocks world, $do(a, \text{puton(x,y)})$, i.e. the agent a putting the block x on the block y.

The gas oven test

Suppose agent A turned on the oven in situation S_0 (call this event E_1) and observes that in the resulting situation S_1 the oven is not lit. Agent A can reason as follows: if the pilot light of the oven had been on in S_0, then in S_1 the oven would be lit, since he turned it on. Since he knows that the oven is not lit in S_1, the pilot light was not on in S_0 (and remains not on in S_1).

at (a, o) : agent a is at the oven o

lit(o) : the oven is lit

pl(o) : the pilot light of the oven is lit

In the example I will use small letters for variables and capital letters for constants. To get rid of some parenthesis, I will write $(f \text{ in } a\text{-}s)$ instead of $(f \text{ in } vp(a,s))$ and $(f \text{ in } vp\text{-}s)$ instead of $(f \text{ in } vp(s))$.

Common knowledge:

1. $\forall\, a\, o\, s .\ (\text{at}(a, o) \text{ in } vp\text{-}s) \Rightarrow$

    $((\text{lit}(o) \text{ in } a\text{-}s) \land (\text{lit}(o) \text{ in } vp\text{-}s)) \lor ((\neg\text{lit}(o) \text{ in } a\text{-}s) \land (\neg\text{lit}(o) \text{ in } vp\text{-}s))$

    If the agent is at the oven, he can observe, therefore he knows, whether the oven is lit.

2a. $\forall\, a\, o\, s_i\, s_f .\ EV(do(a, \text{light}(o)), s_i, s_f) \Rightarrow$

    $(\text{at}(a, o) \text{ in } vp\text{-}s_i) \land ((\text{pl}(o) \text{ in } vp\text{-}s_i) \Rightarrow (\text{lit}(o) \text{ in } vp\text{-}s_f)) \land$

    $((\neg\text{pl}(o) \text{ in } vp\text{-}s_i) \Rightarrow ((\text{lit}(o) \text{ in } vp\text{-}s_i) \Leftrightarrow (\text{lit}(o) \text{ in } vp\text{-}s_f))$

    Action of turning on the oven: what changes.

2b. $\forall\, a\, o\, s_i\, s_f .\ EV(do(a, \text{light}(o)), s_i, s_f) \Rightarrow$

    $\forall\, f .\ SAF(f) \land (\neg(f = \text{'lit}(o)\text{'}) \Rightarrow ((f \text{ in } vp\text{-}s_i) \Leftrightarrow (f \text{ in } vp\text{-}s_f))$

    Action of turning on the oven: what does not change.

The frame axiom, 2b, closely follows the axiomatization in [Konolige, 1982] since the aim is not to offer new insights or contributions to the axiomatization of events or to the frame problem.

Initial conditions:

3. $(\text{at}(A, O) \land \neg\text{lit}(O)) \text{ in } A\text{-}S_0) \land ((\text{at}(A, O) \land \neg\text{lit}(O)) \text{ in } vp\text{-}S_0)$

    A knows in S_0 that he is at the oven and that the oven is not lit.

4. $(EV(do(A, \text{light}(O)), S_0, S_1) \text{ in } A\text{-}S_1) \land (EV(do(A, \text{light}(O)), S_0, S_1) \text{ in } vp\text{-}S_1)$

    A knows in S_1 that the action of lighting the oven in S_0 brings to situation S_1

Agent A can observe whether or not the oven is lit in S_1; the proof goes as follows:

5. EV(do(A, light(O)), S_0, S_1)

6. $\forall$ f . SAF(f) $\wedge \neg$(f = 'lit(O)') $\Rightarrow$ ((f in vp-S_0) $\Leftrightarrow$ (f in vp-S_1))   ($\forall$E, $\Rightarrow$E: 2b, 5)

7. (at(A, O) in vp-S_0)   ($\wedge$E: 3)

8. (at(A, O) in vp-S_1)   ($\forall$E with f = 'at(A, O)', $\Rightarrow$E: 6, 7)

9. ((lit(O) in A-S_1) $\wedge$ (lit(O) in vp-S_1)) $\vee$ ((¬lit(O) in A-S_1) $\wedge$ (¬lit(O) in vp-S_1))

                                                                          ($\forall$E, $\Rightarrow$E: 8, 1)

We now proceed to the proof that A in situation S_1 can use the fact that the oven is lit (or not lit) as a test to deduce whether the pilot light was lit (or not lit) in situation S_0. Reasoning by cases, suppose that the second disjunct of 9 holds, i.e. A observes that the oven is not lit:

10. (¬lit(O) in A-S_1)   (assume)

11. (EV(do(A, light(O)), S_0, S_1) in A-S_1)   ($\wedge$E: 4)

12. (2a in A-S_1)   (common knowledge)

13. (((pl(O) in vp-S_0) $\Rightarrow$ (lit(O) in vp-S_1)) in A-S_1)   ($\forall$E, $\Rightarrow$E, proof in context: 12, 11)

14. ((¬(lit(O) in vp-S_1) $\Rightarrow$ ¬(pl(O) in vp-S_0)) in A-S_1)   (counterpositive:13)

15. ((¬lit(O) in vp-S_1) in A-S_1)   (BS0: 10)

16. (¬(lit(O) in vp-S_1) in A-S_1)   (axiom **D** for situations)

17. ((¬(pl(O) in vp-S_0) in A-S_1)   (proof in context: 16, 14)

18. ((¬pl(O) in vp-S_0) in A-S_1)   (weak completeness of situations)

That is, A believes in situation S_1 that the pilot light was not lit in situation S_0. Analogously, by assuming that A can observe that oven is lit in S1, we can prove that A believes in situation S_1 that the pilot light was lit in situation S_0.

With this example our formalization behaves no better and no worse that other formalizations (see for example [Konolige, 1982]), in the sense that it requires the same axioms and roughly the same inference steps. This is not a bad result considering the gain in simplicity and uniformity of the axiomatization.

8. Conclusions and open problems

The ground was set up for a basic theory of viewpoints. The proof theory behaves reasonably well allowing to deduce a weak axiom **T** for viewpoints, namely ('A' in 'vp') $\Rightarrow$ ($vp \Rightarrow A$), which turns out to be useful for beliefs. Positive introspection is not a theorem, due to the restriction imposed on the reflect up rule in order to keep paradoxes out, but it can be safely added as an axiom.

A uniform characterization was provided for beliefs, truth, knowledge and situations in terms of provability in a viewpoint, by imposing additional constraints on the provability notion for specialized viewpoints. The following table summarizes the constraints imposed for belief, truth and situations.

Belief	**Situations**	**Truth**
Positive introspection	*Positive introspection*	*Positive introspection*
Consistency	*Consistency*	*Consistency*
	Weak Completeness	*Weak Completeness*
		Veridicality

The approach was tested with an example taken from the literature; the gas oven test shows how belief and knowledge are combined with situations in our proposal.

Viewpoints, and in particular the fact that two place predicates are used for belief, truth and knowledge, thus allowing to make a fact relative to the set of assumptions used to derived it, proves to be a valid alternative to standard treatments of beliefs, truth and knowledge with only one argument (and in a multi-agent context one belief predicate for each agent); this solution is more expressive in some cases (see axiom **T** for viewpoints, i.e. Theorem 1) and looks promising also for reasoning in an evolving world where beliefs have to be revised.

The ability to refer to a theory implicitly and give properties of the theory through axioms, is fundamental when dealing with theories that are self referential or mutually referential, but is also important for reasoning about situations. For a full treatment of implicit theories, a non standard semantics is required which gives a notion of model also in case of self referential or mutually referential theories. There are reasons to believe that techniques developed for giving semantics to epistemic or non monotonic theories can be exploited in this context. This will be the object of future work.

Acknowledgements

Giuseppe Attardi has contributed most of the ideas behind the present work. I thank Piero Bonatti for the useful and stimulating discussions and for convincing me that a semantic account of viewpoints is possible.

References

Attardi G., Simi M., "Metalanguage and Reasoning across Viewpoints", in *ECAI–84:Advances in Artificial Intelligence*, T. O'Shea (ed.), Elsevier Science Publishers, Amsterdam, 1984,

Attardi G., Simi M., "Reflections about Reflection", in Allen, J. A., Fikes, R., and Sandewall, E. (eds.) *Principles of Knowledge Representation and Reasoning: Proceedings of the Second International Conference.* San Mateo, CA: Morgan Kaufmann, 1991.

Bowen K.A., Kowalski R.A., "Amalgamating Language and Metalanguage in Logic Programming", in *Logic Programming*, K. Clark and S. Tarnlund (eds.), Academic Press, 1982, 153–172.

Davies N., "Towards a First Order Theory of Reasoning Agents, *Proc. of 9th European Conference on Artificial Intelligence*, Stockholm, 1990, 195-200.

Konolige K., "A First–order Formalization of Knowledge and Action for a Multi–agent Planning System", *Machine Intelligence* 10, 1982.

McCarthy J., "First Order Theories of Individual Concepts and Propositions", *Machine Intelligence* 9, 1979, 129–147.

Montague R., "Syntactical Treatment of Modalities, with Corollaries on Reflexion Principles and Finite Axiomatizability", *Acta Philosoph. Fennica*, (16), 1963, 153–167.

Moore R. C., "Reasoning about Knowledge and Action", Proc. of IJCAI–77, Cambridge, MA, 1977, 223–227.

Perlis D., "Languages with Self–Reference I: Foundations", *Artificial Intelligence*, (25), 1985, 301–322.

Turner R., "Truth and Modality for Knowledge Representation", Pitman Press, London, 1989.

AUTOMATING META-THEORY CREATION AND SYSTEM EXTENSION

David Basin*   Fausto Giunchiglia†   Paolo Traverso‡

Abstract

In this paper we describe a first experiment with a new approach for building theorem provers that can formalize themselves, reason about themselves, and safely extend themselves with new inference procedures. Within the GETFOL system we have built a pair of functions that operate between the system's implementation and a theory about this implementation. The first function *lifts* the actual inference rules to axioms that comprise a theory of GETFOL's inference capabilities. This allows us to turn the prover upon itself whereby we may formally reason about its inference rules and derive new rules. The second function *flattens* new rules back into the underlying system. This provides a novel means of safe system self-extension and an efficient way of executing derived rules.

1 Introduction

Theorem proving systems are generally viewed as static systems or black boxes. One cares not how the underlying rules are implemented, but only that they mimic the inference rules of some desired logic and that they only allow valid formulas to be proven. The focus of this paper is a new approach to automating meta-theory creation and extension in which the black box is opened and the actual implementation of a theorem prover (GETFOL [GT91a]) provides the basis for a formal theory about the prover, a *theory of implementation*.

There are many possible theories of implementation; for example, theories of inference, theories of syntax, and theories of binding. Each corresponds to the axiomatization of a specific part of the underlying system. The previous examples correspond respectively to axiomatizing the procedures that specify the prover's inference rules, term structure, and variable binding. Which theory is formalized determines the kind of theorems one can prove about the system.

In this paper, we formalize a theory of inference where axioms are provided to reason about the system's inference rules. Within the GETFOL system we have built a pair of functions that operate between the system's implementation of inference rules and a theory about this implementation. The first function *lifts* the actual inference rules to axioms that comprise a theory of GETFOL's inference capabilities. The second function *flattens* derived rules back into the underlying system. Within the formalized theory we can turn the prover upon itself, formally reason about its inference rules, and derive new rules. By this means, we may derive any inference rule that corresponds to some finite application of primitive rules. These derived rules are similar to the class of inference rules derivable in Paulson's Isabelle system [Pau89]. And as in Isabelle, we have a guarantee of correctness.

This process of lifting, proving, and flattening, is illustrated in Figure 1. The lifting step

---
*DAI, U. of Edinburgh, EH1 1HN, Scotland. (basin@aipna.ed.ac.uk)
†IRST and DIST, U. of Genoa, Via Opera Pia 11A, Genova, Italy. (fausto%irst@uunet.uu.net)
‡IRST, Povo, 38100 Trento, Italy. (leaf%irst@uunet.uu.net)

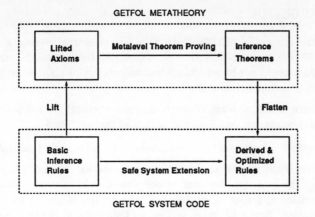

Figure 1: Lifting and Flattening Cycle

builds the metatheory from scratch. Deduction in the metatheory generates theorems about the inference rules. Compilation down expands the system, adding new code that implements the new derived rules. This cycle may be iterated; successive iterations may use rules derived on previous rounds either as inference rules or as axioms to derive further inference rules in the current theory of inference.

This approach provides a foundation for self-reasoning and self-extension. In addition, it can provide considerable efficiency advantages, both intellectual and computational. First, new derived inference rules can be used to shorten subsequent proofs. Second, derived rules may be applied without the overhead of reflection; their flattened images are executed as compiled code like the rest of the system. Third, logical manipulation at the theory level corresponds to program transformation at the system level; hence, the system may be safely optimized via logical manipulation. For example, logical manipulations that shorten the length of a rule or replace functions with simpler counterparts will generally compile to a faster executing rule. Finally, our rules explicitly represent the proof tree data-structure and this allows us to perform optimization in the meta-theory via partial evaluation. We shall later provide examples of such optimizations.

Our paper is organized as follows. Section 2 provides background on GETFOL and indicates the central role of this system in creating a theory of inference. Section 3 describes lifting, the process of automatically generating a theory of the implementation from the implementation. Section 4 shows how new inference rules can be derived in this theory. Section 5 explains flattening, the dual of lifting, whereby new rules are compiled down into the underlying Lisp system and indicates why the entire lifting/deriving/flattening process preserves theorem-hood in GETFOL. Section 6 demonstrates how logical manipulation at the theory level corresponds to function transformation and optimization at the system level. In Section 7, some related work is considered, and in the final section, we draw conclusions and indicate directions for further research.

2 The Role of GETFOL

Our work occurs in the context of GETFOL [GT91a] a reimplementation and extension of the FOL system [Wey80]. GETFOL was carefully coded[1] to facilitate the automatic axiomatization of parts of the system. This would not be possible for an ordinary implementation; we believe that systems of the kind we propose require that

1. the actual inference procedures are coded in a manner whereby these procedures can be given a declarative axiomatic reading (*e.g.*, a clausal manner); and

2. these procedures directly construct and manipulate the actual proof data-structure.

The first point is necessary if we are to be able to generate axioms automatically from the implementation itself. The second is required as our objective is to reason about and modify the GETFOL implementation and control strategy without having to reason about or modify a layer of meta-interpretation. In the following section we indicate that the inference functions of GETFOL do meet these criteria.

These system design requirements, so central to our approach, are non-trivial to achieve simultaneously, although individually each is easily achieved. For example, if GETFOL had been implemented in a pure logic programming language (not Prolog!), the first objective could be satisfied but not the second. On the other hand, one may write inference rules that directly construct and modify proof trees, but considerable care must be taken if these routines are to be automatically axiomatizable. Hence, much care was taken to design GETFOL to not only have proper extensional properties (*i.e.*, the inference rules compute the right proof data structures) but to have these intensional properties as well. After this, the definition and implementation of the lifting and flattening functions was relatively simple.

3 Lifting

```
<C-RULE>  ::=  (DEFLAM <NAME> (<VAR> ...  <VAR>) (IF <C-PROP> <C-PROP>))
<C-PROP>  ::=  (AND <C-PROP> <C-PROP>) |
               (<PRED-CONSTANT> <C-TERM> ...  <C-TERM>)
<C-TERM>  ::=  <VAR> | (<FUNC-CONSTANT> <C-TERM> ...  <C-TERM>)
```

Figure 2: Grammar for Lisp Subset

GETFOL allows the definition of multiple distinct first-order theories, each a Natural Deduction calculus [Pra65]. In this section we describe how we automatically create a theory of inference corresponding to the GETFOL implementation. We proceed as follows. First, we circumscribe the subset of Lisp that liftable GETFOL procedures must be written in; it corresponds to a clausal language. All GETFOL inference rule procedures have been written in this Lisp subset. Second, we define the lifting function as a family of functions that maps programs written in the Lisp subset to axioms in a formal theory. Our description will be brief as these mappings are fairly direct. One subtlety we address is that the procedural distinction between *determining if* a formula holds and *asserting that* a formula holds under assumptions collapse declaratively when there is no notion of execution and evaluation order. Hence, these concepts must be collapsed at the theory level.[2] We conclude with an example.

---

[1]GETFOL was written in a Lisp-like functional language GET. The details of the implementation and the semantics of GET are hinted in [GT91b] but are not relevant here. We will subsequently speak as if Lisp were the implementation language.

[2]Note that this procedural/declarative distinction would be confused in a (semi-)declarative language such as Prolog where one augmented the proof database using the procedural predicate ASSERT.

Figure 2 defines our axiomatizable Lisp subset. Some explanations are in order. `DEFLAM` is the equivalent of Lisp's `DEFUN` and starts a function definition. The `NAME` of a function is a unique (from other function names) character string. Similarly, declared variables (members of `VAR`) must also be unique strings. Variable occurrences in functions are restricted to these named variables. We have not further specified the `PRED-CONSTANT`, and `FUNC-CONSTANT` syntactic categories. These may be any predicate (functions returning `TRUE` or `FALSE`) or function defined in the underlying code. Also not explicitly mentioned is that each such symbol has an associated arity and the number of arguments to which it is applied must respect its arity. Constants are considered to be 0-ary functions. Finally, although only the propositional connective `AND` is used in our current work, others may be easily added.

```
(DEFLAM impe-rule (fact1 fact2 )
  (IF (AND (AND (IS-FACT fact1) (IS-FACT fact2))
       (HYP-OF fact1 fact2))
          (proof-add-theorem (impe fact1 fact2))))

(DEFLAM alli-rule (fact v1 v2)
  (IF (AND (AND (IS-FACT fact) (AND (IS-VAR v1) (IS-VAR v2)))
       (NO-FREE v2 fact))
          (proof-add-theorem (alli fact v1 v2)))))
```

Figure 3: Implication Elimination and All Introduction

For example, Figure 3 contains the code that implements the following Natural Deduction inference rules.

$$\supset E \quad \frac{A \quad A \supset B}{B} \qquad \forall I \quad \frac{A(v_1)}{\forall v_2 A(v_2)} \tag{1}$$

Here `IS-FACT` is a function that evaluates to `TRUE` when its argument is a hypothesis in the current deduction. A *fact* in `GETFOL` is the analogue of a theorem under assumptions. `HYP-OF` evaluates to true when its second argument is a formula whose main symbol is implication and the implicand matches `HYP-OF`'s first argument. `NO-FREE` checks the restriction required by Natural Deduction on $\forall I$. The function `proof-add-theorem` augments the current deduction with a new fact.

Our translation of a program in this language into first order logic is a direct encoding (in Lisp) of the functions recursively defined in Figure 4. In our presentation of these rules the expressions *name*, p_i, f, P, v, and t_i are meta-variables ranging over the syntactic categories `NAME`, `C-PROP`, `FUNC-CONSTANT`, `PRED-CONSTANT`, `VAR`, and `C-TERM` respectively. `T` is a distinct uninterpreted predicate symbol (*i.e.* we assume that there is no system function "T") and signifies the truth of a fact.

The one complication in lifting is that we wish to collapse the distinction between `IS-FACT` and `proof-add-theorem` at the theory level (we map them both to `T`) and restore the distinction upon flattening. To accomplish this we insist that `IS-FACT` only appears on the left hand side of the implication and `proof-add-theorem` on on the right. This is reasonable because in the underlying system the former would never be executed except as precondition to an inference rule and the later is a procedure which would only be executed for its effects. This slightly complicates our lifting and flattening functions though, as we must have both $\mathcal{L}_{prop_l}$ and $\mathcal{L}_{prop_r}$ functions to keep track of which "side" of the implication we are lifting.

As we are describing a theory of inference, all other function symbols and predicate symbols occurring in the lifted inference are uninterpreted; they lift to uninterpreted function and predicate symbols (of the same name) and flatten back down to themselves. It may not be obvious

$$\mathcal{L}_{rule}(\text{DEFLAM } name \ (V_1, ..., V_n) \ (\text{IF } p_1 \ p_2)) =$$
$$\text{axiom } name: \ \forall V_1 ... \forall V_n \ \mathcal{L}_{prop_l}(p_1) \supset \mathcal{L}_{prop_r}(p_2)$$

$$\begin{aligned}
\mathcal{L}_{prop_l}((\text{AND } p_1 \ p_2)) &= \mathcal{L}_{prop_l}(p_1) \wedge \mathcal{L}_{prop_l}(p_2) \\
\mathcal{L}_{prop_l}((\text{IS-FACT } t)) &= \text{T}(\mathcal{L}_{term}(t)) \\
\mathcal{L}_{prop_l}((P \ t_1 \ ... \ t_n)) &= P(\mathcal{L}_{term}(t_1), ..., \mathcal{L}_{term}(t_n)) \\
&\quad for \ P \neq \text{proof-add-theorem}
\end{aligned}$$

$$\begin{aligned}
\mathcal{L}_{prop_r}((\text{AND } p_1 \ p_2)) &= \mathcal{L}_{prop_r}(p_1) \wedge \mathcal{L}_{prop_r}(p_2) \\
\mathcal{L}_{prop_r}((\text{proof-add-theorem } t)) &= \text{T}(\mathcal{L}_{term}(t)) \\
\mathcal{L}_{prop_r}((P \ t_1 \ ... \ t_n)) &= P(\mathcal{L}_{term}(t_1), ..., \mathcal{L}_{term}(t_n)) \\
&\quad for \ P \neq \text{IS-FACT}
\end{aligned}$$

$$\begin{aligned}
\mathcal{L}_{term}(v) &= v \\
\mathcal{L}_{term}((f \ t_1 \ ... \ t_n)) &= f(\mathcal{L}_{term}(t_1), ..., \mathcal{L}_{term}(t_n))
\end{aligned}$$

Figure 4: Lifting Functions

that one can effectively reason about these inference rules without further interpretation (*e.g.*, theories of syntax, variable binding, and the like). This concern is addressed in the next section.

```
axiom impe-rule:
```
$$\forall f_1 \forall f_2 (T(f_1) \wedge T(f_2) \wedge \text{HYP-OF}(f_1, f_2)) \supset T(\text{impe}(f_1, f_2)))$$
```
axiom alli-rule:
```
$$\forall f \forall v_1 \forall v_2 (T(f) \wedge \text{IS-VAR}(v_1) \wedge \text{IS-VAR}(v_2) \wedge \text{NO-FREE}(v_2, f)) \supset T(\text{alli}(f, v_1, v_2)))$$

Figure 5: Translation of $\supset E$ and $\forall I$ Rules

Returning to our example, applying $\mathcal{L}_{rule}$ to the $\supset E$ and $\forall I$ inference rules given in Figure 3 yields the axioms given in Figure 5. Note that the actual code implementing $\mathcal{L}_{rule}$ has to generate automatically the appropriate signature (*e.g.*, sort declarations for the relevant syntactic entities). We do not describe this process as it is straightforward.

The lifting function automatically generates axioms that comprise the meta-theory of GETFOL inference capabilities. We will address the correctness of this procedure after our discussion of flattening in Section 5.

4 Self Reasoning

In [GT90] it is explained how to combine axioms and prove theorems which may be used as new derived rules. To make the paper self contained, we will illustrate self reasoning with a rather simple example: proving that C follows from A, $A \supset B$, and $A \supset (B \supset C)$. The Natural Deduction proof is as follows.

$$\supset E \frac{\supset E \dfrac{A \quad A \supset B}{B} \quad \supset E \dfrac{A \quad A \supset (B \supset C)}{B \supset C}}{C} \tag{2}$$

We can derive this new rule within our GETFOL theory of inference from our axiom impe-rule (Figure 5) in the following way. Let a_1, a_2, and a_3 be free variables ranging over facts. Performing $\forall Es$ on the impe-rule axiom with a_1 and a_2 and again with a_1 and a_3 yields the following formulas.

$$T(a_1) \wedge T(a_2) \wedge \text{HYP-OF}(a_1, a_2) \supset T(\text{impe}(a_1, a_2)) \tag{3}$$

$$T(a_1) \wedge T(a_3) \wedge \text{HYP-OF}(a_1, a_3) \supset T(\text{impe}(a_1, a_3)) \tag{4}$$

Instantiating `impe-rule` again, this time with `impe(a_1, a_2)` and `impe(a_1, a_3)` yields

$$
\begin{aligned}
&T(\text{impe}(a_1, a_2)) \wedge T(\text{impe}(a_1, a_3)) \wedge \text{HYP-OF}(\text{impe}(a_1, a_2), \text{impe}(a_1, a_3)) \\
&\supset T(\text{impe}(\text{impe}(a_1, a_2), \text{impe}(a_1, a_3)))
\end{aligned}
\tag{5}
$$

Notice that the conclusions of Equations 3 and 4 match conjuncts in the hypothesis of Equation 5. Hence, a bit of manipulation will yield the formula

$$
\begin{aligned}
&(T(a_1) \wedge T(a_2) \wedge \text{HYP-OF}(a_1, a_2) \wedge T(a_1) \wedge T(a_3) \wedge \\
&\text{HYP-OF}(a_1, a_3) \wedge \text{HYP-OF}(\text{impe}(a_1, a_2), \text{impe}(a_1, a_3))) \\
&\supset T(\text{impe}(\text{impe}(a_1, a_2), \text{impe}(a_1, a_3)))
\end{aligned}
\tag{6}
$$

Finally, applying $\forall I$ completes the GETFOL derivation

$$
\begin{aligned}
&\forall f_1 \forall f_2 \forall f_3((T(f_1) \wedge T(f_2) \wedge \text{HYP-OF}(f_1, f_2) \wedge T(f_1) \wedge T(f_3) \wedge \\
&\text{HYP-OF}(f_1, f_3) \wedge \text{HYP-OF}(\text{impe}(f_1, f_2), \text{impe}(f_1, f_3))) \\
&\supset T(\text{impe}(\text{impe}(f_1, f_2), \text{impe}(f_1, f_3))))
\end{aligned}
\tag{7}
$$

This new derived inference rule may be used in subsequent proofs in the meta-theory. In the following section we show how it can be flattened back into GETFOL's Lisp source and used directly by the system for proofs in all theories.

5 Flattening

Flattening is the process of compiling formulas derived in the particular theory of implementation back down into GETFOL's Lisp source. It is the dual of lifting and the flattening functions are essentially inverses of their lifting counterparts.[3]

```
<T-RULE>  ::=  ∀ <VAR> ...  ∀ <VAR> (<T-PROP> ⊃ <T-PROP>)
<T-PROP>  ::=  (<T-PROP> ∧ <T-PROP>) |
              <PRED-CONSTANT>(<T-TERM>, ..., <T-TERM>)
<T-TERM>  ::=  <VAR> | <FUNC-CONSTANT>(<T-TERM>, ..., <T-TERM>)
```

Figure 6: Grammar for Formula Subset

Not all formulas have procedural equivalents. The grammar describing the subset of formulas that we flatten is given in Figure 6. This grammar is the dual of the Lisp subset grammar: there is an isomorphism between the syntactic categories C-RULE, C-PROP, and C-TERM, with their theory equivalents T-RULE, T-PROP, and T-TERM. Lifting, like flattening, is straightforward; the only complication is that flattening must reestablish the distinction between IS-FACT and proof-add-theorem at the source level.

Since the flattening functions given in Figure 7 are dual to the lifting functions, then if we were to flatten axioms such as `impe-rule` and `alli-rule` given in Figure 5, we would end up where we started: with their implementation given in Figure 3. By flattening derived rules, we extend the system with new procedures. Flattening Equation 7 and naming the result `impe-3` augments the system with the inference procedure given in Figure 8. Furthermore, if *name*

---

[3]Not quite as the formula flattening function must take an additional argument that provides a name for the function corresponding to the flattened formula.

$$\mathcal{F}_{rule}(\forall V_1...\forall V_n(p_1 \supset p_2)(name) =$$
$$(\texttt{DEFLAM } name \ (V_1...V_n) \ (\texttt{IF } \mathcal{F}_{prop_l}(p_1) \ \mathcal{F}_{prop_r}(p_2))$$

$$
\begin{aligned}
\mathcal{F}_{prop_l}(p_1 \wedge p_2) &= (\texttt{AND } \mathcal{F}_{prop_l}(p_1) \ \mathcal{F}_{prop_l}(p_2)) \\
\mathcal{F}_{prop_l}(T(t)) &= (\texttt{IS-FACT } \mathcal{F}_{term}(t)) \\
\mathcal{F}_{prop_l}(P(t_1,...,t_n)) &= (P \ \mathcal{F}_{term}(t_1) \ ... \ \mathcal{F}_{term}(t_n)) \\
&= \text{for } P \neq T
\end{aligned}
$$

$$
\begin{aligned}
\mathcal{F}_{prop_r}(p_1 \wedge p_2) &= (\texttt{AND } \mathcal{F}_{prop_r}(p_1) \ \mathcal{F}_{prop_r}(p_2)) \\
\mathcal{F}_{prop_r}(T(t)) &= (\texttt{proof-add-theorem } \mathcal{F}_{term}(t)) \\
\mathcal{F}_{prop_r}(P(t_1,...,t_n)) &= (P \ \mathcal{F}_{term}(t_1) \ ... \ \mathcal{F}_{term}(t_n)) \\
&= \text{for } P \neq T
\end{aligned}
$$

$$
\begin{aligned}
\mathcal{F}_{term}(v) &= v \\
\mathcal{F}_{term}(f(t_1,...,t_n)) &= (f \ \mathcal{F}_{term}(t_1) \ ... \ \mathcal{F}_{term}(t_n))
\end{aligned}
$$

Figure 7: Flattening Functions

```
(DEFLAM impe-3 (f1 f2 f3)
 (IF (AND (AND (IS-FACT f1) (AND (IS-FACT f2)
     (AND (HYP-OF f1 f2) (AND (IS-FACT f1) (AND (IS-FACT f3)
     (AND (HYP-OF f1 f3) (AND (HYP-OF (impe f1 f2) (impe f1 f3)))))))))))
        (proof-add-theorem (impe (impe f1 f2) (impe f1 f3)))))
```

Figure 8: Flattening of Derived Rule

refers to an already defined system function, then flattening $\mathcal{F}_{rule}(\forall V_1...\forall V_n(h \supset c)(name)$, modifies the system, replacing *name*, with the new flattened function. This provides a means for self-modification in addition to self-expansion.

Of course it is important to know that any such modifications to the prover are correct. That is, we must know that whenever $\forall V_1...\forall V_n(p_1 \supset p_2)$ is a theorem then extending GETFOL with $\mathcal{F}_{rule}(\forall V_1...\forall V_n(p_1 \supset p_2))$ will not allow the theorem prover to derive any new theorems in any theory it is applied to. This correctness requirement is stated formally and proved in [GT91b]. The proof proceeds by induction on the complexity of the theorem proved in the meta-theory; the various proof cases demonstrate that generated preconditions map down to tests which guarantee that the derived inference rule only proves theorems that would be provable directly using primitive inference rules.

6 Optimization

There may exist many logically equivalent formulas that flatten to procedurally distinct derived inference rules. The procedural distinction between two rules being not that they implement different inference functions (*i.e.*, generating different conclusions from identical premises), but rather their execution efficiency. The correctness of the optimized rules is a trivial consequence of the correctness of the original ones.

The simplest and most direct example of this is logical simplification. Section 4 provides such an example; there, several inference rules were combined in GETFOL to form a new rule. However, the combination generated redundant premises. Because both Equations 3 and 4 have $T(a_1)$

7 Related Work

In GETFOL, reasoning about a logic's inference rules provides a means for deriving new rules. This idea also appears, for example, in Isabelle [Pau89], and systems with reflection principles [CAB+86]. In [GT90, GT91b], Giunchiglia and Traverso show how in GETFOL one can build a uniform hierarchy of theories where theorem proving at one level constructs new inference rules which can be used via a reflection rule at a lower level. In this report, we demonstrated that, by inverting the lifting process, we can safely flatten new derived rules back down into the underlying system. The result is that reflection principles are not required to use these new rules. Hence, our approach is very general.

We have already indicated how our work differs from those working with logic programming meta-interpreters. That is, these system have fixed control strategies that are difficult to reason about and impossible to modify; the underlying Prolog system must be treated as a black box. More closely is the work of Smith [Smi83] who defines a tower of meta-circular Lisp interpreters where modifying the description of a "Lisp processor" at one level can alter the execution of Lisp functions at lower levels. The linkage between the levels is provided by a principle of *procedural reflection*. In contrast, through our lifting and flattening functions, we do not require any kind of reflection principles nor a hierarchy of theories. Moreover, our meta-language is declarative and the "programs" which control proof-search are derived via logical deduction in a formal theory.

Within the theorem proving community, perhaps the work of Boyer and Moore on metafunctions [BM81] most closely resembles our work. In the setting of their inductive theorem prover, users can augment the system by coding term-rewriting functions in Lisp. After proving that these functions essentially preserve the "meaning" of terms, the functions become integrated into the prover and used for subsequent term simplification. Unlike our work, their system extension are effected by explicitly coded procedures as opposed to declarative reasoning about the representation of the underlying system. Their work also takes place within a rather limited logic (quantifier free first-order logic) although they may use induction principles to reason about defined functions.

8 Conclusions and Extensions

We have demonstrated how within the GETFOL theorem prover we can automatically generate a meta-theory for parts of the implementation and use this theory to safely extend GETFOL with derived meta-theoretic rules. This approach is rather general and does not involve reflection or other features of GETFOL.

Our work serves as the starting point for a deeper examination of theories of implementation. As we only lift inference rules, the kind of derived rules we can formalize and prove is limited. For example, the theorem suggested in Weyhrauch [Wey80] — a formula made up of sentential variables and the if-and-only-if connective is valid if and only if each sentential variable occurs an even number of times — would require an additional theory of syntax with appropriate induction principles.

We have recently begun to examine extensions that allow theorems like Weyhrauch's to be proven. One possibility is to use type information given in the implementation to axiomatize induction principles. For example, a type of recursively defined formulas naturally gives rise to a structural induction principle for formulas. This possibility is sketched in [BGT91] and is the subject of a forthcoming research report. We believe that such additions will enable us to extend our theories of implementation to reason about a very large class of recursive functions that should include powerful term simplifiers and decision procedures.

as a premise, in Equation 6, $T(a_1)$ occurs twice. However as conjunction ($\wedge$) is an associative and commutative propositional connective, and for all propositions A, $(A \wedge A) \supset A$, we can eliminate the second occurrence of $T(a_1)$ in this equation. Such a simplified formula would flatten into a function identical to the one given in Figure 8, except there would be only one call to (IS-FACT f1) instead of two. Hence each application of this rule would execute faster. Furthermore, by partially axiomatizing syntactic functions, such as HYP-OF or IS-FREE, more elaborate simplification is possible by reasoning about the relationships between hypotheses.

A more complex and interesting kind of optimization is possible based on transforming the proof-structure component of derived inference rules to a direct syntactic representation of the inference function computed. Specifically, given the structure of primitive inference rules and the way that inference rules are combined into new rules, each rule amounts to a series of tests or preconditions followed by a term that constructs a new proof node (fact) as a function of some encoded proof. For example, the inference function given in Figure 8 directly encodes the proof given in Equation 2. While this construction enables us to reason about the structure of proofs at the meta-level, it can result in slowly executing code as the inference rule must mimic the proof structure in computing the new proof-node. The alternative is to replace the encoded proof-function with a direct syntactic representation of the resulting proof-node. This syntactic representation is similar to those used in systems such as Isabelle. As a simple example, consider the impe-3 rule given in Figure 8 (flattened from the formula given in (7)). Its syntactic representation is

$$
\begin{aligned}
\forall f_1 \forall f_2 \forall f_3 (T(f_1) &\wedge T(f_2) \wedge T(f_3) \wedge \\
\text{HYP-OF}(f_1, f_2) &\wedge \text{HYP-OF}(f_1, f_3) \wedge \\
\text{concl}(\text{wff-of}(f_2)) &= \text{hyp}(\text{concl}(\text{wff-of}(f_3))) \\
&\supset T(\text{mkfact}(\text{concl}(\text{concl}(\text{wff-of}(f_3))), \text{dep3}(f_1, f_2, f_3))))
\end{aligned}
\tag{8}
$$

where mkfact(wff, dep) builds a proof-node, *i.e.*, a formula with the assumptions it depends on, concl and hyp take the conclusion and hypothesis of their formula arguments, wff-of($fact$) takes the formula of a fact, and dep3(f_1, f_2, f_3) builds the union of the assumptions that f_1 f_2 and f_3 depend on.

Complex derived rules can be represented in this way and the representation is independent of how they were proved. That is, all the distinct deductions with the same root and leaves correspond to a unique syntactic representation. Generally, the longer the deduction based representation, the more effective the optimization is. Many more factors not described here contribute to making this operation more or less effective; some of them are: the sequence of rule applications, how introduction and elimination rules intermix, the presence of redundant steps (maximal segments [Pra65]) and so on.

These optimized syntactic inference rules can be derived in the metatheory using the appropriate axioms [GT90]. *E.g.*,

$$
\begin{aligned}
\forall f_1 \forall f_2 (\text{wff-of}(\text{impe}(f_1, f_2)) &= \text{concl}(\text{wff-of}(f_2))) \\
\forall f_1 \forall f_2 (\text{dep-of}(\text{impe}(f_1, f_2)) &= \text{dep2}(f_1, f_2))
\end{aligned}
\tag{9}
$$

and others. Here dep-of($fact$) takes the assumptions the fact depends on and dep2(f_1, f_2) builds the union of the assumptions that f_1 and f_2 depend on.

A very effective way to obtain these optimized representations is by partial evaluation using the GETFOL semantic simplifier [GT91a], which is similar to the old FOL's simplifier [Wey80]. Unfortunately a further discussion of optimization via partial evaluation is beyond the scope of this paper.

References

[BGT91]   D. Basin, F. Giunchiglia, and P. Traverso. Meta-theory as the dual of system imple-
          mentation. Technical Report 9103-015, IRST, Trento, Italy, 1991.

[BM81]   R.S. Boyer and J.S. Moore. Metafunctions: proving them correct and using them
          efficiently as new proof procedures. In R.S. Boyer and J.S. Moore, editors, *The
          correctness problem in computer science*, pages 103–184. Academic Press, 1981.

[CAB+86] R.L. Constable, S.F. Allen, H.M. Bromley, et al. *Implementing Mathematics with
          the NuPRL Proof Development System*. Prentice Hall, 1986.

[GT90]   F. Giunchiglia and P. Traverso. Plan formation and execution in an uniform archi-
          tecture of declarative metatheories. In M. Bruynooghe, editor, *Proc. Workshop on
          Meta-Programming in Logic*, 1990. Also available as IRST Technical Report 9003-12.

[GT91a]   F. Giunchiglia and P. Traverso. GETFOL User Manual - version 1 release 1. Technical
          report, IRST, Trento, Italy, 1991.

[GT91b]   F. Giunchiglia and P. Traverso. Reflective reasoning with and between a declarative
          metatheory and the implementation code. In *Proceedings of the International Joint
          Conference in Artificial Intelligenge (IJCAI)*, 1991. Also IRST-Technical Report no.
          9012-03.

[Pau89]   L. Paulson. The fundation of a generic theorem prover. *Journal of Automated
          Reasoning*, 5:363–396, 1989.

[Pra65]   D. Prawitz. *Natural Deduction - A proof theoretical study*. Almquist and Wiksell,
          Stockholm, 1965.

[Smi83]   B.C. Smith. Reflection and Sematincs in LISP. In *Proc. 11th ACM POPL*, pages
          23–35, 1983.

[Wey80]   R.W. Weyhrauch. Prolegomena to a theory of Mechanized Formal Reasoning. *Arti-
          ficial Intelligence. Special Issue on Non-monotonic Logic*, 13(1), 1980.

Implementing Exceptions in Inheritance by Concept Transforming Actions

Bertram Fronhöfer

Institut für Informatik, Technische Universität München
Arcisstr. 21, Postfach 202420, D-8000 München 2

ABSTRACT

The paper presents a method for handling exceptions in inheritance of properties from concepts to subconcepts, combined with a sorted logic which allows to express *conceptual* information about objects. To this end we split up our universe, and consequently our language, into an *imaginary* part which deals with stereotypic properties of concepts and a *real* part which comprises the concrete properties of (sorted) objects. To model the *imaginary* part we use a modal logic framework of actions which implement the transitions from concepts to subconcepts. To model the *real* part we use a functional framework for reasoning about sorts. To each concept in the *imaginary* part corresponds a sort in the *real* part and vice versa. Property inheritance processes will be (easy) plan generation tasks which take place in the *imaginary* part. Due to the *non-monotonicity* of reasoning about plans, not all properties of a concept are passed on to its subconcepts, i.e. the subconcept *overrides* the superconcept, and consequently, the handling of exceptions in inheritance can be achieved. On the other hand properties can be passed along the sort hierarchy from subsorts to supersorts. In this process no exceptions will occur. Both parts—the *imaginary* and the *real* one—are connected by information specifying for an object its most specific sort membership. This information allows to transport properties of the respective concept from the *imaginary* to the *real* part. Finally, in order to avoid the frame problem in the plan generation processes, the linear proof calculus is chosen as a vehicle for the concept transforming actions.

INTRODUCTION

In [CF88], [Fur89] and [FH89] a technique was proposed which expresses sorts as functions and results in a sort-handling theorem prover through a function handling during unification. It was also shown that inheritance of properties can be implemented easily on this basis, being basically performed by suitable instantiation of formulae. This means that reasoning about concept hierarchies—as required for the implementation of knowledge-based systems—can be carried out with a theorem prover which is also able to handle functions.

However, this approach was not apt to cope with exceptions in the inheritance of properties.

In the present paper we will modify and extend this approach to cover exception handling as well.

- In the first section we review inheritance of properties along functionally represented concept hierarchies—as developed in [CF88], [Fur89] and [FH89]. We will show in particular, how inheritance without exceptions works in this framework, and why inheritance with exceptions is not possible.

- The second section explains the general setting of our approach to coping with exceptions, which consists of a duality between a hierarchy of concepts and an isomorphic hierarchy of sorts.

- The third section presents the relationship between concepts and subconcepts by concept transforming actions, and how we can use this representation to deal with exceptions in property inheritance.
- The fourth section extends the inheritance from (unary) properties to binary relations, so-called roles.
- The fifth section discusses implementational issues.

To avoid misunderstandings, note that in this paper we will not treat the handling of exceptions within a hierarchy of (unstructured) concepts, as e.g. in Touretzky's work on *inferential distance ordering* (see [Tou86]). We will only consider exceptions in the inheritance of properties, as it is found, for instance, in frame systems: the (structured) concepts there are called frames, while properties are usually called slots (see e.g. FLAVORS [Sym85]). In [Tou86] systems of the second type are called *class/property inheritance systems*.

1 Review of Inheritance along Functionally Represented Concept Hierarchies

In this section we want to illustrate the approach to sort-handling via functions which we mentioned above. This shall be done by help of the following example:

Given two sorts: elephants and mammals, denoted by the function symbols eleph and mammal. Using functions to denote sorts, we write a term like $\text{eleph}(x)$ to express that x is a variable of sort elephant, instead of the common notation of sorts which would be: $x : \text{eleph}$.

Let us assume the following facts, which say that mammals are mortal, that elephants are mammals, and that an individual named clyde is an elephant:

Mammals are mortal:	(i)	$\text{Mortal}(\text{mammal}(x))$
Elephants are mammals:	(ii)	$\text{mammal}(\text{eleph}(x)) = \text{eleph}(x)$
clyde is an elephant:	(iii)	$\text{eleph}(\text{clyde}) = \text{clyde}$

Note that these facts would be expressed in the standard sort notation as:

(1)	$\text{Mortal}(x : \text{mammal})$
(2)	$x : \text{eleph} : \text{mammal} = x : \text{eleph}$
(3)	$\text{clyde} : \text{eleph} = \text{clyde}$

We see that sort information—both that an object appertains to a certain sort or that a sort is a subsort of another—is expressed by equations.

We get through easy reasoning with this formalism that elephants are mortal by inheriting this property from the superclass of mammals: First we instantiate x in (i) by $\text{eleph}(x)$ and get:

$$\text{(iv)} \quad \text{Mortal}(\text{mammal}(\text{eleph}(x)))$$

and then we rewrite the term $\text{mammal}(\text{eleph}(x))$ to $\text{eleph}(x)$ by means of equation (ii), which yields: $\text{Mortal}(\text{eleph}(x))$. Furthermore, by instantiating now x by clyde and making use of (iii) we can get that clyde is mortal, i.e. $\text{Mortal}(\text{clyde})$.

Thus a property of an *elephant object* has been derived by inheritance from the respective property of a superclass.

All would be fine, if there were not these (logically) unpleasant royal elephants which, though being elephants, so obstinately resist to be grey, but prefer to be white, i.e. the fact that royal elephants are an exception in the class of elephants. This cannot be handled in the presented framework where we would get the following axiomatizations of royal elephants:

Royal elephants are elephants:	(v)	$\text{eleph}(\text{roy.eleph}(x)) = \text{roy.eleph}(x)$
and elephants are grey:	(vi)	$\text{Grey}(\text{eleph}(x))$
but royal elephants are not grey:	(vii)	$\neg\text{Grey}(\text{roy.eleph}(x))$

Analogously as above we can deduce by means of (v) and (vi) that royal elephants are grey, i.e. Grey(roy.eleph(x)), which is contradictory to (vii).

To allow for exceptions in this framework of inheritance we would have to restrict the instantiation of variables, e.g. not allowing the variable x to be instantiated to roy.eleph(x), if x is in the context Grey(eleph(x)). However, this seems not to be recommended, because it would profoundly impair the underlying logical calculus.

A way out of this dilemma is, intuitively spoken, to *"turn round the order of functions"* in equations like (ii) and (v). Doing that we get the following equations

$$\text{(ii')} \quad \text{eleph(mammal}(x)) = \text{eleph}(x)$$
$$\text{(v')} \quad \text{roy.eleph(eleph}(x)) = \text{roy.eleph}(x)$$

in order to express that elephants are mammals and that royal elephants are elephants. Now in order to deduce that elephants are mortal, because mammals are, we first have to get *somehow* from

$$\text{(i)} \quad \text{Mortal(mammal}(x)) \quad \text{to} \quad \text{(iv')} \quad \text{Mortal(eleph(mammal}(x)))$$

and then by rewriting with (ii') we get: Mortal(eleph(x))

The interesting novelty is that the step from (i) to (iv')—in contrast to the easy instantiation for getting from (i) to (iv)—needs some additional reasoning feature which is not provided by usual logical calculi. To propose an appropriate definition of this additional reasoning feature is the purpose of this paper. This means that apart from allowing inferences as the one just presented, it must be able to preclude undesirable ones, as for instance those which result in grey royal elephants. We will follow this intuition in the next section for the development of an exception handling mechanism.

2 Stereotypic Properties vs. Real Properties

The idea to cope with the destructive aspects of exceptions in inheritance is to model concept/subconcept relationships by actions, which oriented from the concept to the subconcept may change some of the concept's properties, while most of them are just handed on. The actual properties of an object are then given by the properties of the concept which corresponds to the object's sort. This means, that we have to distinguish clearly between the *imaginary* universe of *concepts* and the *real* world of *concrete objects of certain sorts*. To each concept corresponds a certain sort. To the concepts are attached stereotypic properties, while to an object of a certain sort are attached the object's real properties. The stereotypic properties may change when we pass from a concept to a subconcept, but an object's real properties don't change when we pass from a subsort to a supersort. By calling the universe of concepts an imaginary one, we want to express that for each concept we can imagine that it applies to any arbitrary object, e.g. we can imagine that clyde is an elephant, or a royal elephant or a sailing vessel, independently of what kind of object clyde really is, i.e. independently of clyde's sort. If we imagine clyde as a sailing vessel, it shares all stereotypic properties of sailing vessels, and if we imagine clyde as an elephant, it shares all stereotypic properties of elephants. However, if in reality clyde is an elephant, i.e. its sort is *eleph*, its *real* properties are only those of elephants. The calculus which we will present, allows to derive any imagination about any object, but only allows to derive real information for that imagination which is the true one.

To represent both the real and the imaginary world, we work with a pair of *isomorphic* hierarchies: one of them being a hierarchy of *sorts*, while the other one is a hierarchy of *concepts* describing these sorts through their stereotypic properties. To speak about the concepts we will use modal logic and each concept will be represented by a possible world. In the following we will make use of the Herzig-Ohlbach-Wallen treatment of modal logic (see [Her89], [Ohl88] or [Wal87]). Its computationally interesting idea is the transformation of sequences of modal operators into world-paths which are prefixed to logical symbols like predicates, functions, constants and variables. We will skip this transformation process and notate our formulae directly with world-paths attached to the symbols. (Note that this is basically a somewhat peculiar 1-order logic notation, where one argument of the predicates is prefixed to the predicates and is notated as a list instead of a term. How these lists can be transformed in terms, see [Ohl88].)

We denote the most general of these concepts by 0. (It is the world/concept we start from.) It corresponds to the most general sort $\top$. Given further sorts like *eleph* (elephants) and *roy.eleph* (royal elephants) with *roy.eleph* being a subsort of *eleph*, we have corresponding world access functions, denoted by the symbols eleph and roy.eleph, which refer to the access paths to the worlds which correspond to the respective sorts: the world path [0 eleph] corresponds to the sort *eleph*, while the world path [0 eleph roy.eleph] corresponds to the sort *roy.eleph*.

Starting from the most general sort $\top$ or from the starting world 0, we can enter the respective hierarchies, i.e. we build formulae which use the syntactic tools which we just introduced:

- Entering the sort hierarchy, we speak about *concrete* properties of objects (i.e. constants, terms, etc.). For instance, we can build the term Grey(*eleph*(clyde)) which would mean that clyde (really) is a grey elephant. (Note the functional notation of sorts.)
- Entering the concept hierarchy, we speak about *stereotypic* properties of classes of objects. We would build formulae like [0 eleph]Grey([0 eleph]clyde) which mean that clyde *imagined* as an elephant is grey. (Note that this statement says nothing about clyde's real colour.)

Let us emphasize again that there is a huge pragmatical difference between the two literals Grey(*eleph*(clyde)) and [0 eleph]Grey([0 eleph]clyde) :

- A statement containing a sort (function), e.g. *eleph*, states a *"real"* property about its object, e.g. clyde. This means that the formula Grey(*eleph*(clyde)) must be read as: *"The elephant clyde is (really) grey"*, or "clyde *is a grey elephant"*.
- However, a literal with modal prefixes states an *"imaginary"* property about the involved object. This means that the formula [0 eleph]Grey([0 eleph]clyde) must be read as: *"If clyde were an elephant, then it would be grey"*, or "clyde *imagined as an elephant, would entail the stereotypic properties of elephants, i.e. being grey"*.

Modally annotated predicates refer to imaginary/stereotypic properties. This stereotypic information may change when we pass from a concept to a subconcept, e.g. when we pass from grey elephants to white royal elephants. (These are the so-called exceptions in inheritance.[1]) On the other hand, real concrete information doesn't change when we pass from a subsort to one of its supersorts: *a white royal elephant is also a white elephant.*

This means that we have two directions of information passing

- in the conceptual hierarchy from a concept to a subconcept[2].
- and in the sort hierarchy from a subsort to one of its supersorts.

Note that the first one has exceptions, while the second one hasn't.

From this follows that determining the colour of the (now real) royal elephant clyde is a three-phase process:

(α) We must first establish the stereotypic information about royal elephants. Here we get that they are white, i.e. we get the formula   [0 eleph roy.eleph]White([0 eleph roy.eleph]x).
This reasoning step is carried out in the conceptual/imaginary hierarchy.

(β) We have to transport the stereotypic information deduced in step (α) from the *imaginary world* to the *real world*. This means that we transform it into real information about clyde. We get White(*roy.eleph*(clyde))

(γ) We have to *weaken* this information to some less specific sort indication, i.e. to a supersort, e.g. to White(*eleph*(clyde)) or to White(clyde) saying that clyde is a white elephant or simply that clyde is white.

---

[1]This is also called the principle that subclasses/subconcepts override superclasses/superconcepts. [Bre87] calls it the *specialisation principle*. Sometimes it is also called *cancellation of properties*.

[2]In terms of modal logic it is the hierarchy of worlds given by the accessibility relation between these worlds.

How this reasoning process is carried out in full detail is presented in the next section.

3 Exceptions in Property Inheritance

To express that royal elephants are a subconcept of elephants, we define a concept transforming action which expresses this taxonomic knowledge. The important point is that in contrast to a mere substitution and a rewrite rule on terms—as illustrated in the first section—such an action may have side effects which *discard* certain properties, while creating new ones, when passing from a concept to a subconcept.

(act2) $\forall \tau \, \forall x \, (\, [\tau \, \text{eleph}]\text{Conceiv}([\tau \, \text{eleph}]x) \wedge [\tau \, \text{eleph}]\text{Grey}([\tau \, \text{eleph}]x) \longrightarrow$
$[\tau \, \text{eleph} \, \text{roy.eleph}]\text{Conceiv}([\tau \, \text{eleph} \, \text{roy.eleph}]x)$
$\wedge [\tau \, \text{eleph} \, \text{roy.eleph}]\text{White}([\tau \, \text{eleph} \, \text{roy.eleph}]x) \,)$

This reads intuitively that from the imagination, that x is an elephant, we can go over to the imagination that the elephant x is a royal elephant, *and* during this transition the property Grey will disappear and the new property White will be created.[3]

We can also say that this action expresses an act of mental constitution. If we have an *arbitrary* elephant clyde, this action conceives clyde as a royal elephant; this is an imagination which needs not to be real. That it is real must be expressed by an additional formula which says that the imaginary world [0 eleph roy.eleph] is exactly the world which is relevant for clyde, i.e. that clyde is of sort *roy.eleph*.

This idea of mental constitution of the concept eleph *is also reflected in the* Conceiv-*literals*. They express that a certain concept is *conceivable*, e.g. the concept roy.eleph is conceivable from the concept eleph by means of rule (act2). However, their main importance is a computational one; namely, that they will match respective queries concerning the *conceivability* of certain concepts; thus starting a reasoning process which derives the valid properties for this concept, as will be seen with the example discussed in this section[4]. With the use of this action (and some additional information), we can deduce that the *real* royal elephant clyde is white, which would correspond to the query: White(clyde)

But let us even assume a more general query, asking whether there are white elephants, i.e.

(Q) $\exists x \, \text{White}(eleph(x))$

To prove this query we have to reason along the following lines:

(α) We must show that the class of elephants (or a subclass of them) has the property White. This reasoning step is carried out on the conceptual/imaginary level.

(β) We have to transport the information deduced in step (α) from the *imagination* to the *real world*.

(γ) We have to do some additional reasoning in the real world, i.e. weakening the sort.

For these phases we need the following knowledge:

Phase (α) :
In this phase we want to constitute *imaginations* about objects. The basic fact we need for this process is that every object can be imagined, at least in the world we start from:

(1) $[0]\text{Conceiv}([0]x)$

Moreover, we need to know that normal elephants are grey, which is expressed by the following action:

(act1) $\forall \tau \, \forall x \, (\, [\tau]\text{Conceiv}([\tau]x) \longrightarrow [\tau \, \text{eleph}]\text{Conceiv}([\tau \, \text{eleph}]x) \wedge [\tau \, \text{eleph}]\text{Grey}([\tau \, \text{eleph}]x) \,)$

and that royal elephants are white, which is expressed by the following action:

---

[3]This reading is strongly inspired by linear proofs which have this kind of *rewriting property* on literals (see [Fro91] and section five of this paper).

[4]This technical computational aspect of the Conceiv-literals is also of vital importance for the implementation based on Linear Proofs. We will make some remarks about it in section five.

(act2) $\forall \tau \, \forall x \, \Big(\, [\tau \, \text{eleph}]\text{Conceiv}([\tau \, \text{eleph}]x) \wedge [\tau \, \text{eleph}]\text{Grey}([\tau \, \text{eleph}]x) \longrightarrow$
$[\tau \, \text{eleph roy.eleph}]\text{Conceiv}([\tau \, \text{eleph roy.eleph}]x)$
$\wedge \, [\tau \, \text{eleph roy.eleph}]\text{White}([\tau \, \text{eleph roy.eleph}]x) \, \Big)$

Phase (β) :
In this phase we transport our imaginations into the real world. To this end we need a general rule of transportation[5]:

(2) $\forall x \, \forall \tau \, \forall t \, \forall \mathcal{P} \, \Big(\, \mathcal{P}(t(x)) \longleftarrow t(x) = x \wedge [\tau]\text{Conceiv}([\tau]x) \wedge [\tau]\mathcal{P}([\tau]x) \, \Big)$

On this rule we have to impose the additional condition that the symbol t in $t(x)$ refers to a sort symbol which corresponds to the last world in the world path $[\tau]$.
Moreover, we need the concrete knowledge that clyde is really a royal elephant:

(3) $roy.eleph(\text{clyde}) = \text{clyde}$

The last formula says that clyde is not only conceivable/imaginable as a royal elephant, but that it really is one.

Phase (γ) :
In this phase we propagate knowledge in the real world, e.g. if clyde is a white royal elephant, then it is also a white elephant. This is done with the following *weakening* rule:

(4) $\forall y \, (roy.eleph(y) \rightarrow eleph(y))$

Now we will show how we can derive the query (Q) *by forward reasoning.*
Starting from   (1) $[0]\text{Conceiv}([0]x)$
we can deduce by means of (act2) and (act1)

(5) $[0 \, \text{eleph roy.eleph}]\text{Conceiv}([0 \, \text{eleph roy.eleph}]x) \wedge [0 \, \text{eleph roy.eleph}]\text{White}([0 \, \text{eleph roy.eleph}]x)$

Note that this formula constitutes the stereotypic information about royal elephants. This information can be further enriched by reasoning via frame axioms, if necessary. The left part of this formula, together with   (3) $roy.eleph(\text{clyde}) = \text{clyde}$

allows to apply   (2) $\forall x \, \forall \tau \, \forall t \, \forall \mathcal{P} \, \Big(\, \mathcal{P}(t(x)) \longleftarrow t(x) = x \wedge [\tau]\text{Conceiv}([\tau]x) \wedge [\tau]\mathcal{P}([\tau]x) \, \Big)$
to the second literal of (5) and we get: White($roy.eleph(\text{clyde})$)
By means of   (4) $\forall y(roy.eleph(y) \rightarrow eleph(y))$
we obtain   White($eleph(\text{clyde})$)
which matches the query (Q).

Having presented an example of how to handle an exception, we want to show now how normal inheritance is performed in this framework.
Let us assume that all objects of our universe of discourse are mortal, i.e. we have the fact

(6) $\forall x \, ([0]\text{Mortal}([0]x))$

Since elephant and royal elephants too are mortal as well, we have to define respective frame axioms to propagate this stereotypic information:

(act1$_f$) $\forall \tau \forall x ([\tau]\text{Mortal}([\tau]x) \longrightarrow [\tau \, \text{eleph}]\text{Mortal}([\tau \, \text{eleph}]x))$
(act2$_f$) $\forall \tau \forall x ([\tau \, \text{eleph}]\text{Mortal}([\tau \, \text{eleph}]x) \longrightarrow [\tau \, \text{eleph roy.eleph}]\text{Mortal}([\tau \, \text{eleph roy.eleph}]x))$

If we want to know now whether the elephant clyde is mortal, i.e. if we have the query
Mortal($eleph(\text{clyde})$)
We have to constitute first by means of these frame axioms[6] that Mortal is among the stereotypic properties of elephants (or of royal elephants, depending on whether we have

---

[5]Instead of a second order formula we could also use an axiom schema which would be turned into a 1-order formula by instantiating the predicate variable $\mathcal{P}$ by a predicate symbol. See also section five concerning an alternative 1-order the implementation.

[6]Of course, we can deduce this information also without frame axioms by means of a linear proof (see [Fro91] and section five of this paper). But for sake of clarity we also gave the frame axioms which would do and put all considerations concerning efficiency in chapter five.

$eleph(\text{clyde}) = \text{clyde}$ or $roy.eleph(\text{clyde}) = \text{clyde}),$

then this information must be converted into real information about clyde, maybe followed by a respective sort weakening. (Note that a further sort weakening would yield Mortal(clyde) which just states that clyde is mortal, and would not convey any further information about clyde's appertainance to a sort or other.)

Let us finish this section with a general remark. The system presented has no possibility to derive *real* information about undetermined objects, e.g. to derive statements like Grey($eleph(x)$), which would mean that all elephants are *really* grey. Only the formula $[\tau \text{ eleph}]\text{Grey}([\tau \text{ eleph}]x)$, which expresses the stereotypic information about elephants can be derived.

4 Exceptions in Role Inheritance

In this section we want to show how *relations with exceptions* can be inherited in the framework just described. We assume that a relation or role Dominate(x, y) is given, which expresses that x dominates y. Elephants shall not dominate any others, while royal elephants shall dominate elephants, but shall not dominate other royal elephants.

If we want to know, whether clyde dominates ali, we must look which kind of elephants are clyde and ali, and which is the respective stereotypic information, in particular with respect to the relation Dominate. As will be clear from the following example, if the Dominate–literals found in the stereotypic information—if any—*agree*, we can derive the concrete instance Dominate(clyde, ali). As before we have to start from the general imagination:

(1) $[0]\text{Conceiv}([0]x)$

Moreover, we need to know that normal elephants are dominated by royal elephants, which is expressed by the following action:

(act3) $\forall\tau\forall x, y \ \big(\ [\tau]\text{Conceiv}([\tau]x) \longrightarrow$
$[\tau \text{ eleph}]\text{Conceiv}([\tau \text{ eleph}]x) \wedge [\tau \text{ eleph}]\text{Dominate}([\tau \text{ eleph roy.eleph}]y, [\tau \text{ eleph}]x) \ \big)$

and that royal elephants dominate elephants, which is expressed by the following action:

(act4) $\forall\tau\forall x, y \ \big(\ [\tau \text{ eleph}]\text{Conceiv}([\tau \text{ eleph}]x)$
$\wedge [\tau \text{ eleph}]\text{Dominate}([\tau \text{ eleph roy.eleph}]y, [\tau \text{ eleph}]x) \longrightarrow$
$[\tau \text{ eleph roy.eleph}]\text{Conceiv}([\tau \text{ eleph roy.eleph}]x)$
$\wedge [\tau \text{ eleph roy.eleph}]\text{Dominate}([\tau \text{ eleph roy.eleph}]x, [\tau \text{ eleph}]y) \ \big)$

Note that in the first action we get that elephants are dominated by royal elephants. When passing from elephants to royal elephants, the fact of being dominated is *deleted*, and a new fact that royal elephants dominate *normal* elephants is created.

Since we now have to cope with relations, we need a more general rule of transportation:

(2') $\forall x, y \ \forall\tau, \sigma, \tau', \sigma' \ \forall t, s \ \forall\mathcal{P} \ \big(\ \mathcal{P}(t(x), s(y))$
$\longleftarrow \qquad t(x) = x \wedge s(y) = y$
$\wedge [\tau]\text{Conceiv}([\tau]x) \wedge [\sigma]\text{Conceiv}([\sigma]y)$
$\wedge [\tau]\mathcal{P}([\tau]x, [\sigma']y) \wedge [\sigma]\mathcal{P}([\tau']x, [\sigma]y)$
$\wedge \ \sigma' \prec \sigma \wedge \tau' \prec \tau \ \big)$

(Note that, as already before, t in $t(x)$ refers to a sort symbol which corresponds to the last world in the world path $[\tau]$. Analogously for s and $[\sigma]$.) $\sigma' \prec \sigma$ means that σ' is a more general concept than σ, or stated otherwise, σ' corresponds to a shorter world path than σ.

With these rules we can now consider four different cases, given by the facts about clyde and ali:

Case (1) : $eleph(\text{ali}) = \text{ali}$ and $roy.eleph(\text{clyde}) = \text{clyde}$:

We get $[0 \text{ eleph roy.eleph}]\text{Dominate}([0 \text{ eleph roy.eleph}]\text{clyde}, [0 \text{ eleph}]y)$

and $[0 \text{ eleph}]\text{Dominate}([0 \text{ eleph roy.eleph}]x, [0 \text{ eleph}]\text{ali})$

From these two literals we can deduce Dominate(clyde, ali) with the transportation rule given above.

Case (2) : $roy.eleph(ali) = ali$ and $eleph(clyde) = clyde$:

We get the opposite of above [0 eleph roy.eleph]Dominate([0 eleph roy.eleph]ali, [0 eleph]y)

and [0 eleph]Dominate([0 eleph roy.eleph]x, [0 eleph]clyde)

From which we could only deduce the opposite relationship Dominate(ali, clyde), which is not what we were asked for.

Case (3) : $roy.eleph(ali) = ali$ and $roy.eleph(clyde) = clyde$:

We get for both elephants [0 eleph roy.eleph]Dominate([0 eleph roy.eleph]ali, [0 eleph]y)

and [0 eleph roy.eleph]Dominate([0 eleph roy.eleph]clyde, [0 eleph]y)

where our transportation rule does not apply.

Case (4) : $eleph(ali) = ali$ and $eleph(clyde) = clyde$:

We get something contrary to case (3) [0 eleph]Dominate([0 eleph roy.eleph]y, [0 eleph]ali)

and [0 eleph]Dominate([0 eleph roy.eleph]y, [0 eleph]clyde)

where our transportation rule does not apply.

5 Implementation Issues

In this paper we presented a combination of a sorted logic (implemented via functions) and property inheritance (implemented via actions). These actions transport properties and roles from concepts to subconcepts, i.e. the subconcepts inherit properties and roles from their superconcepts. The destructive effects of actions were exploited to cope with exceptions in inheritance. Finally, specific sort information about an object allows us to ascribe to an object properties which are typical for the concept related to this sort. Moreover, we can generalize (or weaken) the sorted statements thus derived to other ones, containing less precise sort information.

We indicated already that the system presented can be implemented using the so-called *linear proofs*, a deductive approach to plan generation. First presented in [Bib86] and further developed in [Fro87] and [BFFH89], it was finally remodeled on the basis of modal logic in [Fro91]. It is this modal logic version which seems best apt for the implementation of the framework presented in this paper. Since the issue of this paper is inheritance with exceptions and linear proofs only play the role of an implementation detail (although an important one, due to efficiency reasons) we tried to exclude linear proofs as much as possible from the preceding sections, and we will only give a brief survey now. The basic idea of linear proofs is to restrict the use of literals: each literal may be used at most one in a proof (see [Bib86]). Restricting the use of literals in such a way is practically equivalent to deleting literals after they have been used for the first time. This allows to model the destructive effects of actions in robot planning problems (and in our present case the exceptions in inheritance). It also allowed to work without frame axioms, thus reducing considerably the search space during a reasoning process. Due to certain problems encountered in the course of a detailed analysis of linear proofs (see [Fro87]) and due to the complicated question of the semantics of linear proofs (see [BFFH89]), the idea grew up to remodel the underlying ideas on the basis of an ordinary modal logic. This resulted in a so-called *default unification* between two literals $[\tau]L_1$ and $[\sigma]L_2$, if the non-modal arguments of L_1 and L_2 unify and if $[\tau]$ unifies with a initial subpath of $[\sigma]$ (see [Fro91] for details). This means *at first* that a literal which is valid in a certain world is also valid in all worlds which can be reached from there. However, this propagation of literals is restricted by the *linearity idea*, which says that a default unification is only admitted, if $[\tau]L_1$ and $[\sigma]L_2$ have not been used otherwise. For instance, the literal [0 eleph roy.eleph]Grey([0 eleph roy.eleph]x) could not be derived by default unification from [0 eleph]Grey([0 eleph]x), because the latter literal has been used in the application of (act2). (The application of (act2) is necessary in order to derive [0 eleph roy.eleph]Conceiv([0 eleph roy.eleph]x) which is a prerequisite for the application of the transportation rule (2).) On the other hand,

[0 eleph roy.eleph]Mortal([0 eleph roy.eleph]x)) could have been derived by default connection, and consequently the frame axioms (act1_f) and (act2_f) are superfluous.

It is in this context of the application of linear proofs, that the Conceiv-literals play a crucial role. Default unifications allow the inheritance of all facts, as long as thay were not used otherwise. Therefore, without the Conceiv-literals, it would be possible, e.g in the setting of the example of section three, to unify [0 eleph]Grey([0 eleph]x) with [0 eleph roy.eleph]Grey([0 eleph roy.eleph]x), as long as the first literal is not used otherwise. Next the property Grey could be transported, e.g. to Grey(*roy.eleph*(clyde)). However, the default unification is blocked by the Conceiv-literals: The derivation of the Conceiv-literal in the transportation rule entails a 'replacement' of the Grey-literal by a White-literal, which is effectuated by the action (act2).

Let us finally discuss a further implementation topic which might appear problematic at first sight, namely that the transportation rules (2) and (2') are of second order logic. Concerning the predicate variable $\mathcal{P}$ we can use Kowalski's trick—invented to reduce the number of frame axioms in plan generation based on McCarthy's situational calculus—see [Kow79]. The idea is to *push everything one step down*: predicate symbols P are replaced by corresponding function symbols f_P and a literal $P(t_1, \ldots, t_n)$ is transformed to $\text{HOLDS}(f_P, t_1, \ldots, t_n)$. In this way a formula like $\forall P\ P(t_1, \ldots, t_n)$ is replaced by $\forall f\ \text{HOLDS}(f, t_1, \ldots, t_n)$ which is first order. (P and f being first-order variables.) Let us remark finally that we didn't apply this trick in the presentation of the preceding sections, because we deem the use of functions for the denotation of properties rather unintuitive, which might reduce the readability of the paper. Concerning the sort variable t we are in a less agreeable situation. We can replace the single transportation rule by a set of rules, one for each sort, respectively by a new rule for each pair of sorts in case of rules like (2').

Conclusion

Let us finish this paper with some remarks about related work.

First of all, we are not aware of any system which combines property inheritance (with exceptions) and sorted logic. The LILOG system [PvL90] uses a sorted logic, but their inheritance system allows no exceptions. On the other hand, the use of sorts in logic is getting increasingly important, because sort information allows tremendous reductions of search spaces during a proof process.

Secondly, up to now there are only few approaches which treat exception handling in a logically satisfactory way. Of course, exception handling is found in many commercial knowledge representation systems, e.g. FLAVORS [Sym85], KEE [KEE86] or Knowledge Craft [LATZ86], where properties of concepts/classes can be simply redefined in subclasses without caring for the semantics of this operation.

The most promising contributions come from the field of non-monotonic reasoning. In spite of the large variety of these approaches, the way they argue is roughly the following: a property can be inherited from a concept to a subconcept, if it can be consistently assumed, if nothing contradicts, if there is no exception, etc. This means practically, that we have to search the space of available knowledge (=formulae) and are successful if we find *nothing*. As we have shown elsewhere (see [Fro91], where for the case of plan generation we compared frame axioms and default logic with respect to the amount of reasoning work to be entailed by each of these two approaches), the work to be carried out with non-monotonic reasoning is nearly the same as when working with frame axioms. In both cases we search the space of formulae, the only difference being that in case of frame axioms we are glad in case of *successful* unifications, while in case of non-monotonic reasoning we are glad in case of *unsuccessful* unifications.

Since the linear proof calculus can work without frame axioms, the inheritance system (including the exception handling) presented in this paper will be computationally a lot more efficient.

Acknowledgements

We want to thank Andreas Strasser, Georg Strobl, Josef Schneeberger, Ulrich Furbach, Nur Erol and Torsten Schaub, as well as all colleagues of our AI group in Munich who commented on various versions of this paper. Anonymous referees also provided interesting comments.

References

[BFFH89] W. Bibel, L. Fariñas del Cerro, B. Fronhöfer, and A. Herzig. Plan Generation by Linear Proofs : On Semantics. In D. Metzing, editor, *GWAI 89, 13th German Workshop on Artificial Intelligence*, volume 216 of *Informatik-Fachberichte*, pages 49–62, Schloß Eringerfeld, Geseke, Germany, September 1989. Springer, Berlin.

[Bib86] W. Bibel. A Deductive Solution for Plan Generation. *New Generation Computing*, 6:115–132, 1986.

[Bre87] Gerhard Brewka. The logic of inheritance in frame systems. In J. McDermott, editor, *IJCAI–87, 10th International Joint Conference on Artificial Intelligence*, pages 483–488, Milan, Italy, August 1987.

[CF88] T. Conrad and U. Furbach. Sorts are nothing but functions. An equational approach to sorts for logic programming. FKI Report 89-88, TUM, 1988.

[FH89] U. Furbach and S. Hölldobler. Order-Sortedness, Inheritance and Equations in Logic Programming. In Wilkerson, editor, *Advances in Logic Programming and Automated Reasoning*. Ablex Publ. Coop., 1989. to appear.

[Fro87] B. Fronhöfer. Linearity and Plan Generation. *New Generation Computing*, 5:213–225, 1987.

[Fro91] B. Fronhöfer. Default Connections a Modal Planning Framework. In *European Workshop on Planning (EWSP-91)*. St.Augustin, Germany, March 18–19 1991.

[Fur89] U. Furbach. An equational approach to sorts for logic programming. In Ganzinger Müller, editor, *Ext. abstracts of the 1st German Workshop Term Rewriting: Theory and Applications*. SEKI Report SR-89-02, 1989.

[Her89] Andreas Herzig. *Raisonnement automatique en logique modale et algorithmes d'unification*. PhD thesis, Université Paul Sabatier, Toulouse, 1989.

[KEE86] Intellicorp, MountainView, California. *KEE Software Development System User's Manual*, 1986.

[Kow79] R. Kowalski. *Logic for Problem Solving*. North Holland, New York, 1979.

[LATZ86] J.-P. Laurent, J. Ayel, F. Thome, and D. Ziebelin. Comparative Evaluation of Three Expert System Development Tools: KEE, Knowledge Craft, ART. *The Knowledge Engineering Review*, 1(4):19–29, 1986.

[Ohl88] H.J. Ohlbach. A Resolution Calculus for Modal Logics. In E. Lusk and R. Overbeek, editors, *CADE–88*, 1988.

[PvL90] Udo Pletat and Kai von Luck. Knowledge representation in LILOG. In K.H. Bläsius, U. Hedstück, and C.-R. Rollinger, editors, *Sorts and Types in Artificial Intelligence*, page 140ff. LNCS 418, 1990.

[Sym85] Symbolics. *Lisp Machine Manual, Vol.3*, 1985.

[Tou86] D.S. Touretzky. *The Mathematics of Inheritance Systems*. Morgan Kaufmanns Publishers, 1986.

[Wal87] L. Wallen. Matrix Proof Methods for Modal Logics. In J. McDermott, editor, *IJCAI–87, 10th International Joint Conference on Artificial Intelligence*, 1987.

Approximate Entailment

Marco Cadoli, Marco Schaerf*
Dipartimento di Informatica e Sistemistica
Università di Roma "La Sapienza"
via Salaria 113, 00198 Roma, Italia
cadoli@vaxrma.infn.it   mschaerf@vaxrma.infn.it

Abstract

Approximation techniques are widely used in many areas of Computer Science for dealing with polynomially intractable problems. The major difficulty about introducing approximation in reasoning problems is in that it is very hard to find a measure of the approximation which is not dependent on the particular problem at hand. Our goal is to introduce the notion of *approximate answers* to reasoning problems which are known to be computationally intractable. We focus our attention on a reasoning problem which is both very general and computationally intractable: checking whether a propositional formula in Conjunctive Normal Form entails a clause. We present two sequences of entailment relations approximating the classical one: the relations of the first sequence are sound but not complete, while the relations of the second one are complete but not sound. Both sequences converge to classical entailment and can be computed in polynomial time under some conditions. Our claim is that both these sequences are an approximation of the entailment relation, since they always provide information clearly related to the original problem. In the last part of the paper, we sketch an algorithm for computing incrementally relations of the two sequences.

1   Introduction

Approximation techniques are widely used in many areas of Computer Science for dealing with polinomially intractable problems. For example, it is known that to provide an optimal solution to an Integer Programming problem is NP-complete (see [3]). Anyway, it is possible to provide sub-optimal solutions in polynomial time by means of the well-known technique of constraints relaxation. Moreover, it is possible to precisely bind the distance between the optimal solution and the sub-optimal ones. The major difficulty about introducing approximation in reasoning problems is in that it is very hard to find a measure of the approximation which is not dependent on the particular problem at hand. When we are faced with a reasoning problem such as the problem of querying a knowledge base represented in a logical language, there is no topology in the information that can help defining an approximation, as the topology provided in integer programming problems by the ordering of real numbers. Nevertheless, the availability of

---

*Supported by a scholarship from IMI Istituto Mobiliare Italiano.

approximation techniques would be very useful in many situations, due to the inherent complexity of all reasonably expressive logical languages, such as propositional logic.

Our goal in this paper is to introduce the notion of *approximate answers* to reasoning problems which are known to be computationally intractable. The requirements of an approximate answer are that:

- it provides semantically clear information about the reasoning problem;
- it can be computed in polynomial time;
- it is defined incrementally: successive levels of approximation provide more specific information; the answer to the reasoning problem is reached –although in exponential time– through the computation of several simple steps.

The first goal is probably the most important one to be accomplished, in fact, any approximate answer would be of little use if there is no precise meaning to assign to it. This is to say that approximate answers must be semantically characterized; they cannot be defined only procedurally.

It is important to point out that we deal with formalisms where the knowledge is precisely defined and certain. We are not analyzing situations involving any form of approximate or fuzzy knowledge, based on probabilistic or numerical representations, such as, for example, Zadeh's fuzzy logics [9]. We are trying instead to formalize the approximation of a logical consequence relation defined by means of an extensional semantics but too difficult to compute, through a sequence of simpler consequence relations, also defined by means of an extensional semantics.

The problem we are interested in is that of querying knowledge bases expressed in a logical language. In this paper we focus our attention on a reasoning problem which is both very general and computationally intractable: that of checking whether a propositional formula in Conjunctive Normal Form entails a clause. This problem adequately generalizes that of querying a propositional knowledge base, since information naturally comes in a conjunctive form and complex queries can be decomposed into several simpler clausal queries. Although it is well known that the above problem is co-NP-complete, little attention has been paid to the characterization of approximate algorithms to solve it. A notable exception is the work of Levesque [4], who proposes an interesting semantical characterization of an incomplete entailment algorithm. He shows that some semantically grounded inferences can be computed in polynomial time. In a more recent paper [5], Levesque raises some points in favour of simple algorithms for the entailment problem. His main point is the following: if we are to model the mental activity of an agent, we cannot assume that it always answers queries by using a method that needs an exponential amount of time. It is more realistic to assume that, when faced with normal problems, the agent only applies simple inference rules; only when faced with extremely important or tricky questions, it moves to what Levesque calls a "puzzle mode" and uses more complex inference procedures.

We go one step further in this analysis and point out that, in very common situations, human beings reason incompletely. Imagine the following situation: an agent has its own knowledge base where all its knowledge is stored; this information involves several different topics, not uncorrelated but somehow semantically distinct. If this agent is asked a question about a specific topic it is very realistic to assume that it will reason in several steps: first of all, it tries to answer the question by only using the knowledge directly related to the specific topic; if this is not enough to provide an answer, it will use the knowledge concerning some related topics. These steps are iterated till a solution is found, or the agent decides that this search is taking too much time. Even if it stops before a final answer is found, the search has not been useless because some important conclusions are obtained. This approach is particularly succesful when taxonomic information is present in the knowledge base: suppose to have a knowledge base containing information about animals and their properties. If we want to prove that cows do not have canine teeth, we may try to prove it by only using knowledge about cows; if this is not sufficient, then we may try to involve the properties of the first superclass of cows, say grass-eaters. This procedure could be iterated until the correct answer is found. This amounts to using the whole knowledge base in the worst case, when the property cannot be proven. Notice that this is a weakness of having only sound but not complete approximating procedures, and points out the usefulness of having two complementary approximating procedures, the second one being complete but not sound.

In this work, we start from the ideas of Levesque and propose a new method for approximation. In Section 2 we present two weak characterizations of the entailment relation: the first one (originally defined by Levesque in [6]) is sound but not complete, while the second one is complete but not sound. The two relations provide limited but semantically clear information; moreover they can be computed in polynomial time. In Section 3 we generalize the two relations in such a way that:

- the generalizations are approximations (either complete or sound) of the entailment relation; these generalizations agree with the entailment relation on a subset S of the language;
- the generalizations can be computed in polynomial time when the size of S is fixed;
- when something is added to S, the generalizations are better characterization of the entailment relation; if S is the whole language, then they are equivalent to the entailment relation. When S is increased of a single item, the time needed to compute the generalizations duplicates.

In Section 4 we sketch a general algorithm for computing the two relations at the same time. The algorithm can also be used to answer the full entailment problem in an incremental fashion, by keeping track of the past unsuccesful computations. If it is stopped after any amount of time, it provides a semantically clear answer in terms of the two relations. The computation of the full entailment problem obviously uses exponential time, but the same amount of time is used by the best known algorithms for checking entailment. Finally, in the last section we draw some conclusions and discuss ongoing research.

2 Preliminaries

We denote with L a set of propositional letters. A literal is a letter l of L or its negation $\neg l$; we denote with L^* the set of all literals associated with the letters of L. A clause is a disjunction of literals of L^*; a formula in Conjunctive Normal Form (CNF formula) is a conjunction of clauses. A truth assignment is a function mapping the set of literals L^* into the set $\{0,1\}$. We now introduce three different forms of truth assignment, in which the mapping is differently restricted.

Definition 1 (1-, 2-, 3-interpretation)

- **(Levesque [6])** *A 3-interpretation of L^* is a truth assignment which does not map both a letter l of L and its negation $\neg l$ into 0;*
- *A 2-interpretation of L^* is a truth assignment which maps every letter l of L and its negation $\neg l$ into opposite values;*
- *An 1-interpretation of L^* is a truth assignment which maps every letter l of L and its negation $\neg l$ into 0.*

The definition of 2-interpretation corresponds to having the two truth values *true* and *false*; 3-interpretations also admit the truth value *contradiction*, while 1-interpretations only admit the value *undefined*. Notice that a 2-interpretation is also a 3-interpretation. Moreover, an 1-interpretation is neither a 2- nor a 3-interpretation.

An 1-, 2- or 3-interpretation *satisfies* a clause iff it maps at least one literal of the clause into 1; it satisfies a CNF formula iff it satisfies all its clauses. A CNF formula is 2-satisfiable iff there exists a 2-interpretation satisfying it. For any other kind of formula, the definition of 2-satisfiability requires a previous transformation into CNF. The same definitions apply to 1- and 3-satisfiability[†]. A CNF formula is always 3-satisfiable, while it is never 1-satisfiable.

We now introduce three different forms of logical entailment, each corresponding to a definition of interpretation. We denote a CNF formula with T and a clause with γ.

Definition 2 (1-, 2-, 3-entailment)

- **(Levesque [6])** *T 3-entails γ ($T \models^3 \gamma$) iff every 3-interpretation satisfying T also satisfies γ;*
- *T 2-entails γ ($T \models^2 \gamma$) iff every 2-interpretation satisfying T also satisfies γ;*
- *T 1-entails γ ($T \models^1 \gamma$) iff every 1-interpretation satisfying T also satisfies γ.*

In order to be consistent with the usual terminology, in the following we omit the decoration 2 for both 2-interpretations and 2-entailment. For the same reason we omit the superscript 2 in the symbol $\models^2$.

Notice that $T \models^1 \gamma$ always holds, because there are no 1-interpretations satisfying T. In the following section we generalize the definition of 1-entailment to make it meaningful and useful to our purposes.

3-interpretations can be considered to be *superficial* descriptions of the world[‡] that can take both a property and its negation to be true. We now show two interesting

---

[†] Notice that our definition of 3-satisfiability has nothing to do with the well known decisional problem 3-SATISFIABILITY (see [3]). The last can be restated in our terms as the problem of checking 2-satisfiability of a CNF formula whose clauses contain at most three literals.

[‡] In [5] 4-interpretations admitting both the truth values *contradiction* and *undefined* are called *surface* interpretations.

properties of the relation $\models^3$, concerning its adequacy to efficiently *approximate* $\models$. Theorems 1 and 2, as well as definitions of 3-interpretation and 3-entailment, originally appeared in [6]. The proofs of all the theorems shown in the sequel will appear in the full paper.

Theorem 1 (soundness of $\models^3$) *If $T \models^3 \gamma$ holds, then $T \models \gamma$ holds.*

Theorem 2 (polynomiality of $\models^3$) *$T \models^3 \gamma$ holds iff either a clause subsumed by γ (i.e. such that all its literals also occur in γ) occurs in T or a pair $p, \neg p$ of literals occurs in γ. Therefore, determining if $T \models^3 \gamma$ holds can be checked in $O(|T| \cdot |\gamma|)$ time.*

Theorems 1 and 2 can be easily extended to the 3-entailment of a CNF formula α. In such case the complexity is $O(|T| \cdot |\alpha|)$.

By taking into account the above results and the fact that the problem of determining if $T \models \gamma$ holds is co-NP-complete, Levesque [5] claims that the relation $\models^3$ can be considered to be a superficial, simplified form of entailment which can be performed before any other inference, because it has the appealing property of being computable in polynomial time. Anyway, Theorem 2 shows that the consequences validated by $\models^3$ are simply those explicitly represented in the knowledge base. The following example clarifies that by $\models^3$ we can only perform very simple forms of reasoning.

Example 1 (*modus ponens* does not hold for 3-entailment)
Let L be the set $\{a, b\}$, and T be $\{a, \neg a \lor b\}$. $T \models b$ holds, but $T \models^3 b$ does not hold: the truth assignment which maps $a, \neg a$ and $\neg b$ to 1 and b to 0 is a 3-intepretation satisfying T. $\Diamond$

As we have seen, 3-entailment cannot account for any reasonable approximation of entailment. For this reason, in the next section, we will generalize the notion of 3-interpretation, by restricting to a subset of L the possibility of mapping a letter to truth value *contradiction*. Notice that the 1-entailment relation $\models^1$ can be considered as a polynomial, complete and not sound approximation of $\models$. As it is, this relation is useless, for this reason in the next section it will be generalized.

3 Two definitions of approximate entailment

In the following we denote with S a subset — even not proper — of the alphabet L.

Definition 3 (S-1-, S-3-interpretation)

- *An S-3-interpretation of L is a truth assignment which maps every letter l of S and its negation $\neg l$ into opposite values. Moreover, it does not map both a letter l of $L \setminus S$ and its negation $\neg l$ into 0.*
- *An S-1-interpretation of L is a truth assignment which maps every letter l of S and its negation $\neg l$ into opposite values. Moreover, it maps every letter l of $L \setminus S$ and its negation $\neg l$ into 0.*

Notice that, for any S, an interpretation is always an S-3-interpretation, while the latter is always a 3-interpretation.

Both definitions of S-1- and S-3-interpretation are equivalent to that of interpretation when $S = L$. On the other hand S-1-interpretations are 1-interpretations when $S = \emptyset$. The same holds for S-3 and 3-interpretations. The notion of satisfaction of clauses and CNF formulae introduced in the previous section applies to S-1- and S-3-interpretation as well: an S-1- or S-3-interpretation satisfies a clause iff it maps at least one literal of the clause into 1; it satisfies a CNF formula iff it satisfies all its clauses. Notice that while a CNF formula is always 3-satisfiable, there are some formulae which are not S-3-satisfiable for a given S. On the other hand, while a CNF formula is never 1-satisfiable, some formulae are S-1-satisfiable.

Definition 4 (S-1-, S-3-entailment)
- T S-3-entails γ ($T \models_S^3 \gamma$) iff all the S-3-interpretations satisfying T also satisfy γ;
- T S-1-entails γ ($T \models_S^1 \gamma$) iff all the S-1-interpretations satisfying T also satisfy γ.

S-3- and S-1-interpretations can be considered to be superficial descriptions of the world, which can take both a property and its negation to be either true or false, only if that property is in the set $L \setminus S$. This kind of description could be adequate when all the properties of interest are in S, that is, are given traditional, 2-valued interpretation.

Example 2
Let L and T be as in Example 1. If $S = \{a\}$ then $T \models_S^3 b$, since every S-3-interpretation satisfying T maps a and b to 1, and $\neg a$ to 0. $\diamond$

We now show some interesting properties of the relations $\models_S^3$ and $\models_S^1$ concerning their adequacy to approximate $\models$.

Theorem 3 (soundness of $\models_S^3$) *For any $S \subseteq L$, if $T \models_S^3 \gamma$ holds, then $T \models \gamma$ holds.*

Theorem 4 (monotonicity of $\models_S^3$) *For any S, S' such that $S \subseteq S' \subseteq L$, if $T \models_S^3 \gamma$ holds, then $T \models_{S'}^3 \gamma$ holds.*

Theorem 5 (completeness of $\models_S^1$) *For any $S \subseteq L$, if $T \models \gamma$ holds and both a letter l of $L \setminus S$ and its negation $\neg l$ do not occur in γ, then $T \models_S^1 \gamma$ holds.*

Theorem 6 (monotonicity of $\not\models_S^1$) *For any S, S' such that $S \subseteq S' \subseteq L$, if $T \not\models_S^1 \gamma$ holds and both a letter l of $S' \setminus S$ and its negation $\neg l$ do not occur in γ, then $T \not\models_{S'}^1 \gamma$ holds.*

Theorems 3 and 4 show that we can consider the relation $\models_S^3$ to be a sound approximation of $\models$ as well as a complete approximation of $\models_{S''}^3$, where S'' is any subset of S. Apart from the trivial case in which γ is a tautology, Theorems 5 and 6 show that we can consider the relation $\models_S^1$ to be a complete approximation of $\models$, as well as a sound approximation of $\models_{S''}^1$, where S'' is any subset of S. This implies that, for any $S \subset L$ we are in exactly one of these three situations:

1. $T \models_S^3 \gamma$ holds; in this case we know that $T \models \gamma$ holds;
2. $T \not\models_S^1 \gamma$ holds; in this case we know that $T \not\models \gamma$ holds;
3. both $T \not\models_S^3 \gamma$ and $T \models_S^1 \gamma$ hold; in this case we do not know whether $T \models \gamma$ or $T \not\models \gamma$ hold. Anyway, we know that γ is not true in any S''-3-interpretations satisfying T and that γ is true in all the S''-1-interpretations satisfying T, where S'' is any subset of S.

In the first two cases the entailment problem, that is the problem of determining whether $T \models \gamma$ holds or not, is completely solved and we do not need any further investigation. In the third case, although we do not know whether $T \models \gamma$ holds or not, we have interesting semantic information. Our claim is that the two relations $\models_S^1$ and $\models_S^3$ are approximations of $\models$.

Since $\models_S^3$ is equivalent to $\models^3$ when $S = \emptyset$ (polynomial problem) and it is equivalent to $\models$ when $S = L$ (co-NP-complete problem), in the generic case when $\emptyset \subset S \subset L$ holds we expect an intermediate complexity for $\models_S^3$. The same considerations apply to the relation $\models_S^1$. Therefore, the relations $\models_S^3$ and $\models_S^1$ can at least be used to provide useful semantic information about the entailment problem in a reasonable amount of time.

We now present two examples, showing the usefulness of our method.

Example 3

We suppose that the following CNF formula T is part of a very large knowledge base containing information about animals and their properties. T uses a small alphabet L, which again we imagine to be part of a very large dictionary. The large knowledge base contains a taxonomy of classes, which is partially present in T.

$L = \{cow, dog, grass\text{-}eater, carnivore, mammal, has\text{-}canine\text{-}teeth,$
$\qquad has\text{-}molar\text{-}teeth, vertebrate, animal\}$
$T = (cow \supset grass\text{-}eater), \quad (dog \supset carnivore),$
$\qquad (grass\text{-}eater \supset mammal), \quad (grass\text{-}eater \supset \neg has\text{-}canine\text{-}teeth),$
$\qquad (mammal \supset has\text{-}canine\text{-}teeth \vee has\text{-}molar\text{-}teeth), \quad (mammal \supset vertebrate),$
$\qquad (vertebrate \supset animal), \quad (carnivore \supset mammal).$

Notice that T is not a Horn formula. We want to prove that $T \models (cow \supset has\text{-}molar\text{-}teeth)$ holds. Since $T \not\models^3 (cow \supset has\text{-}molar\text{-}teeth)$, we try to determine a subset S of L such that $T \models_S^3 (cow \supset has\text{-}molar\text{-}teeth)$ holds. By Theorem 3 this implies our goal. In fact, this happens for $S = \{cow, grass\text{-}eater, mammal, has\text{-}canine\text{-}teeth, has\text{-}molar\text{-}teeth\}$, which is a small subset of the whole dictionary. $\Diamond$

Example 4

$L = \{person, child, youngster, adult, senior, student, pensioner,$
$\qquad worker, unemployed\}$
$T = (person \supset child \vee youngster \vee adult \vee senior),$
$\qquad (youngster \supset student \vee worker), \quad (adult \supset student \vee worker \vee unemployed),$
$\qquad (senior \supset pensioner \vee worker), \quad (student \supset child \vee youngster \vee adult),$
$\qquad (pensioner \supset senior), \quad (pensioner \supset \neg student), \quad (pensioner \supset \neg worker).$

We want to prove that $T \not\models (child \supset pensioner)$. By Theorem 5 we try to determine a subset S of L such that $T \not\models_S^1 (child \supset pensioner)$. In fact this happens for $S = \{worker, pensioner, child\}$ since the S-1-interpretation mapping $worker, \neg pensioner, child$ into 1 and all the other literals into 0 satisfies T but not $(child \supset pensioner)$. $\diamond$

The above examples show that an exact solution to an entailment problem can be reached for a very small S. In the following, we show that we can obtain the solution for an S-entailment problem in $O(|T| \cdot |S| \cdot 2^{|S|})$ time. Obviously the choice of the minimal S having this property is not immediate, but it is worth noticing that there cannot be simple general rules for this choice, due to the inherent complexity of the entailment problem. In fact, if we could know in polynomial time which is the minimal S for which $T \models_S^3 \gamma$ or $T \not\models_S^1 \gamma$ holds, then we would know that an upper bound for the entailment problem is proportional to $2^{|S|}$. Anyway, we can perform some qualitative analyses from the above examples. In the first one, in which taxonomic knowledge is present, it seems that, in order to reach an exact solution, it is useful to extend the set S with concepts of the taxonomy which are superclasses of the concepts appearing in γ. About the second example, in which the knowledge is spread over several indefinite clauses, an useful strategy seems to be that of extending S with classes with several properties, such as $pensioner$, or properties shared by several classes, such as $worker$.

The S-3- and S-1-entailment can be considered mechanisms for creating partial *views* of the knowledge base. These views could be so precise to allow us to perform exact inference, as in the above examples. In all the other cases relevant information can be inferred.

In the following, we show how the two relations can be computed, and that this can be done in polynomial time once S is fixed. By taking into account that $T \models \gamma$ holds iff $T \cup \{\neg\gamma\}$ is unsatisfiable, hence for 2-valued semantics entailment can be reduced to unsatisfiability, we now develop methods for the S-1- and S-3-entailment based on S-1- and S-3-unsatisfiability, respectively. First of all, we introduce a set characterizing the clause γ.

Definition 5 *We denote with* $letters(\gamma)$ *the set* $\{l \in L \mid l$ *occurs in* $\gamma\} \cup \{l \in L \mid \neg l$ *occurs in* $\gamma\}$.

The next lemma shows that, when dealing with S-3-entailment, we can, without loss of generality, choose an S such that $letters(\gamma) \subseteq S$.

Lemma 7 *Suppose* $letters(\gamma) \not\subseteq S$ *holds. Let* S' *be the set* $S \cup letters(\gamma)$. $T \models_S^3 \gamma$ *holds iff* $T \models_{S'}^3 \gamma$ *holds.*

The next two theorems show that S-1- and S-3-entailment can be reduced to S-1- and S-3-unsatisfiability, respectively.

Theorem 8 *Let* γ *be* $\gamma_S \vee \gamma_{\overline{S}}$, *where both* $letters(\gamma_S) \subseteq S$ *and* $letters(\gamma_{\overline{S}}) \cap S = \emptyset$ *hold.* $T \models_S^1 \gamma$ *holds iff* $T \cup \{\neg\gamma_S\}$ *is not* S-1-satisfiable.

Theorem 9 *Let letters*$(\gamma) \subseteq S$ *hold.* $T \models_S^3 \gamma$ *holds iff* $T \cup \{\neg\gamma\}$ *is not S-3-satisfiable.*

Our goal is now to find algorithms for determining S-1 and S-3-satisfiability of a given CNF formula. In the following section we discuss this issue.

4 An algorithm to compute S-satisfiability

As already seen in the last section, we can focus our attention on S-3-unsatisfiability and S-1-satisfiability. The following theorems show that both S-1-satisfiability and S-3-unsatisfiability can be checked in $O(|T| \cdot |S| \cdot 2^{|S|})$ time, which is polynomial once S is fixed.

Theorem 10 *Let S be the set $\{a_1, \ldots, a_m\}$. T is S-3-unsatisfiable iff $T \models^3 (a_1 \wedge \neg a_1) \vee \cdots \vee (a_m \wedge \neg a_m)$ holds, or equivalently $T \models^3 (c_1 \vee \cdots \vee c_m)$ holds for any combination $\{c_1, \ldots, c_m\}$, where each c_i $(1 \leq i \leq m)$ is either a_i or $\neg a_i$.*

Theorem 11 *Let S be the set $\{a_1, \ldots, a_m\}$. T is S-1-satisfiable iff there exists a set $\alpha = \{c_1, \ldots, c_m\}$, where each c_i $(1 \leq i \leq m)$ is either a_i or $\neg a_i$, such that each clause of T contains at least one literal in α.*

We have developed an algorithm for performing the satisfiability check based on the above results. Due to the lack of space we will not present it here and it will appear in the full paper. Our desiderata about the algorithm have been:
- the algorithm must compute at the same time both S-1-satisfiability and S-3-unsatisfiability;
- if for a given S, T is still S-1-unsatisfiable and S-3-satisfiable, we probably want to try with a set $S' \supset S$; this may happen after hours or days, depending on our computing resources; therefore the algorithm must compute satisfiability *incrementally*, using information produced in previous steps;
- although we expect that the algorithm uses time exponential in $|S|$, since for $S = L$ our problems are equivalent to the NP-complete problem of satisfiability, we want that the algorithm uses polynomial space.

By taking into account that we want to accomodate a stepwise extension of the set S, an important issue for an efficient algorithm is that this extension does not require to perform all the computations from scratch. In other words, some form of *history* must be kept from the past computations. In the case where S-3-unsatisfiability is not proved until $S = L$, the incremental use of our algorithm is as efficient as the use of the most efficient methods for checking unsatisfiability. On the other hand, if we restrict this same algorithm to the check of S-1-satisfiability, we do not have this appealing property. This is a shortcoming of our algorithm and we are currently examining other solutions, which can improve its performance.

Satisfiability of CNF formulae is a very well-known problem in 2-valued propositional logic, extensively studied and discussed in the specialized literature. In particular we have studied the relations between our algorithm, Resolution-based algorithms (e.g. [8]) and Enumeration algorithms (e.g. [1]). A detailed analysis of these relations will be reported in the full paper.

5   Conclusions and future research

In this paper we have presented some preliminary results on the issue of finding approximate answers to reasoning problems known to be intractable. We focused on the problem of deciding if a CNF formula logically entails a clause. The idea which has led to the results presented in this paper is very general and we believe that it can be applied in the definition of approximating relations for other reasoning problems already known to be intractable, such as Terminological reasoning (see for example [2]).

There are, however, some issues we have not fully considered in the paper. First of all, to make our algorithm smarter and more efficient, we must provide some methods to help in the choice of the way to enlarge the set S. A possible solution to this problem is the following: if we are capable of determining how far we are from proving 3-unsatisfiability and and how far we are from 1-satisfiability, we can choose an increase of S which moves in the direction of the easiest of the two goals. The characterization of heuristic measures seems a promising direction for the improvement of our method and we are currently investigating on this issue. Secondly, our method shows some similarities with forms of hypothetical reasoning and abduction as defined by Levesque in [6]. We are currently investigating on the relation between S-entailment and Levesque's limited abduction.

Acknowledgements

This work has been supported by the ESPRIT Basic Research Action N.3012-COMPULOG and by the Progetto Finalizzato Sistemi Informatici e Calcolo Parallelo of the CNR (Italian research Council).

References

[1] Davis M., Putnam H., "A Computing Procedure for Quantification Theory", *Journal of ACM*, vol. 7, 1960, pp. 201-215.

[2] Donini F. M., Lenzerini M., Nardi D. and Nutt W., "The Complexity of Concept Languages", *Proc. of KR-91*, 1991, pp.151-162.

[3] Garey M.R., and Johnson D.S., *Computers and Intractability, A Guide to the Theory of NP-Completeness*, W.H. Freeman and Company, San Francisco, 1979.

[4] Levesque H. J., "A Logic of Implicit and Explicit Belief", *Proc. of AAAI-84*, 1984, pp. 198-202.

[5] Levesque H. J., "Logic and the Complexity of Reasoning", *Journal of Philosophical Logic*, vol.17, 1988, pp. 355-389.

[6] Levesque H. J., "A knowledge-level account of abduction", *Proc. of IJCAI-89*, 1989, pp. 1061-1067.

[7] Loveland D., *Automated Theorem Proving: A Logical basis*, North Holland, 1978.

[8] Robinson J. A., "A Machine Oriented Logic Based on the resolution Principle", *JACM*, 12, 1965, pp. 397-415.

[9] Zadeh L. A., "A Theory of Approximate Reasoning", in *Machine Intelligence*, vol. 9, (J. E. Hayes, D. Michie and L. I. Mikulich eds.), Elsevier, New York, 1979, pp. 149-194.

NEGATION AS FAILURE AND CONSTRAINTS THROUGH ABDUCTION AND DEFAULTS[1]

L.Giordano A.Martelli M.L.Sapino
Dipartimento di Informatica - Università di Torino
C.so Svizzera 185 - 10149 TORINO, Italy
E-mail: (laura,mrt,mlsapino)@di.unito.it

ABSTRACT

The paper presents an extension of the abduction framework proposed by Eshghi and Kowalski to give the semantics of negation as failure in logic programming. The extension allows to cope with the presence of integrity constraints, not only for pruning inconsistent solutions, but for computing new solutions. This is achieved by adding constraints to the program and using them as logical formulae. Furthermore a new semantics based on defaults, equivalent to the previous one, is given for logic programs with negation as failure and constraints. Finally a transformation is presented which allows constraints to be eliminated, so that proof procedures for general clauses without constraints will be applicable.

The approach proposed in this paper is applicable not only to logic programs with negation as failure but to other nonmonotonic formalisms as well, and, for instance, it can be used to give a semantic characterization to justification-based Truth Maintenance Systems with dependency-directed backtracking.

1. INTRODUCTION

Logic programming with negation as failure has proven to be in many cases a suitable formalism for nonmonotonic reasoning, in particular in the framework proposed by Eshghi and Kowalski where the semantics of negation as failure is given by means of abduction. Indeed, in [EK89] a transformation is proposed which maps general logic programs into abduction frameworks. In the following, we will call it Eshghi and Kowalski transformation. In that setting negation as failure is "simulated by making negative conditions abducible and by imposing appropriate denials and disjunctions as integrity constraints". The result is a generalization of negation as failure, that is equivalent to the stable model semantics [GL88]. It provides, as alternative solutions for a query, several mutually incompatible collections of hypotheses (abductive solutions) that allow the query to be derived. This happens, for instance, when the program has different stable models.

The formalism used in logic programming with negation as failure, i.e. general clauses of the form

$$C \leftarrow A_1 \wedge ... \wedge A_n \wedge \text{ not } B_1 \wedge ... \wedge \text{ not } B_m,$$

is also the formalism used, at least in the propositional case, for expressing justifications for justification-based Truth Maintenance Systems (JTMS). Given a set J of justifications, the purpose of a JTMS is to assign all propositions in J a label IN (believed) or OUT (disbelieved) in such a way that all the justifications in J are satisfied in the labelling and each proposition labelled IN is justified by a non circular argument (the labelling is well-founded). It turns out that labellings of the JTMS correspond to stable models [PC89]. Therefore negation as failure, extended with abduction, and JTMS labellings can be considered as two alternative but equivalent ways of reasoning with propositional general clauses.

In this paper we will show how it is possible, by slightly modifying Eshghi and Kowalski transformation, to get a framework able to cope also with the presence of general constraints of the form

$$\leftarrow A_1 \wedge ... \wedge A_n \wedge \text{ not } B_1 \wedge ... \wedge \text{ not } B_m$$

which can be regarded as the negated conjunction of literals

$$\neg (A_1 \wedge ... \wedge A_n \wedge \text{ not } B_1 \wedge ... \wedge \text{ not } B_m).$$

---

[1]This work has been partially supported by Progetto Finalizzato Sistemi Informatici e Calcolo Parallelo of CNR, under grant n. 90.00689.PF69.

In this way we obtain a semantics for logic programs with two kinds of negation: the default negation and the classical one (expressed by means of constraints).

Usually constraints are dealt with in a *passive* way, i.e. for pruning solutions which do not satisfy them. For instance, the program

    B ← not A

with the constraint

    ← B   (i.e. ¬B)

has no solution, since the only solution of the program, where A is assumed to be false and B is true, does not satisfy the constraint.

The peculiarity of our treatment of constraints with respect to other proposals is that we do not want simply to use constraints to prune some solution, but we want to use them *actively* to compute new solutions. The meaning of active use of constraints will be made clear in the next section. Intuitively we want to consider constraints as formulae in classical logic, and use them, together with the given program, to make inferences. In particular, since constraints allow (classical) negation to be expressed, it will be meaningful to use also the contrapositives of clauses. For the previous example, starting from the constraint and using the contrapositive of the program clause, it is possible to deduce that A must be true (or, more precisely, that it cannot be assumed to be false).

The goal of actively dealing with constraints is also pursued in [Gef90], where an extension of negation as failure is defined for handling negative information. However, there a somewhat skeptical attitude in accepting solutions is adopted, while here a more credulous one is followed. Another proposal for dealing with negative information is the one in [GL90] in which constraints are not allowed, but classical negation is allowed both in the head and in the body of the clauses.

Other proposals for extending the abductive framework to deal with constraints, presented in [KM90a] and [KM90b], will be discussed in the next section.

In this paper we will also define an interpretation of logic programs as default theories which is equivalent to the abductive characterization and thus well suited for dealing with constraints. The proposed interpretation is different from the ones introduced in [MT89], but equivalent to them when constraints are not present. In this case, in fact, as for the interpretations proposed in [MT89], there is a one-to-one correspondence between the stable models of a logic program and the extensions of the corresponding default theory.

Also JTMSs can be extended to deal with constraints, and the so called process of *dependency-directed backtracking* can be considered as an operational way of using constraints actively. Whenever the JTMS finds a solution which is inconsistent with some constraint, it tries to eliminate the inconsistency by detecting an assumption responsible of the inconsistency and adding a new justification for that assumption (such as A ← in the previous example). It was shown in [GM90a] and [GM90c] that dependency-directed backtracking can also be given a declarative semantics. The two semantics defined in this paper (in terms of abduction and in terms of defaults) can in some way be regarded as alternative characterizations for the JTMS, which share the same idea of actively using constraints.

The outline of this paper is the following. In section 2 after recalling Eshghi and Kowalski transformation from logic programs into abduction frameworks and showing, by an example, that it is not suitable for dealing with general constraints, we propose a modified framework, that is a generalization of the previous one and coincides with it when constraints are not present. In section 3 we'll introduce an interpretation of logic programs as default theories, which is able to accommodate also constraints. Given a logic program with constraints, there is a one-to-one correspondence between the extensions of the associated default theory and the abductive assumptions of the corresponding abduction framework, as defined in section 2. Finally, in section 4, we present a transformation for eliminating constraints, so that we will be able to apply known techniques to find solutions for general clauses without constraints.

2. NEGATION AND CONSTRAINTS THROUGH ABDUCTION

In [EK89] abduction has been proposed to characterize negation as failure in logic programs. In the following we will restrict our attention to propositional logic programs. We will regard a logic program as a set of clauses of the form

$$C \leftarrow A_1 \wedge ... \wedge A_n \wedge \text{not } B_1 \wedge ... \wedge \text{not } B_m,$$

where C, A_i and B_j are propositions and the negation in the body of the clause is the usual negation as failure. Let us recall the Eshghi and Kowalski transformation defined in [EK89] to convert logic programs into abduction frameworks. This transformation essentially replaces negated propositions with abducibles and introduces new constraints.

Given a logic program P, the *abduction framework* $<P^*,I,\mathcal{A}>$ associated with P can be defined as follows:

- P^* is a set of clauses obtained from P by replacing all occurrences of "not B" with a new proposition B^* (B^* represents the negation of B);
- I is a set of *integrity constraints* containing, for each new proposition B^*, the "object-level" constraint

$$\leftarrow B \wedge B^*$$

and the "meta-level" constraint

$$\text{Demo}(B) \vee \text{Demo}(B^*);$$

- $\mathcal{A}$ is the set of the new propositions B^*, called *abducible* propositions.

Given an abduction framework $<P^*,I,\mathcal{A}>$, an *abductive solution* for a goal G is a set Δ of abducibles such that

$P^* \cup \Delta \vdash G$ and

$P^* \cup \Delta \cup I$ is consistent,

that is, $P^* \cup \Delta$ is consistent and satisfies I. The constraint $\leftarrow B \wedge B^*$ is satisfied in Δ if it is not the case that both B and B^* are derivable from $P^* \cup \Delta$. The meta-level constraint $\text{Demo}(B) \vee \text{Demo}(B^*)$ is satisfied Δ if either B^* is in Δ or B is derivable from $P^* \cup \Delta$.

In the following we will also speak of abductive solutions, without mentioning a goal, referring to sets Δ of abducibles such that $P^* \cup \Delta \cup I$ is consistent.

In [EK89] it is claimed that this semantics provides a generalization of negation as failure in several respects, one of them being the fact that a program can have more than one abductive solution. For instance the abductive framework associated with the program

$p \leftarrow \text{not } q$

$q \leftarrow \text{not } p$

has the two solutions $\{p^*\}$ and $\{q^*\}$.

Another advantage of this approach is that integrity constraints can also be accommodated. As a constraint we mean a formula of the form

$\leftarrow A_1 \wedge ... \wedge A_n \wedge \text{not } B_1 \wedge ... \wedge \text{not } B_m$.

In the case where a set IC of constraints is given together with a program P, the abduction framework associated with P and IC can be defined by extending Eshghi and Kowalski transformation in two different ways: either regarding the constraints IC in the same way as the object-level constraints introduced by the transformation, or regarding them as part of the program P itself. We will see that both solutions are not satisfactory and that, in order to cope with the presence of constraints, Eshghi and Kowalski transformation has to be modified more substantially.

Following the first approach, the resulting abduction framework will be $<P^*,IC^* \cup I,\mathcal{A}>$, where IC^* is obtained from IC by replacing each occurrence of "not" B with B^*. In this case, the constraints contained in IC can be regarded as pruning constraints, i.e. they are simply used to get ride of some solutions, the ones not satisfying the constraints. Of course, this is not always what we have in mind when writing a program containing constraints, especially when we want to use constraints to introduce negative facts in a program. To make it clear, let us consider the following example, which we will use throughout the paper:

Example

Let P_1 be the set of clauses:

Dove ← Quaker ∧ not ab_Quaker	Quaker ←
Hawk ← Republican ∧ not ab_Republican	Republican ←

and the set IC containing the only constraint:

  ← Dove ∧ Hawk.

The associated abduction framework obtained by the above transformation is $AF_1 = <P_1^*, IC^* \cup I, \mathcal{A}>$, where $\mathcal{A} = \{$ ab_Quaker*, ab_Republican$^*\}$, $IC^* = IC$ and

P_1^*:
  Dove ← Quaker ∧ ab_Quaker* Quaker ←
  Hawk ← Republican ∧ ab_Republican* Republican ←

I:
  ← ab_Quaker ∧ ab_Quaker* Demo(ab_Quaker) ∨ Demo(ab_Quaker*)
  ← ab_Republican ∧ ab_Republican* Demo(ab_Republican) ∨ Demo(ab_Republican*).

Given the goal G=Dove, there is no abductive solution for this goal in the framework. $\Delta = \{$ab_Quaker$^*\}$ is not a solution since it does not satisfy the meta-level constraint Demo(ab_Republican) ∨ Demo(ab_Republican*): in fact, neither ab_Republican* is in Δ, nor ab_Republican is provable from $P_1^* \cup \Delta$, although this solution is intuitively valid. In the same way, we would like to abductively conclude Hawk from the assumption $\Delta' = \{$ab_Republican$^*\}$. We simply do not want to accept both conclusions together because of the constraint ←Dove∧ Hawk.

This way of dealing with constraints, therefore, does not always correspond to the intended meaning, since sometimes we would like to use them to make inferences and not simply to prune solutions. One could guess that this problem is easily solvable by introducing the original constraints (those in IC) in the program P itself as the other clauses, i.e. to follow the second approach. Indeed, this would allow also the contrapositives of the constraints to be used. However, by the same example, it is easy to see that it is not sufficient to add general constraints to the program to obtain the expected solutions.

Example

Let P be the program $P_1 \cup \{$← Dove ∧ Hawk$\}$. The associated abduction framework obtained by the Eshghi and Kowalski transformation is

$$AF_2 = <P^*, I, \mathcal{A}>,$$

where $P^* = P_1^* \cup \{$← Dove ∧ Hawk$\}$.

However, also in this framework the query G=Dove has no abductive solution, and the reason why it happens is the same as before: the meta-level constraint Demo(ab_Republican) ∨ Demo(ab_Republican*) is not satisfied by the set of assumptions $\Delta = \{$ab_Quaker$^*\}$. Indeed, in this case, neither ab_Republican nor ab_Republican* can be proved from $P^* \cup \Delta$. However, by making use of the constraint, ¬ab_Republican* can be derived from $P^* \cup \Delta$. In fact, since Quaker is in P^* and ab_Quaker* is in Δ, by the first clause in P^*, Dove is provable from $P^* \cup \Delta$. From Dove, by the contrapositive of the constraint (¬Hawk←Dove), ¬Hawk is derivable. Finally, by the contrapositive of the second clause (¬ab_Republican* ← Republican ∧ ¬Hawk) and since Republican is a given fact,

¬ab_Republican* can be derived. So ¬ab_Republican* is derived from P* ∪ Δ, while ab_Republican is not.

This outcome gives a suggestion on how Eshghi and Kowalski transformation can be modified in order to deal with constraints in the program P. We define a transformation which maps the program P with constraints into an abduction framework differing from Eshghi and Kowalski transformation only as regards the object and meta-level constraints that are introduced.

Given a logic program P possibly containing constraints, the *abduction framework* <P*,I,$\mathcal{A}$> associated with P is defined as follows:
- P* is a set of clauses obtained from P by replacing all occurrences of "not B" with a new proposition B* (B* represents the negation of B);
- I is a set of *integrity constraints* containing, for each new proposition B*, the "object-level" constraints

$$\leftarrow B \wedge B^* \qquad\qquad \leftarrow \neg B \wedge \neg B^*$$

and the "meta-level" constraint

$$Demo(B) \vee Demo(B^*) \vee Demo(\neg B^*);$$

- $\mathcal{A}$ is the set of the new propositions B*.

With this modified framework, in the previous example we get the expected solutions.

Example

Given the program P of our example, the associated abduction framework obtained by the new transformation is

$$AF = <P^*, I', \mathcal{A}>,$$

where P* is defined as previously and I' contains the following integrity constraints:

$\leftarrow$ ab_Quaker ∧ ab_Quaker* $\qquad\qquad$ $\leftarrow$ ¬ab_Quaker ∧ ¬ab_Quaker*

$\leftarrow$ ab_Republican ∧ ab_Republican* $\qquad\qquad$ $\leftarrow$ ¬ab_Republican ∧ ¬ab_Republican*

Demo(ab_Quaker) ∨ Demo(ab_Quaker*) ∨ Demo(¬ab_Quaker*)

Demo(ab_Republican) ∨ Demo(ab_Republican*) ∨ Demo(¬ab_Republican*).

The query G=Dove has the abductive solution Δ_1={ab_Quaker*}, since, in this case, the meta-level constraint

Demo(ab_Republican) ∨ Demo(ab_Republican*) ∨ Demo(¬ab_Republican*)

is satisfied, being ¬ab_Republican* derivable from P* ∪ Δ_1. For the same reason, the query G=Hawk has the abductive solution Δ_2={ab_Republican*}. Of course, the goal G=Dove ∧ Hawk has no abductive solution.

From this example it should be clear why the modified meta-level constraints are needed. To explain why the object-level constraints $\leftarrow$ ¬B∧¬B* are also required, consider the program P only containing the following constraints:

$\leftarrow$ b $\qquad$ $\leftarrow$ not b ∧ not a.

The associated abduction framework has the single abductive solution Δ={b*}, which satisfies the meta-level constraints since P* ∪ Δ derives ¬a*. The set of abducibles Δ'={a*} is not an abductive solution, because P* ∪ Δ' derives both ¬b* and ¬b, thus contradicting the constraint $\leftarrow$¬b∧¬b*. In absence of such a constraint, we would accept the unintuitive solution Δ'={a*}.

It is easy to see that this transformation is a generalization of Eshghi and Kowalski transformation. In fact, it can be proved that when constraints are not present in the given program the two transformations coincide, that is, the two different abduction frameworks resulting from the two transformations have the same abductive solutions.

As proved in [EK89], given a general logic program, there is a one to one correspondence between the stable models of the program and the abductive solutions of the abduction framework which is the outcome of Eshghi and Kowalski transformation. Then, for the above equivalence, when the program contains no constraint, there is also a one to one correspondence between the stable models and the abductive solutions of the abduction framework we get by this new transformation.

We have said that the peculiarity of this way of dealing with negation and constraints resides in the fact that constraints are used *actively* to make inferences. This is not true of other proposals like the one in [KM90a], where the case is considered where a program P is given together with a set IC of constraints and a set of abducibles Abd, that is, where an abduction framework <P,IC,Abd> is given, instead of simply a program P. In this case the above transformation gives a new abduction framework <P^*,IC^*∪I,Abd∪$\mathcal{A}$>. However, in [KM90b] it has been shown that, if the constraints are restricted to contain only abducible or negated abducible symbols then, in a certain way, an active use of constraints is made, though retaining the usual abduction framework. Anyway, this restriction imposed on the language is quite severe. Moreover, this solution is not applicable to our case, since we have no abducibles other than those introduced by the transformation.

As a final remark, going back to our example, we want to point out that in the more skeptical view adopted in [Gef90] neither the goal G=Dove nor the goal G=Hawk has any solution.

3. NEGATION AND CONSTRAINTS THROUGH DEFAULTS

In this section we describe another equivalent characterization of logic programs with negation and constraints by means of default theories. As said in the introduction, the proposed interpretation of logic programs as default theories also accommodates constraints, and differs from the ones defined in [MT89] although it can be proved equivalent to them in the case where constraints are not present in the program. In fact, as for them, the extensions of the default theory associated with a program correspond to the stable models of the program. Moreover, our default interpretation is nearer to the abductive interpretation defined before.

We are now going to define a mapping from logic programs to default theories which somewhat resembles the above transformation into abduction frameworks. The idea is to perform the same transformation on the clauses and constraints in the program by replacing the negated propositions with new symbols and, then, to use normal defaults to make the new symbols assumable. Other (non-normal) defaults are required to take the place of the (object-level) integrity constraints present in the abduction framework.

Let P be a general logic program also containing constraints. We define a *default theory* (W,D) associated with it as follows:

- W is a set of clauses obtained from P by replacing all occurrences of "not B" with a new proposition B^* (note that W coincides with P^* and it contains constraints too);
- D is a set of default rules containing, for each new proposition B^*, the three default rules:

$$\frac{: B^*}{B^*} \qquad\qquad \frac{B : \delta}{\neg B^*} \qquad\qquad \frac{\neg B : \delta}{B^*}$$

where δ is a new dummy proposition which only occurs in each non-normal default: $\neg\delta$ cannot be introduced in an extension unless it is an inconsistent one (and so the non-normal defaults are applicable when their antecedents are derivable). The language of the default theory is thus the language of the original program plus the proposition δ and the new propositions B^* (for each proposition B occurring negated in the program).

The normal defaults in D allow the new symbols of the form B^* to be assumed, i.e. added to the extensions. The two non-normal defaults in D play the role of the object-level constraints ←B∧B^* and ← ¬B∧¬ B^*. Let us consider the first non-normal default (similar remarks hold for the second one). It codifies as a default rule the contrapositive $\neg B^* \leftarrow B$ of the constraint ←B∧B^* which gives an inconsistency if B^* is assumed when B is derivable. By introducing $\neg B^*$ in the extension, this default rule allows the rule $:B^*/B^*$ to be blocked when B is derived, so that B^* cannot be assumed. Instead of directly introducing the object level constraint $\leftarrow B \wedge B^*$ in W, we add the corresponding non-normal default to the theory in order to prevent the use of its other contrapositive, namely $\neg B \leftarrow B^*$. In fact, default rules can be used in a single direction.

Notice instead that, since W is a theory in classical propositional logic, the contrapositive use of clauses and constraints in it is allowed; for instance, if W contains the clause $A \leftarrow B^*$ and the constraint $\leftarrow A$ (i.e. the formula $\neg A$), $\neg B^*$ is derivable from W. The constraints present in W provide the starting point for the inferences, through contraposition, of new negative information. It has to be noticed that the kind of negation introduced by the constraints in the program is quite different from the negation in the body of clauses (and of constraints) that we have suppressed by introducing new abducible symbols: it is not a negation by default, but the classical negation. The meaning of B^* is that B can be consistently assumed to be false, while the meaning of $\neg B$ is that B can be proved to be false. The reason why the use of the contrapositive $\neg B \leftarrow B^*$ has to be avoided is that it would allow $\neg B$ to be deduced by assuming B^*.

For this same reason, in this default interpretation, we must introduce the new symbols B^* as in the abduction framework and we cannot simply replace "not B" with $\neg B$ and introduce the default $:\neg B/\neg B$ (otherwise, assuming $\neg B$ could start some contrapositive inference and we would not model negation as failure).

Notice that, in the default theory (W,D) there is nothing playing the role of the meta-level constraints $Demo(B) \vee Demo(B^*) \vee Demo(\neg B^*)$ in the abduction framework. This is because, by definition, to get the default extensions as many as possible defaults are applied, and so the defaults $:B^*/B^*$ are applied whenever it is possible, in particular when neither B nor $\neg B^*$ are present in the extension. Thus the effect of the meta-level constraints is automatically supplied. Let us now consider again the example.

Example
The default theory associated with the program P is (W,D), where

W: Dove $\leftarrow$ Quaker $\wedge$ ab_Quaker*
Hawk $\leftarrow$ Republican $\wedge$ ab_Republican*
Quaker $\leftarrow$
Republican $\leftarrow$
$\leftarrow$ Dove $\wedge$ Hawk

D: $\dfrac{: ab\_Quaker^*}{ab\_Quaker^*}$ $\qquad$ $\dfrac{ab\_Quaker : \delta}{\neg\ ab\_Quaker^*}$ $\qquad$ $\dfrac{\neg ab\_Quaker : \delta}{ab\_Quaker^*}$

$\dfrac{: ab\_Republican^*}{ab\_Republican^*}$ $\qquad$ $\dfrac{ab\_Republican : \delta}{\neg\ ab\_Republican^*}$ $\qquad$ $\dfrac{\neg ab\_Republican : \delta}{ab\_Republican^*}$

The default theory (W,D) has two extensions: the one containing ab_Quaker*, Dove and $\neg$ab_Republican* and the other one containing ab_Republican*, Hawk and $\neg$ ab_Quaker*. These two extensions exactly correspond to the two abductive solutions of the abduction framework $AF=<P^*,I',\mathcal{A}>$.

To see how the non-normal defaults introduced in the default interpretation are used, let us consider the following program
p $\leftarrow$ not q
q $\leftarrow$ not p

which has an associated default theory (W,D), where

W: $p \leftarrow q^*$
       $q \leftarrow p^*$

D: $\dfrac{: q^*}{q^*}$ (i) $\dfrac{q : \delta}{\neg q^*}$ (ii) $\dfrac{\neg q : \delta}{q^*}$ (iii)

       $\dfrac{: p^*}{p^*}$ (iv) $\dfrac{p : \delta}{\neg p^*}$ (v) $\dfrac{\neg p : \delta}{p^*}$ (vi)

(W,D) has two extensions: E_1 containing q^*, p and $\neg p^*$ and E_2 containing p^*, q and $\neg q^*$. Notice that to get the extension E_1, the defaults (i) and (v) are applied; in particular, applying default (v) adds $\neg p^*$ in the extension, thus blocking default (iv).

In general, the following theorem can be proved.

Theorem. Given a logic program P possibly containing constraints, there is a one to one correspondence between the abductive solutions of its associated abduction framework $<P^*,I',\mathcal{A}>$ and the consistent extensions of the associated default theory (W,D).

In particular, in the case where P does not contain any constraint, this correspondence guarantees that the extensions of the default theory (W,D) correspond to the stable models of P. This is because, when P does not contain constraints, the abduction framework defined in [EK89], our modified abduction framework and our default interpretation all provide the same solutions that, as proved in [EK89], do correspond to the stable models of the program P.

For this reason our default interpretation of logic programs can be regarded as another semantics for logic programs with negation which is equivalent to the stable model semantics. With respect to other default interpretations of logic programs as the one defined in [GL88] and those proposed in [MT89] it has the advantage of being also well suited for dealing with constraints in the program, while the others are not. In fact, if each general clause $C \leftarrow A \wedge \neg B$ is represented by means of a non-normal default of the form A :¬B/C, then contraposition is not allowed and, therefore, in the previous example the expected solutions cannot be achieved.

4. PROOF PROCEDURE: ELIMINATING CONSTRAINTS

By now, we haven't said anything about inference procedures for this language with default negation and constraints. From a logic programming standpoint, we would like to have a goal directed procedure that, given a logic program with constraints and given a goal, produces a solution for the goal in the program. What we are thinking of is an abductive procedure in the style of the one defined by Eshghi and Kowalski [EK89] for programs with negation. Given a program, that procedure allows to compute the abductive solutions for a goal in the abduction framework associated with the program. Adapting Eshghi and Kowalski algorithm is not straightforward, since in our case the original program can contain constraints and, moreover, the metalevel constraints in the abduction framework have been modified. Instead of modifying the algorithm, we define a transformation on the abduction framework of Eshghi and Kowalski which allows their original algorithm to be used.

Thus given a program with constraints, and the associated extended abduction framework $AF=<P^*,I',\mathcal{A}>$, we are going to define a transformation from it into another one $<P^\sim,I^\sim,\mathcal{A}>$, where $P^\sim$ must be a set of Horn clauses not containing any constraint, and $I^\sim$ must contain object level constraints of the form $\leftarrow B \wedge B^*$ and meta-level constraints of the form $Demo(B) \vee Demo(B^*)$.

Since the obtained abduction framework has the same form as the one proposed by Eshghi and Kowalski, we can use their algorithm. We will not enter the details of the algorithm here, but we point out that it is neither complete nor correct in general. In particular, it fails in dealing with odd negative cycles within the set of clauses in P^*. (We say that there is an odd negative cycle in the set of clauses when a proposition p depends on its negation p^* by an odd number of negative arcs as, for instance, in the case

$p \leftarrow p^*$). In [EK89] it is shown that, when P^* contains such odd negative cycles, the algorithm is not guaranteed to be correct. In fact, in such cases in the abduction framework a goal can have no solution (when p cannot be proved in any other way than assuming p^*), while the algorithm computes one solution.

The transformation, that is somewhat similar to the one defined in [GM90b] to give a characterization of the TMS in terms of abduction, consists in explicitly introducing the contrapositives of the clauses and constraints in P^* and eliminating the constraints from P^*. To state the contrapositives, new symbols p~ are introduced, one for each proposition p, to represent the fact that p is false. The transformation is the following:

1) if

$$C \leftarrow A_1 \wedge ... \wedge A_n \wedge B_1^* \wedge ... \wedge B_m^*,$$

is in P^*, then

$$C \leftarrow A_1 \wedge ... \wedge A_n \wedge B_1^* \wedge ... \wedge B_m^*,$$
$$A_i{}^\sim \leftarrow C^\sim \wedge A_1 \wedge ... \wedge A_{i-1} \wedge A_{i+1} \wedge ... \wedge A_n \wedge B_1^* \wedge ... \wedge B_m^* \quad i=1,..,n$$
$$B_j^*{}^\sim \leftarrow C^\sim \wedge A_1 \wedge ... \wedge A_n \wedge B_1^* \wedge ... \wedge B_{j-1}^* \wedge B_{j+1}^* \wedge ... \wedge B_m^* \quad j=1,..,m$$

are in P~. If the clause is a constraint (i.e. C is false) then the constraint is not introduced in P~ (moreover, $C^\sim$ is true and it is omitted);

2) for each B^* in P^*, the clause

$B^*{}^\sim \leftarrow B$

is introduced in P~

3) for each B^* in P^*, I~ contains the metalevel constraint

$Demo(B^*) \vee Demo(B^*{}^\sim)$

and the object level constraint

$\leftarrow B^* \wedge B^*{}^\sim$

So, with these changes, the resulting abduction framework $<P^\sim, I^\sim, \mathcal{A}>$ is precisely as we want: modulo the names of the propositions, it is exactly an abduction framework as the one obtained by Eshghi and Kowalski and, therefore, their algorithm can be applied to it.

It can be shown that this transformation is correct only if the initial program P^* is not inconsistent by itself (as P={ $\leftarrow$b, b$\leftarrow$ }). Otherwise the constraints $\leftarrow$B$\wedge$B~ should be added to I~. It can also be seen that the constraints $\leftarrow$B$\wedge$B* are not needed because of the clauses added in step 2.

However, it has to be noted that, in some particular cases, this transformation does not preserve all the solutions of the initial framework, that is, there are some abductive solutions that are lost by the transformation. This happens for instance when in P^* the contradiction depends on the same assumption p^* in more then one way: in such cases the transformation introduces negative odd loops, for which, as we have said before, there is no solution. These cases should anyway be ruled out, because the algorithm does not work correctly with them.

Example

By applying this transformation to our example, we obtain the following program P~ and set of constraints I~:

P~:	
Dove $\leftarrow$ Quaker $\wedge$ ab_Quaker*	Quaker $\leftarrow$
Quaker~ $\leftarrow$ Dove~ $\wedge$ ab_Quaker*	Republican $\leftarrow$
ab_Quaker$^*{}^\sim \leftarrow$ Quaker $\wedge$ Dove~	Dove~ $\leftarrow$ Hawk
Hawk $\leftarrow$ Republican $\wedge$ ab_Republican*	Hawk~ $\leftarrow$ Dove
Republican~ $\leftarrow$ Hawk~ $\wedge$ ab_Republican*	ab_Quaker$^*{}^\sim \leftarrow$ ab_Quaker
ab_Republican$^*{}^\sim \leftarrow$ Republican $\wedge$ Hawk~	ab_Republican$^*{}^\sim \leftarrow$ ab_Republican

Γ: $\leftarrow$ ab_Quaker$^{*\sim}$ $\wedge$ ab_Quaker* $\leftarrow \neg$ab_Republican$^{*\sim}$ $\wedge$ $\neg$ab_Republican*

     $\leftarrow$ ab_Republican$^{*\sim}$ $\wedge$ ab_Republican* Demo(ab_Quaker$^{*\sim}$) $\vee$ Demo(ab_Quaker*)

     $\leftarrow \neg$ab_Quaker$^{*\sim}$ $\wedge$ $\neg$ab_Quaker* Demo(ab_Republican$^{*\sim}$) $\vee$ Demo(ab_Republican*)

It is easy to see that in this framework the query G=Dove has the abductive solution $\Delta=\{$ab_Quaker$^{*}\}$. In fact, from P$\cup\Delta$ we derive ab_Quaker*, Quaker, Republican, Dove, Hawk$^{\sim}$ and ab_Republican$^{*\sim}$, which satisfy the integrity constraints.

If we want to find an abductive solution for the given set of clauses and constraints (or all abductive solutions) without reference to a particular goal, it can be more convenient to use other techniques. For instance, in [GM90b] it is shown that, by replacing meta-level constraints with new clauses, it is possible to transform an Eshghi and Kowalski abductive framework into a set of justifications and (pruning) constraints for an assumption-based TMS (ATMS), which can then be used to find all solutions.

5. CONCLUSIONS

In this paper we have extended the abduction framework defined by Eshghi and Kowalski to actively deal with constraints in logic programs with negation. We only want to mention that this formalism is well suited to deal with practical problems requiring nonmonotonic reasoning such as consistency-based diagnoses. The behaviour of the modelled system and the observations can be described by a set of clauses and constraints, and the non-abnormal behaviour of a system component c_i can be expressed as "not abnormal(c_i)" by making use of negation as failure. The solutions will then consist of maximal sets of non-abnormal components. The abduction framework allows to deal with multiple solutions, whereas the active use of constraints allows to derive from the observations those components which are abnormal.

REFERENCES

[EK89] Eshghi K. and Kowalski R.A., "Abduction Compared with Negation by Failure", in *Proc. Int. Conf. on Logic Programming*, pp.134-154, 1989.

[Gef90] Geffner H., "Beyond Negation as Failure", to appear in *Proc. KR'91*, Cambridge, USA, 1991.

[GL88] Gelfond M.and Lifschitz V., "The Stable Model Semantics for Logic Programming", in *Proc. Fifth Int. Conf. and Symposium on Logic Programming*, pp.1070-1080, Seattle, 1988.

[GL90] Gelfond M.and Lifschitz V., "Logic Programs with Classical Negation", in *Proc. ICLP 90*, pp.579-597, Jerusalem, 1990.

[GM90a] Giordano L. and Martelli A., "Generalized Stable Models, Truth Maintenance and Conflict Resolution", in *Proc. ICLP 90*, pp.427-441, Jerusalem, 1990.

[GM90b] Giordano L. and Martelli A., "An Abductive Characterization of the TMS", in *Proc. ECAI 90*, pp.308-313, Stockholm, 1990.

[GM90c] Giordano L. and Martelli A., "Three-valued Labellings for Truth Maintenance Systems", in *Proc. ISMIS 90*, pp.506-513, Knoxville, 1990.

[KM90a] Kakas A.K. and Mancarella P., "Generalized Stable Models: a Semantics for Abduction", in *Proc. ECAI 90*, pp.385-391, Stockholm, 1990.

[KM90b] Kakas A.K. and Mancarella P., "On the Relation between Truth Maintenance and Abduction", in *Proc. 1st Pacific Rim International Conference on AI, PRICAI90*, Nagoya, Japan, 1990.

[MT89] Marek W. and Truszczynski M., "Stable Semantics for Logic Programs and Default Theories", in *Proc. NACLP 89*, pp.243-256, Cleveland, 1989.

[PC89] Pimentel S.G. and Cuadrado J.L., "A Truth Maintenance System Based on Stable Models", in *Proc. NACLP 89*, pp.274-290, Cleveland, 1989.

A Hybrid System with Datalog and Concept Languages

Francesco M. Donini, Maurizio Lenzerini,
Daniele Nardi, Andrea Schaerf
Dipartimento di Informatica e Sistemistica,
Università di Roma "La Sapienza"
via Salaria 113, I-00198, Roma, Italy

Abstract

We present a hybrid system for knowledge representation, called $\mathcal{AL}$-log, based on the concept language $\mathcal{ALC}$ and the deductive database language Datalog. $\mathcal{AL}$-log embodies two subsystems, called structural and relational. The former allows for the definition of structural knowledge about the classes of interest and the membership relation between objects and classes. The latter allows for the definition of relational knowledge about the objects described in the structural component. The interaction between the two components is obtained by allowing $\mathcal{ALC}$-constraints within Datalog clauses, thus requiring the variables in the clauses to range over the set of instances of a specified concept. We propose a method for hybrid reasoning based on constrained resolution, where the usual deduction procedure defined for Datalog is integrated with a method for reasoning on the structural knowledge.

1 Introduction

Hybrid systems are a special class of knowledge representation systems which are constituted by two or more subsystems dealing with distinct portions of a knowledge base and specific reasoning procedures [2,9]. The characterizing feature of hybrid systems is that the whole system is in charge of a single knowledge base, thus combining the knowledge and the reasoning of the different subsystems in order to answer the user's questions. The motivation for building hybrid sytems is to improve on two basic features of knowledge representation formalisms, namely representational adequacy and deductive power.

It is very often the case that a knowledge representation formalism together with the associated reasoning procedures is adequate for representing certain kinds of information, but unsuited or at least heavy to use for others. The possibility of using different formalisms in the same framework is pursued in hybrid systems in order to overcome the limitations of a single representation paradigm.

The improvement in the deductive power of hybrid systems is in terms of both the inferences the system is able to make, and the efficiency of the deductive process. With

---

This work was partly funded by the ESPRIT BRA 3012 (Compulog) and the Italian CNR under Progetto Finalizzato Sistemi Informatici e Calcolo Parallelo, contract 90.00681.PF69.

regard to the first point, the set of conclusions a hybrid system should be able to draw is not just the union of the conclusions derivable within each subsystem, because any subsystem can take advantage of the results obtained by other subsystems. In addition, the use of specialized reasoners makes it possible to optimize the deduction process, since specialized reasoners typically perform better than general purpose deduction procedures.

Based on the above arguments a group of two-component hybrid systems has been proposed, where the subsystems have been be called terminological and assertional. The terminological subsystem provides the ability to create a hierarchical structure of concepts (or classes) by using a so-called concept language, whereas the assertional subsystem provides the user with a language for expressing properties of individuals. Many of these systems (see for example [4,10]) provide a rather powerful concept language, combined with an assertional language that is sometimes used simply to express facts about individuals. Closely related to terminological/assertional hybrid systems are the proposals arising from the study of many-sorted logics, where the sort language can be regarded as an elementary concept language, combined with a full first order language [5,8].

In this paper we present a two-component hybrid system, named $\mathcal{AL}$-log, whose main feature is to add to the framework of deductive databases the structuring power of concept languages.

More specifically, in $\mathcal{AL}$-log we have a *structural* subsystem based on the concept language $\mathcal{ALC}$ [6] and a *relational* subsystem based on the database language Datalog [13]. The whole knowledge base in $\mathcal{AL}$-log is defined by a set of so-called constrained Datalog clauses, which are clauses modified with additional constraints on variables and individual objects, expressed using $\mathcal{ALC}$. The constraints on the variables require them to range over the set of instances of a specified concept, while the constraints on individual objects require them to belong to the extension of a concept.

The $\mathcal{AL}$-log hybrid reasoner computes answers to queries, based on the specification of both the structural and the relational component of the knowledge base. We propose a resolution-based hybrid reasoner, that finds the refutations like a Datalog top-down reasoner in the relational knowledge base, and collects the constraints for a final check done through a satisfiability check on the structural component.

$\mathcal{AL}$-log is innovative mainly in two respects. First, each subsystem embodies a knowledge base with both an intensional and an extensional level. In fact, the structural subsystem by itself is highly expressive compared with usual terminological systems, since the knowledge base of concepts can be defined by specifying containment assertions between concepts and membership assertions on individual objects.

Second, $\mathcal{AL}$-log makes it available the expressive power of concept languages within the substitutional framework studied for many-sorted logics. In this respect, $\mathcal{AL}$-log follows the approach taken in [3], specializing it to the case where the logical language is a deductive database language, and exploiting the use of the concept language in the definition of the structural component of the knowledge base.

The resulting system provides a form of integration between objects and logic within the framework of databases. Compared with other proposals of this kind (see [1]) $\mathcal{AL}$-

log is more expressive in the structural component, and provides more sophisticated reasoning mechanisms on such component. On the other hand, presently $\mathcal{AL}$-log does not include negation in the relational subsystem. Moreover, since relational knowledge does not play any role in deducing new information about the structure of individual objects, the form of integration between the two subsystems is weaker than the one supported in most deductive object-oriented database languages.

The paper is organized as follows. In Section 2 we describe $\mathcal{AL}$-log, by presenting the main features of the structural and the relational subsystems, and defining the semantics of a knowledge base in our system. In Section 3 we present a method for hybrid reasoning in $\mathcal{AL}$-log. Finally, conclusions are drawn in Section 4.

2   The Hybrid System $\mathcal{AL}$-log

As we said in the introduction, $\mathcal{AL}$-log embodies two subsystems, called structural and relational. The former, described in Subsection 2.1, allows one to express knowledge about concepts, roles and individuals. The latter, described in Subsection 2.2, provides the user with a suitable extension of Datalog in order to express a form of relational knowledge. The characterization of both the semantics of a knowledge base in the hybrid system, and the set of inferences that can be carried out over it, is provided in Subsection 2.3.

2.1   The Structural Subsystem

The structural subsystem of $\mathcal{AL}$-log allows one to define what we call an $\mathcal{ALC}$-knowledge base. An $\mathcal{ALC}$-knowledge base is structured into two levels, intensional and extensional. The intensional level refers to the knowledge about the concepts of interest, and is constituted by a set of statements specifying the relevant properties of such concepts. The extensional level regards the knowledge about individual objects, and is constituted by a set of membership assertions between objects and concepts (e.g. a is an instance of C), and between pairs of objects and roles (e.g. a is related to b by the relation R).

Therefore, the structural subsystem of $\mathcal{AL}$-log can be itself regarded as a terminological/assertional hybrid system, where the terminological component constitutes the intensional level, and the assertional component constitutes the extensional level. We shall see later that the expressive power of the language constructs used in the structural subsystem is greater than in conventional terminological/assertional hybrid systems.

Both at the intensional and the extensional level, there is the need of a specific concept language for building concept expressions. In $\mathcal{AL}$-log, the concept language is $\mathcal{ALC}$ [6]. As in other concept languages, $\mathcal{ALC}$-concepts represent the classes of objects in the domain of interest, while $\mathcal{ALC}$-roles represent binary relations between concepts. Complex concept expressions can be defined by means of a number of operators applied to primitive concepts (concepts denoted simply by a name) and roles. In particular, concept expressions in $\mathcal{ALC}$ can be formed by means of the following syntax (A denotes a primitive concept, R denotes a role, C and D denote arbitrary concepts):

$$C, D \longrightarrow A \mid \top \mid \bot \mid C \sqcap D \mid C \sqcup D \mid \neg C \mid \forall R.C \mid \exists R.C$$

Concepts are interpreted as subsets of a domain and roles are interpreted as binary relations over a domain. More precisely, an *interpretation* $\mathcal{I} = (\Delta^{\mathcal{I}}, \cdot^{\mathcal{I}})$ consists of a set $\Delta^{\mathcal{I}}$ (the *domain* of $\mathcal{I}$) and a function $\cdot^{\mathcal{I}}$ (the *extension (or interpretation) function* of $\mathcal{I}$) that maps every concept to a subset of $\Delta^{\mathcal{I}}$ and every role to a subset of $\Delta^{\mathcal{I}} \times \Delta^{\mathcal{I}}$ such that $\top^{\mathcal{I}} = \Delta^{\mathcal{I}}$, $\bot^{\mathcal{I}} = \emptyset$, $\sqcup, \sqcap, \neg$ are interpreted as union, intersection and complement, respectively, and moreover:

$$
\begin{aligned}
(\forall R.C)^{\mathcal{I}} &= \{d_1 \in \Delta^{\mathcal{I}} \mid \forall (d_1, d_2) \in R^{\mathcal{I}}. d_2 \in C^{\mathcal{I}}\} \\
(\exists R.C)^{\mathcal{I}} &= \{d_1 \in \Delta^{\mathcal{I}} \mid \exists (d_1, d_2) \in R^{\mathcal{I}}. d_2 \in C^{\mathcal{I}}\}
\end{aligned}
$$

We now turn our attention to the problem of defining the intensional level of an $\mathcal{ALC}$-knowledge base. As we said before, the intensional level specifies the properties of the concepts of interest in a particular application. Syntactically, such properties are expressed in terms of a set of so-called *inclusion statements* (see [11]). An inclusion statement (or symply inclusion) has the form

$$
C \sqsubseteq D
$$

where C and D are two arbitrary concepts. Intuitively, the statement specifies that every instance of C is also an instance of D. More precisely, an interpretation $\mathcal{I}$ satisfies the inclusion $C \sqsubseteq D$ if $C^{\mathcal{I}} \subseteq D^{\mathcal{I}}$.

Let $\mathcal{T}$ be a finite set of inclusions. An interpretation $\mathcal{I}$ is a *model* for $\mathcal{T}$ if $\mathcal{I}$ satisfies all inclusions in $\mathcal{T}$. Moreover $\mathcal{T}$ *logically implies* an inclusion statement γ, written $\mathcal{T} \models \gamma$, if γ is satisfied by all the models of $\mathcal{T}$.

Terminological systems usually provide the user with suitable mechanisms for *concept definitions* of the form: $A \sqsubseteq D$ (*inclusion*) or $A \doteq D$ (*equivalence*) [11]. In these systems the definitional mechanisms are limited by the requirement that the left-hand side concept A be a concept name, and at most one statement for each concept is allowed. Note that the language proposed here for defining the intensional level of a concept-based knowledge base is much more powerful, because there is no limitation to the form of the concepts involved in the inclusions. In particular, an equivalence of the form $A \doteq D$ can be easily expressed in our system using the pair of inclusions $A \sqsubseteq D$ and $D \sqsubseteq A$. On the contrary, an inclusion of the form $C \sqsubseteq D$, where C and D are arbitrary concepts, cannot be expressed with the restrictions imposed by other systems.

Moreover, most of the existing systems do not allow cycles in the terminological component, i.e. do not permit a concept name A to occur neither directly nor indirectly within the definition of A. On the other hand, since we do not impose any constraint on the form of inclusions, cycles of this kind may occur in our system.

As shown in [11], there at least three types of semantics for terminological cycles, namely the least fixed point, the greatest fixed point and the descriptive semantics. Among them, the latter is the most general, and is the one used in our system.

We can now turn our attention to the mechanisms offered by the structural subsystem of $\mathcal{AL}$-log for the definition of the extensional level. As we said before, such a subsystem uses a rather limited meachanism, that essentially allows one to specify the instance-of relation between objects and concepts, and between pair of obejcts and roles. Other systems allow for the construction of more complex statements involving the usual logical connectives (see [4]).

Let $\mathcal{O}$ be an alphabet of symbols, called *individuals*. Syntatically, instance-of relationships are expressed in terms of *membership assertions* of the form:

$$C(a), \quad R(a, b)$$

where a and b are individuals, C is a concept, and R is a role. Intuitively, the first form states that a is an instance of C, whereas the second form states that a is related to b by means of the role R.

In order to assign a precise meaning to membership assertions, the extension function $\cdot^{\mathcal{I}}$ of an interpretation $\mathcal{I}$ is extended to individuals by mapping them to elements of $\Delta^{\mathcal{I}}$ in such a way that $a^{\mathcal{I}} \neq b^{\mathcal{I}}$ if $a \neq b$. Notice that this restriction ensures that different individuals denote different objects in the world (unique name assumption).

An interpretation $\mathcal{I}$ *satisfies* the assertion $C(a)$ if $a^{\mathcal{I}} \in C^{\mathcal{I}}$, and satisfies $R(a, b)$ if $(a^{\mathcal{I}}, b^{\mathcal{I}}) \in R^{\mathcal{I}}$. $\mathcal{I}$ is a model for a set of membership assertions $\mathcal{A}$ if $\mathcal{I}$ satisfies all the assertions in $\mathcal{A}$.

We can now summarize the features of the structural subsystem of $\mathcal{AL}$-log as follows. The structural subsystem allows one to define an $\mathcal{ALC}$-knowledge base, that is a pair $\Sigma =< \mathcal{T}, \mathcal{A} >$, where $\mathcal{T}$ (the intensional level) is a set of inclusions, and $\mathcal{A}$ (the extensional level) is a set of assertions. An interpretation $\mathcal{I}$ is a model of Σ if it is both a model of $\mathcal{T}$ and a model of $\mathcal{A}$. Notice that by virtue of the unique name assumption, we can focus on what we call $\mathcal{O}$-interpretations. An $\mathcal{O}$-interpretation for Σ is an interpretation for Σ such that for each $a \in \mathcal{O}$, $a^{\mathcal{I}} = a$. AN $\mathcal{O}$-model is an $\mathcal{O}$-interpretation that is a model. In the sequel, when we refer to interpretations (models) for an $\mathcal{ALC}$-knowledge base, we implicitly assume to deal with $\mathcal{O}$-interpretations ($\mathcal{O}$-models).

Σ is satisfiable if it has a model. Furthermore Σ logically implies Γ (written $\Sigma \models \Gamma$), where Γ is either an inclusion or a membership assertion, if every model of Σ satisfies Γ.

2.2 The Relational Subsystem

The relational subsystem allows one to express relational knowledge in terms of a set of so-called constrained Datalog clauses. A constrained clause is a clause modified with a set of restrictions on its variables and constants, expressed using the language $\mathcal{ALC}$.

More precisely, a constrained Datalog clause has the form:

$$\gamma \ \& \ \beta_1, \ldots, \beta_m$$

where $m \geq 0, \gamma$ is a Datalog clause, and each β_i is a *constraint* of the form

$$s : C$$

where s is either a constant or a variable, and C is an $\mathcal{ALC}$-concept.

Intuitively, a constraint on a variable X restricts the values of X to range over the set of instances of a specified concept. Similarly, a constraint on a constant a, called *ground constraint*, imposes the condition that a denotes an individual which is an instance of a specified concept.

A set of constrained Datalog clauses is called a constrained Datalog program.

2.3 Semantics of a Hybrid Knowledge Base

In $\mathcal{AL}$-log, a knowledge base is partitioned into two components, that we call structural (defined using the structural subsystem) and relational (defined using the relational subsystem).

A knowledge base K is therefore defined as a pair $< \Sigma, \Pi >$, where Σ is an $\mathcal{ALC}$-knowledge base, and Π is a constrained Datalog program. Every knowledge base must satisfy the following conditions:

1. The set of Datalog predicate symbols appearing in Π is disjoint from the set of concept and role symbols appearing in Σ.
2. The alphabet of constants used in Π coincides with the alphabet $\mathcal{O}$ of the individuals of Σ. Moreover, every constant occurring in Π appears also in Σ. Note that this condition can always be satisfied, because for each individual a not appearing in Σ one can add to Σ the assertion $\top(a)$, resulting in an $\mathcal{ALC}$-knowledge base which is equivalent to Σ.
3. For every clause γ & $\beta_1, \ldots, \beta_m$ in Π, every variable appearing in $\beta_1, \ldots, \beta_m$ appears also in γ.

The role played by the constraints in the Datalog clauses is critical for the hybrid system. In particular, the interaction between the structural and the relational components of a knowledge base $K = < \Sigma, \Pi >$ is determined by the constraints specified in clauses of Π. It is easy to see the similarity with many-sorted logics, where constants and variables are sorted. However, the language used in the structural subsystem of $\mathcal{AL}$-log is much more powerful than the ordinary languages for sorts. More specifically, our system follows the idea of the substitutional framework proposed by Frisch [8], but adapting it to concept languages.

With regard to the semantics of a knowldge base $K = < \Sigma, \Pi >$, we define an interpretation $\mathcal{J}$ for a knowledge base K as the union of an $\mathcal{O}$-interpretation $\mathcal{I}$ for Σ and an Herbrand interpretation H for Π_D, where Π_D is the set of Datalog clauses obtained from the clauses of Π by deleting in each clause its constraint part (i.e. the symbol & together with every constraints).

A ground instance of a constrained clause of K is the constrained clause obtained by substituting each variable in the clause with an individual occurring in Σ. $\mathcal{J}$ is called a model of K if it is a model of Σ (i.e. $\mathcal{I}$ is a model of Σ), and for each clause γ & $\beta_1, \ldots, \beta_m$, for each of its ground instances γ' & $\beta_1', \ldots, \beta_m'$, either there exists one $i \in \{1, \ldots, m\}$ such that β_i' is not satisfied by $\mathcal{J}$, or γ' is satisfied by $\mathcal{J}$. K logically implies a ground atom α (resp. a ground constraint β), written $K \models \alpha$ (resp. $K \models \beta$), if every model of K satisfies α (resp. β).

A conjunction of ground atoms and ground constraints $\alpha_1, \ldots, \alpha_n$ & $\beta_1, \ldots, \beta_m$ is a logical consequence of K, written as $K \models \alpha_1, \ldots, \alpha_n$ & $\beta_1, \ldots, \beta_m$ if for each $i \in \{1, \ldots, n\}$, $K \models \alpha_i$ and for each $j \in \{1, \ldots, m\}$, $K \models \beta_j$.

A query q to a knowledge base K is a sentence of the form:

$$g_1, \ldots, g_n \text{ \& } \beta_1, \ldots, \beta_m$$

where $n \geq 0, m \geq 0, n + m > 0$, each g_i is an atom and each β_j is a constraint.

An *answer* to the query q is a substitution θ such that $q\theta$ is ground. The answer θ is *correct* with respect to the knowledge base K if $K \models q\theta$. The *answer set* to a query q is the set of answers to q that are correct with respect to K, i.e. $\{\theta \mid K \models q\theta\}$.

It is easy to verify that if a ground query q contains only constraints (i.e. has the form & $\beta_1, \ldots, \beta_m$), then $K \models q$ if and only if $\Sigma \models q$. In other words, the knowledge expressed in the relational component does not play any role in deducing facts about the structural component.

3 Hybrid Deduction

In this section we describe the method used by $\mathcal{AL}$-log for hybrid deduction, i.e. for answering queries to a knowledge base. In particular, we first describe the notions of constrained SLD-derivation and constrained SLD-refutation, and then exploit such notions for devising a sound and complete method for hybrid deduction.

Let $q = g_1, \ldots, g_n$ & $\beta_1, \ldots, \beta_m$ be a query to a knowledge base K. The *goal* associated with q is the constrained clause $\neg g_1 \vee \cdots \vee \neg g_n$ & $\beta_1, \ldots, \beta_m$.

Let G be a goal of the form γ & $\beta_1, \ldots, \beta_m$, and let E be a constrained Datalog clause of the form γ' & $\beta'_1, \ldots, \beta'_h$. Let $\neg g$ be a literal of G, and let L_0 be the head of E, i.e. the positive literal of E. If θ is a substitution such that $L_0\theta = g\theta$, then the *resolvent* of the goal G and the clause E with substitution θ is the goal: γ'' & $\beta''_1, \ldots, \beta''_k$, where γ'' is the (usual) resolvent of γ and γ' with substitution θ, and the new constraints $\beta''_1, \ldots, \beta''_k$ are obtained from $\beta_1\theta, \ldots, \beta_m\theta, \beta'_1\theta, \ldots, \beta'_h\theta$ by applying the following simplification: if there are two constraints of the form $t\!:\!C, t\!:\!D$ they are replaced by the equivalent constraint $t\!:\!C \sqcap D$. We can now provide the definition of constrained SLD-derivation.

Definition 3.1 *A* constrained SLD-derivation *for a goal* G_0 *in* K *is a derivation constituted by:*

1. *a sequence of goals* $G_0, \ldots, G_n$
2. *a sequence of constrained Datalog clauses* $E_1, \ldots, E_n$
3. *a sequence of substitutions* $\theta_1, \ldots, \theta_n$

such that for each $i \in \{0, \ldots, n-1\}$, G_{i+1} *is the resolvent of* G_i *and* E_{i+1} *with substitution* θ_{i+1}.

A constrained SLD-derivation (or simply derivation) may terminate with the last goal of the form & $\beta_1, \ldots, \beta_m$, which is called *constrained empty clause* (or simply *empty clause*).

As pointed out in [3], a refutation in our framework cannot be simply a derivation whose last goal is an empty clause, since what is actually inferrable from such a derivation is that the goal is satisfied in those models of K that satisfy the constraints associated with the empty clause.

Therefore, in order to prove a goal, we must collect enough derivations ending with a constrained empty clause, such that each model of K satisfies the constraints associated with the last goal of at least one derivation. Let us formalize this notion as follows.

Definition 3.2 *A* constrained SLD-refutation *for a goal G in K is a set of constrained SLD-derivations $d_1, \ldots, d_m$ for G in K such that, denoting as $G_0^i \ldots, G_{n_i}^i$ the sequence of goals of the i-th derivation d_i, the following conditions hold:*

1. *for each i, $G_{n_i}^i$ is of the form $\& \; \beta_1^i, \ldots, \beta_{q_i}^i$, i.e. the last goal of each derivation is a constrained empty clause; note that because of the conditions on the constrained Datalog clauses, for each $j \in \{1, \ldots, q_i\}$, β_j^i is ground, hence it corresponds to an assertion of the form $a: C$;*

2. *for every model $\mathcal{J}$ of K, there exists at least one $i \in \{1, \ldots, m\}$ such that $\mathcal{J} \models G_{n_i}^i$.*

We say that G has a refutation in K, written $K \vdash G$, if there is a constrained SLD-refutation for G in K. Our goal is to devise a method for obtaining a constrained SLD-refutation for a goal, when it exists. To this purpose, we need a method for checking condition 2 of the above definition.

First of all, note that since each $G_{n_i}^i$ is in fact a conjunction of ground constraints $\beta_1^i, \ldots, \beta_{q_i}^i$, such a condition is equivalent to:

2'. For every model $\mathcal{I}$ of Σ, there exists at least one derivation $d_i = G_0^i \ldots, G_{n_i}^i$ (with $G_{n_i}^i = \& \; \beta_1^i, \ldots, \beta_{q_i}^i$) such that for every $j \in \{1, \ldots, q_i\}$, $\mathcal{I} \models \beta_j^i$. If this condition is verified, then we say that Σ logically implies $disj(G_{n_1}^1, \ldots, G_{n_m}^m)$.

Following the lines of Baader et al. [3], we can show that this condition is verified if and only if for every sequence of assertions $a_1: C_1, \ldots, a_k: C_k$ such that $a_i: C_i$ appears as a constraint in $G_{n_i}^i$, $\Sigma \cup \{a_1: \neg C_1, \ldots, a_k: \neg C_k\}$ is unsatisfiable. If this problem is proved to be decidable, then we can also decide condition 2' using at most m^k unsatisfiability checks on Σ, where m is the maximum number of constraints in each $G_{n_i}^i$.

In [7] we show that this problem is decidable, thus extending the results reported in [3,12], where the problem of checking the satisfiability of the intentional level of an $\mathcal{ALC}$-knowledge base was addressed.

The method reported in [7], which takes into account both the intensional and the extensional level, makes use of the notion of constraint system (see [6]), and is based on a tableau-like calculus that tries to build a model of the logical formula F corresponding to $\Sigma \cup \{a_1: \neg C_1, \ldots, a_k: \neg C_k\}$. The correctness of the method is established by proving that the attempt to build the model preserves the satisfiability of F. The completeness of the method is assessed by showing that if no contradiction shows up during the construction, then the constraint system resulting from the calculus can be turned into a model of F. Finally, termination is proved by showing that if a model exists for F, then a finite model also exists.

Let q be a query to a hybrid knowledge base K. Following a standard terminology, an answer θ to q is called a *computed* answer if the goal associated with $q\theta$ has a refutation in K. Moreover, the set of computed answers of q is called the *success set* of q in K.

The next theorem states that every answer in the success set of q in K is correct with respect to K, and vice versa.

Theorem 3.3 *Let q be a query to a hybrid knowledge base K. The success set of q in K coincides with the answer set to q, i.e. for every answer θ to q, $K \vdash q\theta$ if and only if $K \models q\theta$.*

It remains to describe how we check whether a ground query q has a constrained SLD-refutation in a knowledge base K.

Theorem 3.4 *Let q be a ground query to a knowledge base $K =< \Sigma, \Pi >$ and let $d_1, \ldots, d_m$ (with $d_i = G_0^i \ldots, G_{n_i}^i$) be all the possible constrained SLD-derivations for q in K ending with a constrained empty clause. Then q has a constrained SLD-refutation in K if and only if Σ logically implies $disj(G_{n_1}^1, \ldots, G_{n_m}^m)$.*

Notice that it follows from the property of constrained Datalog programs that the set of all possible constrained SLD-derivations for a ground goal G ending with a constrained empty clause is finite. Moreover, it is easy to see that the usual top-down reasoning procedure proposed for Datalog allows us to collect in a finite number of steps (actually in a number of steps which is polynomial with respect to the size of the extensional level of the constrained Datalog program) all the possible constrained SLD-derivations for G in K.

It follows that query answering in $\mathcal{AL}$-log is decidable. In fact, in order to answer a query q to the knowledge base $K =< \Sigma, \Pi >$, one can consider each ground instance q' of q, collect the set of all possible constrained SLD-derivations $d_1, \ldots, d_m$ (with $d_i = G_0^i \ldots, G_{n_i}^i$) for q' in K, and then check whether Σ logically implies $disj(G_{n_1}^1, \ldots, G_{n_m}^m)$.

4 Conclusions

In this paper we have presented $\mathcal{AL}$-log, a hybrid system integrating Datalog with concept languages. We considered a structural subsystem based on the language $\mathcal{ALC}$ and a relational subsystem based on Datalog, extended by allowing $\mathcal{ALC}$-constraints in the body of the clauses.

The main goal of our work was to study a form of hybrid deduction over a knowledge base with two components, one concerning structural knowledge on concepts and objects, and the other one concerning relational knowledge on objects. The resulting reasoning procedure is obtained by adding to the deduction procedure of Datalog special deduction steps on the structural component.

As pointed out in the introduction, while $\mathcal{AL}$-log is highly expressive in the structural subsystem, it is in fact still lacking some of the features of most recent deductive object-oriented database languages, such as the treatment of negation in the relational subsystem, and the ability to derive structural information from the relational knowledge.

In the future, we aim at considering several developments of our work. First of all, an analysis will be carried out in order to single out sublanguages of $\mathcal{ALC}$ that gives rise to polynomial tractability of query answering. Second, we aim at extending the relational language with a stratified form of negation, and to adapt both the semantics and the method for hybrid deduction according to the characteristics of the enhanced relational component. Finally, we plan to consider stronger forms of integration between the two subsystems.

References

[1] S. Abiteboul, "Towards a deductive object-oriented database language". *Data & Knowledge Engineering*, Vol. 5, pp. 263-287, 1990.

[2] L. Aiello, M. Lenzerini, D. Nardi, "La rappresentazione della conoscenza in intelligenza artificiale". *Rivista di Informatica*, Vol. XIX, N. 2, pp. 93-110, 1989 (in Italian).

[3] F. Baader, H.-J. Bürkert, B. Hollunder, W. Nutt, J. Siekmann, "Concept logics". *Computational Logics Symposium Proceedings*, J.W. Lloyd (Ed.), pp. 177-201, Springer-Verlag, 1990.

[4] R.J. Brachman, V. Pigman Gilbert, H.J. Levesque, "An essential hybrid reasoning system: knowledge and symbol level accounts in KRYPTON." *Proceedings of the 8th Int. Joint Conf. on Artificial Intelligence, IJCAI-85*, 1985.

[5] A.G. Cohn, "Taxonomic Reasoning with Many-Sorted Logics". *Artificial Intelligence Review*, 3:89-128, 1989.

[6] F.M. Donini, M. Lenzerini, D. Nardi, W. Nutt, "The complexity of concept languages." *Proceedings of the 2nd Int. Conf. on Principles of Knowledge Representation and Reasoning, KR-91*, 1991.

[7] F.M. Donini, M. Lenzerini, D. Nardi, A. Schaerf, "On the integration of logic programming and concept languages." Esprit-BRA Compulog Report, 1991.

[8] A.M. Frisch, "A general framework for sorted deduction: fundamental results on hybrid reasoning". *Proceedings of the 1st Int. Conf. on Principles of Knowledge Representation and Reasoning, KR-89*, 1989.

[9] A.M. Frisch, A.G. Cohn, "Thought and afterthoughts on the 1988 Workshop on Principles of Hybrid Reasoning". *AI Magazine*, pp. 77-83, 1991.

[10] B. Nebel, K. von Luck, "Hybrid reasoning in BACK". *Proceedings of the Int. Symposium on Methodologies for Intelligent Systems, ISMIS-88*, North-Holland, 1988.

[11] B. Nebel, *Reasoning and revision in hybrid representation systems*, LNAI 422, Springer Verlag, 1990.

[12] K. Schild, "A correspondence theory for terminological logics: Preliminary". To appear in *Proc. of the 12th Int. Joint Conf. on Artificial Intelligence, IJCAI-91*, 1991.

[13] J.D. Ullman, *Principles of database and knowledge-base systems*. Computer Science Press, 1988.

Optimal Search for Conjunctive Goals using Constraints

Jeremy Ellman
Conceptual Services
Via S.Antonio da Padova 9
10121 Torino
Italy

Giancarlo Mezzanatto
Artificial Intelligence Lab.
Alenia Aeronautica - GAD
C.so Marche 41
10146 Torino
Italy

Abstract

OSCG is a general admissible algorithm which finds an optimal path through multiple dependent goals in a labelled directed graph. It uses constraints to turn the problem of solving multiple dependent goals into that of solving multiple independent ones. OSCG arose out of work on MARPLES, a route planning expert system. OSCG's admissibility is proven, and related and further work discussed.

Introduction

The conjunctive goal problem is well known in action planning and typically refers to order selection of goals (see Hendler et al 1990 for review). Here we shall be looking at a variant in the path planning domain where several conjunctive goals have to be solved in a predefined order in a labelled directed graph.

The problem with conjunctive goals is that the solution to one goal may affect solutions to subsequent ones. This is particularly true when there is any interaction between the solutions to various goals. Here a locally optimal solution to the first goal may exclude some solutions to subsequent goals. Thus a global optimum is not necessarily the sum of the local optima. Re-stating this idea in terms of path planning, we can say that the optimal path is not guaranteed to be found by repeatedly applying an admissible best first algorithm (see Pearl 1984 for review). This is because heuristic search algorithms give locally optimal solutions, and are not easily guided to give admissible global solutions.

The algorithm we shall be looking at here is admissible and gives a globally optimal path through a labelled directed graph with interacting conjunctive goals. It arose out of work on MARPLES (Military Aircraft Route Planning Expert System, Gallo et al 1989), which we shall use as our example domain.

The paper proceeds as follows: Firstly we briefly describe MARPLES. Next we reformulate the problem of conjunctive goals in terms of constraint satisfaction introducing the related ideas of the constraint graph and the problem graph. Then we describe the algorithm for optimal search for conjunctive goals (OSCG) and a more efficient variation, OSCG-BEAM and prove their admissibiliy. Finally we describe related and further work.

The MARPLES problem domain

MARPLES is a pilot's route planning aid. Mission details (eg take off airfield, landing, targets) are entered, and an optimal route plan is produced. This is composed of way points (which are map features recognizable from the air) over which course changes are required. Each mission is subdivided into tasks where a task corresponds to a major part of the mission. Examples of tasks are the journey from the take off point to the first target, journey from target to target, or from final target to landing. The mission is planned when each task has been resolved and a global path (from the start, through each goal, to the end) has been constructed.

In MARPLES, the reason why one task's route impinges on another is straightforward: An aircraft may not change course by more than $\alpha°$. Thus if it arrives at its first objective (G_1) on a course of $\beta°$, it must continue on to its second (G_2) at a maximum of $\alpha°\pm\beta°$. In other words, that $\beta°$ course to G_1 has constrained possible routes onwards to G_2 (Fig 1). Needless to say, some of these now forbidden partial routes may have been part of the globally optimal solution. Thus the overall mission plan found is no longer guaranteed to be optimal. Note also that the cost function measures a variety of factors including "grayness" of the route which unpredictably augments the routes' cost, so linear (ie Manhattan) distance is not a useful heuristic.

Fig (1) - The path X-Y-Z is legal, but neither X-Y-P, nor X-Y-Q may be followed as the angular deviation is too great.

It should be clear from the above, that a solution to the MARPLES problem will be generally applicable to the problem of multiple goals route finding in a directed graph (eg such as in a town with a network of one way streets). Therefore we shall present the algorithm as generally as possible, only using MARPLES as an example to clarify the explanation.

Reformulation of the problem

The driving principle behind this work is the reduction of the problem of solving multiple dependent goals to that of solving multiple independent ones. This is done by making explicit the problem constraints and generating multiple partial solutions to satisfy them.

The first step is to re-formulate the problem in terms of constraint satisfaction. This stems from the observation that the partial paths (by which we mean paths from start to the first goal state, or paths from successive to following goal states) restrict (or constrain) our choice of possible further legal partial paths.

Given a set of serial and dependent goals $\{G_1, G_2,....G_n\}$, there are also a set of serial and dependent tasks to reach them. Let there be a variable v_i for each task T_i. Associated with each v_i let there be a domain D_i which represents the set of all possible solutions for a task T_1. The dependencies between two or more tasks are defined by the constraint relations between some specified subsets of their variables.

Note that as binary constraints may be represented in a graph, there are two kinds of graphs here: The graph formalizing the problem to solve, and the constraint graph (which represents the constraint satisfaction problem). The nodes of this graph stand for the variables whose domains include all the possible solutions for each task. That is, all the possible partial paths through the problem graph. The edges of the constraint graph stand for the constraints between the various tasks.

By using consistency algorithms (see Mackworth and Freuder 1985, Mackworth 1987) on the constraint graph the problem graph search space may be reduced without affecting the optimality of the problem's global solution. This is because there are parts of the problem search space which correspond to inconsistent variable assignments in the constraint graph. Consequently they can never form part of a global solution and may be removed from the problem graph.

However, the arc consistency part of our algorithm cannot be run as a pre-processing procedure. This is because the solutions belonging to the variable domains are not known until the actual search on the problem graph is performed. Consequently an algorithm --Optimal Search for Conjunctive Goals (OSCG)-- will be proposed which interleaves search on the problem graph with arc consistency work on the constraint graph.

The algorithm OSCG

The input to the OSCG algorithm consists of a start point, an end point, and a series of ordered goals. Additionally there are constraint definitions and feature groups for each goal $(FG_{1,i}, FG_{2,i})$ which contain features that constrain other tasks, and which differentiate a task's solutions into sets.

Let us define (following Freuder [1982]) an ordered constraint graph as one in which the nodes are linearly ordered to reflect the sequence of variable assignments. A node may be SKIPPED in such a graph if there are arcs leading from nodes before it to nodes following it (see fig2)

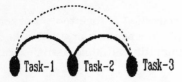
Task-1　Task-2　Task-3

Fig. 2 - Let the direction of instantiation of this ordered constraint graph be (T_1, T_2, T_3). T_2 is skipped while T_1 and T_3 are not.

OCSG also uses AA, which may be any admissible search algorithm which gives a locally optimum path through the problem graph with respect to some constraint(s). Note that we are only concerned here with binary constraints and two sets of feature groups per task: OSCG should be generalizable to more complex constraint and feature group systems but that is not an objective of this paper.

Notation:

n	Total number of tasks
m	number of the feature group (ie 1 or 2)
T_i	Task i
$AA\,(T_i, FP_{x,i})$	Generic admissible search algorithm
$F_{m,i,x}$	Feature x in task i from m
$FG_{1,i}$	Feature group one in task i
$FG_{2,i}$	Feature group two in task i
$FP_{x,i}$	A feature pair x in task i obtained by combining two features taken from feature groups one and two.
D_i	The domain of possible solutions to task i

Constraint definitions: eg.

(1) $(F_{1,i,x}\ ;\ F_{2,j,y})$

(2) $(F_{1,i,x}\ ;\ F_{2,j,y})$

Constraint definitions (1) and (2) say that a path having feature $F_{1,i,x}$ in task i is compatible with paths having features $F_{2,j,p}$ and $F_{2,j,q}$ in task j.

Procedure OSCG

1) For i = n to 1 by -1

    If groups of feature $FG_{1,i}$ and $FG_{2,i}$ are empty

    sol_i <-- $AA\,(T_i,$ nil)   ;*No constraint*

    else (i)   UPDATE-FEATURES ($FG_{1,i}, FG_{2,i}$)   ;*Constraint Propagation*

        (ii) Feature-pairs <-- COMBINE-FEATURES ($FG_{1,i}, FG_{2,i}$)

        (iii) For each feature-pair $FP_{x,i}$ in feature-pairs

            sol_i <-- $AA\,(T_i, FP_{x,i})$

            If sol_i = nil Mark $FP_{x,i}$ as empty

            else PUSH sol_i into D_i

        (iv) If D_i has no Solns FAIL   ; *No solutions for this task*

        (v) SOLUTIONS <-- EXTEND-SOLUTIONS (solutions, D_i)

        (vi) If SOLUTIONS is EMPTY FAIL   ;*No compatible solns*

        (vii) For each $F_{m,i,x}$ in $FG_{1,i}$ and $FG_{2,i}$

            If all $FP_{x,i}$ in feature-pairs

            containing $F_{m,i,x}$ are marked as empty,

            DELETE constraint definitions containing $F_{m,i,x}$

2) For all solutions in solutions,

    find the one with the lowest cost C(x)

Procedure UPDATE-FEATURES ($FG_{1,i}, FG_{2,i}$)

For each $F_{1,i,x}$ in $FG_{1,i}$ do

    If $F_{1,i,x}$ is not included in any constraint definition

    REMOVE $F_{1,i,x}$ from $FG_{1,i}$

For each $F_{2,i,x}$ in $FG_{2,i}$ do

    If $F_{2,i,x}$ is not included in any constraint definition

    REMOVE $F_{2,i,x}$ from $FG_{2,i}$

Procedure COMBINE-FEATURES $(FG_{1,i}, FG_{2,i})$
If $FG_{1,i}$ is empty   ;*At the Initial Goal*
    for each $F_{2,i,x}$ in $FG_{2,i}$
       PUSH pair $[nil, F_{2,i,x}]$ in feature-pairs
else If $FG_{2,i}$ is empty   ;*At the Final Goal*
    For each $F_{1,i,x}$ in $FG_{1,i}$
       PUSH pair $[F_{1,i,x}$ nil] in feature-pairs
else For each $F_{1,i,x}$ in $FG_{1,i}$ do   ;*Intermediate Goals*
      For each $F_{2,i,x}$ in $FG_{2,i}$ do
         PUSH pair $[F_{1,i,x}, F_{2,i,x}]$ in feature-pairs

Procedure EXTEND-SOLUTIONS $($ SOLUTIONS, $D_i)$
If solutions = nil
    for each $sol_{y,i}$ in D_i PUSH $sol_{y,i}$ in SOLUTIONS
else For each sol_x in SOLUTIONS do
    1) For each $sol_{y,i}$ in D_i
       If $sol_{y,i}$ can be combined with sol_x
       according to the constraint definitions
         do SOL <-- JOIN $(sol_x, sol_{y,i})$
           PUSH SOL in SOLUTIONS
    2) REMOVE sol_x from SOLUTIONS

Notes on OSCG

Feature pairs calculated by the procedure COMBINE-FEATURES represent different kinds of partial solutions that, according to the constraint definitions, can affect the partial solutions of successive tasks.

AA is used to find the optimal solution amongst those defined by each feature pair. These optimal partial solutions make up the domain of the variable standing for the current task. When AA does not find any solution with some set of features (step(iii)), subsequent partial solutions depending on those features may be eliminated. This reduces the problem search space of subsequent tasks. This is implemented by steps (vii) and (i).

In step (vii) constraint definitions which refer to path features for which no solution has been found in the current task are removed. Subsequently UPDATE-FEATURES (step (i)) removes all the features no longer referenced by the remaining constraint definitions. (The notions of feature and feature group make explicit what is usually hidsaden in the definition of the constraints as predicates, $P(g_i, g_j)$).

The algorithm OSCG-BEAM

In Marples, partial paths of one task may only constrain their immediate neighbours. For example, if three tasks are to be carried out $(T_1-T_2-T_3)$, paths of T_1 are not linked to paths to T_3 by any constraint relation. Therefore, as only paths of T_2 can constrain partial paths of T_3, for each path to T_2 only one which solves the preceding tasks (with the lowest cost) need be retained

This idea can be generalized. If a node T_i in a ordered constraint graph is not SKIPPED (see fig.2), for all solutions sharing the same local path of T_i, only the best solution need be retained. This variation is called OSCG-BEAM. It is exactly the same as OSCG, apart from one more step in procedure OSCG

(viii) Given the ordered constraint graph
If node T_i is not SKIPPED
    For each $sol_{x,i}$ to T_i
    take all solutions in SOLUTIONS which include $sol_{x,i}$ and prune away all
    but the one with the lowest cost

OSCG-BEAM trades off increased evaluation effort of complex partial solutions with a reduction in their number. Thus the number of partial complex solutions at any goal (including the final one) is equal in size to its constrained feature set. This corresponds to the number of local paths to that goal. Without this step the number of partial solutions grows exponentially with respect to the number of tasks.

The Admissibility Proof

The proof rests on the fact that OSCG reduces the problem search space. Thus we need only show that OSCG never prunes a partial path which could be part of a better global solution. The necessary conditions are that algorithm AA is admissible and that the cost function is order preserving (see Pearl 1984).

The proof is in three steps: Firstly we show that for each local path pruned away one optimal local path is retained that can be part of the same global solutions. Next we show that, if there are global solutions, the best one will be composed of the local paths retained, and therefore, that OSCG is admissible. We then extend this proof to deal with OSCG-BEAM.

Lemma 1. For any partial solution n of task T_i not included in D_i by AA, there is an equivalent partial solution n' where $C(n) \geq C(n')$
Proof. Let n have features $(F_{1,i,x}, F_{2,i,y})$. These are part of a number of constraint definitions. Consequently, the partial path n can be part only of global solutions that satisfy such constraint definitions. However this is also true of the partial path n' produced by AA for the feature-pair characterizing n. As AA is admissible by definition, C(n') is lower than C(n). N' is therefore the partial solution OSCG retains in the domain D_i. Now we can conclude that for a path n characterized by a feature-pair $FP_{x,i}$, there is a path n' with the same features (as far as the feature-pair is involved) but with $C(n) \geq C(n')$. Since every partial path is characterized by the feature-pairs created in step(ii), there can be no other partial path for which what has been proved does not hold.

Theorem 1. If it exists, the best solution is made up of partial solutions pushed in domains $(D_1, D_2 .... D_n)$.

Proof. Since the cost function is order-preserving, this result follows from Lemma 1. For any global solution k which includes a pruned partial solution n_i, there is a global solution k' which includes a partial solution n'_i pushed in the domain D_i, such that $C(k) \geq C(k')$. Therefore no pruned partial solution can be part of the best solution.

Theorem 2. OSCG is admissible

Proof. The procedure EXTEND-SOLUTIONS does no pruning. From this and from Theorem 1 it follows that the best complex path will be in the set of global solutions (SOLUTIONS) at the end of step(1). Thus step(2) will find the optimal global solution from that set.

Theorem 3. OSCG-BEAM is admissible.

Proof. In OSCG-BEAM there is an additional step (viii). As this is a second pruning step, Theorem 3 is proved only if we can show that the solutions removed can not be part of the optimal global solution.

Lemma 2. If K is a solution pruned away by step (viii), it is neither a part of the optimal global solution nor the optimal global solution itself.

Proof. By definition, step (viii) only prunes solutions if the current task is not SKIPPED, that is no local path previously considered may constrain successive ones. This means that only local paths of the current task can admit or reject successive local paths as part of the final global solutions. Therefore, since for each local path the complex solution with the lowest cost is kept (and the cost function is order preserving), no solution pruned away could either be part of a global optimal solution or the final optimal solution itself.

An Application of OSCG in the Marples Domain

Assume that we have the problem in Fig (3): Find the lowest cost route from the start point to a middle point, Target-1, going on to Target-2, to the End. This is composed of three tasks T_1, T_2, and T_3 (Start→Target-1, Target-1→Target-2, and Target-2→End). These tasks are connected by the arrival and departure directions at their ends, and a 90° limit on direction change serves as our sole constraint.

Way Points at which we can change directions constraining (or being constrained by) other tasks serve as our task features ($F_{m,i,x}$). Feature groups 1 and 2 of task i are respectively the set of all way points immediately after the task's start point, and immediately before its end point. A feature pair is made up of a feature from Feature Group 1 and a feature from Feature Group 2. Our constraint definitions are the list of pairs $F_{2,i,x}$,$F_{1,i+1,y}$ which are legal course changes at task i's start or end points. In this example the constraint graph is a simple chain (Fig 2), but this does not show the interraction between the search problem we are solving, and the constraint problem given by the conjunctive goals. Fig (4) better illustrates this.

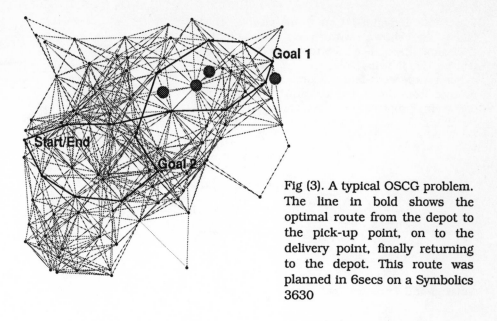

Fig (3). A typical OSCG problem. The line in bold shows the optimal route from the depot to the pick-up point, on to the delivery point, finally returning to the depot. This route was planned in 6secs on a Symbolics 3630

The first conceptual step in OSCG is to use AA to find a set of solutions to the final task with respect to known constraints. This is composed of several steps. Firstly UPDATE-FEATURES is called to remove features which no longer apply (Assuming for simplicity that no tasks' feature groups are empty). In the first instance this will do nothing. Next COMBINE-FEATURES creates every possible feature pair for this task. Then AA is used to find real paths which solve that task for every Feature pair. Note that relatively few connections are shown in the expanded constraint graph. (eg there is no connection F-1-1-2, F-2-1-4) as AA finds no such paths.

The solutions found by AA become the problem's solutions in step(v) of OSCG. Features pairs for which no path was found are then checked against the constraint definitions. Where a constraint definition has no suppporting feature pair it may be deleted. As we proceed to the second task the effect of UPDATE-FEATURES becomes clear. Some Features in task 2 required the now deleted constraint defintions. These may now be deleted. This means that we need not find any paths which would have included these points as they are unreachable from the previous task(s).

The two sets of partial solutions found so far are then merged using EXTEND-SOLUTIONS. In the OSCG-beam variation these are pruned so that each corresponds to only one (the last) feature pair.As the tasks are successively solved the number of features remaining is reduced (see fig 4). This is the effect of constraint propagation allowing the deletion of features, their pairs, and corresponding partial paths.

Fig(4) The Expanded Constraint Graph. The tasks are shown with their end points enclosing their two feature groups. Each feature is labelled as F-X-Y-Z (F-FEATURE-GROUP-**TASK-NUMBER**-*feature-number*). As we proceed from the end to the start the effect of constraint propagation is seen in the reduced number of feature groups.

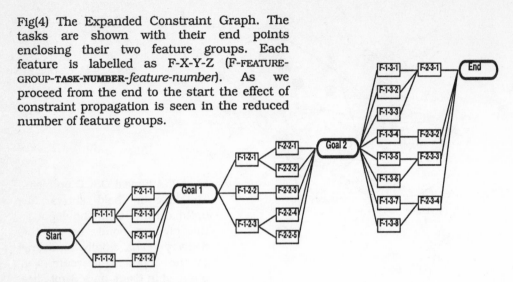

Related and Further Work

OSCG represents a solution to a search problem using constraint satisfaction. However the "conjunctive goals" problem has seen most attention in planning. Nonetheless work in planning on conjunctive goals (see eg Chapman 1987, Joslin & Roach 1989, Hendler et al. 1990) is not directly relevant here, as there the main issues are eg. order selection of goals, goal protection etc, and these are not addressed in OSCG. This is because a part of the OSCG problem definition is that goals have to be reached in a predefined order.

OSCG has nothing to say about traditional search algorithms. The definition of AA permits any algorithm to be used providing that it can be sufficiently controlled. In fact, MARPLES uses an exhaustive approach. This is because search cut-off is low and the evaluation function used is expensive. Thus in searching for a task's constrained partial solutions it is far less costly to find all the solutions and then to prune them, than it would be to repeatedly apply an algorithm such as A* (which would involve far heavier use of the evaluation function). Indeed, one could say that the exhaustive enumeration plus pruning approach used in MARPLES is a version of the well known branch and bounds technique (see Kumar 1987 for review).

The use of constraints in OSCG is straightforward. OSCG is nothing more than a way to achieve directional arc consistency (DAC, Dechter and Pearl (1988). Whilst full arc consistency (FAC, Mackworth 1987) achieves higher consistency of the constraint graph, it would not improve OSCG. This is because whilst DAC processes each arc no more than once, it is this first arc consistency test which requires the use of AA. The full variable domain reduction obtained from FAC (by successive REVISE operations) will not affect the search work done by AA as this must always be done once. Additionally, such a reduction would not make up for the increased time complexity of the work in the constraint graph (from $O(nk^2)$ to $O(nk^3)$ where n is the number of variables and k is the number of possible values (see Dechter & Pearl 1988).

It is likely that in practice there will be some optimum ordering of the constraint graph which will maximize constraint propagation. This will be the case when either one task more heavily constrains the problem graph or when one task requires less search. Such a heuristically ordered task list will not affect the number or quality of the global solutions, but will allow earlier elimination of inconsistent paths. Similar approaches have been reported by eg. Hayes (1987) and Natarajan (1987). There are also strong similarities here with Fox et al's (1989) work on MOLGEN. There, besides using constraints at multiple levels to guide planning, the constraint graph is also manipulated to optimize the ordering of variables and values.

Conclusion

We have outlined an admissible algorithm OSCG which finds an optimal path through multiple interacting goals in a labelled directed graph. OSCG reduces the problem search space by manipulating its corresponding constraint graph, thus reducing the problem of solving multiple dependent goals to that of solving multiple independent ones. The advantage of this approach is particularly seen with the algorithm OSCG-BEAM, where the number of complex solutions remains constant irrespective of the number of goals. OSCG is not domain specific, although the improvements in performance it gives depend on the domain's intrinsic constraints.

Acknowledgements: We would like to thank Federica Luise and Ermanno Girardelli, our collaborators in the Marples project.

References

Chapman, David (1987), *Planning for Conjunctive Goals*,AI 32,pp337-377.
Dechter R. and Pearl J. (1988), *Network based heuristics for Constraint Satisfaction Problems*, AI 34 (1), pp1-38
Fox, M. S., Sadeh N., Baykan C. (1989), *Constrained Heuristic Search*, IJCAI 89
Freuder, E. C. (1982), *A sufficient condition of backtrack-free search*, J. ACM 29 (1)
Gallo, P., Dabbene D., Luise, F., Giordanengo, P. (1989), *Expert System for pilot assistance: The Challenge of an intensive prototyping*, Proc. "Applications of Artificial Intelligence" VII SPIE, Orlando, Florida.
Hayes, Caroline (1987), *Using Goal Interactions to Guide Planning*, AAAI 87.
Hendler, J., Tate A, Drummond M. (1990) *AI Planning: Systems and Techniques* AI Magazine, Summer 1990.
Joslin, David, and Roach, John (1989) *A Theoretical Analysis of Conjunctive-Goal Problems* AI 41, pp97-106.
Kumar V. (1987), *Search, Branch and Bound* in Shapiro and Eckroth eds.
Mackworth A. K.(1987) *Constraint Satisfaction* in Shapiro and Eckroth eds.
Mackworth, A.K. and Freuder E.C. (1985) *The Complexity of Some Polynomial Network Consistency Algorithms for Constraint Satisfaction Problems* AI 25(1), pp65-74.
Natarajan K. S. (1987) *Optimizing Backtrack Search for All Solutions to Conjunctive Problems*, IJCAI 87, pp955-958
Pearl J (1984) *Heuristics* Addison-Wesley, London.
Shapiro and Eckroth (1987) (eds), *Encyclopedia of Artificial Inteligence*, Wiley-Interscience, New York.

FSS-WASTL
Interactive Knowledge Acquisition for a Semantic Lexicon

Roman M. Jansen-Winkeln   Alassane Ndiaye   Norbert Reithinger *

Universität des Saarlandes
D-6600 Saarbrücken 11
Federal Republic of Germany
{roman, ndiaye, bert}@cs.uni-sb.de

Abstract

The following paper describes FSS-WASTL, a system for the acquisition of semantic knowledge within XTRA – a natural language access system to expert systems. Starting from user-supplied example utterances, hypotheses for lexical entries are induced, which then are refined top down through interactive classification. The refinement process of FSS-WASTL is a variant of the well-known KL-ONE classification procedure and is an extension of T. Finin's interactive classifier. The integration of XTRA's natural language generator, which is a highlight of FSS-WASTL, allows for the paraphrasing of the user's input for clarification purposes. FSS-WASTL is compared with other research systems. It is argued that this approach can be transfered to applications beyond the natural language domain.

1 Introduction

A key issue during the development and the application of knowledge-based systems is maintaining and extending their knowledge bases. Hence for adaptable systems, such as transportable natural language systems or expert system shells, there arises the problem of applying these systems to new application areas. Providing special knowledge acquisition tools has proved useful.

We present a tool for KL-ONE-like knowledge representation languages named *interactive classifier*. In the natural language system XTRA it is applied to acquire new semantic knowledge. This module called FSS-WASTL infers new lexical entries from exemplary user input. The interactive classifier provides a comfortable interface with the ability to explain its various reasoning steps. However, the highlight of the interface is the integration of XTRA's natural language generator, which allows for the paraphrasing of the user's input for clarification purposes.

After a short survey of the XTRA system, the interactive classification algorithm will be presented. Then the application of the interactive classifier is shown, and the paraphraser will be explained in particular. The last section refers to similar approaches and gives development perspectives beyond the state of the art.

---
*This research has been supported by the German Science Foundation in its Special Collaborative Research Programme on Artificial Intelligence and Knowledge Based Systems (SFB 314).

2 An Overview of the XTRA System

The XTRA access system to expert systems [Allgayer et al., 89a; Allgayer et al., 89b] is aimed at rendering the interaction with expert systems easier for inexperienced users. XTRA communicates with the user in a natural language (German), extracts data relevant to the expert system from her/his natural language input, answers user queries as to terminology, and provides user-accommodated natural language verbalizations of results and explanations provided by the expert system. Special emphasis is placed upon the separation of linguistic and world knowledge, the bidirectional use of knowledge sources, and the combination of pointing gestures and written natural language.

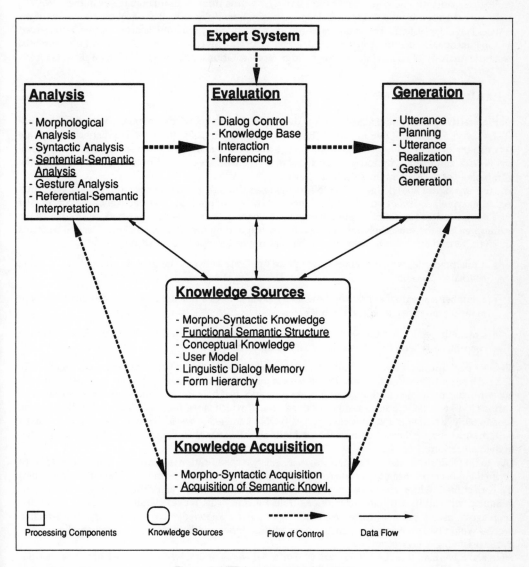

Figure 1: XTRA – system architecture

Processing in the XTRA system can be roughly separated into three phases: analysis, processing, and generation (see figure 1). A user's natural language input is first subjected to a morphological, syntactic and sentential-semantic analysis carried out by the system's parsing components and then transformed into an internal, domain-dependent representation – the conceptual knowledge base (CKB). Based upon this representation, interaction with the respective expert system takes place, the result of which also is represented in the CKB. These results provide the basis for the subsequent generation of natural language output and pointing gestures.

To adapt the XTRA system to different expert systems and to extend existing dictionaries and knowledge bases, research on knowledge acquisition has been carried out. One research goal was to develop an acquisition tool – WASTL [Jansen-Winkeln, 88] –, which learns the various aspects (namely morphological, semantic and contextual aspects) of new words from natural language examples. WASTL makes use of subproblem-specific knowledge acquisition modules as well as of selected modules of the natural language system. The component for the acquisition of semantic lexicon entries, represented within Functional Semantic Structure (FSS), is FSS-WASTL. This component makes use of the sentential semantic Analysis (SSA) module, the knowledge representation language SB-ONE, as well as its tools.

3   Interactive Classification

Our interactive classification algorithm was developed for the knowledge representation language SB-ONE [Kobsa, 91] – a KL-ONE lookalike [Brachman & Schmolze, 85]. In SB-ONE a distinction is made between the definitional knowledge, represented as concepts and roles in the so-called terminological box (TBox), and the description of a specific state of the world, expressed by assertions which use the terminology of the TBox in the so-called assertional box (ABox).

The terminological knowledge in SB-ONE is modeled through *general concepts* and *general roles*. In a logical interpretation[1] they correspond to one- and two-place predicates, respectively. The concepts of the TBox are ordered in a subsumption hierarchy (taxonomy), where the ISA-link between two concepts is interpreted as the subset-relation between the corresponding predicate extensions. General concepts are characterized by attribute descriptions. Each attribute description consists of:

- a role predicate, which denotes a two-place predicate between the domain concept and a value restriction concept

- a number restriction, expressing how many extensions of a role are needed to describe a concept in the minimal, maximal and default case,

- a modality, which indicates whether the attribute is part of the definition of every instance of the concept, i.e. whether the role is necessary or optional.

SB-ONE distinguishes between primitive and defined concepts. In the first case the concept is not fully defined by its attribute descriptions. Primitiveness means that the concept is described by necessary but not sufficient conditions. Defined concepts are fully specified by necessary and sufficient conditions.

Various tools for SB-ONE have been developed, one of which is the matcher [Aue et al., 89]. It can be used to retrieve elements and substructures of SB-ONE knowledge bases. The matching algorithm maps pattern structures – ABox structures enhanced with so-called variable concepts and roles – onto SB-ONE individualizations.

Due to SB-ONE's well defined semantics, there exists a classification algorithm which can be used to verify the subsumption hierarchy and to insert new knowledge – represented as TBox-expressions – into the correct place within the taxonomy. The input of the classification algorithm is a complete concept definition with all its attribute descriptions (roles) given. This makes classification in KL-ONE-like languages a useful, but non-interactive tool. Especially for knowledge acquisition, a more interactive process would be appreciated in which a concept description can be developed incrementally, guided by the reasoning of classification.

Finin and Silverman [Finin & Silverman, 84; Finin, 86] were the first who developed such a procedure, which they called *interactive classifier*. Their classifier works for a representation language similar to

---

[1] First order predicate calculus is assumed

SB-ONE, but more restricted[2]. The algorithm which we developed is an extension of interactive classification to full-scale SB-ONE allowing for subsumption graphs (instead of trees), roles with cardinality and modality attributes, and several kinds of relations between roles (inheritance, restriction, and differentiation). Following Finin we subdivide the interactive classification into three phases: acquisition of the initial concept description, establishing the most specific subsumers (which become the parents in the subsumption graph), and establishing the most general subsumees (which become the children in the subsumption graph).

Within these phases the second is the most important for our approach, because here an interactive top-down refinement of the user's initial concept description takes place. The refinement process is based upon the *structural differences* between concepts which guide the traversal of the graph.

Definition Structural Differences: Let both C_1 and C_2 be concepts, with C_2 being a direct subconcept of C_1. C_1 and C_2 *differ structurally* if at least one of the following conditions occurs:

- C_2 has all roles of C_1 and at least one additional role.

- At least one role of C_1 is restricted in either its value, cardinality or modality at C_2.

- At least one role of C_1 is differentiated at C_2.

- C_2 has at least one primitive superconcept, which does not subsume C_1.

- C_2 is a primitive concept.

The *structural difference* is the collection of all parts of C_2's definition differing structurally from C_1.

The Classification Algorithm

The algorithm starts with a given initial partial concept description C linked to an adequate superconcept S. It is the task of the user to supply these starting conditions, which depends on the application. The algorithm iterates over all subconcepts C_i of S, computes the structural differences between S and C_i, and queries the user as to which of these differences are part of C's definition. Each selected structural difference is added to the description of C, and the interactive step is recursively performed for each of the corresponding C_i as new superconcepts of C. This recursive refinement of C's definition ends, when no more structural difference is added. After that, the user can add new or restrict existing roles to complete C's concept definition. Finally the non-interactive SB-ONE classifier is applied onto the now completed description of concept C in order to (a) verify all established most specific subsumers, (b) detect hidden superconcepts, and (c) find all most general subsumees of C.

4 Acquisition of Semantic Knowledge

We apply the interactive classification as part of the acquisition of new entries for the semantic lexicon of XTRA. The semantic knowledge in XTRA is represented in terms of a generalization of Fillmore's case frames, implemented as a terminological SB-ONE knowledge base, called the Functional Semantic Structure (FSS). The FSS is subdivided in two parts: the generic, domain-independent FSS, and the application-dependent lexical part, which is the object of the knowledge acquisition. The functional semantic structure of the user's utterances are constructed through the sentential-semantic analysis within the corresponding ABox.

The module SEMANTIX performs this sentential-semantic analysis. Based on transformation rules and the semantic lexicon, it translates the syntactic derivation's DAGs[3] into individualizations of the FSS. SEMANTIX interprets successively the constituents of each DAG by looking up the corresponding word stem information from the semantic lexicon and individualizing them into a coherent FSS structure as

---

[2]In [Finin, 86, page 1415] T. Finin describes the underlying representation language as follows: "The KB is constrained to be a tree structure, so each node has at most one parent. Nodes have single-valued attributes which represent components or characteristics that apply to the [...] concept described. Values of attributes can be numbers, intervals, symbols, or sets of symbols. [...] Each node inherits all attributes of its parent node, but its values can be restrictions of the parent attribute's values."

[3]Directed Acyclic Graphs as known from the PATR formalism.

the semantic representation of the example sentence. For our purposes, SEMANTIX was extended to SEMANTIX+ in order to work on only partly interpretable sentences, using variable concepts and roles as placeholders for unknown words.

The acquisition component uses example sentences containing an unknown word as its primary source of information. In a first phase, SEMANTIX is applied to analyse an example sentence semantically. The resulting ABox is matched against the TBox, using the above mentioned TBox-matcher, to dereferentiate the variable parts and find all consistent assignments. The purpose of this phase is to make a good guess for variable-free but possibly partial concept description, which becomes the initial description for the subsequent refinement process. This second phase of the knowledge acquisition is the interactive classification, starting with the most general candidate from the set of assignments, to which our classification algorithm is applied until the concept description is complete and correctly classified. To improve the performance of this classification, we encoded heuristics about how knowledge is represented within the FSS[4]. The resulting description becomes the new lexicon entry. To verify the result and to continue processing, the semantic analysis is restarted. Figure 2 shows the system architecture.

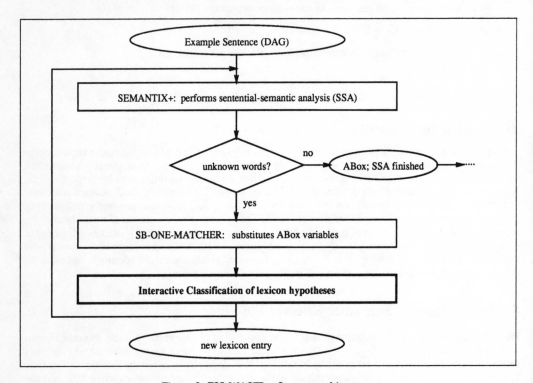

Figure 2: FSS-WASTL – System architecture

An Example

To illustrate our idea of the application of the interactive classifier during the example-driven knowledge acquisition, consider the following user's input[5]:

---

[4]These heuristics encode very general conventions of the FSS's design (e.g., new roles can only be introduced for generic concepts and not for lexicon entries) as well as very specific information (e.g., concepts, which are subconcepts of both PREDICATE and THING, represent verb nominalizations and cannot be meaningful hypotheses for unknown verbs).

[5]The following examples will be given in German with the English translation in parenthesis.

> Der Mann radelt vom Tagungshotel zum Strand.
> (*The man cycles from the conference hotel to the beach.*)

We assume that the system recognizes all words except for radelt (*cycles*). Moreover, we assume, that the sentence successfully passes the morphological analysis[6]. The unification based parser analyzes the user's input sentence syntactically and constructs as a result a derivation graph (DAG). This DAG is the input to the sentential-semantic analysis, during which an error, due to the incomplete lexicon, will arise. Following the acquisition algorithm described above, FSS-WASTL builds an ABox enhanced by variable concepts and roles. The TBox-matcher will be used in order to find TBox concepts consistent with the unknown word. These are MOTION and all its subconcepts, which are established due to the semantic roles agent, source and destination (see figure 3). The final step is the interactive classification, starting the incremental refinement with the most general hypothesis (MOTION). As described above, the interactive classification is guided by the structural differences. Thus, given the TBox in figure 3, the user is asked the following question:

> "Wird die optionale Rolle instrument auf die notwendige Rolle means restringiert?"
> ("Will the optional role instrument be restricted to the necessary role means?")[7]

If the user responds "yes", MOTION-BY-MEANS will become the actual most specific subsumer and the process continues recursively.

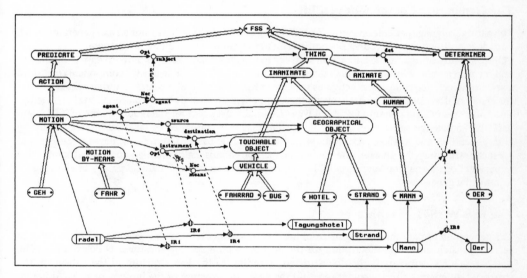

Figure 3: *An extract of the Functional Semantic Structure. The upper part of the TBox contains the generic FSS. Lexicon entries, which are marked with asterisks, can be found in the middle of the picture. The concepts and roles in the lower part form the ABox with variable structures (e.g. radel).*

The results which can be achieved through the application of FSS-WASTL depend on the example sentences. Bad example sentences are those with very limited information about unknown words, e.g. very short sentences: Ich radle. (*I cycle*). In this case the only possible hypothesis for radeln depends on its syntactic category and makes it a subconcept of PREDICATE. On the other hand, the

---

[6] If an error occurs during this phase, the morphologic acquisition component WIMOX [Klein, 90] is activated.

[7] This is an application independent question, which asks for elements of the knowledge base. Another approach is to use the generator in order to verbalize a question like "Is a vehicle used in order to radeln?". This kind of questions, however, can only be generated with additional knowledge about how the respective knowledge base is structured and how to verbalize this additional knowledge.

choice of appropriate examples prunes the search space strongly, as e.g. in `Ich fahre mit dem Bus nach Wemmetsweiler`. (*I go by bus to Wemmetsweiler.*), where `Wemmetsweiler` is the unknown word and the most general hypothesis, which the TBox-matcher finds, is `GEOGRAPHICAL OBJECT`. This initial description leads within one or two steps to a correct lexicon entry.

5 Building Paraphrases

The user interface to the interactive classifier offers some explanation facilities. It supports *Why-* and *How-*questions. The *Why-*option informs about the goal considered at the moment, while the *How-*explanation works like a tracer and lists the steps already performed.

Referring to the example above, we remark that the user has to know the structure of the FSS, viz. the meaning and the interpretation of the concepts and roles within the FSS, in order to sensibly answer the questions of the interactive classifier. Although the interactive classifier has a menu-based interface and an explanation component, we decided to generate example sentences as alternative explanations. The generated sentences, which we call *paraphrases*, have to clarify the structural differences between two concepts. The paraphraser is useful for two purposes: verbalizing the content of the knowledge base, and verifying the consistency and plausibility of new concept definitions[8]. The paraphraser is interfaced to POPEL, the generation component of XTRA.

The Generation Component POPEL

The natural language generation system POPEL[9] [Reithinger, 90] has been designed as a generator which pays special attention to discourse phenomena and integration within an overall system.

POPEL's main features are the interaction between the "what-to-say" and the "how-to-say" components, and the incremental selection and realization of the utterance. The "what-to-say" component consists of a selector which determines and activates the conceptual content, and a context handler which handles the choice of descriptions. The decisions of this component are heavily based on contextual knowledge. The "how-to-say" component POPEL-HOW is especially designed for the requirements of XTRA and uses the knowledge sources of the whole system that were designed to be used bidirectionally by both generation and analysis. Using intermediate linguistic-based descriptions, namely the FSS and syntactic structures, it translates the content of the non-linguistically oriented conceptual knowledge representation into natural language. POPEL is realized on a (simulated) parallel processor allowing for incremental generation.

The FSS-WASTL Paraphraser

The generation of paraphrases begins from the FSS processing level within POPEL-HOW. In order to select a possible structural description for the new concept, a specific subsumer is determined. The paraphrase's FSS-structure is then constructed according to the FSS structure of the subsumer, the structural differences already computed, and the syntactic structure of the input sentence. Although processing in POPEL is based on the SB-ONE knowledge representation language, the generator is not tightly coupled to it; especially word choice is performed independently. This facilitates its use during paraphrase generation: it is possible to separate the words that are to be uttered from the FSS structure. The FSS-WASTL paraphraser verbalizes the content of the knowledge base around the subsumer. In case the user accepts the paraphrase, the new concept is inserted as subconcept of the current subsumer. Let us consider again the example above. We assume that the value restriction of the role `means` from `FAHR` (`RIDE`) should be `FAHRRAD` (`BICYCLE`). For the transition from `MOTION-BY-MEANS` to `FAHR`, the interactive classifier asks the user by means of a menu:

"Wird der Wertebereich der Rolle 'means' von `VEHICLE` auf `FAHRRAD` restringiert?"
("Will the range of the role `means` be restricted from `VEHICLE` to `FAHRRAD`?")

---

[8] A more detailed discussion can be found in [Weischedel et al., 87] or [Ndiaye, 90].
[9] POPEL is the acronym of "Production Of {Perhaps, Possibly, P...} Eloquent Language".

On demand, the FSS-WASTL paraphraser explains the effects of this question by verbalizing the resulting intermediate description. For our example, the input of the generator consists of the TBox-expression corresponding to the individualized part of Figure 3, where the general concept of radel is restricted from MOTION-BY-MEANS to FAHR, and where radel has the additional role means with the value Fahrrad. The paraphraser generates the following sentence:

"Der Mann fährt mit dem Fahrrad vom Tagungshotel zum Strand."
(The man rides a bicycle from the conference hotel to the beach.)

6 Conclusion

The problem FSS-WASTL deals with – the acquisition of new semantic knowledge – arises frequently in natural language systems. Thus several solutions to this problem have already been proposed. IRACQ, developed as part of BBN's IRUS system [Weischedel et al., 87], uses a similar approach. It starts from a natural language example, establishes hypotheses for an unknown word by partly interpreting the example sentence, and then tries an interactive top-down refinement of these hypotheses. Unlike FSS-WASTL, the modules for IRACQ were especially developed for this application and did not evolve from the extension of existing analysis modules (SEMANTIX) and the accommodation of general tools (TBox-matcher and Interactive Classifier). DANTE, developed at the IBM Scientific Center of Rome [Antonacci et al., 89], solves its task in a multiple example sentences, bottom up approach. For DANTE, an induction algorithm was developed which like FSS-WASTL and IRACQ partly analyzes its inputs sentences and then forms lexicon hypotheses which cover all given examples.

The interactive classifier has its origin in the idea of Finin and Silverman in making the major reasoning procedure for KL-ONE-like languages – the classification – an interactive task. Unlike conventional net browsers, the interactive classifier traverses the taxonomy, relying on the defined structure of the concepts and not on their names or the user-ascribed position in the net. This meets the central idea of KL-ONE based knowledge representation languages, thus eliminating a major drawback of other frame-based languages. This approach is useful as a general-purpose, stand-alone tool as well as embedded in a specialized knowledge acquisition module, as was done with FSS-WASTL.

Using structural differences facilitates the natural language feedback during the development of knowledge bases. We demonstrated this within a natural language system, where such a feedback can be integrated easily. Even more important, however, is the ability to interface this algorithm to a natural language generator in order to verbalize example sentences based on the explanations about the internal representation of any new concept. This makes the approach transferable to other applications with arbitrary SB-ONE knowledge bases.

The problem to extending the use of exemplary natural language input to arbitrary SB-ONE knowledge bases is even more serious. In our understanding of natural language processing, an arbitrary SB-ONE knowledge base can only be integrated as the conceptual knowledge of the natural language system. This requires at least one further acquisition step: In addition to the acquisition of lexicon information as described above, which is a prerequisite for further interpretation of an example sentence, the acquisition step for the conceptual information itself is needed. Furthermore, an extension of interpretable natural language input to e.g. definitional sentences as used in dictionaries and as NANOKLAUS [Haas & Hendrix, 84] tried to interpret (e.g. "To cycle means to ride a bicycle") would increase the power of our method. Both problems are topics of our current research.

All systems mentioned are implemented in Common Lisp and work on various hardware platforms. They are integrated into the XTRA system and help to extent the semantic lexicon of XTRA's current application.

Acknowledgments

We would like to thank Jürgen Allgayer as well as John Nerbonne for their proof-reading of this paper and valuable discussions on the classification algorithm.

References

[Allgayer et al., 89a] J. **Allgayer**, K. **Harbusch**, A. **Kobsa**, C. **Reddig**, N. **Reithinger**, and D. **Schmauks**. *XTRA: A natural-language access system to expert systems.* International Journal of Man-Machine Studies., 31(2):161–195, August 1989.

[Allgayer et al., 89b] J. **Allgayer**, R. **Jansen-Winkeln**, C. **Reddig**, and N. **Reithinger**. *Bidirectional use of knowledge in the multi-modal NL access system XTRA.* In: 11th IJCAI, pp. 1492–1497, 1989.

[Antonacci et al., 89] F. **Antonacci**, M. **Russo**, M. T. **Pazienza**, and P. **Velardi**. *A system for text analysis and lexical knowledge acquisition.* Data & Knowledge Engineering, 4(1):1–20, Juli 1989.

[Aue et al., 89] D. **Aue**, S. **Heib**, and A. **Ndiaye**. *SB-ONE Matcher: Systembeschreibung und Benutzeranleitung.* SFB 314, Memo 32, Fachbereich Informatik, Universität des Saarlandes, Saarbrücken, 1989.

[Brachman & Schmolze, 85] R. J. **Brachman** and J. G. **Schmolze**. *An Overview of the KL-ONE Knowledge Representation System.* Cognitive Science, 9(2):171–216, 1985.

[Finin & Silverman, 84] T. **Finin** and D. **Silverman**. *Interactive Classification: A Technique for the Acquistion and Maintenance of Knowledge Bases.* Report ms-cis-84-17, University of Pennsylvania, Computer and Information Science, 1984.

[Finin, 86] T. **Finin**. *Interactive Classification: A Technique for Acquiring and Maintaining Knowledge Bases.* In: IEEE, volume 74, pp. 1414–1421, October 1986.

[Haas & Hendrix, 84] N. **Haas** and G. **Hendrix**. *Learning by being told.* In: R. S. Michalski, J. G. Carbonell, and T. M. Mitchell (eds.), Machine Learning: An Artificial Intelligence Approach, pp. 405–427. Springer-Verlag, 1984.

[Jansen-Winkeln, 88] R. M. **Jansen-Winkeln**. *WASTL: An Approach to Knowledge Acquisition in the NL Domain.* In: EKAW, pp. 22.1–22.15, Bonn, W. Germany, June 1988.

[Klein, 90] H. **Klein**. *WIMOX – ein Wissenserwerbssystem für ein morphologisches Lexikon.* Master thesis, Fachbereich Informatik, Universität des Saarlandes, Saarbrücken, 1990.

[Kobsa, 91] A. **Kobsa**. *Utilizing Knowledge: The Components of the SB-ONE Knowledge Representation Workbench.* In: J. Sowa (ed.), Principles of Semantic Networks: Explorations in the Representation of Knowledge. San Mateo, CA: Morgan Kaufmann, 1991.

[Ndiaye, 90] A. **Ndiaye**. *FSS-WASTL – Ein interaktives Wissensakquisitionssystem zur Erweiterung des semantischen Lexikons in XTRA.* Master thesis, Fachbereich Informatik, Universität des Saarlandes, Saarbrücken, 1990.

[Reithinger, 90] N. **Reithinger**. *POPEL – A parallel and incremental Natural Language Generation System.* In: C. Paris, W. Swartout, and W. Mann (eds.), Natural Language Generation in Artificial Intelligence and Computational Linguistics. Kluwer Academic Publishers, 1990.

[Weischedel et al., 87] R. **Weischedel**, D. **Ayuso**, A. **Haas**, E. **Hinrichs**, R. **Scha**, V. **Shaked**, and D. **Stallard**. *Research and Development in Natural Language Understanding as Part of the Strategic Computing Program.* Annual technical report 6522, BBN Laboratories Incorporated, Cambridge, MA, 1987.

Hybrid Encoding: Constraints on Addressing Structure

Jon M. Slack

Istituto per la Ricerca Scientifica e Tecnologica (I.R.S.T.)
38050 Povo (TN), ITALY
e-mail: slack@irst.it

Abstract

Cognitive models often make recourse to locality constraints as an important determinant of mental functioning. Such constraints are generally assumed to have their source at the hardware, or neuronal, level. However, the paper shows that certain cognitive limitations arise from the hybrid nature of cognitive architecture. In particular, the way symbols address constituent structure represented at the connectionist level limits their access to the encoded information. These limitations are expressed as the constructs of local and address domain and can be shown to provide an explanatory basis for a wide range of cognitive constraints.

Introduction

Researchers have recently turned their attention to the exploration of hybrid symbolic-connectionist architectures (Hendler 1991). At the heart of such systems, however, there remains the problem of structure, and how to encode it in terms of connectionist weights and activation levels (see Hinton 1990; Pollack 1990; Touretzky 1990; Smolensky 1990). As a pre-emptive strike, Fodor and Pylyshyn (1988) have claimed that the explanation of mental functioning is properly located at the symbolic level and that connectionism provides little more than an implementation paradigm for such models, making issues of hybrid encoding irrelevant. However, the paper shows that the hybrid nature of cognitive architecture is itself the source of constraints which have a powerful influence on shaping mental abilities.

As Fodor and McLaughlin (1990) have pointed out connectionist encodings are not directly accessible for symbolic addressing. To overcome this problem it is proposed that symbolic access is only possible through the use of a particular communication protocol, one based on the general view of structural configurations as comprising an address structure and a contents. This particular protocol is forced on hybrid systems by the nature of information representation at the connectionist level. The next section outlines the general properties of connectionist encoding.

Locality constraints are generally explained in terms of hardware limitations or neuronal properties. An alternative explanation can be cast in terms of a restrictive communication protocol mediating between the levels of an hybrid symbolic-connectionist architecture. The third section specifies the form of this protocol.

The basic thesis being proposed is that certain forms of locality imported into symbolic accounts of cognition derive from the fact that symbolic structures are encoded in a medium that imposes natural local restrictions. In the last section, these constraints are derived from the symbolic addressing protocol. Finally, it is suggested that such constraints might underlie a wide range of locality properties originally invoked to account for the observed features of human cognition.

E-Space: Encoding Space

The question of the most appropriate assignment of cognitive phenomena to symbolic and connectionist levels of explanation is left as open. What is being proposed is that the mapping between the two levels provides an appropriate basis for the explanation of locality constraints, even when only minimal assumptions are made concerning the nature of the relationship between them.

Encoding structure in an hybrid symbolic-connectionist architecture involves showing how the notion of combinatorial structure can be preserved in passing from the symbolic level to an encoding medium comprising points in a vector space. Slack (1990) shows how the operations of association and superposition can be used to define a connectionist representation medium, referred to as *Encoding Space*, E-space, consisting of composed connectionist states. Formally, the structure of E-space can be defined as a *semiring*, as follows:

Definition E-space comprises the quintuple $(V,+,**,0,\partial)$

1. $(V,+,0)$ is a commutative monoid defining the superposition operator;

2. $(V,**,\partial)$ is a monoid defining the association operator;

3. ** distributes over +.

V is the set of points, or corners, of a vector space, and the two identity elements, 0 and ∂, correspond to identity vectors for the operations of superposition and association, respectively. It is important to note that the set V is closed under both operations.

We can now define a representational mapping, referred to as the *encoding homomorphism*, f_e, which preserves combinatorial structure in mapping the set of symbolic languages L_X, that can be defined over an alphabet of symbols, X, using the combinatory operations of concatenation, denoted by '.', and union, denoted by '$\cup$', into E-space. The homomorphism is defined as follows:

Definition The encoding homomorphism, f_e, maps the semiring $(L_X,\cup,.,\emptyset,\{\varepsilon\})$ into the semiring $(V,+,**,0,\partial)$, such that

$$f_e(x\cup y) = f_e(x) + f_e(y)$$
$$f_e(x.y) = f_e(x) ** f_e(y), \text{ where } x, y \in L_X.$$

Thus, through f_e the set of languages that can be defined on a symbolic alphabet can be encoded in E-space, preserving their combinatorial structure.

This representational framework establishes a formalism for describing the composition of distributed representations which can encode constituent structure. It is not intended as a specific connectionist representation scheme in that it does not specify the details of particular connectionist operators. Rather, it captures the general properties of an encoding medium comprising a vector space and the operations of association and superposition.

Addressing Encoded Structures

The encoding mapping, f_c, can be used to build composite E-space vectors which encode constituent structure. The problem is that it isn't clear how information encoded in this way can be accessed. For example, consider the structured vector built using the operations of association and superposition whose composition is described by the expression given in (1)

$$[a**[c**w + d**x] + b**[f**y + g**z]] \ . . (1)$$

where the bold letters denote elements of the set V. As an encoding in E-space this composite structure is realised as just another point in vector space, its implicit structure is not apparent in its encoding. This problem is at the heart of Fodor and McLaughlin's (1990) argument against connectionist structure. As Fodor and McLaughlin put it,

...when a complex Classical symbol is tokened, its constituents are tokened. When a tensor product   vector or superposition vector is tokened, its components are not.......the components of tensor product   and superposition vectors can have no causal status as such. (Fodor & McLaughlin 1990, p. 198)

This is illustrated by the complex symbol [[John] [gave [Mary] [the ball]]] where each component is tokened as part of the composed structure's token. With composed vectors, on the other hand, the constituents are not directly accessible. The problem is to specify how the constituents of a composed vector encoding can be accessed such that mental processes can be sensitive to this structure.

In an hybrid architecture mental processes can be defined at two levels; symbolic processes and connectionist processes. The latter class of processes might operate on compound vector encodings exhibiting a form of *systematicity* equivalent to that underlying symbolic processes and structures, as suggested by van Gelder (1990). However, the focus of this paper is on the problem of how structures encoded in E-space can be made accessible to processes defined at the symboilic level. Some view this as a trivial problem of implementation (Fodor and McLaughlin, 1990; van Gelder, 1990), but it will be shown that important cognitive constraints have their origins in this problem of access. To solve this problem it is necessary to show how symbols address the nodes of vector composition trees. The problem is viewed as one of defining an address system for composed E-space encodings such that symbols can access the encoded constituents.

In (1), the vectors, a-g and w-z, might correspond directly under f_e to a set of symbols. This allows the terminal nodes of the derivation tree to be accessed via their corresponding symbols, but leaves the non-terminal nodes inaccessible. This contrasts with complex symbols such as [[John] [gave [Mary] [the ball]]] in which the component structures are made explicit by the parentheses; each pair of parentheses denotes a non-terminal node in the symbolic composition tree. When Fodor and Pylyshyn (1988) speak of mental processes being *sensitive* to the structure of such symbols, they mean that the processes can access the individual constituents on the basis of their structural configuration. The configuration of the symbol is given by the embedding of the parentheses, which expresses the derivation of the symbol string. The problem remains that with E-space encodings the equivalent configuration is not directly accessible to symbolic-level processes. First, we need to develop a general concept of *address structure* which specifies how information encoded in a structure can be accessed, regardless of whether it is encoded symbolically or as an E-space vector.

In general, symbolic structures support two basic forms of addressing, *direct addressing* and *relative addressing*. The former involves direct access to constituents. For example, in the complex symbol the pairs of parentheses distinguish the different components and can be used to access them directly provided they are individuated through some form of indexing or labeling scheme. This is equivalent to uniquely labeling each nonterminal node of the symbol's derivation tree. In addition, the individual words label the terminal nodes of the tree. The parentheses can also be used to define a relative addressing system in terms of their depth of embedding and/or sequential order. For example, the component *Mary* can be located using the address *the first set of paretheses at the second level of embedding*. Such an addressing scheme requires (i) a pre-defined origin to function as a 'zero' address, and (ii) a set of labels for distinguishing the elements of the path connecting the origin to the addressed component. From these examples, it is clear that the address structure comprises a structural basis, the symbol's derivation tree, plus some form of addressing scheme, that is, a set of labels over which a formal language can be defined, for accessing the individual constituents. Whereas direct addressing is insensitive to the structural configuration of the symbol, relative addressing schemes utilise it to encode addresses. Thus, a direct addressing scheme merely comprises a set of labels plus a mapping taking elements from this set onto the set of constituents. A relative addressing scheme, on the other hand, requires both a set of labels and a structural configuration over which to define paths, plus a mapping which assigns the labels to elements of the configuration.

Dual Addressing

E-space encodings require a direct symbolic addressing scheme so that the encoded constituents can be processed as 'chunks'. This type of distal access (Newell, 1980) which is the capacity to address a structure in some remote, abbreviated manner, is fundamental to any notion of compositionality as without it a structure could only be referenced through its full specification. In a classical complex symbol, the parentheses function to indicate the 'chunking' of the symbol into constituents. However, each chunk needs to be uniquely labeled for it to be accessed directly. This reference capability also instantiates *the principle of explicit naming* (Marr, 1982).

Relative addressing schemes are important for expressing the address of one constituent relative to another. This referential capacity is crucial to the notion of constituent structure as it captures the mother-daughter, or dominance, relationship expressed in composition trees. 'Daughter' nodes can be addressed relative to their 'mother' nodes. This capacity is constantly utilised in building composite structures where a constituent can only be identified relative to an existing node in the structure. In such circumstances only a relative addressing scheme is available.

Symbolic access to E-space encodings needs to support both of these referential capacities and thus, an address structure incorporating both direct and relative addressing schemes is required.

Address Structure DAGs

Symbolic addresses access E-space encodings through the operation of *retrieval*. This operation delimits the communication protocol between the levels of the hybrid architecture. In most connectionist systems retrieval is the inverse operation of association. We can define a general retrieval operator, denoted #, as follows: Given the composite vector, $v_1 = [a^{**}b + c^{**}d]$, then

$$a \# v_1 = b \quad \ldots (2)$$

Because the association operator is noncommutative we can distinguish between its arguments, similar to the role-function distinction maintained in Smolensky's representation scheme (1990). The arguments are labeled *address* and *constituent* according to the interpretation given in (3),

$$[\text{address vector}] ** [\text{constituent vector}] \ldots (3)$$

Within this protocol, a is interpreted as the address of the constituent vector, b, in the composite encoding, v_1. Thus, when the composite vector is accessed using the address vector,

a, it retrieves the constituent vector, **b**.

The protocol is independent of the form of the address and thus supports both direct and relative addressing. Direct addressing is achieved by associating each constituent vector of an E-space encoding with an address vector corresponding to a symbolic label. This label can then retrieve the constituent vector through its assigned address vector. Symbolic labels that function in this way are referred to as *global labels*.

Relative addressing is the natural mode of operation of the retrieval operator in the sense that an address vector specifies the address of a constituent vector relative to a particular composite encoding. For example, **a** is the address of **b** relative to v_1, but would not retrieve **b** given a different composite encoding. In this sense, global labels can also be regarded as defining relative addresses; they specify the direct address of constituents relative to the top-level composite encoding, that is, the vector that encodes the complete structure. Symbolic labels assigned to address vectors that retrieve constituents relative to other constituent vectors are referred to as *local labels*.

Via the retrieval operator, the constituents of an E-space encoding can be accessed using both direct and relative symbolic addresses. The full set of such addresses comprises the *address structure* of the composite encoding. Because symbolic addressing is mediated through the address-constituent protocol these structures are restricted to the class of *regular languages*. This allows address structures to be represented as directed acyclic graphs (DAGs), in which the edges and nodes are assigned local labels and global labels, respectively. Figure 1 shows the address structure DAG (AS-DAG) for the compound vector given in (1). The local labels are denoted by the lower-case letters, a-g, and the global labels by the upper-case letters, A-C. The global labels function as direct addresses for the constituent vectors within the composite E-space encoding. The local labels, on the other hand, specify the address of a constituent relative to its superordinate ('mother') constituent.

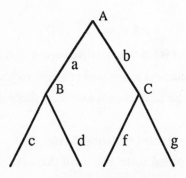

Figure 1 Address Structure Tree
(AS-DAG)

In fact, the AS-DAG shown in figure 1 represents the union of two separate address structures both of which take the global label A as their root-node. It is important to remember that vector composition trees specify the encoding of composed vectors, but are not necessarily accessible at the symbolic level as connected configurations. An AS-DAG corresponds to a symbolic level 'view' of a composite E-space encoding. However, because they have a restricted form, the full address structure for a particular E-space encoding may comprise the union of a set of AS-DAGs, each providing a view of a different part of the composite configuration.

There remains the problem of how the labels of an AS-DAG are assigned vector values under the encoding mapping. Because AS-DAGs incorporate a dual-addressing system the resulting redundancy requires the dynamic assignment of vector values to at least one of the two sets of labels. Local labels capture local structure and the assignment should therefore be both *faithful* and *consistent*, that is, elements of the set of local labels, denoted by L, should map to different elements of V, the set of vectors, and the mapping should be constant, at least local to a given address structure. Global labels are by definition unique relative to a given address structure and so the problem of consistency does not arise. However, the mapping should be *faithful* (elements of the set of global labels, denoted by G, should map to different elements of $V)^1$. These constraints give a higher priority to fixing the vector values of local labels under f_e. In this case, the values of the global labels are determined by (i) assigning a vector value to the root-node of the AS-DAG, and (ii) propogating the vector values down the tree through association with the fixed local label vector values. Thus, an AS-DAG functions both as the component of f_e that maps global labels onto vector values, and as the symbolic 'view' of the local structural relations existing between the constituents the global labels reference.

In summary, hybrid encoding captures combinatorial structure through the association of a composite E-space encoding with a corresponding address structure, the latter specifying the symbolic-level access to constituent encodings. If the address structure is well-formed, then the E-space encoding has a unique decomposition.

---

[1] As defined, the sole function of global labels is to retrieve constituents directly from composite E-space encodings and as such the relationship between their vector values and the constituent vectors they access can be quite arbitrary. There is no necessity for the address labels to comprise partial descriptions of their associated constituents as implemented in some hybrid architectures (Touretzky 1990). This independence allows the vector values of global labels to be determined as a function of the AS-DAG configuration rather than being related to the constituent vectors they access.

Locality Constraints on Address Structures

A number of important locality constraints emergent from the properties of hybrid encoding can be defined on AS-DAGs. These constraints provide the basis for defining the constructs of *local* and *address domain*.

As AS-DAG representations are drawn from the class of regular languages they can be generated by right-linear grammars where each production has the form,

$$A \to \omega B \text{ or } A \to \omega$$

and where $A, B \in G$, $\omega \in L_f$, and $\mathcal{F}$ is the set of labels which have faithful and consistent encodings under f_e. This allows each level of an AS-DAG structure to be defined as a domain local to a particular global label.

Complex relative addresses can be defined on AS-DAGs as strings comprising a global label, functioning as the origin node, followed by a string of local labels of arbitrary length. However, this structural referential capacity is in fact restricted to *nearest neighbour addressing*. That is, AS-DAG nodes can only be addressed relative to their mother node, and relative addresses defined on AS-DAGs comprise the global label of the mother node plus at most one local label (that is, one AS-DAG edge). This is because structural AS-DAG addresses connect points in E-space and between any two such points there are an infinite number of possible paths linking them, but only the minimal path is distinguishable. Thus, unless the intermediate nodes of an E-space path are differentiated through labeling, that is, direct addressing, the path is not recoverable, only the end point is accessible.

These different constraints can be integrated into a single construct, referred to as a local domain, incorporating the following properties:

(a) A local domain is associated with a single **global label**;

(b) associated with each global label is a **finite local structure** comprising local labels (AS-DAG edges) which have vector values fixed relative to the value of the global label; and in addition,

(c) a local domain can dominate upto **one** subordinate local domain.

The full definition is as follows,

Definition A local domain is a labeled AS-DAG comprising a global label at its root node, a fixed local structure, that is, a finite set of descending edges, such that each edge is assigned a local label, with a maximum of one such label addressing a non-terminal AS-DAG node.

In fact, we can distinguish between terminal and non-terminal local domains, with only the latter having property (c). At the intuitive level, local domains can be thought of as the permanent building blocks used to compose structured E-space encodings. All the information encoded in a local domain is accessible from its global label, as the vector value of each daughter node is known relative to the root node.

Composition of local domains: Address domain.

Address structures are built up through the composition of local domains. This operation is schematized in figure 2 in which local domains are represented as productions. In this figure, the domain associated with the global label A_1 specifies the address of a local domain, X, the identity of which is 'unknown' prior to composition. In composing the next level of structure, this address is attached to the new local domain labeled B_1 through the process of *address unification*. In assigning the address of X to B_1, the relative addresses encoded in its local domain become instantiated as E-space encodings. This is because the domain contains local labels which specify E-space addresses relative to the vector value of the domain's global label. Once the global label receives a value, the relative addresses are automatically established.

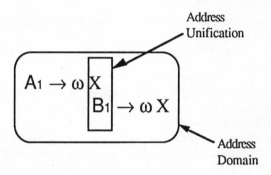

Figure 2. Address domain for A 1

The operation of composition can be viewed from the opposite direction and seen as linking the contents of the constituent B_1 to the address specified by X. In this sense the composition operator instantiates the address-constituent protocol. Hence the protocol spans adjacent local domains. In figure 2, the address part of the protocol is specified relative to A_1 and the constituent part is the local domain B_1. Thus, the protocol through which symbolic processes access E-space encodings can be defined on AS-DAGs as a window spanning two adjacent local domains, indexed to the global label of the most dominant of the two domains. This construct of a symbolic addressing window is referred to as an *address domain* and is defined as follows:

Definition The address domain indexed to an AS-DAG node, A, comprises the local domain of A plus the subordinate adjacent local domain attached through composition.

Conclusions

Elsewhere the construct of a local domain has been used to explain unbounded dependency phenomena (Slack 1990). In the longer version of this paper (Slack 1991) a wide range of locality constraints inherent in natural language phenomena are accounted for in terms of the functions of local and global labels. However, the full range of applicability of these ideas remains to be explored.

References

Fodor, J.A., and McLaughlin. B. P. 1990. Connectionism and the problem of systematicity : Why Smolensky's solution doesn't work. *Cognition* 35: 183-204.

Fodor, J.A., and Pylyshyn. Z.W. 1988. Connectionism and cognitive architecture: A critical analysis. *Cognition* 28: 3-71.

Hendler, J. 1991. Special issue of *Connectionist Science* on hybrid symbolic-connectionist architectures. Forthcoming.

Hinton, G.E. 1990. Mapping part-whole hierarchies into connectionist networks. *Artificial Intelligence* 46: 47-77.

Marr, D. 1982. *Vision*. San Fransisco:Freeman.

Pollack, J.B. 1990. Recursive distributed representations. *Artificial Intelligence* 46: 77-107.

Slack, J.M. 1990. Unbounded Dependency: Tying Strings to Rings. In *Proceedings of COLING-90*, Helsinki, Finland.

Slack, J.M. 1991 Hybrid Encoding as a Source of Cognitive Constraints. Forthcoming.

Smolensky, P. 1990. Tensor product variable binding and the representation of symbolic structures in connectionist systems. *Artificial Intelligence* 46: 159-217.

Touretzky, D.S. 1990. BoltzCONS: Dynamic symbol structures in a connectionist network. *Artificial Intelligence* 46: 5-47.

Uncertainty and cyclic dependencies: a proposal and a network implementation

Andrea Bonarini°, Ernesto Cappelletti°, Antonio Corrao°

^Dipartimento di Elettronica del Politecnico di Milano
°Artificial Intelligence & Robotics Project
Piazza Leonardo da Vinci, 32 - 20133 Milano - Italy
E-Mail: BONARINI@ipmel1.elet.polimi.it

1. Introduction

We propose an Uncertainty Manager (UM) based on belief revision concepts: it maintains automatically the consistency of a knowledge base according to a theory of uncertainty. This type of system can be used both to efficiently support inferential engines in uncertainty management, and as independent what-if advisor.

We represent facts as nodes of a network, whose links stand for cause-effect relationships. We associate to each node a measure of the confidence the UM has in it. The effect of any change in the network (i.e. topological changes, or update of uncertainty measures) is propagated throughout the whole network to preserve consistency. All changes produced in the network are communicated to the inference engine, which considers them as new knowledge. It possibly reacts, generating new facts to be added to the network.

We discuss the motivations to accept cyclic dependencies among propositions in such a network and we present our solution to the so arising problems.

In section 2 we summarize he uncertainty theory we adopted, based on belief intervals [Driankov, 1988]. Section 3 is devoted to the presentation of our approach to Uncertainty and Belief Revision (UBR). In section 4, we will show our solution to cyclic dependencies. A working example is described in section 5. A discussion of our approach and notes about future developments will close the paper. More details on our approach and related issues can be found in [Bonarini, Cappelletti, and Corrao, 1990] and in [Bonarini, in press].

2. An approach to uncertainty representation

It has been pointed out (e.g. [Clark, 1990] or [Buxton, 1989]) that numerical representation of uncertainty suffer for difficulty of interpretation of the numerical measure, impossibility of normalization, and precision problems. To override these drawbacks, some proposals have been issued (e.g. [Bonissone and Decker, 1986]) to represent uncertainty with a small set of ordered linguistic labels, called *linguistic variables*. Each of them corresponds to a *fuzzy number* [Zadeh, 1983] in the interval [0, 1].

In the following we will consider the set of linguistic variables (L_2) defined by Bonissone and Decker composed of nine elements ranging from *impossible* to *certain*. We will refer to the nine elements of this set with the shorter notation E_i with i ranging from 1 to 9. Driankov defines an ordering among these variables as:

$$E_i < E_j \leftrightarrow i < j \quad \text{with } i, j = 1, ..., 9$$

2.1. Belief intervals

Driankov claims that his theory satisfies the requirements proposed by Bonissone [Bonissone, 1987] for uncertainty representation.

He defines a *belief interval* as a set of two parameters varying on L_2:
- *support*: $s(a)$ expresses the positive evidence for the assertion a;
- *plausibility*: $p(a) \equiv certain - s(\neg a)$

Plausibility is defined as the difference between the absolute certainty and the support of the negation of the assertion. Support and plausibility are always updated independently of each other, since they are defined as different kinds of information associated to a proposition, separately acquired and conceptually unrelated. Moreover, representing uncertainty with such a pair of parameters makes it possible to consider also contradictory and unknown belief states, as we will discuss in detail below.

The use of uncertainty measures similar to belief intervals is common to other proposals (e.g. [Shafer, 1990]), but some of the requirements and properties of these theories are relaxed here, since Driankov works on subjective linguistic estimates, while the others deal with set-theoretic numerical (or fuzzy) measures (see [Driankov, 1986] for a detailed discussion).

To make clearer to the user the meaning of a given belief interval, Driankov provides criteria to measure the semantic relevance of the difference between belief intervals. Two distinct belief intervals are significantly different only if they belong to different *belief states*. The defined belief states partition in six areas the 9×9 table (called *BI*) combining all the possible values for support and plausibility:

- Believed (B): this belief state plays a role similar to that played by the value true in boolean logic;
- *Rather Believed than disbelieved* (*RB*);
- *Contradictory* (*C*): both the evidence supporting the proposition and that refuting it are more than significantly positive;
- *Unknown* (*U*): neither the evidence supporting the proposition nor that refuting it are more than significantly positive;
- *Rather Disbelieved than believed* (*RD*);
- *Disbelieved* (*D*): this belief state plays a role similar to the one played by the value *false* in boolean logic.

Table 1 - The *BI* table. We will refer to linguistic labels with their shorter identifiers E_i, ranging from E_1 (= impossible) to E_9 (= certain).

In many situations, it is useful to reason about uncertainty measures in terms of belief states, instead of belief intervals. For instance, when we have to understand qualitatively how an inference network evolves we would prefer to manage only 6 values, instead of 81. This is what we will do in the rest of the paper.

2.2. Operators on belief intervals

In the following, we will include between slashes a logical expression to denote the belief interval associated to it. Therefore, the notation /<*expression*>/ is a shorthand for [s(<*expression*>), p(<*expression*>)]. Moreover, we consider atomic all propositions, and we will refer to them with single small letters.

To compute the belief interval associated to a compound expression, operators have been defined on belief intervals. In the following we will provide the definitions of operators working on L_2.

- *Negation*.

We have to introduce first the definition of the negation of a linguistic variable:

$$N(E_i) = E_9 - E_i = E_{9-(i-1)} \qquad\qquad i = 1,...,9$$

This operator returns the symbol symmetric to its argument with respect to the middle element of the scale (i.e. E_5 for L_2).

The negation operator for a belief interval is:

$NOT(/a/) \equiv [s(\neg a), p(\neg a)] = [N(p(a)), N(s(a))]$

Notice that this operator satisfies the involutive property, defined as:

$NOT(NOT(/a/)) = /a/$ $\qquad\qquad \forall /a/$

In the following we will use the shorthand $/\neg a/$ for the notation $NOT(/a/)$

• *Conjunction.*
Although Driankov defines different conjunction and disjunction operators (based on T-norms and S-norms [Dubois and Prade, 1982]), in this paper we consider only one operator for each kind, for sake of conciseness. Moreover, we will present our versions of these operators, which is slightly different from the Driankov's. The chosen conjunction operator is:

$$AND^* (/a/, /b/) = \begin{cases} [E_1, E_9] & /a/ \in U, /b/ \in C \\ [min(s(a), s(b)), min(p(a), p(b))] & otherwise \end{cases}$$

where $[E_1, E_9]$ is the most representative belief interval of the belief state *Unknown*. In the following we will use also the infix symbol $\wedge$ to refer to conjunction.

• *Disjunction.*
We use the disjunction operator:

$$OR^* (/a/, /b/) = \begin{cases} [E_1, E_9] & /a/ \in U, /b/ \in C \\ [max(s(a), s(b)), max(p(a), p(b))] & otherwise \end{cases}$$

In the following we will use also the infix symbol $\vee$ to refer to disjunction.

To use his theory also with rules, Driankov defined the following operators.
• *Aggregation.*
This operator aggregates the evidence coming from different sources to a single assertion. For instance, it can be used to combine evidence for an assertion which is present in the conclusions of more than one inference rule. It is defined as:

$AGGR(/\{a\}_1/, /\{a\}_2/) = [max(s(\{a\}_1), s(\{a\}_2)), min(p(\{a\}_1), p(\{a\}_2))]$

where the notation $\{a\}_i$ stands for "the evidence pertaining to a and coming from source i".

• *Detachment.*
This operator propagates the evidence pertaining to the premise of an inference rule to its conclusions. We first present the DET_{ns} operator, to be used for rules whose conditions ar necessary and sufficient to infer the conclusion.

$DET_{ns}(/H/, /H \rightarrow T/) \qquad = [s(H)\, s(H \rightarrow T), p(H)\, p(H \rightarrow T)]$

where $/H/$ is the belief interval pertaining to the premises of the rule (i.e. the hypothesis) and $/H \rightarrow T/$ (the *strength* of the rule) is a belief interval expressing the confidence in the deduction. The strength of the rule should belong to the belief state *Believed* in accordance to the common sense principle that a rule makes sense only if it is trustworthy.

A second operator is used for rules whose conditions are sufficient only. We present here our modification of the DET_1 operator proposed by Driankov:

$$DET_s \ (/h/, /h{\rightarrow}t//) = \begin{cases} AND^* \ (/h/, /h{\rightarrow}t//) & /h/{\in}\{B, RB\} \\ [E_1, E_9] & /h/{\in}\{D, RD, U, C\} \end{cases}$$

Our operator propagates only positive evidence, assigning a value *Unknown* to the conclusion if the premise has not meaningful, favourable evidence. These conditions apply only if the hypothesis is trustworthy. In the following we will use also the infix symbol → to refer to the DET_s operator.

3. An approach to Belief Revision on uncertain information

The goal of Belief Revision is to maintain the consistency of a set of propositions with respect to a truth theory. In our case, the truth theory is the outlined uncertainty theory.

To improve readability, we introduce here *dependency networks*. In these networks three types of nodes exist: *external assumptions, propositions*, and *rules* (see figure 1)

Each proposition node represents a proposition p_k. Its only output is the belief interval (y_k) pertaining to the proposition. The node receives in input the external assumption z_k about p_k and the contributions coming from rules having p_k as conclusion (the links marked with u_i).

Each rule node receives in input the belief intervals of its premises, and produces as output the belief interval of its conclusion.

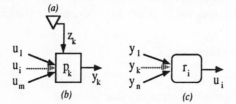

Figure 1 - The *belief network* nodes: *(a)* an external assumption, *(b)* a proposition, *(c)* a rule.

Changes in the network consist either in the insertion of new nodes and links, or in the modification of assumptions. The effects of these changes are propagated through the network to preserve consistency.

3.1. Problems with circular justifications

Now we can discuss problems arising from circular dependencies. When, given a set of rules, at least one proposition is inferentially related to itself, the network representing the set of rules contains at least one loop. Belief interval propagation through loops could suffer from termination problems.

The simplest solution would be to reject a priori those inferences which would cause propositions to justify indirectly themselves, as soon as they are introduced in the network. We cannot accept this solution, otherwise the resulting network topology would depend on the order of insertion of the inferences.

Another possible solution could be to present to the user all the inferences participating to a loop, and to ask him how to change the network to cut the cyclic path. This solution needs human intervention, and the consequent network update might be complex. Moreover, the possible insertion of closing-loop propositions may be performed by an inference engine, which should work without any human mediation. Therefore, also this solution has to be rejected.

A third solution would be to make the system automatically modifying the topology of the network. We believe automatic topological changes should not modify the semantic of the connections present in the network, since both the user and the problem solver had their good reasons to define the network as they did.

We have to accept loops in a system as the one we are discussing about, since they reflect some knowledge coming from external sources, to be considered unquestionable. If the external sources are people, the UM should make them aware of the result of their updates. If they are motivated to insert anyway a proposition, the system should be able to handle the situation. On the other side, if the external source is an inference engine, it could hardly manage possible warnings about problems in its knowledge base. The system should rely on its fact base manager. Moreover, knowledge may come from different agents (either humans or artificial), each one partly contributing to the whole knowledge base. Therefore, although the knowledge introduced by a single agent may be loops-free, the global knowledge base may show cyclic paths. If there are multiple knowledge sources, the solution of presenting to the user the loop to be cut is not viable, since each agent may be responsible of only a part of the loop.

Another motivation to accept loops is that some theories exist that cannot be expressed with acyclic networks. For instance, consider the case in which an expert describes a theory using the following inferences:

$$\begin{cases} a \to b & [1] \\ \neg b \land c \to \neg a & [2] \end{cases}$$

We recall that the symbol $\to$ represents the DET_s operator: therefore information about $\neg b$ does not affect a through inference [1], since $a \to b$ does not imply $\neg b \to \neg a$. Therefore, the theory does make sense.

Moreover, as outlined above, the global confidence in a proposition results from the aggregation of the confidence supplied by *all* its sources. Here, the global confidence values of the propositions cited in the right part of the formulae does not come from the single formula, but from the whole underlying network

The information carried by [1] and [2] is relevant at least for some assumptions about the involved propositions. For instance, if there is no evidence for a, while there is meaningful positive evidence for $\neg b$ and c, then positive evidence is propagated via [2] to $\neg a$. Here, rule [1] does not fire, since initially there is not positive evidence for a and after the activation of [2] the evidence is negative. Moreover, evidence about b does not propagate any value back to a through [1]. On the other side, if there is meaningful positive evidence for a, but not for $\neg b$, then rule [1] will fire, while [2] will not. Therefore, we have shown two possible well-founded executions for the same network topology: there is no reason to forbid the expression of such relationships among propositions.

Given that we have to accept loops, we cannot leave them uncontrolled. Two critical cases may arise:
- the propagation algorithm does not end;
- the propagation algorithm ends, but the results depends on the order of execution.

4. A solution for loop problems

A possible solution consists in the elimination of cyclic dependencies. We do that, without changing the structure of the network, as the inference engine or the user built it.

Loops can be safely represented in the network splitting each proposition node belonging to a loop in two subnodes.

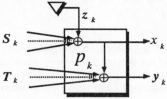

Figure 3 - The node p_k split.

In figure 3 we see the node p_k, split in two subnodes having as exits respectively the x_k and y_k links. The symbol $\oplus$ indicates the aggregation operation while the triangle represents a generic external assumption.This node structure keeps the evidence propagating through loops including p_k, distinct from the evidence propagating through open paths. Evidence coming from loops, enters via the T_k links and the contribution of this node goes toward cyclic paths via the x_k link. Evidence independent from p_k enters via the S_k links, and propagates to non-cyclic paths via the y_k links. This topology physically breaks all loops. Acyclic beliefs propagation flows towards the nodes belonging to some cyclic path which contains the current node, whereas cyclic beliefs are propagated only to those nodes which the current one does not depend on. This is shown in figure 4. Here, you can see the topology changes made when a loop is closing. In *(a)* we have node p_1 dependent on p_2 through an unspecified dependency chain represented by the dashed line. The *(b)* part of the figure shows how the propagation path from p_1 to p_2 changes when p_1 becomes dependent on p_2 (here because the inference $p_1 \rightarrow p_2$ has been inserted).

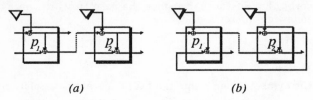

    (a)   *(b)*

Figure 4- Topology changes when a loop is closing.

Whenever the global measure of uncertainty is needed, it can be found at the y_k link. Only the "safe" part of it (given at the x_k exit) is used in a loop.

To appraise the effect of our proposal on the cases discussed above, consider the network resulting from [3] and [4] after loop detection and node splitting (figure 5).

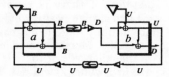

Figure 5 - The belief network from rules [3] and [4] after loop detection.

The same external assumption that caused endless-propagation brings now the topologically changed network to a stable configuration where:
• the confidence status of a is *Believed*, since its loop-external sources (i.e. the external assumption and the contribution coming from the network) are reduced to the external assumption only, which is *Believed*;
• the confidence status of b is *Disbelieved*;
• inference [3] fires using only the loops-external sources of a;
• inference [4] does not fire, since the loops-external support is not enough.

Together with loops, problems coming from the order of firing of the inferences and uneven treatment of the involved propositions disappear.

5. A working example

We implemented the proposed approach in **UBRS** (Uncertainty and Belief Revision System), which now runs both on Xerox 1186 and MacIntosh. We wrote it in **SILK** (Smalltalk In Lisp Kernel), a compact, portable, and efficient object-oriented system that we implemented in standard Common Lisp and implementing Smalltalk-like [Goldberg and Robson, 1983] structures.

In this section we will present a simple example of the system working on heart disease diagnosis. It is a part (adapted to be presented in this paper) of a larger consultant system aimed at supporting the quick diagnosis of heart problems from data which can be observed in a first aid department of a hospital. The setting is: a patient showing chest pain comes to the first aid department and the physician has to identify quickly whether the patient suffers from heartache or not, to adopt the correct therapy in the shortest time. The example we present here considers some simple observations and anamnestic data influencing the confidence in the fact that the patient may run the risk of heartache.

In this example, we represent propositions by (*<predicate>* *<value>*) pairs. Some predicates are boolean, and in the example we will only consider their positive form. Other predicates can take a single value in a larger set of alternative choices. This is a constraint we implemented defining the operator *one-of* working on belief intervals. It has the same semantic of an *exclusive-or*: it gives a result in the classes *Belived* or *Rather Belived* if one and only one of its arguments belongs to the same class. We decided to implement it as though the propositions appearing in the exclusive-or, where partecipating to a set of inference rules like those presented here below:

$$xor(a, b, c) = \begin{cases} or(a, b) \Rightarrow not(c) \\ or(b, c) \Rightarrow not(c) \\ or(c, a) \Rightarrow not(b) \end{cases}$$

The rules of our example are presented here below in the format used to insert them in the network. This format should be familiar to the reader knowing Smalltalk.

```
[ubrs :if '(smokes-a-lot yes)          [ubrs :if '(temperament vehement)
      :then '((heart-risk yes))              :then '((heart-risk yes))
      :explanation 'r1 :strength 8]          :explanation 'r5 :strength 8]
[ubrs :if '(stress yes)                [ubrs :if '(face-color ruby)
      :then '((heart-risk yes))              :then '((temperament vehement))
      :explanation 'r2 :strength 8]          :explanation 'r6 :strength 6]
[ubrs :if '(job manager)               [ubrs :if '(temperament sure)
      :then '((stress yes))                  :then '(('not(heart-risk yes)))
      :explanation 'r3 :strength 6]          :explanation 'r7 :strength 7]
[ubrs :if '('and ('not(stress yes))
                 (temperament shy))
      :then '(('not (job manager)))
      :explanation 'r4 :strength 6]
```

For instance, the first rule can be expressed in natural language as: *it is extremely likely that a person smoking a lot could run the risk of heartache.* Notice the value of the field *strength*, which is *8*, represents the belief interval $[E_8, E_9]$.

The predicate *temperament* may assume one of three alternative values: *sure*, *shy*, or *vehement*. This is expressed by the following expression; using the macro-operator *one-of*:

```
[ubrs :one-of '((temperament sure)(temperament vehement)(temperament shy))]
```

which expands in a set of three rules as described above.

The resulting network is presented in figure 6. Notice the expansion of the macro-operator *one-of* and the fact that only the nodes participating to a loop have been split. Notice also how a graphical representation becomes hard to be understood, when nodes and links are more than few. This is a problem common to all network-based systems: a graphical representation is almost useless if it is used in a real application. So, we did not implement any graphical interface. UBRS supports the user with a set of investigation tools if all the needed information to understand the network behaviour.

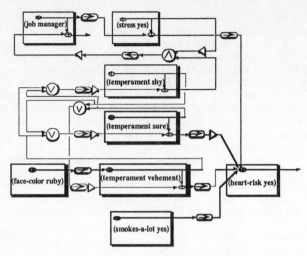

Figure 6 - The network of the example

In our example the first information supplied to the system is that the patient has a ruby face. This fact is judged extremely likely $[E_8, E_9]$. We show here below the insertion of this information, together with the produced effect. Every change in the network is notified by a demon. Here you may see the result of the activation of the demon writing a message on the screen.

```
? [ubrs :assume '((face-color ruby)) :values (list (beint 8 9))]
Proposition (TEMPERAMENT SHY): Evidence was /1, 9/ : U    Now it is /1, 4/ : D
Proposition (HEART-RISK YES): Evidence was /1, 9/ : U    Now it is /6, 9/ : B
Proposition (TEMPERAMENT VEHEMENT): Evidence was /1, 9/ : U    Now it is /6, 9/ : B
Proposition (TEMPERAMENT SURE): Evidence was /1, 9/ : U    Now it is /1, 4/ : D
Proposition (FACE-COLOR RUBY): Evidence was /1, 9/ : U    Now it is /8, 9/ : B
```

The fact that the patient has a ruby face triggers rule r6, which make the system deduce there is a *meaningful chance* $[E_6, E_9]$ that the temperament of the patient be vehement. This fact, in turn, triggers the rules corresponding to the macro-operator one-of which deduces there is a *meaningful chance* that the patient has not a temperament shy, nor sure. This can be seen interpreting the messages about these two facts. Let us consider the first one. It informs us that the belief interval of the fact (*TEMPERAMENT SHY*) is $[E_1, E_4]$, which belongs to the belief state *Disbelieved*. This belief interval means there is no evidence supporting the fact while there is evidence supporting the negation of the fact: the plausibility value E_4 comes from E_9-E_6, where E_6 is the evidence in favour of the negation of the fact coming from the application of the operator *one-of*.

The second observation made by our physician is that the patient seems to be shy.

```
? [ubrs :assume '((temperament shy)) :values (list (beint 6 9))]
Proposition (TEMPERAMENT SHY): Evidence was /1, 4/ : D    Now it is /6, 4/ : C
Proposition (HEART-RISK YES): Evidence was /6, 9/ : B    Now it is /1, 9/ : U
Proposition (TEMPERAMENT VEHEMENT): Evidence was /6, 9/ : B    Now it is /6, 4/ : C
```

The effect of this insertion combines with the previous status of (*TEMPERAMENT SHY*) making it belong to the belief state *Contradictory*: there is meaningful evidence both in favour and against the fact. Because of the *one-of* operator, this reflects on (*TEMPERAMENT VEHEMENT*), making it *Contradictory*, too. Notice that nothing changes for the third element appearing in the *one-of* application, since no evidence is added to it. Since (*HEART-RISK YES*) is no longer supported (the antecedent of rule *r5* is now *Contradictory*) its belief state becomes *Uncertain*.

Our physician starts to ask some information to his patient. She says that she is head of the marketing department at "Pop-corn Machines and Co.". With certainty, the new fact inserted affirms that the patient is a manager. This triggers rule *r3*, making the system assume there is some meaningful chance that the patient is stressed. This, in turn, triggers rule *r2* which rises the belief interval of (*HEART-RISK YES*) to [E_6, E_9].

```
? [ubrs :assume '((job manager)) :values (list (beint 9 9))]
Proposition (STRESS YES): Evidence was /1, 9/ : U   Now it is /6, 9/ : B
Proposition (HEART-RISK YES): Evidence was /1, 9/ : U   Now it is /6, 9/ : B
Proposition (JOB MANAGER): Evidence was /1, 9/ : U   Now it is /9, 9/ : B
```

If now our physician collects some subjective evidence there is a small chance that the patient is not stressed, he adds his observation obtaining that the belief state of (HEART-RISK YES) lowers to *Rather Believed than disbelieved*.

```
? [ubrs :assume '((stress yes)):values (list (beint 1 6))]
Proposition (STRESS YES): Evidence was /6, 9/ : B   Now it is /6, 6/ : RB
Proposition (HEART-RISK YES): Evidence was /6, 9/ : B   Now it is /8, 6/ : RB
```

We may now ask to UBRS an explanation of the current belief interval associated to (HEART-RISK YES). The system supplies the list of all the possible inferences influencing this value, with their status.

```
? [ubrs :explain '(heart-risk yes)]
Proposition (HEART-RISK YES) is RB because:
   rule R7 says ('NOT (HEART-RISK YES)) is U because:  (TEMPERAMENT SURE) is D.
   rule R5 says (HEART-RISK YES) is U because:  (TEMPERAMENT VEHEMENT) is C.
   rule R2 says (HEART-RISK YES) is RB because:  (STRESS YES) is RB.
   rule R1 says (HEART-RISK YES) is U because:  (SMOKES-A-LOT YES) is U.
```

6. Discussion and future developments

We propose an approach to Belief Revision based on uncertainty propagation. We choose to represent uncertainty using a theory based on belief intervals defined in terms of subjective linguistic estimates, since this approach seems the most promising to capture subjective estimates, one of the most important sources of uncertainty. We provide also an extension to cope with cyclic dependencies.

Our work can be compared with causal networks [Lauritzen and Spiegelhaler, 1988] Bayes Belief networks [Pearl, 1986] and in general with network approaches to uncertainty management. Being based on subjective linguistic estimates, we are free both from problems concerning numerical treatment of uncertainty and from Bayes theory requirements. With respect to HUGIN [Andersen, Olesen, Jensen and Jensen, 1989], one of the most assessed causal probabilistic network systems, we can cope with cyclic dependecies, which are not accepted there.

Our system has been designed as an Uncertainty Manager, i.e. a system maintaining the fact base of a problem solver according to the triggered inferences and a theory of uncertainty. However its use as causal network (with modalities similar to those of HUGIN) is possible, since the problem solver role may be played by the expert/user. We are currently designing an interface suitable to test this possibility.

The proposed model is very general: fuzzy numbers can be successfully used to model knowledge features coming from people. However, since we realized UBRS using the object-oriented paradigm, different types of measures for different knowledge features can be easily defined and integrated with the current one. The first successor of UBRS, *CUMa*

(*C*omponents of *U*ncertainty *Ma*nager) [Bonarini, In press] propagates probabilities (represented by numbers), judgements on the knowledge sources (represented by linguistic variables), and subjective judgements on knowledge elements (represented by belief intervals), keeping them distinct, and giving the possibility to summarize the different measures of the uncertainty associated to a node with a single belief interval. It is used to obtain different reactions of the system to the different types of uncertainty may affect a knowledge element.

Although our proposal is focused on uncertainty propagation, the same approach may be used to model the propagation of measures of different knowledge features. Particularly, it is possible to have different conceptual networks (each one modeling a specific feature) coexist on the same set of propositions. Therefore, a proposition *p* can be qualified by its *belief interval*, but also by its *necessity*, by the *cost* needed to assess it, by its *relevance* for the task faced by the problem solver, and so on. Now, we are identifying the most important features, studying the interactions among them and extending the implemented system to cover the functionalities of a more general Quality Manager.

References

[1] Andersen S.K., Olesen K.G., Jensen F.V., Jensen F (1989) HUGIN - a shell for building bayesian belief universes for expert systems. *Proc. 11th IJCAI*, Morgan Kaufman, Los Altos, CA.

[2] Bonarini A., Cappelletti E., Corrao A. (1990) Belief Revision and Uncertainty: a proposal accepting cyclic dependencies. *Report n. 90-067,* Dipartimento di Elettronica, Politecnico di Milano, Milano, Italy

[3] Bonarini A., (In press), Uncertainty components: issues and a proposal for their integrated management in expert systems, *Proceedings The World Congress on Expert Systems*, Pergamon Press, New York.

[3] Bonissone P.P. (1987) Reasoning. Plausible. In S.C. Shapiro (ed.) *Encyclopedia of Artificial Intelligence*, John Wiley & Sons, London.

[4] Bonissone P.P., Decker K.S. (1986) Selecting uncertainty calculi and granularity: an experiment in trading-off precision and complexity. In Kanal L.N. and Lemmer J.F. (eds.) *Uncertainty in Artificial Intelligence*, 217-247, Elsevier Science Publishers B.V., Amsterdam.

[5] Buxton R. (1989) Modelling uncertainty in expert systems. *International Journal of man-machine studies*, 31, 415-476.

[6] Clark D.A. (1990) Numerical and symbolic approaches to uncertainty management in AI. *Artificial Intelligence Review*, 4, 109-146.

[7] Driankov D. (1986) Uncertainty calculus with verbally defined belief-intervals. *Report LITH-ID A-R-86-14*, Department of Computer and Information Science, Linköping University, Sweden.

[8] Driankov D. (1988) Towards a many-valued logic of quantified belief. PhD Thesis No. 192, Department of Computer and Information Science, Linköping University, Sweden.

[9] Dubois D., Prade H. (1982) A class of fuzzy measures based on triangular norms. *International Journal of General Systems*, 8, 1.

[10] A. Goldberg, D. Robson (1983) *Smalltalk-80: the language and its implementation*. Reading, Mass: Addison-Wesley.

[11] Lauritzen S.L., Spiegelhaler D.J. (1988) Local computation with probabilities on graphical structures and their application to expert systems. *J. Royal Statistical Society B*, 50(2), 157-224.

[12] Pearl J. (1986) Fusion, propagation, and structuring in belief networks. *Artificial Intelligence*, 29, 241-288.

[13] Shafer G. (1990) Perspectives on the theory and practice of belief functions. *Int. J. of Approximate Reasoning*, 4, 323-362.

[15] Zadeh L.A. (1983) Commonsense knowledge representation based on fuzzy logic. *IEEE Computer*, 16, 61-65.

Abductive Reasoning in a Multi-theory Framework

Antonio Brogi[1], Evelina Lamma[2], Paolo Mancarella[1], Paola Mello[2]

[1]Dipartimento di Informatica, Università di Pisa
Corso Italia 40, 56125 Pisa, Italy
brogi,paolo@dipisa.di.unipi.it

[2]DEIS, Università di Bologna
Viale Risorgimento 2, 40136 Bologna, Italy
evelina,paola@deis33.cineca.it

Abstract

A multi-theory framework is presented where both abduction and dynamic theory composition are modelled in a logic programming setting. In this framework the evolution of knowledge can be modelled by means of theory composition, while a form of hypothetical reasoning is supported by abduction. The semantics is expressed in terms of the standard semantics of logic programming (Herbrand models), by defining a compositional model-theory. A proof-theory is given in terms of inference rules, and soundness and completeness results are stated.

1 Introduction

One important issue in knowledge representation systems is the handling of some form of incomplete knowledge. In fact, it is often the case that knowledge is not complete both because it can be dynamically assimilated and because there is missing information about some aspects of the system being modelled. In a general setting, these issues raise other important issues such as non-monotonicity and truth maintenance which will not be addressed in this paper. Instead, we will study how to provide mechanisms for dealing with the dynamic assimilation of new knowledge along with some form of hypothetical reasoning in logic programming.

It has been argued in [1,9,10] that the addition of new knowledge can be modelled by providing suitable operators that combine knowledge bases, viewed as logic theories.

Work partially supported by CNR, Progetto Finalizzato "Sistemi Informatici e Calcolo Parallelo" under grants n. 890004269 and n. 8900121

This allows one to consider a knowledge base as a dynamic entity that evolves as further information is provided in the form of new logic theories, which are dynamically combined with the existing ones. On the other hand, some form of hypothetical reasoning seems to be needed in order to cope with incomplete knowledge. Abductive reasoning is an appropriate form of hypothetical reasoning, which captures also other important issues such as reasoning with defaults and beliefs (see for instance [5,8,13]). Incomplete knowledge is handled by designating some pieces of information as abducibles, that is possible hypotheses which can be assumed, provided that they are consistent with the current knowledge base.

The addition of new knowledge can either confirm (i.e. prove definitely true) some of the hypotheses or discard them if they become inconsistent with the new acquired information.

Thus, both abduction and theory composition seem to be appropriate to deal with the dynamic evolution of knowledge. In the literature there exist either proposals which define different policies for theory composition dealing only with deduction [2,9,10,11], or proposals which model different forms of abduction in a single theory framework [4,3,6,7].

The main aim of this paper is to define a general framework where both abduction and dynamic theory composition can be modelled, and to provide it with a single, unified semantics. Abduction, in this setting, can be regarded as a way of finding new hypotheses (explanations) or modifying the previous ones for a given observation when further knowledge is assimilated.

Some remarks are worth making here. First, following the approach of [6,7] we will designate predicate names as abducibles, with the intended meaning that an atom A is abducible if its predicate name is so. The idea is to distinguish two classes of predicates in each theory T, corresponding to hypotheses which can be confirmed by the help of other theories (abducibles) and standard predicates which, when needed, have to be proved only in T (non-abducibles). In other words, abducible predicates are *open* predicates which obey a sort of open world assumption whereas non-abducibles are *closed* predicates on which a closed world assumption [14] is enforced.

In order to model declaratively abductive reasoning, the notion of *admissible* Herbrand model is introduced. Roughly speaking, an Herbrand model M of a theory T is also admissible if there exists a set of hypotheses H (i.e. abducible atoms) such that all the atoms in M can be deduced from H using the clauses of T. In other words, H is a set of hypotheses that, if true, would entail, together with the rules in T, all the atoms in M. The least Herbrand model of a theory T is of course admissible, and it corresponds to the empty set of hypotheses.

In our framework, the cooperation of logic theories is modelled by a suitable *compose* operator defined in [1]. However, the compositional model-theoretic semantics defined in [1] is adapted to cope with abduction, by suitably modifying the notion of admissible hypotheses.

Finally, an operational semantics is given which extends the one defined for the case of a single theory by inheriting the idea of performing abduction through deduction as proposed by several authors (see for instance [6,13] and references therein). Soundness and completeness results are stated with respect to the admissible Herbrand model semantics.

A plan of the paper follows. In section 2, abduction is modelled in a single theory setting both declaratively and operationally. In section 3, the previous modelisation is extended to the case of multiple-theories. Finally, soundness and completeness results are stated.

2 Abduction in a Single Theory

Abduction has been recognized as a powerful mechanism for hypothetical reasoning in the presence of incomplete knowledge [3,5,4,6,7].

Though abduction has been the focus of intensive research, many questions concerning both declarative and operational semantics of abduction still arise. Given a theory T and a formula G, the goal of abduction is to find a set of atoms Δ which together with T allows to prove G, that is $T \cup \Delta \models G$. Operationally, G is derivable in T with "conditional answer" Δ.

As stated in the introduction, we designate some predicate names as abducibles, i.e. *open* predicates which obey a sort of open world assumption as opposed to non-abducibles ones, i.e. *closed* predicates on which a closed world assumption [14] is enforced.

As far as one standard logic theory is concerned, it is well known that its least Herbrand model completely characterizes it [15]. When dealing with abduction, such a modelisation does not suffice any more, since we can have multiple, alternative explanations (abduced atoms) associated with a given goal. To model abductive reasoning, we associate to a theory T a set of its Herbrand models, called *admissible* Herbrand models.

2.1 Model-Theory: Admissible Herbrand Models

In this subsection, abductive reasoning within a single logic theory is declaratively modelled by means of *admissible* Herbrand models, firstly introduced in [1] to deal with theory composition, which will be shown in section 3 to provide a unified semantics for abductive reasoning in a multi-theory framework.

In the following, we will assume that for each theory T a set of predicate names, $ABD(T)$, is given to designate abducible predicates.

Let us now introduce the definition of admissible Herbrand models for a single theory. Roughly speaking, an Herbrand model M of a theory T is also admissible if there exists a set H of abducible atoms (also called hypotheses or explanations) built from predicate symbols in $ABD(T)$ such that all the atoms in M can be deduced from H using the clauses of T. In the following, admissible models will be denoted by M^H to outline the role of the atoms in H as hypotheses.

Given a theory T, a ground observation O is true under the hypotheses (explanations) H ($T \models_H O$) if O belongs to the admissible Herbrand model M^H of T. The formal definition of admissible hypotheses for a program follows.

Definition 2.1 *(Admissible Hypotheses)*
Let T be a theory. A subset H of the Herbrand base of T is an admissible set of hypotheses *for P if and only if for all $p(t) \in H$:*

1. *$p \in ABD(T)$*

2. *there exists a ground instance $h \leftarrow B$ of a clause in T such that $p(t) \in B$*

□

The definition of Admissible Herbrand Models is induced by the former definition of admissible hypotheses.

Definition 2.2 *(Admissible Herbrand Model)*
Let T be a program, M be an Herbrand model of T, and H be an admissible set of hypotheses for T. M is an admissible Herbrand model *of T under the hypotheses H if and only if M is the minimal Herbrand model of $T \cup H$.* □

In practice, we consider *admissible* those Herbrand models which correspond to the assumption of a set of abducible atoms, where each atom must unify with at least one atom in some clause body of the theory.

Notice also that if no abducible predicates are associated with a theory T (i.e. $ABD(T) = \{\}$) the theory T is a *closed* theory in the sense that it is assumed to have a complete knowledge on some domain. This implies that a closed theory will consider only its internal information independently of subsequent addition of knowledge. In terms of the model-theory, a closed theory is described only by its least Herbrand model, i.e. only by the admissible Herbrand model corresponding to the empty set of hypotheses.

Example 2.3 *Let us consider the following theory $t1$, inspired by [12]:*
$grass\_is\_wet \quad \leftarrow \quad rained\_last\_night$
$grass\_is\_wet \quad \leftarrow \quad sprinkler\_was\_on$
$shoes\_are\_wet \leftarrow \quad grass\_is\_wet$
and $ABD(t1) = \{ rained\_last\_night, sprinkler\_was\_on \}$. Its admissible Herbrand models are: $\{\}^{\{\}}$,
$\{shoes\_are\_wet, grass\_is\_wet, rained\_last\_night\}^{\{rained\_last\_night\}}$,
$\{shoes\_are\_wet, grass\_is\_wet, sprinkler\_was\_on\}^{\{sprinkler\_was\_on\}}$,
$\{shoes\_are\_wet, grass\_is\_wet,$
$rained\_last\_night, sprinkler\_was\_on\}^{\{rained\_last\_night, sprinkler\_was\_on\}}$
Notice that no model annotated with $grass\_is\_wet$ exists, since this is not an abducible predicate. In other words, we assume to have in $t1$ a complete knowledge on $grass\_is\_wet$.

□

2.2 Proof-Theory

In this section, a set of inference rules is given to characterize the operational behaviour of abductive reasoning in the case of a single theory. In section 3.2, we will show how to extend it to deal with the more general case of abductive reasoning in a multi-theory framework.

An atomic formula $A\vartheta$ is derivable in the theory T (with substitution ϑ under the hypotheses H) if there exists a proof for $T \vdash_{\vartheta,H} A$. A proof for $T \vdash_{\vartheta,H} A$ is a tree such that:

- The root node is labelled by $T \vdash_{\vartheta,H} A$

- The internal nodes are derived by using the inference rules of definition 2.4

- All thw leaves are labelled by the empty formula ($true$)

Definition 2.4 *(Inference Rules)*
Let T a theory, A, A' atoms, G a (conjunctive) formula, ϑ, γ substitutions, ϵ the empty substitution and Abd, Abd' sets of abducibles.

$$(1) \quad \frac{}{T \vdash_{\epsilon,\{\}} \ true}$$

$$(2) \quad \frac{T \vdash_{\vartheta,Abd} A \wedge T \vdash_{\gamma,Abd'} (G)\vartheta}{T \vdash_{\vartheta\gamma,(Abd)\gamma \cup Abd'} (A,G)}$$

$$(3) \quad \frac{A' \leftarrow G \in T \wedge \vartheta = mgu(A,A') \wedge \ T \vdash_{\gamma,Abd} (G)\vartheta}{T \vdash_{\vartheta\gamma,Abd} A}$$

$$(4) \quad \frac{A = p(t) \wedge \ p \in ABD(T)}{T \vdash_{\epsilon,\{A\}} A}$$

Notice that in rule (2), we merge the sets of hypotheses Abd and Abd', obtained when deriving A and G separately, and suitably applying the substitution for G (i.e. γ) to each element of Abd. Rule (4) allows us to abduce atoms.

Example 2.5 *Let us consider the theory t1 of example 2.3 and the formula shoes_are_wet. We have the two following successful top-down derivations (substitutions are omitted since the theory is propositional):*

$t1 \ \vdash_{Abd} \ shoes\_are\_wet$
$t1 \ \vdash_{Abd} \ grass\_is\_wet$
$t1 \ \vdash_{Abd} \ rained\_last\_night$
success with $Abd = \{rained\_last\_night\}$

$t1 \ \vdash_{Abd} \ shoes\_are\_wet$
$t1 \ \vdash_{Abd} \ grass\_is\_wet$
$t1 \ \vdash_{Abd} \ sprinkler\_was\_on$
success with $Abd = \{sprinkler\_was\_on\}$ □

It is possible to prove that soundness and completeness results hold for this restricted case, that is abductive reasoning in a single theory. We omit here details, since in section 3.3 we will present these results for the more general case of a multi-theory setting. It is worth noting that the two derivations of example 2.5 have a direct correspondence with two admissible Herbrand models of theory $t1$ (see example 2.3). We do not have, instead, any derivation under the set of hypotheses $\{rained\_last\_night, sprinkler\_was\_on\}$. This leads to a weak equivalence between the declarative and the operational semantics which is reflected into the completeness proposition of section 3.3.

It is also worth noting that for abducible atoms we can non-deterministically apply both rule (3) and rule (4). This is due to the fact that in our framework, differently from [6,7], we can have some definitions also for abducible predicates. This kind of more general abductive reasoning is needed in our case since we assume that knowledge undergoes changes by the addition of new facts and rules. It can happen that some definition for an abducible atom is dynamically added, making the corresponding hypothesis definitely true.

3 Extending Abduction to a Multi-Theory Framework

In our framework, new knowledge can be dynamically assimilated by composing new theories with the existing ones, thus increasing the degree of completeness of the description, since something which does not hold in one theory can hold in another one, and the former can exploit this to derive new hypotheses or confirm the previous ones.

In this section, we model this incremental behaviour, both from the declarative and the operational point of view. In our framework, the incremental addition of new knowledge is expressed by a *compose* operator (denoted by $*$) which is similar to the union operator defined in [11,2,1] with the difference that we take into account abduction. Since abducible predicates are *open* predicates which obey a sort of open world assumption, whereas non-abducibles are *closed* predicates, only the former will be taken into account during theory composition.

Let us now give a formal definition of the systems of theories (called *extension formulae*) which are dealt with.

Definition 3.1 *(Extension Formula)*
An extension formula *is defined as follows:*

$$E ::= \perp \mid T \mid E * E$$

where $\perp$ represents the empty extension and T a theory name. □

3.1 Extending the Model Theory

Several approaches have been proposed [11,2,1] in order to define compositional declarative semantics for logic programs. In this section, we present a compositional model-theoretic semantics for modeling abductive reasoning in a multi-theory framework. While the concept of logical consequences (i.e. minimal model) is not compositional (i.e. given two logic theories, the logical consequences that can be drawn from the combination of the two collection of clauses are not derivable straightforwardly from the logical consequences of the single theories), the concept of admissible Herbrand model set as the denotation of a theory is compositional. The denotation of theory combination is obtained directly in terms of the denotation of the involved theories.

As pointed out in section 2, each theory is denoted by a set of admissible Herbrand models. Now we can compose theories, and build up incrementally the admissible Herbrand model set resulting from this composition. The syntactic operator $(*)$ for theory composition is mapped onto a suitable semantic operator $(\otimes)$ working on the admissible Herbrand models of the involved theories. The semantic operator produces a new set of admissible Herbrand models that are all monotonic extensions of those of the theories involved.

Definition 3.2 *(Admissible Herbrand Models of Compose)*
Let $E1$ and $E2$ be two extension formulae. The set of admissible Herbrand models of $E1 * E2$ is:
$$AHM(E1 * E2) = AHM(E1) \otimes AHM(E2)$$
□

The semantic operator $\otimes$ is defined as follows.

Definition 3.3 *(Composition of Admissible Herbrand Models)*
Given two sets of admissible Herbrand models, $S1$ and $S2$, the composition $S1 \otimes S2$ is defined as follows:
$$S1 \otimes S2 = \{M^H \mid M = lfp\ \varphi_S \wedge H \subseteq K\}$$
where:

- $S = S1 \cup S2 \cup \{H^{\{\}}\}$
- $K = \cup\{H' \mid M'^{H'} \in S1 \cup S2\}$
- φ_S *is a monotonic and continuous function (see [1]) working on sets of standard Herbrand interpretations which is defined as follows:*
  $$\varphi_S(I) = \cup\ \{M \mid \exists H'\ s.t.\ M^{H'} \in S\ and\ H' \subseteq I\}$$

□

To help intuition, in the case of the composition of two theories t_1 and t_2, we build each resulting admissible Herbrand model M^H by considering $AHM(t_1)$, $AHM(t_2)$ and the admissible Herbrand model corresponding to the hypotheses H, that is $H^{\{\}}$. The function φ_S builds M^H starting from the empty set, and adding to this set, at each step, each admissible Herbrand model whose hypotheses are subsumed.

Example 3.4 *Let us consider the theory t1 of example 2.3 and the new theory t2 containing the only clause rained_last_night ← which has only one admissible Herbrand model {rained_last_night}$^{\{\}}$. The admissible models of t1 * t2 are:*
$$AHM(t1) \otimes AHM(t2) =$$
{ $\{shoes\_are\_wet, grass\_is\_wet, rained\_last\_night\}^{\{\}},$
$\{shoes\_are\_wet, grass\_is\_wet, rained\_last\_night\}^{\{rained\_last\_night\}},$
$\{shoes\_are\_wet, grass\_is\_wet, sprinkler\_was\_on, rained\_last\_night\}^{\{sprinkler\_was\_on\}},$
$\{shoes\_are\_wet, grass\_is\_wet, rained\_last\_night,$
$sprinkler\_was\_on\}^{\{rained\_last\_night, sprinkler\_was\_on\}}$ }.

□

3.2 Extending the Proof-Theory

In this section, we extend the proof procedure given in section 2.2 to take into account both abduction and the dynamic adding of new knowledge in terms of theory composition. So, we consider an extension formula E instead of a single theory T.

To simplify the formal description of the operational behaviour, we exploit the properties of commutativity, associativity and identity of the $*$ operator. Now, an atomic formula $A\vartheta$ is derivable in the extension formula E (with substitution ϑ under the hypotheses H) if there exists a proof for $E \vdash_{\vartheta,H} A$ (the concepts of proof and proof trees are straightforward extensions of the ones presented for the case of single theories). In the following, with abuse of notation, we will write $E \vdash_{\vartheta,H} G$ to mean that G is derivable in E with substitution ϑ under the hypotheses H.

Definition 3.5 *(Inference Rules)*
Let E be an extension formula, T a theory name, G a (conjunctive) formula, ϑ, γ substitutions, Abd, Abd' sets of abducibles. The following inference rules hold:

$$(5) \quad \frac{T \vdash_{\vartheta,Abd} G \; ; \; T * E \vdash_{\gamma,Abd'} Abd}{T * E \vdash_{\vartheta\gamma,Abd'} G}$$

$$(6) \frac{T \vdash_{\vartheta,Abd} G}{T * E \vdash_{\vartheta,Abd} G}$$

□

Notice that these rules exploit the fact that $*$ is commutative and associative. Rule (5) deals with theory composition while rule (6) deals with abduction in a multi-theory setting.

Example 3.6 *Let us consider the theory t1 and theory t2 of example 3.4. In the extension t1 * t2, for the formula shoes_are_wet we get, among others, the following successful top-down derivation:*

$t1 * t2 \vdash_{Abd'} shoes\_are\_wet \quad by \ rule \ (5)$

$t1 \vdash_{Abd} shoes\_are\_wet \quad by \ rule \ (3)$

$t1 \vdash_{Abd} grass\_is\_wet \quad by \ rule \ (3)$

$t1 \vdash_{Abd} rained\_last\_night \quad by \ rule \ (4)$

$Abd = \{rained\_last\_night\}$

$t1 * t2 \vdash_{Abd'} rained\_last\_night \quad by \ rule \ (5)$

$t2 \vdash_{Abd'} rained\_last\_night \quad by \ rule \ (3)$

$t2 \vdash_{Abd'} true \quad by \ rule \ (1)$

$success \ with \ Abd' = \{\ \}$

Notice the correspondence between the successful top-down derivation and the first admissible Herbrand model of $t1 * t2$ (see example 3.4). □

3.3 Soundness and Completeness

In this section, we state the equivalence between the declarative and the operational semantics presented above.

The soundness and completeness results are straightforward consequences of the corresponding results for SLD resolution, provided that extension formulae are transformed into standard HCL theories. To this purpose, a suitable transformation τ which transforms extensions formulae into "equivalent" HCL theories has to be introduced. For the lack of space proofs for τ-equivalence and soundness and completeness are omitted.

In the following B_E denotes the Herbrand base built from predicate symbols occurring in the extension formula E. Given an extension formula E, a set of abducibles H and a ground atomic formula $g \in B_E$, we will write $E \models_H g$ to denote that there exists $M^H \in AHM(E)$ such that $g \in M$.

Proposition 3.7 *(Soundness)*
Given an extension formula E and an atomic formula g, such that $E \vdash_{\vartheta,H} g$ then $\forall \gamma$ such that $(g)\vartheta\gamma$ and $(H)\vartheta\gamma$ are ground, we have: $E \models_{(H)\vartheta\gamma} (g)\vartheta\gamma$. □

Proposition 3.8 *(Completeness)*
Let E be an extension formula, g a ground atomic formula and $H \subseteq B_E$ a set of ground abducibles. We have:
$$E \models_H g \implies \exists \gamma, \vartheta, H' : (H')\gamma \subseteq H \ and \ E \vdash_{\vartheta,H'} g$$
□

References

[1] A. Brogi, E. Lamma, and P. Mello. Open Logic Theories. In L.-H. Eriksson, P. Krueger, and P. Schroeder-Heister, editors, *Proceedings of Second Workshop on Extensions of Logic Programming, Lectures Notes in Artificial Intelligence*. Springer-Verlag, Kista, January 1991. Forthcoming.

[2] A. Brogi, P. Mancarella, D. Pedreschi, and F. Turini. Composition Operators for Logic Theories. In J.W. Lloyd, editor, *Computational Logic, Symposium Proceedings*, pages 117–134. Springer-Verlag, Brussels, November 1990.

[3] L. Console, D. Theseider Duprè and P. Torasso. Abductive Reasoning Through Direct Deduction from Completed Domains Models. In *Methodologies for Intelligent Systems*, N. 4, page 175, North Holland,1989.

[4] W. Chen and D.H. Warren. Abductive Logic Programming. TR, Dept. of Computer Science, State University of New York, October 1989.

[5] P.T. Cox and T. Pietrzykowski. Causes for events: Their computation and applications. In *Proceedings CADE-86*, page 608, 1986.

[6] K. Eshgi and R.A. Kowalski. Abduction compared with negation by failure. In G. Levi and M. Martelli, editors, *Proc. Sixth International Conference on Logic Programming*, page 234. The MIT Press, 1989.

[7] A.C. Kakas and P. Mancarella. Generalized stable models: a semantics for abduction. In *Proceedings of 9th European Conference on Artificial Intelligence*. Pitman Publishing, 1990.

[8] R.A. Kowalski. Problems and promises of computational logic. In *Proceedings of Symposium on Computational Logic*. Springer-Verlag, November 1990.

[9] D. Miller. A logical analysis of modules in logic programming. *Journal of Logic Programming*, 6:79–108, 1989.

[10] L. Monteiro and A. Porto. Contextual logic programming. In G. Levi and M. Martelli, editors, *Proc. Sixth International Conference on Logic Programming*, pages 284–302. The MIT Press, 1989.

[11] R. O'Keefe. Towards an algebra for constructing logic programs. In *Proceedings of IEEE Symposium on Logic Programming*, pages 152–160, 19856.

[12] J. Pearl. Embracing causality in formal reasoning. *Proc. National Conference on Artificial Intelligence*, Seattle, WA, pages 369-373, 1987.

[13] D.L. Poole. A logical framework for default reasoning. *Artificial Intelligence*, 36:27, 1988.

[14] R. Reiter. On closed world data bases. In H. Gallaire and J.Minker, editors, *Logic and Data Bases*. Plenum, 1978.

[15] M.H. van Emden and R.A. Kowalski. The semantics of predicate logic as a programming language. *Journal of the ACM*, 23(4):733–742, 1976.

The Abstract Interpretation of Hybrid Rule/Frame-based Systems.

Rick Evertsz
Scientia Ltd.,
St John's Innovation Centre,
Cowley Road,
Cambridge, CB4 4WS,
United Kingdom.

Enrico Motta
Human Cognition Research Laboratory,
Walton Hall,
The Open University,
Milton Keynes, MK7 6AA
United Kingdom
email: e_motta@vax.acs.open.ac.uk

Abstract

In this paper, we describe an algorithm for the abstract interpretation of hybrid knowledge bases which comprise both frame and rule-based representations. The program, HybAbs, can automatically analyse hybrid knowledge bases for completeness and correctness, and provides a significant improvement over earlier approaches which can only cope with homogeneous representations. Furthermore, because HybAbs considers the procedural semantics of the hybrid system, it can identify classes of incomplete and incorrect knowledge bases which would elude purely declarative approaches.

1. INTRODUCTION

With the increasing use of knowledge-based systems (KBSs) in safety-critical application areas, it has become very important to develop automatic methods for verifying their correctness and completeness. In particular, a number of techniques have been proposed for the automated analysis of rule-based systems (Suwa et al., 1982; Nguyen et al., 1985; Beauvieux, 1990; Evertsz, 1991), and for the verification and validation of frame-based representations (O'Leary, 1990). However, these techniques exhibit a limited range of applicability, as they cannot cope with the kind of hybrid KBSs which are nowadays developed to tackle real-world problems. In fact, both the current practice of industrial KBS, and the consensus among researchers (Frisch & Cohn, 1991) suggest that hybrid architectures, embedding a number of specialized representations/reasoners, are required to enable knowledge engineers to build efficient and powerful KBs (Frisch & Cohn, 1991).

In particular, frame and rule based programming are now established as the leading AI programming paradigms, as shown by the fact that virtually every present-day commercial AI shell or toolkit combines some sort of frame-based representation with a rule-based inference engine. In fact, while frames "provide a convenient way to organize data objects in a class taxonomy and to inherit their properties from more general classes" (Yen et al., 1988), rules "are appropriate for representing logical implications, or for associating actions with conditions under which the action should be taken" (Yen et al., 1988). Therefore, "because their strengths and weaknesses are complementary to each other, a system that integrates the two will benefit from the advantages of both techniques" (Yen et al., 1988).

Abstract interpretation is a technique commonly used to prove properties about programs. The idea is to gather information about a program by running it on *abstract* rather than concrete inputs. This technique has been used to many ends, including the optimization of Prolog compilers (Mellish, 1986), and the generation of inputs which discriminate between pairs of student models (Evertsz, 1989; 1990). More recently, one of us has shown that abstract interpretation compares favourably with alternative approaches in the context of verifying production systems (Evertsz, 1991).

The work presented here is a natural extension of this previous effort, and describes an algorithm for the abstract interpretation of a hybrid architecture, which comprises both frame and rule representations. This technique enables us to automatically analyse the correctness and completeness of a hybrid knowledge base, thus improving over other existing approaches, which only cope with homogeneous representations.

The paper is organized as follows. Section 2 describes a hybrid architecture, which comprises both a frame and a rule system. In section 3 we describe the algorithm for the abstract interpretation of this hybrid architecture, while in section 4 we outline how our algorithm can provide a solution to the problem of verifying and validating hybrid KBSs. Finally, in section 5 we indicate future areas of research.

2. A HYBRID KBS ARCHITECTURE

2.1 PS, a rule-based language

Our production system language (PS) has much in common with the OPS family of interpreters (Forgy and McDermott, 1977). A PS knowledge base consists of a set of rules and a working memory (WM). The left-hand-side (LHS) and right-hand-side (RHS) of a rule are made up of one or more patterns conjoined by ampersands ('&'). A pattern is a list such as (Pred Arg1......Argn), with n≥0. Variables are prefixed with a question mark. WM is a set of ground patterns (wm-patterns).

On each cycle of the interpreter, PS repeatedly tries to match the LHS of its rules against the contents of WM, to produce rule instantiations. Then, conflict resolution strategies are sequentially applied to the current set of instantiations, to choose one to fire. The conflict resolution strategies used in PS are: 'refractoriness', which prevents the same instantiation from firing twice; 'recency', which selects the instantiations which match the most recently asserted wm-patterns; and 'specificity', which selects the most specific instantiation. These strategies are applied one after the other in the above order. If, after applying these three strategies, more than one instantiation remains, then the ruleset is non-deterministic, and the interpreter generates an error. Although in this paper we show examples based on PS, our approach can be applied to any forward-chaining interpreter which relies on *deterministic* conflict resolution for flow of control.

2.2 FS, a frame-based language

The frame language used in this paper, FS, is a simplified version of Flik (Motta, 1990), a frame-based reasoning tool that is part of the Keats knowledge-engineering workbench (Motta et al., 1990; Eisenstadt et al., 1990). Like Flik, it supports multiple-inheritance hierarchies with exceptions, and has a sound mechanism for non-monotonically invalidating inherited values, which is based on the notion of *blocks* (cf. Nado & Fikes, 1987). Because of space limitations we shall only present a brief and informal description of FS.

The FS user models his or her world by means of a number of domain assertions. A domain assertion in FS is defined as a 6-tuple <Fr, S, Fi, M, T, K>, where Fr and Fi are entities in the domain, S denotes a binary relation. M, T, and K are flags describing the modality (default or definitional), the type (prototype or own), and the kind (slot or block) of the assertion.

For instance, the assertion <elephant, colour, grey, default, prototype, slot> specifies that the filler of slot 'colour' of frame 'elephant' is 'grey'. The meaning of the three classes of flag will be made clear in the course of the discussion.

Two important slots are 'member_of' and 'subclass_of', which are used to structure frames into an *inheritance network*. Intuitively, member_of links relate an individual to the class to which it belongs, while subclass_of links connect a more specific class to a more general one. An inheritance network specifies a number of *inheritance paths*, along which assertions with type 'prototype' are inherited. If an assertion has type 'own', then it is inherited only by the frame with which it is associated. Hence, a knowledge base in FS consists of a number of assertions and a number of *inherited properties* (simply, properties) deduced through inheritance. When there is an inheritance path between two frames, X and Y, we say that the 'isa' relation holds between them. When X isa Y, we say that X is a *descendant* of Y and Y is an *ancestor* of X.

The fact that a property is inherited down an inheritance path does not imply that the property necessarily holds for the frame which has inherited it. In fact, properties with kind 'slot', and modality 'default' can be invalidated by an inherited block whose specification matches the property. A block is a property with kind 'block'. Note that neither blocks nor definitional properties can be *blocked* (made invalid by a block). From now on, we'll use the words 'assertion' and 'property' to refer to assertions and properties with kind 'slot'.

As an example, we give a FS representation of a few facts about elephants, which state (among other things) that elephants are grey by default, while royal elephants are always white. We have an elephant called Clyde, which is both an african and a royal elephant. Both these classes are subclasses of class 'elephant'.

> <royal-elephant, subclass_of, elephant, definitional, own, slot>
> <african-elephant, subclass_of, elephant, definitional, own, slot>
> <clyde, member_of, royal-elephant, definitional, own, slot>
> <clyde, member_of, african-elephant, definitional, own, slot>
> <elephant, colour, grey, default, prototype, slot>
> <royal-elephant, colour, grey, definitional, prototype, block>
> <royal-elephant, colour, white, definitional, prototype, slot>.
> *Figure 1 – Sample FS knowledge base*

If we query this FS knowledge base, asking for the colour of clyde, the answer will be 'white'. In fact, clyde can inherit both white from royal-elephant, and grey from elephant. However, this second property is blocked by the block that clyde inherits from royal-elephant. Therefore only white is a valid value for slot colour of clyde.

In the next section we'll sketch an integrated architecture, where the inference engines of both FS and PS are amalgamated together.

2.3 Integration of frame and rule-based inferences

2.3.1 Integrating FS and PS by means of a generalized working memory

A forward-chaining rule interpreter such as PS performs a match-execute cycle. The integration of PS with FS can be achieved by generalizing both the 'match' and the 'execute' phases, to also deal with properties in FS. This means that when PS attempts to instantiate a rule, in the 'match' phase, it should also check whether the LHS of the rule being tried matches properties in FS. Analogously, during the 'execution' phase firing a rule could also introduce and retract FS assertions. This style of integration can be achieved through the notion of a generalized WM, which includes, together with ordinary wm-patterns, the *image* of the current valid properties in FS (*frame memory*).

In this way, the behaviour of the rule interpreter stays unchanged, as it remains concerned only with fetching, asserting, and retracting wm-patterns. However, a number of these wm-patterns will be 'special', as they will correspond to properties in the frame system. Hence, when asserting or retracting one of these 'special' patterns, the combined frame/rule system will need to ensure that the corresponding assertions in FS are made or deleted, propagation through inheritance is performed, and the WM image of the frame memory is kept consistent with the knowledge base in FS. The wm-patterns associated with properties in FS are called *frame patterns*. As a property in FS can be inherited and then blocked, the combined PS/FS system will need to ensure that only frame patterns corresponding to valid properties are kept in WM. Not all wm-patterns have to be associated with properties in FS. Following the terminology used in KEE, we call this latter type of wm-pattern an *unstructured wm-pattern*.

2.3.2 A protocol for rule/frame communication

A knowledge base in FS consists of a number of properties with the format <Fr, S, Fi, M, T, K>. Given a property such as <Fr, S, Fi, M, T, K>, the associated frame pattern has the format (S Fr Fi). For instance, the assertion <clyde, member_of, elephant, definitional, own, slot> maps to the frame pattern (member_of clyde elephant). Note that the WM image of FS that we construct is incomplete. In particular, flags and blocks are hidden from the rule interpreter. This is for two reasons. First we want to keep a superficial similarity between structured and unstructured wm-patterns. Second, flags and blocks only affect the inheritance mechanism, which is managed by FS, and should therefore be transparent to PS. Moreover, we will not include prototypical properties in the WM image, unless they have been inherited through member_of links. This last constraint is imposed, because we normally want our rules to reason about specific individuals, rather than generic classes.

We will now look in more detail at what happens when a wm-pattern (structured or unstructured) is fetched, asserted, or retracted. For the sake of simplicity, we assume that these operations can only be carried out from PS. That is, FS can only be accessed through PS.

Asserting wm-patterns

Unstructured wm-patterns are simply added to WM. Structured wm-patterns are transformed into frame assertions, these are asserted into FS, the frame memory is updated, and then all the valid properties are (virtually) mapped into WM according to the convention given above.

Below we describe how frame assertions are generated from wm-patterns.

1) If the wm-pattern has the format (member_of Arg1 Arg2) or (subclass_of Arg1, Arg2), then the corresponding frame assertion <Arg1, member_of, Arg2, definitional, own, slot>, or <Arg1, subclass_of, Arg2, definitional, own, slot> is asserted in FS.

2) If the wm-pattern has the format (S Arg1 Arg2), with S ≠ member_of or subclass_of, then the corresponding frame assertion <Arg1, S, Arg2, default, prototype, slot>, is asserted in FS.

3) If the wm-pattern has the format (assertion Fr, S, Fi, M,T, K), then the corresponding frame assertion <Fr, S, Fi, M, T, K> is asserted in FS.

4) All the other formats map to unstructured wm-patterns.

Fetching wm-patterns

This is the same as in the case of PS alone.

Retracting wm-patterns

If the pattern we are retracting matches the templates in 1), 2), or 3) above, then the corresponding frame assertion template is deduced, and all the frame assertions (not properties!) which match it are retracted.

3. THE ABSTRACT INTERPRETATION OF HYBRID KNOWLEDGE BASES

3.1. The abstract interpretation of production systems

To date, all of the work on analysing rule-based systems assumes monotonicity. This means that new facts can never invalidate previously held ones, and no assertions can be retracted. Issues related to conflict resolution are ignored, despite the fact that many rule-based systems rely on conflict resolution for flow of control.

AbsPS is a program that takes a rule-base and an abstract specification of the set of permissible inputs to the rule-base, and generates the set of possible final states (WMs) which can be produced from the given input specification. The algorithm used by AbsPS is complete for rule-bases which do not contain cycles, and is described in detail in (Evertsz, 1990). Figure 2 shows an example of an input specification containing two facts and a constraint on the variable ?y (constraints are prefixed with "c:").

> Input Specification:　(colour ?x ?y), (colour background ?y)
> 　　　　　　　　　　WHERE (c:member ?y {red, green, blue}).
> *Figure 2 – An input specification*

AbsPS commences abstract interpretation by initialising WM with the two initial facts, and annotating the domain label for the variable ?y (i.e. ?y∈ {red,green,blue}). Because we are dealing with abstract data items, AbsPS substitutes unification for the one-way pattern matching of normal forward-chaining interpreters. The process of unification and rule firing generates further constraints on the variables in the input specification and augments WM with new abstract wm-patterns. Note that because AbsPS maintains an abstract description of WM it can also model the effects of retraction. In contrast to interpreters which handle concrete data, the abstract interpreter must explore *all* paths - only then can it yield a complete description of the input-output (I/O) mapping of the rule-base. The set of variable bindings and constraints is carried down the path from cycle to cycle and is *local* to that path. When a path is exhausted (i.e. no further rules can fire), the local environment represents an abstract description of the set of final databases which could be generated when following that path. Figure 3 shows an example of an output description obtained by applying a rule (R4) to the abstract specification in figure 2.

> (def-rule R4
> 　if (colour background ?y) & not (= ?y green)
> 　then (select green))

> Output Description:　(colour ?x ?y), (colour background ?y),
> 　　　　　　　　　　WHERE (c:member ?y {red, blue}).
> *Figure 3 – One possible final database.*

Note that the description of ?y's domain has been refined during the unification of R4. The process of domain refinement for the variables in the input specification enables AbsPS to prune many of the paths whose domain variables do not intersect with the environment collected down the current path. This reduction in the size of the search space is vital if one is to avoid the combinatorial explosion which can result when executing a rule-base on abstract rather than concrete data. Because the rule-base normally *relies* on conflict resolution for flow of control, this pruning is enhanced by incorporating the *procedural semantics* of conflict resolution into the abstract interpreter.

During conflict resolution, AbsPS cannot merely choose one instantiation for expansion and follow that path alone; this is because each instantiation is likely to cover *different subsets* of the abstract domain. Therefore, AbsPS must characterise these disjoint subsets and expand those instantiations with non-empty subsets (an empty subset is a domain which contains no elements and is therefore unsatisfiable).

These disjoint subsets are characterised through the generation of *exclusion clauses*. An exclusion clause is a term which describes the conditions under which those instantiations which appear to lose out during conflict resolution would actually win. For example, if an instantiation of R_i is selected after conflict resolution, this means that it will win for all concrete cases which allow it to be instantiated. However, there may be other data sets which, whilst enabling the losing instantiations to remain instantiated, prevents R_i from being instantiated. This can only happen if one of the constraints generated during the process of unifying R_i with WM is violated. For example, if the constraints on R_i are: $[C_1 \wedge ... \wedge C_n]$, then the exclusion clause which characterises the conditions under which it could not be instantiated would be: $[\neg C_1 \vee ... \vee \neg C_n]$. If we add this clause to the local environments of the losing instantiations then we will get a description of the conditions under which they, and not R_i, are eligible for firing. Some of these instantiations are pruned from the conflict set because adding the exclusion clause leads to a contradiction (this means that there are no concrete instances which would enable these rules to be instantiated when R_i is not). This exclusion-clause-generation process is applied repeatedly to the conflict set until no instantiations remain. Each instantiation, together with its associated exclusion clause, forms a new path emanating from the current state.

Because of specificity, R6 (figure 4) will be preferred in situations where both it and R5 are instantiated. However, AbsPS will also characterise those instances where R5 will fire because R6 is not instantiated at all. The exclusion clause: $?x \notin \{PENGUIN, OSTRICH\}$ describes this situation.

(def-rule R5 if (bird ?x) then (flies ?x))

(def-rule R6 if (bird ?x) & (c:member ?x {PENGUIN,OSTRICH})) then (walks ?x))
Figure 4 – R6 is more specific than R5.

Because of the exclusion clause, the path emanating from R5 would contain: $?x \notin \{PENGUIN,OSTRICH\}$. The analysis of this path shows that rule R7 (figure 5) cannot be eligible for firing after R5, because this would conflict with ?x's current environment, $x \notin \{PENGUIN,OSTRICH\}$.

(def-rule R7 if (bird penguin) then (swims penguin))
Figure 5 – R7 Cannot be selected after R5.

The key point about the role played by the procedural semantics of production systems is that the rule-base will inevitably have been designed with these semantics in mind. The procedural semantics *control* the deductive process and thereby prune the space of possible solutions. AbsPS' power comes from its ability to make use of this very same control information to guide its processing.

3.2 Abstract interpretation in HybAbs

We will now describe how the technique outlined in the previous section can be extended to cope with the hybrid system (henceforth the term 'hybrid' refers to the rule/frame system). In the interests of clarity, we will present an example before explicating the general rules for carrying out abstract interpretation in HybAbs.

3.2.1 An example

We first initialise WM with the following patterns:.

    (subclass_of non-conducting-material material)
    (subclass_of conducting-material material)
    (member_of asbestos non-conducting-material)
    (member_of aluminium conducting-material)
    (conducts material yes)
    (assertion non-conducting-material conducts no definitional prototype slot)
    (assertion non-conducting-material conducts yes definitional prototype block)
    (assertion conducting-material conducts yes definitional prototype slot)
    (assertion conducting-material conducts no definitional prototype block)

As they are all frame patterns, they are processed by FS, which returns this initial (virtual) WM:

    (subclass_of non-conducting-material material)
    (subclass_of conducting-material material)
    (member_of asbestos non-conducting-material)
    (member_of aluminium conducting-material)
    (isa non-conducting-material material)
    (isa conducting-material material)
    (isa asbestos non-conducting-material)
    (isa aluminium conducting-material)
    (isa asbestos material)
    (isa aluminium material)
    (conducts asbestos no)
    (conducts aluminium yes)

Note that WM also includes the 'isa' facts implied by the initial set of assertions. The input specification is as follows:

    (goal (grasp ?A ?B)), (hot ?C), (made-of ?D ?E), (conducts ?F ?G)

and the rules are:

    (def-rule R1
    if (goal (grasp ?x ?y)) & (hot ?y) & (made-of ?z ?w) & (conducts ?w no)
    then (holds ?x ?z))

    (def-rule R2
    if (goal (grasp ?x ?y)) & not (hot ?y)
    then (holds ?x ?y))

    (def-rule R3
    if (goal (grasp ?x ?y)) & (hot ?y) & (holds ?x ?z) & (conducts ?w no)
    then (holds ?x ?y) & retract (goal (grasp ?x ?y)))

R1 is unified with the initial WM as follows: the LHS, (goal (grasp ?x ?y)) & (hot ?y) & (made-of ?z ?w) & (conducts ?w no), matches the abstract patterns (goal (grasp ?A ?B)), (hot ?C), (made-of ?D ?E), (conducts ?F ?G), producing the following constraints:

?C=?B, ?E=?F, and ?G=no.

Therefore, we make the constraints explicit and produce the following abstract wm-patterns:

(goal (grasp ?A ?B)), (hot ?B), (made-of ?D ?F), (conducts ?F no), (holds ?A ?D)

The wm-pattern (conducts ?F no) is partially instantiated; therefore, HybAbs can compute the exclusion clause for it:

(conducts ?F no) UNLESS (isa ?F conducting-material).

On the next cycle, R3 fires, asserting (holds ?A ?B) and retracting (goal (grasp ?x ?y)). The final WM, not counting ground frame patterns, is therefore:

(hot ?B), (made-of ?D ?F), (conducts ?F no), (holds ?A ?D), (holds ?A ?B)

with the exclusion clause:

(conducts ?F no) UNLESS (isa ?F conducting-material).

The path involving R2 is only chosen whenever ?C≠?B is true. There is one further path, which involves no rules firing at all - this occurs when the following constraint is satisfied: ?C=?B ∧ (?E≠?F ∨ ?G≠no). Thus, for the above example, the I/O mapping is as shown in figure 6.

Input Specification:	(goal (grasp ?A ?B)), (hot ?C), (made-of ?D ?E) (conducts ?F ?G).
Output Description:	(hot ?B), (made-of ?D ?F), (conducts ?F no), (holds ?A ?D), (holds ?A ?B), UNLESS (isa ?F conducting-material).
	(goal (grasp ?A ?B)), (hot ?C), (made-of ?D ?E) (conducts ?F ?G) (holds ?A ?B) WHERE ?B≠?C.
	(goal (grasp ?A ?B)), (hot ?C), (made-of ?D ?E) (conducts ?F ?G), WHERE ?C=?B ∧ (?E≠?F ∨ ?G≠no).

Figure 6 – I/O mapping.

This example illustrates that when inserting an abstract frame pattern in WM, the program must also check whether there are any applicable blocks which can invalidate the pattern. In fact, the frame pattern (conducts ?F no) can only be in WM if ?F is not a descendant of conducting-material. Otherwise ?F will inherit a block preventing (conducts ?F no) from being valid. Therefore, we need to compute a particular type of exclusion clause, which enables HybAbs to correctly handle the non-monotonicity induced by blocks.

3.2.2 The HybAbs algorithm

No change needs to be made to AbsPS to enable it to cope with fetching and retracting abstract patterns in HybAbs. The only extension concerns asserting abstract frame patterns. There are three possible cases, which are listed below (the rationale for these cases is discussed in the ensuing paragraph).

Asserting abstract frame-patterns

Here we use uppercase letters to indicate generic frames which are not variables.

1) If the frame-pattern has the format (member_of ?x Y) or (subclass_of ?x Y), then a new frame, ?x, is created in FS and linked through the member_of or subclass_of link to its

parent or superclass Y. ?x inherits all the properties from Y, and for each inherited property the exclusion clause is generated.

2) If the frame-pattern has the format (S ?x Y), where S ≠ member_of or subclass_of, then it is asserted in WM and the exclusion clause is generated.

3) In all the other cases the abstract frame pattern is inserted in WM without notifying FS.

The exclusion clause for a pattern such as (S ?x Y) has the format:

(S ?x Y) UNLESS (isa ?x F1) ∨ ....∨ (isa ?x Fn),

where F1, ... ,Fn are frames with block assertions matching (S ?x Y).

As shown above, only abstract assertions such as (S ?x Y), where S can be any relation including member_of and subclass_of, are notified to FS. The reason for this is that in the other cases the assertions bear too little information to make it worthwhile computing exclusion clauses. For instance, reasoning about an assertion such as (member_of X ?y) implies considering all possible ways of substituting ?y with a class in FS, and then spawning as many scenarios. This is not only too expensive, but also not very useful, as no information which can help reduce the search space can be obtained this way. Therefore, only when we have enough information to perform useful deductions, do we attempt to construct exclusion clauses for abstract frame patterns. This way, the frame-related overhead of the abstract interpretation is kept to a minimum.

4. APPLICATIONS OF ABSTRACT INTERPRETATION

4.1 Verification of hybrid knowledge bases

Hybabs enables us to verify the correctness of a knowledge base by comparing the I/O mapping between initial and final WMs with the (formal) initial specification.

4.2 Checking the completeness of a hybrid knowledge base

HybAbs provides a significant improvement over existing approaches to checking a knowledge base for completeness (Nguyen et al., 1985), as it can cope with hybrid knowledge bases, and take into account the procedural semantics of the knowledge base.

4.3 Refining a knowledge base.

In contrast with purely declarative approaches, HybAbs correctly identifies 'subsumed rules', by only flagging those rules which are truly redundant (i.e. their increased specificity has no effect on the choice of path during conflict resolution).

HybAbs is also able to locate 'unreachable rules', which can never fire, and 'dead-end rules', which are only involved in paths that do not lead to a solution. Again, in contrast with purely declarative approaches, HybAbs is able to flag only the 'true' unreachable and dead-end rules, as it can take into account the effects of conflict resolution strategies and non-monotonicity due to retraction and blocks

5. CONCLUSIONS

A number of research issues still need to be addressed. HybAbs cannot accurately reason about rule cycles, though it can identify them and compute their termination conditions. A more difficult issue is that abstract interpretation is a potentially combinatorial problem. We have found that its ability to make use of the non-monotonicity of the frame-base and the control information implicit in the rule-base enables it to cope with fairly large problems (≈100 rules).

However, more work is needed to improve its performance in analysing very large knowledge bases. Grouping rules into self-contained functional units offers the prospect of interactive use of HybAbs if each group is small in size (of the order of 20 rules). Interestingly, abstract interpretation itself may offer a means by which such rule groups could be generated automatically.

ACKNOWLEDGEMENTS

We would like to thank John Domingue and Marc Eisenstadt for providing helpful comments on earlier drafts of this paper.

REFERENCES

Beauvieux, A. (1990). A General Consistency (Checking and Restoring) Engine for Knowledge Bases. Proceedings of the 9th European Conference on Artificial Intelligence. Stockholm, Sweden.

Eisenstadt, M., Domingue, J., Rajan, T., and Motta, E. (1990). Visual Knowledge Engineering. *IEEE Transactions on Software Engineering, 16(10)*. October 1990.

Evertsz, R. (1989). The Generation of 'Critical Problems' by Abstract Interpretations of Student Models. *Proceedings of the 11th International Joint Conference on Artificial Intelligence*. Detroit, pp 483-488.

Evertsz, R. (1990). The Role of the Crucial Experiment in Student Modelling. *Doctoral Dissertation* (and forthcoming CITE Report), IET, The Open University, U.K.

Evertsz, R. (1991). The Automated Analysis of Rule-based Systems Based on their Procedural Semantics. *Proceedings of the 12th International Joint Conference on Artificial Intelligence*. Sydney, Australia.

Forgy, C.L. and McDermott, J. (1977). OPS, a domain-independent production system language. *Proceedings of the 5th International Joint Conference on Artificial Intelligence*. Cambridge, MA.

Frisch, A. and Cohn, T. (1991). 1988 Workshop on Principles of Hybrid Reasoning, *AI Magazine, 11(5)*.

Mellish, C.S. (1986). Abstract Interpretation of Prolog Programs. *Proceedings of the 3rd International Conference on Logic Programming*. London, Spriger-Verlag, pp463-474.

Motta, E. (1990). The FLIK Handbook. *Technical Report no. 65*, Human Cognition Research Laboratory, The Open University, Milton Keynes, U.K., 1990.

Motta, E., Rajan, T., Domingue, J., and Eisenstadt, M. (1990). Methodological Foundations of KEATS, The Knowledge Engineers'Assistant. *Proceedings of the European Workshop on Knowledge Acquisition,* Amsterdam, The Netherlands, June 1990. Also to appear in the Knowledge Acquisition Journal.

Nado R., and Fikes R. (1987). Semantically Sound Inheritance for a Formally Defined Frame Language with Defaults. *Proceedings of AAAI '87*, Seattle, Washington.

Nguyen, T.A., Perkins, W.A., Laffey, T.J & Pecora, D. (1985). Checking an expert system knowledge base for consistency and completeness *Proceedings of the 9th International Joint Conference on Artificial Intelligence*. Los Angeles, CA.

O' Leary, D.E. (1990). Verification of Frame and Semantic Network Knowledge Bases. *Proceedings of the 5th Knowledge Acquisition for Knowledge-Based Systems Workshop*. Banff, Canada, November 1990.

Suwa, M., Scott, A.C. & Shortliffe, E.H. (1982). An approach to verifying completeness and consistency in a rule-based expert system *AI Magazine*, pp16-21.

Vignollet, L., and Ayel, M. (1990). A Conceptual Model for Building Sets of Test Samples for Knowledge Bases. *Proceedings of the 9th European Conference on Artificial Intelligence*. Stockholm, Sweden.

Yen, J., Neches, R., and MacGregor, R. (1988). Classification-based Programming: A Deep Integration of Frames and Rules. *Tech. Report ISI/RR-83-213*, USC/Information Sciences Institute, March 1988.

TAXONOMIC REASONING IN CONFIGURATION TASKS[1]

Clara Bagnasco, Paola Petrin, Luca Spampinato

Quinary SpA, Via Crivelli, 15/2, 20122 Milano - Italy

ABSTRACT

A taxonomic reasoning procedure, able to deal with a class of configuration tasks is introduced and it is discussed in the case of personal computer configuration. The procedure uses as building blocks the basic mechanisms, i.e. subsumption test and classification, of Querelle a terminological knowledge representation language. Limits and related works are addressed.

1. INTRODUCTION

One of the most stimulating research lines in current knowledge representation studies is about KL-ONE like languages (Brachman andSchmolze, 1985). Several partially overlapping disciplines are often grouped with this name: term subsumption languages, terminological languages, hybrid systems, classification based languages, etc.

The common aim is to define a family of representation tools designed to play as the basic kernel of bigger knowledge based systems (KBS). In particular, the focus of attention is on the very large class of domains in which terminology has an important role. The typical tool of this type provides, in a efficient and semantically founded way, a set of functionalities to represent and manipulate information related with complex terminologies.

Subsumption tests, classification and realization have been devised as the fundamental mechanisms to be provided. The basic assumption is that every time domain terminology is relevant enough to play a key role in the system organization, classification and the other mechanisms are useful to carry out the application tasks.

---

[1]This work has been partially supported by the Italian National Research Council, under Progetto Finalizzato Informatica: "Sistemi Informatici e Calcolo Parallelo"

With respect to the effort devoted to the definition and the analysis of variations on the representation language theme, a limited experimental work has been done with this representation approach(Damiani and Bottarelli, 90; Mays et al., 1987). The experimentation work done has however revealed very important for the research field as a whole(Doyle and Patil, 1989).

These projects often exploit classification as an automatic knowledge base organizer, mainly useful during development. Entities in the domain are represented by means of concepts and instances with the selected representation tools and basic mechanisms are applied in a way often transparent to the rest of application. Domain specific problem solving uses classified concepts but it is not concerned with the dynamics of classification.

Another approach is concerned with classification, realization and the subsumption test as building blocks of taxonomic reasoning schemas (Attardi et al, 1986). In these cases, specific dynamics in the terminological taxonomy are defined for specific types of concepts and/or instances by means of which something typical to the application is represented.

This stimulating research line seems to offer an opportunity to achieve general solutions for large classes of problems, to be easily specialized into applications. This being the way often referred as able to face the nowadays unsolved engineering troubles in KBS development.

In this paper, we introduce an example of this approach. The class of tasks considered is configuration and the specific example used is software and hardware configuration of personal computers.

After some information on Querelle, the representation language used for this exercise, the basic ideas of the proposed solution are introduced. A short example and few notes on implementation are thus reported, together with some observations from a different point of view on the subject[2]. A list of open problems and an overview of other approaches to configuration follow.

2. QUERELLE

Querelle is a Term Description Language, developed in the tradition of hybrid systems such as KL-ONE (Brachman and Schmolze, 1985), Krypton (Brachman, Fikes and Levesque, 1983), dealing with the "querelle" between expressiveness and tractability with respect to terminological knowledge representation.

Querelle provides a set of construction operators (all, all+some, etc.) to build term descriptions, and it is able to organize them in hierarchical structures, based on the

---

[2] For more details see (Bagnasco et al., 1991).

generalization/specialization relation. The basic operations provided by the language are detection of a subsumption relation between two descriptions and classification of a description, namely the computation of all its subsumers and of all its subsumees within a IS-A taxonomy. A detailed description of the language can be found in (Decio et al., 89).

An example of description in this language is:

```
(aqo anything named personal-computer
     with-meta QUERELLE-METACLASS has:
:produced-by = [defining]³
                    (all+some hardware-company)
:memory = [defining] (all+some memory-board)
:graphic = [defining] (all graphic-board)
:colour = [erasable] (all+some gray)
...
)
```

This expression defines the querelle object **personal-computer** trough a set of slots (or roles) describing its structure and its relations with others objects in the taxonomy. In particular, a **personal-computer** is composed by a memory, which must be of class **memory-board**, and, if it presents graphic capabilities by a **graphic-board**. Further, it has a slot :colour, which usually is filled by colour **gray**, but could also be filled by **black** or **jaune**, because the modality is erasable.

Querelle has been implemented using QSL (Decio et al., 90), a frame based environment for knowledge based applications, developed at Quinary on top of Common Lisp. Querelle is an embedded language for QSL: each Querelle entity is a QSL object too, and it is possible to put some QSL stuff in each Querelle entity without influencing the formally justified behaviour of it. In particular, this is intuitively useful for methods and special-purpose data structures.

This feature, together with the QSL meta-level architecture (Maes and Nardi, 1989), made ity easy to specialize the Querelle behaviour for delaing with taxonomic reasoning in configuration tasks as described in the next section. In particular, the relevant issue is the extension of Querelle to homogeneously deal with normal descriptions and requirements descriptions, as well as with normal operations (subsumption test, classification, etc.) and UNIFICATION.

3. TAXONOMIC REASONING FOR CONFIGURATION

The class of configuration task we are focusing can be defined with the following statement: *a set of basic components has to be selected and parametrized from a bigger predefined set,*

---

[3] Square brackets include the reference to metaslots: QSL metalevel entities associated with slots and controlling them. Querelle modalities [Decio et al. 89], express the definitional import of each slot definition, and they have been implemented trough metaslots. A set of QSL metaslots has been defined to implement the different modalities provided by Querelle.

satisfying a list of user requirements and all the predefined constraints among the basic components.

Even if this definition probably entails a far more general sort of problems, the hardware and software configuration of personal computers, and computer in general, is a typical representative of this class, and it is historically used as *the example*. We don't try something new here, but we don't claim that a solution to this problem is a solution for the whole class of tasks.

3.1 KNOWLEDGE REPRESENTATION

Several research experiences (Owsnicky-Klewe, 1988; Attardi et al., 1985) have put into evidence as, in this kind of domain, the structure of the basic components constitutes the terminological knowledge and it is properly and easily represented with a taxonomy. In our example, CPUs, memory boards, disk controllers, etc. are defined and organized in a terminological taxonomy. In practice, it is something like the price list of a multi vendor PC integrator.

One of the nice consequences of this choice is that user requests too can be represented in the same way; for instance "I need a desktop PC with a big mass storage and a good CAD -software". As detailed in the following, we represent user requirements as concept like descriptions.

The constraints among the basic components and in user requirements can be partitioned into two classes:

Structural constraints
> The typical part-of like constrained relations. In our example "A personal computer has a CPU board, a video monitor and a keyboard"and "I need a PC with a numeric keypad".

Operational constraints
> The technological, architectural, physical, etc. constraints. In our example "Windows 3.0 requires EGA graphics"and "All the software I buy must be copy protected".

It is easy to represent structural constraints among components directly with the structure of the terminological descriptions representing component types in the basic terminology. Constraints of part-of like relations, are transformed into restrictions on corresponding roles. This holds for user requirements too.

Operational constraints can be represented as role restrictions (and thus as concepts definitions) but they should not be included in the basic terminology. In a sense, they are a part of the terminology which has to be taken into account only when a structure of related instances is created with a definite shape. For example, "Windows 3.0 requires EGA graphics" is a constraints which must hold when an instance of Windows-3.0 is included in a solution list together with an instance of PC with the proper role filled by an instance of graphic-board.

We represent operational constraints as they were a sort of additive user requirements, which pop up only when the concepts they refer to are considered during the configuration procedure.

As an example of structural constraints representation, consider the following expressions describing personal computers as something produced by an hardware company, and constituted by a memory board, a graphic board, etc... , and EGA-ALR-pc, as an entity produced by Advanced Logic Research Inc.constituted also by a memory board and by the EGA graphic board.

```
(aqo anything named personal-computer has:
:produced-by = [defining](all+some hardware-company)
:memory = [defining] (all memory-board)
:graphic = [defining] (all graphic-board))


(aqo anything named EGA-ALR-pc has:
:produced-by = [defining] (all+some AdvancedLogicResearchInc)
:memory = [defining] (all memory-board)
:graphic = [defining] (all+some EGA))
```

When the description of EGA-ALR-pc is classified, a subsumption relation with the description of personal-computer is detected.

The following example shows the description of the software package Level 5 and its operational requirements.

```
(aqo software-component named level-5 has:
:name = [defining] (all+some "level 5")
:produced-by = [defining] (all+some Information-Builders-Inc)
:running-on = [erasable] (all personal-computer)
...
:requirements = [m-local] (EGA-graphic-board))
```

Level 5 is defined as a software component, produced by Information Builders Corporation, which runs on personal computers. Operational requirements are also expressed: to be operative, it needs a machine with EGA graphic.

Defining informations are represented with Querelle slots :name, :running-on, :produced-by, etc...., while the QSL slot :requirements is used to represent the operational requirement of Level 5. This kind of information is not considered by the classification operations, but it will be used by the configuration procedure.

All the user requirements are represented by means of descriptions called **requirement descriptions**. They are usual terminological concept descriptions which can be tested for subsumption and classified as any other Querelle description. They can nevertheless be recognized as different by the system and combined by unification.

Requirement descriptions always have at least two subsumers: the requested object in the component taxonomy and the concept `requirement-description`, from which they inherit informations used in the configuration process itself.

In each configuration session, user requirements are thus represented by a set of requirement descriptions whose roles are value restricted by other requirement descriptions. Let's call, at each level, **subdescriptions** those used as role fillers and **maindescription** that holding the roles.

A set of requirement descriptions often represents complementary requirements with respect to the solution. In these cases they can be combined into a new requirement representing their common meaning. For example "... with a graphics board"and "... with a EGA graphics board"can be combined in "...with a EGA graphics board".

We call **unifiable** the requirement descriptions representing complementary requirements and **UNIFICATION** the procedure to combine them.

3.2 PROBLEM SOLVING

UNIFICATION is the fundamental operator introduced for requirement descriptions. Two requirement descriptions without subdescriptions are recognized as unifiable when: 1) one of them subsumes the other, or 2) they have a common subsumee. If they have subdescriptions, the subdescriptions restricting corresponding roles must be recursively unifiable.

The UNIFICATION procedure returns the more specific description in the case 1), and the common subsumee in the case 2). This recursively applies to the corresponding subdescriptions.

The basic mechanism of the configuration procedure, called **incremental classification,** is now simple enough and can be abstracted in the following statements:

- All the requirement descriptions are classified "in parallel" with respect to the components taxonomy; as each subdescription proceeds, it is shown to be more specific and, as a role restriction, helps the corresponding maindescription to proceed.

- When a requirement description is shown to be subsumed by a concept with associated operational constraints, the additive requirement descriptions representing the operational constraints are taken into account and take part in the play.

- When two requirement descriptions are shown to be unifiable, they are unified. The maindescriptions of the unifiable descriptions share the unified one. The unified description is more specific and has more chances to proceed down in the taxonomy.

- When a requirement description is shown to have a single subsumer in the components taxonomy, and this has no subsumees (it is a leaf node), the requirement description is instantiated and the new instance is a part of the solution.

- When no requirement description can be better classified in the taxonomy, the procedure stops, returning the list of instances so far created.

Intuitively, each starting requirement description, after a number of unifications, is eventually classified under a leaf node of the components taxonomy and a corresponding "satisfying" instance is inserted in the solution. At each step, all the information available is propagated to all the interested descriptions and all the opportunities to combine different requirements are taken.

4. AN EXAMPLE

The requirement descriptions, representing user requirements and structural and operational constraints, will be grouped in the requirement taxonomy. Requirement descriptions are actual Querelle objects, defined in the same way as component descriptions

Let us suppose the user request be: "I need a notebook computer to use Level 5". This request is split into two linked requests: "I need a notebook computer"and "I need Level 5".

The user requirement produces two descriptions, the first of which translates the requirement about the personal computer:

```
(aqo requirement-description,notebook
  named notebook-req
  with-meta  requirement-meta-class
)
```

The Querelle object **notebook-req** is initially attached to the component taxonomy, as a child of the class notebook-computer, and to the requirement-descriptions taxonomy, as a child of the root requirement description. The request of level 5 is analogously translated.

As a notebook computer is composed, among other things, by a graphic board, the notebook requirement is automatically transformed in a set of linked requirement descriptions, **notebook-req**, **graphic-board-sys-req**, that are classified within the taxonomy.

The next requirement to be considered is **level-5-req**. It refers to a node in the taxonomy that entails some operational requirements. In particular, it requires a personal computer with EGA-graphic-board. A new requirement-description is generated: **level-5-EGA-pc-req**. **level-5** is a bottom node, thus an instance of it will be created and made available for the final configuration. As personal computers are structured components, requirement descriptions are created for each subcomponent; in particular the description **EGA-board-sys-req** is created in order to search for a EGA graphic board, as specified by the operational requirements.

The description **level-5-EGA-pc-req** provides missing informations about the needed personal computer and its graphical capabilities.

First of all, after the classification of its subcomponents descriptions, **level-5-pc-req** will be classified as a personal computer, as it does not bring enough information to be recognized as a notebook, portable or desk-top-computer. The configuration procedure will now realize this description is unifiable with **notebook-req**; they in fact express constraints over the same kind of component (Figure 1).

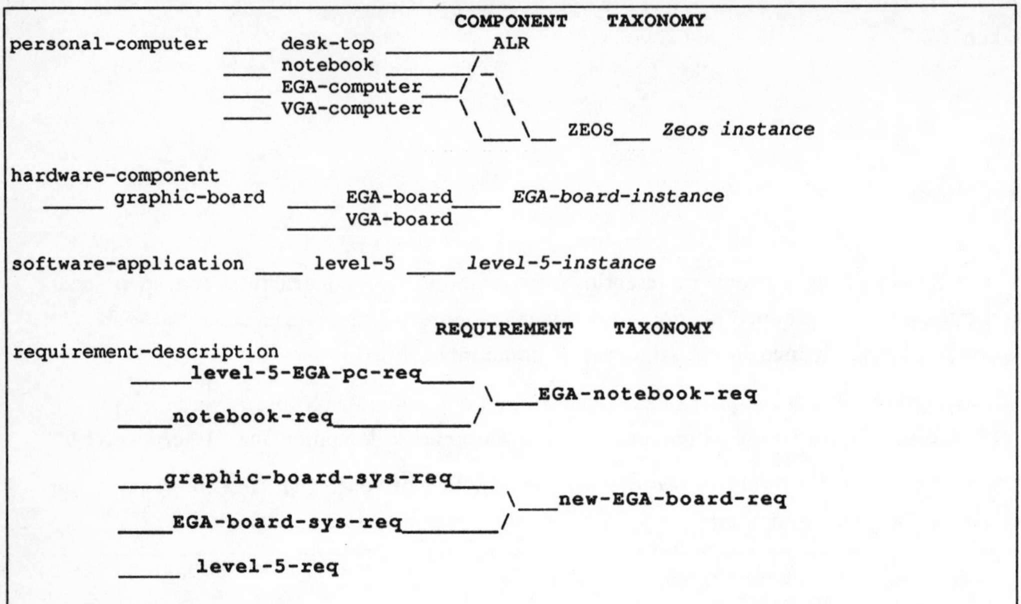

```
                              COMPONENT     TAXONOMY
personal-computer ____ desk-top _____ALR
                  ____ notebook _____/_
                  ____ EGA-computer___/ \
                  ____ VGA-computer  \   \
                                      \___\__ ZEOS___ Zeos instance

hardware-component
     _____ graphic-board ____ EGA-board____ EGA-board-instance
                         ____ VGA-board

software-application ____ level-5 ____ level-5-instance


                              REQUIREMENT   TAXONOMY
requirement-description
         ____level-5-EGA-pc-req____
                                    \___EGA-notebook-req
         ____notebook-req_____/


         ____graphic-board-sys-req___
                                     \___new-EGA-board-req
         _____EGA-board-sys-req_____/

         _____ level-5-req
```

Figure 1

The unification algorithm is recursive, the unification between **level-5-pc-req** and **notebook-req** will thus cause the unification of descriptions referring to the same subcomponents.
The requirement description **new-EGA-notebook-req**, which is the result of unification between **level-5-pc-req** and **notebook-req**, will be classified as a **ZEOS** computer. Among the subcomponents descriptions, **new-EGA-board-req**, resulting from the unification between **graphic-board-sys-req** and **EGA-board-sys-req** will be the description of the **ZEOS** graphic board.

It is clear that the unification of compound descriptions brings as a side effect an information increase at the level of subcomponent descriptions. The subcomponent descriptions are moreover allowed to be integrated with operational constraints on the same kind of components. The increase of information gained at this level can be exploited for discriminating among alternative compound objects.

The result of the configuration process is thus the set of instances *Zeos-instance, EGA-board-instance, level-5-instance,* which provide a description of the components of the final configuration and of the structural relations among them.

5. OPEN PROBLEMS AND RELATED WORKS

Some open problems remain to be solved before candidating our model as a complete solution to the configuration task. The main issue to be tackled in the very near future is search.

The strength of the proposed approach is to reduce search by means of a classification-driven partial choice strategy, making several further steps on the way indicated by (Mittal and Frayman, 87a). At present however, the reasoning algorithm ends without search (maybe proposing a class of solutions) or detects an inconsistency, but it does not handle request of multiple components (e.g. "two printers") and disjointness (e.g. "a matrix or a laser printer"). Some additional limitations concern the expressive power of Querelle, which does not allow the formulation of requests involving existential quantification or disjointeness between concepts.

However, the stage of development it's advanced enough to enable us to make some comparison with some related works.

One of the very first implementation of a computer system configurer is R1/XCON (Mc Dermott, 82). R1 was developed in OPS5 and represents both the knowledge about the components and their connections by means of OPS5 rules. The main problem with this approach regards system extensibility: the difficulty in localizing any modification is, above all, due to the impossibility to keep apart, in a clear way, domain knowledge and processing knowledge.

R1 limitations are overcome by the Cossack system (Mittal and Frayman, 87b), from which we borrowed ideas about the separation of different kind of knowledge and the use of partial choice strategy. Cossack is an object oriented system, in which the knowledge about components is structured in a taxonomy, while goals and constraints are represented with "ad hoc" data structures. The problem of constraints unification is tackled, while the search space is narrowed making partial choices in the components taxonomy. Control is demanded to a centralized algorithm.

A third approach deals with the configuration task exploiting MESON, a hybrid KL-ONE descendant developed at Philips research laboratories (Owsnicky-Klewe, 88). Knowledge about structural and architectural relations among components is expressed by means of the terminological and implicational components, while problem solving is accomplished by the realization algorithm of the assertional component. No constraints unification is provided.

The main common aspect between our approach and the MESON based one is that in both cases configuration is considered as a monotonic inference, which adds knowledge to a knowledge base, reducing the number of possible models. Both of them represent only valid states, while in the rule-based approach every possible state is represented and rules force transitions among valid states.

6. REFERENCES

Attardi G. et al., *Building Expert Systems with Omega*, Tech. Rep. ESP/85/2-3, DELPHI SpA, 1985.

Attardi G. et al., *Taxonomic Reasoning*, Proc. of the European Conference on Artificial Intelligence, ECAI-86, Brighton, UK, 1986.

Bagnasco C., Petrin P. and Spampinato L., Configuring with Querelle, Technical report 7/xx (minor number to be assigned), CNR: Progetto Finalizzato Sistemi Informatici e Calcolo Parallelo, sottoprogetto 7, 1991

Brachman R.J., Fikes R.E.and Levesque H.J., *KRYPTON a functional approach to knowledge representation*, IEEE Computer, **16**(10):67-73, 1983

Brachman R.J., Schmolze J.G., *An overview of the KL-ONE representation system*, Cognitive Science, 9:171-216, 1985

Damiani M., Bottarelli S., *A Terminologicalal Approach to Business Domain Modelling* , Proc. of DEXA 90,Vienna, Austria, August 90

Decio E., Petrin P. and Spampinato L., *Pushing the terminological barrier,* in M. Lenzerini and M. Simi (eds.) Inheritance in Knowledge Representation and Programming Languages, Wiley, 1990.

Decio E., Spampinato L., Gilardoni L., *QSL 4.2 Report*, Quinary Technical Report, Quinary Spa, 1990

Doyle J., Patil R.S., *Two Dogmas of Knowledge Representation*, MIT/LCS/TM-387.b, MIT, MA, 1989

Maes P. and Nardi D. (eds.), *Meta-level architectures and reflection*, North Holland, 1988.

Mays E., Apté C., Griesmer G., Kastner J., *Organizing Knowledge in a Complex Financial Domain* , IEEE Expert, n. 2, 61-70, Fall 1987,

McDermott J., *R1: A Rule-Based Configurer of Computer systems*, Artificial Intelligence, Vol 19, No. 1, September 1982

Mittal S., and Frayman F., *Making Partial Choices in Constraint Reasoning Problems*, Proceedings of 6th National Conference on Artificial Intelligence, Seattle, Washington, 1987 (a)

Frayman F., Mittal S., *Cossack: a constraint-based expert system for configuration tasks*, Proceedings of the 2nd international Conference on Application of AI to Engineering, Boston, MA., August 1987(b)

Owsnicky-Klewe B., *Configuration as Consistency Maintenance Task*, Proceeding of the 12th German Workshop on Artificial Intelligence, Berlin 1988

REPRESENTATION AND USE OF TELEOLOGICAL KNOWLEDGE IN THE MULTI-MODELING APPROACH

Giorgio Brajnik[1], Luca Chittaro[1], Giovanni Guida[2], Carlo Tasso[1], Elio Toppano[1]

[1] Università di Udine, Dipartimento di Matematica e Informatica, Udine, Italy

[2] Università di Brescia, Dipartimento di Automazione Industriale, Brescia, Italy

1. INTRODUCTION

Artifacts are intentionally designed to serve some purpose. These purposes provide important information for understanding and reasoning about their behavior. The teleological analysis of an artifact is aimed at identifying the purposes associated to it by the designer and at explicitly representing their organization. Although teleological knowledge plays a fundamental role in understanding and reasoning about physical systems, the problem of how to represent and use it for activities such as diagnosis, design, simulation, etc. has been faced so far only in a partial and inadequate way. Past work on Qualitative Physics has mostly focused on how the behavior of a system can be derived from its structure using first principles (Bobrow, 1984); therefore, it does not deal with teleology. An exception is represented by the teleological analysis proposed by De Kleer (1984) within the electrical domain. More recently, Downing (1990) has investigated the role of teleological knowledge for the evaluation and explanation of physiological systems in satisfying purposes such as oxygen transport, carbon-dioxide dissipation, and heat conservation in diverse environments. Finally, some attention has been devoted to teleology by researchers focusing on functional representations. Sembugamoorthy and Chandrasekaran (1986), for example, propose a functional representation which is based on the assumption that understanding how a device works can be achieved by showing how an intended function is accomplished through a series of behavioral states. Keuneke (1989) enhances this functional representation including the specification of a taxonomy of function types, or purposes, such as: achieving a state, maintaining a state, preventing an undesirable state, and controlling state change.

Current work on modeling teleological knowledge presents several problems. First, in the literature there is often ambiguity between the terms function and purpose, and some authors do not even distinguish between them. Secondly, the concept of purpose is difficult to formalize in objective terms: it often seems to depend on the observer viewpoint and on the context rather than on well defined features of the physical system at hand. Moreover, usually several different goals are attached to an artifact and their mutual relationships may be very intricate. Finally, it is necessary to explicitly represent the relationships existing between teleology and other types of knowledge which characterize the representation of an artifact, such as function, behavior, and structure.

The research reported in this paper is aimed at exploring the issue of representation and use of teleological knowledge within the frame of the multi-modeling approach proposed in recent years by the authors (Chittaro et al., 1989; Brajnik et al., 1989). The ideas presented in this paper have been tested in DYNAMIS, a research prototype, developed in Quintus Prolog on a SUN 3, dealing with the diagnosis of a thermostat-controlled home heating system.

The paper is organized as follows. After a brief survey of the multi-modeling approach in section 2, we illustrate our concept of function as a bridge between behavior and teleology in section 3. In section 4 we define and discuss in detail the main elements of our teleological model, namely the concepts of goal type, primitive and composite goal types, and the instances of goal types i.e. goals. The issue of goal decomposition and the relationship between goals and phenomena in the functional model are investigated in that section as well. Finally, in section 5 we focus on the contribution of teleological knowledge to diagnosis, i.e. to exclude unproper use of a system as the cause of an unexpected behavior (operator diagnosis) and to focus the diagnostic activity towards missing phenomena and abnormal variables. A summary of the results achieved and an outline of research perspectives conclude the paper.

2. THE MULTI-MODELING APPROACH: A SURVEY

Our multi-modeling approach is based on a systematic and simultaneous exploitation of several types of knowledge. Representation of a physical system is obtained by means of several different models, each one containing only a specific kind of knowledge and organized into a set of (sub)models corresponding to different levels of detail of the representation and to different phenomenological perspectives (Chittaro et al., 1989; Brajnik et al., 1989).

More precisely, in multi-modeling, knowledge relevant to the representation of physical systems is classified according to three criteria, namely: epistemological type, aggregation level, and physical view. These are briefly illustrated below.

By *epistemological type* of a model we mean the class of epistemological features the model represents about the system at hand. More precisely, in our approach we identify five epistemological types:
- *structural knowledge*, i.e. knowledge about system topology. This type of knowledge describes which components constitute the system and how they are connected to each other;
- *behavioral knowledge*, i.e. knowledge about potential behaviors of components. This type of knowledge describes how components can work and interact in terms of the physical quantities that characterize their state (variables and parameters) and the laws that rule their operation;
- *functional knowledge*, i.e. knowledge about the roles components play in the physical processes in which they take part. This type of knowledge relates the behavior of the system to its goals, and deals with functional roles and processes;
- *teleological knowledge*, i.e. knowledge about the goals of the system and the operational conditions which allow their achievement through a correct use. More specifically, this type of knowledge encodes the reasons and intentions of the system designer, that influenced his/her conceivement of system structure and components.
- *empirical knowledge*, i.e. knowledge concerning shallow associations between system properties. This type of knowledge concerns, in particular, compiled knowledge, competence, and subjective experience that usually human experts acquire through direct operation of the system.

The *aggregation level* of a model of a given epistemological type refers to the degree of granularity of the represented knowledge. For example, a structural model of a plant may be detailed to the level of major subsystems or may be further refined to that of elementary components. Of course, given a physical system and focusing on a specific epistemological type, several models featuring different levels of aggregation may generally be considered.

Finally, *physical view* represents a feature of knowledge organization which allows a dynamic control of the focus of attention, in such a way as to take into account at each step of the reasoning process only those parts of a set of models which are relevant to a physical aspect of interest, such as, for example, mechanical, electrical, geometrical, thermal, etc. Views are not new models, but ways of looking at existing ones from a given perspective using an appropriate filter. Of course, views can cross through several models of different epistemological type and aggregation level. The availability of views allows the reasoning process to consider only those parts of the models which are relevant to the task at hand, discarding other details which turn out to be useless or immaterial for the solution of the current subproblem.

Reasoning on a system represented according to the multi-modeling approach is based on two fundamental activities:
- *reasoning inside a model*, which exploits knowledge available within a single model by using specific problem-solving mechanisms;
- *reasoning through models*, which supports opportunistic navigation among models in order to allow each individual step of the overall problem-solving activity to take place in the most appropriate model; of course, this requires an explicit representation of strategies for (i) evaluating the appropriateness of a model with respect to a given task, and (ii) appropriately switching from one model to another, exporting partial results so far obtained.

In the next section we will concentrate on the main features of our functional model in order to illustrate its relationships to the teleological model.

3. FUNCTION AS A BRIDGE BETWEEN BEHAVIOR AND TELEOLOGY

In literature there is often ambiguity between the terms teleology (i.e. intended use or purpose) and function. This section makes explicit the role functional knowledge plays in multi-modeling and gives the reader the necessary background to follow our discussion about teleology.

In our approach we call *function* of a system the relationship between its behavior and the goals assigned to it by the designer. The concept of function is therefore understood as a bridge between behavioral and teleological knowledge. Accordingly, the *functional model* of a system is a conceptualization aimed at describing how the behaviors of individual components cooperate in achieving the behavior of the system as a whole and, ultimately, the designer's goals. The mapping between behavior and teleology has been explicitly represented as follows.

First of all, physical variables in the behavioral model are classified on the basis of the role they play in physical phenomena interpreted as flow-structures. From this perspective, it is possible to identify two types of *generalized variables* common to different physical domains:
- *Generalized substance*, i.e. the abstract entity which flows through a system. The concept of generalized substance can be further decomposed into two subtypes: *generalized displacement* (e.g. electrical charge, heat, volume, position, etc.) and *generalized impulse* (e.g. flux linkage, momentum, etc.).
- *Generalized current*, i.e. the amount of generalized substance which flows through a unitary surface in a time unit. Therefore, according to the type of generalized substance which is flowing, we distinguish between *generalized flow*, i.e. flow of displacement (e.g. electrical current, heat flow, velocity, etc.) and *generalized effort*, i.e. flow of impulse (e.g. voltage, temperature, pressure, force, etc.).

Generalized variables are, of course, independent of any specific physical domain. When they are instantiated in a specific physical domain we obtain the usual physical variables.

This conceptualization can then be interpreted from the perspective of the Tetrahedron of State (Paynter, 1961): an abstract framework common to different physical domains, which describes domain-independent relationships, called *generalized equations*, between generalized variables. The Tetrahedron of State is used to identify a set of *functional roles* which are considered sufficient to interpret the behavior of any component of practical interest. A component role is thus identified by the type of relationship (i.e. the generalized equation) the component behavior satisfies. These roles are: the conduit, the purely conductive conduit, the barrier, the reservoir and the generator. The correspondence thus defined between generalized equations and functional roles constitutes the first pier of the bridge between behavior and teleology which functional knowledge is expected to constitute; more precisely, it represents a first link between behavior (generalized equations) and function (functional roles).

Using functional roles, a set of *generic processes* can be defined, which represent the elementary building blocks necessary to define physical phenomena. For the large class of physical phenomena whose behavioral model can be interpreted in terms of the Tetrahedron of State, we have identified the following generic processes: transporting, reservoir charging, and reservoir discharging. For example, the heating of the water contained in a bowl is an instance of a charging process in the thermal domain, the transmission of rotation from the barrel to the escapement of a mechanical timepiece is an instance of a transporting process (of angular velocity) in the mechanical domain, etc.

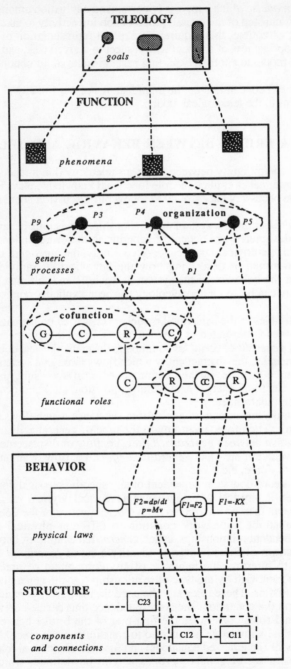

Fig. 1: A schematic diagram of our approach to modeling of physical systems with a detailed insight of the functional model.

The specification of which functional roles are needed to support a generic process and the way they must be related together is called *cofunction*. Cofunction takes part in the definition of generic processes, which also includes their *preconditions*, *effects*, and *posteffects*, expressed in terms of behavioral knowledge. So, generic processes represent a further link between behavior (preconditions, effects, and posteffects) and function (cofunction).

Finally, the concept of *phenomenon* is introduced. A phenomenon is characterized by an *organization* i.e. a network of interrelated generic processes defining i) which generic processes are needed and ii) how they must be related together in order to enable the occurrence of the phenomenon. For example, the organization of the phenomenon of oscillation is represented by four generic processes: the processes of discharging of displacement and charging with impulse and the processes of discharging of impulse and charging with displacement.

The link between the functional and the teleological model is obtained by a correspondence between goal types i.e. classes of goals (as it will be discussed in the following section) and phenomena: in this way the second pier of the bridge between behavior and teleology which functional knowledge is expected to constitute is established. Figure 1 illustrates the above concepts in a schematic diagram. For more details see (Brajnik et al., 1990).

4. THE TELEOLOGICAL MODEL

The *teleological model* of an artifact describes the goals associated to it by the designer. We assume that every artifact is committed to achieve a given set of goals: the teleological model describes these goals (i.e., the intentions of the designer in terms of effects or results obtained by operating the artifact) and their organization.

The fundamental concept of the teleological model is that of goal type. A *goal type* represents a class of goals that share a common generic purpose. Consider, for example, a ram, a pump, and a single phase alternator; all these devices may be considered as power transducers, since they convert power from one physical domain to another. However, the ram specifically converts power from the hydraulic to the mechanical domain, the alternator from the electrical to the mechanical domain, etc. "To transduce power from one domain to another" is, thus, the generic purpose, i.e. the common type, of their goals.

A goal type is characterized by a *name*, which intuitively describes the goal type (e.g., TO_TRANSDUCE), a *purpose*, and a set of *operational conditions*.

The *purpose* specifies the behavioral effects that are expected from the system when the goal has been achieved, i.e. it provides the semantics of the goal type in terms of the intended correct behavior of the system. The term "correct" means here "matching the intentions of the designer". The purpose is represented by specifying: (i) the system variables which are considered relevant to the goal type, (ii) the functional relationships that are expected among the values of these variables and parameters, (iii) a set of constraints on admissible values for the relevant variables (e.g., maximum and/or minimum value, tolerances, etc.).

For example, the purpose associated to the goal type TO_KEEP which intuitively means "to keep a variable at a given reference value" is that a generalized variable VAR achieves and maintains a value that lies within the interval: $X \pm \Delta$, where X represents a parameter (reference value) specified in the operational conditions (see below), and Δ is a tolerance described in the constraints.

The *operational conditions* specify what is necessary for the achievement of the purpose. More specifically, the operational conditions are expressed in terms of:
- *Inputs* which specify what should be provided as input to the system in order to enable it to achieve its purpose. Inputs are expressed in terms of admissible values (or ranges of values) for exogenous variables, i.e. system variables whose values are fixed by the user or by phenomena that are outside the particular system under consideration.
- *settings* which specify how to adjust system parameters in order to enable it to achieve its purpose. Settings refers, for example, to the controls (e.g. knobs, switches, buttons, levers,

etc.) the operator may use to determine the desired behavior. Settings include the specification of:

- ○ *modes*, i.e. qualitative states dividing system behavior into different regions of operation. Each region is specified in terms of inequalities among some relevant system parameters;
- ○ *reference values*, i.e. parameters values which can be set by the operator to calibrate system behavior;
- *Environment* which specifies the admissible values for environmental variables (e.g. force, pressure, temperature, humidity, etc.) outside which the achievement of the goal is no longer guaranteed.

Goal types may be primitive or composite. *Primitive goal types* are goal types whose purposes can be directly achieved by a single generic process. Examples of primitive goal types are:

- TO_TRANSFER: this type represents the class of goals whose purpose is to move a generalized substance from a point to another of a system. Examples of goals of this type are "TO_TRANSFER HEAT FROM THE BOILER TO THE RADIATOR" associated to a heating system, "TO_TRANSFER ELECTRICITY FROM THE BATTERY TO THE LIGHT" associated to an electrical circuit, etc. The purpose can be achieved by a transporting process;
- TO_ACCUMULATE: this type represents the class of goals whose purpose is to increase the amount of a generalized substance inside a system. Examples of goals of this type are "TO_ACCUMULATE HEAT" associated to a boiler, "TO_ACCUMULATE ELECTRICITY" associated to an electrical capacitor, etc. The purpose can be achieved by a reservoir charging process;
- TO_CONSUME: this type represents the class of goals whose purpose is to decrease the amount of a previously accumulated generalized substance inside a system. Examples of goal of this type are "TO_CONSUME WATER" associated to a discharging container, "TO_CONSUME HEAT" associated to a cooling fin, etc. The purpose can be achieved by a reservoir discharging process.

The link between primitive goal types and generic processes in the functional model is represented by the mapping between the arguments of a goal type and the generalized variables associated to the functional roles belonging to the cofunction of the generic process that achieves that goal. This mapping is domain-independent. Figure 2 describes this mapping for the goal type TO_TRANSFER.

Composite goal types represent purposes that can be achieved by phenomena whose organization is usually represented by more than a single generic process. Examples of possible composite goal type are:

- TO_TRANSDUCE: this type represents the class of goals whose purpose is to convert an effort or a flow from a physical domain to another. Examples of goals of this type are "TO_TRANSDUCE FORCE INTO PRESSURE" associated to an hydraulic ram, "TO_TRANSDUCE TORQUE INTO CURRENT" associated to a single phase alternator, etc. The purpose can be achieved, for example, in magnetic or electrostatic actuators by two coupled storage processes (two reservoir charging processes) of electrical and mechanical energy.
- TO_CONTROL: this type represents the class of goals whose generic purpose is to regulate a current flowing out of a system by some substance accumulated inside the system. Examples of goals of this type are "TO_CONTROL ELECTRICAL_CURRENT BY SWITCH_POSITION" associated to an electrical switch, "TO_CONTROL WATER_FLOW BY THE ANGULAR_DISPLACEMENT OF A TAP" associated to a valve, etc. The purpose can be achieved, for example, by a phenomenon whose organization is composed by a reservoir charging process that regulates a transporting process.
- TO_KEEP: this type represents the class of goals whose generic purpose is to maintain a specific partial state in time. This state is described in terms of the values which some relevant physical variable describing the purpose of the system must hold. Examples of goals of this type are "TO_KEEP ROOM_TEMPERATURE AT 18 C°" associated to a

thermostat-controlled home heating system, "TO_KEEP ANGULAR_VELOCITY OF THE PLATTER AT 45 RPM" associated to the control system of a turntable, etc. The purpose can be achieved by a phenomenon whose organization is represented by a complex network of interrelated generic processes.

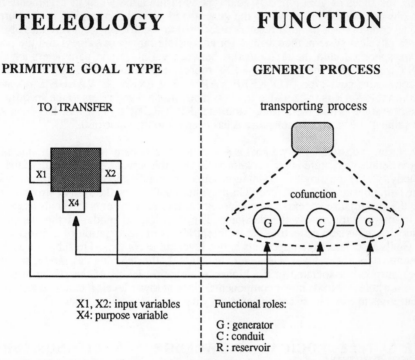

Fig. 2: Relationship between the primitive goal type TO_TRANSFER and the generic transporting process in the functional model.

Composite goal types can be defined by composing together primitive (or composite) goal types. Therefore, a composite goal type may be described through its *decomposition*, i.e. by explicitly specifying the primitive and/or composite types (called subtypes) upon which it is based and the relationships existing among them. Usually, a composite goal type can be decomposed in several different ways. Therefore, a composite goal type may be described, in general, by specifying the set of *alternative decompositions* of the composite type into subtypes. Allowing multiple decompositions for a given goal type is motivated by the fact that, when designing artifacts, in general, several alternatives exist to implement a single purpose. Each of these alternatives can potentially be associated to different decompositions of the goal type, and all the decompositions obtained constitute a library of templates that can be used, for example, in design activities.

Composite goal types are associated to phenomena in the functional model. Since there may exist alternative decompositions of a single composite goal type in subtypes the mapping between goal types and phenomena is, in general, many to many: a goal type can be mapped into a set of alternative phenomena that can achieve that goal. On the other hand, the same phenomenon can participate to more than one goal type decomposition. Each decomposition of a composite goal type leads to a set of interrelated primitive goal types that constitute the leaves of a decomposition tree. Primitive goal types correspond directly to generic processes in the functional model and the relationships existing among the arguments of the primitive goal types are mapped into phenomenological relationships between their corresponding processes. In this way the phenomenon associated to the composite goal type is characterized by an organization that is the network of the generic processes associated to the primitive goal types that constitute the leaves of its decomposition.

Goals are instances of goal types. A goal type is instantiated when its arguments refer to a specific physical situation i.e., when the generalized variables occurring in the purpose and operational conditions of the goal type are associated to specific physical variables of the model of a given physical system, their values (or admissible ranges of values) and the parameters values are specified, and the relationships between variables and parameters are explicitly stated. So, for example, the goal "TO_KEEP room_temperature at $18 \pm 0.5\,°C$" is an instance of the composite goal type "TO_KEEP VAR at REFERENCE_VALUE $\pm \Delta$", where the purpose variable VAR is instantiated in the thermal domain and refers to the specific variable: room_temperature, while the setting parameter REFERENCE_VALUE has been set at the specific value of $18\,°C$ and the tolerance Δ has been set to the value of $0.5\,°C$.

Usually, during a design activity a goal is associated to a system as a whole. In this case, since the system detailed structure is not yet known (in fact, this structure is the result of the "in fieri" design activity), the teleological model represents the specification of the requirements that the structure being designed should meet. On the other hand, when the system structure is known because the system already exists, the teleological model represents the goals associated to it and to its major subparts by the designer. The teleological model of the system may be hierarchically organized reflecting the different levels of aggregation of the structure of the device. Goals associated to components at one level are decomposed in subgoals associated to components at a lower level. However, in general, the teleological model meaningfully describes purposes associated to the higher aggregation levels of the structure (i.e., to the system as a whole and to its major components) since at lower levels it could be very difficult to assign purposes to elementary components: they have only functional roles.

5. USING TELEOLOGICAL KNOWLEDGE FOR DIAGNOSIS IN THE DYNAMIS SYSTEM

Teleological knowledge can be used in diagnostic tasks to support three main activities which are normally performed in the early stages of a diagnostic session:
- *operator diagnosis and guide*: teleological knowledge can be used to identify/exclude unproper use, i.e. abnormal operational conditions or non-admissible goals, as the cause of an unexpected behavior. If an unproper use of the system has been diagnosed, teleological knowledge can then be used to guide the user in the choice of the correct actions to perform;
- *diagnosis focusing*: teleological knowledge can be used to provide hints to focus the diagnostic activity. Knowing which expected goals are unachieved and exploiting the relationships existing between teleology, function and behavior allows to localize areas for diagnostic search in the behavioral and functional models.

In the following, we illustrate in more detail how these activities are performed by DYNAMIS, a prototype system developed in PROLOG to experiment the multi-modeling approach in a thermostat-controlled heating system diagnostic application.

Current approaches to diagnosis are generally based on the assumption that discrepancies between expected and observed behavior of a physical system are always explainable in terms of faulty components. However, there exists an additional aspect to consider which is often not taken into account appropriately by current approaches, i.e. the user. In real-world diagnosis technical service is often called to diagnose faults deriving from wrong use, instead of malfunctioning system components. Users often place systems in unproper environments or feed them unproperly or fail to set system settings as the pursued goal would require. Sometimes, users even try to operate the system to pursue goals not intended by its designer. These problems are dealt with in the first of the above mentioned tasks.

Operator diagnosis and guide starts when DYNAMIS is provided with a) actual operational conditions or b) a set of operator's goals in using the system. In both cases, DYNAMIS tries to validate operator's behavior using the teleological model where admissible goals and expected operational conditions of the system are described.

If the operator provides the system with actual operational conditions then DYNAMIS tries to deduce operator's goals. This is done following this abstract procedure:
1. select a goal in the teleological model of the system. If all goals have already been considered, then go to step 3.
2. match actual operational conditions against the expected operational conditions associated to the selected goal. If the matching succeeds then include the goal in a list of hypothesized operator's goals. Return to step 1.
3. validate the list of hypothesized operator's goals: if the list is empty then terminate operator diagnosis with a failure (this is the case of unproper use, both abnormal or novel) else verify each goal in the list asking the operator if he/she actually wants to pursue it, prevent it or if he/she considers it immaterial (this can be the case of lower level goals). In the case the operator wants actually to prevent some of the hypothesized goals or he/she judges the list incomplete, then terminate operator diagnosis with a failure (abnormal or novel use). Otherwise, terminate operator diagnosis (success) with validation of actual operational conditions.

Analogously, if operator diagnosis starts with the operator's goals as input, DYNAMIS deduces the operational conditions that would be necessary to achieve all the desired goals (hypothesized operational conditions). If the hypothesized operational conditions are not consistent (for example, a tap can be required to be open and closed at the same time), then operator diagnosis terminates with a failure (unproper use caused by non-admissible goals). If the hypothesized operational conditions are consistent, the operator is prompted to check if actual operational conditions matches the hypothesized one. If that is the case, operator diagnosis is completed successfully with validation of operator's goal. Otherwise, it terminates with a failure.

When an unproper use is detected during operator diagnosis and guide, teleological knowledge can be used i) to inform the operator about the proper system operational conditions required to achieve a specific goal, ii) to suggest which actions (e.g. settings, inputs, etc.) to correct after an abnormal use has been diagnosed, iii) to inform the operator about the admissible goals that are achievable by the system.

If operator diagnosis excludes that an unproper use of the system could be the cause of a missing or undesired behavior then teleological knowledge can be used to guide the diagnostic activity in other models (*diagnosis focusing*). In the case of a missing behavior, i.e. a behavior that is expected but not realized, diagnosis focusing is done by i) the identification of unachieved goal(s); and ii) the identification of the candidate phenomena.
Goal achievement is checked by DYNAMIS using the behavioral information represented by the purpose i.e. by comparing observed values of purpose variables with expected values. If the operational conditions are correct, but the purpose is not realized then the goal is considered unachieved. If a goal is unachieved and decomposable, its decomposition is followed and the achievement of its subgoals is assessed too.
The identification of the candidate phenomena is done by DYNAMIS by exploiting the relationship existing between goal types and phenomena in the functional model of the system. Given unachieved goals, the link allows to consider only those phenomena that are relevant to them and thus might be malfunctioning.

At this point diagnosis is carried on by DYNAMIS in the functional, behavioral and structural models using knowledge about the functional roles and the physical laws that underlaid the operation of components in missing processes. A more detailed description of these activities is given in (Chittaro et al.,89).

Note that undesired behaviors may not realize any explicit goal of the design; in this case, searching in the teleological model for unachieved goals is useless. Therefore, it is advisable to use structural and behavioral knowledge to possibly conjecture unforeseen phenomena.

6. CONCLUSIONS AND PERSPECTIVES

The main contributions of the present research are two-fold. First, it focuses on teleological modeling, an issue that has been faced so far in AI research only in a partial way. The paper illustrate the main components of our teleological model and discusses the relationship existing between teleology and function within the multi-modeling approach. The second contribution is to show how teleological knowledge can be used in diagnosis to perform three main activities i.e. operator diagnosis, operator guide and diagnosis focusing.

Future research efforts include the exploration of the use of teleological knowledge for design activities. We will explore the use of the link between goal type and phenomena to automate the proposal of an initial functional organization for an artifact starting from its stated goals as input.

REFERENCES

Bobrow D. (Ed.), Special volume on Qualitative Reasoning about Physical Systems, *Artificial Intelligence 24.*, 1984.

Brajnik G., Chittaro L., Costantini C., Guida G., Tasso C., Toppano E. "Un approccio alla rappresentazione di sistemi fisici basato sull'utilizzo di modelli eterogenei", *Atti Primo Congresso dell'AI*IA*, Trento, 1989, pp. 221-232.

Brajnik G., Chittaro L., Tasso C., Toppano E. "Epistemology, organization and use of functional knowledge for reasoning about physical systems", *Proc. AVIGNON '90: 10th International Workshop on Expert Systems and Their Application: General Conference Second Generation Expert Systems*, Avignon, France, 1990, pp. 53-66.

Chittaro L., Costantini C., Guida G., Tasso C., Toppano E. "Diagnosis based on cooperation of multiple knowledge sources," *Proc. AVIGNON '89: 9th International Workshop on Expert Systems and Their Application: Specialized Conference Second Generation Expert Systems*, Avignon, France, 1989, pp. 19-33.

De Kleer J. "How circuits work," *Artificial Intelligence 24*, 1984, pp. 205-280.

De Kleer J., Brown J.S. "A qualitative physics based on confluences," *Artificial Intelligence 24*, 1984, pp. 7-83.

Downing K. "The qualitative criticism of circulatory models via bipartite teleological analysis," *Artificial Intelligence in Medicine*, vol.2 no.3, 1990, pp. 149-171.

Falkenhainer B., Forbus K.D. "Setting up large scale qualitative models," *Proc. 7th National Conference on Artificial Intelligence*, St. Paul, MN, 1988, pp. 301-306.

Fink P.K., Lusth J.C. "Expert systems and diagnostic expertise in the mechanical and electrical domains," *IEEE Trans. on Systems, Man, and Cybernetics* SMC-17(3), 1987, pp. 340-349.

Keuneke A. "Machine understanding of devices. Causal explanation of diagnostic conclusions" PhD dissertation, Ohio State University, 1989.

Liu Z. and Farley A. M. "Shifting ontological perspectives in reasoning about physical systems," *Proc. 9th National Conference on Artificial Intelligence*, Boston, 1990, pp. 395-400.

Paynter H.M. *Analysis and design of engineering systems*. MIT Press, Cambridge, 1961.

Sembugamoorthy V. and Chandrasekaran B. "Functional representation of devices and compilation of diagnostic problem solving systems," *Experience, Memory and Reasoning*, J.L. Kolodner and C.K. Riesbeck (eds.), Lawrence Erlbaum Assoc., Hillsdale, NJ, 1986, pp. 47-73.

TOWARDS THE INTEGRATION OF DIFFERENT KNOWLEDGE SOURCES IN MODEL-BASED DIAGNOSIS

Luca CONSOLE*, Daniele THESEIDER DUPRE'**, Pietro TORASSO*

* Dipartimento di Matematica e Informatica	** Dipartimento di Informatica
Universita' di Udine	Universita' di Torino
Via Zanon 6 - 33100 Udine	Corso Svizzera 185 - 10149 Torino
E-mail: {lconsole,torasso}@di.unito.it	E-mail: dtd@di.unito.it

ABSTRACT. Over the last few years several attempts have been made to design diagnostic systems which combine more than one model of the system to be diagnosed or more than one reasoning mechanism. In this paper we analyze the integration of different knowledge sources in model-based diagnosis, and, in particular, abductive diagnosis. We consider behavioral models in which the interaction between processes can be represented, enriched with constraints and taxonomic relationships among diagnostic hypotheses. We provide several insights into the role of such forms of knowledge in model-based diagnosis, showing how they can be accommodated both in a meta-level definition of abduction with constraints and in an object-level framework for abduction.

1. INTRODUCTION

The theory of diagnosis has received considerable attention in recent years and various characterizations have been proposed in the literature. Most of the efforts have been devoted initially to investigate a single approach in isolation; however, the attempts to solve complex diagnostic problems using a single approach have been only partially successful. For example, it has been shown [27] that using only a model of the correct behavior of the system to be diagnosed, the consistency-based definition of diagnosis [12, 14, 24] provides some solutions that are physically impossible.

Over the last few years some attempts to design diagnostic systems able to combine more than one formalism or more than one reasoning mechanism have been carried out. On the one hand, in order to reduce the computational burden usually associated with deep formalisms, some proposals for the integration of heuristic and deep reasoning have been made (e.g. the CHECK project [28]). On the other hand, and more recently, several research efforts have been devoted to investigate closer forms of interaction or integration between formalisms or reasoning mechanisms at the deep level: these may vary from the investigation of multiple views of the same device (functional, behavioral, structural, teleological [1, 4]) to the combination of different models (in particular, fault models and models of the correct behavior [10, 15, 27]), or the integration of other forms of knowledge in order to focus the reasoning mechanism (for example, the use of probabilistic information for evaluating only the most plausible diagnoses [15] or the adoption of "exoneration" rules for ruling out some candidates [17, 23]).

Two basic problems in integrating various types of knowledge are whether a unique formalism is able to capture the different knowledge sources and which are the advantages or disadvantages of using a general inference mechanism on a uniform representation. In this paper we do not aim at providing a general solution, but at discussing an instance of the problem in the field of model-based

The research described in this paper has been partially supported by grants from MPI 40% (Automated Reasoning Techniques for Intelligent Systems) and CNR (Progetto Finalizzato "Sistemi Informatici e Calcolo Parallelo", under grant n. 90.00689.PF69).

diagnosis. One of our goals in this field is to provide a framework where different kinds of knowledge can be easily integrated and the basic inferential mechanisms are not committed to a specific logical characterization of diagnosis. Part of this goal has been already achieved and part is under investigation. Most of our recent work has been devoted to formalize the notion of diagnosis when the system to be diagnosed is modeled via a "causal" model. "Structure + function" models [12] differ at the knowledge level from causal models; however, they can be mapped into the same formalism (behavioral models) at the symbol level, and therefore can be dealt with by the same inferential mechanism. Moreover, the common formalism of behavioral models can report the correct and/or the faulty behavior of the system to be diagnosed. A second step towards the integration of different approaches to model-based reasoning has been recently obtained [10] with the unification of different logical definitions of model-based diagnosis: in particular, we showed that consistency-based and abductive [9, 11, 22] diagnosis can be regarded as extremes in a spectrum of definitions, which can be captured with the notion of "abduction with consistency constraints".

However, the analysis of various application domains suggests that such a framework should be enriched by considering several knowledge representation aspects. In particular, different types of knowledge concur to define the model of the system to be diagnosed in real-world domains; a formalization of the diagnostic process should exploit in the correct way all types of available knowledge by taking into account the different roles they play. Our experience suggests that at least the following types of knowledge should be taken into account:

- Knowledge about the interaction between processes, which can be represented using negation in the behavioral model.

- A set of constraints between the entities in the model.

- Taxonomic relationships between diagnostic hypotheses, which can be useful in describing the model at different levels of abstraction.

- "Compiled" knowledge derived taking into account the problem solving strategy, and focusing strategies based on such knowledge.

In this paper we discuss the first three points whereas the last is approached in a companion paper [6]. In particular, we analyze at the knowledge level the different roles of the various knowledge sources. Such knowledge sources are mapped into a uniform logical formalism, but it is useful to maintain them distinct because they have to be used in different ways during diagnostic reasoning. In particular, after a brief presentation of our approach to diagnosis (section 2), this paper analyzes the use of negation in modeling interaction between processes in the behavioral model (section 3) and the role of constraints (section 4) and taxonomic relationships between hypotheses (section 5), using simple examples and discussing how such kinds of knowledge can be accommodated in a meta-level definition of abduction. In section 6 we sketch an object-level formalization of abduction [7, 8] which provides both a declarative specification of the process for generating the solutions to a diagnostic problem and further insights into the role of the different types of knowledge considered in the paper. In section 7 we provide a final example.

2. A GENERAL LOGICAL DEFINITION OF DIAGNOSIS

In this section we briefly recall the general logical definition of diagnosis we provided in [10]. Let MODEL be a set of definite Horn clauses constituting the model of the behavior of the system to be diagnosed. We assume that:

- MODEL is hierarchical [5], i.e. the dependency graph of MODEL (the digraph having the predicates in MODEL as nodes and an arc from p to q if and only if there is a clause of MODEL such that p occurs in its antecedent and q occurs in its consequent) is acyclic (the discussion can be extended to "acyclic" models according to the definition in [2]);

- the predicate symbols in MODEL are partitioned into the two classes of **abducible** and **non-abducible** symbols. The former do not occur in the head of any clause and represent the hypotheses that can be accepted in explanations, e.g. "initial states" in a causal model like the one used in CHECK [9, 28][1], or different behavioral modes of the components of the system to be diagnosed in the "structure + function" models used in GDE-like systems [15, 27] (for example, modes such as "correct", "stuck-at-0", "stuck-at-1" in a model of the behavior of a gate in a digital circuit). Non-abducible symbols are in turn partitioned into **observable** (which represent observable parameters of the system to be diagnosed and do not occur in the body of any clause) and **non-observable** symbols.

At the knowledge level, a diagnostic problem is characterized by different types of data which play very different roles in the diagnostic process (see the discussion in [10] where, in particular, we analyze the roles played by contextual data and normality and abnormality observations[2]). At the symbol level, a diagnostic problem can be reformulated as an abduction problem, which is characterized by a domain theory (the model MODEL of the system to be diagnosed) and a formula Ψ to be explained. In particular, Ψ is a conjunction of observation literals: the positive literals correspond to the observations that must be covered by an explanation (i.e. that must follow from the domain theory and the explanation); the negative literals denote either the values of observable parameters that are different from those observed, and therefore must not be predicted by an explanation, or partial information about observations (e.g., in a medical domain, it can be useful to specify data such as "temperature is not high", to mean that even if the specific value of the parameter "temperature" is not known exactly, it is certainly not high). In any case, negative literals represent constraints that must be satisfied by an explanation.

The correspondence between the data characterizing a diagnostic problem and the literals in Ψ has been deeply discussed in [10] where, in particular, we showed that the different definitions of diagnosis (in particular, consistency-based diagnosis and abductive diagnosis), and therefore different sets of solutions, can be obtained through different mappings between the observations characterizing a diagnostic problem and the formula Ψ. In the following, for the sake of simplicity, we will abstract from the distinction between diagnostic and abduction problems and we shall assume Ψ as primitive, i.e. as the formula characterizing the data of the problem to be solved.

Given an abduction problem, we say that a set E of abducible atoms is an **explanation** for Ψ, given MODEL, if and only if:

1) MODEL $\cup$ E $\vdash$ m, for each positive literal m in Ψ

2) MODEL $\cup$ E $\nvdash$ m, for each negative literal $\neg$m in Ψ,
   i.e. MODEL $\cup$ E $\cup$ Ψ is consistent.

In the following sections we shall extend such a general abductive characterization of diagnosis by considering the role that different types of knowledge play in the diagnostic process.

3. INTERACTION BETWEEN PROCESSES IN BEHAVIORAL MODELS

The expressive power of a language for modeling the behavior of a system should be sufficient to represent the interaction between causes, i.e. situations where two or more events can separately influence another event, and it is necessary to distinguish which combination of the "causing" events is present; in fact, the interaction can lead to the reinforcement or to the cancellation of some effect. As an extreme case, it could be useful to model inhibition phenomena, i.e. processes that can block other processes or evolutions.

Such kinds of qualification can be expressed with the use of negation, stating that a particular effect is present if one (or more) causing event is present and some other events are *absent*. However, we think that it is more useful to have negation as failure rather than classical negation; the motivation is analogous to other uses of negation as failure, and in particular consists in the fact that one ordinarily wants to build only a partial model of a system (e.g. only a fault model). In order to illustrate these issues, let us consider two simple examples.

Example 1. Consider the following behavioral model:

---

[1] Actually, as discussed in [9], in such a kind of model abducible symbols can be used also to deal with incomplete knowledge.

[2] In order to simplify the presentation, in this paper we will not deal with contextual data.

$$MODEL_1 = \{worn\_piston\_rings \rightarrow increased\_oil\_consumption,$$
$$worn\_cylinders \rightarrow increased\_oil\_consumption,$$
$$oil\_cup\_holed \rightarrow oil\_loss,$$
$$oil\_cup\_holed \rightarrow oil\_below\_car,$$
$$increased\_oil\_consumption \wedge \neg oil\_loss \rightarrow oil\_lack(limited),$$
$$oil\_loss \rightarrow oil\_lack(severe)\}$$

(where *worn_piston_rings*, *worn_cylinders* and *oil_cup_holed* are the abducible symbols). In this case both an increased oil consumption and an oil loss have as effect an oil lack, but an oil loss is supposed to override the effect of an increased oil consumption. Notice moreover that if, as in the example, one does not want to provide a model of the correct behavior of the system, the reasons for the *absence* of an oil loss are not explicitly given, and therefore "$\neg$" in the fifth clause has to be interpreted as failure to prove. Consider now the following observation to be explained:

$$\Psi_1 \equiv oil\_lack(limited)$$

In such a case $E_1 = \{worn\_piston\_rings\}$, $E_2 = \{worn\_cylinders\}$ and $E_1 \cup E_2$ are the acceptable explanations (clearly $E_1 \cup E_2$ is redundant) while those explanations containing the abducible *oil_cup_holed* (as, for example, $E_3 = \{worn\_piston\_rings, oil\_cup\_holed\}$) should be rejected. Notice that E_3 would be a redundant explanation in case "$\neg$ *oil_loss*" were omitted from the fifth clause in $MODEL_1$.

According to the definitions in [10] the negative observation "$\neg$ *oil_lack(severe)*" should be added to Ψ_1 to enforce consistency of the solution with the observation. However, this is not necessary since the constraint that an explanation cannot predict both *oil_lack(limited)* and *oil_lack(severe)* is already expressed by the use of negation.

Example 2. Let us consider the following model adapted from ABEL [19]:

$$MODEL_2 = \{hypocapnia \wedge \neg hypobicarbonatemia \rightarrow serum\_pH(increased),$$
$$hypobicarbonatemia \wedge \neg hypocapnia \rightarrow serum\_pH(decreased)\}$$

This is an example of cancellation since the two hypotheses *hypocapnia* and *hypobicarbonatemia* have opposite effects on the *serum_pH*.

Given the interpretation of negation as failure to prove, we can generalize the definition of abductive explanation as follows. A set E of abducible atoms is an **explanation** for Ψ, given MODEL, if and only if:

$$MODEL \cup E \vdash_{NF} \Psi$$

where $\vdash_{NF}$ is the SLDNF query evaluation procedure used in logic programming [5].

It is interesting to notice that, in order to generate explanations, a naive extension of SLDNF-resolution is not sufficient. Two solutions are given in [16, 26]; an alternative approach will be presented in section 6.

4. CONSTRAINTS

In many diagnostic problems it is important to have the possibility of specifying mutual exclusion relationships between different entities of the behavioral model. In the following we first concentrate on the problem of dealing with constraints in the form of denials between abductive hypotheses (abducible predicates), i.e. of the form:

$$\neg(A_1 \wedge ... \wedge A_n)$$

(where A_i are abducible atoms); constraints of this form, with n=2, represent mutual exclusion conditions.

These conditions are necessary in many applications of diagnostic problem solving to prune the set of solutions. For example, in a component-oriented approach such as [15, 27], where the abductive hypotheses correspond to different behavioral modes of the components of the modeled system, it is useful to specify that the different modes of the same component are mutually exclusive. Similarly, in a causal model it is quite common to have mutually exclusive hypotheses, as shown by the following simple example.

Example 3. Let us consider the following behavioral model:

$$\text{MODEL}_3 = \{worn\_piston\_rings \rightarrow decreased\_compression,$$
$$decreased\_compression \rightarrow increased\_fuel\_consumption,$$
$$rich\_mixture \rightarrow increased\_fuel\_consumption,$$
$$lean\_mixture \rightarrow overheating,$$
$$lack\_of\_coolant \rightarrow overheating\}$$

where *worn_piston_rings*, *rich_mixture*, *lean_mixture* and *lack_of_coolant* are the abducible atoms. Notice that the two hypotheses *rich_mixture* and *lean_mixture* are mutually exclusive, since they correspond to two opposite anomalies of the mixture produced by the carburettor. This could be represented with the denial:

$$\neg\ (rich\_mixture \wedge lean\_mixture)$$

Let us consider now the problem of explaining:

$$\Psi_3 \equiv increased\_fuel\_consumption \wedge overheating$$

One should not accept {*rich_mixture*, *lean_mixture*} as an explanation since it violates the constraint and thus the only minimal explanations are {*worn_piston_rings*, *lean_mixture*}, {*worn_piston_rings*, *lack_of_coolant*}, {*rich_mixture*, *lack_of_coolant*}.

In a similar way, one could allow for denials not restricted to abducible predicates, in order to express mutual exclusion relationships between any entity of the modeled system. However, although they can be useful from a modeling point of view (and a knowledge representation language should allow the user to define such general constraints), they are not necessary from a theoretical point of view, since each denial $\neg C$, where C is a conjunction, can be expressed in terms of abducible predicates, finding all the explanations $E_1, \dots, E_n$ for C, and then denying each E_i. Therefore, in the definitions below we shall limit ourselves to the case of denials on abducibles. This restriction is useful to simplify the description of the framework in section 6.

Moreover, there are some interesting interactions between the use of negation as failure and the use of constraints. In example 1, in fact, one could introduce the mutual exclusion condition:

$$\neg(oil\_lack(limited) \wedge oil\_lack(severe))$$

However, if one tries to express it in terms of abductive hypotheses, one obtains no constraint (there is no explanation for *oil_lack(limited)* $\wedge$ *oil_lack(severe)*); as we already noticed, the constraint is implicit in the way negation has been used in the model[3].

Given the possibility of defining a set I of constraints between abducible predicates, we have to modify our definition of explanation, requiring not only that MODEL $\cup$ E $\vdash_{NF} \Psi$, but also that E $\cup$ I is consistent.

5. TAXONOMIC RELATIONSHIPS BETWEEN ABDUCTIVE HYPOTHESES

In this section we consider taxonomic relationships between abductive hypotheses, discussing their importance and showing how they should be used in the diagnostic process. By *taxonomic relationships* we mean a set of implications of the form:

$$A_1 \rightarrow A_2$$

(where A_1 and A_2 are abducible atoms) such that the corresponding dependency graph is acyclic and no atom appears in the antecedent of two distinct taxonomic implications.

As in the previous sections, let us first analyze informally why relationships of such a kind can be useful in diagnostic reasoning. In many cases it can be useful to model hypotheses at different levels of abstraction, in order to build a more concise and readable model. In fact, in a component-oriented model one could introduce general behavioral modes for a component (e.g. "abnormal" and "correct") as well as specific modes (such as "stuck-at-0" for a gate in a digital circuit). Moreover, if

---

[3] A similar relation between constraints and negation as failure has been investigated in [18].

the system is structured in components or subsystems which have subcomponents and so on, such a "part-of" hierarchy naturally induces taxonomic relationships between faults of subcomponents and faults of components. Taxonomic relationships between hypotheses are also useful in cases where a behavioral model is not component-oriented. For example, in the medical domain of liver diseases one could represent the pathophysiological consequences of general hypotheses (such as "cirrhosis" or "hepatitis") as well as the consequences of specific diseases (such as "alcoholic cirrhosis" or "viral hepatitis").

The introduction of taxonomic knowledge allows a system to produce more "clever" explanations: an explanation involves only general hypotheses when no evidence about specific ones is available while in those cases where such pieces of evidence are available, specific hypotheses can be supported and should be preferred.

Example 4. Let us consider the following simple model:

$$MODEL_4 = \{electrical\_problems \rightarrow car\_won't\_start,$$
$$battery\_problems \rightarrow lights\_off\}$$

(where *electrical_problems* and *battery_problems* are abducible atoms). In such a case we have a general hypothesis (*electrical_problems*) and a more specific hypothesis (*battery_problems*); this can be represented by the following taxonomic relationship:

$$battery\_problems \rightarrow electrical\_problems$$

Let us consider now the problem of explaining the following observation:

$$\Psi_{4,1} \equiv car\_won't\_start$$

In such a case one would expect {*electrical_problems*} to be the explanation of the observation. Notice that also {*battery_problems*} would be an explanation (since it implies *electrical_problems* and thus $\Psi_{4,1}$). However, since there is no specific evidence supporting *battery_problems*, the more general explanation, which does not make unnecessary assumptions, should be preferred. This in fact is the *least presumptive* explanation according to the definitions in [21].

On the other hand, consider the following observation to be explained:

$$\Psi_{4,2} \equiv car\_won't\_start \wedge lights\_off$$

In such a case one would expect the explanation {*battery_problems*} and not the explanation {*battery_problems, electrical_problems*}. The latter, in fact, is syntactically redundant and logically equivalent to the former, given the taxonomic relation.

Notice the different treatment of behavioral and taxonomic knowledge: in the generation of explanations, one should trace back from the observations to their explanations on the behavioral theory, but not on the taxonomic relationships: an abducible atom A should not be explained in terms of another abducible atom B unless B has to be assumed for other reasons.

The introduction of taxonomic relationships between hypotheses forces us to modify once again the definition of explanation for an abduction problem. As we noticed in the example, such a form of knowledge should be used to make explicit the preferred (least presumptive [21]) explanations. In fact, syntactic preference criteria (such as minimality) are no more sufficient in case hypotheses are related: it may be the case that two syntactically different explanations are equivalent given the taxonomy (see, e.g., the second part of example 4). We thus have the following definitions. Given:

- a behavioral model MODEL;

- a set I of denials on the abducible predicates of MODEL;

- a set A of taxonomic relations between abducible predicates of MODEL;

a set E of abducible atoms is an **explanation** for Ψ if

1) $MODEL \cup E \cup A \vdash_{NF} \Psi$

2) $E \cup I \cup A$ is consistent

Moreover, in our context, we have that an explanation E_1 is **less presumptive** than E_2 if $E_2 \cup A \models E_1$. Notice that this generalizes set inclusion since $E_2 \models E_1$ follows from $E_1 \subseteq E_2$.

6. AN OBJECT-LEVEL FRAMEWORK FOR ABDUCTION

In this section we shall provide a framework for abduction (and therefore for abductive diagnosis), giving a characterization of the set of solutions to a diagnostic problem described with the types of knowledge discussed above. In such a characterization we shall point out from another point of view how these different types of knowledge should be used.

Our starting point is the object-level account of abduction we proposed in [7], where we discussed its correspondence with more traditional "meta-level" definitions of abduction (like the ones used in previous sections). In the object-level approach, the abductive conclusions are derived deductively at the same level of the domain theory (which, in diagnostic reasoning, is the behavioral model of the system to be diagnosed). The idea of such an approach is the following. Given a set of "cause-effect" relations expressed as definite clauses, if it contains the following clauses having "q" as their consequent:

$$p_1 \rightarrow q$$
$$...$$
$$p_n \rightarrow q$$

then, in order to explain "q", at least one of the "p_i" has to be assumed. This form of reasoning can be reduced to deduction provided that one takes the predicate completion [5] of "q", i.e. adds the formula

$$q \rightarrow p_1 \vee ... \vee p_n$$

One can then reason in the theory resulting from the union of Ψ and the completion $MODEL_C$ of all the non-abducible predicates in the domain theory. In particular, since the completed domain theory is a set of equivalences, and the original domain theory is hierarchical, one can apply the following abstract procedure:

Procedure ABDUCE.

   Rewrite Ψ, substituting each non abducible predicate with its completed definition
   until a formula F (called the **explanation formula**) containing only abducible predicates is
   obtained.

We then have that F follows deductively from $MODEL_C \cup \{\Psi\}$ and moreover:

$$MODEL_C \models \Psi \longleftrightarrow F$$

In example 1 the explanation formula is

   $(worn\_piston\_rings \vee worn\_cylinders) \wedge \neg \; oil\_cup\_holed \equiv$
   $(worn\_piston\_rings \wedge \neg \; oil\_cup\_holed) \vee (worn\_cylinders \wedge \neg \; oil\_cup\_holed)$

As shown in the example, if such a formula is transformed into disjunctive normal form, one obtains conjunctions corresponding to the minimal explanations (provided that one has removed redundant disjuncts) and containing explicit negative information (in the example, the fact that *oil_cup_holed* cannot be added to obtain a redundant explanation). The following correspondence result can be proved:

   E is a meta-level explanation **iff** an interpretation satisfying exactly those abducible atoms
   occurring in E is a model of the explanation formula[4].

Some interesting characteristics of the object-level framework are that it clarifies the relationship between abduction and deduction (i.e. shows that abduction can be regarded as deduction in a completed theory) and that it produces a formula that provides an abstract, model-theoretic characterization of all the explanations, and can be transformed into a canonical syntactical form only if desired.

The analysis in [7] has been restricted to the case where the domain theory is a set of propositional definite clauses in which the abducible symbols are precisely the ones that do not occur in the "head" of any clause (and then no knowledge about abducible atoms is available). In the following, as in [8], we shall consider the case of a domain theory with negation as failure, enriched with

---

[4] Given such a relationship, in the propositional case (or in case the explanations are ground) it can be proved that the prime implicants of the explanation formula F are "kernel" explanations in the sense of [13].

relations between abducible atoms in the forms introduced in section 4 and 5. Moreover, the considerations in the following can be applied not only to the propositional case but also to the case where the facts to be explained are ground and no variables are introduced in tracing back on the model, thus obtaining ground explanations (this is reasonable in a diagnosis context; a more general treatment is given in [8]). In the case of multiple knowledge sources, the generation of explanations can be described as a two-step process:

1) The generation of the explanation formula F, using ABDUCE;

2) The transformation of F according to the knowledge about abducible atoms; in particular, F will be transformed into a formula F^* which is equivalent to F given $A \cup I$. As a result we shall have that

$$MODEL_C \cup A \cup I \models \Psi \longleftrightarrow F^*$$

In particular, the transformation can be described as follows[5].

2.1) The disjunctive normal form of F is simplified by taking into account the constraints I (possibly in conjunction with the taxonomy A); in particular, the main simplification rule concerning the constraints is the following: if $\neg(\alpha_1 \wedge ... \wedge \alpha_n) \in I$ and $A \models \beta_i \rightarrow \alpha_i$ (i=1,..,n), then one can remove disjuncts containing $\beta_1 \wedge ... \wedge \beta_n$, i.e. transform

$$(F'): \quad (\beta_1 \wedge ... \wedge \beta_n \wedge E_1') \vee E_2 \vee ... \vee E_n$$

into

$$(F''): \quad E_2 \vee ... \vee E_n$$

Notice that, in order to prove the equivalence of F' and F" given $A \cup I$, $F'' \models F'$ trivially; the opposite requires $A \cup I$ (i.e. $F' \cup A \cup I \models F''$).
This is the transformation needed in example 3 (in such a case we had $\beta_i \equiv \alpha_i$) to remove the undesired explanation "*rich_mixture $\wedge$ lean_mixture*" from the explanation formula.

2.2) Other simplifications can be performed using the taxonomy A. For example, in case $A \models \alpha \rightarrow \beta$, one can transform:

$$(F'): \quad (\alpha \wedge \beta \wedge E_1') \vee E_2 \vee ... \vee E_n$$

into

$$(F''): \quad (\alpha \wedge E_1') \vee E_2 \vee ... \vee E_n$$

In this case $F' \models F''$ trivially; the opposite requires A (i.e. $F'' \cup A \models F'$).
This is the transformation needed in example 4 (second part) in order to transform the explanation formula "*battery_problems $\wedge$ electrical_problems*" into "*battery_problems*".

The formula F^* obtained at end of such a process characterizes all the solutions to the abduction problem[6]. In particular, keeping A separated from MODEL avoids tracing back on the taxonomic relationships and thus producing explanations that are not least presumptive (see also example 4).

The correspondence between meta-level explanations and models of the formula produced by object-level abduction can be extended to this more general case. The technical details of this correspondence, which are not our main concern here, are given in [8].

7. A FINAL EXAMPLE

As a final example which illustrates the interaction between different forms of knowledge about abductive hypotheses and the use of the object-level framework, consider the theory <$MODEL_5,A_5,I_5$>, where:

$MODEL_5$ = {*lubr_system(normal)* → *oil_level_lamp(off)*,
lamp(broken) → *oil_level_lamp(off)*,
lubr_system(faulty) $\wedge$ lamp(normal) → *oil_level_lamp(on)*,
lubr_system(increased_consumption) → *stack_smoke(black)*,

---

[5] A more detailed description of the simplification rules is reported in [8].

[6] The process above can also be regarded as a procedure (not necessarily an efficient one) for determining the explanations.

$$oil\_cup(holed) \rightarrow oil\_below\_car(present) \}$$

$$A_5 = \{ lubr\_system(increased\_consumption) \rightarrow lubr\_system(faulty),$$
$$lubr\_system(leak) \rightarrow lubr\_system(faulty),$$
$$oil\_cup(holed) \rightarrow lubr\_system(leak) \}$$

$$I_5 = \{ \neg [lubr\_system(normal) \wedge lubr\_system(faulty)] \}$$

(where *lubr_system*, *lamp* and *oil_cup* are the abducible symbols) and the problem of explaining

$$\Psi_5 \equiv oil\_level\_lamp(off) \wedge stack\_smoke(black)$$

Step 1 (ABDUCE) produces

$$[lubr\_system(normal) \vee lamp(broken)] \wedge lubr\_system(increased\_consumption)$$

whose disjunctive normal form is

$$[lubr\_system(normal) \wedge lubr\_system(increased\_consumption)] \vee$$
$$[lamp(broken) \wedge lubr\_system(increased\_consumption)]$$

which can be simplified (applying transformation 2.1) into

$$lamp(broken) \wedge lubr\_system(increased\_consumption)$$

Notice that { *lamp(broken)*, *lubr_system(increased_consumption)* } is the unique least presumptive meta-level explanation.

CONCLUSIONS

In this paper we discussed the integration of different knowledge sources in model-based diagnosis. The knowledge sources considered are: behavioral models in which the interaction between processes can be represented; constraints between the entities in the model; taxonomic relationships between diagnostic hypotheses. We pointed out their role at the knowledge level, and showed how they can be accommodated both in a meta-level definition and an object-level framework for abduction.

The adoption of a logical approach and the fact that the different knowledge sources are taken separate are opposed to an "homogeneous" approach such as the one of "belief networks" [20] and have the advantage of dealing in a natural way with multiple faults problems, providing in any specific case a distinction between hypotheses that have to be necessarily assumed, redundant hypotheses and hypotheses that have to be absent. This advantage is not obtained by imposing severe restrictions on the model; in fact, the reasoning mechanism is able to deal also with incomplete knowledge, as discussed in [9].

It is worth mentioning, in conclusion, that the complexity of some of the forms of abductive reasoning presented in this paper has been deeply investigated in [3, 25]; the latter, in particular, shows that the core of abduction is intrinsically intractable. Although the worst case analysis shows that such forms of reasoning are in general intractable, we agree on the point raised in [3] that several mitigating factors, such as the use of "rule-out" knowledge (i.e. knowledge to rule out hypotheses), can be taken into account in practical cases; in particular, in [6] we showed how the abductive process can be focused using "rule-out" knowledge compiled from the original model; this technique is useful in case there are several alternative explanations having different manifestations that can be used to discriminate among them.

REFERENCES

[1]   Abu-Hanna, A., Benjamins, R., and Jansweijer, W., "Functional Models in Diagnostic Reasoning," pp. 243-256 in *Proc. 11th Int. Work. on Expert Systems and Their Applications (Conf. on 2nd Generation Expert Systems)*, Avignon (1991).

[2]   Apt, K.R. and Bezem, M., "Acyclic programs," pp. 617-633 in *Proc. 7th Int. Conf. on Logic Programming*, MIT Press, Jerusalem (1990).

[3]   Bylander, T., Allemang, D., Tanner, M., and Josephson, J., "Some Results Concerning the Computational Complexity of Abduction," pp. 44-54 in *Proc. 1st Conference on Principles of Knowledge Representation and Reasoning*, Toronto (1989).

[4]   Chittaro, L., Costantini, C., Guida, G., Tasso, C., and Toppano, E., "Diagnosis Based on Cooperation of Multiple Knowledge Sources," pp. 19-33 in *Proc. 9th Int. Work. on Expert Systems and Their Applications (Conf. on 2nd Generation Expert Systems)*, Avignon (1989).

[5]   Clark, K., "Negation as failure," pp. 293-322 in *Logic and Data Bases*, ed. H. Gallaire, J. Minker,Plenum Press, New York (1978).

[6]   Console, L., Portinale, L., and Theseider Dupre´, D., "Focusing Abductive Diagnosis," pp. 231-242 in *Proc. 11th Int. Work. on Expert Systems and Their Applications (Conf. on 2nd Generation Expert Systems)*, Avignon (1991).

[7]   Console, L., Theseider Dupre´, D., and Torasso, P., "Abductive Reasoning through Direct Deduction from Completed Domain Models," pp. 175-182 in *Methodologies for Intelligent Systems 4*, ed. Z. Ras,North Holland (1989).

[8]   Console, L., Theseider Dupre´, D., and Torasso, P., "On the Relationship between Abduction and Deduction," *to appear in Journal of Logic and Computation*, (1991).

[9]   Console, L., Theseider Dupre´, D., and Torasso, P., "A Theory of Diagnosis for Incomplete Causal Models," pp. 1311-1317 in *Proc. 11th IJCAI*, Detroit (1989).

[10]   Console, L. and Torasso, P., "Integrating Models of the Correct Behavior into Abductive Diagnosis," pp. 160-166 in *Proc. 9th ECAI*, Stockholm (1990).

[11]   Cox, P.T. and Pietrzykowski, T., "General Diagnosis by Abductive Inference," pp. 183-189 in *Proc. IEEE Symposium on Logic Programming*, San Francisco (1987).

[12]   Davis, R. and Hamscher, W., "Model-based reasoning: Troubleshooting," pp. 297-346 in *Exploring Artificial Intelligence*, ed. H.E. Shrobe,Morgan Kaufman (1988).

[13]   DeKleer, J., Mackworth, A., and Reiter, R., "Characterizing Diagnoses," pp. 318-323 in *Proc. AAAI 90*, Boston (1990).

[14]   DeKleer, J. and Williams, B.C., "Diagnosing Multiple Faults," *Artificial Intelligence* 32 pp. 97-130 (1987).

[15]   DeKleer, J. and Williams, B.C., "Diagnosis with behavioral modes," pp. 1324-1330 in *Proc. 11th IJCAI*, Detroit (1989).

[16]   Eshghi, K. and Kowalski, R., "Abduction Compared with Negation as Failure," pp. 234-254 in *Proc. 6th Int. Conf. on Logic Programming*, MIT Press, Lisbon (1989).

[17]   Friedrich, G., Gottlob, G., and Nejdl, W., "Physical Impossibility Instead of Fault Models," pp. 331-336 in *Proc. AAAI 90*, Boston (1990).

[18]   Kowalski, R. and Sadri, F., "Knowledge Representation without Integrity Constraints," Technical Report, Department of Computing, Imperial College, London (1988).

[19]   Patil, R., "Causal representation of patient illness for electrolyte and acid-base diagnosis," MIT/LCS/TR-267, Cambridge (1981).

[20]   Pearl, J., *Probabilistic Reasoning in Intelligent Systems*, Morgan Kaufmann (1989).

[21]   Poole, D., "Explanation and Prediction: An Architecture for Default and Abductive Reasoning," *Computational Intelligence* 5(1) pp. 97-110 (1989).

[22]   Poole, D., Goebel, R., and Aleliunas, R., "Theorist: a logical reasoning system for default and diagnosis," pp. 331-352 in *The Knowledge Frontier*, ed. N. Cercone, G. Mc Calla,Springer Verlag (1987).

[23]   Raiman, O., "Diagnosis as a Trial: The Alibi Principle," in *Proc. Int. Workshop on Model-based Diagnosis*, Paris (1988).

[24]   Reiter, R., "A Theory of Diagnosis from First Principles," *Artificial Intelligence* 32 pp. 57-96 (1987).

[25]   Selman, B. and Levesque, H., "Abductive and Default Reasoning: A Computational Core," pp. 343-348 in *Proc. AAAI 90*, Boston (1990).

[26]   Shanahan, M., "Prediction is Deduction but Explanation is Abduction," pp. 1055-1060 in *Proc. 11th IJCAI*, Detroit (1989).

[27]   Struss, P. and Dressler, O., "Physical Negation - Integrating Fault Models into the General Diagnostic Engine," pp. 1318-1323 in *Proc. 11th IJCAI*, Detroit (1989).

[28]   Torasso, P. and Console, L., *Diagnostic Problem Solving: Combining Heuristic, Approximate and Causal Reasoning*, Van Nostrand Reinhold (1989).

Integrating statistics, numerical analysis and dependency-recording in model-based diagnosis

Stefano Cermignani, Giorgio Tornielli
Cise SpA P.O. Box 12081, I-20134 Milano, Italy

Abstract

Research on model-based diagnosis of technical systems has grown enormously in the last few years, producing new basic tools, new algorithms and also some applications. However, the majority of research has dealt with systems described by variables ranging in discrete domains (e.g., digital circuits), and only few attempts have been made at applying such techniques to continuous domains. Continuous systems are characterized by additional problems, such as the unavoidable sensor errors and the need for using more complex models which may consist of simultaneous non-linear equations. The distinctive feature of the approach we present in this paper is the integration of techniques well known in the field of numerical analysis and statistics (e.g., the solution of non-linear systems and the error propagation) with a dependency-recording technique based on ordering the equations and the variables of the model.

1. Introduction

Research on model-based diagnosis of technical systems has progressed enormously in the last few years, thus stimulating the development of tools of general applicability in the AI field (e.g., the ATMS [de Kleer, 1986]), proposing general diagnostic algorithms (e.g., GDE [de Kleer and Williams, 1987], XDE [Hamscher, 1988], Sherlock [de Kleer and Williams, 1989], and GDE+ [Struss and Dressler, 1989]) and also developing some interesting applications (e.g., TEXSYS [Glass and Wong, 1988]). However, the majority of research has addressed the problem of diagnosing faults of discrete systems (e.g., digital circuits), and only few attempts have been made at applying such techniques to diagnosis of continuous systems, i.e., systems where the variables take values from the set of real numbers instead of from a discrete set. Continuous systems (e.g., hydraulic and thermodynamic processes) can be found when modelling physiological systems as well as in many industries such as petrochemical, chemical and electric power generation where process monitoring, malfunction diagnosis and performance evaluation are tasks of paramount importance. Continuous systems are characterized by further problems with respect to discrete ones; among them we find the following:

- sensors may be faulty, hence diagnosing the main process independently from the sensors is unfeasible;

- even if the sensors are working correctly, the value they return always include an unknown error; hence, determining discrepancies between different predicted values obtained from sensors values requires more accuracy;

- the cardinality of the set of components is usually smaller for continuous systems than for discrete ones (e.g., a hydraulic circuit consists of some tenths of components against some thousands of components of a digital circuit), but the models of the former are much more complex than the ones of the latter since, often, they consist of simultaneous non-linear equations.

Diagnosis may be interpreted as an iterative process consisting of two steps: generation of a candidate diagnosis (i.e., an assignment of a mode of behaviour, either correct or faulty, to each component and sensor), and its evaluation. Evaluation of a candidate is performed by checking whether the logical conjunction of the equational model denoted by the candidate and of the observations is consistent: if this is the case, the candidate is a correct diagnosis. The current most popular model-based diagnostic algorithms, yet aiming at being "general", suffer of some drawbacks when applied to continuous systems. One of the causes is the locality of constraint propagation [Sussman and Steele, 1980], the mechanism usually adopted for implementing the evaluator, which prevents solution of simultaneous equations (unless the expensive symbolic constraint propagation is applied [de Kleer and Sussman, 1980]). Finally, these algorithms always assume that the values gathered by the data acquisition system do not include any error.

The candidate evaluator we present in this paper has been designed for coping with the above mentioned difficulties. In particular, for evaluating candidates we adopt well known numerical algorithms (e.g., the Newton-Raphson algorithm), we perform error propagation using techniques based on statistical analysis and, assuming that observations are actually statistical variables of known distribution, we adopt statistical tests for determining discrepancies between different predicted values. These techniques are coupled with a dependency tracing mechanism embedded into the evaluator which allows determining the minimal sets of modes on which a given discrepancy depends on (i.e., conflicts). Conflicts are then used by the candidate generator as a basis for generating new candidates. The dependency mechanism is achieved by arranging the equations of the model into a lattice which represents a partial ordering between the equations and the variables of the model, and exploiting this ordering for determining the sets of conflicting modes.

The aim of this paper is to show how the above mentioned techniques may be combined within the candidate evaluator of a model-based diagnostic system. The paper is organized as follows: section 2 introduces the overall diagnostic strategy; section 3 is focused on the candidate evaluator and describes how the equations are ordered, how the ordering is used for checking the consistency between the observations and the model and for determining conflicts. Finally, section 4 gives our conclusions and discusses on future work.

2. The diagnostic process

For the purpose of our work, we assume that the physical system to be diagnosed is described by a static model and that diagnosis has to determine two different kinds of faults: component and sensor faults.

We interpret diagnosis as an iterative process consisting of two steps: generation of a candidate diagnosis and its subsequent evaluation (the modules actually composing the diagnostic system are shown in Figure 1). Here, a candidate consists of an assignment of a behavioural mode to each component and to each sensor of the system. For instance, a hydraulic pump may be described by two modes of behaviour: the correct behaviour and the faulty behaviour due to blade erosion. In the same way, sensors may be either working correctly, thus the data that they return may be trusted in (even if they are affected by the physiological sensor error), or may be broken and the value that they return is completely un-reliable and has to be discarded.

Generation of candidate diagnoses may be achieved by exploiting several types of knowledge such as the prior fault probability or experiential knowledge. Furthermore, it is important that candidates be conflict free where a conflict is the minimal set of modes which have been used for determining a discrepancy. Conflicts are incrementally computed by the evaluator, and when they are available, the generator has not to generate candidates including already discovered conflict since this candidate would be surely rejected by the evaluator. A longer discussion of the overall diagnostic process and on the candidate generator in particular is outside the scope of this paper.

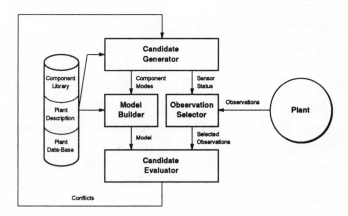

Figure 1.

In summary, the interaction between the generator and the evaluator is as follows: the former feeds the evaluator with a candidate to be evaluated, and the latter returns to the generator the conflict sets that possibly it has discovered. In order to be used by the evaluator, the candidates proposed by the generator have to be translated into a set of equations and into a set of known values and unknown variables. This is achieved by means of the Model Builder and by the Observation Selector modules.

3. The candidate evaluator

As argued in the introduction, designing an evaluator for continuous systems requires to take into account that models often consist of non-linear simultaneous equations, and that the values returned by correctly working sensors include an unknown error. Furthermore, the evaluator has to be designed in such a way that the number of known values be not fixed a priori since different candidates may denote different known values. The approach that we propose for coping with these requirements is herein described.

For the purpose of our work, we assume that each variable assumed to be known (i.e., measurements and parameters) be considered as a statistical variable of known distribution. Thus, the candidate evaluator has to verify whether the equations denoted by a candidate are consistent with the statistical distributions of the known variables, and, if they are not, it has to find the relevant conflict set. In this context, consistency may be defined as follows:

Let S be the set of n_{eq} algebraic equations in n_{var} variables. The variables are partitioned into the sets Kn and Unk, where the statistical distributions of the n_{kn} variables in Kn is known. The equations in S are consistent with the assumed statistical distribution of the variables in Kn if there exists at least one assignment $\underline{Unk}$ of the variables in Unk such that the value of the quantity chosen to represent the global error of the system may be ascribed to chance only.

In other words, writing the equations of the model as

$$f_i (Kn, Unk) = 0, \qquad\qquad\qquad i = 1, n_{eq}$$

the problem is to decide whether there is an $\underline{Unk}$ such that

$$\text{prob} \left(\Sigma\, \varepsilon_i^2 > \Sigma\, \underline{\varepsilon}_i^2 \right) > \alpha$$

where $\varepsilon_i = f_i (Kn, \underline{Unk})$, $\underline{\varepsilon}_i = f_i (\underline{Kn}, \underline{Unk})$, $\underline{Kn}$ is the expected value of Kn and α is the maximum accepted probability for false positive cases, for instance 5%.

In order to determine whether such a $\underline{Unk}$ exists, we have devised a procedure consisting of the following main steps:

1. Consider each equation of S as having the variables in Unk only as unknown quantities, while those in Kn are set to their expected values (i.e., the measured values for the observable variables and the design values for the parameters).

2. Determine a well constrained subset (WC) of the equations of S, i.e., one allowing the computation of all its unknowns. The cardinality of WC has to be the greatest possible.

3. Arrange the equations in WC according to a partial ordering (see section 3.2). The ordering is exploited for two reasons: firstly, it reduces the complexity of the computation by making easier the convergence of the numerical algorithms, and, secondly, it allows the minimal conflict set to be determined.

4. Highlight the subset (OC) of the remaining equations that contains redundant equations only, i.e., equations in which all unknown quantities become known as the equations in WC are solved.

5. Solve the equations in WC with respect to the unknowns exploiting the ordering computed in 3.

6. Estimate the distributions of the computed quantities as functions of the distribution of the variables in Kn.

7. For each equation in OC, verify whether, once the unknown quantities are substituted with their values computed in 5, the outcome error may be ascribed to chance only.

8. If this is the case, then the system may be considered consistent with the assumed statistical distributions for the variables in Kn.

9. Otherwise, select the first equation in OC that does not verify the test in 7 and use the ordering defined in 3 for finding the relevant conflict set.

This procedure becomes tractable if some assumptions about the equations and the statistical properties of the known quantities are considered. Namely, we assume that all the functions associated to the equations are piecewise continuous and provided with left and right partial derivatives with respect to all the variables, at least in the interesting domain. All the errors associated to each known quantity, i.e., the differences between the expected value (which is assumed) and the actual value (which is actually unknown), are supposed to be statistically independent. Each error is also supposed to be distributed according to a gaussian curve with mean equal to zero and known standard deviation. Finally, each difference is supposed to be small enough to allow the linearization of the equations around the expected values. All these assumptions seem to be acceptable for realistic cases. In the following sections the main steps of this procedure are detailed, using the simplified mixing plant described in the next section.

3.1. A reference example

Let us consider the mixing plant shown in Figure 2. This plant consists of twenty interconnected components belonging to two different classes, namely pumps (triangles) and pipes (rectangles). The correct behaviour of each of these components may be expressed as a parameterized relation between input pressure (P_i), output pressure (P_o) and flow rate (G) as follows:

$$\text{Pump} \Rightarrow P_o - P_i - a\,G^2 - b\,G - c = 0$$
$$\text{Pipe} \Rightarrow P_i - P_o - r\,G^2 = 0$$

where a, b and c are the characteristic parameters of each pump and r is the characteristic parameter of each pipe.

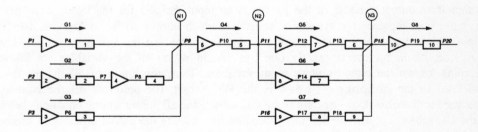

Figure 2.

In addition, in force of the mass balance principle, an equation is associated to each of the nodes as follows:

Node 1 $\Rightarrow$ $G_1 + G_2 + G_3 - G_4 = 0$
Node 2 $\Rightarrow$ $G_4 - G_5 - G_6 = 0$
Node 3 $\Rightarrow$ $G_5 + G_6 + G_7 - G_8 = 0$

Let us assume that P_1, P_2, P_3, P_7, P_9, P_{11}, P_{12}, P_{15}, P_{16}, P_{18} and P_{20} are measured, and let us also assume that the candidate to evaluate states that all the components and all the sensors work correctly (this step actually corresponds to fault detection). In this case the system model consists of 23 equations in 68 variables; the subset Unk consists of 17 variables, since 11 pressures are measured and all the 40 parameters are supposed to be known.

3.2. How to structure the equations (steps 2-3-4)

The n_{eq} equations of the system S can be partitioned into three disjoint, and possibly empty, subsets:

- The subset of the *Well Constrained* (WC) equations, consisting of n_{wc} equations in n_{wc} unknowns. This set has to be chosen with the largest cardinality, i.e., in such a way that there is not another set with the same property and with a larger cardinality. Under the above mentioned assumption about the properties of the f_i's, the equations in WC admit one and only one solution.

- The subset of the *Over Constrained* (OC) equations, consisting of n_{oc} equations, each of them referring only to some of the unknowns belonging to the set computable by the equations in WC. Each of the equations in OC may be used in order to check whether the assumed statistical distributions of the variables in Kn and the values computed by WC is consistent.

- The subset of the *Under Constrained* (UC) equations, consisting of the remaining $(n_{eq} - n_{wc} - n_{oc})$ equations. Our diagnostic algorithm does not use this set.

The procedure for determining these three subsets builds a partial ordering of the equations that can be represented as a directed lattice whose nodes are either `computer-nodes` or `checker-nodes`. A `computer-node` is characterized by a set of input variables, a set of output variables and a set of known quantities, while a `checker-node` has no output variables. All the nodes are connected in such a way that there is a link from a node to another if an output variable of the former is an input variable for the latter. Each `computer-node` represents a system of equations which allows all the unknowns listed as output variables to be computed, given the input variables and the known quantities. Each `checker-node` represents exactly one equation in which all the variables are known, assuming known the ones listed as input variables. Thus, the union of all the equations associated to the `computer-nodes` is the WC subset, the union of all the equations associated to the `checker-nodes` is the OC subset, and all the remaining equations belong to the UC subset. Let us note that this procedure for building the partial ordering is strongly related to the Iwasaki and Simon's procedure for computing a causal ordering among the variables of a well-constrained set of equations [Iwasaki and Simon, 1986]. In fact, our procedure, when supplied with a well-constrained set S of equations, exactly produces Iwasaki and Simon's causal ordering; however, in our case, we have to compute a partial ordering even if S is not well-constrained.

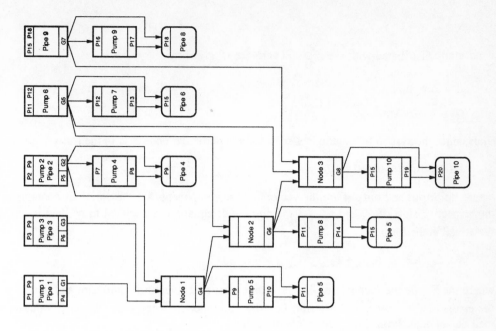

Figure 3.

The output of our procedure applied to the mixing plant is shown in Figure 3. In this picture, checker-nodes are drawn as rounded corner rectangles, while computer-nodes as squared corner rectangles. In the upper side of each node are shown the measured variables of the components associated to that node, in the lower side the output variables and, since in our example there is a one to one relationship between components and equations, the nodes are labelled with the component names only. Furthermore, the parameters associated to each node are unambiguously denoted by the component names and thus are not explicitly shown.

3.3. How to solve the structured system (steps 5-6)

The ordering determined in the previous step of the procedure may now be exploited for computing the expected values of all the computable variables and for estimating the variance of their associated errors. The problem described in this section deals with the processing of the computer-nodes of the lattice. The sequence according to which they are processed is given by the ordering fixed by the lattice. In other words, a particular node may be processed only after that each of its predecessors has been already processed. The expected value of the unknowns listed in the output slot of a node may be computed by solving the equations associated to it by means of a numerical algorithm, such as the Newton-Raphson method.

The variance of the errors may be obtained starting from the variance of the errors associated to the input variables and of the errors associated to the known quantities in Kn. This is easy to be performed if all the errors associated to the variables in Kn are supposed to be normally distributed, and to be small enough to allow the linearization of the system around their expected values. In fact, it is well known that if v_i are n statistical variables normally distributed and mutually independent with means μ_i and variances σ_i^2, then also the statistical variable

$$v = \Sigma \; w_i \; v_i, \qquad\qquad\qquad\qquad\qquad i = 1, n$$

is normally distributed with mean μ and variance σ^2 given by

$$\mu = \Sigma \; w_i \; \mu_i, \qquad\qquad\qquad\qquad i = 1, n \qquad\qquad (1)$$

$$\sigma^2 = \Sigma \; w_i^2 \; \sigma_i^2, \qquad\qquad\qquad\qquad i = 1, n. \qquad\qquad (2)$$

Thus, since the system of equations associated to a particular node N is in the form

$$f_i \; (\mathbf{kn, input, output}) = 0, \qquad\qquad\qquad i = 1, n_{eq\text{-}N},$$

where **kn**, **input** and **output** are the vectors whose components are the variables contained in the respective slots of N, and $n_{eq\text{-}N}$ is the number of equations associated to N, then it can be linearized in the form

$$\mathbf{F}_{kn} \, \Delta_{kn} + \mathbf{F}_{input} \, \Delta_{input} + \mathbf{F}_{output} \, \Delta_{output} = 0, \qquad\qquad (3)$$

where the **F**'s are the Jacobian of the f_i's with respect to the vector in subscript and the Δ's are the errors of the vectors in subscript, i.e., the difference between their expected values and their actual ones. From (3) it can be obtained that

$$\Delta_{output} = - \, \mathbf{F}^{-1}_{output} \, (\mathbf{F}_{kn} \, \Delta_{kn} + \mathbf{F}_{input} \, \Delta_{input}). \qquad\qquad (4)$$

Since **input** is computed by the predecessors of N starting from **kn**, the variables in Δ_{input} are neither mutually independent nor independent from those in Δ_{kn}. Hence, (1) and (2) cannot be used, unless we relate Δ_{input} directly with Δ_{kn}. This may be done associating a vector $\mathbf{w}_v$ to each computed variable v. Each $\mathbf{w}_v$ contains n_{kn} components, representing the value of the partial derivatives of v with respect to every variable in Kn. These derivatives are evaluated in the point corresponding to the expected values of each variable. In order to obtain the $\mathbf{w}_v$'s for the variables computed by the node N, from the $\mathbf{w}_v$'s for the variables computed by its predecessors, it is sufficient to substitute

$$\Delta_{input} = \mathbf{W}_{input} \, \Delta_{kn} \qquad\qquad\qquad\qquad (5)$$

in (4), obtaining:

$$\Delta_{output} = - \, \mathbf{F}^{-1}_{output} \, (\mathbf{F}_{kn} + \mathbf{F}_{input} \, \mathbf{W}_{input}) \, \Delta_{kn},$$

where $\mathbf{W}_{input}$ is defined as the matrix built putting the $\mathbf{w}_v$ associated to each input in each row. Hence, $\mathbf{W}_{output}$ (defined analogously to $\mathbf{W}_{input}$) is given by:

$$\mathbf{W}_{output} = - \, \mathbf{F}^{-1}_{output} \, (\mathbf{F}_{kn} + \mathbf{F}_{input} \, \mathbf{W}_{input}).$$

Since Δ_{output} is represented now as linear combination of the independent variables in Δ_{kn}, the best estimate of the variance of the output errors is given by applying (2)

$$\sigma^2_{output} = \mathbf{W}^2_{output} \, \sigma^2_{kn},$$

where W^2_{output} is the matrix obtained from W_{output}, squaring each of its element. However, as it will be clear in the next section, only the w_v's associated to the output variables are actually computed. Indeed this is the only information needed for detecting discrepancies in the checker-nodes.

3.4. How to detect an inconsistency and the relative conflict set (steps 7-8-9)

As already described, a checker-node N denotes an equation of the following form:

f (**kn**, **input**) = 0,

where **kn** and **input** are the vectors whose components are the variables contained in the respective slots of N. Evaluating the function f in the point denoted by the expected values of **kn** and **input**, an error ε is obtained. Using the previous assumptions about the errors in Kn, ε can be expressed as follows:

$$\varepsilon = F_{kn} \Delta_{kn} + F_{input} \Delta_{input} = 0, \tag{6}$$

where the F's and the Δ's are defined as above. Substituting (5) in (6), it is possible to express ε as a linear combination of Δ_{kn},

$$\varepsilon = (F_{kn} + F_{input} W_{input}) \Delta_{kn} = 0.$$

Hence, defining:

$$W_\varepsilon = F_{kn} + F_{input} W_{input},$$

the best estimate of the variance of ε is given by

$$\sigma^2_\varepsilon = W^2_\varepsilon \sigma^2_{kn},$$

where W^2_ε is the matrix obtained from W_ε, squaring each of its element.

At this point, in order to decide whether the obtained value of ε is consistent with the assumption that it should be equal to zero, it is sufficient to compare the ratio between ε and σ_ε with the characteristic values of a normalized gaussian distribution. For instance, if the maximum accepted probability for false negative cases is 0.05, then the absolute value of this ratio must be less than 1.96.

When a discrepancy is discovered by a given checker-node, the set of components involved in the determination of the discrepancy (i.e., the conflict set) have to be collected. Actually, a conflict is defined as a set of component modes, but here we can unambiguously talk of components since in a candidate each component is associated with one and only one mode. This is achieved by traversing the lattice starting from the checker-node which discovers the discrepancy, back to the root nodes: all the components associated to the computer-nodes found along the path are included in the conflict. Thus, if the checker-node of Figure 3 labelled with component pipe8 discovers a discrepancy, then at least one component among pipe9, pipe8 and pump9 is faulty or one measure among P_{15}, P_{16} and P_{18} is incorrect.

4. Conclusions and future work

The distinctive feature of the approach to diagnosis we have presented in this paper is the integration of techniques well known in the field of numerical analysis and statistics (e.g., solution of non-linear systems and error propagation) with dependency-recording. The latter is a powerful technique adopted by model-based diagnostic algorithms for determining the sources of the observed symptoms, only exploiting the model of the physical system to be diagnosed. The need for this integration arises from the difficulty experimented when applying the most popular model-based diagnostic algorithms (e.g., GDE) to the application domains in which we are interested in, namely, hydraulics and thermodynamics. Our approach may be easily implemented if some simplifying assumptions may be made. These assumptions seem realistic for practical cases.

Future work will consist in applying this algorithm to real size industrial cases. We expect that this activity will better evidence possible limitations of the design and possible areas of improvement. However, we believe that such improvements mainly concerned with optimization of the computation of the partial ordering when the system of equations is over-constrained and with the choice of the best algorithm for solving a given set of numerical equations.

Acknowledgments

The work described in this paper has been funded by the Automatica Research Centre (CRA) of the Italian Electricity Board (ENEL).

References

[de Kleer and Sussman, 1980] de Kleer, J. and Sussman, G.J. Propagation of constraints applied to circuit synthesis. In *Circuit theory and applications*, 8, pages 127-144, 1980.

[de Kleer, 1986] de Kleer, J. An assumption-based truth maintenance system. In *Artificial Intelligence*, 28, pages 127-162, 1986.

[de Kleer and Williams, 1987] de Kleer, J. and Williams, B.C. Diagnosing multiple faults. In *Artificial Intelligence*, 32, pages 97-130, 1987.

[de Kleer and Williams, 1989] de Kleer, J. and Williams, B.C. Diagnosis with behavioral modes. In *Proc. of the 11th International Conference in Artificial Intelligence*, pages 1324-1330, 1989.

[Glass and Wong, 1988] Glass, B.J. and Wong, C.M. A knowledge-based approach to identification and adaptation in dynamic systems control. *Proc. of the 27th IEEE Conference on decision and Control*, Austin, TX., pages 881-886, 1988.

[Hamscher, 1988] Hamscher, W.C. Model-based troubleshooting of digital systems. *Technical Report 1074*, MIT Artificial Intelligence Lab., August 1988.

[Iwasaki ans Simon, 1986] Iwasaki, Y. and Simon, H.A. Causality in device behaviour. *Artificial Intelligence*, 29, pages 3-32, 1986.

[Struss and Dressler, 1989] Struss, P. and Dressler, O. "Physical negation" - Integrating fault models into the General Diagnostic Engine. In *Proc. of the 11th International Conference in Artificial Intelligence*, pages 1318-1323, 1989.

[Sussman and Steele, 1980] Sussman, G.J. and Steele, G.L. CONSTRAINTS - A language for expressing almost-hierarchical descriptions. *Artificial Intelligence*, 14(1), 1980.

Knowledge   Acquisition

VERSION-SPACE INDUCTION WITH MULTIPLE CONCEPT LANGUAGES

Claudio Carpineto

Fondazione Ugo Bordoni, Rome

Abstract

The version space approach suffers from two main problems, i. e. inability of inducing concepts consistent with data due to use of a restricted hypothesis space and lack of computational efficiency. In this paper we investigate the use of *multiple* concept languages in a version space approach. We define a graph of languages ordered by the size of their associated concept sets, and provide a procedure for efficiently inducing version spaces while shifting from small to larger concept languages. We show how this framework can help overcome the two above-mentioned limitations. Also, compared to other work on language shift, our approach suggests an alternative strategy for searching the space of new concepts, which is *not* based on constructive operators.

1 Introduction

The candidate elimination (CE) algorithm [Mitc82] is the best known exemplar of a class of algorithms for incrementally inducing concepts from examples and counter-examples, based on the partial order defined by generality over the concept space. The CE algorithm represents and updates the set of all concepts that are consistent with data (i.e. the version space) by maintaining two sets, the set S containing the maximally specific concepts and the set G containing the maximally general concepts. The procedure to update the version space is as follows. A positive example prunes concepts in G which do not cover it and causes all concepts in S which do not cover the example to be generalized just enough to cover it. A negative example prunes concepts in S that cover it and causes all concepts in G that cover the example to be specialized just enough to exclude it. As more examples are seen, the version space shrinks; it may eventually reduce to the target concept provided that the concept description language is consistent with the data.

This framework has been later improved along several directions. The first is that of incorporating the domain knowledge available to the system in the algorithm; this has resulted in feeding the CE algorithm with analytically-generalized positive examples [Hirs89] and analytically-generalized negative examples [Carp91]. Another research direction is to relax the assumption about the consistency of the concept space with data. In fact, like many other learning algorithms, the CE algorithm uses a restricted concept language to incorporate bias and focus the search on a smaller number of hypotheses. The drawback is that the target concept may be contained in the set of concepts that are inexpressible in the given language, thus being unlearnable. In this case the sets S and G become empty: to restore consistency the bias must be weakened adding new concepts to the concept language [Utgo86]. Thirdly, the CE algorithm suffers from lack of computational efficiency, in that the size of S and G can be exponential in the number of examples and the number of values describing the examples [Haus88]. Changes to the basic algorithm have been proposed that improve efficiency for some concept language [Smit90].

In this paper we investigate the use of *multiple* concept languages in a version space approach. By organizing the concept languages into a graph corresponding to the relation *larger-than* implicitly defined over the sets of concepts covered by each language, we have a framework that allows us to shift from small to larger concept languages in a controlled manner. This provides a powerful basis to handle inconsistency. The idea is to start out with the smallest concept languages and, once the version spaces induced over them have become inconsistent with the data, to move along the graph to the maximally small concept languages that restore consistency. The main focus of the paper is to define a set of languages and a method for inducing the new version spaces after any language shift efficiently. Since this framework supports version-space induction over a set of concept languages, it can also be suitable to improve the efficiency of a version space approach in which the concept language is decomposable into a set of smaller concept languages. This is also discussed in the paper.

The rest of the paper is organized as follows. In the next section we define a graph of conjunctive concept languages and describe the learning problem with respect to it. Then we present the learning method. Finally we compare this work to other approaches to *shift of bias* , pointing out the differences in the search strategies used to find new concepts to add to the concept language.

2 Learning with multiple independent concept languages

We first introduce the notions that characterize our learning problem. In the following concepts are viewed as sets of instances and languages as sets of concepts.

A concept a is *more general than* a concept b if the set of instances covered by a is a proper superset of the set of instances covered by b.

A language L_1 is *larger than* a language L_2 if the set of concepts expressible in L_1 is a proper superset of the set of concepts expressible in L_2.

Two concept languages L_1 and L_2 are *independent* if for every concept c_1 in L_1 and every concept c_2 in L_2 there is an instance that belongs to both L_1 and L_2. For example, if we consider the domain of playing cards, the concept language L_1 = {anysuit, black, red, ♣, ♠, ♥, ♦} and the concept language L_2 = {anyrank, face, numbered, J, Q, K, 1, 2, 3, 4, 5, 6, 7, 8, 9, 10} are independent, for membership in any of the concepts from L_1 does not imply or deny membership in any of the concepts in L_2 (the relation more-general-than over the concepts present in each language is shown in fig1). This definition implies that for every concept c_1 in L_1 and every concept c_2 in L_2 the intersection of c_1 and c_2 is neither empty nor equal to either concept. Two independent concept languages are unordered with respect to the larger-than relation.

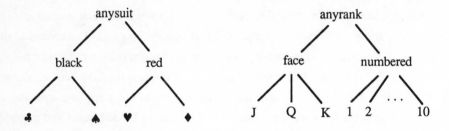

Fig. 1. Two independent concept languages in the playing cards domain.

The *product* $L_{1,2}$ of two independent languages L_1 and L_2 is the set of concepts formed from the conjunctions of concepts from L_1 and L_2 (examples of product concepts are 'anyrank-anysuit', 'anyrank-black', etc). The number of concepts in the product language is therefore the product of the number of concepts in its factors. Also, a concept $c_{c1',c2'}$ in the language $L_{1,2}$ is more general than (>) another concept $c_{c1'',c2''}$ if and only if $c_1' > c_1''$ and $c_2' > c_2''$.

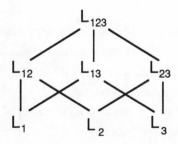

Fig. 2. The graph of product languages with three factor languages.

With n initial independent languages it is possible to generate $\Sigma_{k=1,n}$ n! / (n - k)! k! = 2^n product languages (see fig. 2). Moreover, if each factor language contains the concept 'any', the relation larger than over this set of languages can be immediately established, for each product language is larger than any of its factor languages.

The learning problem can be stated as follows.

Given
  A set of multiple independent concept languages
  A set of positive instances.
  A set of negative instances.

Incrementally Find
  The version spaces in the set of languages that are consistent with data and that contain the smallest number of factors.

3   The learning method

In this approach concept learning and language shift are interleaved. We process one instance at a time, using a standard version space approach to induce consistent concepts over *each* language of the current set (initially, the n independent concept languages). During this inductive phase some concept languages may become inconsistent with the data. When every member of the current set of languages has become inconsistent with data, the language shifting algorithm is invoked. It iteratively selects the set of maximally small concept languages that are larger than the current ones (i.e. the two-factored languages, the three-factored languages, etc.) and computes the new version spaces in these languages. It halts when it finds a consistent set of concept languages (i.e. a set in which there is at least one consistent concept language); then it returns control to the inductive algorithm to process additional examples.The whole process is iterated as long as the set of current languages can be further specialised (i.e. until the n-factored language has been generated).

The core of the method is the algorithm to find the new consistent version spaces in the product languages. The difficulty is that the algorithm for inducing concepts over a language (the inductive algorithm) is usually distinct from the algorithm for adding new terms to the language itself (the constructive algorithm). In general, the inductive algorithm has to be run again over the instance set after any change made by the constructive algorithm ([Utgo86], [Math89], [Paga89], [Wogu89]). In this case, however, in defining the procedure to induce the new consistent concepts after any language shift, we take advantage of the features of the particular inductive learning algorithm considered (i.e. the CE algorithm) and of the properties of language "multiplication". The two key facts are that the CE algorithm makes an explicit use of of concept ordering and that concepts in any product language preserve the order of concepts in its factors. This makes it possible to modify the basic CE algorithm with the aim of computing the set of consistent concepts in a product language as a function of some appropriate concept sets induced in its factors.

The concept sets computed in each factor language which will be utilized during language shift are the following. First, for each language we compute the set S*. S* contains the most specific concepts in the language that cover *all* positive examples, regardless of whether or not they include any negative examples. Second, for each language *and each negative example*, we compute the set G*. G* contains the most general concepts in the language that do not cover the negative example, regardless of whether or not they include all positive examples.

These operations can be better illustrated with an example. Let us consider again the playing cards domain and suppose that we begin with the two independent concept languages introduced above - rank (L_1) and suit (L_2). Let us suppose the system is given one positive example - the Jack of spades - and two negative examples - the Jack of hearts and the Two of spades. We compute the two corresponding version spaces (one for each language), the sets S* (one for each language), and the sets G* (one for each language and for each negative example) in parallel. In particular, the sets S* and G* can be immediately determined, given the ordering over each language's members. The inductive phase is pictured in fig.3 (f stands for face, b for black, etc).

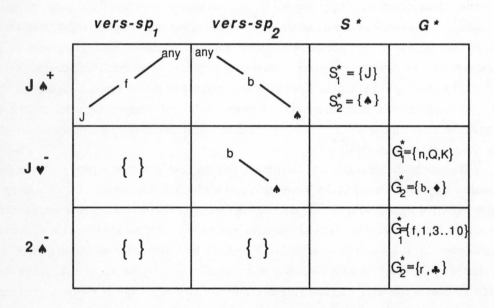

Fig. 3. Concept sets computed during the inductive phase.

The three instances cause both of the version spaces to reduce to the empty set. The next step is therefore to shift to the set of maximally small concept languages that are larger than L_1 and L_2 (in this case the product L_{12}) and check to see if it contains any concepts consistent with data. The problem of finding the version space in the language L_{12} can be subdivided into the two tasks of finding the lower boundary set S_{12} (i.e. the set of the most specific concepts in L_{12} that are consistent with data) and the upper boundary set G_{12} (i.e. the set of the most general concepts in L_{12} that are consistent with data).

Computation of S_{12}

Because a product concept contains an instance if and only if all of its factor concepts contain the instance, the intersection of S_1^* and S_2^* returns the most specific factor concepts that include all positive instances.By discarding those that also cover negative examples, we get just the set S_{12}. If the set becomes empty, then the product language is also inconsistent with the data. More specific concepts, in fact, cannot be consistent because they would rule out some positive example. More general concepts cannot be consistent either, for they would cover some negative examples. In our example, as there is only one positive example, the result is trivial :
$S_{12} = \{J\spadesuit\}$.

Computation of G_{12}

Rather than generating and testing for consistency all the product concepts more general than the members of S_{12}, the set G_{12} is computed using the sets G^*. As for each negative example there must be at least one factor concept in each product concept present in G which does not cover the negative example, the idea is to seek the maximally general factor concepts that do not cover the negative example. The concepts in the sets G^* can be used as upper bounds to find such maximally general factor concepts.

The algorithm is as follows. It begins by dropping from the sets G^* the concepts that can only generate factor concepts that are more specific than those contained in S_{12}. Then, it finds all the conjunctions of concepts in the reduced sets G^* such that (a) each negative instance is ruled out by at least one concept and (b) there are no more-general conjunctions. Step (a) requires computing the conjunction of each factor concept in each G^* (it will rule out some negative example) with all the combinations of factor concepts in the other G^*'s which rule out the remaining negative examples. Step (b) requires generalizing those factor concepts present in the product concepts found at the end of step (a) which do not contribute to rule out any negative example. The resulting set of conjunctions, if any is found, coincides with the set G_{12}, in that there cannot be more general product concepts consistent with data. However, it may not be possible to find a consistent concept conjoining the members of the G^*'s. In this case we are forced to specialise the members of the G*'s to the extent required so that they rule out more negative instances, and to iterate the procedure (in the limit, we will get the set S_{12}).

In our example there are just two factors and only two negative instances. The initial sets G* are:

J ♥ ⁻	{n, Q, K}	{b, ♦ }
2 ♠ ⁻	{f, 1, 3,.., 10}	{r, ♣ }

The simplification with the set S_{12} returns:

J ♥ ⁻	{ }	{b}
2 ♠ ⁻	{f}	{♣}

Step (a) in this case reduces to the *union of* G_1* relative to instance 1 intersected with G_2* relative to instance 2 *and* G_1* relative to instance 2 intersected with G_2* relative to instance 1. The result ({fb}) does not need be generalized (step (b)) for both 'f' and 'b' contribute to rule out (at least) one negative example. Also, in this case, the specialisation procedure is not needed because we have been able to find a consistent conjunction: G_{12}={fb}. The overall version space in the language L_{12} is shown in fig.4. It is worth noting that because the two initial concept languages can be represented as trees, the sets S of their version spaces, as well as of the version space of their product, will never contain more than one element [Bund85]. Even in this case, however, Haussler [Haus88] has shown that the size of the sets G can still be exponential. .

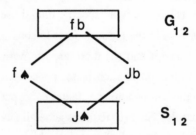

Fig.4. The version space in the product language after the constructive phase.

4 Discussion

We have implicitly assumed that the initial independent concept languages can be processed by a version space approach. The two standard requirements are that the test of whether concepts cover instances and whether one concept definition is more general than another must be tractable. From this point of view, assessing the more-general-than relation over the product concepts does not add any further complexity to that of assessing the same relation over the factor concepts.

Another assumption we have made is that the initial concept languages be independent. It is intended to guarantee that their product languages will contain a number of concepts significatively larger (actually their product) [1]. To illustrate this, consider the concept language L_B we introduced earlier along with the concept language $L_C = \{$anyrank, odd, even, 1, 3, 5, 7, 9, J, K, 2, 4, 6, 8, 10, Q$\}$. These two languages are not independent. For instance, the intersection of the concept "2" in L_B and the concept "odd" in L_C is empty. In general, the product of two concept languages that are not independent will contain a much smaller number of concepts than the product of the number of concepts in the factors. For instance, any intersection of concepts equal to or more specific than "2" and "odd" will also be empty. In the limit, if the intersection of the most general concepts contained in the factor languages is empty, the product language contains no concepts at all.

As mentioned earlier, this work can also be seen as an instance of a general divide-and-conquer strategy to improve the efficiency of a standard version space approach in which the concept description language is factorizable. This is the case, for instance, with a conjunctive concept language defined on a tree-structured attribute-based instance space in which each attribute contains the value 'any' (the description language used in our playing cards example can also be viewed in this way). By testing the concepts individually, before they grow in conjunctions, many inconsistent product concepts are not even generated[2]. Furthermore there is little loss of information, for we are guaranteed to find at least a subset of all n-factored concepts that are consistent with data. The actual gain in efficiency depends on the number of instances that each intermediate language is able to account for before it becomes inconsistent. In the best case all the induction is done within the smallest languages,and language shift to larger languages is not necessary. In the worst case no consistent concepts are induced in the smaller languages, so that all the induction is eventually done within the full concept language. If language shift occurs, the cost of recomputing the version space(s) in the new language(s)

---

[1] Factorization with independent concept languages has also been used by [Subr86] with the aim of improving efficiency of experiment generation in a version space approach. For that purpose, however, the requirement about language independency is much stronger.

[2] The advantage of processing two factor languages instead of their product is striking. If each factor language has r concepts, the size of the hypothesis spaces is 2r and r^2 respectively.

must be added to the standard cost of inducing the version space(s) in the current language(s). There is therefore a trade-off between using few concept languages and using many concept languages in a given range. The fewer the concept languages, the less the amount of computation devoted to language shift. The more the concept languages, the more likely it is that a small amount of induction will be done within the largest concept languages, which are the least convenient. Experimentation might help investigate this kind of trade-off .

5. Search strategies for language shift

Addressing the problem of introducing new concepts to overcome the limitations of a restricted concept language has led to the use of a set of restricted concept languages to constrain the search for new useful concepts. This is a significant departure from the search strategy usually employed in most approaches to language shift. Regardless of the specific goal pursued - many systems deal with improvement of some quality measures of the learned descriptions rather than with their correctness - "the problem of new terms" [Diet82] or "constructive induction" [Mich83] is in general tackled by defining a set of appropriate *constructive operators* and carrying out a depth-first search through the space of the remaining concepts to find useful (e.g., consistent, more concise, more accurate) extensions to be added to the given language. Furthermore, since the number of admissible extensions is generally intractably large, most of the approaches to constructive induction rely on various heuristics to reduce the number of candidate additional concepts and/or to cut down the search (e.g. [Math89], [Paga89], [Wogu89]).

By contrast, we compute and keep all the admissible language extensions that restore consistency with data, rather than considering one or few plausible language extensions at a time. Just as the relation *more general than* that is implicitly defined over the terms of a concept language may allow efficient representation and updating of all consistent concepts [Mitc82], so too the relation *larger than* that is implicitly defined over a set of languages may provide the framework to efficiently organize the small-to-large breadth-first search of useful languages. These considerations suggest that an alternative abstract model for language shift can be formulated, in which the search for new concepts, rather than being based on the use of constructive operators, is driven by the ordering of the candidate concept languages (work in preparation).

6. Conclusion

We have presented a framework for efficiently inducing version spaces over a set of partially-ordered concept languages. The utility of this framework is twofold: inducing consistent version spaces if the initial concept language is inconsistent with data, and improving the efficiency of version-space induction if the initial concept language is consistent with data. One promising insight gained from this work is that the problem of adding new terms to a given restricted concept language can be cast as a search through a space of ordered concept languages.

Acknowledgements

This work was carried out within the framework of the agreement between the Italian PT Administration and the Fondazione Ugo Bordoni. Most of the work was done while at the Computing Science Department of the University of Aberdeen, partially supported by CEC SS project SC1.0048.C(H). I would like to thank Derek Sleeman and Pete Edwards for their support and for useful discussions on this topic.

References

[Bund85]   Bundy, A., Silver, B., Plummer, D. (1985). An analytical comparison of some rule-learning problems. *Artificial Intelligence*, 27.

[Carp91]   Carpineto, C. (1991). Analytical negative generalization and empirical negative generalization are not cumulative: a case study. In *Proceedings of EWSL-91, Lecture Notes on Artificial Intelligence*, Springer-Verlag.

[Diet82]   Dietterich, T.G., London B., Clarkson K., Dromey R.G. (1982). Learning and inductive inference. In Cohen & Feigenbaum (Eds.) *The Handbook of Artificial Intelligence*, Morgan Kaufmann.

[Haus88]   Haussler, D. (1988). Quantifying inductive bias: Artificial Intelligence learning algorithms and Valiant's learning framework. *Artificial Intelligence*, 36.

[Hirs89]   Hirsh, H. (1989). Combining Empirical and Analytical Learning with Version Spaces. In *Proceedings of the sixth international workshop on Machine Learning*. Syracuse, Morgan Kaufmann.

[Math89]   Matheus, C.J., Rendell, L.A. (1989). Constructive induction on decision trees. In *Proceedings of the 11th IJCAI*, Detroit, Morgan Kaufmann.

[Mich83]   Michalski, R.S. (1983). A theory and methodology of inductive learning. *Artificial Intelligence*, 20, 111-161

[Mitc82]   Mitchell, T.M. (1982). Generalization as Search. *Artificial Intelligence*, 18, 203-226.

[Paga89]   Pagallo, G.(1989). Learning DNF by Decision Trees. In *Proceedings of the 11th IJCAI*, Detroit, Morgan Kaufmann.

[Smit90]   Smith, Rosenbloom, P, (1990). Incremental Non-Backtracking Focusing: A Poliniomally Bounded Generalization Algorithm for Version Spaces. In *Proceedings of the eighth AAAI*, Boston, Morgan Kaufmann.

[Subr86]   Subramanian, D., Feigenbaum, J. (1986). Factorization in Experiment Generation. In *Proceedings of the fifth AAAI*, Philadelphia, Morgan Kaufmann.

[Utgo86]   Utgoff, P.E. (1986). Shift of bias for inductive concept learning. In R. Michalski et al. (Eds), *Machine Learning II*. Morgan Kaufmann, Palo Alto, California.

[Wogu89]   Wogulis, J., Langley, P. (1989). Improving efficiency by learning intermediate concepts. In *Proceedings of the 11th IJCAI*, Detroit, Morgan Kaufmann.

Knowledge Compilation to
Speed Up Numerical Optimization

Giuseppe Cerbone

Thomas G. Dietterich

Computer Science Dept.

Oregon State University

Corvallis, OR 97331-3202 (USA)

cerbone@cs.orst.edu

tgd@cs.orst.edu

Abstract

Many important application problems can be formalized as constrained non-linear optimization tasks. However, numerical methods for solving such problems are brittle and do not scale well. This paper describes a method to speed up and increase the reliability of numerical optimization by (a) optimizing the computation of the objective function, and (b) splitting the objective function into special cases that possess differentiable closed forms. This allows us to replace a single inefficient non-gradient-based optimization by a set of efficient numerical gradient-directed optimizations that can be performed in parallel. In the domain of 2-dimensional structural design, this procedure yields a 95% speedup over traditional optimization methods and decreases the dependence of the numerical methods on having a good starting point.

1   INTRODUCTION

Numerical optimization techniques are applied to a variety of engineering problems. For example, we are studying the domain of two-dimensional (2-D) structural design. In this task, the goal is to design a structure of minimum weight that bears a set of loads. In principle, optimal solutions to problems of this kind can be found by numerical optimization techniques. However, in practice [7] these techniques are slow, and the solutions depend on the choice of starting points. Hence, their applicability to real-world problems is severely restricted. To overcome these limitations, we propose to augment numerical optimization with a symbolic compilation stage to produce objective functions that are faster to evaluate and that depend less on the choice of the starting point. These goals are accomplished by successive specializations of the objective function that, in the end, reduce it to a

Table 1: The 2-D Design Task.

Given:	A 2-dimensional region R
	A set of stable points (supports)
	A set of external loads
	A topology specifying the connection points, the number of members, and the interconnections.
Find:	The positions of all intermediate connection points such that the structure has minimum weight and is stable with respect to all external loads.

collection of independent functions that are fast to evaluate, that can be differentiated symbolically, and that represent smaller regions of the overall search space.

Our optimization schema differs from techniques currently used in the machine learning community and relies on the specialization of the problem via incorporation of constraints prior to optimization. Braudaway [1] designed a system along the same principle. However, to our knowledge, very little work has been done in using symbolic techniques and domain knowledge to speed up numerical optimization tasks. In contrast, the current trend in the machine learning community focuses on methods, such as Explanation Based Learning (EBL) [3], capable of generating rules. Minton [5] shows how these methods can result in a slow-down of the overall process. In addition, EBL methods have had little success in the task of optimizing numerical procedures. We conjecture that one of the reasons is the dependence of EBL methods on the trace of the problem solver which, for optimization algorithms, gives little information on the structure of the problem. Therefore, in mathematical domains, EBL-derived rules are too detailed to produce any appreciable speedup.

The remainder of the paper is organized as follows. Section 2 presents the 2-D structural design task. This is followed in Section 3 by an overview of numerical optimization techniques, their limitations, and the proposed method which is applied to a collection of randomly generated examples. The results of the experiments are reported in Section 4. Finally, Section 5 summarizes the benefits and limitations of our method and outlines future work.

2   TASK DESCRIPTION

Table 1 describes the 2-D structural design task that we are attacking, and Figure 1 shows an example problem in which L is the load and S1 and S2 are two supports. The goal of the design process in this example is to find a location for point C that minimizes the weight of the structure.

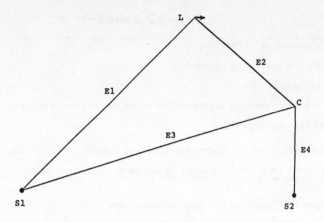

Figure 1: A 2-D structural design problem.

The position shown in the figure gives the minimum-weight solution. Members E1 and E3 are in tension (they are being "stretched"), while members E2 and E4 are in compression.

The task shown in Table 1 is actually only one step in the larger problem of designing good structures. In general, structural design proceeds in three steps [6, 7]. First, the problem solver chooses the topology. Then, the second step is to determine the locations of the connection points (and hence the lengths, locations, and internal forces) so as to minimize the weight of the structure. This is usually accomplished by numerical non-linear optimization techniques and it is the focus of this paper. The third and final step in the process optimizes the shape and the cross-sectional areas of the members.

In addition to focusing only on the second step, we have introduced several simplifying assumptions to provide a tractable testbed for developing and testing knowledge compilation methods. Specifically, we assume that structural members are joined by frictionless pins, only *statically determinate* structures are considered, the cross section of compressive members is square, compressive and tensile members of any length and cross sectional area are available, and supports have no freedom of movement. A statically determinate structure contains no redundant members, and hence, the geometrical layout of the structure completely determines the forces acting in each member.

Given these assumptions, the weight of a candidate solution is usually calculated by a three-step process. The first step is to apply the *method of joints* as outlined in Wang and Salmon [8] to determine the internal forces operating in each member. Once this is known, the second step is to classify each member as compressive or tensile, which is important, because compressive and tensile members have different densities. The third step is to determine the cross-sectional area of each member. The load that a member can bear is assumed to be linearly proportional to its cross-sectional area, hence the weight of each member can be computed as the product of the density of the appropriate material, the length of the member, and the cross-sectional area of the member. The last two steps can be collapsed into a single parameter k: the ratio of the density per-unit-of-force-borne for compressive members to the density per-unit-of-force-borne for tensile members. With this simplification, instead of minimizing the weight, we can minimize the following quantity:

$$V = Volume = \sum_{\substack{tensile \\ members}} \|F_i\| \, l_i + k \sum_{\substack{compressive \\ members}} \|F_i\| \, l_i,$$

where F_i is the force in member i, and l_i is the length of member i. This is the initial objective function for the work described in this paper.

3 OPTIMIZATION

Classical optimization textbooks [7] present a comprehensive survey of optimization methods and of various techniques to search for an optimal solution. Typical domain independent non-linear optimization methods are iterative. Starting at some initial point, they search the space by taking a step of some chosen length in some chosen direction away from the current point. Most optimization algorithms differ primarily in the criteria used to choose the direction along which to optimize. Some optimization methods (e.g., Powell's method [7]) choose the direction and step size using only evaluations of the objective function. Other methods, such as gradient descent and its variations [7], require computation of the partial derivatives of the objective function to choose the new direction of optimization. The primary computational expense of numerical optimization methods is the repeated evaluation of the objective function. An advantage of gradient descent methods is that they need to evaluate the objective function less often, because they are able to take larger, more effective steps. Of course, they incur the additional cost of repeatedly evaluating the partial derivatives of the objective function. Hence, they produce substantial savings only when the reduction in the number of function evaluations offsets the cost of evaluating the derivatives.

In engineering design, the objective function is typically very expensive to evaluate since it reflects many of the specifications for the design problem. Furthermore, it is often the case that the objective function lacks a differentiable closed-form. For example, in our objective function from the previous section, the fact that the constant k is applied only to compressive members makes it impossible to obtain a differentiable closed-form. The signs of the internal forces must be computed before it is possible to determine which members are compressive.

Table 2: Compiled objective function for Figure 1.

$$Volume = \left(2.44\ 10^5 y^3 - 4.08\ 10^{16} + 1.14\ 10^{13} x - 5.66\ 10^9 x^2 + 8.16\ 10^5 x^3 + \right.$$
$$3.28\ 10^{13} y - 3.26\ 10^9 xy + 2.44\ 10^5 x^2 y + 8.16\ 10^5 xy^2 - 6.70\ 10^9 y^2 \left.\right) \Big/$$
$$\left(1.28\ 10^1 xy + 2.56\ 10^4 y - 2.56\ 10^4 x + 6.40\ y^2 - 2.56\ 10^7\right)$$

Given that the speed of numerical optimization is determined by the cost and frequency of evaluating the objective function, we have developed an approach to speed up the process by reducing (a) the cost of each evaluation and (b) the number of evaluations. The approach involves a four-step "compilation" stage prior to numerical optimization.

First, the given topology is incorporated into the objective function. This allows us to specify in symbolic form the system of linear equations expressing the method of joints. We then apply procedures to simplify the system of equations and to obtain a closed-form expression for the internal forces.

The second step is to plug in the givens of the problem and to partially evaluate the resulting mixed symbolic/numeric expression. For our examples, the givens of the problems are the loads and the supports; however, one may wish to analyze a structure subject to different inputs such as various loading conditions or support locations. In such cases, one should leave those values in symbolic form and substitute their numerical values at run-time.

The third step is to split the objective function into several special-case objective functions according to an abstraction called the *stress state*. The *stress state* of a structure is a vector indicating, for each member, whether it is compressive (-1) or tensile ($+1$). It can be considered a generalization of *load path* [4]. Within each special case, the objective function now has a closed-form derivative, because it is now known which forces should be multiplied by k. This allows us to employ gradient descent methods to optimize each of these special cases. Table 2 shows the special-case objective function for the stress state $(+1, -1, +1, -1)$.

The final step of compilation is to compute linear and quadratic approximations of the gradient by truncating its Taylor expansion.

The result of these four compilation steps is a collection of special-case objective functions that can be evaluated in parallel to determine which one gives the lightest-weight solution.

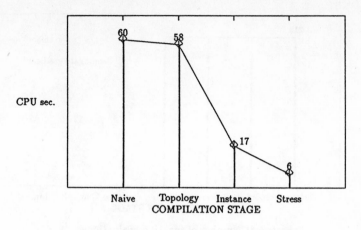

Figure 2: CPU time per function evaluation.

4 EXPERIMENTS

To test the efficacy of this approach, we have solved a series of design problems using an implementation based on Mathematica [9], and we have measured the impact of the compilation stages on the evaluation of the objective function, on the optimization task, and on the reliability of the optimization method. The measurements presented are averages over five randomly generated designs and, for each design, over 25 randomly generated starting points.

Cost of the Objective Function. The objective function of each design problem was evaluated in four different ways and, for each of them, we averaged the CPU[1] time over the different designs and starting points. The volume was first computed using the traditional, naive, numerical procedure with the method of joints. We then compiled the designs incorporating, in three successive stages, topological information, givens of the problems, and stress state. Figure 2 shows the time (per 100 runs) to evaluate the objective function at the various compilation stages. The biggest speedups were obtained in compilation steps 2 and 3. For the stress state special cases, we measured the *parallel* CPU time (i.e., the time to optimize only the *best* special-case objective function). This figure shows that the cost of evaluating the objective function is reduced by a factor of 10.

Number of Evaluations. Figure 3 shows the speedup obtained by reducing the number of times the objective function needs to be evaluated. The values connected by solid lines correspond to cases in which we applied Powell's method, which uses no gradient information. The values connected by

---

[1]On a NeXT Cube with a 68030 board.

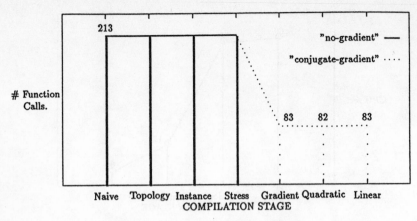

Figure 3: Number of function evaluations.

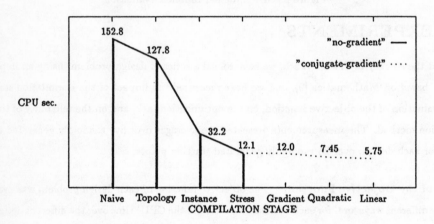

Figure 4: Total CPU time.

dashed lines represent cases in which we applied the conjugate-gradient method (with alternative approximations for the gradient vector). The number of evaluations is reduced by more than a factor of 2.

Total CPU Time. Finally, Figure 4 shows the combined effect of reducing the cost of each objective-function evaluation and of reducing the number of evaluations. In the figure, total (parallel) CPU time is plotted for each compilation stage. Overall CPU time decreases steadily. Note, however, that when we switch to the conjugate-gradient method, there is initially no speedup, because the cost of evaluating the full gradient offsets the decrease in the number of times the objective function must be evaluated. However, additional speedups are obtained by using the quadratic and linear approximations of the gradient. We have found experimentally that there is no appreciable difference between the minima reached using the full gradient vector and the minima computed using quadratic approximations of the partial derivatives. However, the precision of the results obtained with the linear approximation is reduced. Depending on the application, this trade of accuracy for speed may be acceptable. If not, the quadratic approximation should be employed. Another possibility is to employ the linear approximation for the first half of the optimization search, and then switch to the quadratic approximation once the minimum is approached. In other words, the linear approximation can be applied to find a good starting point for performing a more exact search.

Reliability. An optimization method is reliable if it always finds the global minimum regardless of the starting point of the search. Gradient descent methods are reliable only if the objective function is unimodal. However, inspection of plots of the objective function show that even in simple problems, the objective function has multiple "basins". This means that simple gradient-descent methods will be unreliable unless they are started in the right "basin." It is the user's responsibility to provide such a starting point, and this makes numerical optimization methods difficult to use in practice.

Surprisingly, however, further inspection of objective-function plots appear to show that, over each region corresponding to a single stress state, the objective function is unimodal. We conjecture that this is true for most 2-D structural design problems. If this conjecture holds, then starting from *any* point within a stress state our "divide-and-conquer" approach of searching each stress state in parallel will be guaranteed to produce the global optimum. We have tested this conjecture by performing 20 trials of the following procedure. First, a random starting location was chosen from one of the basins of the objective function that did not contain the global minimum. Next, two optimization methods were applied: the non-gradient method and the conjugate gradient method. Finally, our divide-and-conquer method was applied using, for each of the special-case objective functions, a random starting location that exhibited the corresponding stress state. In all cases, our method found the global minimum while the other two methods converged to some other, local minimum.

5 Concluding Remarks

Our overall strategy for speeding up numerical optimization methods relies on successive specializations and simplifications of the objective function. This paper has described two specialization steps: (a) specializing the objective function by incorporating the invariant aspects of the particular problem and (b) splitting the objective function into special cases based on stress states.

In a previous paper [2], we illustrated another source of constraining knowledge that can be incorporated into the objective function. In that paper, inductive learning methods were applied to discover regularities in the solutions found by numerical optimization. These regularities apply to particular classes of problems and include constraints such as $\alpha_1 = \alpha_2$ (i.e., two angles must be equal) and constraints that a member must be tangent to a "forbidden region" (a region into which the structure must not intrude). When regularities of this kind are discovered, they too can be incorporated into the objective function. This often has the effect of reducing the number of independent variables, and hence, the dimensionality of the search space.

The benefits of all of these forms of specialization are great. First, the cost of evaluating the objective function is reduced. Second, the specializations make it possible to obtain differentiable closed forms for the objective function. This allows us to apply gradient-directed optimization methods, which generally require fewer evaluations of the objective function to find the optimum. Third, the specializations create opportunities for parallel execution of the optimization calculations. Existing numerical optimization procedures are inherently serial and contain almost no parallelism.

We are currently attacking the following open problems. First, not all of the 2^m stress states make physical sense. We have developed rules that can exploit this to prune useless stress states. Second, we hope to prove our unimodality conjecture. This would provide a proof of correctness for our divide-and-conquer schema. Finally, we want to tackle the problem of selecting a good topology. Topological optimization is nearly impossible to perform using current numerical methods. However, if we can find reasonable approximations for the special-case objective functions, we believe it will be possible to bound the weight of an optimal design for a given topology without performing the complete optimization process. This would allow us to determine the conditions under which one topology will be lighter than another. Such topology optimization rules would provide a valuable tool for mechanical designers.

Acknowledgements

The authors wish to thank David G. Ullman, Prasad Tadepalli, Igor Rivin, and Jerry Keiper. David Ullman is responsible for suggesting the term "stress state." This work was also presented at the Eighth International Workshop on Machine Learning. This research was supported by NASA Ames Research Center under Grant Number NAG 2-630.

217

References

[1] Wesley Braudaway. Constraint incorporation using constrained reformulation. Tech.Rep. LCSR-TR-100 Computer Science Dept., Rutgers University, April 1988.

[2] Giuseppe Cerbone and Thomas G. Dietterich. Inductive and numerical methods in knowledge compilation. In *Proceedings of the Workshop on Change of Representation and Problem Reformulation*, 1989.

[3] Thomas Ellman. Explanation-based learning: A survey of programs and perspectives. *ACM Computing Surveys*, 21(2):163–222, 1989.

[4] James E. Gordon. *Structures: or, Why things don't fall down*. Plenum Press, New York, 1978.

[5] Steve Minton. Empirical results concerning the utility of explanation-based learning. In *Proceedings AAAI*, 1988.

[6] A.C. Palmer and D.J. Sheppard. Optimizing the shape of pin-jointed structures. In *Proc. of the Institution of Civil Engineers*, pages 363–376, 1970.

[7] Garret N. Vanderplaats. *Numerical Optimization Techniques for engineering design with applications*. New York: McGraw Hill, 1984.

[8] Chu-Kia Wang and Charles G. Salmon. *Introductory Structural Analysis*. Prentice Hall, New Jersey, 1984.

[9] Steven Wolfram. *Mathematica*. Wolfram Research, 1988.

New Perspectives about Default Hierarchies Formation in Learning Classifier Systems

Marco Dorigo

Progetto di Intelligenza Artificiale e Robotica
Dipartimento di Elettronica - Politecnico di Milano
Piazza Leonardo da Vinci 32 - 20133 Milano - Italy
E-mail: dorigo@ipmel1.elet.polimi.it

1 Introduction

In this paper we present some results of research in default hierarchies formation. A default hierarchy is a set of rules that models a set of environmental states in which some default rules cover most of the environmental states while specific ones cover exceptions. It is well known that default hierarchies can be used to categorize environmental states very efficiently. In fact, a default hierarchy implements a quasi-homomorphic model of the world, which usually requires far less rules than a homomorphic one [6] [7]. After a brief introduction to learning classifier systems (LCS), we examine in deep a result [4] widely used to analyze the way default hierarchies behave under the bucket brigade algorithm and we show why it is not correct. A different and more precise analysis is then presented along with simulation results. The second part of the paper will present a different approach to the apportionment of credit problem and an algorithm which inherently creates, when possible, default hierarchies. Again, simulation results are reported to advocate the theoretical study. We show that this approach is different from the notion of message support or message intensity already introduced (e.g., in [6], [1]) and after a brief theoretical analysis we present simulation results in the case of a simple automaton. In this paper a knowledge of basic properties of learning classifier systems is assumed. The novice can refer for example to [3] for an exhaustive introduction.

2 An introduction to learning classifier systems

A learning classifier system is an adaptive system that learns to accomplish a task by means of interaction with an environment. It belongs to the class of *reinforcement learning* systems, i.e. systems in which learning is guided by rewards coming from environment. The system is composed of three main parts

- the performance system (included in it are two conflict resolution modules)
- the apportionment of credit system
- the rule discovery system

The overall learning classifier system resulting from the interaction of these three systems (see Fig.1) is a parallel production system. In LCSs we can observe two different learning processes; in the first the set of rules is given and how to use them is to be learned. In the second, new and possibly useful rules should be created. These two kinds of learning are accomplished by the apportionment of credit algorithm and by the rule discovery algorithm respectively. New rules are learned using past experience and the way to use them is learned using environmental feedback. In this paper we are concerned with learning how to use existing sets of rules. As a consequence, we only briefly outline the performance system and skip the rule discovery system.

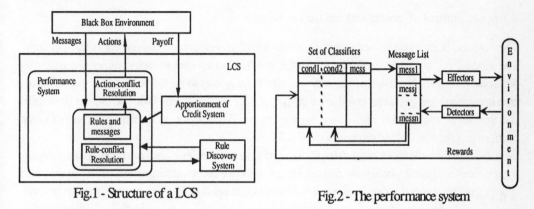

Fig.1 - Structure of a LCS   Fig.2 - The performance system

3 The performance system

The performance system is composed of
- a set of rules, called classifiers
- a list of messages, used to collect messages sent from classifiers and from the environment to other classifiers
- an input and an output interface with the environment (detectors and effectors) to receive/send messages from/to the environment
- a payback mechanism to reward the system when a useful action is performed and to punish it when a wrong action is done.

At time zero a set of classifiers is created (they may be generated randomly or by some algorithm that considers the structure of the problem domain) and the message list is empty. At time 1 environmental messages are appended to the message list, then they are matched against the condition part of classifiers and matched classifiers are set to status active. At time t messages coming from environment and messages sent by classifiers active at time t-1 are appended to the message list. Then they are matched against classifiers in the classifiers set. Matched classifiers are set to active status. The message list is then emptied and the cycle repeated.

The algorithm described would work only if the message list could become infinite in length. In practical systems the message list length has some fixed finite length and therefore some kind of mechanism has to be introduced to decide which classifiers have the right to post messages when the number of messages is bigger than the message list dimensions (this mechanism is implemented in the rule conflict-resolution box, see Fig.1). The need for a rule conflict-resolution system is one of the reasons for the introduction of an apportionment of credit algorithm that redistribute environmental payoff to the rules that caused the performed actions. This allows the performance subsystem to choose which rules to fire according to some measure of their usefulness. Conflict resolution is also used to solve conflicts when effectors propose inconsistent actions (e.g. "go right" and "go left").

4 Apportionment of credit and the bucket brigade

The main task of the credit apportionment algorithm is to classify rules in accordance with their usefulness. The standard way to measure usefulness in classifier systems is to associate to each classifier C a real value Str_C^t (called *strength*). Nevertheless, this is by no means the only way to do it. We could for example associate strength to messages (as proposed in the last part of this paper) or to conditions or even to all of them and then define composition rules to use this information. The solution to the apportionment of credit problem proposed by Holland can be described as follows:

Give each classifier the same initial strength; when an external classifier causes an action on the environment it receives a payoff whose value depends on how good the action performed was with respect to the system goal. This reward is then transmitted backward to internal classifiers that caused the external classifier to fire. The backward transmission mechanism, examined in detail later, causes the strength of the classifiers to change dynamically and to reflect the classifiers relevance to the system performance (with respect to the system goals). Clearly it is not possible to keep track of all the paths of activation followed by the rule chains. In fact, the number of these paths grows exponentially with the path length. A proper algorithm is then necessary to solve the problem using only local, in time and in space, information. Space locality means that changes in a classifier strength are caused only by classifiers directly linked to it (we say that classifiers C_1 and C_2 are linked if the message posted by C_1 matches a condition of C_2). Time locality indicates that the information used at each computational step is coming only from a fixed recent temporal interval. The classical algorithm used to this purpose is the already mentioned bucket brigade algorithm. This algorithm models the classifier system as an economic society, in which each classifier pays an amount of its strength to get the privilege of appending a message to the message list and receives a payment by all the classifiers activated because of the presence in the message list of the message it appended during the preceding time step. In this way payoff flows backward from the environment again to the environment through a chain of classifiers. The net result is that classifiers that participate in chains causing highly rewarded actions tend to increase their strengths.

We present here a formulation of the bucket brigade algorithm

Step 0 • associate an initial - possibly random - strength to each classifier, clear the message list and set all the classifiers to status not-active; then append all the environmental messages

Step 1 • set to status active each classifier which has both conditions matched by messages on the message list and then empty the message list

Step 2 • for each active classifier C compute the quantity Bid_C^t

Step 3 • auction step: choose with a probability functionally related to Bid_C^t the messages to be posted until the message list is full (every message posted memorizes the name of the posting classifier for step 4 purposes)

Step 4 • each classifier that has successfully posted a message pays the quantity Pay_C^t to the classifier that caused its activation; classifiers that have sent messages to the environment receive a reward proportional to the usefulness of the sent message

Step 5 • the status of all classifiers is set to not-active

Step 6 • new environmental messages are read and appended to the message list and the algorithm repeated from step 1

The quantities used in the algorithm are so defined

• $Bid_C^t = f(Str_C^t, \rho_C, Sup_C^t)$

is the quantity offered from classifier C at time t to compete in the auction where Str_C^t is the strength of classifier C at time t, ρ_C is the specificity of classifier C and Sup_C^t is the support of classifier C at time t. Specificity ρ_C is defined as follows

$$\rho_c = \frac{\text{number of non-* positions in C}}{\text{length of classifier C}}$$

• $Pay_C^t = g(Str_C^t, \rho_C)$

is the quantity actually paid by classifier C when allowed to post a message

• R_C^t is the reward classifier C receives at time t

• $Str_C^t = Str_C^{t-1} - Pay_C^t + R_C^t$ is a value intended to be proportional to the classifier C usefulness

• Sup_C^t is a function of the support of messages matching classifier C. Message support is usually considered to be equal to the bid offered by the classifier that posted it. Support measures indirectly how useful a message is, indirectly because the measure uses the classifier strength as a reference.

The form chosen for function f and g can influence the default hierarchies formation process.

5 Default hierarchies

One of the effects of the apportionment of credit algorithm should be to contribute to the formation of default hierarchies, i.e. set of rules that categorizes the set of environmental states into equivalence classes to be treated alike. Default hierarchies have some nice properties. They can be used to build quasi-homomorphic models [7] of the environment which generally require far fewer rules than equivalent homomorphic ones [8]. The difference between the two approaches can be briefly seen as follows: if E is the set of environmental states that the learning system has to learn to categorize, then the system could either try to find a set of rules that partition the whole set E never making mistakes, or build a default hierarchy. With the first approach a homomorphic model of the environment is built, with the second a quasi-homomorphic one. Moreover using default hierarchies the system performance can be improved adding more exceptions and the whole system can learn gracefully, i.e. the performance of the system is not too strongly influenced by the insertion of new rules. An example of default hierarchy is given in Fig.3. In this simple example the two conditions of a rule are constrained to be equal; both the sets of rules implement the logical-OR function on the conditions bits. The first set realizes the function by means of a logical partition of the space state, while the second set achieves the same result using a default hierarchy (i.e., there is a rule, in Fig.3 the first one, called "exception" that fires only in presence of message 00, and a rule, called "default", that fires for every message). It is clear from the example that a default hierarchy requires, in order to categorize the same space, less rules. A default hierarchy, to work correctly, requires a mechanism that, in presence of both an exception and a default rule ready to fire, favours the exception one. Our main interest here is to understand if the proposed approaches to the apportionment of credit problem have the capacity to promote default hierarchies formation, i.e. if the form of the functions f and g actually used by the different approaches give to rules strength values that cause the system to run with the desired performance. We later show that by changing the model to one in which strength is associated to messages, this very same requirement becomes an inherent property of the system.

non-hierarchical set (homomorphic set)	hierarchical set (quasi-homomorphic set)
$00;00 \to 00$	$00;00 \to 00$
$01;01 \to 11$	$**;** \to 11$
$10;10 \to 11$	
$11;11 \to 11$	

Fig.3 - The hierarchical set implements the same state categorisation with fewer rules.

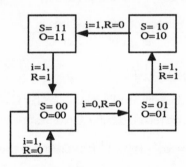

Fig.4 - A finite automaton environment with single-step reward delay (from [4])

6 Default hierarchies formation process

We will examine now the influence that different bidding and paying-out policies (different forms of f and g functions) have on the default hierarchies formation process. In the standard bucket brigade we have $f = g$:

$$Bid_C^t = Pay_C^t = kStr_C^t \rho_C$$

where k is a constant (usually set to some low value between $0.01 \div 0.1$; in our simulations $k = 0.1$)

We can now proceed to analyze the steady-state behaviour of a simple system composed of two classifiers: a default classifier C_d and an exception one C_e. The classical analysis, that we are going to criticize and proposed for example in [5] and in [4], works like this:

Consider a default and an exception rule implementing a default hierarchy. Their strengths will change in time according to the following formulas:

$$Str_d^{t+1} = Str_d^t(1-k\rho_d) + R \qquad (1)$$
$$Str_e^{t+1} = Str_e^t(1-k\rho_e) + R \qquad (2)$$

where d and e suffixes stays for default and exception and R is the mean reward received from a rule.
If we examine the steady-state behaviour of the classifier strength for a single default exception pair we find that

$$Str_d^{ss} = \frac{R}{k\rho_d} \text{ and } Str_e^{ss} = \frac{R}{k\rho_e} \text{ yielding}$$

$$Bid_d^{ss} = Bid_e^{ss} \qquad (3)$$

To see why this analysis is not correct, consider now the following classifier system composed of two rules (this is the simplest possible example of default hierarchy)

0**;1**→111
000;1**→100

and the simple environment as defined in Fig.4 (example from [4]).

The rules implementing the classifier system can be read as follows: in each condition the first bit indicates whether the matching message comes from the environment - value 0 - or it is an internal one - value 1. In messages coming from environment (i.e. the automaton) the other two bits are given by the variable O (automaton output) that in our example is equal to the variable S representing the automaton state. So, given the two rules, our classifier system can maximize the received payoff emulating a logical OR function over the input bits (i.e., variable O; the automaton output is the learning system input). To achieve the required behaviour the classifier system must learn strength values for the two rules, so that the exception rule wins when in competition with the default one. If we apply to this example the preceding analysis, it is easy to show that the implicit hypothesis that the mean reward R received from a rule is equal for each rule is wrong.

We first rewrite equations (1) and (2) giving different names to the two rules rewards:

$$Str_d^{t+1} = Str_d^t(1-k\rho_d) + R_d \qquad (4)$$

$$Str_e^{t+1} = Str_e^t(1-k\rho_e) + R_e \qquad (5)$$

At steady-state we can rewrite formula (5) as

$$Str_e^{ss} = \frac{R_e^{ss}}{k\rho_e} \qquad (6)$$

R_e represents the average reward got from the exception rule. As the exception rule fires only when the automaton goes from state S=00 to state S=01, then its mean reward at steady-state is

$$R_e^{ss} = \frac{k\rho_d Str_d^{ss}}{2} \qquad (7)$$

because the default rule, when activated by the exception one, gives half of its payment to the exception rule (the other half goes to environment).

Substituting (7) in (6) we get

$$Str_e^{ss} = \frac{1}{2}Str_d^{ss}\frac{\rho_d}{\rho_e}$$

In our example $\rho_d = 1/3$ and $\rho_e = 2/3$ ->

$$Str_e^{ss} = \frac{1}{4}Str_d^{ss} \qquad (8)$$

and therefore

$$Bid_e^{ss} = \frac{1}{2}Bid_d^{ss} \qquad (9)$$

From this result we see that the behaviour of the system is still worse than expected using equation (3).

Examining the way the system functions we observed that, in the proposed automaton, the transition from state S=00 to state S=01 happens, in the average, after three auto-cycles (i.e. the default rule fires in the average three times before the exception one fires). This happens because, when looping, the default rule looses strength (during every auto-cycle it pays half of its bid to environment) and finally the default hierarchy is working again. This behaviour (i.e., a default hierarchy that is repeatedly created and destroyed) is the reason for the low level of performance of this system, as shown in Fig.5. It is easy to see that, even if we use the modified version of bucket brigade in which specificity is factored out of actual payoff [5] the same result holds (with a different value for the constants in equations 8 and 9 - see [2]).

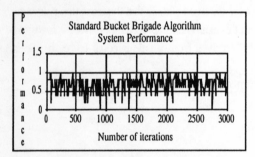

Fig.5 - System performance using the standard bucket brigade:
Average reward: 0.68
Standard deviation: 0.21

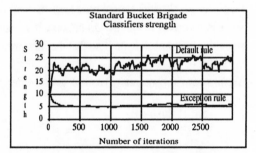

Fig.6 - An experiment supporting equation (7)
Average strength: default rule = 22.27
exception rule = 5.49
Standard deviation: default rule = 1.94
exception rule = 0.38

This analysis has been confirmed by simulations: Fig.6 shows the strength of the default and exception rules (average values: 22.27 and 5.49) confirming equation (7). We are working to better understand the dynamics of classifier systems under the bucket brigade algorithm. We choose here to propose a different approach that removes somewhat more radically the problem of default hierarchy formation and simultaneously improves system performance, as existing default hierarchies do work better.

7 Message-based bucket brigade

As said before it is possible to associate information about rules usefulness to messages. The result is that rule usefulness is computed as a sum of the usefulness of messages which compose it. We present hereafter a modified version of the bucket brigade algorithm in which only messages strength and specificity, without any classifier strength, are used to learn to properly control the system behaviour. We call this algorithm message-based bucket brigade - MBB for short.

- a strength M_j^t is associated to each "generable" message j (a message is said to be generable if it is in the action part of some classifier of the classifier set)
- during competition at time t each matched classifier C offers a bid
  $$\text{M-Bid}_C^t = M_a^t + \rho_1 M_{c1}^t + \rho_2 M_{c2}^t$$
  where M_a^t is the strength associated to the message representing the action part of classifier C, M_{c1}^t and M_{c2}^t are respectively the strength associated to the messages matching the first and second conditions of classifier C, ρ_1 and ρ_2 are the specificities of the two classifier conditions
- a winning message j pays an amount proportional to its strength (kM_j^t, where k is the payout constant) to both the messages that have matched the conditions of the classifier that posted it.
- in the genetic phase the classifier strength is computed in the same way as bid is computed in the competition phase, except for the value of the two conditions is averaged on the value of all the messages that can match them and that have already been generated

The MBB algorithm is then

Step 0 • create a list of all the generable messages and associate them an initial strength; clear the message list, set all the classifiers to status not-active and then append all the environmental messages

Step 1 • set to status active each classifier which has both conditions matched by messages on the message list and then empty the message list; two lists containing the messages that matched the two conditions are maintained for step 4 purposes

Step 2 • for each active classifier C compute the quantity M-Bid_C^t as defined above

Step 3 • choose with a probability proportional to M-Bid_C^t the messages to be posted until the message list is full

Step 4 • each message j successfully posted pays the quantity kM_j^t to the messages that caused its activation (according to the rule explained above)

Step 5 • the status of all the classifiers is set to not-active

Step 6 • new environmental messages are read and appended to the message list and the algorithm is repeated from Step 1.

It is important to point out that messages strength as defined here is different from the already introduced notions of support [6] and intensity [1]. Message strength is a lasting property of the message, dynamically changing with a law given by the MBB algorithm. Support and intensity are temporary values associated to messages and reflect the usefulness of rules that have posted them.

8 Steady-state analysis and simulation results

The major property of MBB is that a classifier with low specificity conditions will be activated with lower probability than one with high specificity, this property being independent of the activating messages strength. This can be easily seen examining the steady-state behaviour of the message strength

$$M_c^{i+1} = M_c^i - kM_c^i + R_c \Rightarrow M_c^{ss} = \frac{R_c}{k}$$

where R_c is the mean value of the reward received by $mess_c$. It is clear that the steady-state strength M_c^{ss} of message $mess_c$ is independent of specificity, while the bid a classifier offers depends on specificity. As a consequence default hierarchies support is an inherent property of the system. In our example

$$0**; \ 1** \rightarrow 111$$
$$000; \ 1** \rightarrow 100$$

if both messages 000 and 111 are in the message list both classifiers become active but the first one will always, independently of how well the strength of matching messages reflects their usefulness, bid less than the more specific one. Although the probability of posting a message is dependent also on the action message, our approach works correctly because either the value of the action message is equal or higher in the more specific rule, and then there is no problem, or it is lower and then it could be sensible to apply a less specific rule that results in a more useful action.

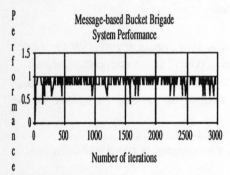

Fig.9 - System performance using the message-based bucket brigade
Average reward: 0.91
Standard deviation: 0.12

Another important feature of the MBB algorithm is that it makes the value of a rule context-dependent, i.e. the rule value depends on the value of matching messages. This means that using MBB a classifier strength can be more precisely tuned than using the classical bucket brigade. A problem with the classical model is that a default classifier can be matched by very different messages and that the resulting action can be only partially influenced by them by means of pass-through characters, i.e. characters that repeat in the action part the value found in the corresponding position of one of the conditions. Our MBB algorithm transcends this problem using rules whose strength is a function of matching messages strength. We made some experiments on the same automaton presented in Fig.2. The performance of the system, as can be seen from Fig.9, is significantly improved (average reward 0.91).

9 Conclusions and further work

In this paper we analyzed the apportionment of credit problem in learning classifier systems. Previous theoretical results used to predict the system behaviour at steady-state have been discussed and a new, more precise analysis has been presented. This analysis has shown that, in order to have working default hierarchies, the current implementations of the bucket brigade needs at least to be modified.

Making strength a property of messages, we solved the problem. The proposed algorithm, called message-based bucket brigade, inherently supports default hierarchies.

We are now investigating the following related topics:

- How extensible is the proposed approach? We are testing the system performance in case of multi-layered default hierarchies. First results are confirming the appropriateness of MBB.
- Could it be useful to use BB and MBB simultaneously?
- What are the effects of the proposed shift from a system in which actions are guided by rule strength to one in which message strength leads the computation on the rule discovery system?

Acknowledgements

This research was supported in part by a grant from CNR - Progetto finalizzato robotica - Sottoobiettivo 2 - Tema: ALPI, and from CNR - Progetto finalizzato sistemi informatici e calcolo parallelo - Sottoprogetto 2 - Tema: Processori dedicati.

References

[1] Booker,L., "Classifier Systems that Learn Internal World Models", Machine Learning, 3(3), p.161-192,1988.

[2] Dorigo,M., "New Perspectives about Default Hierarchies Formation in Learning Classifier Systems", Technical Report No. 91-002, Dip. di Elettronica, Politecnico di Milano, Italy.

[3] Goldberg, D.E., "Genetic Algorithms in Search, Optimization & Machine Learning", 1989, Addison-Wesley.

[4] Goldberg,D.E., Smith, R.E., "Reinforcement Learning with Classifier Systems", Proceedings of Congress on AI, Simulation and Planning in High Autonomous Systems,University of Arizona, Tucson, March-1990, IEEE Computer Society Press.

[5] Goldberg,D.E., Wilson,S.W., "A Critical Review of Classifier Systems", Proceedings of the Third International Conference on Genetic Algorithms, June 4-7 1989, Morgan Kaufmann (pp.244-255).

[6] Holland,J.H.,Holyoak,K.J., Nisbett,R.E.,Thagard,P.A., "Induction, Processes of Inference, Learning and Discovery" The MIT press, Cambridge, MA, 1986.

[7] Holland,J.H.,Holyoak,K.J., Nisbett,R.E., Thagard,P.R., "Classifier Systems, Q-Morphisms, and Induction", in Genetic Algorithms and Simulated Annealing, pp.116-128, Pitman, 1987.

[8] Riolo,R.L., "Bucket Brigade Performance: II. Default Hierarchies", Proceedings of the Second International Conference on Genetic Algorithms, July 28-31 1987, Lawrence Erlbaum (pp.196-201).

[9] Riolo,R.L., "The Emergence of Default Hierarchies in Learning Classifier Systems", Proceedings of the Third International Conference on Genetic Algorithms, June 4-7 1989, Morgan Kaufmann (pp.322-327).

Use of a Causal Model to Learn Diagnostic Knowledge in a Real Domain

M. Botta[*]   F. Brancadori[+]   S. Ravotto[*]   L. Saitta[**]   S. Sperotto[*]

[*] Dipartimento di Informatica, Università di Torino   [+] SOGESTA S.p.A.
Corso Svizzera 185, 10149 - TORINO (Italy)   Località Crocicchia, URBINO (Italy)

[**] Dipartimento di Meccanica Strutturale e Progettazione Automatica, Università di Trento
Via Mesiano 77, 38100 - TRENTO (Italy)

Abstract

This paper presents a system which learns a diagnostic knowledge base using a-priori knowledge and a set of examples. The a-priori knowledge consists of a causal model of the domain and a body of phenomenological theory, describing the links between abstract concepts and their possible manifestations in the world. The phenomenological knowledge is used deductively, the causal model is used abductively and the examples are used inductively. The system has been applied to learn the knowledge base of a diagnostic expert system for mechanical trouble-shooting.

1. Introduction

The recently proposed explanation-based (EBL) approach to learning (Mitchell, Keller & Kedar-Cabelli, 1986; DeJong & Mooney, 1986) had the great merit of focusing the attention of the machine learning community on the importance of justifying the acquired knowledge. However, in this deductive approach, justifications can be obtained at the cost of supplying a complete and consistent domain theory, which is not often available in practice. Furthermore, even if a perfect theory could be possibly encoded, its use would most likely turn out to be intractable. For the mentioned reasons, the explanation-based approach should be widen to accomodate a notion of explanation more comprehensive than logical entailment; furthermore, the domain theory should satisfy the two requisites of being tractable while keeping its explanatory power. In this paper, we suggest that a *causal model* of the domain (used *abductively*) satisfies both requirements. We will rely on the following intuitive notion of the cause-effect relationship: A is the cause of B if a physical mechanism can be specified, which shows how the occurrence of A brings about B (Botta, Giordana & Saitta, in press).

That causality plays a fundamental role in explaining the world is out of doubt; then, we do not need to argue about its explanatory import. Before discussing tractability, let us define what we mean by abduction. In this paper abduction refers to the following reasoning scheme: from the truth of $(\alpha \rightarrow \beta)$ and β, abduce the plausibility of α (Peirce, 1958; Levesque, 1989). Abduction regresses, through chains of cause-effect relations, from observations to a set of axioms, the *first causes,* which are the ultimate hypotheses we are willing to accept. Obviously, the selection of the first causes is task-dependent and can be suggested by an expert of the domain. First causes roughly correspond, in the literature on principled diagnosis, to "abducible predicates" (Eshghi & Kowalski, 1989; Console, Torasso & Theseider-Dupré, 1990).

A detailed discussion of the potential superiority of the causal/abductive approach to explanation, in comparison with a logical/deductive approach is out of the scope of this paper; here, we just mention that it mostly resides in the robustness of causal knowledge and in the possibility of making *assumptions* about the state of the world. In this way, possibly large parts of domain theory can be overlooked, at least in a first stage, strongly reducing the size of the search space. Causal models are particularly useful in updating and refining a knowledge base, because they substantially help locate defective parts of the knowledge and in suggesting motivated changes (Botta & Saitta, 1988; Morris & O'Rorke, 1990). Some authors have recently proposed to use plausible reasoning or abduction in learning, mainly as a way of coping with theory incompleteness and/or intractability within the framework of explanation-based learning (Botta, Ravotto & Saitta, in press; DeJong, 1990; Geffner, 1990; Hartley & Coombs, 1990; Morris & O'Rorke, 1990).

The proposed approach has been applied to the automated acquisition of the knowledge base for a diagnostic expert system, oriented to a mechanical trouble-shooting problem. Diagnosis from first principles has already been advocated as a way of facing expert system brittleness (Genesereth, 1984; Davis, 1984; Reiter, 1984; de Kleer & Seely Brown, 1986, Torasso & Console, 1989; Poole, 1988). Hence, the same causal model can be used both in classification and in learning.

The causal model C plays, in the proposed approach, a prominent role, but also other types of knowledge may contribute. In fact, the causal model is usually too abstract to allow practical diagnostic rules to be learned on its only basis. Then, we consider, beside C, a *phenomenological* theory P. The theory P contains structural information and definitions of relevant categories and their taxonomic organization; but, more importantly, P also contains a set of rules aimed at describing the manifestations of abstractly defined concepts, i.e., re-expressing them in terms of "operational" predicates (Keller, 1988). Pragmatically, however, a phenomenon will be considered *justified* only if it is explained by C, i.e., if it can be traced back to a first cause (For a formal definition, see Botta, Giordana & Saitta, in press). The causal reasoner presented in this paper is not a stand-alone system, but it has been developed within the ML-SMART framework (Bergadano, Giordana & Saitta, 1988a; Bergadano & Giordana, 1988b), in which inductive and deductive techniques have already been integrated to learn classification rules. The global learning strategy envisages two main phases, namely the initial acquisition of a knowledge base and its refinement. In this paper we are only concerned with the first one.

2. The Application

The domain of application was supplied by the ENICHEM chemical plant in Ravenna, where a technique of *on-condition* maintenance has been used for a long time. According to this technique, all the company's electro-mechanical apparata (in this paper we refer to motor-pumps, only) undergo periodical predictive controls. Should the technician detect, during this control, something anomalous in the machine behavior, a more accurate analysis, called *Mechanalysis,* is performed. Mechanalysis requires specially trained experts and is aimed at locating faults through a Fourier analysis of the machine vibrations, measured on the supports of the machine components.

Each mechanalysis provides the basic features of a single example; these features are collected in a table, whose layout is reported in Fig. 1. On each support (A, B, C and D) of the motor-pump, three series of measurements are repeated along three directions: Axial (parallel to the machine's shaft), vertical and horizontal (perpendicular to the former two). For each direction, the amplitude (in micron) and the speed (in mm/s) of the total vibration are first measured. Then, the expert locates in the frequency spectrum peaks of energy (harmonic components of the total vibration). For each peak, the corresponding frequency ω (in cycle per minute = CPM) and the speed are recorded.

Sup-port	Direc-tion	Total Vibration		Fourier Analysis				
		Amplitude [μm]	Speed [mm/s]	ω [CPM]	v [mm/s]	....	ω [CPM]	v [mm/s]
A	Hor	7/11	2.4/2.6	3000	0.7/0.9	....	18,000	0.7
	Vert	4/8	1.2/1.4	3000	0.2/0.7	....	18,000	0.4
	Ax	20	12	3000	3/3.2	....	18,000	0.8/1
	....	....		....		....		....

Fig. 1 – Organization of the data collected during a mechanalysis.

Inside the table the data are arranged into groups of three rows; each group corresponds to a given support and each row to one spatial direction. A first group of two columns (denoted by "Total Vibration") contains measures of amplitude and velocity of the total vibration, whereas a second group (denoted by "Fourier Analysis") contains measures of frequency, velocity and (possibly) phase of the harmonic components of vibrations.

The automatic acquisition of diagnostic knowledge from a set of mechanalyses is a difficult task, because the examples are very noisy and multiple faults are quite frequent.

The motor-pump faults can be grouped into six classes (one containing normal machines):

C_1 = Problems in the joint C_2 = Faulty bearings C_3 = Mechanical loosening
C_4 = Basement distortion C_5 = Unbalance C_6 = Normal operation conditions

Locating the fault is not sufficient for an effective repair. In fact, several phenomena may have caused the same fault. For instance, a bearing may be faulty because of prolonged use or fatigue or because the machine shaft is misaligned. Only changing the bearing may not be the best strategy; in fact, this intervention solves the problem only if the bearing was old, but not if the fault was induced by a shaft distortion: in this case, the bearing will shortly be faulty again. In order to cope with this difficulty, a causal model of the domain, specifying the possible reasons underlying the various faults, has been used.

3. Knowledge Representation

All the used schemes share a first order logic language $\mathcal{L}$ in Horn clause form. Lower case letters predicates are operational (i.e. directly observable on the data), whereas capital letters predicates are non-operational.

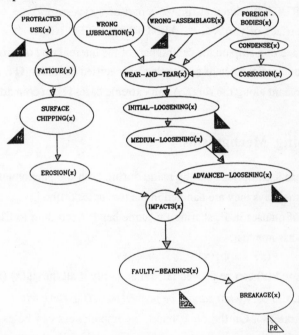

Fig. 2 – Part of the causal model referring to class C_2 (Faulty bearings).

The causal model C consists of a network; in Fig. 2 the subnetwork referring to class C_2 (Faulty bearings) is reported. Ellipses represent processes or states (described as first order atomic formulas) which are linked by means of cause-effect relations (shaded ellipses are first causes), whereas triangles indicate those phenomena which are observable in the world, either directly on the data or indirectly through the phenomenological theory. The global causal network consists of 63 nodes, including constraints and contexts.

The phenomenological theory $\mathcal{P}$ consists of a set of Horn clauses. Predicates associated to nodes in the network shall also occur in some clause of $\mathcal{P}$. The theory $\mathcal{P}$ contains taxonomies, structural information and links between abstract concepts and manifestations. For instance:

ROLLING-BEARING(s)∧ internal-ring(x)∧ part-of(x,s)∧ radius(x, r)∧ cage(z) ∧

part-of(z,s) ∧ external-ring(y)∧ part-of(y,s)∧ radius(y,R) ⇒ RADIUS(z, (r+R)/2)   (1)

Rule (1) defines the radius of the cage as a function of those of the two rings.

When encoding a domain theory, incompleteness may affect almost any part of it and we may not be aware of where and what knowledge is missing. On the other hand, there are cases in which either we know exactly where some information is missing, but we do not know which one, or we want to hide information on purpose (for instance, for tractability reasons). In these case we would like to warn the system about this lack of information. To this aim, the special predicate Ω (unknown) is introduced. For example, the rule:

ROLLING-BEARING(s) ∧ internal-ring(u) ∧ part-of(u,s) ∧ strip(y) ∧

central(y)∧ on-surface-of(y,u) ∧ Ω ⇒ ABNORM-RAD-FORCE(s)   (2)

states that the appearance of a strip on the central part of the internal ring of a rolling bearing is a symptom of an abnormal radial force, if some other unspecified condition Ω holds (the width of the strip should be constant along the ring). As an extreme case, Ω can coincide with the whole body of a clause.

4. Basic Reasoning Mechanisms

In the presented system assumptions can be made during both the phenomenological and the causal reasoning, but the ways they are handled in the two cases differ.

Let us consider a set of clauses in $\mathcal{P}$, sharing the same head. According to Clark's completion (Clark, 1978), we can assume that:

$$P(x) \Leftrightarrow \varphi_1(x) \vee \dots \vee \varphi_n(x) \qquad (3)$$

Using rule (3), predicate $P(x)$ can be proved false if and only if all the $\varphi_k(x)$ ($1 \leq k \leq n$) are false. In the phenomenological theory, *what cannot be proved false is assume true* (the opposite of the negation by failure strategy). On the other hand, incompleteness can be explicitly declared through the predicate Ω. This predicate can occur in the body of a clause, as, for instance, in (2); the effect of Ω is that ABNORM-RAD-FORCE(s) in rule (2) will never be true, but only *assumed* true if the other predicates in the body of the rule are true. In the causal network the symbol Ω may occur only within constraints and contexts. Constraints involve properties whose truth is time invariant, such as physical properties of or structural information about the bodies which are currently the focus of analysis (denoted by the variable x). Contexts, on the contrary, are conditions referring to larger parts (denoted by variables different from x) of the system than the one currently considered; moreover, the truth of these conditions may change if the environment changes. Constraints must be observable, whereas contexts need not be; moreover, predicates associated to nodes of the causal network can only occur in contexts, generating thus recursion. Predicates occurring in constraints and different from Ω are *necessary,* in the sense that they are assumed false if they cannot be proved true. The presence of Ω in a constraint denotes a weakening in the causal relation associated to the corresponding edge: in this case the cause *may* produce the effect, but not necessarily. Effects generated by a cause in a possibilistic way have a status of assumed true even if the cause is true.

Contexts, even without Ω, play a particular role in the assumption strategy; suppose that we are trying to explain why a bearing is faulty. The causal network tells us that there are a number of causes justifying this phenomenon; however, some of these are acceptable only if the environment supplies the conditions to support them: for instance, the presence of extraneous micro-bodies in the bearing occurs when the machine works in a dusty environment. When the causal reasoning is invoked on a given part of the system (in the example the object x), contexts act as defaults and are always assumed true. Then, each of the first causes, hypothesized to explain the phenomenon, has its context hypothesized at the same time. It is up to the general control strategy to decide whether accepting the assumed context by default or to verify it, possibly re-entering the causal network. This strategy closely matches the one often used by human experts and has also the advantage of breaking recursion in the causal reasoning.

Reasoning with the phenomenological theory can be realized through backward and forward deduction: the former is used to find alternative operationalizations of a concept, the latter is used to start the explanation process.

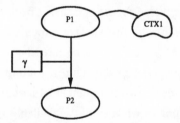

Fig. 3 – Scheme of the relations among nodes in the causal network, allowing two basic reasoning steps to be defined: deduction from causes to effects and abduction from effects to causes. Boxes attached to edges represent constraints which must be verified in order to instantiate the corresponding cause-effect relation. Clouds attached to ellipses represent contextual conditions (concomitant causes) to be added to the cause in order to obtain the effect.

Reasoning with the causal model can be performed (see Fig. 3) by moving from effects to causes (search for explanation via abduction) or from causes to effects (prediction via deduction), changing the truth status of the causal nodes.

- Deduction from a cause to an effect:

$$P_1 \wedge CTX_1 \wedge \gamma \rightarrow P_2$$

If node P_1 is true in the context CTX_1 and the constraints γ are verified, then node P_2 deterministically (if Ω does not occur in γ) or plausibly (if Ω occurs in γ) follows.

* Abduction from an effect to a cause:

$$P_2 \wedge \gamma \rightarrow P_1 \wedge CTX_1$$

If effect P_2 has been observed (or hypothesized) and the constraints γ are verified, then we can hypothesize that P_2 was originated by P_1 in the context CTX_1. In this abductive step, Ω does not have any influence.

Notice that the truth status of a node can also be determined by its observability, i.e., by its evaluation on the data, independently of the presence of its causes and/or effects. This fact constitutes another connection between phenomenological and causal reasoning.

Finally, data can be used inductively, for filling gaps left by theory incompleteness, in much the same way as proposed by Bergadano & Giordana (1988).

5. Building Explanations

The process of acquiring an initial set of diagnostic rules is performed in two steps. First, the available examples (in the limit just one) are justified all at the same time, building up the justification structures: these last consist of an *AND/OR forest* $\mathcal{T}$ of formulas and a set of *causal paths* $\Sigma = \{ \sigma_i \}$.

5.1. Generation of the forest $\mathcal{T}$

Given a set F of examples of the concepts to be discriminated, the rules of the phenomenological theory are activated forwards, starting from a specified set of operational predicates (Botta, Ravotto & Saitta, in press). The process ends when no more rules are applicable or some node of the causal network has been reached. To each node, other pieces of information are associated (not shown in the figure). Among others, the extension of the formula corresponding to the node, with the number of assumptions made so far for each sample included, and the indication of whether all the available alternative operationalizations have already been tried or not. Obviously, the forest $\mathcal{T}$ contains only those parts of the theory $\mathcal{P}$ which have been stimulated by the considered examples. When new examples will be added later, the forest will possibly expand.

5.2. Generation of the Causal Paths Σ

After the process of forward deduction halts, some nodes of the causal network have possibly been activated. Starting from the nodes which are most far from the first causes, the system tries to complete paths in the causal network, by using the abductive inference rule described in

Section 4. This process is done for all the samples at the same time and, for each of them, its status (true or assumed true with k assumptions) is recorded.

When the search for causal paths ends, a first-order formula $\psi \wedge \gamma$ (where γ are necessary conditions and ψ are sufficient conditions), summarizing all the conditions that have been assumed or proved true in building the explanation structure, is associated with each causal path. Starting from these formulas, we want to generate a set of classification rules; the process which performs this task is described in the next section.

6. Generation of the Heuristic Rules

Heuristic rules are derived from formulas associated to causal paths ($\psi \wedge \gamma$) and share the same structure:

$$\varphi \wedge \delta \rightarrow H \qquad (4)$$

In (4), sub-formula φ contains sufficient conditions, obtained as a specialization of the corresponding ψ, the sub-formula δ contains necessary conditions, which may be a generalization of the corresponding γ, and H is a diagnostic hypothesis. The distinction between necessary and sufficient conditions is kept as such in the heuristic rules, because we want the classifier to manage them in different ways: necessary condition must be verified by the instance to be classified, whereas sufficient conditions may be assumed true if they cannot be proved false.

Let us now consider one causal path σ and the associated formula $\psi \wedge \gamma$. The path explains, in terms of cause-effect relationships, why the instances covered by that formula belong to a given class. Should the theory be complete, no counterexample is explained by the causal path. In such a case, the formula $\psi \wedge \gamma$ itself can be used as a heuristic rule, possibly generalizing the necessary conditions γ. In practice, it is unlikely that such a situation arises and, usually, $\psi \wedge \gamma$ will cover some counterexamples; this means that the formula $\psi \wedge \gamma$ is overly general, due to the incompleteness of the theory, which obliged us to make some untrue assumption. A heuristic rule is, then, derived from $\psi \wedge \gamma$ by specializing some predicates in the sufficient conditions ψ. This can be accomplished either by replacing a predicate in ψ with one or more of its operazionalization, descending the AND/OR forest, or by finding, by means of induction, an alternative operationalization of a predicate in ψ.

If we consider the causal path connecting the nodes <u>PROTRACTED-USE</u>(x) and <u>FAULTY-BEARINGS</u>(x), the associated formula is the following:

ROLLING-BEARING(s) $\wedge$ OLD(s) $\wedge$ dang-vibr(x) $\wedge$ measure(x,s) $\wedge$

vel-in(z) $\wedge$ measure(z,s) $\wedge$ high-freq(y) $\wedge$ measure(y, s) $\Rightarrow$ FAULTY-BEARING(s) $\qquad$ (5)

Formula (5) can be paraphrased as follows: "If there is an old bearing inside a support, in which a dangerous vibration has been measured and, moreover, a peak has been detected in the high frequency range, than the bearing in that support is damaged". This rule cover all the examples and also two counter-examples. In order to eliminate these, the system first tries to specialize formula (5) by replacing a predicate with a more specific operationalization. Then, as it does not succeed, the induction module is invoked; this last tries to quantify part of the above formula and successfully outputs the following new rule:

ROLLING-BEARING(s) $\wedge$ OLD(s) $\wedge$ dang-vibr(x) $\wedge$ measure(x,s) $\wedge$

ATL 6 y [vel-in(z)$\wedge$measure(z,s)$\wedge$high-freq(y)$\wedge$measure(y, s)] $\Rightarrow$FAULTY-BEARING(s) (6)

Formula (6) can be paraphrased as follows: "If there is an old bearing inside a support in which a dangerous vibration has been measured and, moreover, at least 6 peaks have been detected in the high frequency range, than the bearing in that support is damaged". Should formula (6) be still inconsistent, the process is iterated until either a consistent formula is found or the AND/OR forest has been exhaustively descended or a formula with an empty (too low) extension is generated. Obviously, from this process more than one heuristic rule might be generated: they are evaluated according to simplicity and completeness criteria, among others, and the best ones are selected.

Notice that the learned heuristic rules may contain non-operational predicates. This results in a much more compact knowledge base, but in a more sophisticated performance system. Moreover, form (6) of the rules is only used to communicate with the user. In fact, the system keeps the rules in their tree form, derived from the justification structure. In this way, when classification fails, all the work necessary to understand why, is already done (because the exact point of failure is already located). This is a first step toward the complete identification of the performance element and the learner, obtaining thus a true self-developing expert system.

7. Conclusions

A system which learns diagnostic rules from a set of examples (by induction), from a phenomenological theory (by deduction) and from a causal model (by abduction) is presented. The system can work automatically or in an interactive mode. The system, applied on a real domain of mechanical trouble-shooting, showed a remarkable robustness: in fact, several among the rules learned from only 30 examples (5 for each class) coincided with the ones acquired previously from 170 examples. The suggested conclusion is that a causal model allows robust and meaningful knowledge to be learned with acceptable computational complexity.

References

F. Bergadano, A. Giordana, L. Saitta (1990), "Automated versus Manual Knowledge Acquisition: A Comparison in a Real Domain", Proc. *First Japanese Knowledge Acquisition for Knowledge-Based Systems Workshop* (Tokyo, Japan), pp. 301-314.

F. Bergadano, A. Giordana, L. Saitta (1988a), "Automated Concept Acquisition in Noisy Environment", *IEEE Trans. PAMI, PAMI-10,* 555-575.

F. Bergadano, A. Giordana (1988b), "A Knowledge Intensive Approach to Concept Induction", Proc. *Machine Learning Conference* (Ann Arbor, MI), pp. 305-317.

M. Botta, L. Saitta (1988), "Improving Knowledge Base System Performances by Experience", Proc. *EWSL-88* (Glasgow, UK), pp. 15-23.

M. Botta, A, Giordana, L. Saitta (1990), "Knowledge Base Refinement using a Causal Model", *Intelligent Systems: State of the Art and Future Trends,* Z. Ras & M. Zemankova (Eds.), Ellis-Horwood Publ. Co.

M. Botta, S. Ravotto, L. Saitta (in press), "Use of Causal Models and Abduction in Learning Diagnostic Knowledge", *Int. J. of Man-Machine Studies,* in press.

L. Console, P. Torasso, D. Theseider Dupré (1990), "A Completion Semantics for Object-Level Abduction", Proc. AAAI Symposium on Automated Abduction (Stanford, CA), pp. 72-75.

R. Davis (1984), "Diagnostic Reasoning based on Structure and Behavior", *Artificial Intelligence, 24,* 347-410.

G. DeJong, R. Mooney (1986), "Explanation based learning: An alternative view", *Machine Learning, 1,* 47-80.

G. DeJong (1990), "Plausible inference vs. abduction", Proc. AAAI Symposium on *Automated Abduction* (Stanford, CA), pp. 48-51.

K. Eshghi, R. Kowalski (1989), "Abduction Compared with Negation by Failure", Proc. 6th Int. Conf. on Logic Programming (Lisbon, Portugal), pp. 234-254.

H. Geffner (1990), "Causal theories for default and abductive reasoning", Proc. AAAI Symposium on *Automated Abduction* (Stanford, CA), pp. 150-154.

M. Genesereth (1984), "The use of design descriptions in automated diagnosis", *Artificial Intelligence, 24,* 411-436.

R. Hartley, M. Coombs (1990), "Abduction in model generative reasoning", Proc. AAAI Symposium on *Automated Abduction* (Stanford, CA), pp. 130-134.

R. Keller (1988), "Defining operationality for EBL", *Artificial Intelligence, 35,* 227-242 .

J. de Kleer, J. Seely Brown (1986), "Theories of causal ordering", *Artificial Intelligence, 29,* 33-61.

H. Levesque (1987), "A knowledge-level account of abduction", Proc. IJCAI (Detroit, MI), pp. 1061-1067.

T. Mitchell, R. Keller, S. Kedar-Cabelli (1986), "Explanation based generalization", *Machine Learning, 1,* 47-80.

S. Morris, P. O'Rorke (1990), "An approach to theory revision using abduction", Proc. AAAI Symposium on *Automated Abduction* (Stanford, CA), pp. 33-37.

C. Peirce (1931-1958), Collected Papers of Charles Sanders Peirce, C. Hartchorne, P. Weiss and A. Burks (Eds.), Harvard University Press (Cambridge, MA).

D. Poole (1988), "Representing knowledge for logic-based diagnosis", Proc. Int. Conf. on Fifth Generation Computer Systems (Tokyo, Japan), pp. 1282-1290.

R. Reiter (1984), "A theory of diagnosis from first principles", *Artificial Intelligence, 32,* 57-95.

P. Torasso, L. Console (1989), *Diagnostic problem solving,* Van Nostrand Reinhold.

EXTENDING INVERSE RESOLUTION TO BUILD UP ABSTRACTIONS

A. Giordana[(*)]   L. Saitta[(+)]
R. Finelli[(*)]   M. Paderni[(*)]   D. Roverso[(**)]

[(*)] Dip. di Informatica, Università di Torino
Corso Svizzera 185, 10149 - Torino, Italy
[(**)] Computing Science Dpt., University of Aberdeen
Aberdeen, Scotland, UK
[(+)] Dip. di Meccanica Strutturale e Progettazione Automatica, Università di Trento
Via Mesiano 77, 38100 - Trento, Italy.
Email: saitta@pianeta.di.unito.it

Abstract

Abstraction is a conceptual framework potentially unifying and integrating different methodologies developed in machine learning and problem solving. According to the common understanding of the term, abstraction is a mapping between languages, and, then, in many learning tasks it can be so formulated. On the contrary, in this paper abstraction is defined as a mapping between models, implicitly extending Tenenberg's *restricted predicate mapping* in order to include more complex abstraction schemes and to cope with the problem of inconsistency in the abstract model.

In our proposal, the abstraction mapping is axiomatized by means of a theory T_A, defining the semantics of the relations in the abstract model starting from the ones in the ground model. Therefore, this form of abstraction is called *semantic* and must be evaluated using a deductive mechanism instead of a purely syntactic rewriting. Afterwards, a restricted class of semantic abstraction (CP-Abstraction) is characterized: it has the property of preserving concept instances, with respect to a given model, and the more-general-than relation between formulas. CP-Abstraction fits in the paradigm of inverse resolution, already proposed as a framework for constructive learning and a restricted form of absorption rule is introduced to compute it.

Inverse resolution, in its original formulation, does not allow important abstraction types, such as the definition of a compound object starting from its parts, to be defined. A new operation, called *term abstraction,* is then introduced.

1. Introduction

Recently the machine learning community begun to pay attention to abstraction as a potentially useful mechanism for learning. Abstraction has been used for problem solving [1-5], for learning heuristics in problem solving [4] and for learning concept descriptions [6-8]. Even though different definitions of abstraction have been given by different authors, all of them agree on the importance of searching for a new representation language "simpler" than the one in which the problem at hand has been originally formulated. Even if abstraction may be involved in many intelligent tasks, we are only concerned, in this paper, with machine learning.

In our view, abstraction is neither a task nor a methodology, but it is, instead, a knowledge-level conceptual framework which tries to capture, formalize and possibly automatize a fundamental aspect of human thought: the ability of changing the level of details in representing knowledge, according to the current reasoner's goals. The first formal definition, in AI, was proposed by Plaisted, who presented abstraction as a syntactic mapping between languages [2]. This definition has been later revised by Tenenberg, who suggested a semantic view [3].

Abstraction, dealing with transformations between representation schemes, offers a new perspective to learning, in that it addresses the fundamental dilemmas involving knowledge simplicity, meaningfulness, predictivity and task-dependency. All the dilemmas are rooted in the problem of choosing a suitable knowledge representation language. Looking from this point of view, different machine learning tasks, apparently different, can be traced back to a common source. Thus, abstraction may act as a common framework for planning [9], conceptual clustering [10], language bias shift [11] and constructive induction [12]. Recognizing commonalities among these tasks rises the hope of being able to design unified methodologies and heuristics for solving them. In the present paper we concentrate the analysis on constructive induction.

Let us consider, for the moment, the intuitive notion of abstraction as a mapping between a ground and an abstract space. Then, constructive learning can be interpreted as the task of building up an abstraction mapping, starting from the ground space. For (partially) solving this task, the methodology of *inverse resolution* is already available [12-13]. Therefore, casting constructive induction into the abstraction framework has a twofold advantage: abstraction can profit of an experimented algorithm to be computed, while constructive induction can exploit the constraints that the abstraction mapping shall satisfy as a general criterion to reduce the choice of possible new predicates, reducing the need for an oracle.

The notion of abstraction as a mapping between representation languages is very general and covers a large variety of tasks. After discussing how inverse resolution can be used in connection with this general notion of abstraction, we will introduce a special kind of abstraction mapping (an extension of Tenenberg's semantic definition), which we think can play a particularly relevant role in learning, because of its properties. More precisely, this mapping, which we call Completeness-Preserving Abstraction (CPA), preserves the extension of formulas and the more-general-than relation between pairs of formulas across the ground and the abstract space. This means that the knowledge acquired in any of the two spaces can be transferred into the other, without bothering about loosing completeness and/or consistency. Abstraction is in no way intended to be an alternative to generalization in acquiring concepts. On the contrary, both mechanisms are needed and each one has its role: generalization works inside a representation space, whereas abstraction works across representation spaces. If generalization could be considered as a special kind of abstraction is a question which deserves further investigation, but will not pursued further here.

After defining CP-Abstraction, the question if inverse resolution can still be used to compute it, spontaneously arises. The answer is yes, under some conditions, a suitable extension to the standard inverse resolution operators is presented.

2. Semantic Abstraction

Plaisted defined abstraction as a *Predicate Mapping,* between a ground and an abstract language, preserving instances and negation [2]. The definition is then extended to clauses. However, predicate mappings or, in general, abstractions based only on syntactic transformations can generate an inconsistent set of abstract clauses, even if the ground set is a consistent one. Tenenberg discussed this problem and showed that renaming the predicates in the abstraction mapping can cause positive and negative assertions to collide, possibly generating contradictions [3]. In order to overcome this problem, Tenenberg defines a *Restricted Predicate Mapping*, which is no longer a purely syntactic one. More precisely, given a set of clauses Θ, a restricted predicate mapping $g(\Theta)$ is a subset of the corresponding predicate mapping $f(\Theta)$; $g(\Theta)$ maps only that subset Θ' of Θ for which consistency is preserved. The set Θ' is determined by checking consistency on the model. However, the restricted predicate mapping is no longer an abstraction in Plaisted's sense. As a consequence, not every proof derivable from Θ has a correspondent proof in $g(\Theta)$, as it happens for an abstraction mapping. Nevertheless, restricted predicate mappings proved useful in problem solving [5].

In this paper we extend Tenenberg's framework to include abstraction schemes more complex than predicate mappings. To this aim, we adopt a different definition of abstraction, which explicitly uses the models associated to the languages. As Tenenberg pointed out, the consistency requirement cannot be satisfied without using models and, hence, abstraction implicitly becomes a mapping between models. In other words, this form of abstraction is semantic and must be evaluated using a deductive mechanism instead of a purely syntactic rewriting.

Abstraction is then defined by means of a theory T_A defining the semantics of the relations in the abstract model from the ones in the ground model. In particular, given a set of sentences Θ in a language L, a language L' and an abstraction theory $T_A \subseteq L \cup L'$, defining the predicates of L' in terms of the predicates in L, the set of sentences Θ' of L', such that :

$$\Theta \cup T_A \ldots \Theta'$$

will be called the *abstraction of Θ through T_A.* Therefore, any minimal model $\mathcal{M}'$ of Θ' will be considered as the abstraction of a model $\mathcal{M}$ of Θ.

The theory T_A consists of a set of definitions of the form:

$$\forall x \, \exists z \, [\psi(x) \leftrightarrow D_1(y) \vee D_2(y) \vee \ldots \vee D_n(y)] \tag{1}$$

where ψ is an atomic formula of the language L', $D_1, ... , D_n$ are conjunctions of predicates in the language $L \cup L'$, X is the set of variables occurring in ψ, Y is the set of variables occurring in $D_1 \vee .... \vee D_n$ and $Z = Y - X$. The variables in the set Z are defined as functions of the variables in the set Y.

In order to exemplify this form of abstraction, we will use a simple example from a block world domain, where the basic components are bricks (of different length) and wheels (of identical size). A ground world M, consisting of an instance of the concept CAR, together with some disconnected elements not pertaining to the concept instance, is represented in Fig. 1(a).

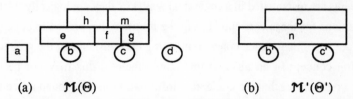

(a) $M(\Theta)$ (b) $M'(\Theta')$

Fig. 1 – Example of semantic abstraction. (a) Ground world $M(\Theta)$, consisting of an instance of the concept CAR plus some disconnected elements. (b) Abstract world $M'(\Theta')$, obtained using the theory reported in Table I. Adjacent bricks have been merged and disconnected elements have been deleted.

Table I

Example of abstraction axiomatization. Predicates of the language L are in lower case letters, predicates of the language L' are in capital letters. In the axioms of Θ and T_A the quantifiers have been omitted.

$\Theta = X \cup T$

$X = \{$brick(a), wheel(b), wheel(c), wheel(d), brick(e), brick(f), brick(g), brick(h), brick(m),   on(e,b), on(g,c), on(h,e), on(h,f), on(m,f), on(m,g), adj(e,f), adj(f,g), adj(h,m),   left-most(h), left-most(e), left-most(a), right-most(m), right-most(g), right-most(a)$\}$

$T = \{$chain([x,y]) ← brick(x) ∧ right-most(y) ∧ brick(y) ∧ adj(x,y),   chain([x,y]) ← brick(x) ∧ chain(y) ∧ adj(x,y),   adj(z,[x,y]) ← chain([x,y]) ∧ adj(z,x), ... $\}$

$T_A = \{$WHEEL(x) ↔ [wheel(x) ∧ on(y,x)] ∨ [wheel(x) ∧ on(x,y)],   BRICK(x) ↔   [left-most(x) ∧ right-most(x) ∧ on(x,y)] ∨   [left-most(x) ∧ right-most(x) ∧ on(y,x)] ∨   chain(x) $\}$

$\Theta' = X' = \{$ WHEEL(b'), WHEEL(c'), BRICK(p), BRICK(n) $\}$

A domain theory Θ, including a factual knowledge X and a set of axioms T, is reported in Table I. T defines composite objects, obtaining by merging chains of adjacent bricks. An abstraction theory T_A, stating which relations are to be kept in the abstract world, is also reported in Table I. Using T_A, the new world $M'(\Theta')$, represented in Fig. 1(b), has been built up by deduction from $\Theta \cup T_A$. It consists of a simplified scene, where the boundaries between bricks chained together disappear and the isolated objects have been deleted.

Semantic Abstraction, as defined in (1), preserves the *more-general-than* relation between formulas (according to the definition given by Buntine [14]). This is an essential property for the task of learning concept descriptions, because it guarantees that concept descriptions can be learned on an abstract model and transferred safely to the ground model and viceversa. Finally, this formulation of semantic abstraction allows many of the schemes already proposed in the literature to captured and, in particular, it can be seen as an extension to the first order logic of the definition adopted by Drastal for learning concept description [6].

3. Completeness Preserving Non-Generalizing Abstraction

In order to justify the abstraction mechanisms introduced in the following, we will refer to a learning problem relevant to robotics and image analysis. Suppose we have a scene, in which several concepts are instantiated in a contextual way, i.e., they are logically related. We want to learn descriptions for these concepts. Using the traditional approach to concept learning, we could learn descriptions for each concept, mapping each instance of the ground space into the corresponding concept in an abstract one. Nevertheless, this may not be what we want, because we would prefer that the contextual information in the ground space be preserved in the abstract one. For instance, if the involved concepts are those of "cube", "on-ground", "flat-bottom" and "stable", we know that a cube which is on-ground and has a flat-bottom is also stable; this can be encoded into a domain theory. Therefore, we need to abstract not only the concepts, but also the domain knowledge expressed in the ground world; in general, we need to define new intermediate concepts, in order to achieve this goal.

The problem above can be stated as follows. Suppose we are given a set of assertions Θ defining a set H of interrelated concepts. Let D be the set of relations derivable from Θ, establishing semantic links among the concepts in H. The relations D are supposed to have the form d_i: $h_i \leftrightarrow \varphi_i$, being $h_i \in H$ and φ_i a formula, expressed in a language $L \supset H$, containing at least another predicate h_j belonging to H. We want to build an abstraction theory T_A, such that:

- $\Theta \cup T_A$ ... ($h_i \leftrightarrow \varphi_i'$) for every sentence in D, being φ_i' a formula expressed in the abstract language $L' \supset H$.
- The set D' of the abstracted sentences be as simple as possible.

Such a theory will be said a Completeness-Preserving Abstraction (CPA) with respect to the set of definitions Θ.

3.1. Inverse Resolution Paradigm

The framework for constructive learning based on inverse resolution is a good start point for dealing with CPA. Inverse Resolution has been first proposed by Muggleton [12] and then was significantly improved by Rouveirol and Puget [13]. This paradigm is based on three basic inference rules:

1) **Absorption:** Given two Horn clauses c_1 : $P \leftarrow \varphi \wedge \psi$ and c_2 : $Q \leftarrow \varphi$, the new clause c_3 : $P \leftarrow Q \wedge \psi$ is generated by replacing in c_1 the formula φ with the head of c_2, provided that

an appropriate unifier σ exists between the terms of the two clauses. Inverse resolution defines the rules for finding σ when it exists.

2) **Intra-construction:** Given two (or more) clauses of the type $c_1 : P \leftarrow \varphi \wedge \psi$ and $c_2 : P \leftarrow \varphi \wedge \xi$, the new predicate $NP \leftarrow \psi \vee \xi$ is defined; then, the new clause $c_3 : P \leftarrow \varphi \wedge NP$ can be generated by absorption.

3) **Truncation:** This is basically the dropping condition rule, according to the definition of generalization based on the θ-subsumption defined by Plotkin [15].

The absorption and truncation rules potentially generalize the clause they are applied to, and, hence, new proofs can be obtained after the transformation. As an example, if we consider the clauses $c_1 : P \leftarrow \varphi \wedge \psi$, $c_2 : Q \leftarrow \varphi$ and $c_3 : Q \leftarrow \xi$, the application of absorption to generate $c_4 : P \leftarrow Q \wedge \psi$ produces a theory which derives also $P \leftarrow \varphi \wedge \xi$. This problem has been solved either by consulting an oracle, in order to check the correctness of the new sentence, or by proving, under the closed world assumption, that no new logical consequences are added with respect to the considered extension. Nevertheless, this last solution frequently leads to an unacceptable complexity.

Then, inverse resolution offers a framework that can be used to compute some kinds of CPA. Nevertheless we want to extend it in two ways. On the one hand, we want to define an inference scheme for computing a more constrained form of CPA, which does not generate generalization, and, on the other, we want to introduce more sophisticated abstraction mechanisms.

3.2. Inverse Resolution Revisited

Given a set Θ of sentences and an abstraction theory T_A, we will define a restricted form of absorption that does not generalize. In the following we suppose that the sentences Θ to be abstracted, as well as the abstraction theory T_A, be in the form of equivalence relations. According to the closed world assumption, any Horn theory can always be transformed into this form by completing it according to the negation as failure strategy. We suppose, moreover, that functors occur only in equality relations, and that no nested functors exists. A theory can always be put in this form by applying a flattening procedure analogous to the one proposed in [13].

Suppose that $\mathbf{A}: [R(x) \leftrightarrow \mathcal{D}_1 \vee \mathcal{D}_2 \vee ... \vee \mathcal{D}_k \vee ... \vee \mathcal{D}_n]$ be a sentence belonging to $\Theta \cup T_A$, being the $\mathcal{D}_j$'s conjunctions of atomic formulas and equality relations. Suppose, moreover, that the right hand side of $\mathbf{A}$ can be set in the form:

$$[R(x) \leftrightarrow [\mathcal{C}_1 \vee \mathcal{C}_2 \vee ... \vee \mathcal{C}_k] \sigma \wedge \varphi \vee ... \vee \mathcal{D}_n] \qquad (2)$$

being $\mathcal{D}_j = \mathcal{C}_j \sigma \wedge \varphi$ where σ is a substitution not renaming the variables x. Then, if another sentence $\mathbf{B}: [P(y) \leftrightarrow \mathcal{C}_1' \vee \mathcal{C}_2' \vee ... \vee \mathcal{C}_m']$ exists, such that every $\mathcal{C}_j$ is subsumed by the corresponding $\mathcal{C}_j'$, the new sentence $\mathbf{A}': [R(x) \leftrightarrow [P(y) \wedge \varphi] \vee ... \vee \mathcal{D}_n]$ can be derived by inverting the resolution simultaneously on all the pairs of disjuncts. We call this form of deduction **Non-Generalizing Absorption** (NGA).

Alternatively, if such an axiom **B** does not exist, it can be constructed by renaming the subformula $[C_1 \vee C_2 \vee ... \vee C_k]$ with a single predicate name, in which the variables are again chosen by inverting the resolution in the formula (2). This operation corresponds to **Intra-Construction**. In order to select among the alternative intra-constructions, a good heuristic criterion can be that of preferring the ones which can be absorbed simultaneously in many different sentences. This criterion captures the idea of inter-construction [16]. Finally, if we can prove that the subformula $[C_1 \vee C_2 \vee ... \vee C_k]$ is always true, the axiom **A** can be simplified, by applying **Truncation**, into **A'**: $[R(X) \leftrightarrow \varphi \vee ... \vee D_n]$.

We will now illustrate NGA through an example. The theory T reported on Table I can be rewritten as follows:

T: {chain([x,y]) $\leftrightarrow$ [brick(x) $\wedge$ right-most(y) $\wedge$ brick(y) $\wedge$ adj(x,y)] $\vee$

$\qquad$ [brick(x) $\wedge$ chain(y) $\wedge$ adj(x,y)]} $\hfill$ (3)

Consider, moreover, the abstraction theory:

$\quad T_A$: {CHAIN(x) $\leftrightarrow$ chain(x); R-BRICK(x) $\leftrightarrow$ right-most(x) $\wedge$ brick(x);

$\qquad$ C-BRICK(x,y) $\leftrightarrow$ brick(x) $\wedge$ adj(x,y)}

It is easy to verify that we can derive, from T and T_A, the sentence:

$\quad$ CHAIN([x,y]) $\leftrightarrow$ [C-BRICK(x,y) $\wedge$ R-BRICK(y)] $\vee$ [C-BRICK(x,y) $\wedge$ CHAIN(y)] $\quad$ (4)

recursively defining a definition the predicate CHAIN(x) in the abstract world. The abstraction (4) does not introduce new proofs and, at the same time, it is completeness preserving with respect to T, because a complete definition of the predicate CHAIN(x) in terms of the predicates C-BRICK(x,y) and R-BRICK(y) has been obtained; in the ground world, the predicate chain(x) was completely defined in terms of the predicates brick(x), adj(x,y) and right-most(x), as well. However, it is easy to verify that abstracting a set of sentences Θ using only NGA and constructive operators, an abstracted set of sentences Θ' will be obtained such that it will remain consistent also with respect to models which are not minimal with respect to Θ, i.e. if we add new ground instances. This kind of abstraction will be called Non-Generalizing CP-Abstraction. In any case, NGA cannot be totally replace absorption. In fact, there exist useful sentences generated by absorption which cannot be generated by CPA; for instance NGA is unable to generate recursive rules, because it cannot absorb the head of a clause in its body.

3.3. Term Abstraction

A fundamental type of abstraction, frequently needed in reasoning, consists in identifying compound objects in such a way that their internal details are hidden. This is what is done, for instance, in programming according to the paradigm of the abstract data types. Is it possible to let a similar mechanism be realized inside an automated abstraction program?

In the following we propose a new constructive operator, which allows such a capability to be introduced in the inverse resolution framework. Suppose we have defined the concept of CAR through the following axiom:

$$car(x_1, x_2, x_3) \leftrightarrow wheel(x_1) \wedge wheel(x_2) \wedge body(x_3) \tag{5}$$

Suppose, moreover, that the 3-arity function $pack(x_1,x_2,x_3)$ be defined through the axiom:

$$pack(x_1,x_2,x_3) = y \tag{6}$$

stating that for every triple x_1, x_2, x_3 there exists a term y defined as a sequence $<x_1, x_2, x_3>$. From axioms (5) and (6) it follows that:

$$car(x_1, x_2, x_3) \wedge [pack(x_1,x_2,x_3) = y] \leftrightarrow [wheel(x_1) \wedge wheel(x_2) \wedge$$
$$\wedge body(x_3) \wedge [pack(x_1,x_2,x_3) = y] \tag{7}$$

Then, by applying intra-construction, we can define the new predicate:

$$CAR(y) \leftrightarrow wheel(x_1) \wedge wheel(x_2) \wedge body(x_3) \wedge [pack(x_1,x_2,x_3) = y]$$

from which the sentence $CAR(y) \leftrightarrow car(x_1,x_2,x_3) \wedge [pack(x_1,x_2,x_3) = y]$ can be obtained. The construction rule (7) will be called **Term-construction** rule. Sentences defined through term abstraction cannot be absorbed in the body of another sentence $\mathbf{A}$ if the new compound term hides components occurring also in other parts of $\mathbf{A}$. It is possible to overcome this drawback if the function which defines the new term is reversible. Suppose that the function $pack(x_1,x_2,x_3)$ is reversible, i.e., there exist three functions: first(y), second(y) and third(y) returning x_1, x_2 and x_3 respectively, when applied to an object built form the function $pack(x_1,x_2,x_3)$. This can be stated through an axiom:

$$[pack(x_1,x_2,x_3) = y] \leftrightarrow [first(y) = x_1] \wedge [second(y) = x_2] \wedge [third(y) = x_3] \tag{8}$$

which we call **Reversibility** axiom. The reversibility axiom, when added to the theory to be abstracted, allows new interesting constructions. Consider, for instance, the sentence:

$$mycar(x_1,x_2,x_3) \leftrightarrow car(x_1,x_2,x_3) \wedge red(x_3) \tag{9}$$

By applying term construction three times, we obtain:

$$mycar(x_1,x_2,x_3) \wedge [pack(x_1,x_2,x_3) = y] \leftrightarrow$$
$$\leftrightarrow car(x_1,x_2,x_3) \wedge red(x_3) \wedge [pack(x_1,x_2,x_3) = y] \wedge [third(y) = x_3]$$

Then, by applying intra-construction two times, we can construct the three following sentences:

$$MYCAR(y) \leftrightarrow CAR(y) \wedge RED\text{-}BODY(y)$$
$$CAR(y) \leftrightarrow car(x_1,x_2,x_3) \wedge [pack(x_1,x_2,x_3) = y] \tag{10}$$
$$RED\text{-}BODY(y) \leftrightarrow red(x_3) \wedge [third(y) = x_3]$$

In this way, by exploiting reversibility, also properties depending on internal details of a compound object can be abstracted. In other words, reversibility axioms allow subformulas, that otherwise would be connected through shared variables, to be isolated.

Finally, global properties of a compound object can be abstracted using NGA (as well as absorption), provided that the closure of the considered property be properly specified. As an example, suppose to have the following axiom:

$$on(x,y) \leftrightarrow on(x_1,y) \wedge on(x_2,y) \wedge on(x_3,y) \wedge [pack(x_1,x_2,x_3) = x] \tag{11}$$

stating the transitivity of the property "on" with respect to the compound built up by the function pack. If, after some term construction steps, the sentence:

trailer(x) $\leftrightarrow$ brick(x$_1$) $\wedge$ brick(x$_2$) $\wedge$ brick(x$_3$) $\wedge$ *[pack*(x$_1$,x$_2$,x$_3$) = z] $\wedge$

wheel(y$_1$) $\wedge$ wheel(y$_2$) $\wedge$ on(x$_1$,y$_1$) $\wedge$ on(x$_2$,y$_1$) $\wedge$ on(x$_3$,y$_1$) $\wedge$

on(x$_1$,y$_2$) $\wedge$ on(x$_2$,y$_2$) $\wedge$ on(x$_3$,y$_2$) $\wedge$ *[pack*(y$_1$,y$_2$,z) = x]

is obtained, the following sentence can be derived:

trailer(x) $\leftrightarrow$ BODY(z) $\wedge$ on(z,y$_1$) $\wedge$ on(z,y$_2$) $\wedge$ wheel(y$_1$) $\wedge$wheel(y$_2$) $\wedge$ *[pack*(y$_1$,y$_2$,z) = x]

In conclusion, we have shown how new interesting abstractions can be obtained just by introducing the new deductive operator term construction.

4. Discussion

In this paper, a formal definition of semantic abstraction, extending the framework of Tenenberg, is given; in particular the abstraction mechanism is axiomatized by means of a theory and the abstraction itself can be obtained by deduction.

Afterwards, we have shown that inverse resolution is a good starting point for computing a kind of semantic abstraction called completeness-preserving abstraction. Moreover, the operator set defined in inverse resolution [12,13] is extended in order to allows term abstraction, i.e. an abstraction mechanism similar to the one used for dealing with abstract data types in programming languages, where the internal structure of the data is hidden and only some of the properties are exported. Term abstraction is still a CPA.

Moreover, we noticed how the absorption rule can introduce inconsistencies which need to be checked through a step of theorem proving, and we introduced a more restricted form of absorption, called NG-absorption, which does not involve generalization and does not require consistency check. Using NGA and constructive operators, such as intra-construction and term construction, a restricted form of CPA can be obtained which has been called Non Generalizing CP-Abstraction.

Non-Generalizing CP-Abstraction maintains its consistency independently on the extension, because it is generated without introducing generalization. This property results particularly important when a universal theory has to be abstracted (the domain theory, for instance). In this case CPA could add new theorems to the abstract theory, whereas Non-Generalizing CP-Abstraction does not.

In conclusion, by defining Non-Generalizing CP-Abstraction, we obtained the possibility of splitting the mechanism for generating abstract representations from the mechanism for learning, which is based on generalization.

References

[1] A. Newell, H. Simon: *Human Problem Solving,* Prentice-Hall, (Englewood Cliffs, NJ, 1972).

[2] D. Plaisted: "Theorem Proving with Abstraction", *Artificial Intelligence, 16,* 47-108 (1981).

[3] J. Tenenberg: "Preserving Consistency across Abstraction Mappings", *Proc IJCAI-87,* (Milano, Italy, 1987), pp. 1011-1014.

[4] C. Knoblock: "Abstractiong the Tower of Hanoi", *Working notes of the AGAA-90 Workshop,* (Boston, MA, 1990), pp. 13-23.

[5] C. Knoblock: "Learning Hierarchies of Abstraction Spaces", *Proc. 6th Int. Workshop on Machine Learning* (Ithaca, NY, 1989).

[6] G. Drastal, G. Czako, S. Raatz: "Induction in an Abstraction Space", *Proc. IJCAI-89,* (Detroit, MI, 1989), pp. 708-712.

[7] I. Mozetic, "Abstractions in Model-Based Diagnosis", *Working notes of the AGAA-90 Workshop,* (Boston, MA, 1990), pp. 64-75.

[8] A.Giordana, L.Saitta, "Abstraction: a General Framework for Learning", *Working notes of the AGAA-90 Workshop,* (Boston, MA, 1990), pp. 245-256.

[9] J. Carbonell, C. Knoblock, S. Minton: "PRODIGY: An Integrated Architecture for Planning and Learning", *Report CMU-CS-89-189,* Carnegie-Mellon Univ. (Pittsbugh, PA), (1989).

[10] R.Stepp, R. Michalski,"Conceptual Clustering, Inventing Goal-Oriented Classifications of Structured Objects", in Michalski R., Carbonell J. & Mitchell T.(Eds) *Machine Learning: An AI Approach,* Vol. *II.* Los Altos, CA: Morgan Kaufmann (1985), pp. 471-498.

[11] P.Utgoff, "Shift of Bias For Inductive Concept Learning", in Michalski R., Carbonell J. & Mitchell T.(Eds) *Machine Learning: An AI Approach,* Vol. *II.* Los Altos, CA: Morgan Kaufmann (1985), pp.107-148.

[12] S.Muggleton, W.Buntine, "Machine Invention of First-Order Predicates by Inverting Resolution", *Proc. Fifth Int. Conf. on Machine Learning,* (Ann Arbor, MI, 1988), pp.339-352.

[13] C.Rouveirol, J.F. Puget,"Beyond Inversion of Resolution", *Proc. Seventh Int. Conf. on Machine Learning,* (Austin, TE, 1990). pp.122-131.

[14] W. Buntine: "Generalized Subsumption and its Applications to Induction and Redundancy", *Artificial Intelligence, 36,* 149-176 (1988).

[15] G.Plotkin, "Automatic Methods of Inductive Inference", *Doctoral thesis,* Edimburg University.

[16] S. Muggleton, "Duce, an Oracle Based Approach to Constructive Induction," in *Proc IJCAI-87,* (Milano, Italy, 1987), pp. 287-292 .

References

Natural Language

USING WORD ASSOCIATION FOR SYNTACTIC DISAMBIGUATION

R. Basili(*) M. T. Pazienza(*) P. Velardi(**)
(*)   Dept. of Electr. Engineering, University of Roma "Tor Vergata", Roma, (Italy)
(**)   Institute of Informatics, University of Ancona, Ancona, (Italy)

Abstract
The study of word co-occurrences is common in linguistics but only recently the availability of on-line corpora and dictionaries made it possible to extensively collect word associations. Several papers published on this topic claim that their results are useful not only for lexicographers and linguists, but also for NLP, particularly for semantic and syntactic disambiguation in sentence analysis, as well as for lexical choice in generation. However such claims have not been convincingly proved so far. In this paper we argue that word associations derived through pure statistical analysis can hardly cope with the problem of syntactic disambiguation. It is shown that better performances are obtained by integrating wide-coverage techniques such as statistics with traditional NLP methods.

1. Introduction

The challenge for next generation NLP systems is to be able to process texts which are not restricted to a few hundred words. A wider diffusion of AI-based text processing techniques depends upon the ability of current systems to improve their robustness, in particular for what concerns knowledge-intensive, low-coverage techniques such as semantic analysis. In this paper we address the problem of automatically extracting from corpora data which can be useful for syntactic disambiguation.

In traditional NLP systems the disambiguation of compounds, prepositional phrases (PPs) and conjunctions is handled by specifying the selectional restrictions to which words must obey. Hence for example in:

> *John goes to Boston by bus*

the PP "*by bus*" is attached to the verb "*go*" rather than to "*to Boston*", because somewhere in the semantic knowledge base it is specified that:

[GO]->(INSTRUMENT)->[VEHICLE]

The task of hand-encoding selectional restrictions is a bottleneck in NLP systems, because it is very time-consuming and it is hard to keep consistency among the data when the lexicon has several hundred or thousand words. The limitations of AI techniques for extensive text processing has been recently stressed in many important linguistic forums [COL 1990],[ACL 1990]. A new tendency is to automatically acquire lexical knowledge from on-line dictionaries and large corpora using statistical methods. However, pure statistics is at the other extreme with respect to pure knowledge-based techniques. In our view, a better compromise should be pursued between breadth and depth.

The algorithm that we propose hereafter to help syntactic disambiguation is based on a mixture of shallow methods, such as the statistical collection of co-occurring words, and more traditional NLP methods, such as syntactic analysis and semantic tagging. Knowledge-intensive techniques are adopted to the extent their demand for manual knowledge codification is time constrained and can be realistically performed on an extensive basis.

The next Section addresses the limitations of statistically collected word co-occurrences for syntactic disambiguation. It is shown that more reliable data are obtained using a syntactic parser. Section 3 illustrates our method in detail, and Section 4 evaluates its performances.

2. *Limitations of statistically collected associations for syntactic disambiguation*

The study of word associations extracted from on-line corpora or dictionaries is a common practice in computational linguistics [Calzolari 1990], [Church 1990], [Smadja 1989], [Tsutsumi 1991],[Zernik 1990]. Word associations are collected by extracting word pairs in a ±5 window. In [Calzolari 1990], [Church 1990] the significance of an association (x,y) is measured by the <u>mutual information</u> $I(x,y)$, i.e. the probability of observing x and y together, compared with the probability of observing x and y independently. In [Smadja 1989], [Zernik 1990], the associations are filtered by selecting the word pairs (x,y) whose frequency of occurrence is above $f+ks$, where f is the average appearance, s is the standard deviation, and k is an empirically determined factor. The results of these studies have had important applications in lexicography to detect lexico-syntactic regularities, for example support verbs (e.g. *"make-decision"*) prepositional verbs (e.g. *"rely-upon"*) idioms and fixed expressions (e.g. *"kick the bucket"*).

It is also claimed that association knowledge is useful in NLP for semantic and syntactic disambiguation in sentence analysis, and for lexical choice in generation, even though such claims are not explicitly addressed in the mentioned papers. There is a clear evidence that lexical choice and semantic disambiguation would benefit from the results of these analyses.

Statistically collected associations provide pragmatic cues for lexical choice in sentence generation. For example, we can learn that *"make-decision"* is a better choice than, say, *"have-decision"* or *"take-decision"*.

It is also learned the <u>semantic domain</u> of words, i.e. the collection of words that typically co-occur in a given context. This is useful for semantic disambiguation. For example, if *"bank"* co-occurs with words such as *"clerk"*, *"money"* or the like, we can infer that the text is about a bank-establishment rather than about a river-bank. What is questionable is the utility of statistically collected associations for syntactic disambiguation. Word pairs like *"bank"* and *"money"*, *"doctor"* and *"nurse"*, etc., are semantically related because they belong to a common conceptual domain, <u>not</u> because they are mutually constrained by some selectional restriction, as for *"go"* and *"bus"*. In other words, the ±5 associations provide a measure of semantic relationship different from the one needed for syntactic disambiguation.

A more useful notion of semantic vicinity is the following:

Two words x and y are <u>selectionally related</u> if for some sense $S(x)$ of x and $S(y)$ of y, there exists a selectional restriction:
$S(x)$-REL-$S(y)$ (e.g.: [GO]->(INSTRUMENT)->[VEHICLE]).
The notion of <u>semantic relationship</u> is wider than that of <u>selectional relationship</u>. Semantically related word pairs include also selectionally related pairs, but the percentage of such co-occurrences is in our view very low, and does not provide a reliable body of data to support syntactic disambiguation.

To experiment on a concrete example, we analyzed a corpus of 25,000 descriptions of economic enterprises registered at the Chambers of Commerce in Italy. The database of these descriptions (in total over 1,000,000) is managed in Italy by the Company CERVED, that cooperates with researchers of the Universities of Ancona and Roma "Tor Vergata" on a project for the extensive acquisition of lexical knowledge [Pazienza 1991], Velardi 1991],[Velardi 1991b]. Sentences describe one or several commercial activities carried out by a given Company. Examples of these descriptions are provided in what follows (see S1), S2), S3), S4)).

To get an idea of the body of knowledge extracted using pure statistical associations, we selected some 100 sentences from which we collected two sets of associations:
With <u>method 1</u>, we collected ordered pairs of content words (noun, verbs and adjectives) in a ±5 window.
With <u>method 2</u>, the ordered word pairs are extracted by a fast syntactic analyzer [Fasolo 1990]. The analyzer extracts syntactically related pairs (e.g. verb-object, noun-adjective, etc.). In case of syntactic ambiguity, all the ambiguous associations are generated.
The word pairs were inspected by hand and classified as follows:
1.   "correct" associations, i.e. <u>selectionally related words</u>
2.   non-selectionally related associations (= <u>errors</u>)
3.   selectionally related associations which are detected with method 2 and missed with method 1 (= <u>good misses</u>)
4.   non-selectionally related associations which are collected with method 2 and missed with method 1 (= <u>wrong misses</u>).
Errors are prefixed with one star (*), "good misses" with two (**), "wrong misses" with three (***). "Wrong misses" are computed as errors for method 2, even though they are highlighted separately. "Good misses" are not computed as errors for method 1. To make an example, we report hereafter the complete list of word pairs extracted from one sentence, and a summary table for four sentences. The sentences selected for this example are representative of typical ambiguous structures that may occur in the domain, i.e. conjunctions and prepositional phrases.

S1)   *Costruire*(1) *ed assemblare*(2) *serramenti*(3), *carpenteria*(4) *leggera*(5), *profilati*(6) *di alluminio*(7), *materiali*(8) *ferrosi*(9) *e non-ferrosi*(10), *serramenti*(11) *ed accessori*(12), *macchine*(13) *utensili*(14).
*   *To build*(1) *and package*(2) *locks*(3), *light*(5) *framing*(4), *[draw pieces]*(6) *in aluminium*(7), *ferrous*(9) *and non-ferrous*(10) *material*(8), *locks*(11) *and fittings*(12), *machine*(13) *tools*(14).

<u>Associations extracted with method 1</u>:

1-2,1-3,1-4,*1-5,1-6,2-3,2-4,*2-5,2-6,*2-7,*3-4,*3-5,*3-6,*3-7,*3-8,

4-5,*4-6,*4-7,*4-8,*4-9,*5-6,*5-7,*5-8,*5-9,*5-10,6-7,*6-8,*6-9,*6-10,
*6-11,*7-8,*7-9,*7-10,*7-11,*7-12,8-9,8-10,*8-11,*8-12,*8-13,9-10,
*9-11,*9-12,*9-13,*9-14,*10-11,*10-12,*10-13,*10-14,11-12,*11-13,
*11-14,*12-13,*12-14,13-4

Associations extracted with method 2:

1-2,1-3,1-4,*1-5,1-6,*1-7,**1-8, **1-11,**1-12,**1-13,2-3,2-4,*2-5,2-6,
*2-7,**2-8,**2-11,**2-12,**2-13, 4-5,6-7,8-9,8-10,11-12,13-14

S2)   *Produzione(1) e commercio(2) di prodotti(3) per il trattamento(4) del cotto(5).*
*   *Production(1) and sale(2) of products(3) for the treating(4) of the brickwork(5).*

S3)   *Imbottigliamento(1) e confezionamento(2) dei prodotti(3) chimici(4) per la pulizia(5) della casa(6) e della persona(7).*
*   *Bottling(1) and manufacturing(2) of chemical(4) products(3) for the cleaning(5) of the house(6) and of the person(7).*

S4)   *Installazione(1) di materiali(2) idraulici(3) e realizzazione(4) di impianti(5) di riscaldamento(6)*
*   *Installation(1) of hydraulic(3) tools(2) and building(4) of heating(6) plants(5).*

Sentence	Method	Totally collected associations	Errors	Good Misses	Wrong Misses
1	1	55	41	-	-
1	2	24	4	8	0
2	1	10	5	-	-
2	2	10	5	0	0
3	1	20	2	-	-
3	2	16	7	0	1
4	1	5	10	-	-
4	2	6	1	0	0

- Fig. 1 : Summary of collected association -

The statistics over the 100 sentences gives about a 55% of errors for method 1 plus an 8% of "good misses" (i.e. selectionally-related pairs of words, not detected by method 1). Method 2 gives only a 25% of errors. An extensive statistics of the percentage of non selectionally related collocates cannot be gathered from the corpus, because the star tagging is done by hand. However, looking at the data we can give some general account of the major sources of errors:

1   With method 1, many errors are due to syntactically wrong associations of adjectives or adverbs with verbs or nouns (e.g. *"hydraulic-heating"*, *"chemical-house"*, *"to package-ferrous"* etc.). In English, many errors would also be produced from sentences with conjunctive compounds. For example:
    House(1) *cleaning*(2) *and sorghum*(3) *blooms*(4)
    give with method 1 the following errors: *1-3, *1-4, *2-3, *2-4.
    These errors are avoided with a syntax that handles noun phrases and conjunctions.
2   With method 1, the ±5 limitation causes some missed attachment for long PP sentences (nested or in conjunction), and VPs with many objects (or subjects) in conjunction. Missed thematic roles (subjects and objects) are always "good misses". In case of PP sentences, it is not possible to determine whether "good misses" (e.g. *"packaging-fittings"*) are more than "wrong misses" (e.g. *"bottling-person"*), even though, in our corpus, there is a strong evidence about. This however is likely to depend upon the syntactic structure of the corpus. In principle, wrong and "good misses" have the same probability.
3   Errors with method 2 are due to prepositional (PP) ambiguity[1] (e.g. *"manufacturing-of the house"* in S3). The same errors are produced with method 1, and only for long PP sequences the +5 limitation avoids the collection of some wrong collocate that is instead collected with method 2 (the only example is *"bottling-person"* in S3).

In general, method 1 performs well for what concerns thematic roles such as object and subject, provided these are attached, or very close (d<5) to the verb. However, in NLP systems the problem is with the attachment of conjunctions and PPs, not with thematic roles. It can be concluded that a statistical collection of word associations hardly gives disambiguation cues for NLP parsers, because the percentage of collected associations that are selectionally related is too low. The use of filtering techniques like the mutual information and the minimum frequency of occurrence are useful at pruning out pairs which are not semantically related, but not at extracting selectionally related pairs. More reliable data are extracted using a syntactic parser. An additional improvement can be obtained with semantic tagging. This is discussed in the next Section, where it is described our method for syntactic disambiguation.

3. A method for syntactic disambiguation

One of the problems with word-pairs collections (both with method 1 and 2) is that reliable data are obtained only for a subset of high-frequency words on very large corpora (for example, Church reports over 20-30 millions words), otherwise the association ratio becomes unstable. In the previous Section we showed that the problem is even worst with method 1, because there are too many sources of errors that add noise to the data. In many practical NLP applications corpora are not so large, and typically span from 100,000 to 1,000,000 words. The analysis of associations could be done on wider domains, but a part for very general words, it is much more desirable to collect data from the application corpus. Information collected from other sources could

---

[1] The main difference in English is that the problem with PP attachment is found also with compounds. The general rule of correspondence between English compounds and Italian PPs is the following:
noun1 noun2 -> noun2 of(=di) noun1
e.g. *house cleaning* -> *pulizia(cleaning) della(of the) casa(house)*

add noise rather than strengthening the data, because in most NLP applications jargon, technical words, and domain-dependent associations are the norm. In [Smadja 1989b] it is shown a table of <u>operational pairs</u> like adjective-noun and verb-object, from which clearly emerges the very different nature of the two source domains (Unix Usenet and Jerusalem Post): for example, the noun-noun pairs with *"tree"* include associations such as *"parse, grammar, decision"* and *"olive, Christmas"*. If the NLP application is about the computer world, associations such as *"olive tree"* or *"Christmas tree"* are (at best) useless.

In order to capitalize on the limited data that can be collected from a given linguistic domain, we give words a semantic tag and use the tag to cluster the collected associations.

The task of hand-tagging words is not at all prohibitive if very few and high-level semantic categories are selected, such as human-entity, action, location, etc. In this case, the task is much easier and can be performed in parallel with the codification of the morphologic lexicon.

In our application, the following categories were adopted:

ACTIVITY (*buy, sell, production, packaging*, etc.)
HUMAN_ENTITY (*shareholder, company, person*, etc.)
ANIMAL (*cow, sheep*, etc.)
VEGETABLE (*carrots, grape*, etc.)
MATERIAL (*wood, iron, water*, etc.)
BUILDING (*mill, farm, greenhouse, house*, etc.)
BY_PRODUCT (*jam, milk, wine, hide*, etc.)
ARTIFACT (*brickwork, can, bottle*, etc.)
MACHINE (*car, tractor, grindstone*, etc.)
PLACE (*ground, field, territory, Italy, sea*, etc.)
QUALITY (*green, chemical, coaxial, flexible, hygiene*, etc.)
MANNER (*chemically, by-hand, wholesale, retail*, etc.)

These categories classify well enough the words which are found in the selected sub-corpus as a test-bed for our research. Some words received two tags: for example, there are sentences in which a BUILDING metonymically refers to the ACTIVITY held in that building (e.g. *"trade mills for the production.."*); some word is both a BY_PRODUCT (e.g. *"wood carving"*) or a MATERIAL (e.g. *"handicrafts in wood"*). Other words, such as *"law"*, *"number"*, *"sector"*, *"economy"* could not be tagged and were just ignored. Unclassified words are less than 10% in our corpus.

Before describing formally the syntactic disambiguation method, we give a concrete example of the type of information we wish to extract from the corpus. Let us consider the following five sentences:
1.*To sell wine in bottles*
2.*To sell wine to the customers*
3.*Cellars with wine in barrels*
4.*To sell fruit to the shareholders*
5.*To sell vegetables in the markets*
All the above sentences give rise to syntactic ambiguity for what concerns the attachment of the prepositional phrase. We want to solve the ambiguity of the first two

sentences. A good clue would be to learn from the corpus that the probability of occurrence of "*sell-in*-ARTIFACT" (1) is significantly lower than "*wine-in*-ARTIFACT" (1 and 3), and "*sell-to*-HUMAN_ENTITY" (2 and 4) is significantly higher than "*wine-to*-HUMAN_ENTITY" (2).

An important difference with the previous works on word associations is that we collect operational pairs or triples, hereafter called <u>syntactic associations</u> (e.g. verb-object: "*sell wine*", noun-preposition-noun: "*wine in barrel*"), rather than simple co-occurrences (e.g. "*sell wine*", "*wine bottle*"). Indeed, the type of syntactic link, and the linking preposition (if any) imply important restrictions on the nature of the semantic relation between co-occurring words. Hence for example "*to sell flats*" and "*to sell..in flats*" give rise to different syntactic associations, which are clustered separately.

Let us describe the method more formally, for the case of a VP NP PP structure. The treatment of other ambiguous structures follows straightforwardly.
Let $V\_N(x,y)$ be a verb-object pair, $V\_p\_N(x,p,y)$ be a verb-prep-noun triple, and $N\_p\_N(x,p,y)$ be a noun-prep-noun triple. Let W be the set of semantic tags. For any verb v, such that the number of occurrences in the corpus $N_V > \beta$[2]

1. Let X_V be the set of objects of v, i. e.:

$$X_V = \{ x : \exists \ V\_N(v, x) \}[3]$$

and P_V the set of prepositional phrase modifiers of v

$$P_V = \{ (p,y) : \exists \ V\_p\_N(v, p, y) \}$$

2. For any object $x \varepsilon X_V$, and preposition p such that it exists at least one y, with $(p,y)\varepsilon P_V$
    a. for all $w \varepsilon W$, let Y_W' be the cluster of y such that it exists at least one $N\_p\_N(x, p, y)$, and they have the same semantic tag w.
    Let N_W' be the cardinality of the set Y_W', i.e. $N_W' = card(Y_W')$
    b. for all $w \varepsilon W$, let Y_W'' be the cluster of y, such that it exists at least one $V\_p\_N(v, p, y)$ and they have the same semantic tag w.
    Let $N_W'' = card(Y_W'')$.
    c. for all $w \varepsilon W$, let $D_W = N_W'' - N_W'$
3. for any sentence of the type

$$v - x - p - y$$

where y has the tag $w \varepsilon W$, prefer the attachment:
    i) $v - p - y$ if $D_W > \alpha$ $\alpha \varepsilon R^+$
    ii) $x - p - y$ if $D_W < -\alpha$
The decision is not reliable when $| D_W | \leq \alpha$.
Step 3 establishes the preference criterion.

4. Evaluation of results

The above method was applied on about 25,000 descriptions, for a total of 420.000 words, 427 lemmata in the class ACTIVITY, 15 prepositions (*di, a, da, per, con, mediante, su,*

---

[2] The value of β depends upon the corpus size.
[3] The symbol $\exists$ refers to the existence of the association collected from the corpus.

senza, fra, tra, sotto, secondo, entro, presso, attraverso). Words like "*production*" and "*to produce*" have been considered as a single activity. Accordingly, the syntactic associations $N\_p\_N(A,of,x)$ where A is an activity, are considered the same as $V\_N(A,x)$ (e.g. *production of wine = to produce wine*).

The morphologic and syntactic analyzers used to extract associations are described in [Fasolo 1990]. The morphologic lexicon has now some 6000 lemmata, but keeps growing. The syntactic analyzer uses heuristic techniques to cut long sentences into phrases with the structure: <ACTIVITY> <DESCRIPTION>. A fast noun-phrase parser runs on the DESCRIPTION segments. The parser does not produce a structured tree, but only a list of syntactic associations, e.g. $V\_N(to\_sell,wine)$. Overall, we have:
2847 different V_N associations, 38592 V_p_N, and 4783 N_p_N (including the "*A of x*"). The preference criterion of step 3 is applied provided $N_W''+N_W'>10$, $\alpha=0.3\times(N_W''+N_W')$. These values have been experimentally selected.

The results of the algorithm are summarized in tables like Tables 1 and 2. Each table refers to an activity A and a preposition P. The first column gives the distribution of the collected $V\_p\_N(A,P,x)$ among semantic classes. The subsequent columns give the distribution of $N\_p\_N(X_i,P,y)$ among semantic classes. The X_i are those extracted in Step 1 of the algorithm, and the distributions are computed according to Step 2. For example, Table 1 gives a preference criterion for phrase structures like: "*Costruire (To build) Y con (with) X*" and Table 2 for phrase structures like: "*Acquistare (to buy) Y per (for) X*". Table 1, rows 7 and 8, suggests that the PP modifiers "*with MATERIAL*" (e.g. *wood, cement, iron,* etc.) or "*with MACHINE*" (*crane, press, lathe,* etc.) should be attached to the verb rather than to its object. Row 6 of Table 2 suggests that "*for ACTIVITY*" is more likely to specify the destination of the object to be sold (e.g. "*attrezzature per la pesca*" "**equipments for fishing*", "*macchine per l'edilizia*" "**machinery for the building-industry*" etc.).

From the 25,000 sentences, the algorithm produced 650 tables for about 250 activities, such that at least some row of each table allows a reliable decision according to the preference criterion in Step 3. The number of columns is variable in each table. The interpretation of the tables is not always straightforward and one must look at the corpus to verify the plausibility of the data. For example, the associations like "*to build with ACTIVITY*" (row 6 in Table 1) are collected because in Italian the preposition "*con*" (with) is also used like a conjunction (e.g. "*costruzione [di qualcosa] con vendita..*" "**construction [of something] with sale..*"). A manual evaluation of the results was performed on the following 9 more frequent verbs: *build, breed, trash, commercialize, work, manage, produce, cultivate, buy.* We selected from the corpus 150 sentences where these verbs appear in a VP NP PP structure. The tables could provide a reliable preference criterion in 93 cases out of the 150, and the criterion was manually verified as correct in the 90% of such 93 cases.
It is hard to classify the sources of errors. In many cases, it is just a matter of noise in the data or odd sentences. For some errors, a further clustering of the data could improve the reliability of the results. For example, consider in Table 3 ("*Costruire Y per X*") the crosspoints of row 6 (ACTIVITY) with column 2 (*house*). The table suggests that in sentences like: "*costruire case per il ricovero..*" ("**to build houses for [destined to] the sheltering..*"), the PP should be attached to the verb. The problem here is that "*house*" has a limited number of occurrences. By merging in Table 3 the data in the columns

belonging to the class BUILDING (e.g. 2, 3, and 6) we would learn a more general rule, i.e. that in sentences like: "*to build* BUILDINGS *for* ACTIVITY", the PP modifier should preferably be attached to the verb object. The current state of our experimental research however does not allow a full evaluation of the pros and contras of a further data clustering. A wider experimentation on a larger corpus is needed.

5. *Concluding remarks*

The method presented in this paper to solve syntactic ambiguity has several advantages:
1   the disambiguation criteria are automatically derived form the application corpus;
2   the method relies on "robust" NLP techniques, like morphologic and syntactic parsing, and on shallow, wide-coverage techniques like statistics;
3   manual codification of deep knowledge (semantics) is needed to a very limited extent;
4   it is not necessary to process very large corpora, as for standard   co-occurrences analysis, because the use of NLP techniques improves the reliability of the data.

One obvious drawback (common to all statistically-based methods) is that the algorithm provides a decision criterion only for frequent cases, and in some case it provides the wrong answer. More experimental work is needed to fully evaluate the algorithm. We plan to extend our analysis to different and wider corpora. Despite these limitations, we believe that   a better compromise between depth and breadth in NLP systems can only be obtained with a mixture of shallow and AI based techniques. Finding the best cocktail among heuristics, statistics, syntactic and semantic parsing, reasoning etc. is a matter of experiments and evaluations. No single method is likely to produce amazing performance improvements, but even a 10% improvement should not be misregarded. NLP is nowadays a mature discipline that must demonstrate a more incisive impact on applications.

Acknowledgments

This work has been in part supported under grant PRO_ART 1991 by the European Community and in part by the CERVED. We thank the NLP group at the CERVEDomani who developed the morphologic and syntactic analyzers.

References

[ACL 1990], Proceedings of ACL 90, Philadelfia, Pennsylvania, 1990.
[Calzolari 1990], N. Calzolari, R. Bindi, *Acquisition of Lexical Information from Corpus*, Proc. of COLING 90, Helsinki 1990.
[Church 1990], K.W.Church , P. Hanks, *Word Association Norms, Mutual Information, and Lexicography*, Computational Linguistics vol 16, n. 1, March 1990.
[COL 1990], Proceedings of COLING 90, Helsinki 1990.
[Fasolo 1990], M.Fasolo, L.Garbuio, N.Guarino, *Comprensione di descrizioni di attivita' economico-produttive espresse in linguaggio naturale*, Proc. of GULP Conference, Padova 1990.

[Smadja 1989], F. A. Smadja, *Lexical Co-occurrence: The Missing Link*, Literary and Linguistic Computing, vol. 4, n.3, 1989.

[Pazienza 1991], M.T. Pazienza, P.Velardi, *Knowledge Acquisition for NLP: Tools and Methods*, Proc. of The Int. Conference on Current Issues in Computational Linguistics, Penang, Malaysia, June, 1991.

[Smadja 1989b] F. Smadja, *Macrocoding the Lexicon with Co-occurrence Knowledge*, in First Lexical Acquisition Workshop, August 1989, Detroit.

[Tsutsumi 1991], T.Tsutsumi, *Word sense disambiguation by examples*, Proc. of The Int. Conference on Current Issues in Computational Linguistics, Penang, Malaysia, June, 1991.

[Velardi 1991], P. Velardi, M.T. Pazienza, M. Fasolo, *How to encode linguistic knowledge: a method for meaning representation and computer-aided acquisition*, Computational Linguistics, 1991 (forthcoming).

[Velardi 1991b], P. Velardi, *Acquiring a semantic lexicon for natural language processing*, in "Lexical Acquisition Using On-line Resources" U.Zernik editor, Lawrence Erlbaum ed., 1991 (in press).

[Zernik 1990], U. Zernik, P. Jacobs, *Tagging for Learning: Collecting Thematic Relations from Corpus*, Proc. of COLING 90, Helsinki, August 1990.

TABLE 1   Verb: Costruire   (to Build)
          Prep.: con (with)

	to Build	Hotel	bid	work	house	machine
Hum. Entity	–	–	–	–	–	–
Veg.	–	–	–	–	–	–
Build..	–	15	–	–	–	–
By_prod.	–	–	15	20	–	12
Place	–	–	–	–	–	–
Activity	60	15	15	23	50	10
Material	26	–	–	–	10	–
Mach.	22	–	–	–	–	28

TABLE 2 Verb: Acquistare (to Buy)
Prep.: per (for)

	to Buy	product	building	equipment	machine	
Hum. Entity	—	—	—	—	12	—
Veg.	—	—	—	—	—	—
Build..	—	14	40	36	—	—
By_prod.	—	15	—	—	—	—
Place	—		10	20	24	—
Activity	39	120	50	42	95	—
Material	—	—	—	—	40	—
Mach.	—	—	—	—	—	—

TABLE 3 Verb: Costruire (to Build)
Prep.: per (for)

	to Build	house	building	product	machine	hotel	article
Hum. Entity	24	—	—	—	15	12	15
Veg.	—	—	—	—	—	—	—
Build..	50	—	36	40	12	30	48
By_prod.	—	30	—	—	—	—	26
Place	10	15	10	20	24	10	22
Activity	70	12	39	540	95	25	350
Material	—	—	—	—	—	—	—
Mach.	—	—	—	—	—	—	—

A COMPUTATIONAL MODEL OF TENSE SELECTION AND ITS EXPERIMENTATION WITHIN AN INTELLIGENT TUTOR

D. Fum[1], C. Tasso[2], L. Tiepolo[2], A. Tramontini[2]

[1] Dipartimento di Psicologia - Universita' di Trieste
[2] Laboratorio di Intelligenza Artificiale - Universita' di Udine

ABSTRACT. The paper presents a new computational model for the selection of verb tenses aimed at supporting the choice and conjugation of the appropriate tense in English sentences. The work has been developed within the framework of the ET research project whose purpose is the experimentation of intelligent tutoring systems for foreign language teaching. The model has been validated and experimentally tested through the development of TEN-EX (TENse EXpert), a prototype system which receives in input a representation of an English sentence and is capable of finding and conjugating the appropriate tense(s) for it. The model originates from the functional-systemic approach to tense from which it inherits the basic ideas of tense opposition and seriality. The model is characterized by some original assumptions such as the partitioning of the tense selection process in two separate phases aimed at discovering the 'objective' tense, relating speaking time to event time, and at mapping the objective tense into the actual grammatical tense. This bipartite organization corresponds to the idea that the tense selection process is influenced by both the temporal semantics of the situation a speaker intends to describe and the pragmatic and syntactic features which act as a filter in mapping the objective tense into the grammatical resources of the language at hand. TEN-EX is a fully implemented system which is currently capable of solving more than 80 exercises covering all the English indicative tenses.

1. Introduction

The study of the verb tense has traditionally arisen the interest of linguists and philosophers concerned with the semantics of natural language. Linguists have tried to describe the properties (at the morphological, syntactical or semantic level) of the tense in the different languages, while the philosophers have attempted to characterize its usage conditions. More recently, however, the issue of tense has attracted the attention of people interested in the construction of systems capable of automatic natural language processing since the tense of the verb plays a major role in the possibility of describing - and in understanding the description of - complex events. (For some recent collection of papers on this topic see: Dahl 1985; Dowty, 1986; Tedeschi and Zaenen 1981; Webber, 1988).

Our interest for the issue of tense has a different source since it originates from the efforts to construct intelligent tutoring systems for foreign languages. In the last few years we have built different versions of ET, a prototype tutor capable of supporting the learning of the English tense system (Fum, Giangrandi, and Tasso 1988, 1990; Fum, Pani and Tasso 1991, in press). As it is known, a fundamental component of a tutoring system is represented by the so called domain-expert module which incorporates the knowledge constituting the system expertise that has to be transmitted to the student. In the domain of tutoring systems for foreign languages, this module is supposed to incorporate the knowledge underlying the competence of a native speaker, in our case the system of rules supporting the use of English tenses.

In the paper we present a new computational model for the selection of tense which has been validated and experimentally tested through the development of TEN-EX, a prototype system capable of solving the tense generation problem. More particularly, the system, after receiving in input a schematic representation of an English sentence, finds and conjugates the appropriate tense(s) for it. The model originates from the functional-systemic approach to tense from which it inherits the basic ideas of tense opposition and seriality. The model is characterized by some original assumptions such as the partitioning of the tense selection process in two separate phases aimed at discovering the 'objective' tense relating speaking time to event time, and at mapping the objective tense into the actual grammatical tense, respectively. This bipartite organization corresponds to the idea that the tense selection process is influenced by both the temporal semantics of the situation a speaker intends to describe and the pragmatic and syntactic features which act as a filter in mapping the objective tense into the grammatical resources of the language at hand.

The paper is organized as follows: The next section illustrates the systemic approach to tense developed theoretically by Halliday (1976) and, from a computational point of view, by Matthiessen (1983, 1984). In the section some criticisms to the Matthiessen's approach are raised which motivate the development of our original model. Section 3 is devoted to the presentation of the new model from the theoretic point of view, to the discussion of its basic assumptions, and to the description of the knowledge it relies upon. Section 4 deals with the implementational aspects of TEN-EX in which the theoretical model has been realized, and provides an example of interaction with the system giving an idea of its capabilities. Section 5 ends the paper by making a general evaluation of the model and by suggesting some guidelines for future research.

2. The Systemic Theory of Tense

In this section the systemic approach to the problem of tense selection is briefly described. What follows is based on the work of Halliday (1976) and, in particular, of Matthiessen (1983, 1984).

According to the systemic approach, two assumptions are made concerning the grammar of the English tense. These assumptions are:
a) *Tense opposition:* the tense in English is considered as a three term opposition of past vs. present vs. future.
b) *Seriality:* complex tense combinations can be constructed by repeatedly selecting among the three term opposition.

The two assumptions reduce the process of tense selection to a series of iterative choices within the three terms option. In other words, a tense combination like *'is going to have built'* is chosen by picking up the first time *(primary tense)* the present, then *(secondary tense)* the future and finally *(ternary tense)* the past. The name for a tense combination in the systemic approach is determined by considering the inverted order of the choices: in our case the tense combination is a *past-in-future-in-present*.

Halliday identifies a series of 'stop rules' which capture the restrictions that the English grammar puts on the usage of tense and state which possible tense combinations are admissible. An important consequence of the rules is the fact that up to quinary tenses (like: *'will have been going to have been taking'* : a present-in-past-in-future-in-past-in-past) are allowed by the grammar. The rules define whether a tense combination is legitimate but they do not indicate *how* a given tense combination is selected. To this end, a significant contribution has been given by Matthiessen with his notion of *chooser*. To each option concerning the tense, Matthiessen assigns a procedure (or chooser) that states how the selection among the options specified is controlled.

According to this point of view, a verb tense essentially indicates the temporal relationship which holds between the so called *speaking time Ts* (i.e., the moment in which a sentence is uttered) and the *event time Te* (i.e., the moment in which the action or event described in the sentence is supposed to happen), and the tense selection process is based on such a relation. More particularly, for each iteration step, the choosers take into account a relation of precedence (anteriority) - that we symbolize through $'<'$ - between two different temporal variables called the *reference time (Tr)* and the *comparison time (Tc)*, respectively. If:
- *Tr* come after *Tc* $(Tc < Tr)$, then the past is chosen;
- *Tr* comes before *Tc* $(Tr < Tc)$, then the future is chosen;
- otherwise the chosen tense is the present.
The process starts by setting the time variable *Tr* to the speaking time *Ts* and by looking for the comparison time *Tc*, i.e., the time interval the speaking time is related to. At this point it is possible to choose the primary tense according to the relation which holds between the values

of Tr and Tc. If the comparison time matches the event time $Te,$ then the temporal link between Ts and Te has been found, and the resulting tense combination consists only of a primary tense (a simple present or a simple past or a simple future). If, on the other hand, the comparison time is different from the event time, the process cannot terminate since no temporal link has been established between the speaking time and the event time. A new iteration cycle starts by assigning the old value of Tc to Tr, which becomes the new *reference time*, and by looking for a new value of the comparison time Tc. The choice of the secondary tense is made again according to the relation holding between Tr and $Tc,$ and the process terminates if Tc matches Te. If this is not the case, the process goes on according to the same modalities with a tertiary, quaternary or quinary tense, until a link between the speaking time and the event time is found.

Two points should be emphasized at the end of this description of the systemic grammar of tense. The first concerns the fact that, in the Matthiessen's approach (1983, 1984) the identification of the comparison time - which represents, according to our point of view, the most critical step in the tense selection process - is a process that falls outside the grammar since it is a question that ultimately concerns text planning: the choice of the temporal relations among different times depends in fact on the meaning a given utterance is intended to convey. This will represent, as we shall see below, a critical issue in our treatment of tense.

The second point concerns the semantics of tense. According to Matthiessen, the verb tense expresses a temporal link between the speaking time and the event time. These two times are directly connected in the case of a primary tense; they are associated through the mediation of one, two, three, or four intervening times in the case of secondary, ternary, quaternary and quinary tenses, respectively. Differently from Halliday, however, the fact that no tense exists beyond the quinary depends on reasons of meaning and text planning, not on grammatical motives. Other approaches (among these the classic account of Reichenbach (1947) claim that the temporal structure is restricted to three elements, i.e, the speaking time, the event time, and *one* reference time. According to Matthiessen, a three time account is inadequate for English for two reasons: First, it would limit the coverage of the grammar to secondary tenses. Second, there is no logical basis for arbitrarily restricting the temporal structure to three (instead of, say, five, two or six) different times.

The ideas which Matthiessen's proposal is grounded upon (i.e., the temporal chaining, and the criteria for selecting the tense and terminating the process) are simple and appealing. There are however some difficulties with this approach.

The main criticism which can be raised against the model concerns one of its major assumptions, i.e. the fact that the selection of a given tense in each iteration step depends on the precedence relation which exists between the current reference and the comparison times. Taken in its strong form (the selection depends *only* on the precedence relation) this assumption is simply wrong since it does not allow to capture all the subtleties and nuances of meaning which can be expressed through the appropriate use of English tenses. Taken in its weaker form (the selection depends *primarily* on the the precedence relation - allowing thus the exploitation of other kinds of knowledge) it conflicts with the orthodox systemic approach in which the roles of the different features are clearly defined and ordered. Let us clarify this point through some examples.

If we look at how the Matthiessen's chooser of the primary tense really works, we realize that the first test the chooser makes about the incoming clause concerns its counterfactuality (which is obviously a non-temporal aspect). If the clause expresses a counterfactual meaning, then the chosen tense is the past, otherwise a new test concerning whether the clause denotes any logical or temporal restriction is made. Only after this second test has been executed, a direct comparison between the Tr and Tc is performed. It is clear that the criterion of counterfactuality and the existence of logical or temporal restrictions introduce in the process of tense selection some factors that go beyond the precedence relation between the current reference and comparison time.

Another critical case for the model concerns the so-called futurate use of the simple present in sentences like:*We live home at six, arrive in London at midnight and take a plane to Amsterdam*. According to the model, since the event time comes after the speaking time, the future tense, instead of the present, should be chosen. The explanation Matthiessen gives to this 'anomaly' is not completely convincing: "My claim is that one reason for choosing the present is that there is a plan (which is executed at some time in the future, often adverbially specified) and what is important is that the plan is present. In other words, the relevant time is the time of planning not the time of execution and it is the relevant time that is *present* (i.e., located at *Ts*) " (1984, pg. 92). Matthiessen thus introduces a time associated with the planning activity and, in order to terminate the selection process with the simple present, forces the time of planning to coincide with the speaking time. The event in such a way almost disappears being substituted by its planning.

In summary, Matthiessen's model constitutes a useful approach to a computational treatment of the English tense within the systemic framework but, by concentrating almost exclusively on the role of a particular temporal relation, it falls short of providing a clear picture of the factors that play a significant role in the process of tense selection. It is on this point that we provide our original contribution.

3. A New Computational Model of Tense Selection

The computational model we propose divides the tense selection process in two separate phases, each phase exploiting knowledge of a different kind.

The first phase is devoted to determine the relationship a speaker intends to establish between the speaking time and the event time. This phase ends with the identification of the so-called *objective tense,* a conceptual, extra-linguistic entity which reflects the semantics of the situation the clause (or sentence) is intended to convey. The procedure for the determination of the objective tense follows the systemic model, i.e. it is performed through an iterative process whose choices are made sequentially within the opposition past vs. present vs. future according to the precedence relation between a given reference time and its comparison time. The process obviously terminates when the comparison time matches the time of the event, thus indicating that a link between the speaking time and the event time has been found. Depending on the number of intervening times, the objective tense - as it has been demonstrated by Matthiessen (1984) - can theoretically range from the primary to the quinary.

The main problem to be solved in this phase is that of identifying, for each iteration step, the time to which the reference time has to be compared. Once the reference time and the comparison time have been determined, in fact, the choice within the three term opposition is performed - following Matthiessen's algorithm - according to the precedence relation existing between them. However, while Matthiessen considers the identification of the comparison time as concerning the text planning activity, and does not therefore include it in his model, in our approach we deal directly with this problem. In particular, we solve it by relying on a set of rules which exploit a group of features of exclusively semantic nature. The most important among these features are those involving the temporal relations between the actions or events described in the sentence. These relation are expressed utilizing the temporal logic developed by Allen (1984). Other features that are taken into account by the rules identifying the comparison time concern the aspectual perspective, i.e., the point of view the speaker adopts in order to describe the situation, and the conceptual status of the events or states described in the sentence (for instance a state can be a consequence of an event, it can represent an enablement condition for the occurrence of an action, etc).

The second phase of the tense selection process is devoted to map the objective tense into the grammatical one. In this phase, the temporal link which exists between the speaking time and the event time is expressed through one of the tenses allowed by the grammar of the language at hand. This is a purely linguistic process and is deeply influenced by the resources of the language. Different languages have in fact different tense systems, and the mapping between the objective and the grammatical tense is generally not one-to-one. Sometimes, in absence of the appropriate grammatical tense, in order to express a given objective tense it is necessary to resort to some periphrastic expression. For example a present-in-past-in-present can be directly realized in English through a present perfect continuous *(I have been trying to finish this letter)* while in Italian the speaker has to choose between a 'passato prossimo' *(Ho tentato di finire questa lettera)* and a periphrasis *(Sto tentando di finire questa lettera)*, conveying thus different nuances of meaning.

The choice of a given grammatical tense, however, does not express (and is not determined by) only the objective tense. Through the usage of a given grammatical tense it is possible to indicate some subtle distinctions and pragmatic implications. We have examined in the previous section the case of the futurate use of the present to suggest the idea that the action expressed by the verb has been already planned. To make another example, in English the use of the present continuous to describe an habitual action *(You are always asking me silly questions)* implies that the action annoys or seems unreasonable to the hearer.

The mapping between the objective and the grammatical tense is performed in the model by another set of rules which exploit a series of language-dependent features of morphologic, syntactic and pragmatic nature that act as a filter in translating a semantic relation into the idiosyncratic characteristics of the language. Among these feature we mention, in the case of English, whether the verb accepts the ing-form (a morphological feature), whether the sentence is a subordinate temporal (a syntactic feature), and whether the register is formal or informal (a pragmatic feature). The existence of these features influences how a given objective tense can be expressed. So, for example, a future event described in a temporal subordinate can be represented through the simple present *(I will stay in bed till the clock strikes seven),* and in the informal context the present continuous can be used to refer to a future action *(We are getting married in June).*

4. The TEN-EX Prototype

The model has been experimented and validated by developing a new prototype (called TEN-EX) of the domain expert for the English tense system. TEN-EX is capable of solving exercises which contain some verbs in infinitive form that have to be substituted by the correctly conjugated tense. The coverage of the system includes only tenses of the indicative form, up to the ternary level (quaternary and quinary tenses, although possible, are very uncommon).

For validating the performance of TEN-EX, a specific corpus has been developed, which includes 80 exercises selected from English textbooks, which have been certified with respect to the following requirements: non-ambiguity of the solution, full coverage of the indicative tenses, reliability of the contextual definition. In TEN-EX the exercises are internally represented by means of an *exercise description* containing a (sub)set of the features necessary for the tense generation process.

The functional architecture of TEN-EX (illustrated in figure 1) is organized around seven *Experts,* each one devoted to a specific part of the overall processing. The Experts are grouped into the following four main modules:
1. *Pre-processing Module,* devoted to augment the (partial) exercise description stored in the Exercise Database with other features which are automatically derived by the system. More specifically, the extension is performed by:
   - a *Temporal Expert,* which is capable of inferring all the temporal relations which exist among the states or events (and the temporal expressions) mentioned in the current exercise and that are not covered by the description. The Temporal Expert is also capable of checking the consistency and the completeness of such temporal relations. The overall temporal description of the exercise can also be transferred to the *User Interface,* in order to be displayed to the user.
   - an *Action Kind Expert,* which determines the correct class of each verb present in the current exercise on the base of the lexical information present in the Dictionary and of the specific contextual information extracted from the exercise description.
2. *Semantic Module,* which constitutes, together with the Linguistic Module, the kernel of the TEN-EX prototype. The operation of this module is based on the temporal relations and on the other semantic features characterizing the exercise (in accordance to the model presented in the previous section) and is aimed at performing the successive choices between past, present, and future which allow the identification of the objective tense. As already mentioned, we have limited the coverage of TEN-EX to ternary tenses, and therefore three

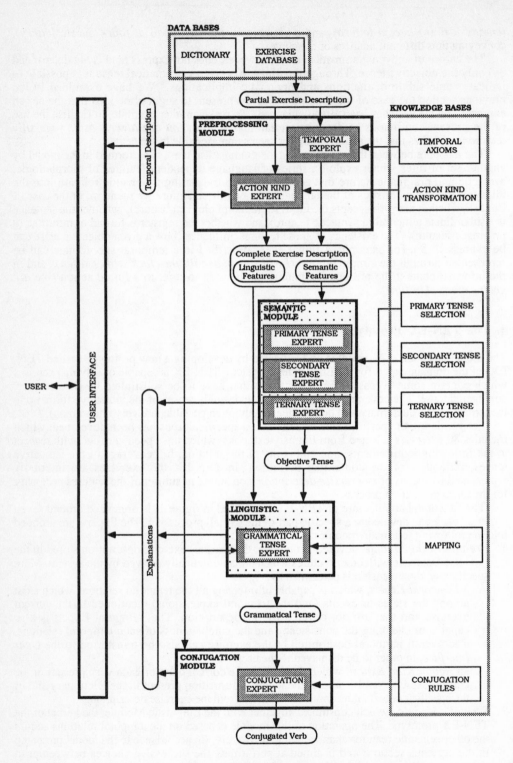

Figure 1. TEN-EX functional architecture.

specific Experts have been utilized, called *Primary, Secondary,* and *Ternary Tense Expert,* respectively. Each expert is in charge of identifying the correct comparison time, to perform the comparison with the reference time and the subsequent temporal selection, and to check whether the full link between speaking time and the event time has been established by verifying if the comparison time coincides with the event time. The Semantic Module has also the capability to provide detailed explanations on its behavior by tracing the derivation process of the objective tense.

3. *Linguistic Module,* devoted to perform the linguistic filtering mentioned in the previous section. The Linguistic Module includes a *Grammatical Tense Expert,* which is capable of mapping the objective tense into the correct grammatical one by taking into account the specificity of the language. It operates by considering the linguistic features describing the exercise together with Dictionary information. This module is also capable of producing explanations about the inferences carried on.

4. *Conjugating Module,* devoted to generate the final form of the verb considered in the solution process. It includes a *Conjugation Expert,* devoted to conjugate the verb into the appropriate tense.

The architecture includes also:

- a *User Interface,* which manages the interaction with the user and is capable of: (i) accepting from the user his/her choices about the specific exercise to be solved; (ii) graphically displaying to the user the temporal description of the exercise; (iii) showing to the user intermediate and final results of each processing phase; and (iv) displaying to the user (possibly at two different levels of abstraction) explanations about the internal inferences. This last capability has received a lot of attention, since the TEN-EX prototype has to be integrated within the ET environment where the capability of explaining how a result is obtained plays a fundamental role. The interface is implemented by means of multiple windows, pop-up menus, and mouse.

The operation of TEN-EX is supported by several knowledge bases devoted to specific tasks within the overall processing. All the knowledge is represented by means of production rules. In particular, as illustrated in Figure 1, for each Expert a specific knowledge base has been utilized, which contains only the knowledge relevant to it. We concentrate here only on the knowledge bases supporting the Semantic and the Linguistic Modules. More specifically, the three knowledge bases devoted to the identification of the objective tense are constituted by the rules in charge of the choice of the comparison times. An example of such a rule is the following:

IF   *the proposition introduces a new temporal context*
     the action described is a process
     the event time includes the speaking time
THEN *the comparison time is NOW.*

As far as the Linguistic Module is concerned, most of its rules utilize the standard correspondence between systemic tenses and grammatical tenses. Specific rules, derived from English grammars, have also been included which capture morphologic, syntactic, and pragmatic knowledge about the usage (limitations, restrictions, exceptions, etc.) of tenses. An example of such a rule is the following:

IF   *the objective tense is present*
     the action described is habitual
     the action described is insistent
     the verb accepts the ing-form
THEN *the grammatical tense is the present continuous*

The system includes also the following two databases:

- the *Exercise Data Base,* which contains texts and descriptions of the exercises included in the above mentioned corpus, and
- a *Dictionary,* storing all the lexical information needed during the processing.

The TEN-EX prototype has been developed in LPA PROLOG on a Macintosh. At the implementation level (not shown in figure 1), the reasoning activity of the Experts is supported by two inference engines (one working in forward chaining and the other in backward chaining) and by a common working memory for the input and output data. A specific module, called *Supervisor*, is in charge of managing the overall operation of the system by assigning control to the expert currently exploited.

We conclude the section by briefly describing the overall operation of TEN-EX. In figure 2, 3, 4, and 5 we show some screens during a working session with TEN-EX. Operations are started by the Supervisor which assigns control to the User Interface in order to let the user choose the exercise to work with (this step will be modified when TEN-EX will be fully integrated with the ET tutoring system, and a specific module will take care of the selection of exercises) and the desired level of explanation. Then the exercise description is extracted from the Exercise Database and stored in the working memory. Control is subsequently assigned to all the Experts in the same order used in the above illustration. Each expert finds in the working memory the partial results produced by the previous one and, by exploiting an inference engine on the relevant knowledge base, contributes to the final solution. These partial solutions are displayed to the user, which may possibly ask for further explanations about the specific rules utilized. The operation terminates when the Conjugation Expert produces the final answer to the exercise.

The figures 2 to 5 refer to the solution of the exercise: "*He was busy packing, for he (leave) that night*". Figure 2 shows the temporal description of the exercise. Figure 3 shows some of the successive steps of the identification of the objective tense. In this case the objective tense is the future-in-past which, according to the standard correspondence between systemic tenses and grammatical tenses, should be mapped into the *'to be going to' (past)* form. However, the Linguistic Expert modifies this choice since verbs indicating movement or position (like *to leave*) prefer the past continuous (provided that the sentence includes a specific temporal expression), as illustrated in Figure 4. Figure 5 shows the final solution to the exercise.

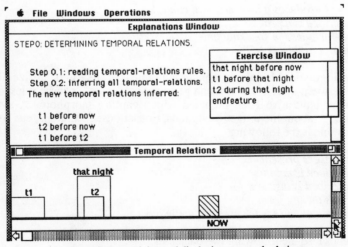

Figure 2. Determining and displaying temporal relations.

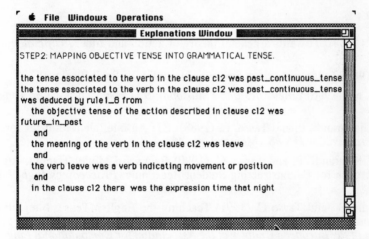

Figure 3. Identifying the objective tense.

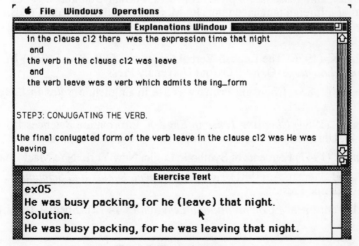

Figure 4. Mapping the objective tense into the grammatical tense.

```
 File  Windows  Operations
▓▓▓▓▓▓▓▓▓▓▓▓▓ Explanations Window ▓▓▓▓▓▓▓▓▓▓▓▓▓
  in the clause c12 there  was the expression time that night
     and
  the verb in the clause c12 was leave
     and
  the verb leave was a verb which admits the ing_form


STEP3: CONJUGATING THE VERB.

the final conjugated form of the verb leave in the clause c12 was He was
leaving
▓▓▓▓▓▓▓▓▓▓▓▓▓▓▓▓▓ Exercise Text ▓▓▓▓▓▓▓▓▓▓▓▓▓▓▓▓▓
  ex05
  He was busy packing, for he (leave) that night.
  Solution:
  He was busy packing, for he was leaving that night.
```

Figure 5. The conjugated tense.

5. Conclusions and Guidelines for Future Research

In the paper a new model for tense selection has been presented which has been implemented into the TEN-EX prototype, a system capable of selecting and conjugating the appropriate tense for English sentences. In comparison with existing models based on the systemic approach, our model clearly separates the identification of the semantic relations existing between the speaking time and the event time from the mapping of such relations into the grammatical tense and moreover it clearly specifies the role of the morphological, syntactic, semantic, and pragmatic features in the process of tense selection.

As a result of the bipartite organization, a level of generality has been achieved which should facilitate the portability of the model to other languages. Building an expert for a language different from English, in fact, would require only the of the construction of a new linguistic filter, being the semantic module left untouched. Several future research perspectives have been disclosed by the development of the model, including (a) the need to validate the approach from a pedagogic point of view; (b) the extension to other languages; and (c) the extension of the system capabilities with respect to the automatic derivation of the exercise description from the natural language text.

References

Allen, J.F. (1984) Towards a general theory of action and time. *Artificial Intelligence* **23**, 123-154.

Dahl, O. (1985) *Tense and Aspect Systems*. Oxford, UK: Basil Blackwell.

Dowty, D., ed. (1986) *Linguistics and Philosophy* **9** (1). Special Issue on Tense and Aspect in Discourse.

Fum, D., Giangrandi, P. and Tasso, C. (1988) ET: An intelligent tutor for foreign language teaching. *Proceedings ITS-88,* Montreal, pp. 462-468.

Fum, D., Giangrandi, P. and Tasso, C. (1990) Backward Model Tracing: An Explanation-Based Approach for Reconstructing Student Reasoning. *Proceedings Eight AAAI,* Boston, 426-433.

Fum D., Pani B., and Tasso C. (1991) Teaching the English Tense: Integrating Naive and Formal Grammars in an Intelligent Tutor for Foreign Language Teaching. *Proceedings Fifth Conference of the European Chapter of the Association for Computational Linguistics,* Berlin, April 9-11.

Fum D., Pani B., and Tasso C. (in press) Naive vs. Formal Grammars: A case for integration in the design of a foreign language tutor. In: M. Swartz and M. Yazdani (Eds.) *The Bridge to International Communication: Intelligent tutoring systems for foreign language teaching.* New York: Springer.

Halliday, M.A.K. (1976) The English Verbal Group. In: G.R. Kress, (Ed.) *Halliday: System and Function in Language.* Oxford: Oxford University Press

Matthiessen, C. (1983) Choosing Primary Tense in English. *Studies in Language* **7**, 369-429.

Matthiessen, C. (1984) *Choosing Tense in English.* Information Sciences Institute Research Report 84-143, University of Southern California, Marina del Rey, CA.

Reichenbach, H. (1947) Elements of Symbolic Logic. New York, NY: MacMillan.

Tedeschi, P. and Zaenen, A. (1981) *Tense and Aspect. Syntax and Semantics: vol. 14.* New York, NY: Academic Press.

Webber, B.L., ed. (1988) *Computational Linguistics* **14** (2). Special Issue on Tense and Aspect.

An Efficient Context-Free Parsing Algorithm with Semantic Actions

Marco Piastra, Roberto Bolognesi
CARES - Viale Monte Grappa, 15, I - 27100 Pavia

Abstract - As M. Tomita [5] has demonstrated, the LR parsing algorithm can be extended so that it will handle acyclic context-free grammars in a very efficient way, producing a *parse forest*, a set of all possible parsing trees for a given input sentence. In this paper we aim to show how Tomita's parsing algorithm can be extended to support *semantic actions*, that is, procedural segments associated with grammar production rules, that are executed contextually during the parsing procedure.

Key Words: computational linguistics, context-free grammars, parallel parsing, semantic actions.

1. Introduction

Roughly speaking, the key idea behind the LR parsing technique is anticipating as much computation as possible and storing the result in a numerical table (Fig. 1). The major advantage of this technique derives from the fact that all application conflicts between different production rules in the input grammar are detected and solved during the compilation of this numerical table. With a few minor exceptions, the LR parsing technique works, however, only with unambiguous grammars since, when translated into numerical tables, ambiguous grammars will lead to ambiguous entries (i.e. entries with more than one value). The basic idea of Tomita's extension to the LR technique is to have an LR parsing algorithm that can deal with ambiguous entries by spawning itself, as soon as an ambiguous entry is encountered, into many parallel LR parsing processes, each following a single unambiguous parse of the input sentence. Moreover, in certain circumstances, some processes join up again to form a single process thus obtaining substantial savings in both memory and CPU time. As we shall see later, this rejoining action is formally justified by Tomita with the concept of the *local ambiguity* of a sentence. As demonstrated experimentally in [5], this technique can lead to a very high level of performance, in particular when it is recalled that a *complete* representation of the *parse forest* is obtained.

From an applicational standpoint, however, the major shortcoming of this technique is that, unlike other parsing techniques such as ATN, semantic processing will necessarily be deferred until the completion of the parsing process. This causes Tomita's parser to suffer from the classic limitations of context-free parsers such as the poor handling of gender/number/person agreement or the inherent intractability of conjunction coupling and long-distance attachments. Besides providing a method by which to cope with the above problems, the execution of semantic actions, together with a proper value-passing mechanism, might also be so structured as to cause the simultaneous translation of the input sentence into a more practical, application-dependent semantic formalism that can greatly ease any subsequent semantic processing.

Grammar
1: S -> NP VP
2: S -> S PP
3: NP -> *det *n
4: PP -> *prep NP
5: VP -> *v NP

Action table

state	*det	*n	*v	*prep	$	NP	PP	VP	S
0	shift 3					2			1
1				shift 5	accept		4		
2			shift 6					7	
3		shift 8							
4				reduce 2	reduce 2				
5	shift 3					9			
6	shift 3					10			
7				reduce 1	reduce 1				
8			reduce 3	reduce 3	reduce 3				
9				reduce 4	reduce 4				
10				reduce 5	reduce 5				

Goto table (NP PP VP S columns)

Fig. 1: A simple unambiguous grammar and its translation into an LR table

2. The Yacc paradigm

The idea of semantic actions associated with grammar rules comes from Yacc (Yet another compiler compiler), the UNIX tool, which is used to describe the synctatic structure of the input of a generic computer program. A Yacc input description incorporates two kinds of items: *production rules* and *semantic actions* associated to production rules, that are invoked when these rules are recognized. These semantic actions may return values and receive values returned by previous actions.

Consider the following sample production rule relating to arithmetic expressions of addition:

EXPR   -> *number '+' *number
                { $$ = $1 + $3; };

In this production rule EXPR is a non-terminal symbol in a grammar while *number is a token (i.e. a basic item in the input string). The semantic action (between braces) is expressed in a host language, in this case, C, and may contain special variables corresponding either to returned or received values. In this case, each $i refers to the value returned by the ith component on the right side of the rule, reading from left to right, while the symbol $$ refers to the value returned by the semantic action. This returned value may in turn be used by higher level production rules in the grammar with an EXPR symbol on their right side.

Due to this value-passing mechanism, it is appropriate to talk of semantic values *associated* to each node in the parse tree. If we take a simple arithmetic expression like '2 + 2' as an example, we obtain the following parse tree (semantic values between braces):

EXPR {4} ——— *number {2} ——————— 2
         ——— '+ ' {nil} ——————— +
         ——— *number {2} ——————— 2

The execution of semantic actions in Yacc may also influence the parsing process by forcing the *acceptance* or *rejection* of the input string. This feature is of great help in building compilers dealing with problems that are inherently intractable using pure context-free grammars, such as checking that variables are declared before their use or checking that the number of actual parameters in a procedure call agrees with the number of formal parameters in the procedure declaration. In both these cases the use of semantic actions will provide a solution by first building, and then looking up, declaration tables in order to ensure consistency.

The use of semantic actions can also greatly simplify the description of syntax-oriented translation procedures. Yacc semantic actions are often used to translate a high level syntactic formalism into a lower level form. However, Yacc is totally unsuitable for natural language parsing since it works with a proper subset of LR grammars which, in its turn, is a proper subset of unambiguous context-free grammars.

3. Extending Tomita's algorithm

Tomita's algorithm works with any acyclic context-free grammar, including ambiguous grammars. Since Tomita's algorithm and the Yacc parsing algorithm are both based on an LR parsing algorithm, the question arises as to whether Tomita's algorithm could be extended to support semantic actions.

The LR parsing algorithm, described in Fig. 2, is deterministically guided by a parsing table that is obtained by automatic translation from a context-free phrase structure grammar. Each row in this table (Fig. 1) corresponds to a *state* of the parsing machine. For the LR algorithm, the order in which these rows are sorted is not meaningful except for the first row which corresponds to the initial state of the machine. Note that the only memory structure used by this algorithm, besides a few working variables, is a *stack*.

As pointed out above, only a proper subset of unambiguous context-free grammars can be translated into an unambiguous table, that is a table with a single value for each entry. Tomita's algorithm makes use of a memory structure called a *graph-structured stack*. This

---

Let $w\$$ be the input string of symbols, $\$$ being the string termination symbol.
Let the symbol 0 be the only value in the stack.

set *ip* to point to the first symbol of $w\$$;
repeat forever begin
    let *s* be the state on the top of the stack and *a* the symbol pointed to by *ip*;

    if *Action*[*s*, *a*] = *shift s'* **then begin**
        push *a* and *s'* to the top of the stack;
        advance *ip* to the next input symbol;
    end
    else if *Action*[*s*, *a*] = *reduce n* **then begin**
        let *l* be the length of the right side of rule *n*;
        let *c* be the left side symbol of rule *n*;

        pop 2 * *l* symbols off the stack;
        let *s'* be the state now on the top of the stack;
        push *c* and *Goto*[*s'*, *c*] to the top of the stack
    end
    else if *Action*[*s*, *a*] = *accept* **then**
        return
end

Fig. 2: The standard LR parsing algorithm [3].

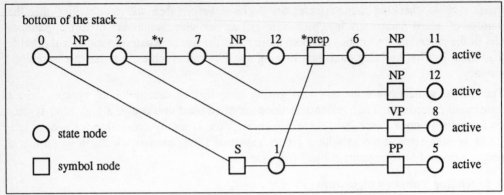

Fig. 3: A typical graph-structured stack (adapted from [5])

graph-structured stack is an efficient way of keeping track of all the parsing processes that are being executed in parallel.

When a multiple entry in the table is encountered, the original process in the standard LR parsing algorithm spawns into more separated processes. This is actually accomplished by spawning the current stack top into as many new nodes as is the number of spawned processes. In certain circumstances these parallel processes may rejoin, in particular when any two or more processes have parsed the same part of a sentence in different ways but have reached the same machine state. In this case the nodes corresponding to these processes are also rejoined in a new (unique) stack node. A typical condition of the graph-structured stack during the execution of Tomita's algorithm is shown in Fig. 3.

The algorithm shown in Fig. 2 is also the basic Yacc algorithm, with the difference that semantic actions are invoked before first executing *reduce* actions and that returned values are stored in the program stack. Previously returned values can thus be retrieved by reading the stack in reverse fashion. Following this approach, we might be led into thinking that Tomita's parsing algorithm could be extended to ensure that the graph-structured stack will hold returned values in much the same way as Yacc does.

4. Synchronization issues

Unfortunately, this extension cannot be carried out in this way as the individual parsing processes in Tomita's algorithm are not completely synchronized.

In discussing this problem, we need to bear in mind the definition, given by Tomita himself, of the *local ambiguity* of a sentence: a fragment of a sentence is *locally ambiguous* if the fragment can be reduced to the same non-terminal symbol in two or more different ways. Loosely speaking, the fork-and-rejoin of two or more parsing processes described above corresponds to these sentence fragments. In this way, even heavily ambiguous sentences can be treated by the algorithm avoiding the combinatorial explosion of processes that would otherwise ensue. This feature also helps reduce the overall use of memory by representing the parse forest as a single tree with many different subtrees corresponding to local ambiguities. Fig. 4 shows two different parse trees relating to the same sentence 'the clever policeman sees a man with a telescope'. The two parse trees differ only as regards the nodes below the *local ambiguity node* (the node marked by square brackets). The in-memory representation of the common part of the parse tree will be unique.

The way the various parse trees are built in parallel is closely related to the way in which semantic actions can be executed. In parsing this sample sentence, Tomita's algorithm drives a single parsing process until the ambiguous fragment 'sees a man with a telescope' is encountered. Imagine that from now on, the two spawned processes are executed sequentially, one after the other: in this way the first process might, for example, build the first parse tree completely, and thereafter the second process would build only the second *subtree*, connecting it to the local ambiguity node VP just before halting. None of this can be done if the execution of semantic actions is desired: the action would be executed just once for all nodes above the ambiguity node and thus the only value associated would be the one derived from the first process, since the second halts at a lower level.

Following another approach, in which there is no rejoining, the second process could continue to work by 'rebuilding' the part of the tree above the ambiguity node so as to be able to execute semantic actions properly. But this causes the problem of combinatorial explosion to resurface. Moreover, this procedure makes it impossible to define semantic actions that handle *multiple* returned values, since all these values are not in general available at the time when actions are executed.

In actual fact, the synchronization problem in Tomita's algorithm is not so dramatic, since the algorithm operates on the input strictly from left to right: all running parsing processes must in fact *shift* the input symbols at the same time. Nevertheless, the *reduce* actions performed by the various processes between two consecutive *shifts* can take place in an unpredictable order. To illustrate this important aspect further, we must look at the execution of the two parsing processes in the example in more detail. After all the symbols in the input sentence have been *shift*ed, the two stacks in the processes might look like this:

Process 1:   0 NP *<state>* VP *<state>* PP *<state>*
Process 2:   0 NP *<state>* *v *<state>* NP *<state>*

At this point Process 1 can perform a *reduce* with rule VP –> VP PP while Process 2 can perform a *reduce* with rule VP –> *v NP. The order of these two *reduce*s is not important

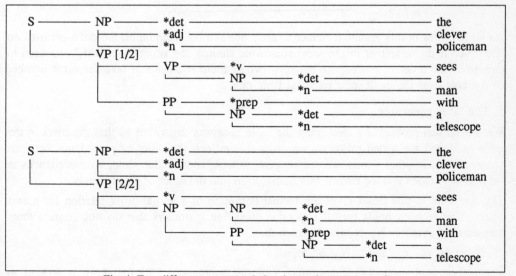

Fig. 4: Two different parse trees belonging to the same parse forest

now, so we may assume that Process 1 performs first. After the *reduce*, the two stacks look like this:

Process 1:   0 NP *<state>* VP *<state>*
Process 2:   0 NP *<state>* *v *<state>* NP *<state>*

Process 1 can now perform a *reduce* with rule S –> NP VP while Process 2 is still waiting to perform its own *reduce*. In this hypothesis, the *reduce* performed by Process 2 would complete both the construction of the second subtree and the execution of Process 2 itself. If we could now allow Process 2 to take precedence, then Process 1 would perform its own *reduce* only after the two subtrees have been connected in a unique local ambiguity node VP. This node could, in turn, be associated with *two* distinct returned values. Before performing the last *reduce* which generates the top node S we could now either execute the semantic action associated with rule S –> NP VP *twice* or, alternatively, simply execute the same semantic action just once, provided, of course, the latter contains code for *multiple-value handling*.

The key feature that ought to make it possible to determine precedence among the various *reduces* is the number of input symbols which are reduced by the rule involved: in the case in point, the *reduce* with rule S –> NP VP takes 9 symbols while the *reduce* with rule VP –> *v NP takes only 6, so the second *reduce* must be performed first. In formal terms, the justification is that, since the derivation is rightmost (in reverse), the shorter fragment is properly contained in the longer one.

This criterion, however, is not decisive in all cases. Consider, for example, the following elementary grammar:

S –> N ,   N –> N' ,   N –> *t ,   N' –> *t

For any sentence made up of a single symbol of category *t, the grammar admits the following parse trees:

S ——— N [1/2] —— *t ————————— *<symbol>*
S ——— N [2/2] —— N' ——— *t ——— *<symbol>*

As all the rules in this grammar reduce exactly one symbol from input, the criterion is of no use. Even if this grammar might seem somewhat strange, the situation in which we need to determine the order of precedence between two or more *reduces* that take the same number of symbols from the input sentence is far from rare.

5. The table generator

We solved this problem by modifying the table generator algorithm so that the rows in the table produced are sorted following an order that reflects the order of precedence between such *reduces*. In other words, we precompute, at table construction time, all precedences in these critical cases and we encode this information into the order of parser *states*.

The appendix to this paper gives the formal definition of a partial-order relation for parser states. This relation holds for all acyclic context-free grammars that do **not** contain three non-terminal symbols N_1, N_2 and N_3 such that:

$$N_1 \Rightarrow N_2 \Rightarrow^+ \varepsilon \quad \text{and} \quad N_2 \Rightarrow^+ N_3$$

The authors call these SALR grammars (Simply Ambiguous LR) for short. It is hard to figure a situation in which these restrictions can result in serious practical limitations.

6. Experimental results

In his paper, Tomita gives no formal analysis of the complexity of his own algorithm and neither do we. Unquestionably, the solution proposed, which entails determining precedences between the various *reduces*, increases the overall complexity of the algorithm. Nevertheless, the empirical results reported here suggest that this increase in complexity, partially counterbalanced by careful implementation procedures, will not, in practice, prevent very satisfactory levels of performance from being obtained. The comparison we give in the figures between parsing times must be seen qualitatively, as a support for the above claim. We report absolute 80286-12Mhz CPU times for our program (a compiled C code), while Tomita [5] reports CPU times minus the time spent in garbage collections, with a MacLisp interpreter on a DEC 20 computer. We measured the performance of a full version of the program, constructing the complete representation of the parse forest, but with no execution of semantic actions, since the performance of a parser executing semantic actions depends strictly on how the semantic actions themselves are defined (e.g. efficiency of the interpreted/compiled host language, semantic actions complexity, etc.).

Figs. 5 and 6 compare the CPU time between our program and Tomita's program using the same grammar and the two different sentence sets reported in [5]. Fig. 7 shows the overall dynamic memory use by our program. Another 64 Kbyte of memory was used to store the table produced using a 245-rule grammar. The compiled code for the parsing program itself, together with a lexical analyzer, takes up slightly more than 64 Kbyte.

7. Conclusions & future work

What we present here is a new and highly efficient technique for dealing with syntactic issues in natural language processing. In this sense, the technique described here provides an improved tool that can be successfully integrated into almost all applications, due to its frugal use of memory and CPU time. We are now working on the integration of this parsing method into a Smalltalk environment where semantic actions can be expressed as code *blocks* using many powerful Smalltalk primitives to handle multiple values. The ultimate goal is to build an environment for the development of high-level educational software, where natural language interaction with the users is a fundamental feature.

Acknowledgements - This research work has been carried out as a part of a research project called OOPSE (Object Oriented Programming System for Education), a joint research project involving Istituto di Farmacologia II, University of Pavia, and CARES. The final program was developed with the co-operation of F. Bolognesi and A. De Giovanni. Special thanks are due to A. P. Baldry from the Dipartimento di Lingue e Letterature Straniere of the University of Pavia whose suggestions and criticisms were of great help in the development of the prototype. He also patiently revised the English of this paper.

References

[1] Aho, A.V., Johnson, S.C., LR Parsing. *Computing Surveys 6*, 2 (June 1974).

[2] Aho, A.V., Johnson, S.C., Ullman, J.D., Deterministic Parsing of Ambiguous Grammars. *Commun. ACM 18*, 8 (Aug. 1975).

[3] Aho, A.V., Sethi, R., Ullman, J.D. *Compilers - Principles, Techniques and Tools.* Addison Wesley Publishing Co., Reading, Mass., 1986.

[4] Blank, G.D. A Finite and Real-Time Processor for Natural Language. *Commun. ACM 32*, 10 (Oct. 1989).

[5] Tomita, M. An Efficient Context-Free Parsing Algorithm for Natural Languages and Its Applications. *Ph.D. thesis*, Carnegie-Mellon University, 1985.

[6] Tomita, M. *Efficient Parsing for Natural Language.* Kluwer Academic Publishers, Norwell, Mass., 1987.

[7] Winograd, T. *Language as a Cognitive Process - Volume 1: Syntax.* Addison Wesley Publishing Co., Reading, Mass., 1983.

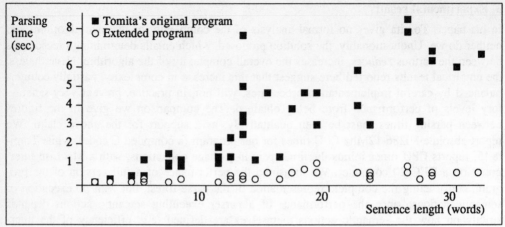

Fig. 5: Time against sentence length (Tomita's grammar III and sentence set I)

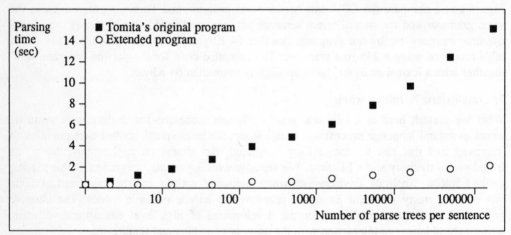

Fig. 6: Time against ambiguity (Tomita's grammar III and sentence set II)

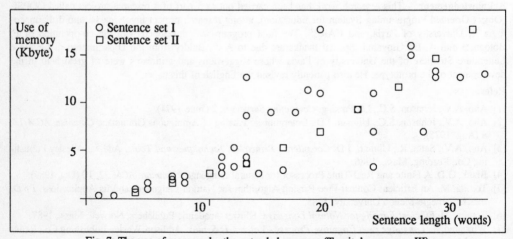

Fig. 7: The use of memory by the extended program (Tomita's grammar III)

Appendix: Formal definition of SALR grammars

Definition 1

A context-free grammar G is acyclic iff it does not admit a derivation of the form $N \Rightarrow^+ N$, where N is a non-terminal symbol of G.

Definition 2

Let N_1 and N_2 be two non-terminal symbols of G. We say that N_1 *precedes* N_2 and we write $N_1 >^* N_2$ iff G admits a derivation of the form $N_1 \Rightarrow^+ N_2$. If neither N_1 precedes N_2 nor N_2 precedes N_1, we say that N_1 and N_2 are equal in precedence and we write $N_1 =^* N_2$.

Proposition 1

The relation $>^*$ is a partial-order relation for all non-terminal symbols of an acyclic context-free grammar G.

Proof:

A binary relation on a set is a partial-order relation if it is non-reflexive, asymmetric and transitive.

- *Non-reflexivity* - Since G is an acyclic grammar, $N \Rightarrow^+ N$ is not a valid derivation.
- *Asymmetry* - Let $N_1 \Rightarrow^+ N_2$ be a possible derivation following G. The reverse derivation $N_2 \Rightarrow^+ N_1$ would cause the grammar to be cyclic.
- *Transitivity* - From $N_1 \Rightarrow^+ N_2$ and $N_2 \Rightarrow^+ N_3$ follows that $N_1 \Rightarrow^+ N_3$.

Definition 3

Let $r_1 : K \rightarrow \alpha N \beta$ and $r_2 : K' \rightarrow \alpha' N' \beta'$ be two production rules of G, where $\alpha\beta \Rightarrow^* \varepsilon$ and $\alpha'\beta' \Rightarrow^* \varepsilon$. We say that r_1 *precedes* r_2 and we write $r_1 >^* r_2$ iff either $N \equiv K'$ or $N >^* K'$. Clearly, this is a partial-order relation for the set of production rules of G.

Definition 4

Let N be a non-terminal symbol of G and γ any string of terminal symbols such that $N \Rightarrow^+ \gamma$. We say that G admits a *local ambiguity for an individual non-terminal symbol* N when G admits two different derivations of the following form:

$$N \Rightarrow^+ N_1 \Rightarrow^+ \gamma \qquad \text{and} \qquad N \Rightarrow^+ N_2 \Rightarrow^+ \gamma$$

where N_1 and N_2 are both non-terminal symbols of G. It follows immediately that an ambiguity of this kind entails the existence of two other non-terminal symbols of G such that $N >^* N_1$ and $N >^* N_2$.

Definition 5

We say that an acyclic context-free grammar G is also *simply ambiguous* if it does **not** contain three different non-terminals N_1, N_2 and N_3 such that:

$$N_1 \Rightarrow N_2 \Rightarrow^+ \varepsilon \qquad \text{and} \qquad N_2 \Rightarrow^+ N_3.$$

We call such grammars SALR grammars (Simply Ambiguous LR) for short.

Definition 6

The relation $>^*$ can be extended straightforwardly from production rules to the LR(0) items (see [3]) that have the dot at the right end.

Proposition 2

Let I_i be an LR(0) set of items produced from an SALR grammar G. If I_i contains two items of the form:

$$i_1 : \quad K \rightarrow \alpha N \beta \cdot$$
$$i_2 : \quad K' \rightarrow \alpha' N' \beta' \cdot$$

(i.e. if this set of items contains a *reduce/reduce* conflict). Then it follows $i_1 =^* i_2$.

Proof:

If the two items i_1 and i_2 belong to the same set of items, one of the two right-hand sides must be a substring of the other.

To see this, we may think of how LR(0) sets of items are produced through the use of CLOSURE and GOTO operators (see also [3][1]). Each GOTO step takes all items with the same symbol at the right of the dot from a given set and produces a new kernel with only these items, advancing the dot one position to the right. Clearly, any two items in the same set with the dot at the right end must have 'survived' at least for the last n GOTO steps, n being the length of the shortest of the two right sides.

Now let us assume that $\alpha N \beta \supseteq \alpha' N' \beta'$. Note that if $N \equiv N'$ both $i_1 >^* i_2$ and $i_2 >^* i_1$ are impossible since the grammar ought to be cyclic. So we will focus on the case $N \neq N'$ (note that this entails $N' \Rightarrow^+ \varepsilon$, since N' must be included either in α or in β).

We will show that both $i_2 >^* i_1$ and $i_1 >^* i_2$ are impossible.

- Case $i_2 >^* i_1$:
  if $N' >^* K$, we would obtain that $K' \Rightarrow N' \Rightarrow^+ \varepsilon$ and $N' \Rightarrow N$, violating Definition 5.
- Case $i_1 >^* i_2$:
  for $i_1 >^* i_2$ to be true, $N >^* N'$ ought to be true, and in this case we would have $K \Rightarrow N \Rightarrow^+ \varepsilon$ and $N \Rightarrow^+ N'$, again violating Definition 5.

Definition 7
The relation $>^*$ between sets of LR(0) items is defined in the following way: we say that a set I_i *precedes* a set I_j and we write $I_i >^* I_j$ iff I_i contains an item i_i and I_j contains an item i_j such that $i_i >^* i_j$.

Lemma 2.1
Consider two set of LR(0) items I_1 and I_2 containing respectively the items i_1 and i'_1 the item i_2. Let these items be of the following form:

$$i_1 \ : \quad K_1 \to \alpha_1 N_1 \beta_1.$$
$$i'_1 \ : \quad K'_1 \to \alpha'_1 N'_1 \beta'_1.$$
$$i_2 \ : \quad K_2 \to \alpha_2 N_2 \beta_2.$$

If $N_1 \neq N'_1$ and $i_2 >^* i'_1$, then $\alpha_1 N_1 \beta_1 \subset \alpha'_1 N'_1 \beta'_1$.

Proof:
Let us assume the reverse case $\alpha_1 N_1 \beta_1 \supseteq \alpha'_1 N'_1 \beta'_1$. We would have $N'_1 \Rightarrow^+ \varepsilon$ (this is because N'_1 would be included either in α_1 or in β_1). But this would entail $K_2 \Rightarrow N_2 \Rightarrow^+ \varepsilon$ and $N_2 \Rightarrow N'_1$, which violates Definition 5.

Lemma 2.2
Consider two set of LR(0) items I_1 and I_2 containing respectively the items i_1 and i'_1 and the item i'_2. Let these items be of the following form:

$$i_1 \ : \quad K_1 \to \alpha_1 N_1 \beta_1.$$
$$i'_1 \ : \quad K'_1 \to \alpha'_1 N'_1 \beta'_1.$$
$$i'_2 \ : \quad K'_2 \to \alpha'_2 N'_2 \beta'_2.$$

If $N_1 \neq N'_1$ and $i_1 >^* i'_2$, then $\alpha_1 N_1 \beta_1 \supset \alpha'_1 N'_1 \beta'_1$.

Proof:
Let us assume the reverse case, $\alpha_1 N_1 \beta_1 \subseteq \alpha'_1 N'_1 \beta'_1$. We would have $N_1 \Rightarrow^+ \varepsilon$. But this, in turn, would entail $K_1 \Rightarrow N_1 \Rightarrow^+ \varepsilon$ and $N_1 \Rightarrow N'_2$, which violates Definition 5.

Definition 8
The relation $>^*$ for sets of LR(0) items is transitive.

Proposition 3
The binary relation $>^*$ is a partial-order relation on the sets of LR(0) items produced from an SALR grammar G.

Proof:
As the last step, we must now show that the relation, extended by Definition 8, does not admit a cycle like the following: $I_1 >^* ... I_k >^* I_1$ ($k \geq 2$).
First, let us note that such a cycle would involve more than one item for each set. This is because for $i_1 >^* ... i_k >^* i_1$ to be true, the grammar ought to be cyclic. Thus, let us assume the existence in the cycle of a set I_j containing at least *two* items of the following form:

$$i_j \ : \quad K_j \to \alpha_j N_j \beta_j.$$
$$i'_j \ : \quad K'_j \to \alpha'_j N'_j \beta'_j.$$

We would also have two other sets I_{j-1} and I_{j+1} such that $I_{j-1} >^* I_j >^* I_{j+1}$, entailing $i_{j-1} >^* i'_j$ and $i_j >^* i_{j+1}$ for some items i_{j-1} and i_{j+1}. Obviously, in order to avoid cyclicity, we must have $N_j \neq N'_j$.
Now, following Lemma 2.1 we would have $\alpha_j N_j \beta_j \subset \alpha'_j N'_j \beta'_j$ and following Lemma 2.2 we would have $\alpha_j N_j \beta_j \supset \alpha'_j N'_j \beta'_j$. Of course, this is impossible.

Final Remarks
It can be shown that the condition of Definition 5 is sufficient but not necessary for a grammar to admit such a partial-order relation for the produced sets of LR(0) items. Nevertheless, this condition is easy to verify either automatically or 'by hand' and introduces no significant limitations in practical use.
Note that the sets of LR(0) items produced from an SALR grammar can be topologically sorted simply comparing their kernels.

From Scopings to Interpretation: The Semantic Interpretation within the AlFresco System.

Carlo Strapparava
IRST -Istituto per la Ricerca Scientifica e Tecnologica
I-38050 Povo Trento
e-mail: strappa@irst.it

Abstract

This work describes two of the interpretation modules in the multilevel semantic architecture of the AlFresco system: quantifier scopings resolution and interpretation of a meaning representation form. The paper overviews the main ideas of the techniques followed in the implementation of such modules. In particular for the scopings resolution a set of heuristic rules borrowed from linguistic analysis is given in order to cut the excessive number of readings proposed by some known mechanisms for scopings generation (Cooper Storage, Hobbs-Shieber algorithm). As far as interpretation is concerned, a semantics for logical operators, including natural quantifiers, in a meaning representation language is explained in full detail.

1. Introduction

Developing a meaning interpretation module that deals at a single level with all the complex problems in natural language processing is at least difficult and probably constructively wrong. A better strategy is to have a multilevel modular semantics, featuring explicitly defined interface languages among the modules and precise definitions of the tasks. Two levels that can be recognized in a cognitive architecture of this kind are: scopings resolution of the quantified noun phrases (NPs) in the sentence and interpretation of the resulting logical form. This work describes these two levels as studied and implemented in the AlFresco multimedial dialogue system. Importance will be given to both theoretical and computational aspects, so as not to assign denotations to expressions of logical/linguistic forms without regard to computational complexity of their interpretation. In particular some techniques that reduce the excessive number of readings in scopings generation algorithms such as the Cooper Storage or Hobbs-Shieber algorithm will be described in full detail. Logical operators of a meaning representation language will then be described stressing their semantic interpretation. We start with a brief overview of AlFresco's environment in which the work has been developed.

2. Overview of the AlFresco system

AlFresco is an interactive system for a user interested in Italian Art History. It is implemented in Xerox Common Lisp and runs on a SUN4 connected to a videodisc unit and a touchscreen. The videodisc contains films and images about Fourteenth Century Italian frescoes and monuments that can be shown on the touchscreen. The system understands language, gives answers and shows images and sequences. The images on the touchscreen are active: the user may refer to a fresco's content combining pointing with linguistic expressions.

The AlFresco system is composed of a number of well-formed modules. A general description of the functionalities and finalities of the AlFresco system can be found in [Stock91].

Putting our attention for the present purpose just to the language understanding side (AlFresco has also a generation side), the most relevant components are:

1) WEDNESDAY 2, a parser for the Italian language [Stock89]. The parser can cope with complex sentences, idiomatic expressions, ellipsis, and so on.

2) the lexical semantic analyzer, which provides incremental semantic discriminations through interacting with the parser and the knowledge base. It resolves some lexical ambiguities, e.g.ambiguities created by prepositions that map appropriate roles in the KB, and makes other checks of lexical coherence. It provides a first kind of semantic representation [Lavelli&Magnini91].

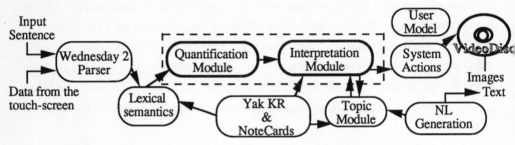

Role of the interpretation modules in the AlFresco architecture

3) the quantification module, which resolves the problems of quantifier scopings, and the interpretation module, which 'understands' the sentences. Its tasks are : finding the correct interpretation of the quantifier, identifying which part of the sentences to extensionalize, giving a set of possible candidates that logically satisfies the sentence for each NP, calculating the logical dependences of the retrieved references, deciding the attributive/referential interpretation of a given NP etc...

4) a topic module that suitably organizes the mentioned referents and with which the interpretation module interacts to find referents for some operators (demonstratives, some definite NPs) [Samek&Strapparava90].

The domain knowledge is represented in different ways:

5) YAK, a hybrid knowledge based system expressed in a KLOne-like language [Franconi90]. An assertional box consisting of instances is connected to the terminological box. The KB provides the main base for the reasoning capabilities of the system.

6) NoteCards, a hypermedia system containing unformalized knowledge such as art critics' opinions on the frescoes and the painters.

3. Scopings

A main characteristic of the quantification phenomenon is the existence of readings in which an NP is considered as a variable that can assume a number of different values in the universe of the discourse. The number of variable values is partly defined by the type of the quantification operator used (some, all, many, etc...) that acts as multiplier of the variable singularity. However the range of such effects spreads also to other elements of the sentence. The set of such elements is called the scope of the quantifier. As not all elements of a sentence are multipliable one has to distinguish in the formulation of the logical form of a sentence which elements are quantifiable and which are not.

An algorithm for the resolution of quantifier scopings has to generate all possible readings and for each quantifier it has to show its range over the rest of the sentence. The naive algorithm for generating quantifier scopings with all the possible permutations of the quantifiers generates n! readings with n quantifiers and it is clearly unacceptable. Indeed the use of an algorithm or a mechanism that makes use of structural considerations about complex NPs drastically reduces the generation of readings ([Cooper83] [Hobbs&Shieber87]). These techniques exploit the idea that in general a quantifier from elsewhere in a sentence cannot come after (i.e. be under the scope of) the quantifier associated with an NP and before (i.e. have scope on) the quantifier associated with a complement of the head of the above NP. The reduction achieved by these techniques is not really satisfying, especially if we are talking about a component of a dialogue system. It needs to add some heuristics based on linguistic/semantic knowledge to get an acceptable number of readings (possibly only one).

Some rules can be:

1) lexical relevance

2) syntactic position of NP

3) scope markers

4) distributive/collective semantics of predicate.

Below the first three rules will be discussed in full detail.

3.1 The structure of the logical forms in AlFresco.

The algorithm must work on a logical representation of the input sentence. The logical form has to reflect that structural information that allows the recognition of the ill-formedness of some forms. This issue is made formal using a logical language that separates the notion of range of quantified expression from its scope, putting information about the range in a part of the logical expression called restriction and the one about the scope in a part called body. The distinction in the syntax of the logical form between two semantic roles (restriction and body) is common with the most relevant approaches in a logical representation form: procedural semantics ([Woods77] [Woods81]) and the model-theoretic approach of generalized quantifiers ([Barwise &Cooper81], [Westerdahl86]).

The logical form built from the output of lexical semantics and constituing the representational level for the scopings resolution module is still neutral with respect to quantifier scopings and the ambiguity for distributive/collective readings. It is called first logical form. Now we shall give some examples of the first logical form used by AlFresco. The form uses a predicate-arguments notation with the possibility to abstract from time and context. Omitting for the moment the intensional aspects, four relevant constructs for the resolution of quantifiers and definite/deictic referents are:

> (complex-term <features><quantifier><variable><restriction>)
>
> (ref-term <features><variable><restriction>)
>
> (demonstr-term <features><variable><restriction>)
>
> (pronoun-term <features><variable><pred-restriction>)

A complex-term represents a quantified NP, for example:

'Molti pittori di Siena hanno dipinto un affresco'
Many painters of Siena painted a fresco

this results after passing through the lexical semantics and a module of logical form construction:

(1) (paint
       (complex-term <features> many x
                             (and (painter x)(in-place x Siena)))
       (complex-term <features> indef y (fresco y)))

A ref-term represents a definite NP. It plays an important role at interpretation level (see below).

A demonstr-term has the task of representing a demonstrative NP. The representation has to take into account the multimediality that the system treats at this level (the touch on the touchscreen for a deictic reference).

A pronoun-term represents a pronoun. The lexical semantics gives a suggestion with <pred-restriction> on the type of semantic restriction that can have the bound variable. Then this information will be used by the interpretation module.

The <features> keep syntactic information of the NP ready for use during semantic interpretation.

The scopings resolution algorithm generates the possible readings and produces a second logical form in which all complex-terms are resolved, making their scope and body explicit. Then in the second logical form for each quantifier a quantified formula appears with this structure

(quant var restriction body)

For example a possible reading for (1) can be:

(many x (and (painter x)(in-place x Siena))
                   (indef y (fresco y)(paint x y)))

3.2 Heuristic rules for scopings generation.

The scopings generation algorithm takes advantage of the idea of Cooper storage improved by some linguistic heuristics. These rules must be seen as a whole, i.e. they strictly interact with each other. It is also important to note that these rules apply for Italian, and obviously some configurations, correct in Italian, are not grammatical in other languages. Finally, these rules *suggest* a disambiguation, they don't always ensure it.

Lexical relevance

What makes the quantified NPs different from other NPs is their non-singularity, i.e.the multiplicity or the lack of referential values that interpret the considered NP. Following Longobardi [Longobardi88] one can divide, from a lexical point of view, the quantification operators into two classes: intrinsic quantifiers and non-intrinsic quantifiers. Intrinsic quantifiers are those that show a singular grammatical number but can denote sets with cardinality $N \neq 1$ (where N is the number of elements of the set denoted by the quantified NP) : n = 0 for negative quantifiers, n > 1 for others. The name 'intrinsic' comes from the fact that the operator, by its intrinsic meaning, quantifies (multiplies) the number of values of the bound variable and then it modifies the intrinsic singularity of the grammatical number. Examples of intrinsic Italian quantifiers are: qualche (some), ciascuno (each), ogni (every), nessuno (none), qualsiasi (whichever)...

The non-intrinsic quantifiers are those that show plural grammatical number and they are introduced by molti (many), pochi (few), tutti (all), alcuni (a few), entrambi (both), `numeral + NP` etc... (There are also non-intrinsic quantifiers without plural morphology, such as coordinated singular NP, ex. 'Giotto and Orcagna'; coordination of plural NPs produces interesting effects of multilevel plurals [Scha & Stallard88]). The rule of lexical conditioning says that among the NPs in a sentence the intrinsic quantifiers always tend to promote a dependent reading, both forcing their scope and enduring the effect of the scope of another quantifier. (Clearly definite NPs resist this tendency, preserving an independent reading).

As an example, in the sentence

'Ogni pittore ha dipinto due quadri nel Palazzo del Governo'
Every painter painted two frescoes in the Palazzo del Governo

the scope of 'ogni' over the rest of the sentence seems clear. (Actually there is also an effect of syntactic position as we'll see in the following section). After scopings resolution we get the following second logical form, rejecting other possible readings provided by Cooper storage.

```
(2) (every x (painter x)
            (two y (and (fresco y)
                        (in-place y Palazzo_del_Governo))
            (paint x y)))
```

Syntactic position

The most important conditioning on the scope relation between two quantified NPs depends on their syntactic position. The relevant positions to scope effects are three. In order of importance they are: 1) preverbal subject, 2) right positioning of NP 3) left positioning of NP (topicalization).

The strongest position is preverbal subject. Therefore, reading (2) is chosen applying both the lexical conditioning rule and the syntactic position that, in this case, strengthen each other. For example

'Un affresco è stato dipinto da tre pittori'.
A fresco has been painted by three painters

Applying the rules we get the following reading:

```
(indef x (fresco x)
            (three y (painter y) (paint y x))
```

that in fact is the most plausible.

Another important position is the right positioning of NP.

'Sono stati mostrati due affreschi ad ogni visitatore'
Two frescoes have been shown to every visitor

for which the most plausible reading seems to be

```
(every x (visitor x)
            (two y (fresco y)
                   (show <speaker> y x))
```

Note that the heuristic of the left/right ordering of the quantifiers at the same syntactic level suggested in many systems is in fact rather weak, at least for Italian.

3.3 Scope markers

The scope markers are particular disambiguating expressions by means of which the dependent reading of an NP can be forced. In Italian there are at least two distributive expressions: 'ciascuno' (each) and 'diverso' (different). The scope markers, when present, give a strong contribution to disambiguation of scope effects. Here 'ciascuno' is meant not as quantifier but as distributive marker right after NP. For example

'Tutti gli affreschi di Giotto contengono un santo ciascuno'
All Giotto's frescoes contain a saint each.

its first logical form is

(contain
        (complex-term <features> all x
                (and (fresco x)(has-painted x Giotto))
        (complex-term <features> indef y
                (and (saint x)(<u>marker</u> ciascuno x))))

that resolves into

(all x (and (fresco x)(has-painted x Giotto))
                        (indef y (saint x)(contain x y)))

The marker 'diverso' behaves syntactically as a regular adjective. It is worth noting that these markers tend also to violate the preverbal subject rule.

'Un pittore diverso ha dipinto ogni affresco nel Palazzo del Governo'.
A different painter painted every fresco in the Palazzo del Governo.

where one prefers

(every x
        (and (fresco x)(in-place x Palazzo_del_Governo))
                (indef y (painter y)(paint y x)))

It is worth noting that the distributive capability of scope markers can be exploited in the natural language generation module, part of the dialogue system. Markers can help make the intended scopes of quantifiers more precise, when the latter were lexically chosen but would perform poorly in relation to the aforementioned rules.

4. Interpretation

As said before, in the AlFresco system the treatment of linguistic expression meaning takes advantage of the notion of multilevel semantics. The interpretation of the second logical form built by scopings resolution makes up a level in which the soundness of a sentence is detected and eventually the relative referents are retrieved (in the literature this level is often called Meaning Representation Language (MRL) or World Model Language (WML)).

Verifying the soundness of a logical form and producing the correct interpretation is not a trivial task. We want the semantic interpreter to be independent of the domain of the knowledge representation system and of the different media through which a linguistic expression can be built. The ease of dealing with some semantic constructs depends on the power of the knowledge base formalism. In case of limited knowledge formalisms, simplification and transformation levels of logical form become necessary (PHLIQA1 [Scha83], BBN 85 [Stallard86]), increasing the architectural complexity of the multilevel semantics. Historically, this increase occured when the domain representation was little more than a database. Now this whole view becomes of the utmost importance in a multiple underlying systems approach ([Bobrow90], [Resnik89]). In this case the knowledge base is not the only underlying system with which the logical form interacts. It becomes necessary to choose which representation or reasoning subsystem will be involved in the interpretation and behaviour generation for a certain logical form or for its subparts. Applications that take advantage of this approach are under development at IRST with MAIA, an integrated system of artificial intelligence that provides for some office automation and interactions with visitors to the institute.

4.1 Semantics of quantification operators

The elements of the logical form are constants corresponding to proper nouns in the input sentence and to individuals in the knowledge base, predicates corresponding to concepts and roles in the knowledge base, interpretation operators being the glue of the logical form (quantifier operator, ref-term, demonstr-term, logical operator etc...).

The notation that will be used in discussing the semantics of quantification operators is given below:

pred[x] indicates a well-formed form in which the variable x appears free.

$\text{ext}(p[x])$ indicates the the extension of p in a representation domain D
$\mathbb{P}(p[x])$ indicates the set of the parts of the extension denoted by p[x].

Be I a set, |I| indicates its cardinality.

We shall show how semantics is assigned to each quantification operator in the logical form. Particular relevance will be given to natural quantifiers.

As seen above a quantifier is syntactically represented with the wff

$$(\textbf{quant } x \text{ restriction}[x] \text{ body}[x])$$

that has a semantic interpretation

$$\{a \in \mathbb{P}_{\textbf{quant}}(\text{restriction}[x]) \mid D \models \text{body}[a] \}$$

where $\mathbb{P}_{\textbf{quant}}(\text{restriction}[x])$ is appropiately defined for each treated quantifier.

Exist

$$\mathbb{P}_{\text{exist}}(p[x]) = \{P \in \mathbb{P}(p[x]): |P| = 1\}$$

in the eventuality that many referents satisfy semantically the form, there are expected interactions with the pragmatic module and with the user modeling. If the suggested referent is not very accurate from a pragmatic point of view (although semantically correct), the interpretation can suggest another one, always keeping the semantic correctness. An analogous interaction can happen in the interpretation of the generic 'qualche' (some).

All

$$\mathbb{P}_{\text{all}}(p[x]) = \{P \in \mathbb{P}(p[x]): |P| = |[\text{ext}(p[x])]|\}$$

Especially in the interpretation of natural quantifiers it becomes essential to computational purpose and conceptual clarity to have the support of a knowledge representation that can cope with sets [Allgayer90]. In the knowledge base of AlFresco a treatment of sets in the assertional part has been implemented.

Numerals 'two three ...'

$$\mathbb{P}_{N \in \mathbf{N}}(p[x]) = \{P \in \mathbb{P}(p[x]): |P| = N\}$$

Exception operators 'all except three...'

$$\mathbb{P}_{except(N)}(p[x]) = \{P \in \mathbb{P}(p[x]): |P| = |[ext(p[x])]| - N\}$$

$$\text{if } |[ext(p[x])]| \geq N \qquad\qquad \mathbb{P}_{except(N)}(p[x]) = \varnothing \text{ otherwise}$$

$$\mathbb{P}_{except \text{ at most } N\%}(p[x]) = \{P \in \mathbb{P}(p[x]): |P| \geq |[ext(p[x])]| (1 - N/100)\}$$

Many

About 'molti' (many) there can be two attitudes: either one excludes this type of quantification by an extensional treatment [Keenan&Stavi86] or one tries to get what 'many' means in a fixed context [Barwise&Cooper81]. In AlFresco his second consideration was followed. Therefore

$$\mathbb{P}_{many}(p[x]) = \{P \in \mathbb{P}(p[x]): |P| = k|[ext(p[x])]|\}$$

where the multiplier k may be fixed, for example 0.6, or may depend on pragmatic aspects or on inferences on the semantic structure of the dialogue.

Vague operators (several, most of, etc...)

Also to interpret vague operators extensionally, it is necessary to make a stipulation of cardinality (fixed or dynamic), depending on the inferential capabilities on dialogue structure at our disposal. For example almost all, most of may be interpreted as semantically similar to 'except at most K', where for K considerations similar to those made for 'many' hold.

4.2 Determinate NPs

The ref-terms, demonstr-terms, pronoun-terms have a special treatment. The demonstr-terms coming from a deictic touch on the touchscreen contain the entities which the user intended to refer to. These are passed to the interpretation module in order to verify the semantic consistency. The demonstr-terms without touch, the pronoun-terms and some ref-terms are resolved with strict interaction with the topic module. The topic module organizes the mentioned referents so that it offers plausible candidates for these operators and the interpretation module verifies their semantic soundness. For a description in detail of the topic module, see [Samek&Strapparava90]. Some details on the logical form structures of some ref-terms for which one doesn't resort to topic module are now given. These ref-terms come from complex NPs such as 'the painter of a fresco in the Cappella degli Scrovegni' in which the referent for the NP 'the painter' is a function of the interpretation of the indefinite 'a fresco in the Cappella degli Scrovegni'. These complex NPs are resolved entirely in the interpretation module and are called ref-term-exs. The ref-term-exs are determined statically before the interpretative phase, with a structural check on their logical form. One looks for a free variable in respect to the ref-term into the restriction of the ref-term. For example

........(indef y (and (fresco y)(in-place y Cappella...))....

...(ref-term <features> x (and (painter x)(paint x y)))).....
                                                ↑

where y is free in respect to the ref-term.

4.3 Main phases of the algorithm.

In the following the main phases of the interpretation algorithm are listed.

• construction of the first logical form from the output of the lexical semantics. The translation takes advantage of a set of rules, one for each linguistic phenomenon then one for each operator in the resulting logical form. (the translation may be not trivial; for example here one may want to choose resolving such ambiguity as coordinated PP attached to coordinated NP at this level).

• scopings resolution. The first logical form is neutral to quantifier scopings. In AlFresco a Hobbs-Shieber type algorithm is used for the structural resolution of the scopings. Heuristic cuts are applied to the resulting readings. The readings are put in order of soundness according to a hierarchy of the rules. In our domain the most plausible reading suggested by the scopings resolution is almost always the correct one.

• construction of the second logical form. In terms of data structures a wff has a scopings completely resolved when no complex-terms appear in it. Then a second logical form is a form in which all complex-terms are resolved in quantifier wffs. The second logical form is the data structure of the interpretation module.

• scanning of the form to initialize the data structures of the interpretation algorithm. For example in a completely referential reading for each variable in the form there must be a set of referents that interprets it. Hence in such case the interpretation module has to give not only an indication about the validity of the sentence, but given a set of referents that verify the form, it has to show all the dependences among such referents.

• notification of the constants (i.e. Giotto, La_Fuga_in_Egitto ...) in the form to the topic module. Checking for the ref-term-exs. Testing the deictic touching about the present demonstr-terms. The interpretation tries to resolve the reference of pronoun-terms, the other demonstr-terms and ref-terms: the topic module gives a set of probable candidates to the interpretation. The interpretation then will test their consistency.

• interpretation of the logical form's operators. In particular for the quantifier operators the steps Calculate-Range and Verify-in-Body are crucial. Calculate-Range calculates the restriction of the quantifier wff according to the semantics of its operator. Verify-in-Body verifies the logical validity of the result. Since there may be an arbitrary nesting of quantifier wff, the algorithm has to provide an arbitrary deep recursion of such functionalities.

• extensionalization of some parts of the logical form. This can be done with an appropriate construction in the Abox language of a query to the knowledge representation. At this level there are all the interactions with the knowledge base, including eventually a treatment of attributive/referential readings (see below).

• resolution of the logic dependencies about the referents found during the interpretation of the sentence. Notification of the interpretation to other modules of AlFresco. In particular the pragmatic component decides on showing a film or a fresco about the focused entities of the sentence. The answer to the user is given in a multimedia way in that s/he can click on the entities of the answer to see a fresco mentioned on the screen or to know what critics say about the subject by means of hypertext cards.

5. Conclusions and future developments

We have explained the main ideas that lie at the basis of two interpretation modules in the multilevel hierarchy of the AlFresco dialogue system: the quantifier scopings resolution module and the interpretation module of a meaning representation logical form. In particular we have discussed some heuristics that have been proven useful in reducing the number of readings in the scopings resolution part. As far as interpretation is concerned, a semantics for a set of natural quantifiers and an interpretation algorithm have been given in full detail.

About scopings resolution, further developments involve a reasoning capability on the collective-distributive semantics of the predicates and the design of an algorithm useful also in the generation of natural language. For the latter, a unification-based algorithm seems to be useful in the structural disambiguation. For the interpretation module, work will focus on referential/attributive readings and full treatment of intensionality with appropriate temporal and contextual structures in the underlying knowledge representation systems. Approaches that try to fix up some ambiguities along the attributive/referential dimension from a computational point of view taking advantage of Fauconnier's theoretical setting are [Magnini&Strapparava90] [Lesmo&Terenziani89].

References

[Allgayer90] Allgayer J. "SB-ONE+ dealing with sets efficiently", *Proceedings of ECAI*, Stockholm, 1990

[Barwise&Cooper81].Barwise J., Cooper R. "Generalized quantifiers and natural language", *Linguistics and Philosophy*, 4, 1981

[Bobrow90] Bobrow R., Resnik P., Weischedel R., "Multiple Underlying Systems: Translating User Requests into Programs to Produce Answers", *Proceedings of the 28th Annual Meeting of the ACL*, 1990

[Cooper87] Cooper R. "Quantification and Syntactic Theory", Reidel, Dordrecth, 1983

[Franconi90] Franconi E., "The YAK Manual: Yet Another Krapfen", *IRST-Manual #9003-01*, Trento, Italy, 1990.

[Hobbs&Shieber87] Hobbs J., Shieber S. "An Algorithm for Generating Quantifier Scopings", *Computational Linguistics*, 13, January 1987

[Keenan&Stavi86] Keenan E., Stavi J., "A semantic characterization of natural language determiners", *Linguistics and Philosophy*, 9, 1986

[Lavelli&Magnini91] Lavelli A., Magnini B., "Lexical Discrimination within a multilevel semantics approach", *Proceedings of AIIA*, 1991

[Lesmo&Terenziani89] Lesmo L., Terenziani P., "Interpretation of Noun Phrases in Intensional Contexts", *Proceedings of Coling 88*, Budapest, 1988

[Longobardi 88] Longobardi G., "I Quantificatori", in *Grande grammatica italiana di consultazione*, Il Mulino, Bologna, 1988

[Magnini&Strapparava90] Magnini B., Strapparava C., "Computational Representation of Mental Spaces: a Functional Approach", *Proceedings of ECAI*, Stockholm, 1990.

[Resnik89] Resnik P. "Access to Multiple Underlying Systems in Janus", BBN Report No. 7142, 1989

[Samek&Strapparava90] Samek-Lodovici V., Strapparava C., "Identifying Noun Phrase References: The Topic Module of the AlFresco System", *Proceedings of ECAI*, Stockholm, 1990.

[Scha&Stallard88] Scha R., Stallard D., "Multilevel Plural and Distributivity", *Proceedings of the 26th Annual Meeting of the ACL*, 1988

[Scha83] Scha R., "Logical Foundations for Question Answering", Philips Research Laboratories, Eindhoven 1983, M.S. 12.331.

[Stallard86] Stallard D. "A Terminological Simplification Transformation for Natural Language Question Answering System", *Proceedings of ACL*, 1986

[Stock89] Stock O., "Parsing with Flexibility, Dynamic Strategies and Idioms in Mind", *Computational Linguistics*, 15, 1989.

[Stock91] Stock O., "Natural Language and Exploration of a Information Spaces: The AlFresco Interactive System", To appear in *Proceedings of IJCAI*, 1991

[Westerstahl86] Westerstahl D. "Quantifier in Formal and Natural Language", Report No. CSLI-86-55, June 1986

[Woods77] Woods W, "Semantics and Quantification in Natural Language Question Answering", *Advances in Computers*, 17, Academic Press, 1977.

[Woods81] Woods W, "Procedural Semantics as a Theory of Meaning", in Joshi et al. (eds.) *Elements of Discourse Understanding*, Cambridge University Press, 1981

PARSING DEPENDENCY GRAMMARS

Vincenzo Lombardo
Dipartimento di Informatica - Universita' di Torino
C.so Svizzera 185 - 10149 Torino - Italy - Tel. 39 - 11 - 7712002
e-mail: vincenzo@di.unito.it

Abstract

The paper deals with a parser for dependency grammars. An intuitive and clear representation of the grammar is introduced: the formalism, that originates from the ID/LP constituency grammar, expresses the constraints of well-formedness of the sentences via two tables of relations of immediate dominance and linear precedence for pairs of syntactic categories. The tables are then compiled in order to generate information structures, called diamonds, that guide the parsing process, whose overall control strategy is described by an algorithm of navigation among the diamond structures. In the paper the grammar for a fragment of Italian is presented: this natural language, because of its high degree of freedom in the sentential order, reveals to be suitable for a dependency analysis.

1. Introduction

There is a huge number of formalisms aiming to express the syntactic constraints that govern the form of the sentences of natural languages, but almost all of them can be assigned to one of two classes. The leading paradigm (Phrase Structure Grammar) conceives of a sentence as decomposable into groups of words, each of which is in turn decomposed into subgroups, down to the basic elements (mainly words, but in some cases endings, dummies, etc.): each group is a "constituent" and the parsing tree specifies how each constituent is decomposed into subconstituents.

The second alternative is to use dependency structures. In this case, it is assumed that the words of a sentence are related via a binary relation (that can be called Immediate Dominance - ID) between a governor and a governed word. The structural tree specifies which is the top-level word (usually a verb), which are the words immediately governed by it, and for the latter which are the words they govern, and so on. The most evident difference between the two approaches is that in constituency trees the surface words appear only as leaves of the tree, while in dependency trees each node is associated with a word.

This is not the place for a discussion of the respective merits of the two alternatives (see [Sgall, Panevova 89], [Kac, Manaster-Ramer 86]), but we must note that the success of constituent structures is largely due to the seminal work of Noam Chomsky on the theory of grammars, which started up a vast body of research on the expressive power of phrase structure grammars. On the contrary, formal systems based on dependency grammar are rare (see [Hudson 84] [Sgall et al. 86] [Mel'cuk 87]). The same can be claimed of dependency parsers (noticeable exception [Nelimarkka et al. 84]).

One of the features of dependency grammars that deserves a mention is the stress they put on the role of the "head". A recent constituency formalism (Head Phrase Structure Grammar) has acknowledged the need of explicitly stating which is the head of a constituent [Pollard 84]. It is an evolution of the ID/LP (Immediate Dominance/ Linear Precedence) approach [Gazdar et al. 85]. In dependency grammars the immediate dominance and the linear precedence between constituents featuring a head are reasonably restated as dominance and precedence between heads.

The next section introduces a formalism for expressing dependency grammars, while the third describes the parser, that operates on the diamond structures, which are the result of the translation phase (not included because of the space constraints).

2. A Dependency Grammar

The structure we associate with a sentence is a dependency tree. Some authors associate a dependency tree to the deep level of the sentence: for instance, in the Prague School [Sgall et al. 86], the Tectogrammatical Representation (TR) generated by the Functional Generative Description (FGD) represents the sentence in its articulation between topic and focus, with the edges labelled with the deep cases involved. Such a TR can be translated into a linearized sentence by the transductive components. The left-to-right order of the elements in a TR is related to Communicative Dinamism (CD) rather than surface order. [Hudson 84] proposes a framework that is intended to cope with surface phenomena in natural language, like word order, multiple dependencies and unbounded dependencies. The structure associated with a sentence is obtained from the rules that state the head&modifier relation for categories of words.

The dependency structure considered is closer to the latter view. In particular, the nodes of the tree keep the information about the surface order of the words, while the arcs represent the dependency relations. The dependency tree in figure 1 is associated with the sentence:

Il ragazzo che viaggio' con Luisa compro' una enciclopedia.
The boy who travelled with Luisa bought an encyclopedia.

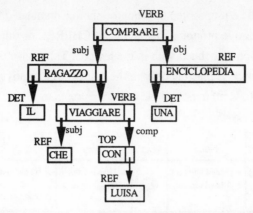

fig.1 An example of a dependency tree. Bold arrows represent standard dependency relations, simple arrows are only structural arcs that do not involve dependency but propagate it from the upper levels. The grammatical relations are assigned by a further set of rules that use clues of syntactic and semantic flavour. A complete description of such a representation can be found in [Lesmo, Lombardo 91].

A very readable and intuitive way to represent a dependency grammar is via ID/LP rules. ID/LP grammars have been introduced within the GPSG framework, in order to avoid many redundancies especially in the case of free-word order languages [Shieber 83]. ID rules specify the relation of Immediate Dominance, while LP rules represent the Linear Precedence, in order to split the two components, that are usually represented together by the rewriting rules of a phrase-structure grammar.

Even dependency grammars can be described via ID/LP rules, that are expressed via the entries of two tables, that represent the ID/LP relations between any pair of categories. In the figures 2 and 3 the grammar for a fragment of Italian is presented. The set of grammatical categories appearing in the tables do not necessarily correspond to the classical categories. New categories have been introduced in order to account for peculiar distributional behaviours (e.g. CHEREL, associated with the relative pronoun "che" - *who, which, that*). Each entry in the ID-table states the relation of immediate dominance between the categories on the row and the column respectively. The entry in the table is empty for pairs of categories that are not "dependency" related. For instance, a determiner will never dominate another word, so its row in the ID-table is empty. The precedence for two categories that stand in an ID-relation is also specified, in order to know whether the dominated category (the modifier) is allowed to appear on the left ($>$), on the right ($<$), or on both sides ($=$) of the head simultaneously. Each precedence sign in a square is associated with a number of constraints on the features' values. For example, the constraint ($\downarrow$e1.RELATIVE,+) in the entry for noun-verb dominance, means that the feature RELATIVE must be present in the first element of the verb node beneath the noun. Such a feature will be propagated up from the subtree dominated by the verb, once it has been originated by a relative pronoun (belonging to CHEREL or other relative categories), which has this information associated with in the lexicon. This constraint is necessary to state that a noun-verb dominance is feasible only in the context of a relative sentence; the leftmost subtree of the root node (a verb) must include a relative pronoun.

Modifier / Head	Verb	Noun	Det	Prep	Adj	Cherel
Verb	> (↑head.tense,+) < (↓head.tense,-)	= (↑head.tense,+) < (↑head.tense,-)	●	= (↑head.tense,+) < (↑head.tense,-)	> (↑head.tense,+) < (↑head.copula,+)	> (↑head.tense,+)
Noun	< (↓head.tense,+) (↓e1.relative,+) (↑head.proper,-)	●	>	< (↑head.proper,-)	=	●
Det	●	●	●	●	●	●
Prep	< (↓head.tense,-)	<	●	●	●	●
Adj	●	●	●	<	●	●
Cherel	●	●	●	●	●	●

fig.2- The Immediate Dominance table.
●: immediate dominance is not allowed; < : the dominant category must precede the dominated one; > : the dominant category must follow the dominated one; = : both orders are allowed simultaneously
Constraints related to an order sign apply only if that order is realized
Constraints appearing apart apply independently of the order
Constraints appearing in the same entry are intended to be in XOR relation.

While the ID-table includes information about the respective order of the head and its modifiers, the LP table describes the precedence constraints among the modifiers at the same level. This information is required to reject, as ill-formed, sequences such as

*bianco il cavallo

white the horse

where the adjectival modifier precedes the determiner. Each entry in the LP-table specifies the linear precedence between two nodes of the specified categories. In many cases the LP-relation between two categories varies according to the dominant category. The constraint <up:Category> associated with the precedence sign accounts for the latter variant.

	Verb	Noun	Det	Prep	Adj	Cherel
Verb	●	= up: Verb	●	= up: Verb > up: Noun	= up: Verb > up: Noun	> up: Verb
Noun		= up: Verb	●	= up: Verb	= up: Verb	> up: Verb
Det			●	●	< up: Noun	●
Prep				= up: Noun/ Verb	= up: Noun/ Verb	> up: Verb
Adj					= up: Noun	> up: Verb
Cherel						●

fig.3 - The Linear Precedence table.

< : the category on the row must precede the one on the column; > : the category on the row must follow the one on the column; = : both orders are allowed; ● : the two categories cannot depend on the same node, on the same side of the head

The table also includes information about the categories that must dominate the pair which linear order relation refers to.

3. The parser

In principle, it would be possible to build a parser that analyzes input sentences directly on the basis of the grammatical constraints stored in the ID/LP tables. But this would be highly inefficient, since it would involve a repetitive examination of the tables, in order to know which kind of relationship may exist between two successive words. They are not always related via an ID relationship: one of them may happen to be many levels below the other (in the dependency tree). Thus, the intermediate nodes (that correspond to actual words in the sentence) must be hypothesized by the parser and this requires a search in the tables for all the possible connections between the two words. The approach is to compile the syntactic knowledge of the tables, in order to yield a different information structure that is able to drive the operations of the parser more directly. This section is divided into two subsections: the first introduces these structures, that are called **diamonds** because of the form they assume in their graphical representation; the second describes the actual parsing algorithm.

3.1 Diamonds

Once a node of category CAT has been created, the parsing (that depends on the following input word) can continue toward several directions in the tree. The next step has many possibilities:

- The node has no head yet: it means that the parser has hypothesized the existence (see below) of such a node during the analysis of the previous words in the sentence. Modifiers of this node that precede the head must exist (the ones whose presence caused the introduction of this node). Then we need to know which are the other modifiers that can also precede the head and can be attached to the current node before the head is found. The information about them is stored in the diamond for CAT in its "backward down" part.

- The node has a head: what follows could be other modifiers of the node that, of course, come after the head. The "forward down" part of the diamond says which modifiers can follow the head of a given CAT.

- The node has a head but what follows cannot start one of its modifiers: this means that the substructure headed by the current node is completed. The attachment point of the new subtree must be found at a higher level in the tree. The current node may be the "sister" of a new substructure having its immediate dominant node (which perhaps is still to be created) as a common parent. Whether this is possible or not is said in the "forward up" part of the diamond of CAT. Actually, this part also covers the case where the next word is the head of the parent of the current node.

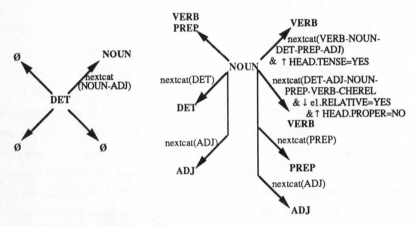

fig.4. The diamonds for the categories NOUN and DET. Many details are ignored in these diagrams: in particular the indication that some arcs in a diamond are mutually exclusive and the relative precedence of the arcs in the same direction, such that, once an arc with a precedence x has been followed, other arcs with a smaller number cannot be followed any more (e.g. DET has value 1 and ADJ has value 2 in the backward-down part of the NOUN diamond).

- The last case accomplishes the task of moving more than one level up in the structure. The "backward up" part of the diamond says what are the diamonds that can be considered in moving upwards.

The diamonds (fig.4) consist in a **center**, that represents the category of the current node, and in four sets of links, one for each direction that has been informally discussed above. Each set (represented in the drawings as a single multiple link that can have more than one arrowhead) identifies a set of categories: they are the categories that are "relevant" during the processing, if the direction associated with the set has been selected. A set of "conditions" is associated with each arc: they state when a substructure having as root the category pointed to by the link can be hypothesized (except for the "backward up" part, whose interpretation is slightly different). The categories which are the arguments of the "nextcat" predicate specify what are the possible "first" categories of a substructure. Other predicates introduce further constraints on the features' values.

Let us examine the diamond associated with the category NOUN (see fig.4). We see immediately that the modifiers that can appear on the left of a nominal head are DET and ADJ and that a DET can be hypothesized only when it is actually found ("nextcat(DET)"), since it cannot have any substructure associated with it, while an ADJ can be assumed if the ADJ itself is found. The same thing happens for the modifiers that can appear on the right of the head: VERB, PREP, and ADJ. Note that the conditions associated with VERB are somewhat strange: the only way to attach a VERB to a NOUN is to have it as the "head" of a relative clause. So, it seems that only CHEREL (in the fragment considered) can start such a substructure. The condition "↓e1.RELATIVE=YES" states that the first element of the modifying verb must have the value YES for the feature "relative"; the "nextcat" predicate simply lists all the categories that can start a substructure headed by a tensed verb. The "forward up" part of the diamond says that in case the parser finds a VERB, a NOUN, an ADJ, etc. it must consider as completed the current noun and move to the next higher node (a verb). The distinction between being the head of the parent vs. being a sister of the current NOUN will be handled by the diamond of the VERB, activated immediately after. Finally, in the case that no other possibilities exist, the parser can proceed upward in the tree. The only legal moves, starting from a NOUN are to pass to a PREP or VERB above ("backward-up").

3.2 The parsing algorithm

The parsing algorithm (figure 5) navigates on the diamonds created by the translation step, which examines the two tables in order to find the categories that are the arguments of the nextcat predicate. The algorithm describes the operations to carry out at the activation of a diamond and the control strategy that is responsible for the subsequent activations. The three arguments used are: CAT, the center of the current diamond, MODE (BACKWARD or FORWARD) and VERSUS (UP or DOWN). Moreover, the global variable CURRENT individuates the node which is currently being considered in the partial tree already built. The parser is started up with:

```
begin
    CAT:= category of the first input word
    NODE:= CREATE (CAT)
    NODE.HEAD:= first input word
    ADVANCE the input pointer
```

```
CURRENT:= NODE
ACTIVATE DIAMOND (CAT,FORWARD,DOWN)
end.
```

The assignment of an input word to the HEAD of a node involves the storing of the lexical information associated with it. The function CREATE, takes as input a category and generates a node of the appropriate type. CREATE is coupled (except for the starting node) with the procedure ATTACH, that links the newly created node, according to the value of the parameter VERSUS, that specifies in which direction we are moving inside the dependency tree: if we are going upwards, the new node will be the parent of the current one, otherwise it will be its daughter.

MODE and VERSUS enable the algorithm to select a set of arcs from the diamond associated with CAT. In case of FORWARD-DOWN, if there is a link for which the conditions are satisfied, a new node of the type associated with NEWCAT (the category found on the selected link) is created and attached beneath the current node. Now, there are two possibilities: the next word is of category NEWCAT (so, it is hypothesized to be the first of itself) or it is of a different category. In the former case, the head of the newly created node is assigned with the lexical data of the input word, and the analysis proceeds on the new node: the NEWCAT diamond will be activated and the FORWARD-DOWN movement is selected (what follows in the input can be modifiers of NEWCAT that follow their governor). In the latter case, the input pointer is kept on the current word, the NEWCAT diamond is activated, but now in BACKWARD-DOWN modality, since the newly created node has no head yet, therefore it has modifiers that precede it. The other cases are similar and are left to the reader (LINKUPorCREATE&ATTACH returns the parent node, if it exists, or creates and attaches a new one; HAS-HEAD is a self explanatory predicate).

4. Conclusions

A parser for dependency grammars represented via ID/LP tables has been presented. The tables are compiled into structures called diamonds that guide the parsing of sentences.

As far as I know this is the first attempt to build a parser for a dependency grammar based on efficient data structures built automatically via a compilation step. Other experiences of this kind have been carried out for constituency grammars. DCG formalism itself [Warren, Pereira 80] can be viewed as the translation of the rules of phrase structure grammars into logical clauses, with the adjunct of further arguments (e.g. gender and number for nouns) for the check of features' values constraints. [Eisele, Dorre 86] presents a parser for the LFG framework, that relies on DCG and features a compilation step of the grammar into Prolog clauses, subsequently interpreted. The appealing of dependency grammars for free word order languages has lead [Nelimarkka et al. 84] to propose a parser for Finnish that is similar to this

DIAMOND(CAT,MODE,VERSUS)

● MODE=FORWARD & VERSUS=DOWN
  IF an arc (CAT,NEWCAT) exists such that the conditions are satisfied THEN
   NODE:= CREATE(NEWCAT); ATTACH(NODE);
   IF the category of the next input word =NEWCAT & the arc constraints are satisfied THEN
     NODE.HEAD:= input word; ADVANCE the input pointer;
     ACTIVATE DIAMOND(NEWCAT,FORWARD,DOWN)
   ELSE ACTIVATE DIAMOND(NEWCAT,BACKWARD,DOWN)
   FI
   CURRENT:= NODE
  ELSE ACTIVATE DIAMOND(CAT,FORWARD,UP)
  FI
● MODE=BACKWARD & VERSUS=DOWN
  IF an arc (CAT,NEWCAT) exists such that the conditions are satisfied THEN
   NODE:= CREATE(NEWCAT); ATTACH(NODE);
   IF the category of the next input word =NEWCAT & the arc constraints are satisfied THEN
    NODE.HEAD:= input word; ADVANCE the input pointer;
    ACTIVATE DIAMOND(NEWCAT,FORWARD,DOWN)
   ELSE ACTIVATE DIAMOND(NEWCAT,BACKWARD,DOWN)
   FI
   CURRENT:= NODE
  ELSE FAIL
  FI
● MODE=FORWARD & VERSUS=UP
  IF an arc (CAT,NEWCAT) exists such that the arc conditions are satisfied THEN
   NODE:= LINKUPorCREATE&ATTACH(CURRENT,NEWCAT);
   CURRENT:= NODE
   IF HAS-HEAD(CURRENT) THEN ACTIVATE DIAMOND(NEWCAT,FORWARD,DOWN)
   ELSE IF the category of the next input word=NEWCAT & the arc constraints are satisfied THEN
     CURRENT:= input word; ADVANCE the input pointer;
     ACTIVATE DIAMOND(NEWCAT,FORWARD,DOWN)
     ELSE ACTIVATE DIAMOND(NEWCAT,BACKWARD,DOWN)
     FI
   FI
  ELSE ACTIVATE DIAMOND(CAT,BACKWARD,UP)
  FI
● MODE=BACKWARD & VERSUS=UP
  IF LINKUP(CURRENT).category=NEWCAT THEN
   ACTIVATE DIAMOND(NEWCAT,FORWARD,UP)
  ELSE IF End of input sentence THEN OK
    ELSE FAIL
    FI
  FI

fig.5 The parsing algorithm: the procedure calls ACTIVATE pass the control to another
diamond. A diamond is associated to a node of the same category in the dependency tree.
The algorithm shows the behaviour of a diamond which is activated. The details described in
the caption of figure 4 about diamonds are not taken into account.

in the strategy of parsing: for every input word a two-step finite automaton tries to attach the word as a dependent on a current head, or a subsequent one in the sentence, by shifting the focus of attention. This parser does not make use of an explicit grammar and therefore no compilation step is required.

Further improvements will be the analysis of the efficiency of the parser and a comparison with the more deeply studied techniques of constituency grammars parsing, like Earley's algorithm [Earley 70], and others that have been derived from it, especially those based on ID/LP grammars [Shieber 83][Barton et al. 87]. The current coverage of the grammar must be extended and the parser must also be improved in order to reduce the non-determinism: the final goal is to make it works quasi-deterministically (perhaps introducing natural changes and restructuring rules [Lesmo, Torasso 83]). The parser and the translator are implemented in C-Prolog 1.5 and run on a SUN workstation under the UNIX operating system.

Acknowledgements

I would like to thank prof. Leonardo Lesmo for his active and precious support.

References
[Barton et al. 87] Barton G.E., Berwick R.C., Ristad E.S., *Computational Complexity and Natural Language*, The MIT Press, Cambridge, Mass., 1987.
[Earley 70] Earley J., *An Efficient Context-Free Parsing Algorithm*, Communications of the ACM 13 (2), 1970.
[Eisele, Dorre 86] Eisele A., Dorre J., *A Lexical Functional Grammar System in Prolog*, Proceedings COLING 86, Bonn, 1986.
[Gazdar et al. 85] Gazdar G., Klein E., Pullum G., Sag I., *Generalizad Phrase Structure Grammar*, Basil Blackwell, Oxford, 1985.
[Hudson 84] Hudson R., *Word Grammar*, Basil Blackwell, Oxford, 1984.
[Kac, Manaster-Ramer 86] Kac M.B., Manaster-Ramer A., *Parsing Without (Much) Phrase Structure*, Proceedings COLING 86, Bonn, 1986.
[Lesmo, Lombardo 91] Lesmo L., Lombardo V., *A Dependency Syntax for the Surface Structure of Sentences*, to appear in proceedings of the WOCFAI Conference, July 1991.
[Lesmo, Torasso 83] Lesmo L., Torasso P., *A Flexible Natural Language Parser based on a two-level Representation of Syntax*, Proc. of the 1st Conference EACL, Pisa, Italy, 1983, pp.114-121.
[Mel'cuk 87] Mel'cuk I., *Dependency Syntax: Theory and Practice*, State University of New York Press, Albany, NY, 1987.
[Nelimarkka et al. 84] Nelimarkka E., Jappinen H., Lehtola A., *Parsing an Inflectional Free-Word-Order Language with Two-Way Finite Automata*, ECAI-84: Advances in Artificial Intelligence, North Holland, 1984.
[Pollard 84] Pollard C.J., *Generalized Phrase Structure Grammars, Head Grammars, and Natural Language*, Ph.D. Thesis, Stanford University, 1984.
[Sgall et al. 86] Sgall P., Haijcova E., Panevova J., *The Meaning of the Sentence in its Semantic and Pragmatic Aspects*, D. Reidel Publishing Company, 1986.
[Sgall, Panevova 89] Sgall P., Panevova J., *Dependency Syntax - A Challenge*, Theoretical Linguistics, vol.15, No. 1/2, 1989.
[Shieber 83] Shieber S.M., *Direct Parsing of ID/LP Grammars*, Technical Note 291R, SRI International, November 1983 (also in Linguistics and Philosophy, vol.7, issue2).
[Warren, Pereira 80] Warren D.H.D., Pereira F.C.N., *Definite Clause Grammars for Language Analysis - A Survey of the Formalism and a Comparison with Augmented Transition Networks*, in Artificial Intelligence 13, 1980.

Perception and Robotics

A SYSTEM BASED ON NEURAL ARCHITECTURES
FOR THE RECONSTRUCTION OF 3-D SHAPES FROM IMAGES

E. Ardizzone, A. Chella*, R. Pirrone, F. Sorbello

DIE - Dipartimento di Ingegneria Elettrica
University of Palermo
Viale delle Scienze 90128 Palermo, Italy

*DIE - Dipartimento di Ingegneria Elettrica
and
CRES - Centro per la Ricerca Elettronica in Sicilia
Monreale (Palermo), Italy

Abstract

The connectionist approach to the recovery of 3-D shape information from 2-D images developed by the authors, is based on a system made up by two cascaded neural networks. The first network is an implementation of the BCS, an architecture which derives from a biological model of the low level visual processes developed by Grossberg and Mingolla: this architecture extracts a sort of brightness gradient map from the image. The second network is a backpropagation architecture that supplies an estimate of the geometric parameters of the objects in the scene under consideration, starting from the outputs of the BCS. A detailed description of the system and the experimental results obtained by simulating it are reported in the paper.

1. Description of the system

An original approach has been developed, as a part of the visual perception model proposed by the authors in [1].The proposed architecture directly recovers 3-D shapes from 2-D images making use of two cascaded neural networks. The first one (called BCS) derives o sort of brightness gradient map of the image, employing a cooperative-competitive interaction among simple neural units [3,4]. This map (called boundary web) is supplied as input to the second stage of the architecture which is based on the backpropagation learning algorithm [6]. This network performs an estimate of the shape factors of the objects that are present in the scene in terms of the best fitting superquadrics parameters. Superquadrics are the primitives of the adopted solid modeling system. The proposed system allows to directly recover

3-D shapes information. The whole architecture has been simulated in C language on a HP9000/825SRX system running under UNIX HP-UX.

The first stage of the system (see figure 1) is a multilayer neural architecture which is called Boundary Contour System (BCS) based on the theories developed by Grossberg and Mingolla leading to a formulation of a mathematical model of low level visual processes (see appendix A for a detailed description).

The BCS allows a substantial data compression without loss of information about the shapes of the visualized objects, providing an image map made up by segments that displace themselves along constant brightness lines and resulting sensitive not only to the sharp luminance variations corresponding to the real edges of the objects, but also to the smooth variations related to the surface shading, because the input sensors of the architecture are approximately sensitive to the brightness gradient. In this way it is possible to determine a map of the brightness gradient over the whole image. This architecture is essentially based on biological and psychological considerations and results in a strongly parallel implementation, showing a good behaviour with respect to the noise sensitivity. On the contrary, computational classical approaches to shape from shading (see for example [5]) generally represent a heavy load. The implementation of the BCS allows to obtain a good low level representation of the displayed objects together with a sufficient degree of spontaneous segmentation of the scene as a result of its intrinsic ability to determine the edges of the objects in the presented scene. The system derives a global estimate of the image contrast through a sort of statistical correlation of several local estimates over an object surface region, to obtain a sharp contour along points with the same luminance. So, an occluding boundary completion is induced by the brightness gradient of the occluding object surface and is very little affected by the brightness gradient of the occluded object surface. This is an important characteristic of the system: in fact a pictorial scene is made up by several elements and it is necessary to perform a segmentation to analyze them correctly. In particular, the BCS theory has been implemented to extract 3-D informations from suitably synthesized images representing superquadrics. In fact the model of the

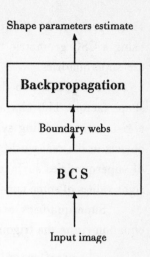

FIGURE 1: The proposed syatem structure. The BCS filters the input image in order to obtain a brightness gradient map (boundary web) that is supplyed as input to the second stage which extracts an estimate of the shape parameters of the objects displayed in the scene.

visual process, to which this architecture belongs, reconstructs the perceived scene using a CSG geometric model (CSG, Constructive Solid Geometry) whose primitives are superquadrics.

It is possible to deform a superquadric surface in several ways, modifying its shape factors. This characteristic makes the superquadrics very suitable primitives for a geometric modeling system because they can easily approximate the shapes of the objects in the real world. In order to make the BCS able to detect the great variability of superquadrics surface curvature of the superquadrics, the determination of the right values of some constant parameters has been necessary.

Superquadrics are geometric shapes derived from the quadrics' parametric equation rising the trigonometric functions to two real exponents [3]:

$$\bar{x}(\eta,\omega) = \begin{vmatrix} a_1\cos\eta^{\varepsilon_1}\cos\omega^{\varepsilon_2} \\ a_2\cos\eta^{\varepsilon_1}\sin\omega^{\varepsilon_2} \\ a_3\sin\eta^{\varepsilon_1} \end{vmatrix} -\pi/2 \leq \eta \leq \pi/2; \ -\pi \leq \omega \leq \pi \tag{1.1}$$

where η and ω are the latitude and longitude parameters. The a-parameters are the superquadric semiaxes lengths, while the exponents ε_1 and ε_2 are called *shape factors* and affect the appearance of the surface of the superquadric respectively in latitude and longitude. If these factors assume values less than 1, then the shape is somewhat squared. If the value is nearly 1 the shape is rounded; if the exponents approach 2 the shape is locally flat with some sharp edges. Finally, if the values of these factors are greater than 2 the surface exhibits some cusps. The (1.1) is the canonic form parametric equation of a superellipsoid that is characterized by only 5 parameters. Three orientation parameters and the center coordinates are to be added to these quantities to completely describe a generically displaced superquadric.

The second stage of the system derives an estimate of the geometric parameters of the objects in the scene, starting from the boundary webs. A suitable way to perform this mapping is making use of an associative mechanism based on an adaptive architecture. A system like this is able to generalize the learned correspondences when tested with unknown input patterns, even if not providing a strictly correct parametrs estimate. To this aim a backpropagation neural network has been used that has been trained to determine the geometric parameters of the best fitting superquadric to the object surface portion used as input. The global estimate of the object shape derives from a series of these local curvature estimates.

2 Simulations and experimental results

2.1 The BCS stage

Some images filtered by the BCS are shown in figures 2 and 3. Generally, they represent a single shaded superquadric referred to its own axes in a suitable reference system.

Due to the need of generating a number of patterns to train the backpropagation architecture as large as possible, the BCS has been used for a great number of images and shapes with satisfactory results (see figure 2 for an example).

The model's equations have been analyzed so as to determine the right values for a series of constant parameters in order to allow a good behaviour of the model relative to the used images. Several trials have been made to determine in which way the parameters values could affect the activations of the units of a particular layer and how the activations of different layers could affect each other.The results have been satisfactory, leading to convergence after a few iterations.

Some side effects have been noted that take place near the edges of the displayed object, in particular in the case of high values of the shape factors (when the surface exhibits some cusps). These effects are due to an intrinsic limitation of the BCS: in fact the need to collect all the pixels of the image leads the input receptive fields to overlap each other. Thus, a receptive field spatially located out of edges of the object image can be excited by pixels belonging to the image itself. However, these side effects did not affect the results of the BCS filtering as regards the quality of the input supplied to the backpropagation net. The implemented architecture has been

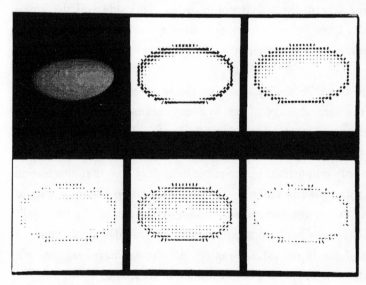

FIGURE 2: A tipical output of the BCS. The graphic display shows the input image and the activation levels of each layer of the network. It can be noted that the segments are displaced along constant brightness contours and, obviously, along the real edges of the displayed object.

applied in an original way to the scene segmentation with satisfactory results. To this aim a simple scene made up by two superquadrics has been synthesized (see figure 3). Different views of the scene have been set up, fixing the distance of the observer from the origin of the reference system and moving all around the objects in latitude and longitude. It is to be noted that a

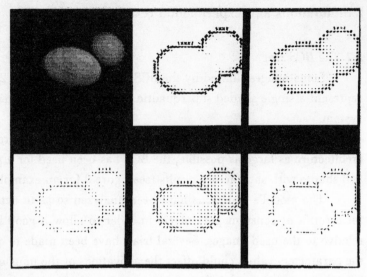

FIGURE 3: An example of the BCS segmentation ability. From the observation of the displacement of the segments, it can be noted that the BCS individuates two separate objects and, reveals the occluding boundary. The scene was made up by a sphere placed behind a superellipsoid that was centered at the origin of the reference system.

latitude and a longitude of 0° correspond, in this reference system, to a view in which the x axis points out of the screen, the y axis points to its right side and the z axis points to its top. The results seem rather independent from the relative position of the observer and the light source, so the segmentation is acceptable even under critical luminance conditions.

As a consequence of this BCS ability, only images representing a single object have been used to train the second stage of the system, because, generally, several properly processed primitives are necessary to correctly approximate a real object, so only local estimates of the object shape parameters are possible. Moreover, the estimates have been made only on portions of the scene boundary web that correspond to proper regions of the superquadric surface. The final aim is to obtain a sort of window that moves across the image and collects different regions of the boundary web, step by step; at each step, the backpropagation network provides the estimate of the geometric parameters of the input surface region. All the estimates regarding a particular object are correlated to supply a global estimate of its shape.

2.2 The backpropagation stage

The employed backpropagation architecture is made up by 400 input units, 8 output units and a set of 10 hidden units. The input units correspond to the collected portion of the boundary web of the image, while the output units correspond to the geometric parameters describing a superquadric referred to its own axes namely 2 shape factors, 3 center coordinates and 3 lengths of the superquadric axes.

Different training sets have been generated corresponding to higher and higher generalization degrees in the network learning. All these training sets are based on images showing a single shaded superquadric with fixed axes lengths (0.5 along the x direction, 1 along y and 0.7 along z) For each image six views have been made, varying the observer position in the following way: its latitude has been fixed to 60°, the longitude has been varied by steps of 60°, starting from 0° and its normalized position has been fixed to 1. The first training set has been built as follows. Seven superquadrics have been synthesized, differing only for the values of the shape factors; thus, 42 different images have been set up fixing to 1 the value of ε_1 and varying ε_2 as it is shown in table 2. For each image, the z-layer activations have been considered to obtain the input data. These activations are ordered as a three indexes matrix in which the first and the second one are related to the spatial location of the corresponding cluster of z units, while the third index is related to the orientations inside the cluster. In particular, 12 different orientations have been implemented for each cluster. If N represents the number of orientations for a particular spatial location and MAX represents the dimension of the activation matrix relative to the first two indexes, it is possible to derive an average orientation and activation for each cluster of units:

$$k_o = (\Sigma_k \, k \, z_{ijk})/ N \qquad (2.2.1)$$
$$z_{ij} = (\Sigma_k \, z_{ijk} \, e^{ -| k - ko | })/ N \qquad (2.2.2)$$

where k_o and z_{ij} are the mean values, while k and z_{ijk} are the values of the current unit orientation and activation. A reference system with the origin in the low left corner of the image has been considered and the coordinates of the position of the current unit have been calculated, i and j being the indexes of the activation matrix:

$$x = j / (MAX - 1) \qquad (2.2.3)$$
$$y = (MAX - 1 - i) / (MAX - 1) \qquad (2.2.4)$$

Finally, for each cluster of 12 units, 4 values have been obtained namely k_o , z_{ij} , x and y.These values represent a sort of average boundary web of the object and form the real input of the backpropagation architecture. The effective input to the architecture is made up by a squared portion of the average boundary web whose area covers 10 spatial locations along both the x and y axes so that each input pattern consists of exactly 400 real values. Every output pattern is made up by 8 real numbers that correspond to the geometric parameters of the superquadric corresponding to the input boundary web . All the values of a pattern are scaled and bounded in the range [0,1]. This is due to the characteristic shape of the logistic function that has been used as activation function of the units in the network and takes values in the range [0,1]. In fact, a local coding has been adopted, so the value of each input unit activation is directly dependent on the parameter that has been supplied to the unit itself. The first training set has been set up selecting 5 regions of the average boundary web, for each image: 4 portions are placed near the corners of the image itself, while the last one is placed in its center. Due to the particular class of employed images, such a choice of the regions displacement allows the system to analyze the most significant parts of the image as regards to the surface curvature of the displayed object. Finally the training set has resulted to be made up by 210 patterns. In order to avoid the problems arising in an ordered training, that is characterized by patterns with increasing ε_2 values, a random pattern presentation has been adopted. After a first trial with 20 hidden units, a simpler architecture using only 10 hidden units has been chosen. With this architecture, different simulations have been run varying the learning rate value from 0.1 to 0.5 and with a momentum fixed to 0.9. Besides, all these choices have been applied in running simulations over 500, 1000 and 2000 learning epochs, with a weight range [-5, +5] (see table 1). In all the simulations a particular measure of the error has been minimized that is called *tss* (total sum of squared errors) and has the following form:

$$TSS = \sum_p \sum_j (t_{jp} - o_{jp})^2 \qquad (3.2.5)$$

where t_{jp} and o_{jp} are respectively the target value and the real output value of the unit j when the pattern p is presented to the network; the first sum is over the set of patterns belonging to the training set and the second sum is over the set of output units. The tss values, that are shown in table 2 have been obtained as the result of a test over the entire training set, after the network had been trained.

Setting up the right momentum value has proved to be a critical matter: decreasing it from 0.9 to 0.6 has resulted in a not significant learning degree, while increasing it to 1 has led the network to near a local minimum of the error function in the weight space. Finally the value 0.9 has been chosen that is the default value of the employed simulator. Figures 4-a,b show the results of the simulations run with the first training set. As a result of all the simulations carried out using the

TABLE 1

EPOCHS	TSS (x0.001)
500	0.1108
1000	0.0928
2000	0.0416

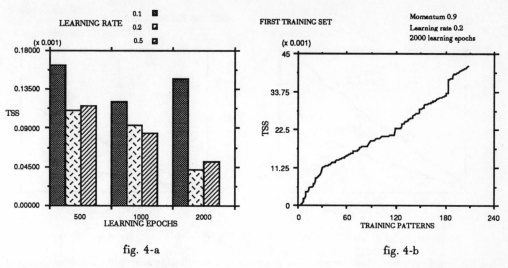

fig. 4-a   fig. 4-b

FIGURE 4 a: Tss versus learning epochs number, for three different values of learning rate, using the first training set. The 0.2 learning rate value provides the best results .b: Tss behaviour, for a sequential presentation of the training patterns for the best simulation,using the first training set.

first training set, it has been observed that increasing the number of learning epochs results in an improvement of the network performance and, in particular, among each group of simulations run over the same epochs number, the best results have been obtained with a learning rate value of 0.2 (see figures 4-a,b). It can be noted that the network best learns those patterns that are characterized by shape factors whose values are round 1, while a less satisfactory learning takes place when ε_1 and ε_2 are near to 0 or more than 1. This effect is due to an intrinsic limitation of the BCS whose input receptive fields are not able to capture sharp surface variations in very little image portions, because they are thought to calculate a mean local image contrast over their area, while sharp edges or cusps arise when the ε_1 and ε_2 values are very different from 1.After these first simulations, a second training set has been set up.It is made up by 630 pattern and has been obtained in the same way as the first training set, starting with 21 superquadrics. In particular, both ε_1 and ε_2 have been varied, following the scheme presented in table 2. Different simulations have been run with this training set.

All these simulations have been run over 2000 and 5000 learning epochs, using a learning rate 0.2 and a momentum 0.9; the weight range has been fixed to [-5, +5]. First, an architecture using 10 hidden units has been employed, starting with a random weight distribution. Then, a second architecture has been checked that uses 20 hidden units and random weight distribution. The aim was to obtain a more structured internal representation of the problem due to the higher complexity of the

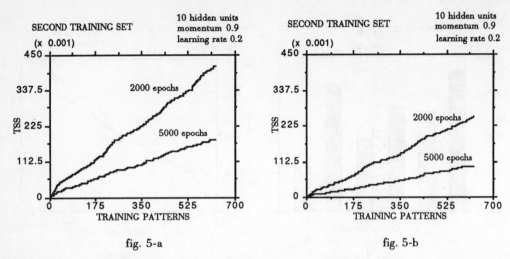

fig. 5-a   fig. 5-b

FIGURE 5-a, b: A comparison between the results of two simulations over 2000 and 5000 learning epochs with a 10 hidden units (a) and a 20 hidden units (b) architecture. It can be noted that the network learns all the patterns approximately at the same way: in fact, there is no sharp variation in the tss slope. The 20 hidden units net exhibits the best learning degree due to its more complex internal representation of the problem.

second training set with respect to the first one. The results are shown in figures 5-a,b and in table 3.

4. Conclusions

The proposed system has exhibited a satisfactory behaviour as regards to the reconstruction of the shapes present in a scene, thus providing suitable data to the remaining part of the visual perception model described in [1]. At present time, we are analyzing the behaviour of the tss versus the number of hidden units and searching an optimal strategy to collect the image regions at the input of the network, in order to obtain a sort of moving receptor providing the network with a collection of inputs it may use to obtain a series of local estimates of the object surface. All these local estimates are correlated each other to derive a global estimate of the object's shape parameters.

Also architectures with weight distributions resulting from preceeding simulations are studied to analyze the network generalization ability. Finally, some work is currently spent to enhance the spontaneous segmentation ability of the BCS.

TABLE 2

ε_1	ε_2
0.5	0.2
1	0.4
1.5	0.6
	0.8
	1
	1.5
	2

TABLE 3

HIDDEN	EPOCHS	TSS (x0.001)
10	2000	0.4141
10	5000	0.1823
20	2000	0.2530
20	5000	0.0981

Appendix A: Brief remarks on BCS

Inside the BCS, it is possible to recognise two blocks: the OC Filter and the CC Loop [5,6]. The OC Filter is made up by the layer of the input receptive fields of the so called J units. These sensitive cells , with elongated and symmetric shape, are suitably displaced to cover the whole image and detect the amount and the direction of contrast across their symmetry axis. The J units activations feed the first competitive stage (w stage) where an on-center-off-sorround interaction takes place: The J units excite like-orientatied units with the same spatial position, and inhibit like-orientated units, but in contigous position. The w units activations are the input for the second competitive stage, namely the y stage. In this stage a push-pull interactions takes place among units in the same spatial position, but with perpendicular orientation. These competitive mechanisms allow a first rough boundary completion. The y units activations feed the cooperative stage: the z stage. Every z unit is made up by two big elongated receptive field that are displaced along the sensitivity direction of the unit. Each receptive field is essentially excited by the activations of all the y units that are spatially placed within the field's area and have its orientation. When both of the receptive fields are excited the unit will be active. The cooperative units' activations are the input for the v stage which is the feedback stage whose outputs feed the first competitive stage, closing the loop. Even in this stage an on-center-off-sorround interaction takes place. The cooperative interaction within the z stage and the feedback through the v stage allow the formation of sharp global contours along the isophotes of the scene.

Acknowledgements
This work has been partially supported by the Italian "Consiglio Nazionale delle Ricerche" (CNR) and by the Italian "Ministero dell'Universita' e della Ricerca Scientifica e Tecnologica" (MURST).

References

[1] Ardizzone, E., Gaglio, S., Sorbello, F. (1989). Geometric and Conceptual Knowledge Representation within a Generative Model of Visual Perception, *Journal of Intelligent and Robotic Systems*, 2, 381-409.
[2] Barr , A.H. (1981). Superquadrics and Angle-Preserving Trasformations, *IEEE Computer Graphics and Applications*, 1, 11-23.
[3] Grossberg, S., Mingolla, E. (1986). Computer Simulation of Neural Networks for Perceptual Psychology. *Behavior Research Methods, Instruments and Computers*, 18 (6), 601-607.
[4] Grossberg, S., Mingolla, E., (1987). Neural Dynamics of Surface Perception: Boundary Webs, Illuminants, and Shape-from-Shading. *Computer Vision, Graphics and Image Processing*, 37, 116-165.
[5] Horn, B.K.P. (1986). *Robot Vision*. MIT Press, Cambridge, MA, USA.
[6] Rumelhart, D. E., McClelland, J. L. (ed.s) & PDP Research Group (1986), *Parallel Distributed Processing*, Vol 1, MIT Press, Cambridge, MA, USA.

Retrieval of High-Level Data Structures from Stereo Vision Data

Fidenzio Burbello[¥], S. B. Pollard[*], J. Porrill[*], J.E.W. Mayhew[*]

[¥] C.E.C. Joint Research Centre, Institute for Systems Engineering and Informatics
TP 321, 21020 Ispra VA, Italy, E-mail: F_Burbello@cen.jrc.it
[*] Artificial Intelligence Vision Research Unit, University of Sheffield
Sheffield S10 2TN, U.K., E-mail: sbp@aivru.sheffield.ac.uk

ABSTRACT

We describe our intermediate level representation and processing of partial 3D wire frame data, obtained from edge-based stereo depth reconstruction systems. We use a double representation schema, based both on CAD winged-edge-like data-structures and on frames. We also use a goal-oriented grouping mechanism combining a data-drive bottom-up indexing, mainly in the form of a potential connect graph, and a knowledge-driven top-down grouping, whose methods are distributed along the structural hierarchy of the knowledge-base. The best candidate instances of higher-level geometrical structures are sought using these grouping mechanisms. They are then matched against their template-class and, when possible, completed using WFRL [Burbello 1991], a knowledge-based system capable of verifying and imposing constraints on incomplete wire frame structures.

INTRODUCTION

The application target in our group at J.R.C.-Ispra is the capture of the 3D geometry of the envelope of buildings in the form of a so called "3D wire frame" model using the results of an edge-based stereo processing of the building images.

Indeed any kind of 3D reconstruction module based on visual informations (e.g. stereo vision), however sophisticated, will deliver output data that need to be:
1. interpreted according to a specific domain-dependent model;
2. completed, as there will always be noise, occlusions, or missing details, non obtainable from image objective features, affecting the data for model reconstruction.

The two problems are tightly connected and non-sequential, since in real complex images most of the completion task cannot be performed without an interpretation of the structure that is to be completed, and vice-versa.

In this paper we focus our attention on the representation of generic 2D and 3D wire frame data, suitable for subsequent reasoning and completion, and on the intermediate level vision grouping techniques that we are using. This work has been undertaken in collaboration with the AI & Vision Research Unit of the University of Sheffield.

UNSTRUCTURED DEPTH-MAPS FROM STEREO VISION

We have been using binocular stereo processing, based on edges as primitives to match, to obtain depth maps from the observed scenes. The depth maps obtained are in the form of 3D straight edge segments. We have been using two separate stereo modules: (a) TINA , a stereo vision system developed at AIVRU and (b) TRICS, a smaller stereo module suitable for PC-level applications developed at JRC.

In the TINA system [Porrill 1987] edges are obtained, to sub pixel acuity, by a single scale high frequency application of the Canny operator ($\sigma = 1$ *pixel*).
The stereo algorithm, called PMF, essentially prefers matches between edges from the left and the right images if they mutually support each other through a disparity gradient constraint (the ratio of the difference in their disparity to their physical separation is below a threshold of 0.5) and if they satisfy a number of higher level constraints (uniqueness, ordering along epipolars, figural continuity, etc.). The 3D scene geometry is recovered by grouping high level features (edge strings, straight lines, conic sections, etc.) prior to disparity detection. Optimal estimates of disparity for each matched edge point are obtained along the intersection of their 2D geometrical descriptors with the epipolar corresponding to the location of the matched point. Position estimates are then obtained by subsequent fitting from the optimal disparity values obtained. The system delivers both straight lines and circular arcs as 3D sparse wire frame descriptors. For the purpose of the work described in this paper only straight line segments are used.

TRICS (ThRee dimensional Input by Colour Stereo) is based on a previous PC-based stereo system [Peckham 1986] which used manually aided digitisation of straight line features, and takes advantage of our experiences with a short straight-line segment stereo matcher, using a Marr-Hildreth edge detector followed by a dynamic-programming matcher [Trucco 1989]. It makes use of straight line features only and stereo matching is performed on short line segments obtained by intersecting line features with pairs of epipolar lines. These are extracted from the stereo pairs through filtering with an approximation to a Laplacian of a Gaussian ($\sigma = 1.5$ *pixels*), zero-crossing location to sub-pixel accuracy and least squares fitting of the edge points to straight lines.
The TRICS system can use colour attributes to aid in the stereo matching process: these are found by calculating the average intensity differences across the lines in the total intensity, red and green component images. A cost function for the match of each couple of left-right segments is computed on the basis of their difference in orientation and in the colour attributes, plus a prohibitively high value added if the match violates a set of constraints (disparity range, etc.). For each epipolar stripe a matrix of costs is built, based on the ordered list of segments. Possible matches next to each other support each other by halving their costs. The final match is found by selecting iteratively those whose cost is the minimum both in the column and in the row which contain them them.

PARTIAL WIRE-FRAMES REPRESENTATION

The unstructured depth data, or other partially segmented data, are not sufficient for many computer vision tasks and especially for all those involving searches of high-level data structures. Therefore in image understanding systems it is rather common to resort to an intermediate representation level, enough structured to be more meaningful but still easy to be manipulated and reconfigured.

Since we start from the output of edge-based stereo, our intermediate-level primitives must include pure 2D and 3D straight line segments enriched by some sort of relational structure. We have chosen to keep a double intermediate-level representation for our primitives:

- Partial 3D Wire-Frames, PWF, which host a precise data-geometry and allow easy access to topological information,
- Wire-frame Frame-based Representation, WFR, which uses approximate geometry and provides a natural connection to a frame-based description of the modelled domain.

Correspondent WFR frames and PWF generics are permanently doubly linked. This double representation allows for an effective interaction between data- and knowledge-suggested structuring and the exploitation of the "down-propagation" of the generative capabilities of the frame-based representation.

Partial 3D Wire-Frames is a prototype representation of partial wire frame structures in edge based stereo data. It has been developed at AIVRU and was inspired by the CAD winged-edge-like data structures. It allows the addition of grouping data such as intersection, continuation, parallelism, loops, links, same faces, etc.

The representation is both 2 and 3 dimensional, at least for the basic data, and is built on a basic data type, the *generic*, which can host information on any chosen wire frame primitive and offers facilities for storing and efficiently retrieving its attached properties.

Two basic properties are necessary to represent a wire frame primitive: topology and geometry. The former is a structure specifying the relationship of the primitive to other primitives to which it is connected, either directly or indirectly. The latter specifies the geometrical occupancy of the primitive in 2, or 2 and 3 dimensions, as appropriate.

The wire frames from stereo are organised into a *connect graph* which collects lists of edges, end-points, vertices, faces and their connections.

WFR is a frame-based representation of the basic stereo wire frame primitives, edges and edge end points, carrying no topological information and built on the same tool, WFRL, as the knowledge base of our system. Therefore it constitutes the domain where instances of the bottom level of a hierarchical representation (in the structural sense) of the modelled domain, i.e. line and point frames, are to be searched (see figure 1).

Expressing the wire frame primitives with the same representation schema of the knowledge base allows a natural knowledge-directed imposition of constraints, when needed.

While the geometry of PWF primitives directly represent that of the wire frames obtained by the images, the WFR frames have a more relaxed approach to it. The geometrical features represented in the slots of WFR primitives, initially taken from the PWF generics, can be modified during the interpretation and completion process while preserving the original data in the generic counterparts of the primitive frames.

WFR primitives also keep a parallel "interpretation-oriented" geometry, what we call *symbolic-geometry* and which is shared with the high-level structure description in WFRL.

Symbolic geometry is a way to implement an approximate geometry indexing schema: each of the symbolic-geometry feature slots of a WFR instance is filled with one or more symbols denoting its belonging to one of the equivalence classes singled out for that geometrical feature during the top-down grouping (see *top-down grouping* section).

The underlying idea is that the geometry to be used for interpretation is intrinsically approximate and this is also more plausible in biological vision systems recognition.

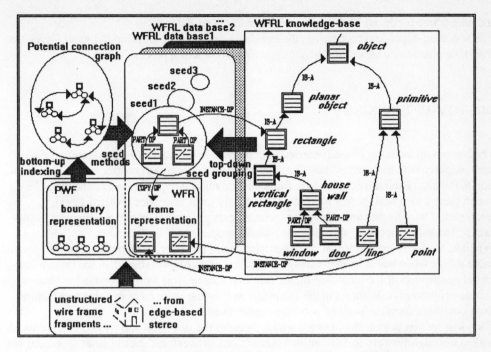

Figure 1: Intermediate Level Representation and WFRL

Once it has been satisfactorily matched we can use the constraints coming from the interpretation to correct the geometry of data, using e.g. Geomstat [Porrill 1987].

REPRESENTATION AND RETRIEVAL OF HIGH-LEVEL STRUCTURES

We call high-level structures all the constructs built upon the basic straight-line segment primitives. The wire frame interpretation and completion system we are developing expresses both its knowledge base and the WFR data base with what we call Wire frame Frame-based Representation Language, WFRL.

WFRL [Burbello 1991] is a frame-based and object-oriented language meant to provide a convenient representation of, and reasoning about, complete/incomplete 2D/3D wire frames. It is inspired by the representation schema for geometrical reasoning used in 3D FORM [Walker 1988] and developed on top of the XRL frame representation module [Charniak 1987] running under Common-Lisp.

The language, not described in this paper, offers tools for representing high-level constructs and relations as frames, specifying, verifying and imposing constraints, both in the geometry and in the application-specific domains. The frames are organized in a semantic network, expressing both structural and specialization hierarchies of the modelled domain.

The strategy for building relations between the wire frames primitives and searching for a specified high-level structure combines semantic-dependent and independent processing. The semantic-independent processing is a bottom-up structuring phase, completely data-driven that we call *bottom-up indexing* and which is currently performed once only on the wire frame produced by the stereo reconstruction module.

The semantic-dependent processing, the *top-down grouping*, is knowledge/model driven and may take place any time during the interpretation/completion process.

BOTTOM-UP INDEXING

The bottom up indexing phase is carried out completely on the PWF representation and simultaneously with its construction. The goal of this process is the construction of a description that makes explicit potential wire frame primitives and hypothesized connections between them and is built purely bottom up using only local heuristics [Pollard 1991].

Such partial wire frames are allowed to include descriptions that arise from changes in surface reflectance properties, shadows, etc., whilst proper wire frames are not.

We have found the generation of PWF descriptions to be easier, computationally cheaper and more robust when based upon the image projection of an object rather than the three dimensional description of the identified image primitives alone. It is straightforward to choose simple neighbourhood criteria in the 2D image as it is less vulnerable to noise and feature drop out; these form the basis of potential connectivities.

Each line section is treated as a triple which includes the line itself and its two end points, this makes it straightforward to differentiate connections between the ends of lines (potential vertices, etc.) and other forms of connection. A few simple heuristics in the image data can be used to identify various vertex and connectivity (e.g. colinearity) types.

When used in conjunction with WFRL high-level structure representation and reasoning, the partial 3D wire frame structure is built by identifying 3 main types of connectivity:

1. Potential Vertex Connections, PVC, or otherwise called Y-connections; a Y connector is put between two line end points which are: (a) within a local neighbourhood ρ, expressed in image pixels, (b) close to the point of line intersection, (c) closer than the other end of the same line to the point of intersection and (d) the two segments to which the end points belong form an angle greater than a threshold ϕ.
2. Colinear connections, abbreviated C-connections; a C-connector is set between two end points which are: (a) within a local neighbourhood ρ, (b) the greatest angle formed between the four possible lines joining the 4 end points of the two line segments is smaller than a threshold θ and (c) they are the closest end points of the considered segments.
3. Line-end connections, otherwise called T-connections; a T-connection is identified when: (a) the end point of one segment is within a local neighbourhood ρ from the *body* of another segment, (b) the end point is not within neighbourhood ρ from any of the segment end points and (c) the two segments to which the end points belong form an angle greater than a threshold ϕ.

We have chosen to represent a T-connection not using a specific type of connector but by using a combination of a C-connector and two Y-connectors. This is achieved by breaking the potentially intersected segment into two smaller segments, sharing the potential intersection point as end point. This representation allows for a more explicit search of high-level structures when any of the successive top-down grouping processes traverse of the connectivity graph established onto PWF.

TOP-DOWN GROUPING

The top-down grouping is inspired by the *probe action* model. The probe behaviour is a largely diffused action-pattern in the biological domain, both microscopic and macroscopic: it basically consists of a limited set of probes cast from the starting status or domain and reaching a target by a nimble path, possibly exploiting the action of some pre-existing, stable, external attractive fields or actions. These "bridges" act as a basis for much more complete and complex connection structures that often hide the initial origin of the link.

The top-down grouping is therefore organised around the concept of *seeds*. The seeds of a class are defined as its very likely candidate instances within the current (wire frame) data. These candidate instances are only SEEDS of instances of the object class wanted; this means that they are intrinsically:

1. incomplete in their parts,
2. an incomplete list of candidates (only the most promising ones...).

Every class can have a specific *find-seeds* method. In order to exploit the power of the structural hierarchy in which the knowledge is organized, the domains on which the method-function operates are the seeds obtained by its ancestor class.

This last feature assures that the method-function works by specialising the seeds of the class of which the current class is the most direct specialisation. The most general class on top of the IS-A hierarchy , the *object* class, will return the most general seed-set, that is all the basic elements of the current wire frame (the complete set of the 3D line frames).

In figure 2 an example of the IS-A hierarchy-driven grouping is given, using a part of an hypothetical class specialization hierarchy in WFRL.

We now sketch some of the grouping methods, associated to WFRL classes, that we have exploited for finding seeds of simple high-level structures in real wire frames and subsequently complete them.

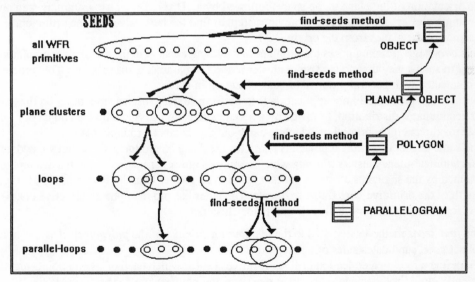

Figure 2: example of IS-A hierarchy-directed grouping

The plane-grouping *find-seeds* method is associated to the feature-slot *atomic-part-list* of the *planar-object* class. It is meant to collect all the *line* primitive-frames that lie on the same planar surface.

Multiple classification of a single line-frame must be allowed, since the line could be either actually shared by the two planes (it is a "corner" line) or could lie in-between two planes separated by a small angle. In this last case there is no reliable data-driven criterion to assign the line unambiguously to one plane and some semantic-driven reasoning must be provided. It is worthwhile remembering that the choice of dealing with approximate geometry at WFR and higher-level WFRL structures definitively frees us from any plane geometrical-optimisation problem and leaves a pure classification task: we want to detect clusters of lines laying roughly on the same plane.

Since the location of an ideal for each class is not known and furthermore we have a specific geometrical model to be searched, with rather relaxed constraints on geometrical precision, Hough-like transform approaches have been a natural choice.

The Hough transform, HT [Illingworth 1988], is a technique belonging the model instanciation class of parameter space decision problems and can be viewed as an evidence gathering procedure. Each image space feature votes for all the parameter combinations that could have produced it, if it were part of the sought-after shape-model. The votes are counted in an accumulator array and the final totals indicate the relative likelihood of shapes-models described by parameters within the corresponding parameter cell.

Plane detection through line segments involves therfore the use of a 3D parameter space and of the parameters of the straight-line passing through the segment in a 3D "image" space as data features.

We represent the planes through their normals or better through the point defined by the intersection of the normal to the plane passing trough the origin and the plane itself.

Representing the intersection point on the plane with spherical coordinates allows the decomposition of the 3D HT into a 2D HT used for finding estimates of the angles corresponding to the orientation of the plane in the space, followed by a 1D HT, i.e. a histogramming step on the angle-clusters identified in the previous step, to find the best values for the orthogonal distance of the planes from the origin.

This two-stage grouping poses the problem of detecting clusters in the angular accumulator array in such a way that no consistent cluster in the full parameter space is lost. This problem is connected with general problem of peak detection in HT.

The solution proposed in our application is to perform first a gaussian smoothing on the angular accumulator distribution, followed by a maxima detection pass and by the choice of a suitable maxima neighbourhood on which to carry out the distance grouping pass.

The same cluster detection approach is taken for the distance grouping stage, but we add a final candidate-plane clusters filtering which requires a quick estimation of the maximum area spanned by the segments clustered for that plane to be greater than the square of the average length of the primitive wire frame segments. The latter has proven to be an effective condition for selecting the physically relevant plane clusters.

The *find-seeds* method associated to the feature-slot *side-list* of the *polygon* class is meant to collect good candidates sides of a polygon.

We define a *loop* as a collection of line primitives (a) for which each of its end points are sufficiently close, in the image space, to at most one end point of another primitive in the loop, (b) laying roughly on the same plane and (c) having at least 3 line primitives in it. Loops will be the seeds for the polygon class. Condition (c) expresses the idea that an incomplete polygon with only two sides is too ambiguously specified to give rise to a limited and meaningful set of knowledge-driven interpretations and completions.

In figure 3 (c) the seeds of the vertical polygon class are shown as an example. Figure 3 (a) contains the left image of the stereo pair and figure 3 (b) the partial 3D wire frame obtained.

In devising a loop-grouping method we exploit two facts:

1. the polygon class is the direct descendant of the planar-object class in the IS-A hierarchy of the knowledge base. This implies that its seeds will be searched only among those of its father class, i.e. the plane-seeds of the planar-object class.

   Hence condition (b) of the loop definition is already implied in the IS-A directed grouping mechanism and we do not need to do any extra work for it.

2. the bottom up indexing phase has already built a potential connection graph based on local neighbourhood in the image space and conditions (a) and (c) simply identify a number of sub-graphs in it.

Therefore the loop-grouping method is reduced to an appropriate search in each of the sub-graphs defined by the restriction of the PWF potential-connect-graph to the PWF edge and edge and end point nodes identified by each of the ancestor class seeds.

The target of the search are chains of edge nodes, of cardinality greater than or equal to three, whose corresponding end point nodes are singly linked to other end point nodes.

As a last example we consider the *find-seeds* method associated to the feature-slot *atomic-part-list* of the *parallelogram* class, which is a direct sub-class of the polygon class.

The seeds chosen are parallel-loops, i.e. a collection of line primitives which satisfies the same (a), (b) and (c) properties as specified before for the loop, plus the property that (d) there are at most two equivalence classes, defined by the "roughly-parallel" relation, within each parallel-loop.

Again the hierarchical top-down grouping mechanism gives us as starting domain the loop instances identified as seeds of the polygon class: we only need to check condition (d) for each of them.

Although this could be performed directly using the vector associated to each WFR or PWF line primitive, we have accomplished it through the symbolic-vector feature-slot associated to each WFR line primitive. We promote a loop to a parallel-loop when the union of all the symbolic-vector features of the line primitives in the loop have at most cardinality two.

Actually the very first access to the symbolic-vector slot of a WFR line triggers, through an if-needed daemon, a clustering process involving all the WFR lines sharing the same plane seed and based on the vector orientation. This clustering is performed in the same fashion as in the distance grouping phase of the plane grouping method and provides the required symbol-denoted equivalence classes.

We can observe that, owing to the grouping structured over the IS-A hierarchy, the trend of the complexity of the top-down seed-grouping methods is to decrease as one moves further down in the structural hierarchy.

Once the seeds for a specific class have been collected, through the mechanism just seen, they are matched against the template represented by the class and a completed, whenever possible, instance of each seed is returned [Burbello 1991].

In figure 3 (d) an attempt to complete the seeds for the vertical polygon class is shown. The faults in this example are due to the loop grouping method which does not yet process the T-junctions and to the seed-extension method which is currently based on the potential connection graph only. In fact the vertical edge of the left wall is not considered as possible extension just because it is not connected to the "wall-loop" in the initial graph.

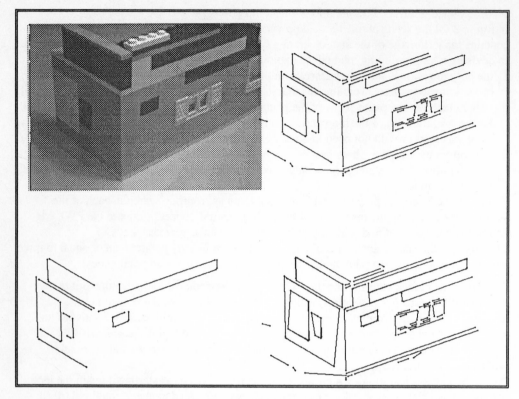

Figure 3: (a) left image of a stereo pair, (b) 3D wire frame primitives,
(c) seeds of the vertical polygon class, (d) attempt to complete them

CONCLUSIONS AND FUTURE DIRECTIONS

We have conjectured that full wire frame descriptions, as boundary descriptions of physically realisable objects, can only be reliably recovered in the presence of domain knowledge. This is why we have concentrated on the design of an effective interface between partial, data-driven and domain-suggested wire frame intermediate structuring.

On one side the double-representation schema allows (a) the down-propagation of the generative power carried by the higher-level WFRL constructs in the knowledge-base, when needed, (b) the exploitation of the effective encoding and retrieval of the topology offered by PWF and (c) the co-existence of symbolic-geometry features and "relaxed" geometry management with image-anchored geometry.

On the other side the feature grouping (a) embodies in its top-down part the "probe" metaphor, building "interpretation islands", therefore (b) allowing a very aimed use of the WFRL matching verification and imposition mechanisms, which alone would easily overload the interpretation task, (c) exploits the IS-A hierarchy-based seed-finding mechanism to minimize the development of grouping functions and (d) easily integrates bottom-up and top-

321

down control flows.
The direction for current and future developments are, on the intermediate-level side, towards the development of a seed-extension mechanism combining general strategies, applicable to all the seed-endowed classes in our knowledge-base, and class-specific methods.
On the higher-level side we are looking for methods of extending and integrating these interpretation seeds, exploiting mutual support between super-, sub- and fellow-parts discovered as seeds. Much work also needs to be done on the knowledge-base, whose semantics are currently restricted to a world of simple geometrical shapes and on WFRL itself to assess its applicability in the context of wire frames of real buildings.

ACKNOWLEDGEMENTS

Special thanks to R.J. Peckham for help with his TRICS stereo module, the valuable discussions and suggestions on the grouping methods and the review of this paper.

REFERENCES

[Burbello 1991] Burbello F.
Wire Frame Representation Language: status of the experiment
C.E.C. Joint Research Centre Working Paper,ISEI-SER 2031-91, Ispra, April 1991
[Charniak 1987] E. Charniak, C.K. Riesbeck, D. McDermott, J.R. Meehan
Artificial Intelligence Programming
Lawrence Erlbaum Assoc. USA, 1987, pp. 276-303
[Illingworth 1988] Illingworth J., Kittler J.
A Survey of the Hough Transform
in *Computer Vision Graphics Image Processing*, vol 44, 1988, pp. 87-116
[Peckham 1986] Peckham R.J., Cooper D., Green C.
From Stereo Images to Thermal Models: a Prototype System
Commiss. of Eur. Comm. Euroreport, EUR, Ispra, 1986
[Pollard 1990] Pollard S.B., Porrill J., Mayhew J.E.W.
Recovering Partial 3D Wire Frames Descriptions from Stereo Data
in *Image and Vision Computing*, Vol. 9, No. 1, 1991, pp. 58-65
[Porrill 1987] Porrill J., Pollard S.B., Mayhew J.E.W.
The Optimal Combination of Multiple Sensors Including Stereo Vision
in *Image and Vision Computing*, Vol. 2, No. 5, 1987, pp. 174-180
[Trucco 1989] Trucco E., Burbello F., Groppello P.
Experiments with Segment-Based Stereo Using Dynamic Programming
in *Proc. 1st AI*IA National Congress*, Trento, 1989, pp. 87-94
[Walker 1988] E.L. Walker, M. Herman, T. Kanade
A Framework for Representing and Reasoning about 3-Dimensional Objects for Vision
in *AI Magazine*, Summer 1988, pp. 47-58

High-Level and Low-Level Computer Vision: towards an integrated approach *

G. Adorni[†], A. Broggi[‡], G. Conte[†], V. D'Andrea[‡] and C. Sansoè[§]

[†]DIST- Università di Genova, [‡]DII - Università di Parma, [§]DE - Politecnico di Torino

Abstract

The term perception refers to the means by which information acquired from the environment via the sense organs is transformed into experiences of objects, events, sounds, tastes, etc. In this paper, we shall focus on the problem of object perception dealing exclusively with the visual modality. More precisely we will present a system, SVL - Symbolic Vision Lab, which is a development environment for object perception algorithms. SVL is mainly devoted to symbolic computation and can exploit for low level tasks a massively parallel computer, such as the general purpose Connection Machine, or an *ad hoc* specific VLSI architectures whose efficiency can be simulated in advance on the Connection Machine itself.

1 Introduction

In order to see an object, the light reflected from it must reach our eyes' retina. To recognize such object from the information contained in the retinal image, we also need some sort of knowledge.

In our everyday world, we have an expectancy of the kind of scenes we will see from one glance to the next. Also, many of the scenes that we do see are familiar, i.e. they have been experienced before. Prior expectancy and familiarity are two factors that could reduce the range of possible scenes before the eye actually fixates on one specific scene.

This leads to having preexisting stereotyped structures, which could be of extraordinary value for the resolution of the complexity of a scene. There are studies in this direction [7], experimentally supporting the idea that prior expectations of a scene could influence its perception.

However, there are many different views about the nature of these stored representations and the precise role they play in processing inputs. For instance, a class of theories assumes a sequences of stages beginning with a low-level analysis of the retinal image and building up gradually to an *interpretation* based on a comparison with stored knowledge

*This work was supported by CNR-Progetto Finalizzato Trasporti-Prometheus under contract n.89.01458.93 and n.89.01446.93

(bottom-up or data-driven processing). According to this bottom-up approach, stored knowledge about the properties of objects, scenes, etc., plays no role in processing the input until the final stage during which an interpretation is made.

Some theorists have instead argued that since the information in the retinal image is ambiguous or fragmentary, this bottom-up, data-driven processing would be insufficient to permit the perception of objects, scenes, etc.. According to this second view, stored knowledge exerts an influence at an early stage in the processing of input, providing additional information which helps to resolve ambiguities or inadequacies in the input, thus permitting suitable interpretations to be made (top-down or conceptually-driven processing).

This difference between bottom-up, data-driven processing and top-down, conceptually-driven processing is a rather rudimentary way of distinguishing theories about operating principles. Many of these theories imply that processing is not exclusively bottom-up or top-down, but a complex interaction of the two.

This paper, for reasons stemming from some of the previous considerations, presents a system which is a development environment for object perception algorithms: SVL - Symbolic Vision Lab. SVL is organized as a blackboard system, whose control flow is a cooperation between bottom-up (data-driven) and top-down (conceptually-driven) processes. SVL is mainly devoted to symbolic computation and can interact with a massively parallel computer, such as the general purpose Connection Machine, or with an *ad hoc* specific VLSI architecture, PAPRICA, very efficient for operations on large matrix of simple data (an image). PAPRICA (PArallel PRocessor for Image Check and Analysis), is mainly devoted to sub-symbolic computation; it is currently simulated on a Connection Machine, and a first prototype of the chip is under testing. Next section describes the overall architecture of SVL, focusing on top-down processes. Section 3 is devoted to low-level bottom-up processes. Section 4 presents the PAPRICA processor as well as some PAPRICA performance analysis. In the last section, some concluding remarks are given.

2 High-Level processes

In the present section we discuss a blackboard architecture [9], whose control system is a cooperation between bottom-up and top-down processes. The system's architecture is depicted in figure 1.

Figure 1 shows a scheme of data and control flows between the four active modules, (Image Reasoner - IR, Low Level Processes - LLP, Perceptual Processes - PP, Conceptual Processes - CP) and the two passive parts (Symbolic Data Base - SDB, Long Term Memory - LTM) of the system. Besides these modules the SVL also includes a Symbolic/Graphic Editor that allows the creation of synthetic images and the manipulation of stored information and images.

The active modules are organized as production systems whose rules are logically subdivided as shown in figure 2 and interact through the data structure of the SDB. Information in the SDB is initially created on the basis of the LLP analysis, and then managed and manipulated by all the active modules. The LTM is used for storing all the information removed (or modified) from the SDB, which can then be used in later backtracking.

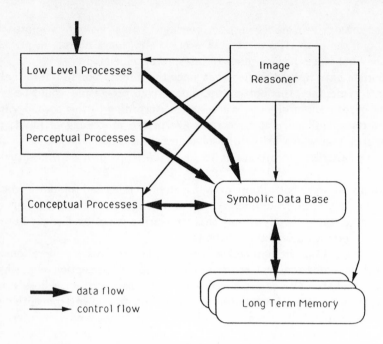

Figure 1: Architecture of the Symbolic Vision Lab.

In the proposed computational model the LLP (i.e., *line detection, region growing, stereo volumetric vision*) use local knowledge in order to pilot a selection and a first aggregation of the low-level data. For example, the aggregation of *edges* into lines can be driven by expectations on the typical edges of a given environment. This kind of knowledge concerns small groups of pixels. The data so obtained constitute a set of *frames* of different kinds, because each of them represents a first segmentation of the image by lines/ by regions/ by volumes [14]. Already at this level, the volumetric representation constitutes the history of the visual process. It contains explicitly the information regarding the three-dimensional structure of the scene as achieved by the peripheral processing stages, and then modified by perceptive and conceptual reasoning. The segmentation by regions and by edges further characterizes some parts of the volumetric representation. The PP are committed to data aggregation according to perceptive rules. The knowledge required at this level concerns both the methods of aggregation of elements of the same kind (for example, the aggregation of several lines into one line), and the matching among different kinds (Segment_Rules and Region_Rules) [4]. The basic criteria are the principles indicated by the Gestalt psychology [11] such as, for example, good continuation, proximity, symmetry. At this point is active the identification of the occlusions among objects and their resolution which, if possible, should take place without making use of information concerning the objects. Therefore the outcome of perceptive reasoning is a scene segmentation based on global knowledge, together with aggregation laws operating on information from different sources. In general, unsettled ambiguities will be due to situations which require more specific knowledge of the objects in the scene. Such ambiguities can be settled by the CP, thanks to the general knowledge of the system, to its reasoning capabilities, and to its expectations about the environment. This kind

325

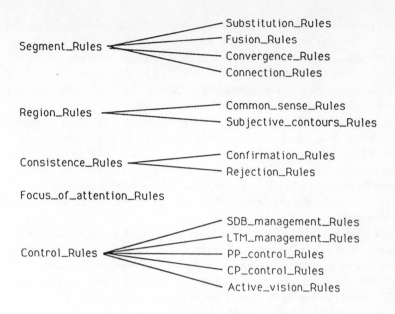

Figure 2: Hierarchy rules of the Symbolic Vision Lab.

of knowledge includes environment organization, spatial relationships among objects, and qualitative physical knowledge [1] (for example, relating to the equilibrium among objects and their function, and the spatial constraints set by their shapes.)

The information produced by the LLP is fed into the SDB, which is the data structure common to all processes. Here, the data are organized into three mutually connected levels: segments, regions, elementary objects [3].

The analysis of this representation requires a hierarchical organization. Considering that the information organized as above has a dominant structural characteristic, it is believed that the hierarchy, if any, should be based on structural information. This is the reason why the information representation has been organized so as to privilege the segments according to their length (both on its own and together with contrast). This does not mean that we suggest the possibility of singling out a length threshold in order to reduce the quantity of information. Rather, in subsequent processing and in the absence of different priority indications (such as, for example, the definition by the IR, of an attention area where information is denser and more aggregated: Focus_of_attention_Rules), processing should initially consider longer segments. At present, the system performs four iterations with four different length thresholds (which are determined experimentally). The results of computations with higher level of detail are used by the IR in order to confirm (by increasing the value of the confidence factor) or to discard the results of previous computations (if the value of a confidence factor drops below a given threshold) (Consistence_Rules). In the latter case the IR retrieves from the LTM the *best* results so far or, if no other information is present in the LTM, returns control to the LLP, providing them with indications as to how to improve the image acquisition (Active_Vision_Rules).

The goal of the perceptual processes is to reconstruct regions which are apparently occluded and, possibly, to set up hypotheses on basic objects (thereby filling the third level of the SDB). The rules on which the PP are based are those of the psychology of perception; in particular, they encode principles of structural information theory [12] developed in cooperation with the Department of Psychology of the University of Nijmegen (Holland). They also encode some elements of psychology of Gestalt developed in cooperation with the Institute of Applied Psychology of Padova [2].

The control system of the PP works in the following way: once a region is selected, it checks whether this region can be considered as occluded; if not, on the basis of the contiguous regions (if any) it checks whether it is possible to envisage the presence of elementary regions, otherwise it selects another region or it returns control to the IR. If an occlusion hypothesis is identified, the system tries to eliminate such occlusion on the basis of its knowledge, by assuming one or more solutions (completions) with different *fuzziness* values [15]:

the higher values correspond to the most plausible interpretation from a perceptual point of view. The other interpretations are not discarded but can be retrieved for subsequent processing if inconsistencies occur during the consistency analysis of the current completion with immediately contiguous regions or elementary objects (Control_Rules).

The CP operate following the paradigm *What is an object for.* A functional analysis of this kind seems to enjoy several advantages with respect to a recognition process based on object prototypes. A treatment of this subject is beyond the scope of the present paper, and we will limit ourselves to remarking that in order to perform a functional analysis it is necessary to define functional primitives to be related to objects (or to classes of objects) and to find strategies which allow the functions and the shapes of the objects to be associated [1].

The CP may be activated by the PP each time the presence of an elementary object (or groups of elementary objects) is hypothesized, or directly by the user if he or she explicitly requires the recognition of a given object. In both cases, starting from the knowledge of a particular object and on the basis of the functional primitives, the CP drive the PP and allow attention to be focused so as to recognize the shapes (elementary objects) which are related to the current function.

SVL is currently implemented on an Explorer Lisp Machine, using KEE.

3 Low-Level Processes

The LLP module executes the early processing of the images. The present implementation of the LLP module is a conventional/procedural one, by mean of the Virtual Image System (VIS) [14], which is conceived as a tool for investigating low-level visual processes. VIS uses a menu-based user/system dialogue. All menu selections are supported by on-line help texts or by a programming language, VISICL - VIS Interpretative Control Language. VIS is currently implemented on a Unix workstation under X-Windows. SVL interacts with VIS by specialized rules (Active_vision_Rules) which generate VISICL instructions if necessary. The VISICL instructions are submitted to VIS from SVL through a LAN connection.

The computation efficiency of the LLP tasks can be greatly improved if a computational model, more adequate to the data structure and to the operation that must be done on it, is adopted. To this purpose a Cellular Automata parallel computational model has been considered together with its implementation on the special purpose processor PAPRICA, or on a Connection Machine [10].

Cellular Automata (CA) provide a paradigm for solving intrinsically parallel problems by the use of *local* computation rules [13].

A CA is made of three components: a set of elements (cells), a dynamic mapping, and scheduling model. Each element is characterized by a value (belonging to a finite set of states) and is a node of a network, which defines the CA topology (usually a two-dimensional grid for image processing applications) and the neighborhood of every node. The dynamic mapping defines a mapping from the neighborhood in the set of states. The mapping has to be uniform (each element is submitted to the same rule) and local (the results of the mapping depend only on the neighborhood values). The scheduling model is needed for the synchronization of the CA: time flows in discrete steps and all the elements of the CA must be updated synchronously. The state of a cell at time t_i depends only on the states of neighboring cells at time t_{i-1}. Let S be the set of states; let n be the number of elements in the neighborhood I; if X and Y are the values, of the elements x and y, the dynamic map D is characterized as follows:

$$D : S^n \to S$$

$$X(t_i) = D(Y(t_{i-1}) : y \in I(x))$$

As an example, relevant for artificial vision applications, let us consider a gradient-like filter for extracting region's contours [5]. It is defined by local rules and thus it can be directly translated into the CA paradigm. The overall hypothesis is that the borderline between two regions is characterized by a rapid variation of some image parameters. The gradient operator calculates the intensity of brightness variation in every pixel. The CA implementing such filtering is defined as follows: the elements of the CA correspond to the pixels of the input image, the set of values corresponds to the set of possible brightness values. The dynamic map is defined as follows:

```
gr_vert  = abs( top - bottom )
gr_horiz = abs( left - right )
gr_value = max(gr_vert, gr_horiz)
```

where the variables top, bottom, left, right indicate the values of cells belonging to the 4-neighborhood of a cell. A single time step (a *one shot* computation) is enough for completing the filtering. The rule can also be extended with a threshold value, which allows discarding noise-generated and irrelevant contours.

The CA computational model can be efficiently implemented on parallel machines with SIMD architecture if the neighborhood structure is well supported by the interconnection topology of the SIMD itself. In order to test CA algorithms, the LLP module makes use of a Connection Machine CM-2. The CM-2 is a *general purpose* massively parallel SIMD computer that allows dynamical reconfiguration of the topology of the network interconnecting the processing elements. One of the supported topologies is the two dimensional grid needed for image processing CA. The Connection Machine is also used for the software simulation of PAPRICA, a special purpose SIMD machine described in the next section. PAPRICA, now under testing, is planned to be part of the LLP module of the SVL. The filtering algorithms, developed on the Connection Machine will also be the guidelines for the next hardware implementation of PAPRICA. Figure 3 shows an example of gradient filtering performed on the CM-2 using the CA paradigm.

Figure 3: Example of gradient filtering using CA.

4 PAPRICA Architecture

PAPRICA [6] [8] is a massively parallel coprocessor designed for low-level image processing applications; it consists of four functional blocks: the program memory, the image
memory, the processor array and the control unit. The program and the image memories
are dual port memories that can be loaded and read by the host computer. The control
unit reads the program from the memory and drives the processor array. The data to be
processed is taken from the image memory, processed in the array and then stored back
into the image memory.

The dimension of the processing array (16 × 16 processing elements (PE), in the
version currently under testing at the Politecnico di Torino) is in general smaller than the
dimension of the data array to be processed (usually greater than 64 kpixels). Therefore
the processor array has to operate on a smaller window which sequentially scans the whole
image (a possible increase in the number of processing elements - 32 × 32 or 64 × 64 - does
not modify substantially the problem). The window that is processed in parallel has the
same size as the processing array, and therefore a support memory is needed to store the
complete image to be processed. The time to transfer data between the image memory
and the processor array (the typical bottleneck of this kind of systems) is sensibly reduced
by locating both of them on the same board.

The processor array is a set of computing cells that forms the kernel of the PAPRICA
architecture. Each PE can record the information (up to 64 bits) related to the associated
pixel; the array can thus memorize the information related to 64 memory planes or layers.

The basic PAPRICA instruction, executed synchronously by all the PE, is the sequence
of a graphic operation and a logic operation, as shown below:

$$Dest \leftarrow GOP(Src_1) \; [LOP \; Src_2]$$

The input data for the graphic operation (GOP) are the 8 neighbors bits and the central bit of Src_1 layer; the output consists of 1 bit, which is pipelined into the logic operator (LOP), together with another central bit belonging to a different memory plane (Src_2). The final output bit is stored back into the central bit of a third layer.

The data dependency, namely the fact that a result is a function of neighboring data, introduces a dependency between the sub-array processing and makes impossible to process completely the single sub-array. It is therefore mandatory to suspend the processing of a sub-array, to store it into the image memory, and to load an adjacent sub-array (the UPDATE instruction forces this behavior).

Since the inputs to PAPRICA instructions are the status of the eight neighboring elements and the status of the central element, PAPRICA can be classified as a cellular architecture. PAPRICA graphic operator (GOP) instruction set comprises the more frequently used one bit CA (such as expansion, erosion, mov, ...); using a specific sequence of shift and logic operations, every CA can be synthesized, with a few constraints on the neighborhood extension and on the number of states (depending on the size of the image memory). As an example, the gradient CA filtering described in the previous section can be implemented on PAPRICA with about 80 instructions (for 4 bit images). PAPRICA is actually a SIMD processing array whose elements are 1 bit Von Newman processors and it's use as a CA is just one among its many possible applications. In contrast, CAM-6 (Cellular Automata Machine [13]) can perform high speed CA filtering even on a PC, but its field of application is restricted only to CA. CAM-6 does not have real processing elements, but uses look-up tables to evaluate CA results. The number of states of the single cell is another CAM-6 limit that PAPRICA can bypass: due to the increasing complexity of look-up tables, CAM-6 can handle only 4 bits cells, while PAPRICA has no constraints at all on the number of bits per pixel. PAPRICA implements in hardware only a few simple CA and needs software algorithms to perform more complex CA; on the other hand, CAM-6 architecture can compute general CA filtering (with undefined neighborhood) in a time independent of the image dimensions (CAM-6 consists of a number of pseudo-PE which is a function of the number of cells).

4.1 CA performance analysis on PAPRICA

The maximum processing speed can be obviously reached when the processor array can contain the complete image or when the sequence of instructions does not reduce the validity area (i.e. only logic instructions). The processing time T_{pr} is expressed by:

$$T_{pr} = Loading\_time + Execution\_time + Saving\_time$$

The loading time and the saving time can be assumed equal and given by the number of elementary transfer operations (i.e. the number of processors in the array) time the elementary transfer duration. The execution time is given by the number of the instructions time the instruction duration (a single clock cycle) and therefore:

$$T_{pr} = (T_M \cdot Q^2) + (L \cdot T_C) + (T_M \cdot Q^2) = 2 \cdot T_M \cdot Q^2 + L \cdot T_C$$

where T_M denotes the duration of the basic transfer operation, Q^2 is the number of available processors (here assumed equal to the number of pixels in the image), L is the number of instructions, and T_C is the clock period.

The execution speed is then given by:

$$S_{pr} = \frac{Number\_of\_pixels\_processed}{Processing\_time} = \frac{Q^2}{2 \cdot T_M \cdot Q^2 + L \cdot T_C}$$

We can observe that actually T_C and T_M are of the same order of magnitude and if L (≈ 100) is negligible compared to $2 \cdot Q^2$ (≈ 2048), the previous expression assuming $T_M = T_C \simeq 100$ns reduces to:

$$S_{pr} \simeq \frac{Q^2}{2 \cdot T_M \cdot Q^2} = \frac{1}{2 \cdot T_M} = \frac{1}{2 \cdot 10^{-7}} = 5 \cdot 10^6 \; pixel/s$$

When the number of processors is less than the number of pixels in the image and when the program contains also graphic instructions, responsible of the reduction of the validity area, S_{pr} assumes the following expression [6]:

$$S_{pr} = \frac{(Q - \frac{2 \cdot G}{n_{upd}})^2}{(2 \cdot Q^2 \cdot T_M \cdot n_{upd} + L \cdot T_C)} \simeq \frac{(Q - \frac{2 \cdot G}{n_{upd}})^2}{2 \cdot Q^2 \cdot T_M \cdot n_{upd}}$$

where G is a function of the number and of the kind of the graphic operators used, and n_{upd} indicates the number of UPDATE instructions in the program.

Like in the previous case, the processing speed does not depend noticeably on the length of the program (the term L is negligible compared to $2 \cdot Q^2 \cdot n_{upd}$ as soon as Q is reasonably large). This approximation is always true when using PAPRICA as a CA engine: in fact to implement CA on PAPRICA only a few graphic operators are needed, usually at the beginning of the program, whereas the body of the filter is made of logic operators, not reducing the validity area. This structure is in general used in the case of CA computations, in which the parameter G is a function of the CA neighborhood: CA with 3×3 neighborhood have $G = 1$. Since G is normally small, the previous expression can be reduced to the approximation obtained in the case of $G = 0$, by assuming $G << Q$ and $n_{upd} = 1$ (one at the end of the program). Various tests show that in the case of G small, the processing speed with PAPRICA is two order of magnitude greater than the processing speed on a conventional computer (i.e. SUN-4).

5 Conclusions

In the paper we presented an environment under development to test procedures and algorithms devoted to low-level and high-level perception. The present implementation is based on different computational approaches (procedural, sub-symbolic and symbolic) running on a Lisp Machine and on a Unix workstation and suffering efficiency problems. The efficiency of the overall procedures can be greatly improved if a Cellular Automata computational model is realized by execution on massively parallel architectures, thus exploiting the benefit of the data locality of the computational model. To this purpose the use of the CM-2, available at the Università di Parma, can first allow verifying the hypothesis, and subsequently the use of PAPRICA, a special purpose engine, can be the first step toward a real time solution.

This work has been done in the frame of the PROMETHEUS project, a European effort set up to increase the safety of road traffic. In this case the medium-term goal of the activity is to prove the feasibility of a computer vision approach to help the driver task. As always in the case of automotive electronics, cost factors and real-time constraints are key points for the adoption of a solution. The project described in this paper is a contribution in this direction: SVL is devoted to study and verify, using AI technologies, algorithms which could be subsequently implemented on specialized low-cost hardware. The Connection Machine CM-2, connected via Ethernet with the SVL host, is devoted to simulate specialized hardware before its actual implementation.

References

[1] G.Adorni and M.DiManzo, "Object Recognition through Functional Modeling," *The CC-AI journal*, vol. 3, no. 17, 1987.

[2] G.Adorni, L.Massone and M.Sambin, "Subjective Contours: a Computational Approach," in *Proc. 7th International Congress of Cybernetics and Systems*, 1987.

[3] G.Adorni, L.Massone, G.Sandini and M.Immovilli, "From Early Processing to Conceptual Reasoning: an attempt to fill the gap," in *Proc. 10th IJCAI*, pp. 775-778, 1985.

[4] G.Adorni and E.Trucco, "A Quantitative Theory of Visual Perception: a case study," in *Advances in Image Processing and Pattern Recognition*, V.Capellini and R.Marconi, Eds., Amsterdam: Elsevier, 1986.

[5] D.Ballard and C.Brown, *Computer Vision*. Englewood Cliffs: Prentice-Hall, 1982.

[6] A.Broggi, G.Conte, F.Gregoretti, L.Reyneri, L.Rigazio, C.Sansoè and C.Zamiri, "PAPRICA," in *MADESS Report*, Rome: CNR, 1990.

[7] J.S.Bruner, "On Perceptual Readiness," *Psychological Review*, vol. 64, pp. 132-157, 1957.

[8] G.Conte, F.Gregoretti, L.M.Reyneri and C.Sansoè, "PAPRICA - A Parallel Architecture for VLSI CAD," in *Cad Accelerators. Proc. of the Int. Workshop on Hardware for CAD*. Oxford, 1989.

[9] R.Engelmore and T.Morgan, *Blackboard Systems*. Englewood Cliffs: Addison-Wesley, 1988.

[10] W.D.Hillis, *The Connection Machine*. Cambridge, Mass.: MIT Press, 1985.

[11] K.Koffka, *Principles of Gestalt Psychology*. New York: Hartcourt, 1935.

[12] E.L.J.Leeuwemberg and H.F.J.M.Buffart, *Formal Theories of Visual Perception*. New York: John Wiley and Sons, 1978.

[13] T.Toffoli and N.Margolous, *Cellular Automata Machines*. Cambridge, Mass.: MIT Press, 1987.

[14] D.Vernon and G.Sandini, "VIS: A Virtual Image System for Image Understanding," *Software Practice and Experience*, vol. 18, no. 5, pp. 395-414, 1988.

[15] L.A.Zadeh, "Fuzzy Sets," *Information and Control*, vol. 8, pp. 338-353, 1965.

An associative link from geometric to symbolic representations in artificial vision

E. Ardizzone, F. Callari, A. Chella*, M. Frixione**.

DIE - Dipartimento di Ingegneria Elettrica, University of Palermo
Viale delle Scienze 90128 Palermo, Italy,
Email: ardizzone@vlsipa.cres.it

*DIE - Dipartimento di Ingegneria Elettrica, University of Palermo
and
CRES - Centro per la Ricerca Elettronica in Sicilia, Monreale (Palermo), Italy

**Dipartimento di Filosofia
and
DIST - Dipartimento di Informatica, Sistemistica e Telematica,
University of Genova, Genova, Italy

Abstract

Recent approaches to modelling the reference of internal symbolic representations of intelligent systems suggest to consider a computational level of a subsymbolic kind. In this paper the integration between symbolic and subsymbolic processing is approached in the framework of the research work currently carried on by the authors in the field of artificial vision. An associative mapping mechanism is defined in order to relate the constructs of the symbolic representation to a geometric model of the observed scene..

The implementation of the mapping mechanism by means of a neural network architecture is described taking into account both the backpropagation architecture and the Boltzmann machine architecture. Promising experimental results are discussed.

1. Introduction

In a previous paper [Frixione et al. 1989], it has been suggested that one case in which some kind of subsymbolic computation seems necessary, even within a "classical" compositional symbolic paradigm context, is the modellization, from a cognitive point of view, of the way in which the reference of mental symbols is established. A subsymbolic level, for example as theorized by [Smolensky 1988], could be adopted to model that non-symbolic activity of the mind which arranges that symbols refer to something.

Even if the reference of mental symbols in a real intelligent system involves a complex interaction between different sensory and motor modalities, in this paper the emphasis is on the visual perception, the long-term authors' aim being the construction of an artificial vision system to be included into an autonomous abstract intelligent system.

The visual perception is generally modelled as a process in which information and knowledge are represented and processed at different levels of abstraction, from the lowest one, directly related to features of perceived images, to highest levels where the knowledge about the perceived objects is of a symbolic kind, through a somewhat analog representation level where the geometric features of the scene are explicitly treated.

In previous papers [Gaglio et al. 1984, Ardizzone et al. 1989], a general model of the visual perception system has been proposed in which the above mentioned different levels coexist and integrate.

In that model, the geometric representation of the perceived scene is built by utilizing a solid modelling system based on geometric primitives known as superquadrics. Superquadrics are mathematical shapes based on the parametric form of quadric surfaces, which, owing to the possibility of easily controlling their form, have been proposed [Pentland 1986] as basic shapes (or primitives) suitable for the representation of "building blocks" of real objects and scenes. A methodology for the extraction of the parameters of the superquadrics approximating the objects in the scene has been described in [Ardizzone et al. 1989.

The link between the described geometrical representation and the conceptual representation of a perceived scene has been investigated from the authors [Ardizzone et al. 1989] in the framework of fuzzy logic, to take into account uncertainty, similarity and approximation typical of reasoning capabilities of intelligent systems. However, this approach requires an explicit representation of fuzziness and therefore a precise definition of its parameters; this generally may be obtained only by choices somewhat arbitrary.

A subsymbolic approach based on connectionist architectures, like the one presented in this paper, may represent an attempt to get over this problem, owing to peculiarities of such architectures like associativity, robustness, adaptive learning capabilities and intrinsic parallelism.

2. The mapping between the geometric and the symbolic representation

The aim of the proposed architectures is the identification and the classification of the objects present in a scene described at the geometric level by a set of relevant parameters.

Considering the large variety of real world objects usually corresponding to a given concept, it it is clear that the problem is not a mere attribution of a group of parameters to a class. It is rather a question of providing a quantitative measure of the similarity of a given object to the prototype defining a class at the conceptual level. Moreover, information about an object may be somewhat limited, as in the case of an object occluded by another object or when the information about the scene is heavily affected by noise due to the characteristics of the scene, to the type of the data acquisition, and so on.

An associative mechanism of a connectionist type can be used to face the above problem in a satisfactory way. First, it allows to avoid exhaustive descriptions of prototypes at the symbolic level as in a fuzzy logic approach : the connectionist mechanism learns upon meaningful examples how to associate the geometric and symbolic representations, then exploiting its ability to generalize from those sample associations when tested with unpreviously seen objects. Second, a similarity measure between prototype and actual object (which, applying fuzzy logic concepts, must be defined a priori and explicitly by means of a membership function) is implicit in the behaviour of the network and is determined during the learning phases.

A scheme of the mapping between the geometric model and the symbolic representation is shown in fig. 1. The associative mechanism is realized by a neural network interacting, via the input/output units, with both the symbolic level

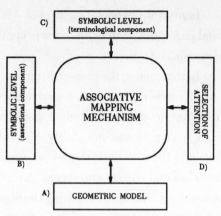

Fig. 1. A schematic view of the proposed associative mapping mechanism between geometric and symbolic representations of a perceived scene.

(terminological and assertional components) and the geometric model. At the geometric level, the external units are clamped to the parameters defining the geometric primitives. At the symbolic level, the external units are connected to the nodes of the semantic network representing the terminological knowledge. Similarly, other external units are connected to the symbolic constants of the assertional component making up the names of the objects in the scene.

In particular, referring to the figure, A) includes the neural network units related to the geometric representation of the scene; B) includes the units corresponding to the constants defining the objects in the scene; C) comprises the units corresponding to the conceptual description, i.e. to concepts and roles in the semantic network; finally D) includes the units for the implementation of the selection of attention mechanism. Each D) unit maps a primitive representing a portion of the scene; the activation of a set of these units realizes the selection of attention on the matching primitives in A). When some D) units are activated, selecting the attention on the corresponding primitives, the associative mechanism attempts the identification and classification of the corresponding objects. If the identification is successful, the units mapping the object names in B) are activated. Simultaneously in C) the units mapping the conceptual description that classifies the selected portion of the scene are activated.

Furthermore, the units present in B) and C) can also be used as input units; e.g. activating a concept or an assertional constant the associative mechanism will attempt to identify the corresponding object (objects) by selecting the attention on the corresponding superquadrics. Analogously the activations of the units corresponding to a role will cause the activation of the pairs of constants in B) and of the corresponding superquadrics in A).

The network can thus exploit the main characteristic of the associative approach: those object features which are interesting to their classification are acquired by the network in an adaptive manner during the learning phase. The system does not infer via membership functions expressly defined, but via the connectivity patterns of network units: the activation level of external units interacting with the symbolic level represents in fact a parametrization of the certainty of the classification and naming.

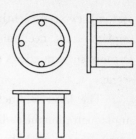

Experimentations on the implementation of the scheme reported in fig.1 have been carried on by using both the Boltzmann machines architecture and the backpropagation architecture. The implementations have been developed on a SUN3/Unix workstation as a C program, making use of callable routines of the Rochester Connectionist Simulator V4.2 [Goddard et al. 1989].

Fig. 2. An example object the architectures have been trained to classify and/or recognize. The corresponding superquadric parameters may be found in tab. 1.

The training set for networks has been made as follows. First, a basic set of a few individual objects is built, each object being described as boolean union of superquadrics. Second, this set is vastly enlarged including translated, scaled, noise-corrupted and attention-selected objects making use of a purposely written Pattern Description Language (PDL), based on the Unix tools lex and yacc. Fig. 2 shows an example of table along with the related superquadric parameters reported in tab. 1.

3. The implementation of the mapping mechanism based on backpropagation architecture

In fig. 3 the schematic representation of a quick neural network architecture partially implementing the above described link is shown. The architecture is a feed-forward architecture based on the backpropagation learning algorithm. The layer A) is made up by the inputs units receiving the information coming from the geometric level (i.e. the superquadric parameters). Each cluster $a\_1, a\_2, \ldots, a\_n$ represents a block of input units coding the parameters of a single superquadric and the related units for the selection of the attention ($s\_1, \ldots, s\_n$, shown in gray in the figure). Beside the selection of attention unit, each cluster $a\_1, \ldots, a\_n$ is made up by eight units: three representing the coordinates of the centre of the superquadric, three representing the lengths of the sides of the superquadric (whose principal axes are assumed parallel to the axes of the general reference

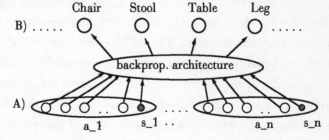

Fig. 3. The proposed backpropagation classifier; $a\_1, a\_2, \ldots, a\_n$ represent input units clamped to superquadric parameter values; $s\_1, s\_2, \ldots, s\_n$ represent input units for the selection of attention mechanism.

system), two representing the form parameters e1 and e2. Units s_1, ..., s_n in layer A) implement the mechanism of selection of attention. These units allow the selection of one or more superquadrics to be considered, when the analysis is limited to a portion of the scene.

The layer B) includes the output units of the neural network. In the current implementation the coding is local, i.e. these units directly match the nodes of the semantic network at the symbolic level. The output units make available their activation level, which may be considered a measure of the certainty of the recognition of the object.

The experimentations showed that very acceptable results may be obtained by using a network without hidden units. This simple kind of network, in spite of its well known computational limits, gives in fact good results on the simple chosen training set, while more complex networks give no better outcomes. This is probably due to the following facts: i) superquadrics represent geometrical entities with continuity, in the sense that small changes in the represented objects correspond to small changes of their parameters; ii) the training set is homogeneous. i) and ii) involve that such classes are, as a matter of fact, linearly separable. i) is a further confirmation about our choice of superquadrics as representation primitives (in a voxel representation, for example, small changes in the object shape or position could imply strong changes in the geometric model). ii) is in fact a simplification adopted as a provisional assumption: the choice of more complex training sets would imply that the classes of objects are not more linearly separable, thus requiring one or more layers of hidden units.

In order to carry on experimentations with the architecture, a large test set made up with 125 patterns has been built; each pattern is a set of superquadrics representing a piece of furniture (chairs, tables and stools), variously positioned and scaled.

Six tests have been carried on; during each test the network has been trained with a training set made up by randomly choosing a number of patterns within the test set. The learning time for each test has been fixed to 1000 epochs with intermediate checks performed after 10, 50, 100, 200, 300, 500 epochs. The tests have been carried on by presenting the whole test set to the network and calculating the APSS (Average Pattern Summed of Squared errors). The APSS is the sum over the output set of the squared differences between output and teach values, divided by 2, and averaged over the test set.

The size of the six training sets along with the corresponding APSS after 1000 training epochs is described in tab. 2. It should be noted that the best result is related shown on training set #2 whose size is only the 20% of the test set one. When the training set become larger, it has been noted the phenomenon of overlearning: the network become too specialized over the learned patterns and it shows a bad generalization over the unknown ones. Note also that no generalization is performed after larning training set #6, which is the same as the test set: this explains the low APSS value.

Fig. 4 shows the behaviour of the network during the training phase when the training set #2 is presented to the network. It is to be noted that after about 400 training epochs in which the APSS is high, the network is about to reach the convergence.

Fig. 5 shows a screen output of the simulator; each unit is represented by a circle whose size is proportional to unit activation. White circles stand for positive activations while black circles for null activations. The input units and the selection of attention units are shown on the bottom of the figure: the first eight units of each row correspond to the superquadric parameters, while the last unit is the selection of attention unit. The output units are shown on the top of the figure. In particular this figure shows the activation of the output units corresponding to an input pattern related to a table; it should be noted that the most active output unit is the one related to the class of tables.

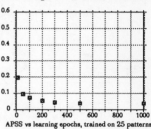

APSS vs learning epochs, trained on 25 patterns

The mechanism of selection of attention, as previously described, allow to select the attention on a particular group of superquadrics. As an example, fig. 6 shows the activation pattern when an example representing a chair is shown to the network while the activation of selection of attention unit related to a chair leg is activated at same time. Note that the most active output unit is the one representing the class of legs.

Fig.4. APSS measure related to the classification task for the backpropagation architecture, showing the ability of the network to generalize over the 125 pattern test set when trained on a subset of 25 patterns.

4. The implementation of the mapping mechanism based on Boltzmann machine architecture

The general structure of the network based on the Boltzmann machine architecture, implementing more closely the general scheme of fig. 1, is shown in fig. 7. Several methodologies and techniques have been proposed in the literature to speed up the Boltzmann learning algorithm. In our implementation we made use of asymmetrical architecture and of the deterministic learning methodology suggested in [Galland and Hinton 1989], thus achieving training speed comparable to the backpropagation architecture.

The implemented network is made up by a set of visible units and by a set of hidden units. The visible units are subdivided into two groups, respectively representing the geometric level and the symbolic level of the associative mechanism in fig. 1.

Units of the first group are in turn subdivided into two blocks. The first block is made up by clusters of units, each representing the geometric parameters of one single superquadric. The second block is composed by units allowing the selection of attention: each unit of this block selects the attention on one superquadric. Units of the second group are subdivided into two blocks too: units of the first block are related to assertional constants (A-Box), while

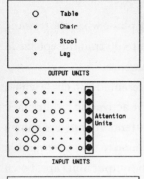

OUTPUT UNITS

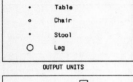

INPUT UNITS

Fig. 5. Screen dump of the simulator graphic output, showing the ability to well classify an input pattern representing a table.
The size of the circles is representative of the activations of their associated units (black = 0, white means positive).
Input unit activations equal the superquadric parameters of the object on which the net is tested.
Output unit activations show the classification performed by the net. The selection of attention mechanism (see text) is not active.

units of the second block are related to generic concepts (T-Box).

The network interface with the environment is realized by the visible units. Once the state of some of some visible units have been clamped, the network produces a complete visible pattern of activation, by estimating the state of the unclamped units.

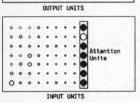

OUTPUT UNITS

INPUT UNITS

Fig. 6. Screen dump of the simulator graphic output, showing the ability to well classify an input pattern representing a table when the selection of attention mechanism is activated on a table leg by switching on the associated attention unit.

The classification is, by definition, independent of position and scale, while scaling affect individual recognition. Therefore, during the learning phase, superquadric parameters related to different positions of the same object are given, while still the same unit related to the object class and/or name is activated at the terminological level. Only the class unit is activated instead when a scaled object is shown to the network.

It is also possible to exploit the feature of the Boltzmann machine that all visible units may be input/output units: it is thus possible to activate some superquadric units, some terminological units and some assertional units: in this case the task of the network is to estimate the state of the remaining units on the basis of its own internal model.

A set of preliminary learning test has been performed by evaluating the various APSS measures over an object set of 315 patterns, after training the network on a much smaller subset (30 patterns only), so to check the net's ability to generalize. APSS measures computed include: total APSS, evaluated over the whole test set; class APSS, over tests not requiring geometric parameters' reconstruction; individual APSS, over tests performed with objects whose names the net was supposed to learn; geometric APSS . All these error figures have been measured after 10, 50, 100, 200 and 500 training epochs. The result of the above tests are summarized in fig. 8.

In subsequent figures, which are hardcopies of the graphical output of the

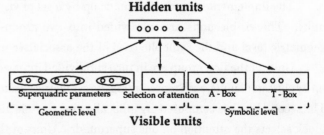

Fig. 7. The proposed deterministic asymmetric Boltzmann machine classifier (see text for description).

simulator, the bottom box includes units related to geometric level and attention units. An unit in the attention unit box, if activated, selects the attention on the corresponding superquadric. The middle box includes visible units representing the individuals. Similarly, the upper box represents the classes. In all the boxes, the size of small squares is representative of the activation level of the corresponding unit.

In fig 9, a chair named chair4 is presented (scaled and translated with respect to the same chair presented during the learning phase) and recognized. In fig 10, a chair named chair0 has been presented and the attention is activated on the second superquadric (representing a chair leg); the units of the semantic level for classes chair and leg and individual chair0 are activated by the network.

Finally, tab. 3 show the ability of the network to complete an incomplete input pattern. In particular, the network is shown with all but one parameters of superquadrics of a table, and simultaneously the units corresponding to the class table and to the individual table0 are activated. The output of units related to the missing superquadric are reported in the column labelled "Output" of table A, while the actual parameters of the superquadric are reported in the column labelled "State" (the other columns are related to the internal operation of the simulator, and have no meaning in the present discussion). As it should be noted the actual superquadric parameters are very similar to the desired ones.

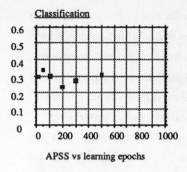

Classification

APSS vs learning epochs

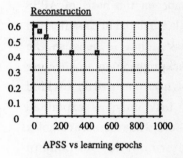

Reconstruction

APSS vs learning epochs

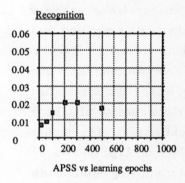

Recognition

APSS vs learning epochs

Fig. 8. APSS measures related to the classification, reconstruction and recognition tasks for the Boltzmann architecture, showing the ability of the network to generalize over the 315 pattern test set when trained on a subset of 30 patterns.

5. A comparison between the two implementations

The backpropagation architecture may be considered a quick and simple implementation of the scheme in fig. 1.

However, a full implementation of the scheme of fig.1 by a backpropagation architecture revealed itself very expensive in terms of computational load: in fact an autoassociator built up by a feed-forward architecture needs to duplicate the whole net while this is not necessary in the Boltzmann machine, where there is no distinction between input and output units, allowing for simple autoassociative processing.

A comparison between the two architectures can be made on the basis of APSS values related to classification tasks; that is because the backpropagation architecture has been operated on this kind of task only, as explained before, while the more complex deterministic Boltzmann architecture is also capable of individual recognition and geometric reconstruction tasks.

In particular fig. 4 and fig. 8 show the classification performances of both architectures. The higher values in APSS shown by deterministic Boltzmann architecture may be explained

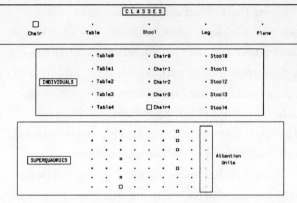

Fig. 9. Screen dump of the simulator graphic output, showing the ability to well classify and recognize an input pattern representing a chair named "chair4".
The size of the small squares is representative of the activations of their associated units.
Unit activations in the lowest box equal the superquadric parameters of the object on which the net is tested.
The selection of attention mechanism (see text) is not active.

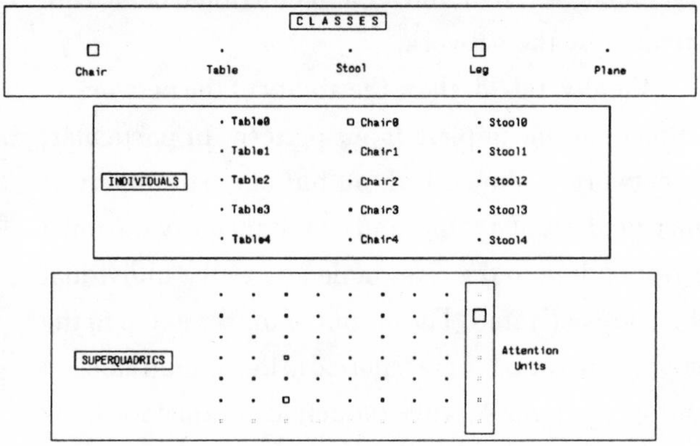

Fig. 10 Selection of attention: a leg of chair0 is well recognized

taking into account the higher complexity of both the network architecture and the required learning tasks. Even with these higher values of APSS, however, the Boltzmann network proved able to well classify its training set, that was more complex and varied with respect to the backpropagation one, as it is clearly visible, for example, in fig.s 11 and 12.

Moreover fig. 8 shows the satisfactory performances of this architecture as far as the simpler task of individual recognition: the APSS measures produced herein are indeed comparable with those of backpropagation classification tasks.

6. Conclusions

In the current implementation of the mapping mechanism the relations of an object with its parts and with other objects in the scene play no role in its classification.

	x	y	z	a	b	c	e1	e2
Leg 1	27	90	65	7	7	65	500	1
Leg 2	90	27	65	7	7	65	500	1
Leg 3	153	90	65	7	7	65	500	1
Leg 4	80	180	65	7	7	65	500	1
Inf.plane	90	90	140	70	70	10	500	1
Sup.plane	90	90	153	90	90	3	500	1

Tab. 1 Superquadric parameters of the object shown in fig. 2

Index	Name	Type	Output	State
0	geoinput[0]	DBM	86	100
9	geoinput[9]	DBM	412	380
18	geoinput[18]	DBM	264	240
27	geoinput[27]	DBM	188	240
36	geoinput[36]	DBM	89	100
45	geoinput[45]	DBM	455	380
54	geoinput[54]	DBM	5	0

Tab. 3 Output of a geometric reconstruction test for the Boltzmann architecture. Target values are labeled as "State", reconstructed values as "Output" (i.e. geometric layer units activation values).

Training set	Size	APSS
#1	10	0.059
#2	25	0.038
#3	50	0.044
#4	75	0.049
#5	100	0.046
#6	125	0.020

Tab. 2 Size of the training sets and corresponding APSS measure after 1000 training epochs.

This heavy restriction has been accepted only as a "temporary assumption", and will be discharged in next implementations. Nevertheless, even in the current implementation, the mechanism of selection of attention permits to stress some relations between an object and its parts; for example, if an object belonging to the class chair is presented to the network and simultaneously the attention is focused on a particular superquadric (e.g. corresponding to a leg), the network activates both the class chair and the class leg, so establishing a sort of "part-of" relation. Of course, this conclusion cannot be generalized, being strongly dependent on the particular nature of this relation.

The inclusion of general roles into the mapping mechanism will give the proposed model the capability to form contexts and expectations, that can properly guide and tune the processing of the underlying subsymbolic levels, acting as a sort of top-down feedback.

Acknowledgements
This work has been partially supported by the Italian "Consiglio Nazionale delle Ricerche" (CNR) and by the Italian "Ministero dell'Universita' e della Ricerca Scientifica e Tecnologica" (MURST).

References
[1] Ardizzone, E., Gaglio, S., Sorbello, F. (1989). Geometric and Conceptual Knowledge Representation within a Generative Model of Visual Perception, *Journal of Intelligent and Robotic Systems*, 2, 381-409.
[2] Ardizzone, E., Chella, A., Frixione, M., Gaglio, S. (1990). Integrating Subsymbolic and Symbolic Processing in Artificial Vision, submitted to *Journal of Intelligent Systems*.
[3] Brachman, R.J., Schmolze, J. (1985). An overview of the KL-ONE knowledge representation system, *Cognitive Science*, 9, 171-216.
[4] Frixione, M., Spinelli, G., Gaglio, S. (1989). Symbols and subsymbols for representing knowledge: a catalogue raisonne', Proc. of the Tenth IJCAI, 3-7, Detroit, USA.
[5] Gaglio, S., Spinelli, G., Tagliasco, V. (1984). Visual Perception: an Outline of a Generative Theory of Information Flow Organization, *Theoretical Linguistics*, 11, 21-43.
[6] Galland, C.C., Hinton, G.E. (1989). Deterministic Boltzmann Learning in Networks with Asymmetric Connectivity, Techn. Rep. CRG-TR-89-6, University of Toronto, Canada.
[7] Goddard, N.H., Lynne, K.J., Mintz, T., Bukys, L. (1989). Rochester Connectionist Simulator, Techn. Rep. 233, University of Rochester, New York, USA.
[8] Pentland, A.P. (1986). Perceptual Organization and the Representation of Natural Form, *Artificial Intelligence*, 28, 293-331.
[9] Smolensky, P. (1988). On the hypotheses underying connectionism, *Behavioral and Brain Sciences*, 11, 1.

A Theory of Sensor-Based Robot Navigation using Local Information

G. Vercelli, R.Zaccaria, and P. Morasso

DIST - Dipartimento di Informatica, Sistemistica e Telematica
Università di Genova, Via Opera Pia 11a, I-16145 Genova, Italia
E-mail: {gianni,renato,piero}@dist.unige.it

Abstract - A definition of the general, multi- robots navigation problem is introduced. Successively, algorithms are described able to solve some subclasses of the problem, describing a new algorithm which guarantees a solution for the simplest case. This algorithm (the *Wild Rover Algorithm*), as well as the entire approach, stands on the idea that it is possible to integrate the *analogical representation* (easy to operate on-line on real sensors, with no problems of local consistency, but which does not guarantee, *per se*, about finding a solution) with a *symbolic representation*, on which sound search algorithms (particular forms of graph-search) can carry out the planning itself and, eventually, optimization. With respect to the existing literature, our approach gives two relevant results: i) it defines an algorithm that, at the same time, under defined assumptions, is complete (it finds a solution if it exists), and is suitable for operating on a real robot in a real world; ii) generalizes navigation problem showing a formal way to face the multi robot problem, with possible partial solutions based on heuristics.

1   Introduction

In Robotic and AI literature, the term *navigation* indicates an intelligent activity of multiple agents for generating a path in a space $\mathbf{R}^N$ starting from a set of initial points $\{\vec{P_0}\}$ towards a set of goal points $\{\vec{P_G}\}$, avoiding forbidden regions of the space (e.g., obstacles in R^3, joint limits in a *configuration space* R^6, actuators power limits in some *control space* and so on).

Although not much present in pure AI literature, the navigation problem should be formalized in a sound way, with the aim of defining an important part of *Cognitive Action Representations* for a robot operating in real time in the real world. Safe, goal driven motions are the most elementary components of such knowledge: therefore, navigation is a relevant base point for the whole theory.

On the other hand, the robotic literature is rich of works on navigation and related topics, but they develop, generally speaking, either specific algorithms, or particular applications, or self-contained heuristics, rather than a formal description of the problem[1].

The existing literature about navigation, path planning, obstacle avoidance and trajectory formation is wide and difficult to classify. For our purposes, we may consider the following classification items:

i. *on-line vs. off-line*: some methods stand on a *a priori* knowledge of the environment and perform on it an optimal search; other methods do not, and the planning process is *distributed* during the navigation;

---

[1] A well founded formalization of the navigation problem exists in Robotics for the *Configuration Space* approach to robot movement. However, we consider it too specific, as well as its related algorithms, to be used in the general case.

ii. *global vs. local knowledge*: this distinction focuses on the nature of the state representation for the agent. It may be either a global map with more or less uniform resolution, or a local memory, centered on the robot, on which sensors accumulate a local description. It has been shown [LS87] that a purely local method is not able to guarantee to reach the goal; nevertheless, advantages of local approaches are straightforward;

iii. *symbolic vs. analogical*: in symbolic approaches the problem is discretized, and search is carried out on a graph representation of the plan; in analogical approaches, continuous mathematical models are used, in which some kind of global energy is defined, and the problem of finding a good trajectory becomes the problem of letting the system "relax" towards a minimum of that energy. Artificial Potential methods [Kha86] use this kind of *metaphor*. Another example is the use of complex dynamics [Ste88], in which paths are like particles of a fluid in a stream. Analogical methods are computationally simple and homogeneous with local strategies, and do not suffer from *consistency problems* like pure symbolic representations do, when the model of the environment is updated in real time.

In the next sections, a definition of a general, multi- robots navigation problem is introduced. Successively, algorithms are described able to solve some subclasses of the problem. The main algorithm (the *Wild Rover Algorithm*), as well as the entire approach, stands on the idea that it is possible to integrate a *local analogical representation* (easy to operate on-line on real sensors, with no problems of local consistency, but which does not guarantees, *per se*, about finding a solution) with a *symbolic representation*, on which a suitable search algorithm (particular forms of graphsearch) can carry out the planning itself and, eventually, optimization.

With respect to the existing literature, our approach gives two relevant results: i) it defines an algorithm that, at the same time, under defined assumptions, is complete (it finds a solution if it exists), and is suitable for operating on a real robot in a real world; ii) generalizes the navigation problem showing a formal way to face the multi robot problem.

It is worthnoting that current results in literature fail to meet the requirements of both completeness and feasibility. As an example, the well known algorithms BUG1 and BUG2 by Lumelsky [LS87] assume a global knowledge that, although apparently poor, is difficult to obtain in real cases, and no idea of exploring the space is present. Our algorithm uses a minimal global information and is able to construct, incrementally, a unique exploration graph for the problem, so that it is suitable for extensions towards multi robot problems and so on, having, at the same time, a low complexity.

2 The Navigation Problem

Given a world W composed by objects OBJ_i, that can be either: (i) fixed obstacles O_i; (ii) robots and mobile obstacles R_i; (iii) target positions T_i; we can define the following problem:

Problem A - For each robot $R_i \subset W$, find a path $\vec{P}_i(t)$ from the initial given position towards its own target position T_i.[2]

We call $\vec{P}_i(t)$ the *PLANNED PATH* for robot R_i, and we assume that each R_i is allowed to move only inside the *free space* FS, defined as the subset of the world not belonging to obstacles nor robots:

---

[2]We assume for simplicity that the robots and mobile obstacles have no kinematic constraints, This is not a trivial problem, and must be taken into account in further investigations.

Def. 1: **FS** (Free Space): $\mathbf{W} - \{O_i\} - \{R_i\} - \{T_i\}$

Def. 2: **OS** (Occupied Space): $\{O_i\} + \{R_i\} + \{T_i\}$

The problem A is a pure navigation problem, that is difficult to solve with classical AI methods if we allow a wide generality for the shapes of the OBJ_i and for the interactions among R_i. Let us define more precisely the objects defined in $\mathbf{W}$:

OBSTACLES An obstacle O_i is a *fixed*, closed, continuous contour, with either a convex or a concave shape; the function defining the contour belongs to a piecewise of class C_k (its derivatives up to the kth order are continuous functions, except for a finite number of singular points). Each O_i is defined in terms of: *shape*(O_i), *position*(O_i).

ROBOTS A robot R_i is a closed, continuous contour similar to O_i; furthermore, three robot types are defined:

1. a *mobile* robot, which has the capability of deciding its law of motion on the basis of its own internal and external sensing equipment, and of its own local and global knowledge of the environment;

2. a *movable* obstacle, which has the capability of passively reacting to external actions (e.g., a pushing action made by another robot) by changing its position;

3. a *mobile* obstacle, which has its own law of motion, but with an *a priori*, independent behavior in $\mathbf{W}$.

Without loss of generality, a given robot R_i can be described in terms of: *shape*(R_i), *initial_position*(R_i), *current_position*(R_i), *speed*(R_i), *motion_strategy*(R_i).

TARGETS A target T_i is a particular position and orientation in the free space **FS**. A target T_i is defined as the final "desired" position of the robot R_i, or a "ghost" shape to be reached by R_i. Each R_i has a unique target, whereas a single T_j can be targeted by several robots. A target T_i is defined in terms of: *shape*(T_i) (the "ghost" shape for R_i), *position*(T_i).

Presently we are not yet able to give a formal solution for the problem A. We will introduce a heuristic solution for a problem, A', which is a subset of A, and a complete solution for a problem, A'', which is a subset of A'. If all robots are of type 1, we define:

Def. 3: **Goal position** : $G_i = T_i(R_i)$.

Def. 4: **Starting position:** $S_i = $ *initial_position*(R_i).

so that the problem A can be replaced by the following:

Problem A' (only for mobile robots inside fixed obstacles) - For each robot $R_i \subset \mathbf{W}$, find a trajectory $\vec{P}_i(t) \subset \mathbf{FS}$ where $(\vec{P}_i(0) = \vec{S}_i) \wedge (\vec{P}_i(T) = \vec{G}_i)$, where T is a finite time instant.

Note that each pair (S_i, G_i) related to a given R_i defines an absolute minimum path (if it exists):

Def. 5: Direct Path for robot R_i: $\mathbf{D\vec{P}}_i = \vec{G}_i - \vec{S}_i$.

If $\forall \vec{P}_i(t) : \vec{P}_i(t) \subset (D\vec{P}_i \cap FS)$, then $\{ D\vec{P}_i \}$ is the (trivial) optimal solution of problem A', since the straight line between the starting point $\vec{S}_i$ and the goal $\vec{G}_i$ is the minimum path by definition.

Def. 5a: Goal Direction for robot R_i: $\vec{GD}_i = \frac{\vec{DP_i}}{\|\vec{DP_i}\|}$.

This versor is crucial for the algorithms described in the following, since it represents the only global information available, comparable to information given by a *compass* always pointing towards the target.

Def. 5b: Compass Direction for robot R_i at any instant t: $\vec{CD}_i(t) = \frac{\vec{G_i} - \vec{P_i}(t)}{\|\vec{G_i} - \vec{P_i}(t)\|}$.

In the following, we will define a formal approach to problems A' and A'' using a hybrid methodology (analogical and symbolic) based on the metaphor of *exploring a force field associated to* W *and constructing a graph for improving the planning capabilities*.

3 Shapes and Abstract Force Fields

Defining a *force field* as an abstraction of objects is a well known technique in Robotics. As described in [Til90], [War89], a mathematical definition of an *Artificial Potential*, as to say, a conservative scalar function $U(x, y)$, can be associated to shapes so that, in any point of **FS**, a force vector $\vec{F}(x, y) = -\nabla U(x, y)$ is defined, resulting from a repulsive component generated by objects and an attractive component generated by the target. The navigation problem may therefore reduced to a passive movement of R_i inside the field, usually driven by a mathematical function linking together $\vec{F}(x, y)$ and $\dot{P}(t)$ (instant speed). This kind of path planning is completely *analogical* and based on local information. Unfortunately, it is known how it is not able to always find a solution, because of the occurrencies of *local minima* of $U(x, y)$. We can extend the concept of *Artificial Potential* to *Abstract Potential*, or *Abstract Force Field (AFF)*, in which the dimensionality of **W** extends from the 3-D world and to more general variables, including dynamics and force; in this case [ZVM89], the navigation paradigm may be used as an alternative to the C-space in planning movements of a redundant system (e.g., a redundant arm) in presence of compliance and forces, or as a metaphor for solving planning problems [CFVZ90].

The shapes of the objects involved in **W** are responsible of the creation of an AFF, so that the given problems becomes a navigation problem using AFFs. The shape defines a repulsive abstract force field, called F_{rep}; F_{rep} may be given by a physical sensor process (e.g., distance measurements) as well as by an *a priori* knowledge about shapes. An F_{rep} can be associated to every agent, both objects and robots:

$$O_i \iff F_{rep_i}(shape(O_i), pos(O_i))$$

$$R_i \iff F_{rep_i}(shape(R_i), current\_position(R_i))$$

A mobile robot, say, R_i, moves in the repulsive field defined as the composition of all repulsion forces. Moreover, R_i has its *compass direction* $\vec{CD}_i$, which indicates at any instant the direction towards G_i; in this sense we have another constant attractive force field (a sort of *magnetic field*)

$$F_{att_i}(G_i, current\_position(R_i))$$

superimposed with a compound repulsive field (a sort af *electric field*)

$$F_{rep_i} = \sum_{k=1}^{M} F_{rep_k}^{obs} + \sum_{j \neq i}^{N} F_{rep_j}^{rob}$$

Unlike conventional artificial potential techniques, each mobile robot is *active*, as to say, it decides at any instant where to go and with which law of motion.

It is important to note that the intelligent behavior of R_i is mostly due to two different skills in navigation:

- the capability of going directly to G_i along $C\vec{D}_i$ at the max possible speed;

- the capability of moving along a given equipotential curve of F_{rep_i}.

4 A sub-problem of A'

Before giving a heuristic temptative solution for A', we introduce the smallest subset of A, for which a complete solution can be devised so far:

Problem A'' (for one robot inside fixed obstacles) - Given $\mathbf{W} = \{R, \{O_i\}, S, G, FS\}$, find a path $\vec{P}(t) \subset FS$ where $(\vec{P}(0) = S) \wedge (\vec{P}(\mathcal{T}) = G)$.

The three problems defined correspond to different level of generality, with the relation

$$A \supseteq A' \supseteq A''$$

so that a solution for a more general problem is also solution for a less general problem and not vice versa.

The problem A'' is a pure navigation problem for a single robot of type 1 inside fixed obstacles, which is the most investigated in literature, and for which several solutions have been found [Lat91]; however, as stated previously, all solutions proposed have some drawback when used in a real time planning system for navigation. In the next section we introduce a novel algorithm for solving a problem of type A''.

4.1 The Wild Rover Algorithm (WRA)

The mobile robot R is able to plan $\vec{P}(t)$ by exploring the analogical map with an algorithm that we call **Wild Rover Algorithm (WRA)**. The main features of WRA are the following:

- it takes as input an analogic map that describes a scene of the world in terms of AFFs, so that real data are treated in the same manner as those derived from the *a priori* representation (if available);

- it computes the next movement on the basis of *local* measurements (F_{rep}, created by obstacles in the neighborough, gives a possible direction for next step referred in WRA as *tangentdir*), taking into account as the unique *global* information F_{att} generated by the goal (the *compass-direction* $C\vec{D}_i$);

- it can be used either for static situations and also in dynamic environments, like the problem A', simply by adding some "ad hoc" skills to each robot (some additional heuristics superimposed to existing behaviors in a concurrent manner).

The WRA algorithm works for a robot R as follows:

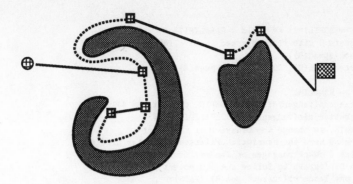

Figure 1: Example of navigation of a robot R using WRA

```
repeat a cycle composed by two tasks:
    T1) measure the two fields (Frep and Fatt) related to R;
    T2) decide the next movement of R:
        climb the field
        or move along an equipotential curve (tangentdir);
until the goal of R is not reached.
```

The main idea is that exploring a given environment *analogically* (i.e., making local measurements on an analogical map), is equivalent, in terms of navigation, to build a discrete *decision graph* over the map (in particular, an OR graph). Each time the robot takes a *decision* (task T2), (a spatio-temporal important point during navigation), it is stored in a graph: we call such a decision point a **landmark**. So far, the purpose of WRA is to produce a graph of landmarks, each of them belonging to the free space **FS**.

If possible, the actor moves directly towards the goal; if not, we consider two different thresholds (HARDLIMIT and SOFTLIMIT) related to the field, which allow us to safety decide the action to do: *climbing the field* or *moving along an equipotential curve*. These thresholds can be dinamically updated on the basis of the movements of objects into the scene. Each time the robot: e1) collides with an hardlimited obstacle, or e2) overtakes and leaves an obstacle, then a *landmark* in that position is created (fig. 1).

Def. 6 - A **landmark** is a decision node of the incremental graph representing the (possible) solution.

Note that the graph is created in a *depth-first* manner. If the robot passes near a landmark for more than 1 time, (like in the case of concavity explored in both ways or in cycling around an obstacle) the *compass-direction* is no more convenient, and a backtracking recovery action to the previous landmark must be taken. The events e1 and e2 are not the only two cases to monitor; also the events e3) end of the recovery action, must create a landmark in the last actual position of R.

The algorithm WRA can be described by the following code:

```
while ( not_in_goal(current_pos(R),G) ) {
    switch ( field = measure_field(Frep, current_pos(R), Oi) ) {
    case (field < SOFTLIMIT) : /* direct path for a step */
        speed_up(speed(R));
        move(current_pos(R), COMPASSDIR, speed(R));
```

```
            break;
    case (field >= SOFTLIMIT && field < HARDLIMIT) :
        /* go toward G with reduced speed (hill climbing of Frep) */
        speed_down(speed(R));
        move(current_pos(R), COMPASSDIR, speed(R));
        break;
    case (field >= HARDLIMIT) :
        choose_tangent(tangentdir, COMPASSDIR, current_pos(R));
        if ( is_better_dir(tangentdir, COMPASSDIR) ) {
            /* NOTE: we change the behavior of the robot
            changing here the heuristic criterion is_better_dir()*/
            switch ( check_passages_on_landmark(current_pos(R)) ) {
            case 0: /*start to follow the equipotential line */
                put_landmark(current_pos(R),1PASS);
                move(current_pos(R), tangentdir, speed(R));
                break;
            case 1: /*continue to follow the equipotential line */
                move(current_pos(R), tangentdir, speed(R));
                break;
            case 2: /* the found landmark was passed
                once and R has to do inversion and to
                follow the equipotential line in the other
                sense */
                mark_landmark(current_pos(R),2PASS);
                move(current_pos(R), -tangentdir, speed(R));
                break;
            case 3: /* the found landmark was passed
                more than one time and R has to
                come back to the previous landmark */
                mark_landmark(current_pos(R),NOMOREPASS);
                move(current_pos(R),dir_prev_landmark,speed(R));
                break;
            } /* end switch */
        } /* end if */
        else { /* leaving the equipotential line */
            put_landmark(current_pos(R),LEAVING);
            speed_up(speed(R));
            move(current_pos(R),COMPASSDIR,speed(R));
        } /* end else */
        break;
    } /* end switch */
} /* end while */
```

The WRA algorithm considers each robot as independent, hence it is not complete, as to say, it is not able to solve the general case in which two or more robots have strong interferences (like trying to pass simultaneously along a narrow corridor and so on). Nevertheless it is important for two reasons:

Proposition. The WRA can heuristically solve the problem A', in which several mobile robots among fixed obstacles are considered.

Proposition. The WRA always solves the problem A'', in which only one mobile robot among fixed obstacles is considered.

4.2 Heuristic solution of A'

To solve the A' problem, so far only heuristics are available. In particular, we sketch here a solution of A' that uses two cooperating concurrent algorithms:

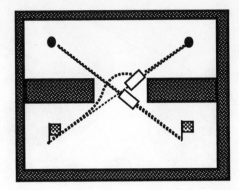

Figure 2: Concurrent navigation of two robots

i. a navigation algorithm (WRA) for *each robot* within *fixed obstacles* (see the solution of A'');

ii. a *deadlock manager* algorithm for couples of robots (generalization of A'' towards A').

In effects, multi robots coordination is an open problem, where a relevant point is the role of the communication between robots in order to escape from what we call *deadlock situations*, such as cluttered passages (doors or tunnels), cross-roads and so on [3], in which two agents, having interacting goals and independent behavior, block each other. If robots communicate, special, rule-based, algorithms could be applied in order to significantly improve the overall navigation planning (fig. 2). A deeper discussion of this approach can be found in [VZM91].

4.3 Discussion about *WRA*

The main advantage of WRA is that the robot R moves among the obstacles O_i in **W** that obstruct its path, leaving landmarks back, and finding incrementally one promising solution with respect to the heuristic criterion used for the choice of the direction when an obstacle is encountered. This characteristic makes WRA very smart and simple to implement in a real mobile robot, provided that the robot have a good odometric system. There are a few known situations in which WRA can fail:

a) when there is an obstacle O_i with infinite shape,

b) when there are obstacles with a particular shape of alternate convex/concave contour patches, in a particular spatial configuration able to drive the robot to an endless cycling.

Apart from these two situations, it is worthnoting that WRA makes a depth-first construction of the graph, by interleaving the exploration of the environment and path finding; "bad" situations like a) and b) above are to be solved only by means of a backtracking triggered by a (heuristic) depth threshold.

On the contrary, expanding the exploration process in the environment, it is possible to discover all possible paths in the class covered by the algorithm (shifting from a depth first

---

[3]The term *deadlock* is borrowed from the terminology of concurrent algorithms, since the situation is functionally similar. In (more formal) mathematical terms, it corresponds to a *local minimum* inside an Artificial Potential Field.

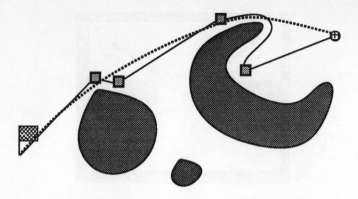

Figure 3: Applying the Ariadne's Thread Algorithm

to a bredth first search, or, if additional heuristics are available, to a A^* algorithm). This is an interesting problem, whose solution is not only useful *per se* (exploration of unknown environments), but also to discover optimal or sub-optimal solutions (minimum path in the graph). Physically, it corresponds to making the robot to explore successively several (or all possible) paths.

It is also posible to define a paradigm in which multiple, cooperating agents explore concurrently W. A suitable algorithm, an extension of WRA, called **MEA** (*Multiple Explorers Algorithm*), that can be easily parallelized, is described in [VZM91], in which a demonstration of the completeness of WRA is also sketched.

An important result about WRA (of which we omit here the demonstration for sake of briefness) is a good complexity figure.

Proposition. If L is the number of convex obstacles (curves)[4], the number of landmarks N_L and the number of arcs (paths between two landmarks) N_A are bounded to:

$$2 + 3L \leq N_L \leq 1 + 4L$$
$$1 + 5L \leq N_A \leq 6L$$

5 Conclusions

A theory for describing and solving navigation problems has been described. Algorithms have been presented and discussed for subclasses of the general multi robot navigation problem.

Two points are still to be discussed:

- As defined, the algorithms are able to find only sub-optimal solutions in terms of metric costs; this is not a real drawback, since eligible paths can be successively improved with simple, concurrent optimization processes that recall a sort of learning;

- The algorithms can be implemented in a real robot using commercially available sensors, like proximity sensors of ultrasonic and infrared type, and a very limited amount of computational power.

---

[4]Concave shapes can always be decomposed into a finite number of convex shapes

For the first point, a successive algorithm based on a relaxation of an analogical model of paths has been defined; it is based on the metaphor of considering a chosen path (which is piecewise for construction) as an elastic thread, which can be pulled until it reaches an equilibrium posture which is, by definition, of minimum length. This algorithm (*Ariadne's Thread Algorithm*) is very fast and suitable for total parallelization. It cannot be described here for briefness; in figure 3 a planned path is shown before and after the Ariadne algorithm. This further process can also generate new paths that extend the exploration of the environment, so that, iteratively, the graph can be expanded with new solutions and so on.

For the second point, a navigation environment has been implemented including the solution of a class of problems like A'', and an experimental setup using a mobile robot with sonar and infrared sensors is in progress.

Acknowledgements

This work was supported by the Progetto Finalizzato Robotica of the Italian National Research Council, Obiettivo ALPI, and by Esprit Basic Research Action FIRST.

References

[CFVZ90] A. Camurri, M. Frixione, G. Vercelli, and R. Zaccaria. Some concepts of analogic planning in assembly tasks. In *Proceedings of ECAI'90*, 1990. August 7-10, Stockholm, Sweden.

[Kha86] O. Khatib. Real-time obstacle avoidance for manipulators and mobile robots. *The Intl J of Robotics Research*, 5:90–99, 1986.

[Lat91] J.C. Latombe. *Robot Motion Planning*. Kluwer Academic Publishers, Boston, 1991.

[LS87] V. Lumelsky and A. Stepanov. Path-planning strategies for a point mobile automaton moving amidst unknown obstacles of arbitrary shape. *Algorithmica*, 2:403–430, 1987.

[Ste88] L. Steels. A step towards common sense. In *Proceedings of the Eighth European Conference on Artificial Intelligence*, 1988. Munich, GFR.

[Til90] R.B. Tilove. Local obstacle avoidance for mobile robots based on the method of artificial potentials. In *Proceedings IEEE Conf Robotics and Automation*, pages 566–571, 1990. Cincinnati, Ohio, May 13-18.

[VZM91] G. Vercelli, R. Zaccaria, and P. Morasso. Robot navigation. Technical report, LIRA Lab - DIST - University of Genoa, 1991. 3/91.

[War89] C.W. Warren. Global path planning using artificial potential fields. In *IEEE International Conference on Robotics and Automation*, pages 316–321, Scottsdale, USA, 1989.

[ZVM89] R. Zaccaria, G. Vercelli, and P. Morasso. Analogic models for robot programming. In Editor G. Sandini, editor, *Nato ASI Series on Robotics*. Springer-Verlag, Il Ciocco, 1989.

Architectures and Technologies

INSIGHTS INTO COOPERATIVE GROUP DESIGN: EXPERIENCE WITH THE LAN DESIGNER SYSTEM

Mark Klein
Boeing Computer Services
PO Box 24346, 7L-64
Seattle, WA 98124-0346
mklein@atc.boeing.com

Stephen C-Y. Lu
Knowledge-Based Engineering Systems Research Laboratory
Department of Mechanical and Industrial Engineering
University of Illinois
Urbana, IL 61820 USA
lu@kbesrl.me.uiuc.edu

Introduction

The design of complex artifacts has become, increasingly, a *cooperative* endeavor carried out by multiple agents with diverse kinds of expertise. For example, the design of a car may require experts on potential markets, function, manufacturability and so on. The development of tools and underlying theories for supporting cooperative group design has lagged, however, behind the growing needs implied by this evolution [18]. In particular, while conflict-free cooperation has been well-studied (e.g. [33], [23], [21], [2]), how design agents can interact when conflict occurs has received little attention.

The goal of our research in this area has been to develop a system for supporting cooperative group design based on a model of how human design agents actually interact; in particular on how they cooperatively detect and resolve conflicts. This development has consisted to date of two major phases. The first phase involved studies of cooperative group design in human groups in two different domains (Architectural and Local Area Network design). These studies led us to develop a model of the cooperative group design process that, in the second phase, was realized as an implemented cooperative group design system (the LAN Designer) that designs Local Area Networks (LANs) using machine-based design agents.

The purpose of this paper is to describe what our experience with designing and implementing the LAN Designer system has revealed about conflict detection (CD) and conflict resolution (CR) in cooperative group design and how computers can support it. These insights can be summarized as follows. Conflict resolution plays a central role in cooperative group design. Conflict resolution can be effectively operationalized by instantiating general CR expertise via interaction with domain expertise. Cooperative group design systems should use a design model designed to support conflict avoidance, early conflict detection and effective use of CR expertise, as well as explanation and modification of design actions.

In the remainder of this paper we describe these insights, including the evidence supporting them, the implications for cooperative group design system development, the strengths and deficiencies of relevant research to date, and how we incorporated each insight into the LAN Designer system. We conclude by discussing directions for future work.

The Central Role of Conflict Resolution

Studies we performed of human cooperative group design in the domain of Architectural design (described in full in [19]) suggest that conflicts, rather than being avoided at all costs, actually play a central role in the cooperative group design process. In these studies, statements made by architects cooperating to design a house (i.e. components of the design *protocol*) were collected and then categorized. These statements fell into four major categories: tentative design *commitments* made by design agents, identification of a positive aspect of a design (i.e. a *positive critique*), identification of a problem in a design (i.e. a *negative critique*), and potential *resolutions* for a conflict. A tabulation of the number of statements in each category revealed the following pattern (Figure 1):

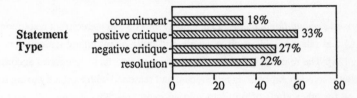

Figure 1: Counts of Different Statement Types

There were actually more critiquing statements (positive *and* negative) as well as more conflict resolution statements than there were design commitments. Conflict identification (negative critiques) and conflict resolution together accounted for *half* of the statements made by the architects during the design sessions.

Close analysis of the protocols suggests that the architects adhere to the following model of interaction:

1. Design agents generate potential solutions for a given design subtask, usually based on "default" or "standard" solutions for that kind of problem.
2. They then evaluate the design, identifying its pros and cons. Cons include conflicting design commitments from different agents as well as negative critiques by one agent of commitments made by other agents. Pros are added to the rationale supporting the positively evaluated design decisions.
3. The design is then modified to resolve the conflicts identified.

The design process thus can be viewed as an iterative generate-and-test process, wherein candidate designs are generated by design agents using default knowledge, evaluated by the agents, and then "tweaked" as needed, in response to conflicts, to make them consonant with each agent's view of the specific demands of the given task. A related study [18] suggests that cooperative group design of Local Area Networks is also characterized by a central role for conflict resolution. We believe this is true, in fact, for a wide range of cooperative group design domains.

Computer systems that aim to support cooperative group design, therefore, must support the process of conflict resolution. In particular, they must support the kind of design process described above, including providing design agents with the ability to make and critique design commitments as well as detect and resolve inter-agent conflicts. A comprehensive review of existing work in this area is included in [18]; this literature is summarized briefly below.

A large body of work is devoted to *analyzing* human conflict resolution behavior [9]. This work highlights the importance of conflict in group interactions, but provides few prescriptions for how conflict resolution can be facilitated. There is in addition some work on *supporting* human conflict resolution (e.g. [16], [29]). This work focuses, however, on competitive conflicts and/or limits itself to structuring interactions among group members, rather than applying conflict resolution expertise to help resolve the conflicts. The conflict resolution expertise is thus still expected to reside in the human participants.

To find work on *computational models* that actually encode and use conflict resolution expertise, we need to turn to AI and related fields such as single and multi-agent planning/design as well as concurrent engineering [22]. The relevant literature can be grouped into three categories according to the extent to which conflict resolution expertise is represented and reasoned with explicitly using formalisms as robust as those used for other kinds of problem-solving expertise. "Development-Time Conflict Resolution" (compiling potential conflicts out by exhaustive discussions during knowledge base development) is used with almost all expert systems currently. "Knowledge-Poor Run-Time Conflict Resolution" systems (e.g. [24], [35], [11], [10], [6]) allow conflicts to be asserted and resolved as the system runs. These approaches incorporate little CR expertise and use restrictive formalisms to represent it. "General Conflict Resolution" systems come closest to providing conflict resolution expertise with first-class status, and include implemented systems (e.g. [36], [13]) as well as unimplemented proposals (e.g. [14], [40]). None of this work, however, constitutes a comprehensive computational model of conflict resolution for cooperative group design.

In general, work on conflict resolution has evolved towards making CR expertise more explicit and using it to support cooperative problem solving. The LAN Designer system is the first system, however, to provide first-class knowledge-intensive support for conflict resolution in cooperative group design contexts. How this system does so is described in the sections below.

The Existence of General Heuristic CR Expertise

The instances of conflict resolution identified in the Architecture and LAN domains were analyzed, to see if we could extract any general principles of how the CR process works. It was found that CR suggestions can be viewed as instantiations of domain-independent general strategies such as the following:

1) **If** two plans for achieving two different agents' goals conflict
   Then find an alternate way of achieving one goal that does not conflict with the other agent's plan for achieving its goal

2) **If** excessive summer insolation through south-facing windows is a concern
   Then provide overhangs to block the sun

3) **If** propagation of some unwanted entity over a shared conduit is a concern
   Then add a filter to the conduit to reduce or eliminate the propagation of that entity

Such general conflict resolution expertise can be expressed in a way specific at most to *classes* of conflicts. Strategy 1, for example, applies to any conflict where the design agents involved have alternate plans for achieving their design goals. Strategy 3 applies to any conflict where a design component that can be abstractly viewed as a conduit currently allows propagation of some undesired but filterable entity. This CR expertise is also largely *heuristic* [14], so we must be able to respond appropriately if CR advice fails.

The implication of these insights is simple: rather than building design agents that inextricably mix CR and design domain expertise in their knowledge bases, it makes more sense to separate these into design and CR components with distinct roles. If we do so, individual design agents do not have anticipate and avoid conflicts with all other potentially relevant design agents. They can focus solely on representing their own concerns as ably as possible, relying on the conflict resolution mechanism to handle disagreements with other design agents as they occur (i.e. at run-time).The division of labour allows a relatively compact corpus of general CR expertise to be applied to a wide variety of design conflicts. The CR expertise can be augmented or changed easily at any time without requiring coordinated changes in the domain expertise of all potentially affected design agents. Existing design systems, for the most part, conflate design and CR expertise (e.g. [12], [24], [6]). Approaches that use distinct CR expertise also exist (e.g. [36], [13]), but suffer from a number of important limitations including trying to encode fundamentally heuristic CR expertise in deductive or domain-idiosyncratic form and using little actual CR expertise.

Our insights into cooperative group design were elaborated into a computational model implemented in the LAN Designer system [20]. In this model, general CR expertise is instantiated, via interaction with domain-level design expertise, to produce specific suggestions for resolving a given conflict. The CR expertise currently included covers a wide range of conflict types, oriented mainly towards design of artifacts for managing and transporting resources (such as data on a Local Area Network). Conflict classes for dealing with failed conflict resolution advice are also included. Note that the LAN Designer effectively resolves LAN domain conflicts using *no* domain-specific CR expertise.

A Design Model That Supports Conflict Management

A cooperative group design system that supports conflict resolution should, ideally, provide support for all aspects of conflict management, including avoiding unnecessary conflicts, detecting them when they do occur and facilitating the conflict resolution process. The LAN Designer system is based on a model of the design process that synthesizes existing work with novel notions regarding conflict detection, and was designed to effectively support conflict management [18]. This model is described below.

The LAN Designer uses a *routine least-commitment refine-and-evaluate* design model. Design tasks can be divided into several categories according to the innate difficulty of the task [5], ranging from "routine" design (where the components and plans for combining them are known) to "innovative" design (where neither components nor plans are available). To date, only routine design models have been implemented with any success for real-world design problems (e.g. R1 [25], VT [24], AIR-CYL [6] and PRIDE [27]). Fortunately, many important real-world design tasks fall into this category [5].

The LAN Designer uses a *least-commitment* [35] design model. All designed artifacts are represented as collections of known components each with characteristic features, connected to each other via a defined set of interfaces with known properties. Components may provide as well as use up different kinds of resources. Agents describe design additions and critiques using a language that allows indefinite commitments. Such committments can include constraints on the component's *class* (selected from an abstraction hierarchy of component types) and *features* (expressed using a constraint language [37]). The least commitment approach (also known as the Refinement plus Constraint Propagation approach) has been used successfully in a wide range of domains including design of VLSI circuits ([26], [38]) genetics experiments [35], alloys [30], buildings ([34], [7]) single-board computers [4] and V-belts [15].

Note that the least-commitment approach supports conflict avoidance. Since the designer is not forced to arbitrarily choose from a set of acceptable alternatives simply to make a definite commitment, conflicts from that kind of arbitrary choice can be avoided.

The "refine" part of the design process begins by asserting a set of abstract specifications (i.e. an indefinite description of the desired design) which the design agents then refine by posting increasingly specific constraints until eventually they describe a set of definitely-defined available components. This can involve either configuring the component by constraining the value of its features, allocating resources, connecting the interfaces of two components as well as specializing or decomposing a component/connection into sub-component/connection(s). This entire process is goal-driven; creating a component automatically leads to the instantiation of the goal to refine the component; these goals trigger design plans that execute refinement actions and create subgoals.

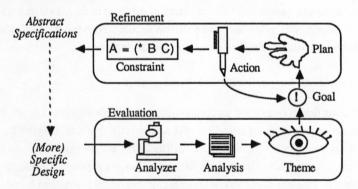

Figure 3: LAN Designer's Hypothesis and Test Cycle

The "evaluate" part of the design process allows design agents to continually check the viability of the current design state. Entities known as "themes" look (with the help of "analyzers" that produce design state analyses) for problems or fortuitous opportunities and create goals accordingly (Figure 3).

Goals trigger plans that create goals or execute actions that in turn add constraints to the design, making it more specific. The design state is monitored by themes, aided by analyzers; the themes create new goals as appropriate. Meta-level reasoning (i.e. reasoning about the state of the *designer* as opposed to the state of the *design*) also uses this model [40]. Note that this approach allows us to maintain the rationale for design decisions in terms of design goals, the themes that create them and the plans that attempt to achieve them.The importance of design rationale will be explored further below. Variants of this refine/evaluate approach have been used successfully in a large variety of domains (e.g. [40], [39], [31], [8]).

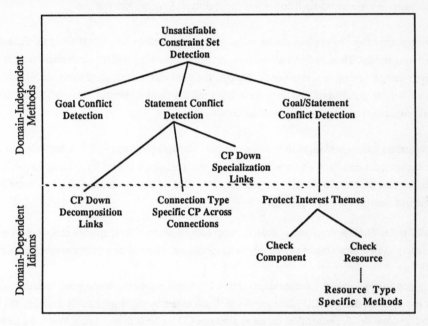

Figure 4: Conflict Detection Tools Provided by LAN Designer

The LAN Designer design model supports conflict detection (CD). In general, when different agents give incompatible specifications for a given design component, or one agent has a negative critique of specifications asserted by another agent, we can say that a conflict has occurred. Some design conflicts can be detected in a domain-dependent fashion. Design experts have in addition a lot of domain-specific expertise concerning the kinds of design situations that represent problems from their particular perspectives. Support for conflict detection thus requires providing both a complete domain-independent conflict detection mechanism as well as making it easy for domain experts to express their domain-dependent conflict detection expertise (Figure 4).

Domain-Independent Methods: In a least-commitment model such as that used in the LAN Designer, all conflicts eventually manifest as unsatisfiable constraint sets on a given design parameter. Underlying all CD methods, therefore, is an unsatisfiable constraint set detection mechanism. This is implemented as constraint combination (i.e. simplifying constraint sets by finding their consequences) coupled with detection of individual unsatisfiable constraints. Conflicts can be detected while the design is still indefinitely described, thus avoiding investing design effort uselessly on inconsistent designs.

Built on top of this is support for detecting conflicts between the two kinds of assertions made by design agents: constraints on component features ("statements") and goals. The LAN Designer's design model uses three types of goals: refine-component (the goal to refine an indefinitely described component), constrain-value (the goal to constrain a given component feature), and achieve-value (the goal to achieve a given value for a given component feature). There are thus three kinds of conflicts at this level: conflicts between achieve-value goals (inconsistent desired constraints on a component feature), conflicts between statements (inconsistent constraints on a component feature), and conflicts between achieve-value goals and statements (inconsistent desired and actual constraints on a component feature).

Constraints asserted by design plans can be propagated through design description along the different links created during design. Thus, to find the complete set of constraints on a given component feature implied by a given design description, one needs to union the constraints asserted directly on the component feature with those constraints that propagate from related design features. The following link types propagate constraints in a domain-independent fashion:

- *configuration links:* Configuration links inter-relate component features within or between components. For example, the constraint on the voltage drop across a resistor is related by a configuration link to the constraint on the current through the resistor. This kind of link is used in design systems based on constraint networks (e.g. [37], [24]).

- *specialization links:* Specialization links connect components and their specializations. All constraints that apply to an abstract component apply to its specialization, so all constraints are propagated down.

Domain-Dependent Idioms: Domain-dependent CD idioms represent stereotyped techniques domain experts use to check designs. CD idioms make their job easier by requiring merely that they fill in some domain-dependent details, rather than create appropriate CD methods from scratch. While the idioms used probably vary somewhat from domain to domain, we suspect that at least some idioms are likely to have wide applicability. As a result, a library of such idioms may prove useful. The CD idioms found useful in the LAN design system are described below:

- *propagation across connection links:* Connection links connect the interfaces of components to each other. The constraints that propagate through a connection depend on the kind of connection. An electrical connection, for example, propagates constraints on voltage and current. The LAN Designer includes a hierarchy of connection types along with a description of what constraints propagate through each type. The knowledge engineer can use an existing connection type or define a new one as a refinement of an existing type.

- *propagation down decomposition links:* One can often use the mapping between abstract and more specific connections to simplify describing this kind of propagation. For example, an abstract LAN trunk component is usually connected to abstract LAN trunk connector components. When the abstract LAN Trunk is refined to a particular trunk technology, the constraints that propagate over connections to the abstract component's interfaces also apply to the corresponding connections in the specific Trunk instance. This is called "Structural" knowledge in MICON [4].

• *protect interests themes:* Protect interests themes monitor the current design state for a state threatening to the interests of a design agent, and make assertions that lead to a conflict being asserted if a threatening design state should ever come to pass. A protect-interest theme works by creating two new goals: (1) an achieve-value goal that must be satisfied for interest to be safe, and (2) a constrain-value goal to find whether the design state satisfies the achieve-value goal. We have identified two kinds of useful protect-interest CD idioms to date: *check-component* and *check-resource*. The former kind of idiom checks that interests relating to individual components are satisfied, while the latter looks for situations where some kind of resource budget is exceeded. Resource over-utilization, however, is detected differently depending on the kind of resource involved. The LAN Designer supports this by maintaining a taxonomy of the different abstract types of resources and associating resource over-utilization detection templates with each type.

The methods described above represent a superset of the conflict detection methods utilized in the other approaches to conflict management (e.g. those incorporated in TROPIC, VT, AIR-CYL, MOLGEN or BARGAINER), and provide a complete set of basic mechanisms for conflict detection given the nature of the cooperative group design model used in the LAN Designer. The notion of an abstract resource-type hierarchy has been previously discussed in [40] as has the conflict-detection advantages of using a least-commitment design model [35]. Previous work has not discussed, however, the use of domain-independent connection-type and resource hierarchies to support conflict detection, nor the notion of instantiable CD idioms.

Improved Design Agent Models

The demands of cooperative group design imply the need for improved computational models for how individual design agents work, so we can build machine-based design agents that effectively cooperate with each other. We have identified four major challenges for such improved design agent models:

• *Representing Design Rationale:* We have found that design agents must be able to answer questions concerning the reasoning underlying a conflict (i.e. the design *rationale*) to effectively find applicable strategies. The LAN Designer represents the rationale for domain and meta-level (i.e. control and conflict resolution) decisions using the meta-planning formalism described above, coupled with typing of resources, interfaces, components and component features. See [3] and [17] for related work.

• *Flexible Redesign:* Once the CR component of a design agent has produced a suggestion for resolving a conflict, the domain component has to be able to respond to this suggestion by producing a new, internally consistent design commitment that implements the suggestion. The language used to express CR suggestions has four primitives: try-deeper-model, try-new-plan-for-goal, modify-value and add-component. Try-new-plan-for-goal is implemented simply by running a different plan for a given triggering goal. Add-component suggestions are implemented by creating an add-component goal, which triggers a plan that changes the appropriate parameters to the refinement plan for the component to which another component is to be added. The other two CR primitives are currently handled in a domain-idiosyncratic way. Related work: [1], [6] [15], [28], [32].

- *Bidirectionality:* Due to the asynchronous and unpredictable nature of design assertions made by different agents in a cooperative group design context, individual design agents need to be able to both add commitments to as well as critique existing design commitments, which implies being able to use the same domain expertise in both directions. i.e. for both analysis *and* synthesis. The LAN Designer implements this by essentially duplicating versions of the same expertise as design plans (for commitment-making) and themes (for design-state critiquing).

- *Analyzing Indefinite Descriptions:* Design agents should be able to operate on indefinite descriptions. While this is often fairly straightforward for the "hypothesize" part of the design cycle, the need to be able to *analyze* abstractly defined components during the "test" part of the design cycle represents a significant challenge. How can commonly-used analysis techniques such as finite-element analysis, for example, be applied to indefinitely described designs, if at all? The LAN Designer currently uses domain-idiosyncratic techniques for this problem.

These challenges imply a central role for design plans in the design process. In the LAN Designer, plans represents the smallest unit that the CR component asks questions about. Plans are also the smallest unit that can make consistent additions to the design, and should be able to change in response to suggestions to produce different self-consistent design additions. This suggests, in general, that plans take on a rich internal structure, acting more as primitive "agents within agents" rather than simple static structures [5].

Conclusions

Our experience with implementing the LAN Designer system for cooperative group design of local area networks has led to a number of insights into how cooperative group design systems can be structured to effectively support this process. Support for conflict management appears to be critical for real-world cooperative design; general conflict detection and resolution heuristics can effectively support this; and future progress in supporting cooperative design requires design models that support self-understanding (i.e. rich design rationale) and self-modifiability (i.e. a powerful replanning facility) as well as the ability to analyze and critique indefinitely described designs. The LAN Designer system is an instantiation of a generic cooperative group design support shell we have developed. We are currently extending this shell to support the interaction of both human and machine-based design agents, and to learn from the process of doing so. We plan to instantiate the shell in a number of different cooperative design and planning domains in order to evaluate and enhance its effectiveness and breadth of applicability.

References

[1] Acosta, R.D., Huhns, M.N., and Liuh, S.L. Analogical Reasoning for Digital System Synthesis. In *Proceedings ICED,* IEEE, November 1986, Pps. 173-176.

[2] Balzer, R., Erman, L., London, P., and Williams, C. Hearsay-II: A Domain-Independent Framework For Expert Systems. *Proceedings of the First Annual National Conference on AI* (August 1980) Pps. 108-110.

[3] Batali, J. Dependency Maintenance In The Design Process. *IEEE Int Conf Computer Design: VLSI in Computers* (1983) Pps. 459-462.

[4] Birmingham, W.P. and Siewiorek, D.P. Automated Knowledge Acquisition for a Computer Hardware Synthesis System. *Knowledge Acquisition 1*(1989) Pps. 321-340.

[5] Brown, D.C. and Chandrasekaran, B. Expert Systems For A Class Of Mechanical Design Activity. *Proc of IFIP WG5.2 Working Conference on Knowledge Representation in Computer Aided Design* (Sept 1984).

[6] Brown, D.C. *Failure Handling In A Design Expert System*, Butterworth and Co. (November 1985).

[7] Chan, W.T. and Paulson, B.C. Exploratory Design Using Constraints. *AI EDAM 1*, 1 (1987) Pps. 59-71.

[8] Chapman, D. Planning For Conjunctive Goals. Tech. Report Massachusetts Institute of Technology, May 1985.

[9] Coombs, C.H. and Avrunin, G.S. *The Structure of Conflict*, Lawrence Erlbaum Associates (1988).

[10] Descotte, Y. and Latombe, J.C. Making Compromises Among Antagonist Constraints In A Planner. *Artificial Intelligence 27*(1985) Pps. 183-217.

[11] Fox, M.S., Allen, B., and Strohm, G. Job-Shop Scheduling: An Investigation In Constraint-Directed Reasoning. *AAAI-82* (1982) Pps. 155-158.

[12] Fox, M.S. and Smith, S.F. Isis - A Knowledge-Based System For Factory Scheduling. *Expert Systems* (July 1984).

[13] Goldstein, I.P. Bargaining Between Goals. Tech. Report Massachusetts Institute of Technology Artificial Intelligence Laboratory, 1975.

[14] Hewitt, C. Offices Are Open Systems. *ACM Transactions on Office Information Systems 4*, 3 (July 1986) Pps. 271-287.

[15] Howard, A.E., Cohen, P.R., Dixon, J.R., and Simmons, M.K. Dominic: A Domain-Independent Program For Mechanical Engineering Design. *Artificial Intelligence 1*, 1 (1986) Pps. 23-28.

[16] Johansen, J., Vallee, V., and Springer, S. *Electronic Meetings: Technical Alternatives and Social Choices*, Addison-Wesley (1979).

[17] Kellog, C., Jr., R.A.G., Mark, W., McGuire, J.G., Pontecorvo, M., Sclossberg, J.L., and , J.W.S. The Acquisition, Verification and Explanation of Design Knowledge. *SIGART Newsletter*, 108 (April 1989) Pps. 163-165.

[18] Klein, M. *Conflict Resolution in Cooperative Design*, Ph.D. dissertation, University of Illinois at Urbana-Champaign, January 1990.

[19] Klein, M. and Lu, S.C.Y. Conflict Resolution in Cooperative Design. *International Journal for Artificial Intelligence in Engineering* (1990).

[20] Klein, M. A Computational Model of Conflict Resolution in Integrated Design. In *Proceedings of the ASME Symposium on Integrated Product Design and Manufacturing*, November 1990.

[21] Lenat, D.B. Beings: Knowledge As Interacting Experts. *IJCAI-75* (September 1975) Pps. 126-133.

[22] Lu, S.C.Y., Subramanyam, S., Thompson, J.B., and Klein, M. A Cooperative Product Development Environment To Realize The Simultaneous Engineering Concept. In *Proceedings of the 1989 ASME Computers in Engineering Conference*, Anaheim, CA, July 1989.

[23] Malone, T.W., Fikes, R.E., and Howard, M.T. Enterprise: A Market-Like Task Scheduler For Distributed Computing Environments. Tech. Report Cognitive and Instructional Sciences Group, Xerox Palo Alto Research Center, October 1983.

[24] Marcus, S., Stout, J., and McDermott, J. VT: An Expert Elevator Designer. *Artificial Intelligence Magazine 8*, 4 (Winter 1987) Pps. 39-58.

[25] Mcdermott, J. R1: A Rule-Based Configurer Of Computer Systems. *Artificial Intelligence 19*(1982) Pps. 39-88.

[26] Mitchell, T.M., Mahadevan, S., and Steinberg, L.I. LEAP: A Learning Apprentice For VLSI Design. In *Proceedings of .IJCAI*, IJCAI, 1985, Pps. 573-580.

[27] Mittal, S. and Araya, A. A Knowledge-Based Framework For Design. *AAAI 2*(1986) Pps. 856-865.

[28] Mostow, J. and Barley, M. Automated Reuse of Design Plans. In *Proceedings ICED*, IEEE, August 1987, Pps. 632-647.

[29] Nunamaker, J.F., Applegate, A., and Konsynski, K. Facilitating Group Creativity: Experience with a Group Decision Support System. In *Proceedings of the Twentieth Hawaii International Conference on System Sciences*, 1987, Pps. 422-430.

[30] Rychener, M.D., Farinacci, M.L., Hulthage, I., and Fox, M.S. Integration Of Multiple Knowledge Sources In Aladin, An Alloy Design System. *AAAI 2*(1986) Pps. 878-882.

[31] Schank, R.C. and Abelson, R.P. *Scripts, Plans, Goals And Understanding*, Lawrence Erlbaum Associates (1977).

[32] Simoudis, E. Learning Redesign Knowledge. In *Banff Knowledge Acquisition for Knowledge-Based Systems Workshop*, AAAI, November 1988.

[33] Smith, R.G. and Davis, R. Cooperation In Distributed Problem Solving. *IEEE Proceedings of the International Conference on Cybernetics and Society* (1979) Pps. 366-371.

[34] Sriram, D. All-Rise: A Case Study Of Constraint-Based Design. *Artificial Intelligence in Engineering 2*, 4 (1987) Pps. 186-203.

[35] Stefik, M.J. Planning With Constraints (Molgen: Part 1 & 2). *Artificial Intelligence 16*, 2 (1981) Pps. 111-170.

[36] Sussman, G.J. A Computational Model Of Skill Acquistion. Tech. Report PhD Thesis. AI Lab, MIT, 1973., 1973.

[37] Sussman, G.J. and Steele, G.L. Constraints - A Language For Expressing Almost-Hierachical Descriptions. *Artificial Intelligence 14*(1980) Pps. 1-40.

[38] Tong, C. Ai In Engineering Design. *Artificial Intelligence in Engineering 2*, 3 (1987) Pps. 130-166.

[39] Wilensky, R. Meta-Planning. *AAAI* (1980) Pps. 334-336.

[40] Wilensky, R. *Planning And Understanding*, Addison-Wesley (1983).

Direct interaction among active data structures: a tool for building AI systems[*]

F. Abbruzzese, and E. Minicozzi
Dipartimento di Scienze Fisiche, Università di Napoli "Federico II", Mostra
d'Oltremare Padiglione 19 I-80125, Napoli. Ph. -39-81-7253410; Fax. -39-81-
614508; e-mail ELIMI@NAPOLI.INFN.IT.BITNET

Summary.
A model of computation and a specific language embodying it are presented. Both are
called ALM and are inspired by a physical metaphor. In ALM computation is carried
on by independent interacting active data structures called active entities. Active
entities, like physical particles, interact with "fields" created by other active entities
and eventually "collide". Field interactions and collisions are achieved by means of
both an Influence and a Filter; the former is the external display of an active entity
internal structure, and the later represents the influences an active entity is sensitive
to. These interactions strongly affect the active entities structure. Due to them, an
active entity "feels" the world in which it is, and of which it has no knowledge. Active
entities evolve following their own prescriptions and then die leaving their sons in
their place. Alm entities and their features are proposed as building blocks for
constructing reliable artificial intelligence systems whose main characteristics are
parallelism, massive distribution of control, maximum availability of distributed
knowledge, robustness with respect to changes in their environment, and capability to
accommodate unscheduled events. Maximum knowledge availability is achieved by
"fields", while "collisions", being a powerful synchronization mechanism, allow
entities to reach any kind of agreement. Examples are given to show how ALM works
with AI problems. Finally, ALM is compared with message-passing and shared
memory systems.
Keywords: Parallel languages, Distribution of control, Architectures, Changing
environment, Artificial Intelligence, Spontaneous Cooperation, Communication
primitives.
Scientific Area: Architectures, Languages and Environments.

1. Introduction.

The complexity of problems that AI is faced with asks more and more for parallel
architectures. Besides, a massive distribution of control is also required to allow the
heterogeneous processing of big amounts of heterogeneous data. Moreover, advanced
AI applications have to deal with quick changing environments and unscheduled

---

[*] Work supported in part by progetto finalizzato 4 C.N.R. 90.00406.PF67.

inputs. Therefore, AI systems have to exhibit robustness with respect to their conditions of operation and adaptability to the external environment. To meet the above needs, new architectures based on independent cooperating agents have been conceived [3, 4, 6, 10, 11, 12, 13]. ALM must be seen in this context. It is a new paradigm, inspired by a physical metaphor. Here agents, like particles, interact with "fields" created by other agents and eventually "collide". While "fields" ensure mainly maximum knowledge availability, "collisions" warrant synchronization. In ALM paradigm agents are active data structures called active entities and both "fields" and "collisions" are due to an Influence attached to each of them. ALM paradigm and the relative ALM language are exhaustively discussed in [1]. Here, we are mainly concerned with those ALM features relevant to AI. In the next paragraph we summarize ALM paradigm and we sketch ALM language. More details on the language may be found in the appendix.

2. Overview of ALM.

2.1. Interaction among active entities.
As we already stated, the ingredients which ALM relies on are active entities and influences. Active entities are completely autonomous chunks of knowledge that affect each other by means of their influences. Inside them they have no explicit reference to other entities, so denotation, as defined by Newell in [14], is not achieved any more by using names but by using compatibility constraints. Such compatibility constraints are encoded into a boundary which both defines the influence associated to its entity and specifies the influences which the entity is sensitive to. More precisely, the component of the boundary defining the Influence is called Influencer, while the component of the boundary defining the influences that can affect the entity is called Filter. An Influence compatible with a given Filter may "pass through" the boundary thus modifying the structure of the concerned entity. An interaction may be either symmetric or asymmetric depending on the Influencers of the involved entities. A symmetric Influencer constrains the interaction to be two-way, that is, the concerned active entity must be simultaneously influenced by the entity it affects. In this way, two entities hit each other as in a collision between physical particles. Asymmetric Influencers have no similar constraints, so they can affect simultaneously several entities. Therefore, asymmetric influence like a physical "field" creates a context that is perceived by all entities sensitive to it. Both Influencer and Filter are represented by attribute-value pairs. Each Filter is composed by many Simple-filters. For an Influencer to be compatible with a Filter it is required that it matches at least one Simple-filter. Such match occurs if each attribute-value pairs of the Simple-filter matches a corresponding attribute-value pair in the Influencer. As a consequence of the match some unbound values of the Filter become bounded. Since attributes stand for "places" within the entities, the internal structure of entities may considerably change because of the perceived influence. Entities may affect each other only if they belong to the same Computational Island. Computational Islands, which are denoted by sequences of attribute-value pairs, were conceived to "detach" groups of tightly interacting entities from the remainder of the system, and to protect them from undesired interactions. Whether an entity is influenced or there is no influence compatible with its Filter, the entity evolves following its own prescriptions. The final

act of an entity evolution is always its death, and the possible creation of new entities. The lenght of the evolution of each entity, while limited is not a-priori determined, due to the complex nature of the entities creation mechanism. Then, due to efficiency considerations and ALM philosophy, entities can not be constrained to simultaneously update. Briefly, entities, once created, influence other entities, are influenced by other ones, and finally die leaving their sons in their place.

When an entity Filter is compatible with more influences, only one is chosen in a not deterministic fashion. No priority mechanism is provided, but it can be easily implemented using the entity evolution. Priority gives entities the capability to accept "interrupts" effectively responding to unscheduled events and changes.

Graphical pictures of interactions among active entities and related evolutions are shown in Fig. 1. There, circles, continuous arrows, dashed arrows, dotted arrows and splitting arrows represent respectively active entities, influences, evolutions caused by influences, free evolutions (evolutions that aren't caused by influences), and evolutions yielding many entities.

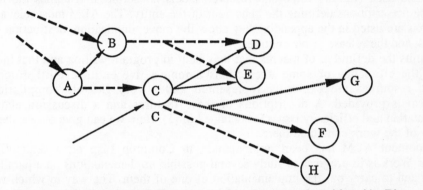

Because of symmetric influence two newly created entities (A, B) evolve respectively into one entity and into two entities. While the first (C) may create either two entities (F,G) via free evolution or one entity (H) if it is influenced, the last two (D, E) die because of asymmetric influence.

Fig. 1 Evolutions of interacting active entities

2.2. The structure of active entities.

The evolution of each entity is an "editing" of its internal structure; parts of the entity are moved, duplicated or destroyed, to yield new entities. The building blocks that compose the parts of an ALM entity are data structures called named-lists. Informally, a named-list is a usual list with a label attached to it; it is written: [list-name (el1, el2,..., eln)]. Each element of a named-list may be, in turn, a named-list; the whole active entity itself is a named-list. By means of named-lists the structure of an ALM entity is hierarchically decomposed into parts having names that allow their manipulation during the "editing" process.

In the hierarchy of parts that characterizes each active entity, places are denoted by paths from the root of the entity. In turn, paths are specified by sequences of list-names and integers representing positions within lists. Such sequences are not required to contain all labels, or all positions along the denoted path, but only the ones needed to identify it unambiguously. A typical denotation is self->my_part->my_subpart->1. There, the denoted element is the first one in the list named my_subpart which is a subpart of the list named my_part; the whole entity is denoted by the label self. Several denotation macros allow the use of default paths which could be linked to simpler denotations. The described denotation mechanism is very flexible and has proved to be very useful for handling partially unknown structures.

Summing up, an ALM entity is just a tree with labels on some of its nodes. New subtrees may be added to it because of perceived influences, while its evolution causes it to be substituted by new trees obtained as result of an editing process. As a consequence, both an ALM program, and an ALM state of the computation are a forest of labelled trees.

All entities contain some reserved labels. One of them is "boundary" that names the list containing the definition of the entity boundary. Attributes in this list specify named-lists within the entity, while their values are represented by the contents of these named-lists. Another important reserved labels is "script" that names the list containing prescriptions defining the behaviour of the entity. The ALM most relevant instructions are listed in the appendix, they allow the move, duplication, destruction of structures, and the release of new entities.

ALM admits the definition of macros that may help in program writing and that may increase the efficiency of some interactions among active entities. Furthermore, hardware resources are explicitly represented and a very flexible compilation mechanism is provided. A descriptions of these features and a discussion about implementation and efficiency issues is contained in [1]. Here we can give only a short summary of the work contained there.

At the moment ALM has been implemented in Common Lisp on a sequential computer. Work is in progress to study several possible implementations on a parallel machine, and to carry out the implementation of one of them. The way in which we describe an architecture adequate for an ALM system is based on two key concepts, the Node and the Group. The Node is the finest hardware resource ALM is able to discriminate, it represents a place where one or more entities may be allocated. Many Nodes are aggregate into a Group which is the place where a Computational Islands may be allocated. Groups, that are temporary structures, are assembled by Group Headers that are permanent structures. Each Group Header has access to several Nodes; when it is requested to allocate a Computational Island it arranges adequately some of them. In general, a Node may fall under the range of action of many Group Headers. Connections among Nodes and Group Headers depend strictly on the implementation and are no way accessible to the ALM system. In addition to the allocation of Computational Islands, Group Headers perform the control and accounting of hardware resources utilization.

Interactions among Nodes mainly rely on buses. The choice of a bus to transmit on or to listen to is done by first, considering the Computational Island, second, hashing adequately the entity Boundary, last, looking at the free buses corresponding to the computed hashes. To reduce conflicts buses, on which communication among Nodes of the same Group takes place, have to be private resources of that Group.

Interactions among entities are verified as soon as they are created. While arbitrations to choose just one asymmetric Influence among the ones compatible with an entity Filter may be performed locally on the Node that hosts the concerned entity, arbitrations involving symmetric Influences that are requested to be two-way need to be global. However, a centralized arbiter would be a bottleneck and would cause unacceptable inefficiencies, so we have conceived a distributed global arbiter, whose description is given in [1].

3. ALM in Artificial Intelligence applications.

3.1. Most relevant features.
In all languages we know of, it is possible to dynamically classify the various "ingredients" involved in the computation as passive or active; the only kind of interaction that is permitted consists in active ingredients acting upon passive ones. On the contrary, ALM entities are always active, they simultaneously act and are acted upon by other entities. In particular, in interactions due to symmetric influence two entities reciprocally modify each other; so each of them accomplishes simultaneously a transmission and a reception act.

In ALM the computation results from the spontaneous cooperation of active entities that "feel" the context they are in, and behave accordingly. This gives to the system a self-organizing capability that results in a great flexibility.

Entities share no structure among them, and no pointers to external places exist. These last assertions together with the capability of ALM entities to "ingest" parts of other entities and to evolve consequently make ALM well suited for quick changing environments.

All ALM features we mentioned, furnish adequate building blocks for the construction of Artificial Intelligence systems based on the new principles needed to overcome the limits of current applications; some of these principles were discussed by Hewitt in [10]. In particular ALM offers a great flexibility in knowledge accessibility. Indeed it achieves maximum knowledge availability by means of asymmetric influence and pattern-directed interaction while it restricts access to knowledge through both Computational Islands and the reciprocal catch caused by symmetric Influence.

Furthermore, ALM offers tools for dealing with problems affecting distributed control systems like those arising when several entities compete on shared resources. In ALM there is no master that can arbitrate such contentions, but symmetric influence can effectively solve them, since it immediately arbitrates competing "aggregations" of two entities and it is an effective building block for achieving the aggregation of more than two entities. The efficiency of the solutions to "aggregation" problems provided by symmetric influence is peculiar and can in no way be obtained with interactions based on message passing or shared memory. In fact, these latter require complex algorithms to prevent or to break deadlocks because they haven't an adequate synchronization power. Moreover, deadlock-free algorithms don't solve completely all problems connected to resource aggregation and mutual exclusion. In fact, partial aggregates may take resources apart, blocking other activities that need them, so that parallelism may suffer considerably. In [1], ALM solution to the "dining philosophers" problem [8], is compared with the ones of other languages and of paradigms such as Actors [2, 9], Linda, and Parlog86 [15]. ALM solution is the only one that warrant the maximum number of philosophers to eat simultaneously. This result is achieved by exploiting the possibility to aggregate resources offered by simmetric influence. Philosophers succeed in taking simultaneously both chopsticks they need, because chopsticks previously aggregate into couples. In this way, no philosopher unfruitfully subtracts a chopstick to another.

The aggregation of an arbitrary number of resources is a generalization of symmetric influence and it can be implemented with ALM primitives. From now on, we will handle aggregation as it were a primitive operation, and we'll graphically represent it with a star of arrows.

In the next paragraph we will sketch some applications of ALM features.

3.2. How all these things work.

Several entities may spontaneously interact trying to solve a specific task. We may represent the task, and all information defining the framework in which it is embedded, with influences that cause the "adequate entities" to interact for producing the right solution. The "adequate entities" are the ones sensitive to those influences that can give an useful contribution to the accomplishment of the task in the given framework. Unscheduled events may cause task and context updatings. As a consequence, new interactions may take place. An informal example may help to clarify the mentioned concepts. Let us suppose that a man is in a French restaurant with his girl-friend and that he wants to order lunch. Fig. 2 shows some relevant features that may characterize the framework in which such task has to be solved.

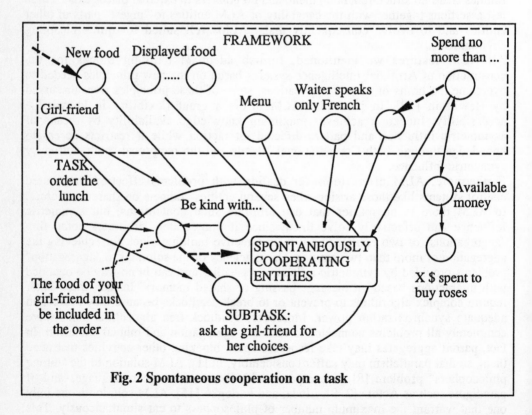

Fig. 2 Spontaneous cooperation on a task

Asymmetric influences of both the task, and the framework cause some active entities to spontaneously cooperate in order to accomplish the task. Because of the simultaneous presence of the task and the girl-friend, the subtask of asking the girl for her choices is created. The menu, and the displayed food influence the choice; while both the fact that the waiter only speaks french and the limited availability of money put constraints on the possible orders. Suddenly, a man selling flowers enters the restaurant enticing our man to buy roses for his girl-friend. This event causes the framework to update because of some changes in the amount of available money. The solution that was going to be built "feels" these changes and evolves in a different way. Some already created entities may become obsolete and either update themselves or die, while others take their place. Something similar takes place if a new food is displayed or other unscheduled inputs occur.

In ALM we can also have groups of entities working on different tasks that may cooperate by using each other results. In fact, both persistence and pattern-directed interaction of influence ensure that once a result is found, it can always be used by whatever entity might need it. Such kind of cross-cooperation could be very useful in graph-search. Here, direct interaction among nodes may allow the expansion of just one of a group of "equivalent" nodes. Furthermore, nodes may use heuristics gathered by other nodes, and may delegate the exploration of the situations they represent to groups of nodes "similar" to them that is to nodes sharing specific features with them. For instance, in a chess-game program, the possibility of "opening a column" may be explored by just one of many similar nodes and the sharing of some features may be recognized using compatibility between Filters and Influencers. Moreover, we can avoid to explore exhaustively a position by recognizing, via influence, that all moves that are relevant in that situation are being explored by similar nodes. Thus, it is enough to collect the results when they are found, and to analyze them if it is the case.

All the forms of croos-cooperation we have discussed can be easily accomplished due to the direct cooperation among data. It's worthwhile to point out that an interaction among data that is mediated by rules cannot substitute direct interaction, because it would require a prohibitive number of rules to take into account all possible couplings of data. In fact, while the situations described by the active entity boundaries are discovered during the computation, all prototypal situations must be encoded in the rules. Moreover, if several rules were activated in parallel, contentions on the same data may cause them to block partially filled, so harmful "wait for" situations might occur. Finally, rules are bottlenecks that data must pass through, and they impose constraints both on the representation of data and on the flow of control.

Direct interaction among data may be very useful in interpretation problems such those arising in Image Understanding and Natural Language Understanding. In fact, symmetric influence may be used to make lower level features to aggregate to yield higher level ones. Moreover, contextual information and "a priori knowledge" may asymmetrically influence all entities involved in the computation circumscribing the search-space. For instance, in the case of Natural Language Understanding, words may couple because of symmetric influence. Instead, contextual information coming from already analyzed phrases may provide, through asymmetric influence, both heuristics to select useful aggregations and constraints to possible word meanings and syntactic patterns.

If one needs to try alternative interpretations, one can introduce "justifications" and "worlds". In this way it is possible to implement in ALM an ATMS-like [6, 7] dependency directed backtracking. All promising alternatives can be explored in parallel, creating an adequate number of copies of the involved entities, and allocating, for each of them, by means of a symmetric interaction a new assumption from an assumption database. In case of failure, direct interactions among "justifications" and "failure reports" may yield other alternatives.

3.3. Comparison with message-passing and shared memory systems.

At this point it is worthwhile to make a short comparison among ALM and both message-passing and shared-memory systems. In fact, ALM includes and improves all their peculiarities. On the one hand asymmetric influence warrants the kind of knowledge availability that is typical of shared memory-system with pattern-directed access, such as Blackboard systems and Linda, on the other symmetric influence achieves a private communication like the one given by message-passing systems.

Neither message-passing nor shared memory systems have the synchronization power provided by ALM symmetric influence. In them, contention and agreement problems may lead to harmful "wait for" situations. In Actors [2, 9], it is proposed to "help" a busy agent with a replacement that, among other things, may solve "wait for" conditions. In this way, deadlocks may be prevented or broken, but slowdowns caused by "wait for" conditions aren't avoided.

Moreover, most of message-passing systems rely on names to identify interlocutors, so they haven't the flexibility of ALM pattern-directed communication. Negotiation [5, 16] overcomes this problem using task announcement to select appropriate interlocutors, but here, only a master-server organization is allowed.

Furthermore, messages have to be sent to already existing targets, while influence is always available. Shared-memory systems with pattern-directed access overcome this problem, but don't deal effectively with contentions of several agents on data. Linda proposes some synchronization primitives, but they haven't the same power of ALM symmetric influence because data are passive and cannot directly interact. Moreover, passivity of data doesn't allow the autonomous updating that is one of the peculiarities of ALM.

Finally, ALM entities, unlike Actors and Linda, have the capability of bulding new living structures by editing their structure rather than using predefined prototypes.

4. Conclusions.

At a first glance, ALM philosophy may appear somehow unusual. A look to an ALM environment would show entities committed to incorporate pieces of other entities and to edit their own structure, while spreading their characteristics all over. Some of them die, some others are created, while others spontaneously group together. Nothing controls their behaviour because it depends only on their internal structure.

How may ALM entities accomplish activities that require organization, coordination, planning etc.? We suggest that similar questions arise each time a parallel architecture characterized by a massive distribution of control is proposed for the implementation of "intelligent" behaviour. However, in ALM the things are a bit worse, in that active entities have neither pointers to the external environment, nor masters orchestrating their independent behaviour. On the other hand, the above mentioned characteristics make ALM well suited for complex and quick changing environments. Here, both adaptability and self-updating capability prove to be more effective than an a priori knowledge. In fact, the use of pointers in unstable and intricate situations may result in unpleasant surprises, while masters lead to bottlenecks and lack of flexibility.

ALM interaction capabilities are then the result of our attempt to answer the question just posed. In fact, while influences achieve maximum knowledge availability, Filters constrain the interacting possibility of an ALM entity, warranting coherence of the overall behaviour. Moreover, active entities administrate their influences keeping up-to-date the knowledge encoded in them. Furthermore, symmetric influence is a powerful synchronization mechanism. Spontaneous cooperation, aggregation and solution to resource contentions and agreement problems, all rely on this useful primitive. Last but not least, Computational Islands protect group of active entities from unwanted interactions, creating in this way private environments.

Appendix.

Fundamental ALM instructions.

(Copy <named-list>) *It returns a copy of its argument.*

(Move <named-list> <TOP or BOTTOM> <denotation>) *It removes the named-list passed as its first argument and adds it to the beginning or to the end of the named-list denoted by its third argument. If the third argument is an empty list, the first argument is removed and returned as value.*

(Create <identifier> [<integer>]) *It returns a new empty named-list whose label is its unique argument. The optional integer specifies the number of element that are likely to be inserted into the named-list.*

(label <named-list>) *It returns the label of its argument*

(Set <denotation> <named-list>) *It removes all elements of its second argument and replaces with them all elements of the named-list denoted by its first arguments.*

(Quote <instruction, macro, or denotation keyword> <named-list>*) *It quotes executable statements defined by its first argument. The successive named-lists are used as arguments of these statements.*

(Gensym) *It returns a new identifier. A total order relation, which is implementation dependent, is defined on identifiers.*

(Newentity <named-list> [<list of attribute-value pairs>]) *It removes its argument and turns it into a new entity. The second argument is optional and specifies hereditary attribute-value pairs.*

(Seq <instruction>*) *It executes all instructions passed as arguments.*

(if <condition> <then-instruction> <else-instruction>) *If <condition> evaluates to the identifier "TRUE" the then-instruction is executed, otherwise the else-instruction is executed. Conditions may involve the usual order and equality predicates and the OR, AND, and NOT logical operators.*

Usual mathematical and string manipulation instructions are included, but will not be listed here.

References.

[1] F. Abbruzzese and E. Minicozzi, "ALM: A parallel language aimed at massive distribution of control", submitted for publication.

[2] G. A. Agha, *Actors: a model of concurrent computation in distributed systems*, The MIT press, Cambridge, 1981.

[3] N. Carriero and D. Gelernter, "Linda in context", *Communication ACM*, vol.32, pp. 444-458, April 1989.

[4] N. Carriero and D. Gelernter, "How to write parallel programs: a guide to perplexed", *ACM Computing Surveys* ,vol.21, pp. 323-357, Sept. 1989.

[5] R. Davis and R. G. Smith, "Negotiation as a metaphor for distributed problem solving", *Artificial Intelligence*, vol. 20, pp. 63-109, 1983.

[6] J. De Kleer, "An assumption-based TMS", *Artificial Intelligence*, vol. 28, pp. 127-162, 1986.

[7] J. De Kleer, "Extending the ATMS", *Artificial Intelligence*, vol. 28, pp. 163-1196, 1986.

[8] E.W. Dijkstra, "Hierarchical ordering of sequential processes", *Acta Inf.*, vol.1, pp. 115-138, 1971.

[9] C. Hewitt, "Viewing control structures as patterns of passing messages", *Artificial Intelligence*, vol. 8, pp. 323-364, 1977.

[10] C. Hewitt, "The challenge of Open Systems", *Byte*, vol. 10, pp. 223-242, April, 1985.

[11] B. Hayes-Roth, "A blackboard architecture for control", *Artificial Intelligence*, vol. 26, pp. 251-321, 1985.

[12] V. R. Lesser, R. D. Fennel, L. D. Erman, and D. R. Reddy, "Organization of the HERSAY II speech understanding system", *IEEE Trans. Acoust., speech, Signal Processing*, vol. ASSP-23, pp. 11-24, Feb. 1975.

[13] H. P. Nee and E. A. Feigenbaum, "Rule-based understanding of signals", in *Pattern-Directed Inference Systems*, D. A. Waterman and F. Hayes-Roth, Eds. Academic, New York, 1978, pp. 483-501.

[14] A. Newell, "Physical symbol systems", *Cognitive Science*, vol.4, pp. 135-183, 1980.

[15] G. A. Ringwood, "Parlog86 and the dining logicians", *Communication ACM*, vol.31, pp. 10-25, Jan. 1988.

[16] R. G. Smith and R. Davis, "Frameworks for cooperation in distributed problem solving", *IEEE Trans. System, Man, and Cybernetics*, vol. SMC-11, pp. 61-70, Jan. 1981.

Introducing Knowledge Representation Techniques in Database Models[*]

A. Artale, F. Cesarini, G. Soda

Dipartimento di Sistemi e Informatica - Università di Firenze
via S. Marta, 3 - 50139 Firenze - Italy
E-mail: Giovanni@IFIIDG.BITNET

Abstract

This paper deals with endowing object-oriented data models with taxonomic reasoning, i.e., an inference capability characteristic of the knowledge representation systems developed within the KL-ONE family. For this purpose, the main point is to introduce the concept of defined class, i.e., class whose structural description gives necessary and sufficient conditions for an object to belong to it. Object-oriented data models usually don't refer to this concept, because only necessary conditions are expressed by the type descriptions. We take into account a data model, developed in a database environment, and show how a uniform formal framework can be defined in order that this model fit taxonomic reasoning.

1 Introduction

This study deals with a way of introducing some inference techniques common to Knowledge Representation systems into object-oriented data models, and, in this context, particular attention is given to taxonomic reasoning. This ability is a feature of the object-based knowledge representation models [18] resulting from the ideas expressed in KL-ONE [8]. A suitable language is used for describing the object's structure and the terms used in the description are associated with an external denotational semantics. The object class defined by a description corresponds to the object set whose structure conforms to that description. Classes can be **primitive** or **defined**: the description of a primitive class indicates the conditions necessary for an object to belong to that class, while that of a defined class specify the necessary and sufficient conditions for an object to belong to it. Subsumption and classification perform deductive reasoning regarding the object definitions. By means of **subsumption** it is possible to determine whether or not a class is a subclass of another one according to the descriptions given. In these derivations, the concept of defined class is fundamental because it allows us to deal with descriptions capable of expressing a class's extension in a complete way. By means of **classification** it is possible to arrange class descriptions into a taxonomy by determining all the subsumers and subsumees of each class. In this environment, particular attention is given to studying the relationships existing

---

[*]This research was partially supported by CNR in the framework of "Progetto Finalizzato Sistemi Informatici e Calcolo Parallelo" - Sottoprogetto 5: "Sistemi Evoluti per Basi di Dati Obiettivo Logidata+"

between the model definition language's expressive power and the related algorithms' complexity [7, 11, 14, 15, 16, 17] in order to obtain tractable systems.

However, there are some features generally common to semantic and object-oriented database models [1, 3, 12, 13] that regard the possibility of treating objects of a structured type (i.e., objects having a complex structure) and managing ISA relationships (i.e., subset relationships among classes); moreover, ISA relationships can only be stated among classes having type descriptions that refine each other. We believe that these database systems could benefit from the use of taxonomic reasoning in various applications. For example, in conceptual design [5, 10] it could be used for finding all the ISA relationships that exist because of the way the classes are defined, whether or not there are any explicit statements present. The whole schema's consistency can then be checked and all cycles and empty classes removed from it. It is also possible to assure schema minimality by only maintaining direct links. At an extensional level, instances can be recognized and classified directly by the system. Moreover, by using taxonomic reasoning in query answering [4, 6] it is possible to: 1) deduce relationships not mentioned in the user's query; 2) give answers at both an intensional and extensional level; 3) optimize query execution.

As previously pointed out, taxonomic reasoning is based on the concept of defined class; this concept is not usually found in object-oriented systems because the type description of a class only specifies necessary conditions and, consequently, ISA relationships must be explicitly stated. We can say that object-oriented database models only take primitive classes into account, while object-based knowledge representation systems are more flexible because they provide a well-founded basis for managing both primitive and defined classes. In this paper, we propose introducing taxonomic reasoning into the object-oriented database field. When it is possible to describe classes as being primitive or defined, taxonomic reasoning can be profitably used for all the above-mentioned purposes, at both an intensional and extensional level.

There are some data models, such as CLASSIC [6] and CANDIDE [4] that are developed directly in a knowledge representation system environment and therefore possess this feature intrinsically. However, in our study, we begin with a data model developed in an object-oriented database environment, and furnish it with the features necessary for taxonomic reasoning. We use the LOGIDATA+ model [3] and give it a formal framework suitable for dealing with defined classes. LOGIDATA+ is able to handle complex structures and represent ISA relationships among classes; its logical component determines its deductive ability, while an object-oriented component makes it possible to structure data at a static level. This model is endowed with a number of advanced features (such as a variety of type constructors and the fact that is both value- and object-based) that are also present in other recent models (see, for example, the last version of O_2 [13]). The deductive ability provided by taxonomic reasoning is limited compared to some logical languages but it provides a well-founded and uniform inferential service with computational tractability that can be exploited for all the previously-mentioned applications.

In our formalization, we deal with the features of LOGIDATA+ that are directly involved in subsumption computation and modify some definitions according to our needs; we call LOGIDATA* the data model we investigate. The intensional and extensional aspects of LOGIDATA* are defined in section 2, together with an interpretation function that associates both levels with each other; schema coherence is defined in section 3. Section 4 is devoted to syntactic characterization of subsumption, and the syntactic constraints for coherence are illustrated in section 5. Some concluding remarks are reported in section 6. The Appendix illustrates an example of schema definition and interpretation.

2 The LOGIDATA* model

The LOGIDATA* model derives from LOGIDATA+ [3], but presents some relevant differences in order to fit taxonomic reasoning.

The main structure of LOGIDATA* is the *Class* that denotes sets of *Objects*, each of which is identified by an *Object Identifier* (OID). Objects in classes can have complex structures obtained by repeatedly using the *tuple* and *set* constructors. Furthermore, *type names* are provided to simplify user declarations. The *type system* is based on two type constructors that are also used in other systems, for example in O_2 [12, 13]. As regards classes, we make difference between *primitive* and *defined* classes.

2.1 Schemata

We assume the existence of predefined and disjoint base types (such as string, integer, etc.). Let **B** be a countable set of *base type names*, **CP** a countable set of *primitive class names*, **CD** a countable set of *defined class names*, **C** = **CP**∪**CD**, **T** a countable set of *type names*, **L** a countable set of *labels*; sets **B**, **CP**, **CD** and **T** are pairwise disjoint. We indicate by Γ(**L,B,C,T**) the whole set of *type descriptors*, or, briefly, *types* over **L,B,C,T** defined as follows:

def: Type
- -each base type name ∈ **B** is a type;
- -each class name ∈ **C** is a type;
- -each type name ∈ **T** is a type;
- -if t is a type, then $\{t\}_{min,max}$ is also a type called **set-type**, where *min* is a not-negative integer, *max* is a not-negative integer or ∞, and *max*≥*min*;
- -if $t_1....t_k$, with k≥0, are types and $l_1....l_k$ are distinct labels, then $[l_1:t_1.....l_k:t_k]$ is also a type, called **tuple-type**. ♦

Note: The type $\{t\}_{1,1}$ is equivalent to t; in the following we assume that the system recognizes this type equivalence.

Let **ISA** be a relationship representing a user-given inheritance hierarchy: C1**ISA**C2 states that each object belonging to class C1 also belongs to class C2, i.e., class C1 is a *subclass* (or a *specialization*) of C2. We note that **ISA** is a *transitive* and *reflexive* relationship.

Let TYP() be a function from **T**∪**C** to the set of *type descriptors* in Γ(**L,B,C,T**). TYP() is such that:
- -for each T ∈ **T**, TYP(T) is a tuple- or set-type descriptor of Γ;
- -for each C ∈ **C**, TYP(C) is a tuple-type descriptor of Γ.

Let Φ:**C**→P^{**}(CP) be a function that associates to each class C∈**C** the set of all its primitive superclasses: Φ(C) = {Cp ∈ **CP**| C**ISA**Cp}.

We can now give the definition of a LOGIDATA* *schema*:

def: LOGIDATA* Schema
A LOGIDATA* *schema* is a six-tuple S=(**T,CP,CD,ISA,TYP,Φ**) where **T**, **CP**, **CD**, **ISA**, **TYP** and Φ are defined as above. ♦

$^{**}P$(X) denotes the powerset of X

<declaration> := <type-declaration> | <class-declaration>
<type-declaration> := **TYPE** <identifier> = <type-constructor>
<class-declaration> := Thing |
          CLASS <identifier> <prim-def> (**ISA** <class-id>+) <type-id> |
          CLASS <identifier> <prim-def> (**ISA** <class-id>+) (<tuple-type>)
<type-constructor> := <tuple-type> | <set-type>
<type> := <type-constructor> | <class-id> | <type-id> | <basic-type>
<tuple-type> := [<component>*]
<component> := <label> : <type>
<set-type> := {<type>}$_{(<card>)}$
<card> := <min>,<max>
<basic-type> := string | integer | ......
<label> := <identifier>
<class-id> := <identifier>
<type-id> := <identifier>
<prim-def> := ⇒ | ⇔
<min> := "an integer ≥ 0"
<max> := "an integer ≥ 0" | ∞

<type-declaration> and <class-declaration> can't be defined recursively. "+" indicates one or more repetitions, "*" indicates zero or more repetitions. Items enclosed in "()" are optional.

Fig 1- LOGIDATA* syntax

2.2 Schema Definition Language

A LOGIDATA* schema can be defined by means of the syntax illustrated in figure 1. We note that we don't take any recursive definitions into account, in accordance with the approach usually used by the KRMs we refer to [16]. As far as <basic-type> is concerned, the actual base types depend on the implementation used. For maintaining the class hierarchy we introduce the universal class *Thing* such that, for each object *o* present in the KB, we can say that *o* is a member of the universal class *Thing*. Furthermore, the type associated with the <type-id> appearing in the <class-declaration> must be a tuple-type.

The ISA clause allows the system to exploit the mechanism of *inheritance*; *multiple inheritance* is allowed, with some restrictions assuring type compatibility (see section 5). We show an example of schema definition in the Appendix.

2.3 Values

While *type* is the basic element of the intensional level of the Knowledge-Base, the *value* is the basic element of the extensional level.

Let D_i be the set of values associated with the base type name $B_i \in \mathbf{B}$. Let $\mathbf{D}$ be $\mathbf{D}=D_1\cup......\cup D_n$, $n\geq 1$. Each element $v \in \mathbf{D}$ is a *basic value*. A particular B_i is *Nil* whose only element is the *nil* value. We assume that sets D_i are pairwise disjoint. Let **O** be a countable set of symbols called *object identifiers* (o is a generic object identifier), disjoint from **D**.

def: Value

A set Ω of *values* is:

$$\Omega = D \cup O \cup VT \cup VS \cup \{nil\} \quad ; \text{ where}$$

- **VT** is the set of *tuple-values*: $VT = \{ v_t \mid v_t \text{ is a mapping}, v_t:L \to \Omega \}$.
  We denote with $[l_1:v_1.........l_k:v_k]$ the total mapping defined on $\{l_1,.........,l_k\}$ such that $v_t(l_i) = v_i \in \Omega$, $\forall i=1,.....,k$.
- **VS** is the set of *set-values*: $VS = \{ v_s \mid v_s \subseteq \Omega \}$.
  A set-value is denoted by $\{v_1,......,v_k\}$, with $v_i \in \Omega$, $\forall i=1,....,k$. The symbol $\{\}$ denotes the empty set and $\{nil\}$ the set whose elements are undefined. ♦

We note that the object identifiers are values, too. Since objects are usually considered to be pairs of identifiers and values, we assume the existence of a function that assignes values to object identifiers:

def: Value Assignment

Value assignment is a total mapping, denoted by δ, that associates a value with each object-identifier: $\delta:O \to \Omega$. ♦

In the following, whenever a set $V \subseteq \Omega$ is considered, we assume that V is associated with a suitable value assignment; we call such a couple *domain*:

def: Domain

A *domain* Σ is a couple $\Sigma = (V,\delta)$ such that $V \subseteq \Omega$ and δ is a value assignment that associates a value $v \in V$ with each $o \in V$. ♦

Note: Both δ and v_t are defined as a total mapping assuming that 1) $\delta(o) = nil$ when an object is created but is not assigned to any class because nothing is known about its properties (in this case o is a member of the universal class *Thing*); 2) $v_t(l) = nil$ for labels with undefined value. The *nil* element makes it possible to treat uncomplete knowledge.

2.4 Interpretation

The LOGIDATA* syntax is associated with a *semantics* which regulates the relationship between the intensional and extensional levels of the model.

def: Interpretation

Given a LOGIDATA* schema S, let Σ be a domain and I a function defined from type descriptors in S to $P(V)$ (i.e., $I:\Gamma \to P(V)$); I is an *interpretation function* of S over Σ if and only if:

1. If type = basic-type
   $I(\text{basic-type}) = I(B_i) \equiv D_i$, $\forall B_i \in B$.
2. If type = tuple-type
   $I(\text{tuple-type}) = I([l_1:t_1.............l_k:t_k]) =$
   $=\{v_t \in VT \mid v_t \text{ is defined } atleast \text{ on } \{l_1,...,l_k\} \text{ and } v_t(l_i) \in I(t_i) \cup \{nil\} \; \forall i=1,......,k\}$.
3. If type = set-type
   a. $I(\{t\}_{m,n}) = \{v_s \in VS \mid m \leq |v_s \subseteq I(t)| \leq n \text{ or } v_s=\{nil\} \}$
   b. $I(\{t\}) = \{v_s \in VS \mid v_s \subseteq I(t) \cup \{nil\} \}$
   c. $I(\{t\}_{1,1}) \equiv I(t)$.
4. If type = type-id
   $I(\text{type-id}) = I(\text{TYPE type-id} = \text{type}) = I(\text{type})$.
5. If type = *Thing*
   $I(Thing) \equiv O$.
6. If type = class-id = C
   $I(\text{class-id}) = I(C) \subseteq O$, $\forall C \in C$ and:
   a. if $C=Cd \in CD$, described as:
   CLASS Cd $\Leftrightarrow$ **ISA** C_1..................C_n <tuple-type>

where $\Phi(Cd) = \{Cp_1,.............,Cp_m\}$, with $m \geq 0$, then:
$I(Cd) = \cap_{i=1}^{m} I(Cp_i) \cap \{o \in O \mid \delta(o) \in I(TYP(Cd))\}$
b. if $C=Cp \in \mathbf{CP}$, described as:
CLASS $Cp \Rightarrow \mathbf{ISA}$ C_1.................C_n <tuple-type>
where $\Phi(Cp) = \{Cp_1,.............,Cp_m\}$, with $m \geq 0$, then:
$I(Cp) \subseteq \cap_{i=1}^{m} I(Cp_i) \cap \{o \in O \mid \delta(o) \in I(TYP(Cp))\}$. ◆
For the interpretation of TYP(C) we have the following recursive definition.
def: Interpretation of TYP(C)
Given the class declarations
CLASS C_0 <prim-def> tuple-type$_0$
CLASS C_1 <prim-def> **ISA** C_0 tuple-type$_1$
....
CLASS C_{n+1} <prim-def> **ISA** C_0..........C_n tuple-type$_{n+1}$
we have
$I(TYP(C_0)) = I(\text{tuple-type}_0)$
$I(TYP(C_1)) = I(TYP(C_0)) \cap I(\text{tuple-type}_1)$
....
$I(TYP(C_{n+1})) = \cap_{i=1}^{n} I(TYP(C_i)) \cap I(\text{tuple-type}_{n+1})$. ◆
This semantics, allows us to consider the **ISA** relationship as an inclusion between classes. Moreover, each value can have more than one type [9]: when a value is of type τ, then it is of type τ', too, in the case that $I(\tau) \subseteq I(\tau')$. In the Appendix we show an example of interpretation.

3 Disjointness and Schema Coherence

An interesting property of classes is *disjointness* [10], i.e., whether two class descriptions denote necessarily mutually exclusive sets. In LOGIDATA* two class descriptions are disjoint because of non-overlapping number restrictions over the same label. In the following schema:
CLASS Person $\Rightarrow$ [name:string birthdate:string]
CLASS Fertile-Person $\Leftrightarrow$ **ISA** Person [children:{Person}$_{1,5}$]
CLASS Inseminator $\Leftrightarrow$ **ISA** Person [children:{Person}$_{10,100}$]
Fertile-Person and Inseminator are disjoint classes given that:
$I([\text{children}:\{Person\}_{1,5}]) \cap I([\text{children}:\{Person\}_{10,100}]) = \varnothing$
In general, the following definition holds.
def: Disjoint types
Given a schema **S**, two types τ_1 and τ_2 are *disjoint* if and only if for each domain Σ and for each interpretation function I defined over Σ, $I(\tau_1) \cap I(\tau_2) = \varnothing$. ◆
An *incoherent type description* contains two or more disjoint types. For example, the following class descriptions are incoherent:
CLASS C1 $\Leftrightarrow$ **ISA** Fertile-Person Inseminator
CLASS C2 $\Leftrightarrow$ **ISA** Person [birthdate:{string}$_{0,0}$]
def: Incoherent type
Given a schema **S**, a type τ in **S** is *incoherent* if and only if for each domain Σ and for each interpretation function I defined over Σ, $I(\tau) = \varnothing$. ◆
We say that a schema **S** is *coherent* if it doesn't contain incoherent types. LOGIDATA* does not permit to create such types in order to always enforce a consistent knowledge state (see section 5, where the above definition is translated into syntactic constraints).

4 Subsumption

The introduction of the interpretation function, together with the notion of defined class, allows us to formalize the concept of *subsumption* between classes and define an algorithm for its computation.

def: Subsumption
Given classes C1 and C2, C2 *subsumes* C1 if and only if for each domain Σ and for each interpretation function I defined over Σ, $I(C1) \subseteq I(C2)$ holds. ♦

In our framework, every **ISA** clause corresponds to a subsumption relationship: if C1ISAC2 then C2 subsumes C1. The opposite is not necessarily true; a class can subsume another one even if subsumption is not esplicitly defined by means of an **ISA** clause.

Because our interpretation function is totally based on structural characteristics, the meaning of a structured description is only determined by its internal structure. This allows us to make an algorithm to deduce all the subsumption relationships among classes implicitly given by the *structural conditions* appearing in the class descriptions. For this purpose we introduce an ordering on $\Gamma(\mathbf{L,B,C,T})$, called *refinement* (in symbols "≤"), based on type's syntactic features.

def: Refinement
Type t is a *refinement* of type t', t≤t', if and only if:
  R1. $t \in \mathbf{T} \cup \mathbf{C} \cup \mathbf{B}$ and t = t' ;
  R2a. $t \in \mathbf{T}$ and $TYP(t) \le t'$;
  R2b. $t' \in \mathbf{T}$ and $t \le TYP(t')$;
  R2c. $t, t' \in \mathbf{T}$ and $TYP(t) \le TYP(t')$;
  R3a. $t \in \mathbf{CP} \cup \mathbf{CD}$ and $t' \in \mathbf{CP}$ and tISAt';
  R3b. $t \in \mathbf{CP} \cup \mathbf{CD}$ and $t' \in \mathbf{CD}$ and:
         i. $\forall Cp' \in \Phi(t')$ then $Cp' \in \Phi(t)$, too
         ii. $TYP(t) \le TYP(t')$;
  R4. $t = [l_1:t_1.....l_k:t_k......l_{k+p}:t_{k+p}]$, $t' = [l_1:t'_1..........l_k:t'_k]$ with $k \ge 0$, $p \ge 0$, and $t_i \le t'_i$, for i=1,..,k;
  R5. $t = \{t_1\}_{m,n}$ and $t' = \{t'_1\}_{p,q}$, with $t_1 \le t'_1$, $m \ge p$ and $n \le q$. ♦

The following theorem, based on refinement, characterizes subsumption syntactically.

Theorem
Given classes C1 and C2, C1 *subsumes* C2, SUBS(C1,C2), if and only if C2 refines C1 (i.e., C2≤C1).

Proof
The proof that the theorem agrees with the above-given subsumption definition (i.e., sound and complete) is in [2]. ♦

Due to the formalism previously introduced (i.e., syntax + semantics + subsumption), we obtain an o-o data model based on classification; in other words, *all* the subsumption relationships are computed by the system, independently of user-given **ISA** links.

As far as the complexity of SUBS(C1,C2) is concerned, we can repeat the same considerations made in [15] about the intractability of terminological reasoning. In the general case, SUBS(C1,C2) performs subsequent expansions of both classes until it is possible to calculate SUBS($\hat{C}$1,$\hat{C}$2), with $\hat{C}$1 and $\hat{C}$2 being *completely expanded classes*. $\hat{C}$ is a completely expanded class if TYP($\hat{C}$) doesn't contain any type–name or defined-class-names: these names are replaced by their descriptions. We note that the transformation from C into $\hat{C}$ is possible in a finite number of steps because our language doesn't have any recursive definitions (acyclic terminology), but induces expressions $\hat{C}$ of size $O(m^n)$, where m is the size of C [1, 15].

The following theorem holds [2]:
Theorem: Subsumption Between C.E.C. is Tractable
SUBS($\hat{C}$1,$\hat{C}$2) runs in $O(|\hat{C}1| \times |\hat{C}2|)$ time. ♦

5 Syntactic Constraints for Coherence

In this section we characterize the notion of *coherent type* from a syntactic point of view by means of giving the definition of *correct type description*. Furthermore, as regards *multiple inheritance*, some syntactic constraints are added to a class description using the **ISA** clause in order for the type of the subclass elements to be compatible with the superclass type [3].

The following definition gives rise to an algorithm looking for correct type descriptions that can be shown to be consistent with respect to the language semantics (see sect. 2.4 and 3).

def: Correct type description

- $t = B_i$, with $B_i \in \mathbf{B}$ (where t = <basic-type>):
  the description of t is correct.
- $t = [l_1:t_1.......l_n:t_n]$:
  the description of t is correct if $l_i \neq l_j$ $\forall i,j=1,......,n$ with i≠j, and each t_i is a correct type description.
- $t = \{t'\}_{min,max}$:
  the description of t is correct if t' is a correct type description and $min \leq max$.
- **TYPE** t = t' (where t = <type-id>):
  the description of t is correct if t' is a correct type description.
- **CLASS** C <prim-def> **ISA** $C_1....C_n$ <tuple-type> (where C and C_i are <class-id>):
  the description of class C is correct if <tuple-type> is a correct type description. Furthermore, for labels appearing in some C_i belonging to the **ISA** clause and in <tuple-type>, the type associated with such labels in <tuple-type> must be a refinement of the type associated with the omologous labels in C_i. Moreover, if the same label appears in more than one C_i with different types, then it must explicitly appear in <tuple-type> with a type that is the refinement of all the previous ones. ♦

The following theorem shows the soundness of the above-given definition with respect to the definition of incoherent type (see section 3).

Theorem: Soundness of correct type description

Given a schema S and a correct type description t in S then there exists a domain Σ and an interpretation function I defined over Σ such that $I(t) \neq \emptyset$. ♦

The definition of Supervisor shows a correct example of multiple inheritance; the *budget* label is present in Supervisor with a type that refines both types appearing in Prj_leader and Prj_manager, respectively.

We can now characterize syntactically the function TYP(), with respect to both the definition of semantics (see section 2.4) and the above-given definition of correct type description. TYP() associates with each symbol $\in \mathbf{C} \cup \mathbf{T}$ the type descriptor defined by the expansion of the non-terminal symbol appearing in the corresponding declaration, with the following exception: if a class is described by means of an **ISA** clause, then TYP(C) is a tuple-type with all the labels that appear in the superclass descriptions and in the tuple-type that describes the class. In the case that the same label appears in the tuple-type that describes the class and in one or more superclass descriptions, then TYP(C) presents such label as it is defined in the tuple-type describing the class.

Using **ISA** makes it possible to exploit *inheritance*, i.e., the mechanism that allows a class to inherit properties of its superclasses. From the above definitions, it is clear that multiple inheritance is only allowed in a framework of "re-definition", and re-definition is subjected to some type refinement constraints; a similar approach also appears in O_2 [13]. We show some results obtained by the function TYP evaluation:

TYP(Date) = [day:int month:int year:int]

TYP(Rsch_leader) = [name:string birthdate:Date emp_code:string salary:int prj:{Rsch_project}$_{1,2}$ budget:[prj_amount:int]]

TYP(Supervisor) = [name:string birthdate:Date emp_code:string salary:int prj:{Project}$_{1,3}$

has_secretary:Secretary budget:[prj_amount:int external_amount:int budget_plan:int]
TYP(Person) = [name:string birthdate:Date].

6 Conclusions

Our study aims at endowing an object-oriented database model with the inference capabilities related to subsumption. Subsumption and its applications have been throughly investigated in the field of Knowledge Representation systems. While database models usually refer to different deductive paradigms, such as logic, recent studies pointed out usefulness of taxonomic reasoning for dealing with data management at both an intensional and extensional level. The main result of our paper is to show how this capability can be added to an object-oriented data model, proposed in a database environment, increasing then its features still maintaining the original ones; as a matter of fact, we develop a formal framework for treating values and objects, and types and classes in a well-founded and uniform way that agrees with taxonomic reasoning. It is worth noting that we really enrich the data model with respect to its original characteristics without distorting it. For example, if schemas only consisting of primitive classes are considered, all the formal definitions and properties stated agree with the proposal of the original framework; furthermore, defined classes can be used in order to exploit the full abilities of taxonomic reasoning. Another important point refers to the characteristics of the model we take into account; it presents the main features of most recent database models, such as structured types and being both value- and object-based. For this reason we believe that our study is a valuable trace for introducing taxonomic reasoning in other object-oriented data models, too.

References

[1]   S.Abiteboul, R.Hull. *IFO: A Formal Semantic Database Model*. ACM Transactions on Database Systems, vol.12, n.4, 1987.

[2]   A.Artale, F.Cesarini, G.Soda. *Subsumption Computation in an Object-Oriented Data Model*. Proc. of PDK91, Kaiserslautern, July 1991.

[3]   P.Atzeni, L.Tanca. *The LOGIDATA+ model and Language*. Workshop "Information Systems 90", Kiev, Oct. 1990, to appear in Lecture Notes in Computer Science, Springer-Verlag.

[4]   H.W.Beck, S.K.Gala, S.B.Navathe. *Classification as a query processing technique in the CANDIDE semantic data model*. Fifth IEEE International Conference on Data Engineering, Los Angeles, 1989.

[5]   S.Bergamaschi, C.Sartori, P.Tiberio. *On Taxonomic Reasoning in Conceptual Design*. Rapporto Tecnico CIOC CNR n.68, Bologna, 1990.

[6]   A.Borgida, R.J.Brachman, D.L.MacGuinness, L.A.Resnick. *CLASSIC: a structural data model for objects*. Proceedings of the 1989 ACM SIGMOD International Conference on Management of Data, Portland, Oreg., June 1989.

[7]   R.J.Brachman, H.J.Lévesque. *The tractability of subsumption in Frame-Based description languages*. AAAI National Conference on Artificial Intelligence, Austin, Texas, 1984.

[8]   R.J.Brachman, J.G.Schmolze. *An overview of the KL-ONE knowledge representation system*. Cognitve science, 9, 1985.

[9]   L.Cardelli. *A Semantic of Multiple Inheritance*. Semantics of Data Type, Lecture Notes in Computer science, Vol. 173, Springer Verlag, 1984.

[10] L.M.L.Delcambre, K.C.Davis. *Automatic Validation of Object-Oriented Database Structures.* proc. of int. conf. Data Engineering, 1989.

[11] F.M.Donini, B.Hollunder, M.Lenzerini, A.Marchetti Spaccamela, D.Nardi, W.Nutt. *The complexity of existential quantification in concept languages.* rap.01.91, Dipartimento di Informatica e Sistemistica, Roma, 1991.

[12] C.Lécluse, P.Richard, F.Velez. *O₂, an Object-Orieted Data Model.* Proceedings ACM SIGMOD, 1988.

[13] C.Lecluse, P.Richard. *Modeling Complex Structures in Object-Oriented Databases,* proc. of PODS89, 1989.

[14] H.J.Lévesque, R.J.Brachman. *Expressiveness and tractability in knowledge representation and reasoning.* Computational Intelligence, 3:78-93, 1987.

[15] B.Nebel. *Terminological reasoning is inherently intractable.* IWBS Report 82, September 1989.

[16] B.Nebel. *Reasoning and Revision in Hybrid Representation Systems.* Lecture Notes in Artificial Intelligence, n. 422, Springer-Verlag, 1990.

[17] P.F.Patel-Schneider. *Undecidability of subsumption in NIKL.* Artificial Intelligence, 39:263-272, 1989.

[18] P.F.Patel-Schneider. *Practical, Object-Based Knowledge Representation for Knowledge-Based Systems.* Information Systems, vol.15, n.1, 1990.

Appendix

Schema specification

TYPE Date = [day:int month:int year:int]

CLASS Project ⇔ [proj_code:string description:string]

CLASS Person ⇒ [name:string birthdate:Date]

CLASS Woman ⇒ **ISA** Person

CLASS Secretary ⇒ **ISA** Woman [emp_code:string salary:int]

CLASS Prj_leader ⇔ **ISA** Person [emp_code:string salary:int prj:{Project}$_{1,3}$ budget:[prj_amount:int]]

CLASS Prj_manager ⇔ **ISA** Person [emp_code:string salary:int has_secretary:Secretary budget:[prj_amount:int external_amount:int]]

CLASS Supervisor ⇔ **ISA** Prj_leader Prj_manager [budget: [prj_amount:int external_amount:int budget_plan:int]]

Schema interpretation

Given the following domain: O={#LogDB, #Anne, #Roland}; where

δ(#LogDB) = [prj_code:DB14 description:deductive_database]

δ(#Anne) = [name:Anne birthdate:[day:22 month:11 year:1964] emp_code:I769 salary:1200]

δ(#Roland) = [name:Roland birthdate:[day:2 month:6 year:1947] emp_code:I302 salary:4000 external_amount:500 budget_plan:3000]]

Fixed the interpretation for the primitive classes:

I(Person) = {#Anne, #Roland};

I(Woman) = I(Secretary) = {#Anne}

The interpretation of the definite classes is unambiguously determined:

I(Project) = {#LogDB};

I(Prj_leader) = I(Prj_manager) = I(Supervisor) = {#Roland}

SELF-ORGANIZING MAPS: A NEW DIGITAL ARCHITECTURE

M. Gioiello, G. Vassallo*, A. Chella**, F. Sorbello,

DIE - Dipartimento di Ingegneria Elettrica
Universita' di Palermo
Viale delle Scienze, 90128 Palermo, Italy

*CRES - Centro per la Ricerca Elettronica in Sicilia
Monreale (Palermo) Italy

**DIE and CRES

Abstract

An original hardware architecture implementing the self-organizing feature maps, which is one of the most powerful and efficent neural network algorithm, is presented. The architecture, contrary to the most investigated hardware implementations of neural networks, is a full digital one and it may be easily built by using the standard VLSI techniques.

Simulations of the architecture at a functional/logic level are carried on, showing the interesting capabilties of the architecture. An extensive application to the task of recognition of very noisy patterns is also described.

1. INTRODUCTION

An important feature of the human brain is its ability to spontaneously develop an efficient representation of concepts, images and actions. It has in fact observed in the brain the existence of maps related to visual, tactual and auditorial stimuli. Those maps allow for a ordered and compress representations of the external stimuli: e.g. in the auditory cortex tonotopic maps exist in which the spatial order of neurons correspond to frequency or pitch of perceived sounds.

Many mathematical models exist about the processes of delevopment of the maps; Kohonen [1] proposed a simple but powerful model of the self-organizing maps easily implementable as a computer algorithm. Several theoretical studies, simulations and applications to concrete problems show the importance of this model in fiels like statistical pattern recognition, control of robot arms, control of diffusion processes during the production of semiconductor substrates, adaptive devices for semiconductor tasks, combinatorial problems such as the Traveling Salesman Problem, and so on.

The second step of the algorithm consists in the improvement of the match between the input pattern and the units belonging to the set of neighbourhoods of the winner unit c.

In the euclidean metric:

$$m_i(t_{k+1}) = m_i(t_k) + \alpha(t_k)[x(t_k) - m_i(t_k)] \quad \text{for } i \in N_c$$
$$m_i(t_{k+1}) = m_i(t_k) \qquad\qquad\qquad\qquad \text{for } i \notin N_c$$

where a is the learning step and Nc is the set of neighbourhoods units of the winner unit c. These parameters are monotonically decreasing with the iteration step t_k. The algorithm iterates these two steps until the process convergence is reached.

The two basic processes of the self-organization are: i) the competition between units for locating the best-matching unit with respect to the input pattern as the winner unit; ii) the increase of the matching for the winner unit and its topological neighbours. Note that this is a unsupervised learning algorithm carrying out the self-organizations of the unit weights.

The self-organizing test algorithm consists on the location of the best-matching unit with respect to the input and it is the same as the first step of the learning algorithm. In the euclidean metric the best-matching unit c is defined as:

$$\left\| x(t_k) - m_c(t_k) \right\| = \min_i \left\| x(t_k) - m_i(t_k) \right\|$$

Kohonen [1] showed that, once the convergence of the process is reached, if the input pattern is a random variable with a stationary probability density function $p(x)$, an ordered image of $p(x)$ will be formed onto the weights of the units. The image is ordered in the sense of the chosen metric, e.g. euclidean metric.

Therefore the algorithm create a map of the input pattern space with two main characteristics: i) the preservation of the topology of the input pattern space over the weights vectors of the network and ii) the optimum choice of the reference vectors of the input pattern space as the weights vectors of the network.

2.2 A brief review of the N-tuple theory

The n-tuple theory [2] is a pattern recognition technique allowing to represent a binary pattern by a vector.

A binary pattern x is randomly divided into t mutually exclusive ordered sets of n binary elements called n-tuples. The binary value of the n-tuple is the state of the n-tuple. The pattern x may then be described by a vector $\overline{x}$ listing the t occurrences of states of the t n-tuples.

A class of patterns is described by a vector X constructed by collecting for each pattern the t occurrences of the n-tuples.

The classification process is carried out by comparing the unknown pattern with all the pattern classes previously defined, storing the number of matching n-tuple for each class and assigning the unknown pattern to the class with the best score.

The n-tuple theory may be used not only as a pattern recognition scheme but also as a coding scheme between the space of patterns x and the space of n-tuples $\overline{x}$. The interesting characteristic of the n-tuple theory is that a pattern is described by a set of random features (the n-tuples) with no semantic meaning and the classification is accomplished by the presence or absence of these features.

Aleksander et al. [3,4] proposed a simple digital implementation of the n-tuple discriminator. In the pattern class discriminator the state of each n-tuple is the address of a RAM. During the learning phase all the patterns belonging to the same class are presented to the discriminator; for each pattern and for each RAM a 1 is written at the corresponding address. During the recognizing phase, the unknown pattern is shown to the discriminator and the corresponding RAM are read; the sum of the outputs from the RAMs is the score of the given pattern, and allows to decide for the belonging of the pattern to a certain class.

This simple digital circuit may be considered as a RAM neuron in the sense that it works in the same way than an analogical neuron, maintaining all the capabilities of associativity, adaptivity, noise tolerance and so on.

3. THE PROPOSED ARCHITECTURE

In order to implement the self-organizing maps algorithm by digital hardware it is necessary to suitably code the input patterns vectors and the weights vectors and to define a distance between patterns. The n-tuple theory suggests a coding of patterns allowing for a very simple digital implementation. A simple measure of the matching degree between a pattern $\overline{x}$ and a class of patterns X may be defined by the number of matching n-tuples.

According to the described coding and metric, the adapted self-organizing map learning algorithm is the following. Given an array of units, let the unit i be individuated by the pattern class vector X_i. The first step of the algorithm is the same than the recognizing phase of the n-tuple theory and it consists in the search of the unit c performing the best-match with respect to the the input pattern x_p; this corresponds to find the pattern class vector X_c with the maximum number of matching n-tuples with respect to $\overline{x_p}$. In matrix notation:

$$S_p^T = [S_{p1} \vdots S_{p2} \vdots \cdots \vdots S_{pn}]$$

where S_p^T is the collection of S_{pi} representing the scores of $\overline{x_p}$ against the pattern classes X_j. The pattern x_p performs the best-match with the pattern class X_c if:

$$S_{pc} = \max S_p^T$$

The second step of the algorithm consists in improving the match between the input pattern and the units belonging to the neighbourhood Nc of the winner unit c; according to the metric this corresponds to adding some of the n-tuple of the input pattern to the winner pattern class and its neighbours pattern classes.

The operator **extract** $(m, \overline{x})$ is defined as the operator extracting m randomly chosen occurrences of n-tuples in vector $\overline{x}$. By using the defined operator this step is described as:

$$X_i(t_{k+1}) = \text{extract } (m, \overline{x_p}) + X_i(t_k) \quad \text{for } i \in N_c$$
$$X_i(t_{k+1}) = X_i(t_k) \qquad\qquad\qquad \text{for } i \notin N_c$$

The learning algorithm iteratively repeats these two steps until the convergence of the process is reached.

The test algorithm, as explained above, coincides with the recognition step of the learning algorithm.

It may be noted that input pattern x is a random variable; therefore from the theory of self-organizing maps follows: i) the algorithm chooses the X_j vectors by preserving the topology of the input pattern space, and ii) the X_j vectors are the optimum choice as samples of the input pattern space. These characteristics therefore represent a net improvement with respect to the n-tuple theory: in the n-tuple theory the X_i vectors are simply a collection of the n-tuples of patterns belonging to class i, while in the implemented architecture the X_i

vectors are optimally chosen as the prototypes best describing the input training set.

The outline of the proposed digital architecture is shown in fig. 1. The input is made up by a pixel matrix representing the binary pattern. In the current implementation, square t x t matrices, with t = 8, are used. The operation of the architecture is the following: t non-overlapping n-tuples are randomly selected from the input matrix and sent to every unit of the architecture, each unit acting as a pattern class discriminator.

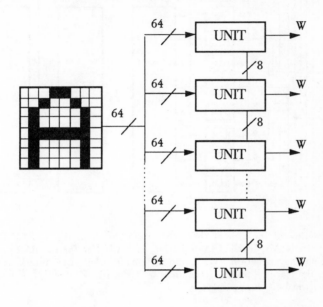

Fig. 1. The overall structure of the proposed architecture for a 8x8 input matrix.

Fig. 2 shows the structure of the unit; this is the basic block of the architecture. The operations of the unit of the architecture is subdivided into two steps corresponding to the two steps of the self-organizing learning algorithm.

During the first step, the operations involved in the first block (the RAMsBLOCK) are similar to those ones of the n-tuple discriminator: each n-tuple is used as an address to a 1-bit RAM of each unit; the number of RAMs whose output is 1 corresponds to the number of matching n-tuples between the input pattern and the pattern class. This number is the whole output of this first block.

The second block, named RBUF (RAM Buffer) is a buffer for the outputs of the RAMsBLOCK. This buffer is also accessed by the block controlling the learning phase, as described later.

The output of the RBUF block is sent to the block named S1 (Sigma 1), a simple PLA, that code the activation level in BCD; the output of this block is then a 4-bit bus.

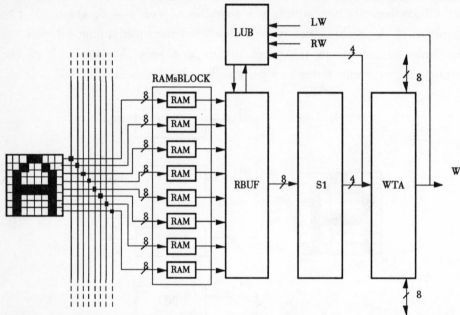

Fig. 2. The structure of the unit of the architecture shown in fig. 1. RAMsBLOCK is the block containing the RAMs, RBUF (RAMs Buffer) is the buffer for the RAMs, S1 (Sigma 1) is the block coding the activation level to the BCD code, LUB (Learning Unit Block) is the block controlling the learning phase of the unit. W is the winner signal, LW and RW are the Right Winner and the Left Winner signals.

The outputs of the previous block are sent to the WTA (Winner Takes All) block. The WTA block interacts with the WTAs of the other units by the WTA bus to individuate the winner unit which is the unit with the higher matching degree with the input pattern; when two or more units present the same matching degree, a simple circuit selects only one winner; in the present implementation the winner unit with the lower cardinality is chosen. This concludes the first step of the learning algorithm and also the whole test phase of the algorithm.

During the second step of the algorithm, the matching degree, of the winner and its neighbours, is increased by augmenting the number of matching n-tuples between the input pattern and the pattern classes. This is obtained by writing a 1 as the contents of some RAMs belonging to the winner unit and to the neighbours, when they are still addressed by the n-tuples of the input pattern. In the current implementation only the left and the right neighbours of the winner unit are considered. According to the theory[1] the matching degree is more increased in the winner unit than in the neighbours units.

This operation is carried on by the LUB (Learning Unit Block). During the learning phase the winner unit sends the signal W to its LUB and the signals LW (Left Winner) and RW (Right Winner) to the LUBs of the neighbours units.

The LUBs solicited by one of the signals W, LW, RW, increase the matching degree between the input pattern and the pattern class by accessing the corresponding RBUFs and by suitably switching some 0 to 1 in its content; the number of 0 switched to 1 is higher for the winner than its neighbours. At the end of the cycle the new content of RBUF is written to the corresponding RAMs of the units, while they are still addressed by the input pattern.

This concludes the second step of the learning algorithm. The operation during the learning phase of the architecture iteratively repeats these two step.

The test phase consists in the first step of the learning algorithm. It is to be noted that while the learning phase is an iterative process, the test phase is a single step process allowing for a quick classification of input patterns while the network is trained.

The simulations have been carried on by using the functional/logic simulator System Hilo of GenRad, Inc.

Fig. 3 shows a hardcopy output from the simulator. The first four lines (ROMBUFFERTRE[1], ... , ROMBUFFERTRE[4]) show the output waveform of the activation level of the 3rd unit of an architecture made up by 5 units. The last line shows the signal RAMREAD, which controls the read phase of the RAMs.

The activation level is obtained from the S1 block and it is therefore coded in BCD: the line ROMBUFFERTRE[1] represents the most significant bit.

The figure refers to the learning phase of the training set (described later) of fig. 4a. During each pulse of RAMREAD, one of the patterns belonging to the training set are presented to the network, in the same order as in fig. 4a.

At the beginning of the reported time slice, the map is already roughly self-organized; the unit under consideration is the winner when the 3rd pattern of the training set is presented but it is also sensitive, although in a weaker manner, to the 2nd and the 4th patterns.

Referring to the figure, when the 2nd pattern is presented to the network for the 1st time in the reported time slice the activation level of the unit is 1, when the 3rd pattern is presented for the 1st time in the reported time slice the activation level of the unit is 2 and when the 4th pattern is presented for the 1st time in the reported time slice the activation level of the unit is 1.

At the same time, the matching degree to the presented patterns increases: when the patterns are presented for the second time the activation levels sequence is 2,4,2, when they are presented for the third time the activation levels sequence is 3,6,3 and so on.

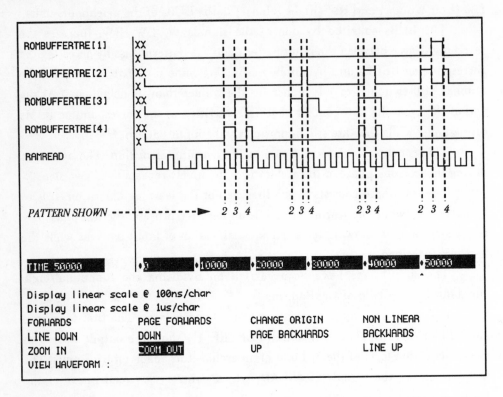

Fig.3. A screen hardcopy from the functional/logical simulator System Hilo. To help comprehension some comments in italics are outlined (see text for description).

The reported unit then reinforces, in an hard manner, its matching degree with the 3rd pattern of the training set, but also it reinforces in a weaker manner, the matching degree with the 2nd and the 4th patterns of the training set.

At the end of the reported time slice the architecture reaches the stable state: the unit is sensitive to the 3rd pattern and other presentations of patterns give no reinforcements of the activation of the unit.

4. EXPERIMENTAL RESULTS

Fig. 4 shows the final results of simulations of the architecture with 5 units. Each training set is made up by 5 classes of input patterns; for each training set 25 presentations of patterns have been carried out in order to reach a stable state of the network. The figure shows the organization of the map along with the representation of the prototypes for each class. In particular, fig. 4a is related to a training set made up by bars with different width; fig. 4b is related to a training set made up by rectangles with different dimensions and in different positions;it is to be noted in fig 4b that the 4th prototype collapses into the 3rd one by allowing the creation of a single class for both prototypes due to high degree of similarity in terms of n-tuples between the 3rd and 4th pattern classes.

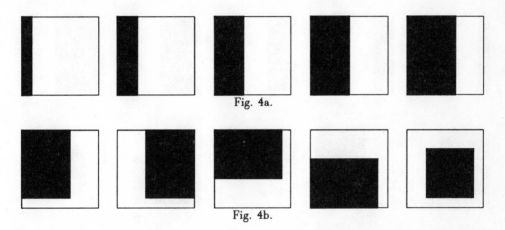

Fig. 4a.

Fig. 4b.

Fig. 4. Results of self-organizations of the proposed architecture when simple training sets are presented. Fig. 4a is related to a training set made up by bars with different width; fig. 4b is related to a training set made up by rectangles with different dimensions and in different positions: the 4th prototype collapses into the 3rd one by allowing the creation of a single class for both prototypes.

It should be noted that also in these simple training sets the basic characteristics of the self-organizing maps algorithm are exploited: i) the preservation of the topology of the input pattern space over the weights vectors of the network and ii) the optimum choice of the reference vectors of the input pattern space as the weights vectors of the network.

For the first point, as pointed out before, the topological ordering of the architecture reflects the chosen matching degree criterion: the class prototypes are ordered on the basis of their similarity, according to the number of matching n-tuples.

For the second point, it is to be noted that the self-organizing algorithm always chooses the optimum prototype for each class, thus improving the n-tuple pattern recognition scheme in which the pattern class is formed only by the sum of all the n-tuples belonging to the elements of the class.

training set 25 presentations of patterns have been carried out in order to reach a stable state of the network. The figure shows the organization of the map along with the representation of the prototypes for each class. In particular, fig. 4a is related to a training set made up by bars with different width; fig. 4b is related to a training set made up by rectangles with different dimensions and in different positions;it is to be noted in fig 4b that the 4th prototype collapses into the 3rd one by allowing the creation of a single class for both prototypes due to high degree of similarity in terms of n-tuples between the 3rd and 4th pattern classes.

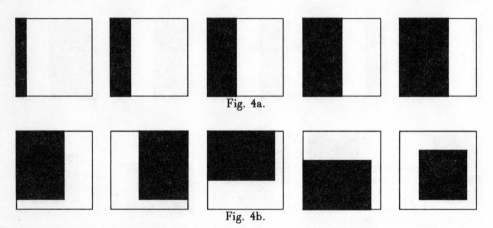

Fig. 4a.

Fig. 4b.

Fig. 4. Results of self-organizations of the proposed architecture when simple training sets are presented. Fig. 4a is related to a training set made up by bars with different width; fig. 4b is related to a training set made up by rectangles with different dimensions and in different positions: the 4th prototype collapses into the 3rd one by allowing the creation of a single class for both prototypes.

It should be noted that also in these simple training sets the basic characteristics of the self-organizing maps algorithm are exploited: i) the preservation of the topology of the input pattern space over the weights vectors of the network and ii) the optimum choice of the reference vectors of the input pattern space as the weights vectors of the network.

For the first point, as pointed out before, the topological ordering of the architecture reflects the chosen matching degree criterion: the class prototypes are ordered on the basis of their similarity, according to the number of matching n-tuples.

For the second point, it is to be noted that the self-organizing algorithm always chooses the optimum prototype for each class, thus improving the n-tuple pattern recognition scheme in which the pattern class is formed only by the sum of all the n-tuples belonging to the elements of the class.

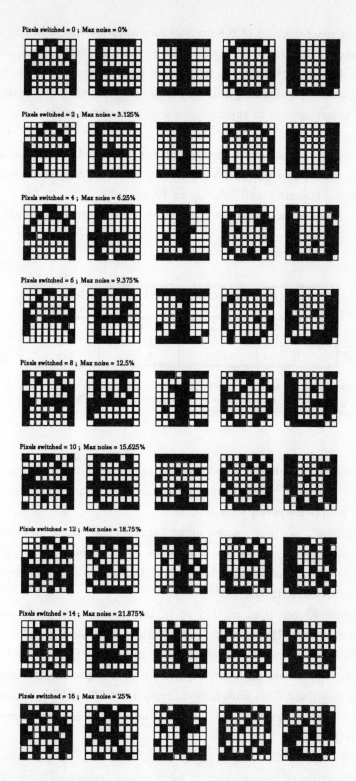

Fig. 5. Examples of vowels with superimposed noise obtained by random switching a number of pixels. The numer of pixel switched is in the range 0 - 16, corresponding to a range of noise of 0% - 25%.

A more extensive test of the proposed architecture has been carried on in order to recognize patterns representing vowels when noise has been superimposed. The superimposed noise may be measured both in % and in number of randomly switched pixels: in fact a random switch of m pixels in the input matrix corresponds to superimposing an amount of noise equal to m/64 %.

Fig. 5 shows examples of vowels with superimposed noise ranging from 0 to 25%; it is to be noted that it is hard also for a human observer to recognize a character with a superimposed noise up to 12.5%.

Three training methods have been tested; their characteristics are outlined in fig. 6.

Training set #	Dimension	Max noise %	Max # of switches
0	25	0	0
1	75	3.125	2
2	125	6.25	4

Fig. 6. Descriptions of the training sets tested for the recognition of noisy vowels. For each training set are specified its dimension, the maximum noise % and the corresponding maximum number of random pixel switched.

Training #1 has been carried on by presenting 25 times an input pattern chosen from the set of pattern prototypes; each prototype is thus presented 5 times with no superimposed noise.

Training #2 has been carried on by presenting 75 times an input pattern obtained from the set of pattern prototypes by randomly switching up to 2 pixels; this operation corresponds to the superimposition of an amount of noise ranging from 0% to 3.125%.

Training #3 has been carried on in the same way, but the number of presented patterns is 125 and the max number of random switch is up to 4 pixels in the input matrix, corresponding a noise ranging from 0% to 6.25%.

The test phase has been carried on by presenting to the architecture 100 patterns for any fixed noise with noise ranging from 0% to 25%, corresponding to random switch up to 16 pixels; the total number of patterns generated for such tests is 1600.

Fig. 7 shows the results of tests when the test sets with increasing noise uniformly distributed are presented to the architecture. The x-axis is the maximum random noise occurring in the training set while the y-axis represents the recognition % when the corresponding test set is presented to the architecture. The 3 curves are related to the 3 training sets above described.

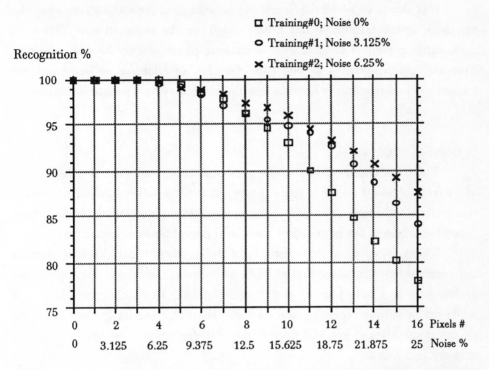

Fig. 7. Results of the tests obtained by presenting to the network 100 patterns for any fixed noise with noise ranging from 0% to 25%. The three curves are related to three training sets, each with a specified noise. In the x-axis are represented the max noise in the training set, either as noise% and in terms of random pixels switched; in the y-axis is represented the recognition %.

In all the cases a satisfactory behaviour of this simple architecture is observed showing its extreme robustness with respect to the noise: in fact the recognition % is up to 95% with "normal" noise less than 12.5% but the recognition maintains an high % of about 80 % also when pattern are very corrupted by noise as in the case of an amount of noise of 25%.

It is also to be noted the clear improvement of the recognition characteristics when an amount of noise has been added to the training set, in particular when patterns with noise greater than 12.5% are presented: when the superimposed noise is up to 25% the improvement of recognition is about 8% in training#2 and 12% in training#3.

The trade-off of superimposing noise in the training set mainly consists in a confused self-organization when the training patterns present a great amount of similarity in terms of n-tuples. In this case the architecture does not discriminate between different noisy patterns belonging to different classes and collapsing of different patterns in the same class may occur.

It is also to be noted the interesting behaviour of the architecture when the extremely quick training#0 has been carried on: the recognition is 78% with noise ranging from 0 to 25% after a training phase of only 25 presentations. This architecture is thus a good candidate for an adaptive on-line character recognition architecture, where the learning time may be a serious limitation.

5. CONCLUSION

The main characteristics of the presented architecture are that the coding of patterns is based on the n-tuple theory, which is a well-consolidated pattern recognition technique. The architecture implements the self-organizing map algorithm which is one of the most successful neural network algorithm.

The proposed architecture is a fully digital architecture simply implementable by standard digital VLSI techniques; the design of the proposed architecture is a fully parallel and distributed one. The architecture is in fact made up by simply repeating several times the described basic block allowing all the capabilities of graceful degradation and fault tolerance typical of neural network architectures.

REFERENCES

[1]   Kohonen, T., *Self-Organization and Associative Memory*. Springer-Verlag, Berlin, 1989.

[2]   Aleksander, I., Stonham, T.J., A Guide to Pattern Recognition Using Random Access Memories, *IEE J. Comput. & Digital Tech.* 2 (1), 29-40, 1979.

[3]   Aleksander, I., (ed.) *Neural Computing Architectures*. North Oxford Academic, London, 1989.

[4]   Steck, G.P., Stochastic model for the Browning-Bledsoe pattern Recognition Scheme, *IRE Trans. Electronic Computers*, EC-11, 274-282, 1962.

[5]   Chella, A., Gioiello, M., Sorbello, F., A New Digital Architecture Implementing the Kohonen Maps, in: Cappellini, V., Constantinides, A.G. (eds.), *Digital Signal Processing '91 - Proceedings of the 1991 International Conference on Digital Signal Processing*, Elsevier Science Publishers B.V., Amsterdam, The Netherlands (in press).

[6]   Ardizzone, E., Chella, A., Sorbello, F., A Digital Architecture Implementing the Self-Organizing Feature Maps, in: T. Kohonen, K. Makisara, O. Simula, J. Kangas (eds.), *Artificial Neural Networks, ICANN-91*, North-Holland, Amsterdam, 1991, pag. 721-727.

ELECTRICAL EQUIPMENT MAINTENANCE TRAINING: AN ITS APPLICATION IN INDUSTRIAL ENVIRONMENT

Alberta Bertin, Fabio Buciol, Giovanna Dondossola, Cristina Lanza
CISE Tecnologie Innovative S.p.A., P.O.Box 12081, I - 20134 Milano

Abstract

The paper reports objectives and results of a research and development activity aimed at designing Intelligent Training Systems (ITS) in industrial environments. The Electrical Equipment Maintenance Training (EEMT) system focuses on recurrent training of technical personnel employed in maintenance of electrical devices, the target being to sensitize experienced technician to safety problems.

Trainees are offered an environment free from real electrical risks in which they can learn how to cope with practical maintenance problems: the model of the electrical equipment coupled with a simulation mechanism provides the physical system behaviour; the explicit representation of the correct maintenance procedures and of the safety regulations support the monitoring and the evaluation of trainee's actions as well as explanations. Adaptability to the trainee needs and preferences is achieved by offering different training strategies and methods, session planning taking into account individual training objectives, and different levels of explanations. Replanning is based on the misconceptions and lacks of knowledge recognized by the diagnosis of detected trainee errors using an implicit cognitive model of his reasoning process. The human computer interface offers a 3D-graphics representation of the working scenario and a highly ergonomic and interactive dialogue system basing on Artificial Reality paradigm.

The work has been undertaken within Esprit Project p2615 which is funded by the Commission of the European Community and by the Electricity Board of Italy.

1. Introduction

This paper describes an Intelligent Training System to support recurrent training courses for expert maintenance personnel of electric distribution networks. The system has been designed within a collaborative project, ITSIE (Intelligent Training Systems in Industrial Environments), partially funded by the European Commission in the ESPRIT2 programme.

The aim of ITSIE is to provide a set of general tools for building Intelligent Training Systems in Industrial Environments and a related development methodology. Both the toolkit and the specification methodology are to be validated through the design and implementation of two demonstrators.

The Electrical Equipment Maintenance Training (EEMT) demonstrator presented in this paper has been designed using the ITSIE toolkit and is now being developed.

The scope of the EEMT system concerns maintenance and repair of electrical equipment of the electricity distribution network. These tasks are to be carried out on live devices. The aim of the system is to support the current training practice by improving trainee skill and background knowledge. Particular care is devoted to stimulating trainee risk awareness, and the conscious application of appropriate safety precautions.

The EEMT offers a simulated environment free from real electrical risks designed according to the Artificial Reality paradigm (Degli Antoni, 1990). The trainee can perform operations on the device to accomplish maintenance tasks by means of direct manipulation, whereas the tutorial dialogue is carried out through a set of predefined menus. A simulation of the behaviour of the electrical equipment underlies the training session to support maintenance operation.

Moreover, the trainee experience and learning needs play a significant role, affecting the training session and both the tutorial interaction and dialogue. The didactic module offers multiple training strategies, individual training objectives, different training methods, and different levels of explanation. The diagnostic module generates error hypotheses using a cognitive model of the error and individual trainee features, and supplies new training objectives to replan the session.

In the next section the overall system architecture is presented, explaining how the different modules are organized and integrated to constitute the whole system. The main features of the EEMT domain will be described in section 3, the adaptive behaviour of the training system with respect to trainee needs and preferences will be detailed in section 4, and the underlying concepts of the simulated laboratory provided to the trainee will be explained in section 5.

2. The EEMT System Architecture

The architecture of an ITS is usually composed of three main subsystems: the Domain, the Tutor and the Human Computer Interface (Wenger, 1987). In designing the EEMT they have been further subdivided identifying constituent submodules which encapsulate specific functionalities.

The EEMT Domain subsystem includes knowledge representation of the subject matter to be taught; this is organized in structural, functional and behavioural models of the equipment and procedural and/or associational models specifying how to operate on the equipment.

Three main modules have been identified: *Simulation*, *Supporting Expertise* and *Executable Expertise*:

-   the purpose of the *Simulation* module is to generate the behaviour of the electrical system subject of training. It consists of a structural and functional model of the physical system and a quantitative simulation mechanism;

-   the *Supporting Expertise* supports the animated environment provided on the Trainee Interface. It comprises a description of the physical environment as it appears to the trainee, including the electrical equipment, working tools and protective clothing to be chosen for accomplishing specific actions, and the management of the trainee operations;

- the *Executable Expertise* refers to the knowledge which can be executed to simulate the *expert behaviour*. It includes maintenance procedures and safety rules which specify the precautions to follow while operating. Executable Expertise is run both for expert behaviour simulation and for trainee monitoring and evaluation.

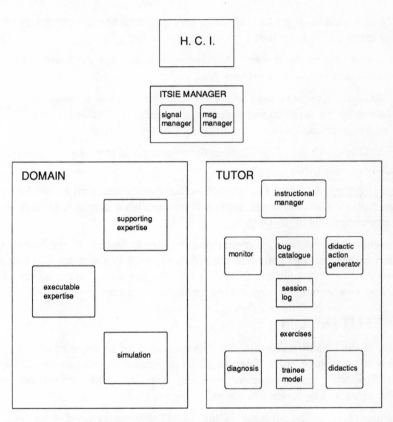

Figure 1 - EEMT System Architecture

The Tutor subsystem simulates the behaviour of a human instructor. It includes a didactic component for planning a training session tailored on the trainee learning needs, a component for monitoring the trainee performances, a diagnostic component which recognizes errors and infers possible misconceptions and lack of knowledge, and finally a trainee model and a set of knowledge bases supporting both the didactic and the diagnostic activities.

The EEMT Tutor is composed of five main functional modules: the *Instructional Manager*, the *Didactics*, the *Didactic Action Generator*, the *Monitor* and the *Diagnosis*:

- the *Instructional Manager* controls the overall training process, co-ordinating the other Tutor modules by sending specific messages in order to adapt the session to the individual trainee learning needs (e.g. providing error remedies to be applied in session re-planning);

- the *Didactics* creates and executes a *plan* for the session to achieve the training objectives, and adapts the plan basing on the interaction with the trainee according to the information provided by the Instructional Manager. The Didactics provides three levels of assistance depending on the attitude of the trainee and his competence, several methods to reach the same training objective, and different levels of explanation (see section 4);

- the *Didactic Action Generator* generates appropriate error explanations and responses to trainee queries or help requests;

- the *Monitor* verifies the trainee behaviour against the expert behaviour and classifies it as optimal, acceptable or incorrect;

- the *Diagnosis* interprets a trainee error and generates diagnostic hypotheses to be considered by the Instructional Manager to propose a suitable remedy. The remedy is applied by the Didactics causing a replanning of the session.

The Tutor modules make use of the Domain for teaching, for generating explanations, and for evaluating trainee behaviour.

The Human Computer Interface implements the interaction specified by the Didactics in the session plan and takes trainee inputs: actions to accomplish a maintenance task, answers to a test or a dialogue, queries to the Didactics.

It interfaces the system to both the trainee and the human instructor: the trainee interface is characterized by textual and graphical presentations, exercises and tests to accomplish the teaching process; the instructor interface allows the human trainer to access the ITS modules and the trainee representation for system maintenance and training supervision.

3. The EEMT Domain

The analysis of the EEMT problem and the identification of its requirements have led to the specification of the three main Domain areas presented in the above architecture, i.e. Simulation, Supporting Expertise and Executable Expertise. The information pertaining to each of these areas will be detailed in the following.

The Simulation part of the Domain in the EEMT system is needed for generating the behaviour of the electrical equipment subject of training. An *interactive* and *inspectable* simulation is provided: it allows the trainee to modify its electrical model while operating on it during maintenance, as well as to get the values of the electrical variables thus making explicit the current state of the device and the safety precautions to be applied. The effectiveness of interactive and inspectable simulations in training has been proved for developing the trainee cognitive model of the physical system he has to cope with (Hollan et al., 1984; Woolf et al., 1986).

Two main parts can be highlighted:

- a structural and functional model of the whole electrical system, including both the electrical circuit of the device and external agents which can intervene during maintenance tasks, such as the operator, the adopted working tools and protections;

- a quantitative simulation mechanism to be applied to the model for generating the system behaviour, and for giving the values of the significant physical variables.

The *model of the electrical system* has been built using a component-based language (Gallanti et al., 1987). This allows to generate the model from a library of electrical components that are to be chosen and connected to form the circuit. The components of the model are represented in terms of physical laws (e.g. the Ohm's law for resistors) and parameter values characterizing each component. In Fig.2 the model for a metering unit is reported. It consists of four main components: Generator, Meter, Limiter, User Load.

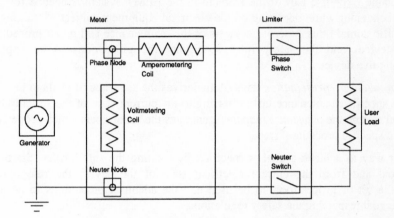

Figure 2 - Electrical Model of the Metering Unit

The model of the physical system is given to the quantitative *simulation mechanism* which takes the physical relations characterizing the circuit and solves the resulting system of equations to find out the values of the significant electrical variables. The result of simulation is used at least for two different purposes: first, variable values must be available when the trainee takes measures on the electrical device, or makes queries about them; in addition, they are used to detect dangerous contact events, short-circuits and any other possible accident caused by the trainee.

The Supporting Expertise is mainly intended to support the simulated laboratory (see section 5 below) provided by the graphical interface where the trainee is allowed to practice maintenance tasks being free from real electrical risks. It consists of a structural model of the physical system subject of training including a representation of the tools and the protective clothing to be adopted while operating. Moreover, a mechanism mapping the user manipulations on the graphical representation into maintenance actions and then modifications of the structural model is provided.

The *structural representation of the physical system* reflects the viewpoint of the operator acting on it: components relevant for the maintenance task simulation are represented, their current state being specified and mirrored in the graphical representation. Relations occurring among components of the physical system are created and released accordingly to the trainee manipulations: they support the propagation of the action effects through the structural model of the physical system.

The *actions managing mechanism* consists of three main functionalities:

- an analyzer of the trainee manipulations which filters them rejecting meaningless ones;

- a mechanism for the identification of the trainee's action starting from the tools currently in use and the state of the device components;

- finally the trainee's action execution is supported: modifications of the structural model of the physical system are triggered and then echoed at the graphical interface; moreover, if the action affects the electrical circuit underlying the device, the modification of the model of the electrical system is performed as well.

The Executable Expertise part of the Domain in the EEMT system is needed for generating the expert behaviour while operating on the electrical equipment subject of training. Because of the specific domain this expertise consists of the maintenance and repair procedures of the electrical devices and the safety rules specifying the precautions to be applied while manipulating live devices.

From the *procedure representation* the system derives the sequence of goals to be achieved to carry out a specific maintenance task: referring to the current state of the structural model of the physical system the *procedure manager* generates the set of goals which properly carry on the task at a specific procedural step.

The proper way to achieve a goal is specified by running the *safety rules*. Starting from a specific goal and from the current electrical state of the device the rule interpretation generates the set of proper tools to be used and the adequate protections to be adopted to achieve the goal respecting the safety regulations.

Thus coupling the procedural goals generation and the safety precautions specification the expert behaviour is provided both for supporting the monitoring of the trainee and for exemplifying the expert performances for training purposes.

4. The Adaptive Training

A main feature of an ITS is the capability of tailoring instruction to the individual needs of the trainee. The ability of an ITS of adapting the training process to the incoming learning needs and the trainee own style is mainly provided by a planning facility guided by an individual trainee model, and by the separation between the content of instruction and the way to teach it (Peachey and McCalla, 1986; Murray, 1989).

The *adaptive training* in the EEMT system is obtained through three basic functionalities offered by the Tutor: the possibility of selecting among three modes of interaction between the trainee and the system; *planning* and replanning facilities for a training session; different *levels of explanations* tailored on the trainee knowledge and needs.

Three *training strategies* are provided as *modes of interaction*: *Tutoring*, *Coaching* and *Self-Teaching*. They differ for the degree of assistance offered by the system and the degree of freedom allowed to the trainee and establish the teaching style taking into account the learning features and the expertise of the trainee:

- the *Tutoring* strategy offers the highest level of assistance intervening with explanations and suggestions whenever the trainee makes a mistake or does not know how to carry on. It particularly suits the needs of an inexperienced trainee;

- the *Coaching* strategy is addressed to expert trainees showing mastery of the subject of teaching, as it intervenes for hints and explanations only when the trainee does not respect safety rules.

- the *Self-Teaching* strategy allows the trainee to choose the topic, the objectives and the methods for the next training session. It is devoted to those users which are conscious of their knowledge and needs, and can autonomously determine the training session development. Self-Teaching also meets a specific requirement of recurrent training, that is letting human instructors be completely free in configuring all the main features of a session.

Planning of a training session is based on individual training *objectives* and on a defined library of training *methods*. The teaching material is provided by the domain knowledge while the form to present it is determined by a set of suitable training methods.

The *cognitive area* of the Bloom's taxonomy results particularly suitable for the specification of *training objectives* in designing training applications for industrial environments (Bloom, 1956). The main training objectives of the EEMT have been identified in that area and are classified as: technical background *knowledge*, its *application* in maintenance working tasks, and the *evaluation* of the existing danger in manipulating electrical equipments.

The human instructor decides the objectives the system has to deal with in accordance to the trainee learning needs; then the Tutor establishes a set of training methods to achieve each objective on the basis of information about their effectiveness represented in the trainee model. EEMT supplies skeletal plans for the following *methods*: *problem-driven*, *example-driven*, *explanation-driven* and *assessment*:

- the *problem-driven* method lets the trainee cope with a training problem acting on the simulation of the physical system. It allows to improve his application skills on working tasks in an environment free from risks;

- the *example-driven* method shows the expert behaviour during the execution of a maintenance task. The trainee can interrupt the system to query about the observed operations in order to know the general underlying criteria;

- the *explanation-driven* method consists of giving a lecture on technical background knowledge (e.g. structural, functional and behavioural knowledge on the physical system, as well as working methods and safety precautions). It is useful both for introducing a new topic and for reviewing previously acquired knowledge;

- the *assessment* method evaluates trainee theoretical knowledge by means of tests, such as multiple-choice questions or specific queries (e.g. "Where is component X?", "What is this?", "What is the functionality of X?").

A skeletal plan is defined as a sequence of training goals to be achieved by the Didactics. Training goals can be either refinable into more specific training goals or directly executable, the refinement depending on individual trainee features and on previous occurred didactic events (e.g. trainee queries, errors, etc).

A session plan may be modified during the interaction with the trainee in order to cope with new learning needs found out through the *diagnosis* of trainee errors.

Evaluation of student performance is carried out by monitoring the behaviour of the trainee and comparing it with the expert behaviour provided by the domain knowledge. Whenever a discrepancy is detected the diagnostic process is activated to interpret the error and to identify its deep causes. EEMT adopts a *classification-based* diagnosis based on a bug catalogue of general error *phenotypes* to support the interpretation of the detected error (Clancey, 1985). Each phenotype can be associated to a set of causal hypotheses (error *genotypes*). These associations constitute an implicit cognitive model of the operator reasoning process, based on information about the trainee working experience, such as records of instances from previous sessions, state of knowledge, experienced accidents. The resulting most probable causal hypothesis is used to replan the session with the aim of giving a remedy to the recognized lacks of knowledge or misconceptions.

Error and query *explanations* can be given at different levels of detail (Nicolosi and Bertin, 1990). Two are the significant parameters to choose the level of explanation suitable to the trainee: an evaluation of the observed performances and the frequency in querying the system about further detailed explanations. The facility of switching between different levels of explanation results in a way of tuning the tutorial dialogue, adapting it to the trainee comprehension capabilities, to his attitudes and preferred training style.

5. The EEMT Simulated Laboratory

A typical training session of the EEMT system is based on the simulation of a maintenance task on a specific electrical equipment: the system provides a simulated laboratory, where the trainee can practice and improve his capabilities. The EEMT simulated laboratory is based on partial simulation, oriented to give the user a subset of the sensorial stimuli (i.e. mainly visual stimuli) by exploiting sophisticated 3D graphic techniques.

The simulated laboratory is built according to the *Artificial Reality* (AR) paradigm which consists of representing a physical system at a level of realism adequate to the specific purpose of the system (Degli Antoni, 1990). The user can act on this representation and modify it by interactive hardware devices according to the rules and the methods of the simulated world. Thus an AR System is characterized by a model of the artificial world with an external (pictorial) and internal (structural) representation, a model of the interaction occurring between the user and the artificial world enabled by a set of specified hardware devices, and finally by a set of symbols and signs to make explicit the world internal status.

The interaction between the user and the artificial world is based on the *direct manipulation* paradigm (Cohen et al., 1989): each represented entity is an object which the user can "touch" and which reacts according to its own methods.

Object Oriented programming techniques have been adopted to implement the EEMT laboratory (Meyer, 1988). Entities of the artificial world, including components of the electrical equipment, working tools and protective clothing, are objects characterized by both a pictorial and a structural identity (see section 3).

Geometric and visual properties and methods allowing movement, like rotation and translation, belong to the pictorial identity, whereas the intrinsic properties of the entity, the state and methods for its modification are ascribed to the structural characterization.

The interaction mechanism allows the user to manipulate pictorial entities of the artificial world for simulating maintenance actions, typically assembly and disassembly of equipment components. Such actions modify the structural representation of the artificial world which is consequently mirrored on to the model of the electrical system. These modifications trigger in turn a pictorial feedback showing to the trainee the effect of the performed action.

The resulting EEMT dialogue system is highly ergonomic and interactive; its effectiveness derives from exploiting sophisticated graphic techniques, which make the representation very close to reality, and from implementing a simple and intuitive interaction mechanism.

6. Conclusions

The results of our research project have shown how the introduction of AI techniques can effectively enhance the design and development technology of computer based training systems in industrial environment specially in the following four areas:

- the simulation techniques exploiting component based models of the plants are getting both closer to the operator cognitive models and more effective in the formulation of explanations;
- the training interaction is made more flexible by adapting subject matter and selecting training strategies and methods according to the trainee learning needs and style on the basis of an explicit trainee representation;
- the diagnosis can effectively support the planning of the training session by making use of cognitive models of the operator behaviour and his errors;
- the dialogue system increases its effectiveness and ergonomics by exploiting 3D-graphic coupled to object oriented techniques to implement Artificial Reality and direct manipulation systems.

In the paper we have presented the current state of the work on the EEMT system which is still under development: the functional specification of the whole system have been completed, the implementation is in course. We intend to verify the effectiveness of the system basing on the final users feedback before long. Our research will continue on the formalization of the cognitive aspects of human learning in order to improve the student model, the explanation mechanism and the diagnostic process. Furthermore, the role of qualitative simulation techniques in training and learning activities will be analyzed.

Though the EEMT system has been designed for dealing with a particular industrial training problem, it has been conceived with the aim of being significative in the larger area of industrial applications of ITSs. The presented architecture highlights the underlying idea of keeping domain knowledge completely separated from the tutoring functionalities, thus pursuing general validity. In this way our application project offers a domain independent system capable of dealing with other problems of training in industrial environments. Furthermore, the proposed domain knowledge organization reflects a conceptual subdivision based on the nature and on the type of knowledge, thus allowing to clearly establish how the knowledge about the subject of training must be introduced in order to be easily available to the tutoring modules.

Acknowledgements

The work described in this paper has been undertaken in ESPRIT Project P2615 - ITSIE. The project is partly supported by the C.E.C. under the ESPRIT programme, and by the E.N.E.L., Electricity Board of Italy.

ITSIE is developed by a consortium composed of the following partners: Marconi Simulation, CISE, Iberduero, (with support from Labein and the Basque Country University), Alcatel Alsthom Recherche, CRI, Heriot Watt University. The authors wish to acknowledge the contribution of all the members of the project team to the work presented.

We also wish to acknowledge D. Marini of Università degli Studi di Milano, and M. Casanova and F. Grasso of CISE for the contribution provided on the Artificial Reality design.

References

Bertin, A., Buciol, F., Casanova, M., Mirandola, P., Nicolosi, E. (1990) *Knowledge-based system techniques applied to training to sensitize personnel to safety problem*, Proceedings BIAS 1990 - System Approach to Automation, Milano: ANIPLA.

Bloom, B.S. (1956) *Taxonomy of Educational Objectives: Book1. Cognitive Domain*, New York: Longmans Green.

Clancey, W.J. (1985) Heuristic Classification, *Artificial Intelligence* 27, 289-350.

Cohen, P.R. et al. (1989) *Synergistic Use of Direct Manipulation and Natural Language*, Proceedings CHI 89.

Degli Antoni, G. (1990) *Realtà Artificiale: una Silenziosa Rivoluzione Cognitiva*, Internal Report n.81/90, Dipartimento di Scienze dell'Informazione, Università degli Studi di Milano.

Gallanti, M., Gilardoni, L., Klausen, B., Levin, M., Malaureille, P., Routin, J., Stefanini, A., Tomada, L. (1987) *Representation Languages Specification*, Deliverable Report D2.1, Esprit Project P820, CISE 3625.

Hollan, J.D., Hutchins, E.L., Weitzman, L. (1984) STEAMER: An Interactive Inspectable Simulation-Based Training System, *AI Magazine* 5, 15-27.

Kearsley, G. (ed.) (1987) *Artificial Intelligence and Instruction*, Addison Wesley Publishing Company.

Meyer, B. (1988) *Object Oriented Software Construction*, Prentice Hall.

Murray, W.R. (1989) *Control for Intelligent Tutoring Systems: A Blackboard-based Dynamic Instructional Planner*, Proceedings of the 4th International Conference on AI and Education, Amsterdam: IOS.

Nicolosi, E., Bertin, A. (1990) *An Analysis of Explanation Types in Intelligent Tutoring Systems*, Proceedings of the 5th Workshop on Explanation, Manchester.

Peachey, D.R., McCalla, G.I. (1986) Using planning techniques in intelligent tutoring systems, *Int. J. Man-Machine Studies* 24, 77-9.

Reason, J. (1987) Generic Error-Modelling System (GEMS): A Cognitive Framework for Locating Common Human Error Forms, in J. Rasmussen, K. Duncan and J. Leplat (eds.) *New Technology and Human Error*, John Wiley & Sons Ltd.

Sleeman, D., Brown, J.S. (eds.) (1982) *Intelligent Tutoring Systems*, London: Academic Press Inc.

Wenger, E. (1987) *Artificial Intelligence and Tutoring Systems*, Los Altos: Morgan Kaufmann Publishers Inc.

Woolf, B., Blagen, D., Jansen, J.H., Verloop, A. (1986) *Teaching a Complex Industrial Process*, Proceedings AAAI-86, Philadelphia: Morgan Kaufmann Publishers Inc.

Short Papers

TEMPORAL AND SPATIAL DATA AND DEFAULT ASSUMPTIONS IN DIPSY-E SYSTEM

M.Kantardžić, V. Okanović, S. Rizvić, A.Filipović, H. Glavić

Faculty of Electrical Engineering

Toplička bb

71000 Sarajevo

Yugoslavia

ABSTRACT

DIPSY-E is software environment for development of real-time expert systems. Since time varying events or space distribution dependent objects appear in these systems, the temporal and spatial data is included in DIPSY-E. Problems of incomplete information and unreachable data in such systems can be solved by means of DIPSY-E default assumptions mechanisms.

The temporal componenet is defined on the level of object attributes, while the spatial component is defined on the level of objects. Besides an absolute temporal component, taken from a real clock, a relative component taken from a symbolic clock is introduced.

The temporal and spatial relations, functions and procedures are introduced.

The default assumptions are based on default values. These can be defined on levels of either an attribute value, a rule condition or a rule conclusion.

1. INTRODUCTION

There are many problems for which, in order to solve them, we have to analyse time-varying events or parameters, space distribution dependent objects or incomplete informations. This is the reason why the systems, handling this problems, should contain temporal, spatial and default reasoning capabilities [3,4,9,11].

The domain where time and space characteristics and default assumptions are extreamly important is engineer systems design, as well as knowledge based monitoring and control of real-time systems.

Temporal, spatial and default components enable us to:

- establish the relations among the current and the previous values of variables

- examine if two objects are close or far to each other, adjacent or abreast

-generate conclusion when there is no complete information and enables use of common-sense knowledge [20,21].

These components are theoreticly defined and applied in production planning, robotics, expert systems development etc. [3,5,6,8,10,12,14].

Starting with previous ideas applied in expert systems development , we extended the previous version of DIPSY-E system [4] with temporal, spatial and default reasoning capabilities, thereby giving objects and their attributes a time and space dimension, introducing the temporal and the spatial relations and functions upon them and implementation of data structures used in situations of default reasoning activation in DIPSY-E system as well as management of these structures .

2. Temporal data representation in DIPSY-E system

Temporal data are in DIPSY-E system stored discrete as time instants and defined on the level of object attributes [4]. Every object-attribute pair can have a time-tag component.

Object attribute becomes temporal if we define that it is TIME_DEPENDENT. The global parameters are defined on the system level and they refer to all TIME_DEPENDENT attributes in the system.

Introducing temporal data on a concept level means defining following global parameters [2,5,7]:

- TIME - can be absolute or relative. The absolute time is the real time taken from a computer real-time clock, while a relative time is taken from a symbolic clock.

- TIME_FORMAT - for an absolute time can be SEC, MIN, HOUR, DAY or YEAR, while for a relative time, format is integer determining only the order of time instances, but not their absolute values. Since format mostly depends on a particular application, system is initialised with time format used in that application.

- DURATION_TYPE - typical duration types for one datum are : **instant** (the value is undefined between the specified points), **valid_for_an_interval, valid_until_changed** and **interpolated.**

It is specific in modeling of continual values of real-time process parameters, that the values are approximated with data valid until next measurement, so we introduce a new duration type, VALID_UNTIL_MEASURED

*   Research supported by *SIZ nauke Bosne i Hercegovine* under grant Information Technologies (Productica)-DCIX-TO5-NP4

- IIISTORY - determines the number of previous values being kept. Taking care of history of some variable means memorising a definite number of its previous values. Various functions can be applied to these values, like variation rate, trend, changes in time (increasing, decreasing etc.). Number of values contained in the history is also introduced as one of time attributes in DIPSY-E system.

All the defined parameters except TIME and DURATION_TYPE have equal values for all TIME_DEPENDENT attributes in the system.

An absolute temporal component can be taken from computer **real clock** along with data from a monitored process, from the external procedures called from rules and (eventualy) from the user. Relative temporal component is taken when symbolic clock is activated. **Symbolic (local) clock** is a mechanism that generates integer values used to establish temporal correlations among events in the knowledge base. Thus it is possible to define what happend "before", "after" or "simultaneous" to something else. Yet, it is not possible to find the real time distance among the events. Activation can be initiated by an external procedure executed by a rule.

3. Spatial data representation in DIPSY-E system

In difference to temporal attributes, defined at object attribute level, spatial attributes are defined at object level.

Objects can be static and dynamic. Static objects coordinates are not changeable, but dynamic objects can change their place, that is they are at one place in one moment, and at different place in another moment. It means that dynamic objects are also time-dependant beside being space-dependent.

Spatial determined data belong to SPACE_DEPENDANT class which contains following attributes :

- x coordinate (X_CO)
- y coordinate (Y_CO)
- z coordinate (Z_CO)
- data storage format (SPACE_FORMAT) - defined on systems level similar as temporal data format. Can be MM, CM, M or KM.
- spatial data position variability (SPACE_VARYING) - depending on capability of the object to change its position in time, this attribut has values YES or NO.

4. Temporal and spatial relations, functions and procedures

Relations and functions introduced in DIPSY-E system are presented in the following table:

	relations		functions	procedures
temporal	upon	BEFORE	DURATION	GET TREND
	time instances	AFTER	CHANGE FORMAT	
		SIMULTANEOUS	VARIATION RATE	
	upon	BEFORE I	TREND	
	time intervals	AFTER I	CORRELATION	
		OVERLAPS	INCREASE START	
	upon time	LONGER	DECREASE START	
	interval durations	SHORTER	CHANGE START	
		EQUAL		
spatial		NEAR	DISTANCE	
		FAR	ADJACENT OBJ	
		ADJACENT	ABREAST OBJ	
		ABREAST		

The relations, functions and procedures are realised in a form of library. Their parameters are not listed, for the matter of simplicity.

The use of temporal relations and functions upon time varying attributes is ilustrated by following example :

> RULE crankshaft_bearings_damage:
>
> IF [x] {motors} (no_of_rotations 4000,
> working_temperature 70)
> AND damage_manifestations (sound > banging)
> AND SIMULTANEOUS (INCREASE_START([x].no_of_rotations),
> INCREASE_START([x].working_temperature))
> THEN damage (possible :+ {crankshaft_bearings});
> needed (action :+ {crankshaft_replacement});

Rule crankshaft_bearings_damage means that if we have an object which belongs to motors class and has the no_of_rotations larger then 4000 rpm and the working_temperature higher then 70 degrees, and also the object damage_manifestations says that the set of sounds we hear when motor is working contains banging and the working_temperature started to increase at the same time with the *no_of_rotations*, then conclude that the set of possible damages contains damage on crankshaft bearings, and add replacement of the crankshaft to needed actions.

The use of spatial relations is ilustrated by the rule from our CSP-TSS system [6] :

> RULE *adjacent_sensor_value_overflow:*
> IF *[x] {sensor} (signal_value treshold)*
> AND *[y] {sensor} (signal_value treshold)*
> AND *[x] [y]*
> THEN *IF ADJACENT([x],[y])*
> THEN *activation_causes_equal*
> ELSE *activation causes_different;*

It means that if activated sensors are adjacent, then conclude that activation causes are equal, else conclude that activation causes are different.

5. Default assumptions

By default assumptions, we mean assumptions defined thus they represent some common-sense knowledge that can be used when there is no complete information, needed in the reasoning process. There are three types of default assumptions in DIPSY-E system[12, 13, 14]:

The structure 'list' containing introduced and concluded default assumptions, will be used in examples describing default assumptions use.

a) **Default assumption on an attribute value level**: if a particular object attribute value is not known, a common-sense value is assumed. This value we call **default attribute value**. Collection of all such values represent **default assumptions base**.

Scenario 1: Example of reasoning based on an attribute value:

Let there be an engine on a test in a factory. If an environment temperature of the testing place is unknown, we will assume that it has a value of 20 (centigrade degree). If environmental agents are represented by an object 'environment' then this assumption, written in DIPSY-E language, looks like:

> **default** environment (temperature 20)

Let this be an element of a default attribute value assumptions base. Let there be the following two rules in the knowledge base (in the rules all the conditions and conclusions irrelevant to the example, i.e. with no interference to default reasoning process, are omitted):

RULE1: IF	RULE2: IF
.	.
environment (temperature >15)	engine (temperature 70)
.	.
THEN	THEN
.	.
engine (temperature 80)	engine (oil_pressure 5)
.	

Let the rule1 be analyzed in a reasoning process. Let there be no *environment temperature* entry in the base of facts. In this case a list is created with the assumption

> *environment (temperature 20)*

as a root. Thus we have:

List = { environment (temperature 20) }

Assuming that all the other conditions of the rule1 are satisfied, the fact

> *engine (temperature 80)*

will be concluded. This fact is valid only if the assumption

> *environment (temperature 20)*

is valid. Thus the concluded fact differs from the facts generated without default assumptions. In order to denote this difference we include the fact

> *engine (temperature 80)*

as the second node of the list. Thus we have:

List = { *environment (temperature 20), environment (temperature 80)* }

Now let the rule2 be analyzed in the reasoning process. The condition is obviously satisfied. Suppose that all the other conditions of the rule2 are satisfied. Then the fact

> *engine (oil_pressure 5)*

is concluded.

Since this conclusion depends on the fact

engine (temperature 80)

which also depends on the introduced assumption

environment (temperature 20)

it appears that the last conclusion also depends, thou indirectly, on the assumption

environment (temperature 20)

Thus this fact becomes the next element of the list. Now we have:

List = { *environment (temperature 20), environment (temperature 80) , engine (oil_pressure 5)* }
Let us analyze a different case. Let the condition of the rule1 now have the form

environment (temperature 15)

If all the other assumptions from the previous example are unchanged, since the assumption

environment (temperature 20)

does not satisfy the condition

environment (temperature 15)

The reasoning process continues as if there were no default assumptions, i.e. the list is not created at all.

b) **Default assumption on a rule condition level**: if there are no facts in the base, needed for a particular condition analysis, an assumption is introduced that the condition is satisfied. This condition we call **default condition. Default condition** is labeled by an additional word '**default**' after the text of condition thus differing from non **default condition.**

Scenario 2: Example of reasoning based on a rule condition:
Let the rule1 from the scenario1, have the following form:

RULE1: IF

.

environment (temperature >15 **default**)

.

THEN

.

engine (temperature 80)

.

The condition of the rule becomes default condition, because the word '**default**' is specified behind the condition. Let the reasoning process analyze the rule1 and let there not be the fact *environment temperetute* in the base of facts . A list is created with the assumption

environment (temperature >15) default

as a root. Thus we have:

List = { environment (temperature>15) }
Assuming that all the other conditions of the rule1 are satisfied, the fact

engine (temperature 80)

will be concluded. This fact is valid only if the assumption

environment (temperature>15)

is valid. Thus the concluded fact differs from the facts generated without default assumptions. In order to denote this diference we include the fact

engine (temperature 80)

as the second node. Thus we have:

List = { (environment (temperature 15), *engine (temperature 80)* }
Using the knowledge base from the scenario1, the reasoning process is continued identically to the reasoning process described in scenario1 from the point where the rule2 have been analyzed.

c) **Default assumption on a rule conclusion level**: there are common-sense knowledge rules in a reasoning process, able to generate data. Such a datum we call **default conclusion. Default conclusion** is labeled by an additional word '**default**' after the text of conclusion, thus differing from non **default conclusion**. It can be used in the reasoning process as a **default attribute value.** This type of **default assumptions** is, in fact, the most commonly found with other authors[12, 13, 14].

Scenario3: Example of reasoning based on a rule conclusion:
Let us introduce a rule0 as a common-sense rule meaning:
"If, among the weather conditions, we do not no anything about the temperature, but we know that the season is a spring, we shall assume that the temperature is 20". If the weather conditions are represented by the object 'environment', we can describe this assumption, using DIPSY-E language, as:

RULE0: IF

environment (season spring)
THEN
environment (temperature 20default)

A conclusion of a rule becomes default conclusion specifying the word 'default' behind the conclusion. Reasoning process using a default conclusion can be described on the example of the knowledge base from scenario1 as follows:

Let the reasoning process analyzes the rule0 and let the condition of the rule0 is satisfied. A list is created, having the concluded fact as a root:

List = { environment (temperature 20) }

The reasoning process is continued identically to the reasoning process described in scenario1 from the point where the list have been created.

The definition of the default assumptions is performed trough a knowledge base editor available in DIPSY-E system. During the edition of knowledge base, default attribute values are defined in the default assumptions base, while default condition and default conclusion are defined in rules.

6. CONCLUSION

The possibilities of implementation of default, temporal and spatial component in expert systems are considered in this paper.

Temporal and spatial data are implemented in DIPSY-E system by introducing temporal and spatial object attributes and corresponding standard relations and functions upon these attributes.

An approach, based on introduction of three types of default assumptions in DIPSY-E system is given.

All the functions and relations in DIPSY-E system are implemented as compiled C procedures, in form of a library. The library is a part of the complete DIPSY-e system, thus the library elements become elements of the language, ensuring maximum run-time efficiency. It is possible to extend the library with new relations and functions, depending on concrete applications of DIPSY-e system.

Reasoning mechanisms, based on these data and assumptions, are developed and implemented, and described in [14].

REFERENCES:
1. Allen J.F., "Toward a General Model of Action and Time ", Artifical Intelligence, Vol. 23, No 2., 1984.
2. Adorni G., Cammuri A., Poggi A., Zaccaria R., "Integrating Spatio-Temporal Knowledge, A Hybrid Approach", ECAI, Munich, August 1988.
3. Dean T.L., McDermott V.D., " Temporal Data Base Management", Artifical Intelligence, Vol. 27, No 1., 1987.
4. Filipović A., Kantardžić M., Glavić H., Gujić N., Okanović V., "DIPSY-E: Expert System Development Tool (Overview, Expiriences and Development Directions)", 1. Conference on Achievements and Implementations of AI, Dubrovnik, October 1989.
5. Huber A., Becker S., "Production Planning using a Temporal Planning Component", ECAI, Munich, August 1988.
6. Kantardžić M., Glavić H., Filipović A., " Computer Aided Design of Technical Security Systems: Knowledge-Base Founded Approach", ETAN, XXXII Yugoslav Conference, 1988.
7. Laasri H., Maitre B., Mondot T., Charpillet F. and Haton J.P., "ATOME : A Blackboard Architecture with Temporal and Hypothetical Reasoning", ECAI, Munich, August 1988.
8. Marc V., Kautz H., " Constraint propagation algorithms for temporal reasoning ", Proceedings 5.th AAAI, Philadelphia, USA, 1986
9. Perkins W.A. and Austin A., "Adding Temporal Reasoning to Expert-System-Buliding Environments", IEEE Expert, Vol. 5, No. 1, February 1990.
10. Petrović S., "The Temporal logic of artifical inteligence", Automatika 29 (1988) 5-6, 187-196, december 1988.
11. D. Poole, 'A Logical Framework for Default Reasoning ', Artificial Intelligence 36, Elsevier Science Publishers B.V. North-Holand, 1988.
12. Marie-Odile Cordier, ' Sherlock : Hypothetical Reasoning in an Expert System Shell ', Proceedings "ECAI '88", Minhen, August, 1988.
13. D. McDermott, ' Nonmonotonic Logic II: Nonmonotonic Modal Theories', Journal of the Association for Computing Machinery, Vol 29, No 1, January, 1982.
14. M.Kantardžić, S. Rizvić, V. Okanović, A. Filipović, H. Glavić: "Temporal, Spatial and Default Reasoning in DIPSY-E System", The World Congress on Expert System, Orlando, Florida, December, 1991.

Visual indexing with an attentive system[*]

Ruggero Milanese   Jean-Marc Bost   Thierry Pun

Computer Science Centre
University of Geneva
12, rue du Lac
1207 Geneva – Switzerland
E–mail: *milanese@cui.unige.ch*

Abstract

In this paper we propose a new architecture for a general–purpose computer vision system whose design principles have been inspired by the study of human vision. Two important components are an object recognition module and a focus of attention module, respectively called "what" and "where" subsystems. The "what" subsystem is implemented through a set of agents that cooperate towards the interpretation of the image features. The "where" subsystem acts as a control module by detecting locations in the image which contain features that are likely to belong to interesting objects. A succession of attention windows is then generated for such locations and used to gate the parts of the image that are analyzed by the agents.

1   Motivations

To date there are two main approaches to the design of computer vision systems: the most traditional one, based on the hypothesize–and–test paradigm, and the one that exploits parallel architectures, based on artificial neural networks. Although the former, classical approach is still the most suitable for most applications, it suffers from the computational complexity of the matching problem [8]. On the other hand, neural network systems can achieve fast and reliable recognition only for very constrained applications.

In order to overcome the previous limitations we have considered some design principles suggested by cognitive neurosciences:

- **Visual indexing:** the process of object recognition is structured into two main phases. The first, called *primal access*, consists of a direct indexing into a database of models using the low–level primitives that have *non–accidental* features [1]. A second phase then refines the results. However, the heaviest part of the matching problem is attacked during the first, bottom–up process.

---

[*]Acknowledgements: This research is supported by a grant from the Swiss National Fund for Scientific Research, National Research Program NFP/PNR 23 (*AI and Robotics*, 4023-027036).

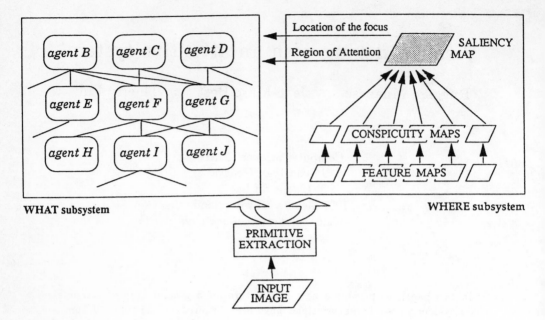

Figure 1: System architecture.

- **Focus of attention:** despite the highly parallel organization of the brain, forms of information selection appears at all stages of processing. Many visual tasks also imply sequential behaviors that are based on the concept of a focus of attention. Such focus is moved to parts of the image which contain the most interesting information, which is selected for detailed processing and object recognition [5].

The architecture we propose exploits the idea of having two cooperating modules that perform these functions. One is responsible for the primal access, i.e. for object recognition and is called *what* subsystem. The other is the focus–of–attention module, called *where* subsystem, and detects the likely location of interesting objects.

2   Overview of the system

The operation of the system is a two–stage process. In the first stage a set of low–level primitives are extracted from the input image. The second stage is a loop, in which the *where* subsystem defines regions of attention and selects the corresponding input primitives for the *what* subsystem [7] (see figure 1).

The extraction of low–level primitives is performed in parallel by a set of image–processing modules. At the current stage of the system, two such modules are implemented, respectively for the extraction of contours and regions. Work is in progress to add modules for corner detection and for the extraction of intrinsic color properties. Contour detection is based on Deriche's recursive edge detection operator [3]. A list of edge chains is then obtained by a peak following algorithm; the chains are split at peaks of the

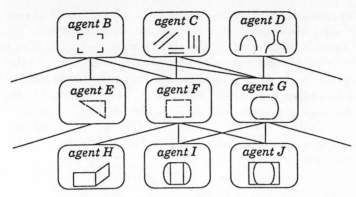

Figure 2: A network of discriminating agents.

local curvature function [4]. Regions are extracted by a classical recursive region–splitting algorithm for color images [6].

The primitives computed in the first stage are used by the *where* subsystem to detect regions of interest in the image. This is a bottom–up process which plays a key role in human vision attention [5]. The general idea is that any primitive which has a "singular" attribute (such as length, orientation, or size) is a potentially interesting primitive. To this end, the hierarchy of data structures represented on the right–hand side of figure 1 is built from the low–level primitives, and a sequence of regions that contain the most singular attributes is extracted. Each region of interest detected by the attention module is used to select a subset of low–level primitives for the *what* subsystem. This in turn is implemented by a set of *agents*, which run discrimination tests that reduce in parallel the possible interpretations [2]. In the next sections the functioning of the *what* and *where* subsystems is described in more details.

3   The *what* subsystem

The goal of the *what* subsystem, which is responsible for object recognition, is to consider a set of primitives extracted from the image and to reduce as much as possible the set of (a–priori known) possible interpretations. To this end, a set of properties are evaluated on the input primitives, with particular emphasis to the *non–accidental* ones [1].

Checking visual properties requires several sequential tests. For example, to determine if a set of segments forms a pair of adjacent rectangles, parallelism is first checked for pairs of segments, then rectangularity, then adjacency between rectangles. By grouping properties that require common tests, a classification hierarchy is defined. Subclasses contain further tests and are used to characterize more specialized properties. As the goal of the tests is to discriminate among objects, they are called *discrimination tests*.

Discrimination tests are defined through frame structures. Each frame contains a list of labels which are consistent if the test is verified, a list of inconsistent labels, a discrimination procedure with pointers to the input primitives and links to ancestors and descendants. This hierarchy is translated into a network of *agents* (see figure 2). Ancestor and descendant links specify connections between agents, whereas the other slots are used to define their behaviors.

The identification process starts by triggering all agents at the top level of the hierarchy, which simultaneously evaluate their tests to reduce the set of possible labels. If the test is successful, the resulting lists of labels are transmitted to the successors. If the test fails, the agent is deactivated. If the agent is unsettled, reductions made by other agents allow to decide whether it should have been successful or not. In this manner, even independent agents cooperate. A successor is in turn triggered as soon as it receives all the expected information, i.e. when all its ancestors have completed their job.

A major advantage of this organization is that agents that are not linked together are independent and can be activated in parallel. In addition, when noisy features affect the behavior of some agents, other agents can still reduce the solution set, thereby ensuring a graceful degradation of the performance.

4   The *where* subsystem

The goal of the *where* subsystem is to define regions of attention that contain the most "interesting" primitives. To this end, some features are computed for all the primitives, and compared with each other. The following ones are currently evaluated:

- Contours: length, orientation, average contrast, average curvature;
- Regions: area, elongation, average color.

Each of these features is represented into a different *feature map* and is analyzed to determined the degree of singularity of each location. Such measure is then used to rank the interest for the corresponding primitive. In order to evaluate the degree of singularity, a neighborhood function is defined and each primitive is compared with all other primitives that are contained in its neighborhood. More precisely, the following expression is evaluated for every location (i, j) of the k-th feature map F^k:

$$C_{i,j}^k = \frac{1}{\| N_{i,j} \|} \sum_{(m,n) \in N_{i,j}} | F_{i,j}^k - F_{m,n}^k |$$

where $N_{i,j}$ is the neighborhood centered on (i, j), and $\| N \|$ is the number of primitive points contained in the neighborhood. The results of this computation are stored into a set of *conspicuity maps* $\{C^k\}_k$. Each conspicuity map then represents for each location a degree of interest related to a specific feature. Once the conspicuity maps are computed, a single *saliency map* S is built to conjoin them. To this end, the values of the conspicuity maps are first amplified through an exponential function in order to enhance the locations with high conspicuity. The amplified values are then combined with a weighted sum. An additional operation which appears to further improve the quality of the results is the multiplication by the contrast conspicuity map:

$$S_{i,j} = C_{i,j}^{contrast} \sum_k a_k e^{C_{i,j}^k}.$$

Figure 3 reports the results obtained using only the contour conspicuity maps. As it can be seen, the three most interesting objects have a different size from the objects of the background and their contour is also more regular. For this reason, the weights used for the saliency map (fig. 3.c) emphasize the length and curvature conspicuity maps (respectively 1/3, 1/3, 1/6, 1/6 for length, curvature, orientation and contrast). The results show that the most salient locations correspond well with what is perceived as the most interesting primitives of the image.

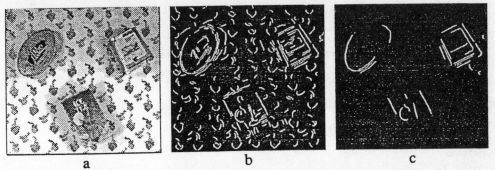

a   b   c

Figure 3: (a) Input image; (b) image contours; (c) saliency map obtained from the contour conspicuity maps. For display purposes, a binary version of the saliency map is shown by selecting the pixels with the highest values (upper 95% of the dynamic range).

5 Conclusions and future work

In this paper the architecture of a computer vision system has been described, which couples two main modules: an object recognition system and a focus of attention system. Experiments run on non–trivial examples show that the bottom–up attention process is robust enough to detect the salient objects of the scene. In the future we want to make it more powerful by adding a top–down component, which will be generated by the agents whenever the features they analyze are either incomplete or inconsistent. These are the cases when the region of attention is respectively too small or too large. This information will thus be used to generate a new focus which better complies with the requirements of the agents.

References

[1] I. Biederman, "Aspects and Extensions of a Theory of Human Image Understanding", in: Z.W. Pylyshyn, ed., *Computational Processes in Human Vision: An Interdisciplinary Perspective*, Ablex Publishing, 1988, pp. 370-428.

[2] J.-M. Bost, "A Distributed Architecture for Visual Indexing", University of Geneva, Computer Science Center, Technical Report in preparation.

[3] R. Deriche, "Fast Algorithms for Low–Level Vision", *IEEE Transactions on Pattern Analysis and Machine Intelligence*, Vol. 12, No. 1, January 1990, pp. 78-87.

[4] D.G. Lowe, "Organization of Smooth Image Curves at Multiple Scales", *Int. Journ. of Computer Vision*, Vol. 3, 1989, pp. 119-130.

[5] R. Milanese, "Focus of Attention in Human Vision: A Survey", University of Geneva, Computer Science Center, A.I. and Vision Group, Technical Report 90-03, 1990.

[6] R. Ohlander, K.E. Price and D.R. Reddy, "Picture Segmentation Using a Recursive Splitting Method", *Computer Graphics and Image Proc.*, Vol. 8, 1978, pp. 313-333.

[7] T. Pun, "The Geneva Vision System: Modules, Integration, and Primal Access", University of Geneva, Computer Science Center, A.I. and Vision Group, Technical Report 90-06, 1990.

[8] J.K. Tsotsos, "Analyzing Vision at the Complexity Level", *Behavioral and Brain Sciences*, Vol. 13, 1990, pp. 423-469.

ON NEURAL NETWORK PROGRAMMING

P. De Pinto and M. Sette
Istituto per la Ricerca sui Sistemi Informatici Paralleli – CNR Napoli

Keywords: Neural network, Parallel processing, Parallel architectures.

Scientific topic: Architectures, languages and environments.

Abstract

In this paper we investigate how a neural network can be regarded as a massive parallel computer architecture. To this end, we focus our attention not on a stochastic asynchronous model, but on the McCulloch and Pitts network [MP43], as modified by Caianiello [Cai61], and we specify what we mean for the environment in which the network operates: it is essentially the entity assigning meaning to the network input and output nodes. Changing the environment definition implies dealing with different neural architectures.

To show how to program a neural architecture, we introduce a model of environment helping us in choosing functions suitable to be pipelined, as in a data flow architecture. As an example, we sketch the working of a parallel multiplier function.

1. The network and its environment

The neural system we are going to consider is a deterministic, synchronous network (see [Lau88, Lau89, DPLS90, Set90]) of simple processing elements u_i, whose activation function is:

$$f_i(t) = \delta \left(\sum_{jl} C_{ijl} f_j(t - l\tau) - \theta \right) \tag{1}$$

where θ is a threshold, C_{ijl} is the weight of the l-dalayed connection between node u_i and u_j, τ is the time unit and $\delta(x)$ is 1 if $x \geq 0$, it is 0 otherwise.

As we want to characterize our network as a parallel distributed processing system [RM86], it isn't enough to specify its internal function, but we need to define also its environment and the relationship between network and environment. This is an often disregarded field, that is crucial for us in defining a network that is non closed to itself but opened and interacting with other entities [Hew85].

We point out that a *parallel computer architecture* is made up of an environment whose evolution is controlled by a neural network with suitable connection weights, input (sensor) and output (motor) nodes. Changing the environment definition implies changing the neural controller and so the computer architecture.

In the following we want to characterize the environment for a neural architecture. It is made of:

- a knowledge base, representing the external world structures. It is better to choose it as close as possible, so to have more constraints to the problem, but nothing limits us to build an open and unpredictable one;

- an interpreter, modifying the knowledge base according to the network output patterns.

Now we define the input and output nodes. The neural program identifies a subset of nodes, called output nodes: they are the only way the network has to control its environment, i.e. their activation values act as procedure calls to the environment interpreter.

The node activation function is not sufficient to characterize the network-environment interactions. While the hidden and the output nodes have a linear threshold activation function (1), the input nodes (sensors) have an activation function dependent on the environment instantaneous configuration. So they represent properties of the environment.

Now let us discuss the *control problem*. At each cycle the environment interpreter modifies the knowledge base. The modifications might be either simple or complex ones: simple or complex in respect to the atomic (symbolic) structure of the knowledge base. More complex are the modifications, less fine tuned is the network control.

Our goal is to transfer more control to the neural network, by using environments that at each cycle perform infinitesimal (sub-symbolic [Tra91]) transformations on the knowledge base. This means handling

Authors address: Dipartimento di Scienze Fisiche, Università degli Studi di Napoli, Pad. 19 Mostra d'Oltremare, I-80125 NAPOLI (Italy). Email: depinto@napoli.infn.it or sette@napoli.infn.it.

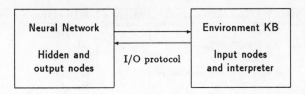

Figure 1: Neural Network + Environment = Parallel Computer Architecture.

neural networks with very large number of nodes, to get, in a very large number of cycles, the same wanted complex modification of the environment.

In conclusion, for *neural network programming*, we mean:

1. definition of the knowledge base that represents the environment, if it is not given physically;

2. definition of the interpreter that executes the procedures called by the motor nodes;

3. definition of the sensors and of their activation function, by giving the properties they represent;

4. definition of the network internal structure: hidden nodes, connections and weights. To make easier this step, an assembly-like programming language, called NNL, has been developed. By means of NNL user specifies names as nodes identifiers and Boolean functions as an equivalent form of (1). For a syntactic and semantic definition of NNL see [DP90].

We stress that these steps are strongly interdependent. They can not be developed separately. A small change of one often propagates to the others and implies a global redefinition.

As an example, we build a neural architecture computing the arithmetic functions on floating point numerals. In section 2 we discuss the definition of a suitable environment, while in section 3 we build a network controlling the concurrent execution of the multiplication.

2. Outline of the environment

We define an environment that enhances the parallel capabilities of the neural network.
Let $\mathcal{A}$ be the alphabet:

$$\mathcal{A} = \{+, -, 0, 1, \#\}$$

The environment knowledge base is a finite set of string in $\mathcal{A}^*$. To each string we associate a subset of input and output nodes. In the input and output node definition we give also the node names. They will be conventionally the same used by NNL in assigning the network internal structure. If $<stringname>$ is a name for a string and $<symbol>$ is an element of $\mathcal{A}$, we introduce:

- $<stringname>$l$<symbol>$
  Sensor activated when the leftmost symbol of $<stringname>$ is $<symbol>$;

- $<stringname>$r$<symbol>$
  Sensor activated when the rightmost symbol of $<stringname>$ is $<symbol>$;

- $<stringname>$empty
  Sensor activated when $<stringname>$ is empty;

- out$<stringname>$l$<symbol>$
  Motor whose activation implies replacement of $<stringname>$ with $<symbol><stringname>$;

- out$<stringname>$r$<symbol>$
  Motor whose activation implies replacement of $<stringname>$ with $<stringname><symbol>$;

- out$<stringname>$lmove
  Motor whose activation implies removing the leftmost symbol of $<stringname>$;

- out$<stringname>$rmove
  Motor whose activation implies removing the rightmost symbol of $<stringname>$.

Table 1 shows the time evolution of the string a and of the related input nodes, according to the related output nodes pattern.

Procedures activated by output nodes at the same time will be executed in parallel; their effect will be undefined if they affect the same string side (e.g. if an insertion and a deletion are activated at the same time on the left side of a string), because in this case they are executed sequentially in an unknown order.

Time	Active output nodes	String a	Active input nodes
1	outal1	ε	aempty
2	outal0, outar0	1	al1, ar1
3	outarmove	010	al0, ar0
4	outarmove, outalmove	01	al0, ar1
5		ε	aempty

Table 1: Time evolution of a sample string a (ε is the empty string).

Two subsets of nodes of the neural network are independent if string sides affected by their output nodes are different; processes associated to independent subsets work properly in a parallel way.
It can be easily shown that the neural architecture so far defined is equivalent (isomorphic) to a multitape Turing machine [HU79], in which the finite control is related to the neural network and the set of tapes and heads is related to our set of strings (with two virtual heads at the boundaries of each one). But, while in a Turing machine control is centralized, here control is distributed in the neural architecture.

3. A parallel arithmetic co-processor

With this kind of environment, we build a neural network controlling the execution of the arithmetic functions on the floating point binary numerals. Our aim is to parallelize and speed up these functions and to manage numerals with unlimited number of digits.
To stress the neural network intrinsic parallelism, we plan arithmetic functions as asynchronous operators, processing their input digit by digit, starting from the leftmost one, as soon as it is available.
Operators can be organized in a data flow graph [Den80] if we connect the output arc of one with the input arc of others. We represent an arc connecting two operators as a string: output nodes relative to the string right side belong to the first operator, while those relative to the string left side belong to the second one. According to the definitions in section 2, operators so far defined are independent and run in parallel.
In subsection 3.1 we introduce the chosen floating point representation and in 3.2 an algorithm for a multiplier operator that satisfies our request. In appendix we give some hints on the implementation.

3.1 Floating point numerals representation

A floating point numeral is represented, according to a normalized exponential notation, by two strings: one to keep the signed binary exponent and the other to keep the signed binary mantissa, with the radix point at the left of the most significant digit (e.g. the decimal numeral 5.25 is represented as: mantissa $\equiv +10101$, exponent $\equiv +11$).
With this convention it is easy to realize either the add operator, as mantissas are left aligned, or the divide operator, as it computes starting from the leftmost digit.

3.2 The multiplier operator

For sake of simplicity, we consider only products of mantissas with the same number of digits, but results can be easily extended.
In this subsection we use the following conventions regarding symbols, strings and elementary operators.

1. The upper-case letters X, Y, Z, eventually with subscripts, denote symbols in $\{0,1\}$.

2. The lower-case letters x, y, z denote strings in $\{0,1\}^*$; x_i, y_i, z_i, denote strings of length i.

3. There exists a shift function, defined over strings. The value of $Sh(z)$ is $z0$ (the concatenation of z and 0).

4. There exists an add function. The value of $Add(x,y)$ is the string that represents the number obtained by adding the numbers represented by x and y.

5. There exists a test function. The value of $Test(X,y)$ is y if X is 1, otherwise it is the empty string.

In our algorithm, the product of two n-length mantissas is one $2n$-length mantissa.
If we suppose that input strings, fed in a left to right direction, are:

$$x_n = X_1 X_2 \ldots X_n \qquad y_n = Y_1 Y_2 \ldots Y_n$$

and if at each step i the couple (X_i, Y_i) arrives, then the product z_{2i} is:

$$
\begin{aligned}
z_0 &= \varepsilon \\
z_{2i} &= Add\big(Sh\big(Add\big(Sh\,(z_{2i-2}),\, Test(Y_i, x_{i-1})\big)\big),\, Test(X_i, y_i)\big)
\end{aligned}
\tag{2}
$$

It can be shown that, during the execution, some of the leftmost bits of z are no longer affected by the carries of the Add functions. So they are digits belonging to the multiplier definitive result. Ready to feed the next operator.

At last we present the algorithm, implementing equation 2:

1. $z := \varepsilon;\quad i := 1.$
2. While a couple (X_i, Y_i) arrives do steps $3\ldots8$.
3. $\quad z := Sh\,(z).$
4. $\quad$ If $Y_i = 1$ then $z := Add\,(z, x_{i-1}).$
5. $\quad z := Sh\,(z).$
6. $\quad$ If $X_i = 1$ then $z := Add\,(z, y_i).$
7. $\quad$ Now z is $Z_k \ldots Z_{n-1} Z_n Z_{n+1} \ldots Z_{2n}$, for some k.
   $\quad$ If $Z_n = Z_{n+1} = 0$, then output the string $Z_k \ldots Z_{n-1}$ and set $z := Z_n \ldots Z_{2n}$.
8. $\quad i := i + 1.$
9. Output z.

4. Implementing the multiplier

Here we show what are the network and the environment that realize the multiplier algorithm.

4.1 The environment

The environment is made of the following strings:

- *fact1, fact2*: input strings.
- *buf1, buf2, buf3*: to store the intermediate results of additions (*buf1* and *buf2*) and to store the sub-string of z (*buf3*) that is going to be output.
- *part1, part2*: to store the partial input factors, after they are fed from *fact1* and *fact2*.
- *prd*: output string.

4.2 The network

To describe the internal structure of the network, we first need to introduce some of NNL.

If <node1>, <node2> and <node3> are node names, <delay1> and <delay2> are integers, an NNL elementary expression is one of the following:

a)   <node3> : &(<node1>(<delay1>), <node2>(<delay2>))
   which means the network:

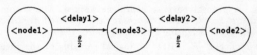

b)   <node3> : v(<node1>(<delay1>), <node2>(<delay2>))
   which means the network:

c)   <node3> : v(<node1>(<delay1>), -<node2>(<delay2>))
   which means the network:

424

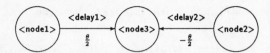

Any other expression is a composition of simple expressions and has a composite meaning. Here is the network controlling the string *prd*:

```
outprdrminus : &( mulget(3), v( &( fact1lminus(3), fact2lplus(3)),
                                 &( fact1lplus(3), fact2lminus(3))))

outprdrplus  : &( mulget(3), v( &( fact1lminus(3), fact2lminus(3)),
                                 &( fact1lplus(3), fact2lplus(3))))

outprdrzero  : &( outbuf3lmove(1), buf3lzero(1))

outprdrone   : &( outbuf3lmove(1), buf3lone(1))

outprdrstar  : v( mulempty2stop(1), mulempty2stop(1))
```

where `mulget` is the node that states the feeding of a couple of symbols from strings *fact1* and *fact2*, and `mulempty2stop` is the node that states the end of the multiplication.
Similar programs have been developed to control the other strings.

Acknowledgments

This research was supported in part through the MPI 40% fund, two CNR contracts: one for the "Progetto finalizzato Informatica" and another for the "Progetto finalizzato Robotica" and a CNR grant on the "Progetto Strategico *Reti Neurali*".

References

[Cai61] E. R. Caianiello. Outline of a theory of thought processes and thinking machines. *J. of Theor. Biol.*, (2):204–235, 1961.

[Den80] J. B. Dennis. Data flow supercomputers. *Computer*, 48–56, november 1980.

[DP90]   P. De Pinto. The implementation of the assembler associated to a general purpose neural network. In *Third Italian Workshop on "Parallel Architectures and Neural Networks"*, Vietri sul Mare (SA), May 1990.

[DPLS90] P. De Pinto, F. E. Lauria, and M. Sette. On the Hebb rule and unlimited precision arithmetic in a MacCulloch and Pitts network. In R. Eckmiller, editor, *Advanced neural computers*, pages 121–128, International Symposium on: Neural Networks for Sensory and Motor Systems, Elsevier Sci., Amsterdam, 1990.

[Hew85] C. Hewitt. The challenge of open systems. *BYTE*, 223–242, April 1985.

[HU79]   J. E. Hopcroft and J. D. Ullman. *Introduction to automata theory, languages and computation.* Addison-Wesley Pub. Co., 1979.

[Lau88] F. E. Lauria. A connectionist approach to knowledge acquisition. *Cybernetics and Systems: an Intern. Journ.*, (5):19–35, 1988.

[Lau89] F. E. Lauria. A general purpose neural network as a new computing paradigm. In E. R. Caianiello, editor, *Second Italian Workshop on "Parallel Architectures and Neural Networks"*, pages 131–144, World Scientific Pub., Singapore, 1989.

[MP43]   W. S. McCulloch and W. Pitts. A logical calculus of the ideas immanent in the nervous activity. *Bull. Math. Bioph.*, 115–143, 1943.

[RM86]   D. E. Rumelhart and J. L. McClelland. *Parallel distributed processing.* Volume 1, MIT Press, Cambridge, MA, 1986.

[Set90] M. Sette. An OCCAM simulation of a general purpose neural network. In *Third Italian Workshop on "Parallel Architectures and Neural Networks"*, Vietri sul Mare (SA), May 1990.

[Tra91] G. Trautteur. Problems with Symbols. A commentary to: Herbert Simon, "Scientific Discovery as Problem Solving". *RISESST*, (1), 1991. To be published.

A LOGIC FOR THE REPRESENTATION OF SPATIAL KNOWLEDGE

Massimo Abbati, Stefano Odoardi[1]

Istituto di Informatica, Facoltà di Ingegneria,
Università di Ancona
Via Brecce Bianche, 60131 Ancona

1-INTRODUCTION

In this introduction we start speaking about temporal logic. In fact, while a wide corpus of studies about temporal logic exists, it is obvious that in a universe where modern relativistic physics has been written down in the book space and time are related both in conceptualization and in formal theories about them. Besides and most important spatial and temporal logic are placed in the same category from the fact of being both topologic logics, that is logics in which a particular collocation of the entities of the universe in an abstract space has a particular relevance. In the philosophy tradition there are two approaches to the representation of time in logic, the first-order and the modal, or intensional, one. First-order supporters sustain the theory that time, while being an important one, is just yet another variable, and so we do not need a particular logic built around time in order to expose the temporal properties of the entities described. The theoretical background of such scientists is generally the study of the logic foundations of mathematics. In opposition when logic is used to analyze the formal properties of the language the tense structure becomes a relevant topic. The first modern philosopher to propose a modal logic for the analysis of the language was Prior, in its Tense Logic [Prior 1955]. In his work, from the proposition p the modal assertions Fp (it will be the case that p) Pp (it has been the case that p) and other ones can be derived, where F and P are the modal operators. In the eighties temporal logic has been investigated in the artificial intelligence field in order to build a theory of events and actions. Here too we can see the use of standard first-order logic and of the intensional one. The intensional temporal logic that we can find in

---

[1]The research whose results are partly presented in this paper is supported by the EEC project PROMETHEUS/PRO-ART.

Artificial Intelligence literature always uses one intensional 'reifing' operator that localizes in a particular temporal segment or instant a first-order well formed formula. The typical stricture of such a temporal atomic formula is the following: T(time-entity, fopc-wff). Examples of works in this field are the ones of McDermott and Shoham [Shoham 1988]. In this paper we will describe a logic for the representation of the knowledge about space and objects having a spatial extension. The research presented here has ultimately the aim of creating a knowledge representation theory that can be used in a computer vision system. Most modern Computer vision systems are model-based, that is the object to be recognized are described in some geometric or mathematic form. Those models are classified as using 2D, 2(1/2)D and 3D shape feature [Chin and Dyer 1986]. Our logic can be particularized for building descriptions of 2D and 3D environments.

2-FIRST-ORDER, INTENSIONAL OR WHAT ELSE ?

The differences of a spatial logic with respect to the temporal one are implied from a formal, mathematic, point of view by the presence in the universe of three dimensions instead of one, which in turn implies the absence of one ordering among the space points which exists in the temporal one, and from an ontological point of view by the absence of one favourite direction which is implicit in the notion of the flow of time. Anyway most structures remains the same, and so remains the question of intensional vs. fopc. At the beginning of our research we did not have any preferred answer, and we think that our solution is particularly tailored for our use, because our real aim was tho build a formalism apt to solve a particular problem.

2.1 Rescher's and Garson's Topologic Logic

Rescher and Garson proposed in 1968 the Topologic, or Positional logic as a generalization of the intensional temporal logic [Rescher and Garson 1968]. That logic is based on the introduction of the generalized intensional parametric operator $P\alpha$, where $P\alpha(p)$ is to be read as 'proposition p is to be realized in position α'. The following two axioms hold in Topologic Logic:

(P1) $P\alpha(\neg p) \equiv \neg P\alpha(p)$

(P2) $P\alpha(p \wedge q) \equiv P\alpha(p) \wedge P\alpha(p)$

Axioms P1 and P2 guarantee that the P-operator distributes over a set of connectives which is functionally complete, and so the following principle results:

(DP) The P-operator distributes over every truth-functional
connective.

The following inference rule is proposed:

(R) If ⊢ A, then ⊢ Pα(A)

Using topologic logic you can build a standard fopc theory, and then you can make it intensional with the use of the P-operator. The limitation of that approach, which is shared by every intensional formalism, is the one that you cannot perform deduction on the reifing context α when having knowledge on the reified context A, since you do not have the rules.

2.2 Shoham's Logic of Time Intervals

The Shoham's Logic of Time Intervals is a recent intensional temporal logic [Shoham 1987], based on the notion of the time interval defined by its terminal points and having a stated semantics where the interpretation function is time-dipendent. There are two types of basic wff: the ones built using the temporal relationships <= and = between time intervals, and the ones built using the reifing operator TRUE. Shoham's logic allows functions to take value in the temporal domain, but the arguments of those functions are restricted to take value in the reifing temporal domain context. This restriction is similar to the one implicit in the one found in Rescher's and Galton's Topologic Logic but is more explicit due to the well-defined nature of the reifing domain. Anyway the result is the same: you cannot reason between reifing context and individuals domain.

2.3-Bacchus', Tenenberg's and Koomen's BTK

BTK is a double sorted temporal logic [Wang 1952] which has been proved to subsume Shoham's Logic of Time Intervals [Bacchus, Tenenberg and Koomen 1989]. The BTK two sorts are one for temporal variables and one for individual ones. Function and predicates are (n,m)-ary, where n is the temporal arguments arity while m is the individual arguments arity. Semantics follows the line exposed above, and two ways of automated the deduction process are suggested: the first is to translate the double sorted theory in fopc using a process called relativization, the second is to use a many sorted theorem prover like the one provided by Walther [Walther 1987]. This logic has at least the same expressive power of the Shoham Logic of Time Interval, because it has been proven that a sentence syntactically and semantically correct in the latter logic can be translated in a correct sentence of the former, while the problem of the separation between the contexts does not exist.

3-A SPATIAL LOGIC

Our spatial logic, which we call SSL (Sorted Spatial Logic) is a double sorted logic. We want to use logic not only to describe a scene, but to reason about it too, so we have to use a logic with a proof theory that can be automated. In the comparison of plain fopc with SSL two things emerge: first a sorted theorem prover is more efficient than an unsorted one; second we use low and intermediate level vision primitives that are guided by a bounding box, that is when the search for an individual is performed it will not happen on the whole scene, but only in a part of it. So our primitives will be sorted in the sense that they will have spatial and individual parameters. The intensional paradigm, as we have briefly already shown, seems to impose too strong a bind to the expressive and deductive power of the logic. It is worth noting that our criticism to the use of the intensional paradigm is not conceptual and general, but only relative to our application, that is to say we found in intensional temporal logic formalisms as it is a lack of descriptive power for the application to spatial logic. From an ontological point of view, while it is obvious for a predicate, that is semantically speaking a relation among individuals, to exist in a particular time, and while it is clear what means for an individual to exist in a particular space, it seems less obvious the meaning of the existence of a relation among individuals in the space. The answer we gave to the meaning question was the containment, total or partial, of the objects involved in the relation in a topologically connected or not portion of the space. In the next paragraphs we informally describe SSL syntax and semantics and then present an example of the axiomatization of some the properties of the objects and of the relations among them in the space which has been developed.

3.1-Syntax and semantics

SSL syntax is much like first order one, with the exceptions that variables must belong to one of the two sets: SV for spatial variables and V for individual ones; functions must belong to the SF set for functions returning spatial values and to the F set for function returning individual values. The sort of a term is determined by the sort of its outermost function or variable. A spatial constant is a 0-ary spatial function and an individual constant is a 0-ary individual function. All argument position of predicates and functions are to be occupied by a term of a specific sort. A predicate or function is said to be (n,m)-ary if it has n spatial arguments and m individual arguments.

The SSL domain is the couple <S,U> where S is the power set of SU, a continuous universe of points in the space, and U is an universe of individuals. An SSL interpretation is the triple <S,U,M> where M is a meaning function that maps SV to S, V to U, each (n,m)-ary SF function in a function from $S^n \times U^m$ to S, each (n,m)-ary F function in a function from $S^n \times U^m$ to U, each (n,m)-ary predicate in a relation over $S^n \times U^m$. The model theory is completed by the standard interpretation of wff with truth-functional connectives and quantifiers, having stated that quantified variables take value in the proper sub-domain.

3.2-The axiomatization of the properties of the space

We developed a set of axioms that capture the knowledge about the space we think is useful for our purposes. The formulae are axiom schemata, since they include predicates not individually specified, but represented by the schematic letter P, where P is a metatheoretic predicative variable which requires the argument in the first place to be a spatial segment. The predicate is false if the first-place spatial argument does not contain the individual arguments in the following places. In applications each axiom schema is to be substituted with its instance relative to the predicates defined and used in the theory. S-named variables are of sort space, X-named variables are of sort individuals. What follows is an example of the axiom schemata.

forall   S,S1,X1,..,Xn [P(S,X1,..,Xn)) *and* IN(S,S1)] *imp* P(S1,X1,..,Xn)

BIBLIOGRAPHY

Bacchus, F., Tenenberg, J. and Koomen, J. A. (1989), 'A non-reified temporal logic', in *Procs. of the 1st Int. Conf. on Principles. of Knowledge. Representation and Reasoning*, 2-10.
Chin, R. T. and Dyer, C. R. (1986), 'Model-Based recognition in Robot Vision', *Computing Surveys*, 18, 67-108.
Prior, A. N. (1955), 'Diodoran modalities', *Philosophical Quarterly*, 5, 205-213.
Rescher, N. and Garson, J. (1968), 'Topological Logic', *Journal of symbolic Logic*, 33, 537-548.
Shoham, Y. (1988), *Reasoning about change*, Cambridge: MIT Press.
Walther, C. (1983), 'A many sorted calculus based on resolution and paramodulation', in *Proceedings of the 8th IJCAI*, 882-899.
Wang, H. (1952), 'Logic of Many-Sorted Theories', *Journal of symbolic Logic*, 17, 105-116.

TRUTH MAINTENANCE IN APPROXIMATE REASONING

Bruno Fringuelli, Stefano Marcugini, Alfredo Milani, Silvano Rivoira
Dipartimento di Matematica, Università di Perugia
via Vanvitelli, 1 - 06100 Perugia, ITALY

Abstract

A reason maintenance system which extends an ATMS through Mukaidono's fuzzy logic is described. It supports a problem solver in situations affected by incomplete information and vague data, by allowing nonmonotonic inferences and the revision of previous conclusions when contradictions are detected.

INTRODUCTION

In recent years truth maintenance systems have been proposed as powerful tools able to perform belief revision at a general level.

Justification-based TMS [1, 2, 3] maintain a single context of belief and support nonmonotonic justifications, while assumption-based TMS [4, 5] avoid the restriction that the overall set of premises is contradiction free, maintaining multiple contexts of belief.

Early truth maintenance systems dealt with certain beliefs only, but several successive works extended them in order to allow handling of some kind of uncertainty [6, 7, 8, 9, 10, 11].

In this paper we describe a Fuzzy Truth Maintenance System (FTMS) obtained by extending an ATMS through a fuzzy logic for which the resolution principle [12] has been proved to be complete [13, 14, 15].

The general idea and motivations of our approach are very close to those of Dubois et al. [11].

The main difference from their work lies in the fact that in our system propositions involve vague predicates which may have intermediary degrees of truth and the underlying logic is truth-functional, while Dubois et al. consider propositions which are true or false, but due to the lack of precision of the available information it can only be estimated to what extent it is possible or necessary that a proposition is true.

DEFINITION OF A FUZZY TRUTH MAINTENANCE SYSTEM

Extending De Kleer 's definition of ATMS [4], by means of the concepts introduced by Mukaidono [15], we define an FTMS in the following way.

Every fuzzy formula introduced or derived by the attached problem solver corresponds to an FTMS **node**.

A special kind of node is represented by the atom $\perp$, corresponding to "falsity", for which $[\perp] = 0$ holds in any interpretation.

A **justification** is a triple: $<j,c(n),c_r(n)>$

where $j: x_1,x_2,...,x_m \rightarrow n$ is a propositional Horn clause asserting that the consequent node n is derivable from the conjunction of the antecedent nodes $x_1,...,x_m$ and where $c(n)$ and $c_r(n)$ are respectively the confidence and the confidence of resolution [15] established by j for the node n and represent, in the closed interval $[-1,1]$, respectively the truth value of the fuzzy predicate associated to n and its degree of derivability from the assumptions.

A justification $<j,-1,c_r(\perp)>$, where the derived node is **falsity**, is communicated by the problem solver every time a contradiction is detected.

An **assumption** is a self-justifying node representing the decision of introducing an hypothesis; it is connected to the assumed data through justifications.

An **environment** is a set of logically conjuncted assumptions .

An environment E has **consistency** $cs(E)$ equal to the opposite of the maximal confidence of resolution with which falsity can be derived from E and the current set J of justifications:

$$cs(E) = - \max_{J} c_r(\perp)_E$$

An FTMS **context** is defined as the set formed by the assumptions of an environment and all the nodes derivable from those assumptions.

The goal of FTMS is to efficiently update the contexts when new assumptions or justifications are provided by the problem solver.

This goal is achieved by associating with every node a description (**label**) of every context in which the node holds.

More formally, a label L_n of the node n is defined as the set of all the environments from which n can be derived:

$$L_n = \{E_i : E_i \underset{J}{\Rightarrow} n\}$$

In order to save space and time, a problem solver may wish to consider only environments whose consistency is greater than some threshold α and/or from which nodes can be derived with a degree of derivability greater than some threshold β, where α and β depend on the problem domain.

Therefore, given the two lower bounds α and β, four important properties can be defined for the labels:

a label L_n is α-**consistent** if the consistency of each of its environments is not less than α;

a label L_n is β-**sound** if n is derivable from each of its environments with a confidence of resolution not less than β;

a label L_n is α-β-**complete** if every α-consistent environment from which n can be derived with a confidence of resolution not less than β is a superset of some environment in L_n;

a label L_n is **minimal** if no environment E_i in L_n is a superset of another environment E_k in L_n with $c_{rc_i}(n) \leq c_{rc_k}(n)$, where $c_{rc}(n)$ is the confidence of resolved consequence [15], defined as $c_{rc}(n)= c(n) * c_r(n)$.

The task of FTMS is to ensure that each label in each node is α-consistent, β-sound, α-β-complete and minimal with respect to the current set of justifications.

This task is performed by invoking a label-updating algorithm every time the problem solver adds a new justification.

Only the **minimal environment database** (MEDB) is maintained, for environments with consistency less than 1, in the sense that an environment E_2 is recorded in the database only if $cs(E_2)<1$ and no environment E_1 exists such that:

$(E_1 \subset E_2)$ and $(cs(E_1) > cs(E_2))$.

The main mechanisms for updating labels and confidences and their possible effects on the reasoning process are illustrated by the following example.

Let us suppose that the problem solver, on the basis of its own domain knowledge (partially reported in fig.1) and inference procedures, has already derived and communicated to FTMS the justifications reported in figure 1 (where π, ρ, σ, τ are assumptions and $\perp$ indicates falsity) from which FTMS has determined the labels and the minimal environment database also reported in figure.

Rules:	Justifications:
R_5: A,B $\rightarrow$ E, {w5= 0.2}	J_1: $< \pi \rightarrow A, c(A) = 0.6, c_r(A) = 1>$
R_6: A,C $\rightarrow$ F, {w6= 0.3}	J_2: $< \rho \rightarrow B, c(B) = 0.4, c_r(B) = 1>$
R_7: E,F $\rightarrow$ H, {w7= 0.4}	J3: $< \sigma \rightarrow D, c(C) = 0.4, c_r(C) = 1>$
R_8: C,D $\rightarrow$ F, {w8= 0.4}	J_4: $< \tau \rightarrow D, c(D) = 0.4, c_r(D) = 1>$
R_9: B,F $\rightarrow$ E, {w9= 0.3}	J_5: $<A,B \rightarrow E, c(E) = 0.5, c_r(E) = 0.5>$
R_{10}: C,B $\rightarrow$ $\perp$, {w10= 0.2}	J_6: $<A,C \rightarrow F, c(F) = 0.75, c_r(F) = 0.75>$
R_{11}: F,D $\rightarrow$ G, {w11= 0.2}	J_7: $<E,F \rightarrow H, c(H) = 0.8, c_r(H) = 0.8>$
R_{12}: A,H $\rightarrow$ G, {w12= 0.4}	J_8: $<C,D \rightarrow F, c(F) = 1, \quad c_r(F) = 1>$
R_{13}: F,G $\rightarrow$ E, {w13= 0.4}	J_9: $<B,F \rightarrow E, c(E) = 0.75, c_r(E) = 0.75>$
R_{14}: D,E $\rightarrow$ $\perp$, {w14= 0.5}	J_{10}: $<C,B \rightarrow \perp, -1, c_r(\perp) = 0.5>$
	J_{11}: $<F,D \rightarrow G, c(G) = 0.75, c_r(G) = 0.75>$
	J_{12}: $<A,H \rightarrow G, c(G) = 0.76, c_r(G) = 0.53>$

Labels:

$L_A = \{[(\pi), cs=1]\}$ $L_B = \{[(\rho), cs=1]\}$

$L_C = \{[(\sigma), cs=1]\}$ $L_D = \{[(\tau), cs=1]$

$L_E = \{[(\pi,\rho), cs=1], [(\rho,\sigma,\tau), cs=-0.5]\}$ $L_F = \{[(\pi,\sigma), cs=1], [(\sigma,\tau), cs=1]\}$

$L_G = \{[(\pi,\rho,\sigma), cs=-0.5], [(\sigma,\tau), cs=1]\}$ $L_H = \{[(\pi,\rho,\sigma), cs=-0.5],[(\rho,\sigma,\tau), cs=-0.5]\}$

MEDB: $[(\rho,\sigma), cs=-0.5]$

figure 1: An FTMS state.

Let now the problem solver add a new contradiction, represented by the justification J_{13} of fig.2. This justification modifies the minimal environment database, introducing two new entries, which are shown in fig.2 with the updated labels.

Justification: J_{13}: $<D,E \rightarrow \perp, -1, c_r(\perp) = 0.4>$

Updated Labels:	**Updated MEDB:**
$L_E = \{[(\pi,\rho), cs=1], [(\rho,\sigma,\tau), cs=-0.4]\}$	$[(\rho,\sigma), cs=-0.5]$
$L_F = \{[(\pi,\sigma), cs=1], [(\sigma,\tau), cs= 1]\}$	$[(\pi,\rho,\tau), cs=-0.4]$
$L_G = \{[(\pi,\rho,\sigma), cs=-0.5], [(\sigma,\tau), cs= 1]\}$	$[(\rho,\sigma,\tau), cs=-0.4]$
$L_H = \{[(\pi,\rho,\sigma), cs=-0.5], [(\rho,\sigma,\tau), cs = -0.4]\}$	

figure 2: Updated labels.

It must be outlined that, in contrast with ATMS, where inconsistent environments are removed from every node label, FTMS always keeps the environments in their labels, since consistency can be changed by successive justifications.

At each step of the reasoning process, the problem solver can rank the partial solutions currently available on the basis of several ordering criteria (truth value, degree of derivability, consistency of the hypotheses), discarding or eliminating solutions which are not enough founded.

ACKNOWLEDGEMENTS

The authors wish to thank Settimo Termini for the valuable discussions about many valued logics. This work has been supported by P.F. Robotica - Consiglio Nazionale delle Ricerche, grant n.90.00403.67 and M.U.R.S.T.- 40% "Tecniche di Ragionamento Automatico in Sistemi Intelligenti".

REFERENCES

[1].Doyle (1979). A Truth Maintenance System. In *Artificial Intelligence*, 12 (3) ,pp 231- 272.

[2] D.McAllester (1980). An Outlook on Truth Maintenance. In *AI Memo* 551, AI Lab., MIT, Cambridge (MA).

[3] D.McDermott (1983). Context and Data Dependencies. In *A Synthesis*, IEEE Trans. Pattern Anal.Mach. Intell., 5 (3), pp. 237-246.

[4] J.de Kleer (1986). An Assumption-based TMS. In *Artificial Intelligence* , 28 (2) , pp.127-162.

[5] J.P.Martins, S.C.Shapiro (1988). A Model for Belief Revision. In *Artificial Intelligence* , 35, pp. 25-79.

[6] J.de Kleer, B.C.Williams (1987). Diagnosing Multiple Faults. In *Artificial Intelligence* , 32, pp. 97-130.

[7] B.Falkenheiner (1988). Towards a General Purpose Belief Maintenance System. In J.F.Lemmer, L.N.Kanal (eds.) *Uncertainty in Artificial Intelligence: 2nd Conference*, North-Holland, pp.125-132.

[8] B.D'Ambrosio (1989). A Hybrid Approach to Reasoning Under Uncertainty. In L.N.Kanal, T.S.Levitt, J.F.Lemmer (eds.) *Uncertainty in Artificial Intelligence: 3rd Conference*, North-Holland, pp.267-283.

[9] G.M. Provan (1989). An Analysis of ATMS-based Techniques for Computing Dempster-Shafer Belief Functions. In *Proceedings of the.9th IJCAI* , Detroit Aug. 1989 , pp. 1115-1120.

[10] K.B.Laskey, P.E. Lehner(1989). Assumptions, Beliefs and Probabilities. In *Artificial Intelligence* 41, pp. 65-77.

[11] D.Dubois, J.Lang, H.Prade (1990). Handling Uncertain Knowledge in an ATMS Using Possibilistic Logic. In *Proceeding of ECAI Workshop on Truth Maintenance Systems* ,Stockolm.

[12] J.A.Robinson (1965). A Machine-oriented Logic Based on the Resolution Principle. In *Journal of ACM*, 12 (1), pp. 23-41.

[13] R.C.T.Lee (1972). Fuzzy Logic and the Resolution Principle. In *Journal of ACM*, 19 (1), pp.109-119.

[14] M.Mukaidono (1982). Fuzzy Inference of Resolution Style. In R.R.Yager (Ed.) *Fuzzy Set and Possibility Theory*, Pergamon Press, New York , pp. 224-231.

[15] M.Mukaidono, Z. Shen, L. Ding (1989). Fundamentals of Fuzzy Prolog. In *International Journal of Approximate Reasoning*, 3, pp. 179-193.

A strategy for design and development of complex knowledge-systems.

Angus McIntyre
Knowledge Technologies N.V., Pelikaanstraat 28
Brussels/Belgium

1. Introduction

One of the most difficult stages in the development of a knowledge-based system (KBS) is the acquisition and encoding of the knowledge to be placed in the system. For any domain where the relevant knowledge is not previously available in a form that is sufficiently structured, detailed and complete, the system designer will have to appeal to human experts to provide the requisite knowledge. (c.f. [Neale 88] for a summary of current acquisition techniques) This raises the problem of how the designer can ensure that the expert's knowledge of the domain can be elicited and transferred to the formalism used in the system. To guarantee the value of the information acquired, the expert must also be comfortable with the acquisition environment and the tasks s/he must perform, and the environment should provide a familiar context in order to favour the elicitation of unformalised or unconscious knowledge.

Work done in the CEC DELTA project Nat*Lab [Nat*Lab 91] led to the proposal of a methodology for knowledge acquisition in KBS construction, based on the use of architectures based on multiple, communicating agents. The first section of the paper briefly explains some agent architectures relevant for this approach, while the second section sketches a prototype architecture for an agent-management shell for knowledge-acquisition. The third section describes how the shell can be used for developing complex knowledge-systems.

2. Agents

The idea of agents, discrete elements of a system realising different areas of expertise, has been widely used in AI, in applications where a system must draw on distinct areas of expertise - for instance, the natural separation between disease and drug expertise in a medical expert system. Dividing a monolithic system into separate modules improves the declarative semantics of the system architecture, leads to systems that are easier to implement and maintain, and permits the use of multiple representation or inference mechanisms within a single system.

In our approach, which is knowledge-oriented, agents are seen as possessors of discrete sub-areas of knowledge. An agent is thus a system element embodying a particular definable area of ·expertise or performing a particular set of activities. A complex knowledge-system can be built up out of a set of such agents in communication with each other, under the control of a kind of super-agent and optionally each containing sub-agents representing further decompositions of their field of expertise.

Agents interact with other agents only through well-defined communications protocols, which not only simplifies the implementation, but also allows one agent to be substituted for another transparently. We can describe agents in terms of three factors; first, the agent's private knowledge, inaccessible from outside; second, a list of *roles* that that agent may play, and third, the messages or *requests* that an agent may send and receive. Agents may also have an implicit internal structure in terms of sub-agents, which may optionally be shared with other agents.

3. An agent-based shell for knowledge acquisition.

The approach to system development that we propose in this paper is based on the idea of a shell for combining and manipulating agents, and for monitoring their interactions. Because all agents must adhere to a strict communications protocol, the shell can record requests made to agents and responses given, creating a highly contextualised record of agent interactions. Strict typing of agents in terms of their roles and supported requests also permits automatic checking to ensure that a given assembly of agents represents an executable system. Conformant agents capable of supporting a given role may also be substituted for each other transparently; a given agent can be 'popped-out' and another 'plugged-in' in its place without necessitating any changes in the rest of the system.

The shell proposed should provide three functions as a minimum; the capability of monitoring and recording the communications between agents, runtime support and consistency checking for a group of agents assembled as a system, and an interface allowing users to select and substitute particular agents. These functions will form the core of the proposed methodology.

The approach described here is based on the idea that during the initial stages of construction of a system, agents might simply consist of a framework for receiving requests and communicating them to a human expert via an interface. The request made and the response given are monitored and recorded by the shell, leading to the build of a database of expert responses structured in terms of requests and the context in which they were made.

Consider the case of a consultant taking the role of the drug prescription agent in a medical expert system. The expert system issues a request:

(prescribe-drug-for <patient #2> <disease #6>)

to the drug prescription agent, here substituted by a human user, who is shown the request via an appropriate interface, and who responds by selecting one drug from a menu. The response and the context that gave rise to it are then recorded by the system. In this way, the system builds up a set of highly contextualised judgements made by the expert, which can then be used either directly or indirectly as the basis for developing the system. Highly-specific 'primitive' requests might even support automatic system construction using machine-learning techniques. In other cases, generalisations might be extracted from a database of contextualised responses automatically and submitted to the expert's approval, or used as a starting point for conventional knowledge acquisition techniques such as interviews, with the advantage that questions put by the interviewer can be given a precise context.

The approach assumes a rapid-prototyping methodology, where knowledge acquired is fed back into the system in the form of partial implementations of agents, which can then participate in new interactions aimed at confirming and refining the new knowledge. To support the system designer, extensible libraries of predefined agent types can be made available, which could be adapted to the needs of a particular system.

4. Developing systems with the support of multi-agent shells.

The shell is envisaged as a tool to help in the incremental development of knowledge-based systems, specifically complex knowledge-systems with multiple interacting knowledge bases. As such, it supports rather than replaces conventional programming and knowledge-acquisition techniques.

The development of a new knowledge-based system using the tool will be an incremental process. The initial stage of the process involves the sketching of the overall architecture of the system to be developed. The major agents of the system are identified and their interactions with each other are described in terms of communications protocols. This part of the design process is relatively free of domain-specific knowledge, and generic task and knowledge structures provided by the libraries should provide a good basis for the initial architecture.

Once the major components of the system have been identified, together with the possible interactions between these components and their likely control structures, the components can be implemented as simplified, under-defined agents and inserted into a system configuration.

In the first interaction, the majority of the agents in the system will be 'hollow', consisting of little more than an interface between the requests issued and a user interface for presenting them to the expert. The expert 'sits behind' the skeleton of the system, and acts as the system's knowledge-base during an interaction with a user. Each response given by the expert during the interaction is then added to a structured database for use in the construction of the system. The figure below summarises the process.

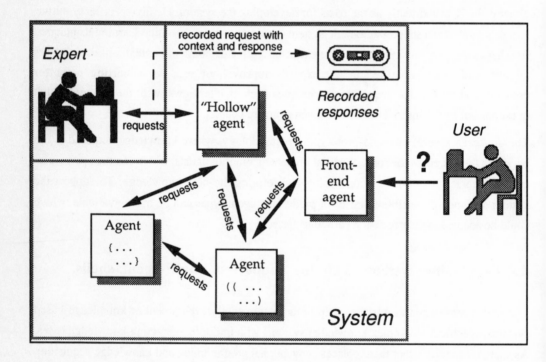

During the early interactions, new agents can be created. When the expert receives a request such as "What disease is this patient suffering from?", s/he will need to know certain things in order to answer the question. The system designer can note down the extra information that the expert asks for, and use it to structure new agents and sub-agents with appropriate communication protocols. In this way, the substructure of the agents of the system can be gradually filled in.

As new agents are implemented the expert's role can be refined, until s/he is acting the part of only one agent at a time. At this point, the expert is responding to a small and well-defined set of requests so some quite detailed knowledge can be acquired, always in a highly structured and contextualised form. This knowledge in turn can be built into a new agent and inserted into the system for testing. To test the system, the expert simply switches roles and acts the part of the user, confirming that the behaviour of the system conforms to his/her expectations.

The final product of the shell, built up over a long series of interactions with several experts will consist of a structured set of agents, each incorporating some detailed knowledge acquired from the expert, which can then be re-coded if necessary to maximise speed and efficiency. The development process is highly incremental, involving repeated interactions which each introduce a small refinement to the system, and capitalize on the results of preceding interactions. It should also be supported by conventional knowledge-engineering techniques such as interviewing, on-line note-taking and so forth, and has been conceived to exploit existing programming techniques such as object-oriented programming and the task-method paradigm [Chandrasekaran 83, Steels 90].

6. Conclusion

The full approach as presented here exists only at a theoretical stage, although it is founded in the concrete work done on communicating agents and role-reversal in the Nat*Lab project, and in particular on experience gained during the implementation of the "NOBILE" prototype [McIntyre & Cheli 90]. Nevertheless, it appears to represent a promising possible line of research, in that it offers a means of acquiring knowledge from experts within the context of familiar yet highly-structured activities, and allows the knowledge acquired to be automatically organised in a structured fashion, suitable for subsequent implementation in a knowledge-representation formalism.

References

[Chandrasekaran 83]   "Towards a taxonomy of problem-solving types". Chandrasekaran, B. in AI Magazine, Vol. 4 nr. 1

[Cheli & McIntyre 90]   "NOBILE: An Object-Based User Model Acquisition Shell". Cheli, E. & McIntyre, A. Proceedings of 'Delta & Beyond' Conference. Den Haag, The Netherlands, October 1990. (forthcoming)

[Nat*Lab 91]   "A Methodology for Student Model Acquisition", Nat*Lab Consortium, Deliverable ND/8 CEC DELTA Nat*Lab project, April 1991

[Neale 88]   "First generation expert systems: a review of knowledge acquisition". Neale, I. in 'The Knowledge Engineering Review', vol.3 no.2, 1988.

[Steels 90]   "Components of Expertise", Steels, L. AI Magazine, Summer 1990

Efficient Compilation of First Order Predicates

Giuseppe Attardi, Mauro Gaspari, Pietro Iglio

Dipartimento di Informatica, Corso Italia 40, I-56125 Pisa, Italy

Abstract

We have developed a theorem prover for the full first order logic, by compiling clauses into proof procedures. These procedures exploit a set of abstract machine primitives for full unification and primitives which provide completeness and soundness for the proof procedure. These primitives are part of a Common Runtime Support which enables mixing code from various high level languages. Our theorem prover can thus be used as a component in a larger application, which may be written in any mixture of C, Lisp and Prolog. We show first how to compile Horn clauses along the lines of Prolog. A full first-order logic theorem prover is then produced by compiling predicates into code which uses full unification, a complete search strategy and a complete inference procedure.

1. Introduction

The need of highly efficient theorem provers is growing to allow their use outside the purely experimental field: a theorem prover may be needed as part of a more general automated reasoning system, for example an expert system. Many systems use an interpreted inference engine to perform deductions but a compilative solution is the obvious approach to obtain higher performance. Presently there are many well-engineered compilers for logic programming languages such as Prolog: these compilers use particular techniques to achieve good performance, such as efficient representation of variable substitutions and the use of specialized primitives for unifications. Unfortunately the Prolog proof procedure is not complete due to a depth-first search strategy and not sound due to the lack of occur checks in unification. We present a theorem prover for the full first order predicate calculus based on compilation techniques and suggest how it could be used as part of a more general automated deduction system. Our solution is essentially based on the Stickel's idea of Prolog Technology Theorem Prover (PTTP) [Stickel 88].

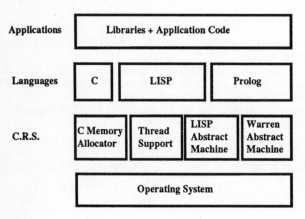

Our work has been developed within an advanced programming environment based on a Common Runtime Support (CRS), an intermediate layer between the operating system and the high level programming languages, which enables interoperability among languages such as Prolog, Lisp and C [Attardi 91]. The CRS provides the essential functionalities which can be abstracted from modern high level languages. The CRS uses C as the common intermediate form for all languages. The diagram represents the relations between the various components. The Lisp Abstract Machine as well as the Warren Abstract Machine [Warren 83] are implemented in C. The COMMON LISP compiler translates Lisp code to C, which is then handed over to the native C compiler to produce executable code. Similarly Prolog is translated to C through an intermediate Lisp form. We introduce a new abstract machine, the Unification Abstract Machine (UAM), which is an extension to the WAM supporting full unification. The theorem prover for full first order logic is implemented as an extension of the Prolog compiler using UAM.

2. Prolog on the CRS

In [Attardi 90] we described how Prolog code is translated into an intermediate Lisp form enriched with the primitives provided by the CRS. In particular we use WAM like primitives and support for logic variables to perform efficient unification and the technique of *success continuations* for non determinism. A predicate is translated into a boolean function with as many arguments as the predicate plus an extra one, the continuation, which is a function of zero arguments, representing any additional goals that were carried over from previous calls. If one clause of the predicate succeeds, the continuation is invoked to carry out the remaining goals. The boolean function returns T whenever the Prolog predicate would succeed and NIL otherwise. As an example, for the Prolog predicate concat:

```
concat([], X, X).
concat([X1|X2], Y, [X1|Z2]) :- concat(X2,Y,Z2).
```

a simple-minded translation into an intermediate Lisp function is:

```
(defun concat (x y z cont)
   (trail-mark)
   (prog1
     (or
       (and
           (get-nil x)              ; concat([],
           (get-value y z)          ;            X, X)
           (funcall cont))          ;                    .
       (trail-restore)
       (let (x1 x2 z2)
         (and
           (get-cons x)             ; concat([
           (unify-variable x1)      ;            X1|
           (unify-variable x2)      ;                X2],
                                    ;            Y,
           (get-cons z)             ;            [
           (unify-value x1)         ;              X1|
           (unify-variable z2)      ;                  Z2])
           (concat x2 y z2 cont)))) ; :- concat(X1, Y, Z2) .
      (trail-unmark))))
```

The function trail-mark sets up a choice point by placing a mark on the trail for backtracking. The function trail-restore unwinds the trail stack up to the latest choice point, undoing the bindings for variables recorded in the trail, while trail-unmark performs a trail-restore and removes the choice point mark from the trail.

3. A Complete and Sound Theorem Prover

A theorem prover which is sound and complete for the full first order logic can be obtained with the technique developed by Stickel [Stickel 88]. This technique can be summarized as follows:
  •   unification performs occur checks for soundness;

- a new inference rule (model-elimination reduction) is added to achieve completeness of the proof system;
- consecutively bounded depth-first search strategy is used instead of usual unbounded depth-first search, to achieve completeness of the search strategy.

Usually Prolog implementations do not perform the occur check during unification for efficiency reasons, but in our case it is necessary to avoid unsound results or nonterminating unifications. However our compiler is smart enough to incorporate the occur checks only when necessary, as we explain later.

A theorem prover for full first order logic must have a complete inference system, and we are interested in inference systems which are amenable to highly efficient compilation. We know that the use of input resolution facilitates the compilation of Prolog programs, but this inference rule is incomplete for non-Horn clause. In input resolution there is a given set of input clauses such that these clauses are always used as one of the two inputs to each resolution operation. It is thus quite natural to compile this given set of input clauses. This suggests to employ a complete inference system that is also an input procedure: Stickel uses, in fact, the *model-elimination* procedure [Loveland 69]. The normal Prolog inference operation is the ME-extension operation, while the new inference operation, the ME-reduction, is the following:

"If the current goal matches the complement of one of its ancestor goals, then apply the matching substitution and treat the current goal as if it were solved."

The reduction operation is a form of reasoning by contradiction. If, in trying to prove P, we discover that P is true if Q is true (i.e., $Q \Rightarrow P$) and also that Q is true if $\neg P$ is true (i.e., $\neg P \Rightarrow Q$), then P must be true. The use of model elimination requires the generation of contrapositives for each clause, therefore for each clause with n literals, n clauses in Prolog form are generated.

The last requirement to achieve completeness is the use of a complete search strategy. The depth first search is incomplete, because we can find an infinite branch in the search tree before finding the solutions, and this can happen, for instance, in the presence of axioms like commutativity. The breadth first strategy is complete, but is unusable because it grows exponentially in space and therefore only solutions in the first few levels of the search tree can be reached. A viable solution is to adopt a consecutively bounded depth first strategy: an initial bound for the depth is chosen, the entire search space up to the current depth bound is explored completely, causing backtracking when this depth is reached; a greater depth bound is then chosen, and so on, repeating each time the steps of previous levels. Because of the exponential growth in size of the search space as the depth bound increases, the number of recomputed results is small in comparison with the size of the search space. In particular, analysis shows that this search strategy performs only about $b/(b-1)$ times as many operations as breadth-first search, where b is the branching factor.

4. Implementation

The techniques described in the previous section allow us to get an automated theorem prover complete for the first order logic. Stickel has given two implementations of PTTP, one based on Prolog [Stickel 90] and one based on an extended Prolog to Lisp compiler [Stickel 88].

Our implementation is based on an extension of the WAM, called UAM (Unification Abstract Machine). In the UAM atoms, lists and terms are represented with the same data structures for symbols, lists and structures in Lisp, respectively. Logic variables are represented through *locatives*, a special data type which represents a pointer to the location which contains either the object to which the variable is bound or a special value denoting unbound. Structure-copying is the only possibility for the UAM, since we want compatibility of representation with Lisp.

Unification is performed through a set of get and unify primitives, similar to those of the WAM, but the new primitives perform full unification. Whenever a variable is to be bound to a term we must check that this term does not contain the variable itself, searching in all his subterms.

Like the WAM, the UAM operates in two states, *read mode* and *write mode*, entered from a get instruction. When in write mode, all unify instructions in the WAM just assigns a value to the slot of a term. In the UAM instead, the `unify-value` instruction performs the occur check before assignement, while the `unify-variable` does not. A similar difference exists for instructions in the read mode. The difference of behaviour between `unify-value` and `unify-variable` is exploited by the compiler, which produces code which avoids unnecessary occur checks.

In fact the occur check must done only for variables which appear more than once in the head of a clause: the first occurrence of a variable may never be bound to a term containing that same variable, since the actual and the formal arguments are initially variable disjoint. For example, in the unification of a goal with the clause head `p([X|Y], [X|Z])` only for the second occurrence of X we must test whether it occurs in the corresponding subterm of the goal, while for the other variables there is no risk of circularity. Here is the code generated for this example:

```
(let (t1 t2 t3)
    (and (get-cons arg1)           ; first arg
        (unify-variable t1)
        (unify-variable t2)
        (get-cons arg2)            ; second arg
        (unify-value t1)
        (unify-variable t3)
        ...
```

In general, we need to use `unify-variable` for the first occurrence of a variable and `unify-value` for any further occurrence. Since Prolog compilers use the same criteria for selecting between these two unify primitives, the code above is the same that a Prolog compiler based on WAM would produce, and the difference remains hidden in the implementation of the primitives.

For the Model-elimination rule we use a set of primitives that store the actual arguments for which unification succeeds in the ancestors list of the corresponding predicate. Since the actual arguments will be used as ancestors only in later calls to other Lisp functions representing Prolog clauses, in order to save memory the current arguments are stored as ancestors in the C stack extending the Lisp compiler with a special construct, `stack-let`, that works like the Lisp `let`, except that cons cell are allocated on the C stack. A run time procedure `reduce-by-ancestors` is used, before trying to match with the head literal of some clause, to check if be the reduction-rule can be applied: it examines the list of all ancestors of the current predicate and, if an ancestor matches with the current goal, then this goal succeeds. Instead of a simple unification match, our implementation uses a subsumption test which allows us to reduce the search space.

The consecutively bounded depth first search is implemented by means of two functions, `begin_search` and `end_search`. `begin_search` has 3 arguments: the maximum level to which to explore, the depth bound for the first search and the successive depth increments. To use this search strategy, we encapsulate the query as follows:

```
:- begin_search(max,min,def), GOAL, end_search().
```

In the generated code the compiler puts a special test on the actual depth level before each unification: if the body of a clause has a number of literals greater of the number of the remaining levels, it fails (remember that at least an inference for each literal is required). Therefore the code generated for each clause, except for atomic ones, is encapsulated in a test, as follows:

```
(test-depth-bound length-of-body
    (and unifications and invocation for the body))
```

At each failure of GOAL, begin_search increases the depth bound and starts the search all over. Since the search is repeated several times, the purpose of end_search is to discard any solution which had been already reached in a previous search with a lower depth bound.

4.1. Performance

We have performed comparative benchmarks between our theorem prover (Elda) and Stickel's PTTP. The measurements were done on a relatively slow (2 Mips) minicomputer.

Benchmark	Inferences	PTTP sec	PTTP inf./sec	Elda sec	Elda inf./sec	PTTP/Elda %
chang&lee2	1590	1.03	1.54 K	0.75	2.12 K	137
chang&lee3	206	0.16	1.28 K	0.11	1.87 K	145
chang&lee8	3105	1.58	1.96 K	1.00	3.10 K	158
steamroller	11073	2.92	3.78 K	2.21	5.01 K	132

The steamroller benchmark was run with a depth bound of 25. The number of inferences performed by our prover was lower then Stickel's, since several branches of the search were cut off by the subsumption test.

Stickel prover uses an indexing scheme within predicates, which improves the efficiency, but doubles the size of the code. We are still considering whether to adopt this solution.

The time to compile a set of clauses should be considered in the performance estimate, but due to the exponential complexity of the proof search procedure, it becomes less relevant when the size of the problem increases.

5. Conclusions

We have presented an approach to build an efficient theorem prover for the full first order predicate calculus by compiling predicates into procedures which perform the appropriate inference steps. Special care has been placed in the efficiency of the solution, though the use of inferencing primitives built-in as part of a C-based Common Runtime Support. This solution has the advantages that ordinary Prolog predicates can be exploited in theorem-proving (and viceversa) because of the compatibility of the intermediate code produced by the theorem prover and the Prolog compiler. The same interoperability is possible also between the theorem prover and Lisp, as provided by the CRS. It is therefore feasible to develop AI applications that exploit interoperability in a sensible way.

References

[Attardi 90]   G. Attardi, M. Gaspari, F. Saracco, Interoperability of AI Languages, Proocedings of 9th European Conference on Artificial Intelligence, 1990, 41-46.

[Attardi 91]   G. Attardi, M. Gaspari, Multilanguage Interoperability, *Third International Symposium on Programming Language Implementation and Logic Programming*, Passau, 1991.

[Loveland 69] D. W. Loveland, A simplified format for the model elimination procedure, *J. ACM*, **16**(3), 1969, 349-363.

[Stickel 88]   M.E. Stickel, A Prolog technology theorem prover: implementation by an extended Prolog compiler, *J. of Automated Reasoning*, **4**(4), 1988, 353-380.

[Stickel 90]   M.E. Stickel, A Prolog technology theorem prover: a new exposition and implementation in Prolog, in *Design and Implementation of Symbolic Computation Systems, Lecture Notes in Computer Science* **429** 1990, 154-163.

[Warren 83]   D.H.D. Warren, An abstract Prolog instruction set, Tech. Note 309, SRI International, Menlo Park, Oct. 1983.

A FLEXIBLE TOOL FOR ASSUMPTION-BASED USER MODELING

Giorgio Brajnik, Carlo Tasso, Antonio Vaccher
Laboratorio di Intelligenza Artificiale
Dipartimento di Matematica e Informatica
Università di Udine

ABSTRACT. The aim of this paper is to present a new flexible general-purpose shell, called UMT2 (User Modeling Tool 2), which supports the design and development process of user modeling applications and which features an original strategy for performing the modeling activity in a nonmonotonic way. More specifically, UMT2 utilizes a modeling approach called assumption-based user modeling which exploits an ATMS-like mechanism for maintaining the consistency of the user model. The modeling task is thus divided into two separate activities, one devoted to user classification and user model management, and the other devoted to consistency maintenance of the models. Modeling knowledge is represented by means of stereotypes and production rules. The ATMS mechanism is capable of identifying, at any given moment during an interaction, all the possible alternative models which are internally consistent. The choice of the most plausible one among them is then performed according to a procedure exploiting an explicit preference criterion. UMT2 is also characterized by a very well defined and easy-to-use interface with the rest of the application, and by a specialized development interface which supports the knowledge engineer during the construction of specific applications. UMT2 has been developed in CLOS Common LISP.

1. INTRODUCTION

User modeling has been recognized as a very important and useful feature in several man-machine systems where the interaction with the user plays a crucial role (Kobsa and Wahlster, 1989). A user modeling component allows flexible and profitable adaptation of the system behavior to the specific characteristics and nuances of an individual user, improving in such a way the usability of the system, the economy of the interaction, and the capabilities of the system of understanding and processing user requests beyond the pure content of his/her utterances or commands. The application of user modeling techniques have been reported in many fields, such as dialog systems (Wahlster and Kobsa, 1989), and intelligent tutoring systems (Wenger, 1987). An area where user modeling has been considered a fundamental requirement is that of information retrieval systems (Belkin et al., 1987; Daniels, 1986; Brajnik, Guida and Tasso, 1987b).

Nevertheless the design and development of user modeling systems constitutes a very ad-hoc and demanding process and for this reason the idea of exploiting generic shells specifically devoted to user modeling has emerged, and a few systems have been developed along this line, such as GUMS (Finin, 1989), UM-tool (Brajnik, Guida and Tasso, 1990), and BGP-MS (Kobsa, 1990), which can be integrated within a specific application in order to provide user modeling services. Even if no established and general theories underlying the user modeling task exist, all the above mentioned tools have been designed following some common idea. More specifically, all of them are based on an explicit information structure, called user model, for storing the individual representation of the current user of the system, and all of them exploit the idea of stereotypes (Rich, 1983) for representing different classes of users.

However, none of them includes satisfactory mechanisms for approaching one of the most typical features of the user modeling task, i.e. its non-monotonicity. In fact user models usually contain two main kinds of information: known, observed facts about the user and assumptions about the user. Information belonging to this last category may be possibly subjected to revisions, if evidence against the specific assumption is collected. The need of explicitly including such mechanisms within user modeling systems has been recognized by several researches (Finin, 1989; Rich, 1989; Kobsa, 1990; Brajnik, Guida and Tasso, 1990).

The aim of this paper is to present a new flexible general-purpose shell, called *UMT2* (*User Modeling Tool* 2), which supports the design and development process of user modeling applications and which features an original strategy for performing the modeling activity in a nonmonotonic way. More specifically, UMT2 utilizes an ATMS-like mechanism (DeKleer, 1986) for maintaining the consistency of the user model, and for this reason the modeling strategy has been called *assumption-based user modeling*. The modeling task is thus divided into two separate activities, one devoted to user classification and user model management, and the other devoted to consistency maintenance of the modeling process. Modeling knowledge is represented by means of stereotypes and production rules. The ATMS mechanism is capable of identifying, at any given moment during an interaction, all the possible alternative models which are internally consistent. The choice of the most plausible one among them is then performed according to a procedure using an explicit preference criterion. UMT2 is also characterized by a very well defined and easy-to-use interface with (the rest of) the application, and by a specialized development interface which supports the knowledge engineer during the construction of specific applications.

UMT2 has been developed and experimented within IRNLI, an expert interface between casual users and information retrieval systems (Brajnik, Guida and Tasso, 1987a). A previous version of IRNLI already included a generic user modeling shell (the UM-tool system already mentioned above), which however utilized only ad-hoc procedures for dealing with possible inconsistencies arising during the modeling process.

The paper is organized in the following way. Section 2 discusses the main concepts underlying the assumption-based user modeling approach. Section 3 illustrates the UMT2 shell, its architecture and mode of operation. Section 4 concludes the paper.

2. ASSUMPTION-BASED USER MODELING

The main original contribution of UMT2 concerns a new approach to the modeling activity which is based on the use of an assumption-based mechanism for building and maintaining user models. Some of the general features of UMT2 have been derived from UM-tool (Brajnik, Guida and Tasso, 1990), and are briefly summarized at the beginning of this section. In the rest of the section we will focus on assumption-based user modeling.

In our approach, the modeling activity is devoted to modeling single individual users, by means of an explicit inferential process, capable of repeatedly classifying the user during a single session.

The main knowledge sources utilized in our approach are taxonomies of the potential user population and empirical associations of features typical of certain classes of users. Classes (possibly overlapping) of users are described by a finite set of (possibly multivalued) attributes, they are characterized by necessary and sufficient conditions, and a set of rules constrain the possible user descriptions. Domain specific knowledge is used in order to derive the values of some user properties on the basis of values of other properties.

A number of basic hypotheses is made concerning the assumption-based user modeling process. We assume that (i) the information about the user at any moment is inherently incomplete; (ii) that user modeling is an incremental process, based on iterative extension, refinement and revision activities, which can take into account any new piece of user information as soon as it becomes available; and (iii) that the information contained in the model can never be considered as definitive, since new information may be acquired which is not compatible with the old one.

It appears very clearly from the above hypotheses that the modeling process features a *nonmonotonic* nature, which motivates the utilization of some kind of belief revision system. As already mentioned, in UMT2 we have adopted an assumption-based TMS mechanism.

3. USER MODELING TOOL 2

The architecture of UMT2 is constituted by two modules:
- the MODEL MANAGER, devoted to carry on the model management activity. More specifically the Model Manager carries out the following tasks: (i) handling the interaction of UMT2 with the knowledge engineer and the main application program; (ii) performing user classification; (iii) modifying the user models after a user reclassification or when new data about the user are available; (iv) choosing the Current User Model among the Alternative User Models provided by the other module.
- the CONSISTENCY MANAGER, devoted to assuring that the current user model and the alternative user models are all in a consistent state. The Consistency Manager is based on an ATMS.

The operation of UMT2 is supported by the following knowledge bases:
- the STEREOTYPES knowledge base, containing all the descriptions, called stereotypes, of user classes. Stereotypes are organized in a multiple inheritance hierarchy through an IS-A relation defined by the inclusion relation holding between corresponding classes. The root of the hierarchy is the *Generic User Stereotype*, which is a very general description of a potential user and is used to define the set of user attributes. All other stereotypes are called *Class Stereotypes*.
  Each stereotype is divided in two parts: a *trigger*, which is a predicate expressing necessary and sufficient membership conditions of a specific user with respect to the class denoted by the stereotype, and the *defaults*, a list of multivalued attributes along with their values representing typical traits of the users belonging to the class. A stereotype is said to be *active* if and only if its trigger is satisfied or the stereotype is the parent (through the IS-A relation) of an active stereotype.
- the MODELING RULES base, containing *(i) constraints* on the admissible values of a single attribute or combinations of attributes, and *(ii) inference rules* allowing the derivation of some attribute values given certain values of other attributes. When a constraint is not satisfied, an inconsistency is raised.
- the DERIVATION SOURCES base, containing a list of the *derivation sources*, which intuitively represent the possible sources from which an assumption has been derived. Each derivation source is associated to a priority weight which represents a preference relation on derivation sources and it is used for choosing the most plausible model among those made available by the CONSISTENCY MANAGER module.

UMT2, during its operation, exploits two working memories:
- the CURRENT USER MODEL: a representation of the current user as it is perceived, up to that moment, by UMT2. It is constituted by a collection of attributes/values pairs being either:
  * individual facts (e.g. the user's age) supplied by the main application program;
  * default information inherited from the Generic User Stereotype;
  * default information inherited from the active class stereotypes;
  * the result of internal derivation performed by applying some modeling rule.
- the set of ALTERNATIVE USER MODELS: a set of alternative models of the current user generated by the assumption-based modeling process. They represent alternative, plausible, consistent and less preferred representations of the current user.

Finally, UMT2 includes also the USER MODELS database, storing the individual models of all the users that used in the past the application. These models are appropriately retrieved at the beginning of each interaction, and stored back at the end.

3.3 THE MODELING PROCESS

The main activity performed during the assumption-based modeling process is the modification of the user model, performed throughout the session in a demand-driven fashion and aimed at integrating in the user models new data about the user provided by the main application program and at managing inconsistencies. More specifically:
1. when new data about the user are asserted, all the applicable Modeling Rules are fired; maximality and consistency of each user model are automatically handled by the Consistency Manager module;
2. when inconsistencies are signalled by the main application program to UMT2, these are notified to the Consistency Manager module that manages it through standard ATMS procedures;
3. when active stereotypes are identified, their instantiation causes the assumption of their default values and the firing of applicable Modeling Rules. Analogously for non-active stereotypes and their deistanciation.

Whenever an inconsistency among two or more assertions is discovered (either internally to UMT2 during model modification or signalled by the main application program) the ATMS algorithms resolve it by identifying the underlying assumptions and generating new user models which are maximal and internally consistent.
Since the Consistency Manager provides several possible model of the user at the time and, on the other hand, the Model Manager has to consider only one user model, a selection has to take place, which identifies the Current User Model out of the available user models so far computed, called Alternative User Models. The selection is performed by the Model Manager whenever a reclassification takes place or an inconsistency has been dealt with by the Consistency Manager. The decision is based upon an order relation induced on the Alternative User Models by the priority weights associated to each derivation sources. Informally defined, the *most plausible* model is the one which features the highest number of occurrences of the most preferable derivation source, or, when such number is the same for two or more models, the highest number of occurrences of the second preferable derivation source, and so on.

4. CONCLUSIONS

In this paper we have illustrated the organization of UMT2, a flexible tool for building user modeling subsystems, which is centered on an assumption-based user modeling process. The main advantage of such a modeling process derive from the very concise, simple and abstract interface of the module devoted to maintaining the consistency and from the possibility to choose the most plausible model according to a general, explicit and customizable criterion. These features reflect on the easiness with which a knowledge engineer can design and construct the user modeling knowledge (stereotypes and rules); in particular, the knowledge engineer is not asked to deal with explicit mechanisms for handling inconsistencies, ubiquitous in user modeling processes.
Two main limitations of UMT2 are: (i) the combinatorial explosion of the number of alternative models, and (ii) the monotonic growth of the graph internally handled by the Consistency Manager and representing all believed assertions and all justifications among them. We plan to approach both problems by adopting a heuristic criterion for pruning those models that are likely to never become very plausible. Other planned extensions of UMT2 concern the definition of a powerful and declarative language to specify the inheritance network of stereotypes, and the definition of a declarative language to specify choice criteria for the Current User Model among the available ones.

UMT2 is implemented in Common Lisp with the CLOS extension. It was initially developed on a Symbolics Mac-Ivory machine, and later ported to other Common Lisps. The testbed application utilized for experimentation concerns a touristic advice giving system.

Future research openings concern the development and experimentation of a user modeling subsystem based on UMT2 included in the FIRE prototype, a flexible environment for developing interfaces to information retrieval systems. After a laboratory validation of such a user modeling subsystem, an experimentation of FIRE with real users will be carried out in order to evaluate the benefits offered by the inclusion of a user modeling component within an expert interface for on-line bibliographic databases.

REFERENCES

Belkin, N et al. 1987. Distributed expert based information systems: an interdisciplinary approach. *Information Processing & Management* vol. 23(5).

Brajnik G., Guida G., and Tasso, C. 1987a. Design and experimentation of IR-NLI: an intelligent user interface to bibliographic data bases. in L. Kerschberg (Ed.), *Expert Data Base Systems*. Menlo Park, CA: The Benjamin/Cummings Publishing Company, pp. 151-162.

Brajnik G., Guida G., and Tasso, C. 1987b. User modeling in intelligent information retrieval, *Information Processing & Management* , vol. 23(4), pp. 305-320.

Brajnik, G. , Guida, G. and Tasso, C. 1990. User Modeling in Expert Man-Machine Interfaces: A Case Study in Intelligent Information Retrieval. *IEEE Transactions on Systems, Man, and Cybernetics* Vol. 20(1), 166-185.

Daniels, P.J. 1986. The user modelling function of an intelligent interface for document retrieval systems, in *Proc. IRFIS 6: Intelligent Information Systems for the Information Society*, Amsterdam, NL: North-Holland, pp. 162-176.

De Kleer, J. 1986. An Assumption-based Truth Maintenance System. *Artificial Intelligence* 28, 127-162.

Finin, T. W. 1989. GUMS - A General User Modeling Shell. In: *User Models in Dialog Systems*. A. Kobsa, W. Wahlster (Eds.), Springer Verlag, pp. 411-430.

Kobsa, A and Wahlster, W. (Editors) 1989. *User Modeling in Dialog Systems*. Springer Verlag, Berlin, Germany.

Kobsa, A. 1990. Modeling the user's conceptual knowledge in BGP-MS, a user modeling shell system. *Computational Intelligence* 6, 193-208.

Rich, E. 1983. Users are individuals: individualizing user models. *Int. Journal of man-Machine Studies* vol. 18, 199-214.

Rich, E. 1989. Stereotypes and User Modeling. In: *User Models in Dialog Systems*. A. Kobsa, W. Wahlster (Eds.), Springer Verlag, pp. 35-51.

Wahlster, W. and Kobsa, A. 1989. User Models in Dialog Systems. In: *User Models in Dialog Systems*. A. Kobsa, W. Wahlster (Eds.), Springer Verlag, pp. 4-34.

Wenger, E. 1987. *Artificial Intelligence and Tutoring Systems*. Morgan Kaufman, Los Altos, CA.

KL: A NEURAL MODEL FOR CAPTURING STRUCTURE IN SPEECH*

P. Frasconi, M. Gori, M. Maggini, G. Soda

Dipartimento di Sistemi e Informatica
Via S. Marta, 3 - 50139 Firenze
Tel. 055-4796265 - Fax 055-4796363
giovanni@ifiidg.bitnet

Abstract. *In this paper we propose a neural model conceived for problems of word recognition and understanding of small protocol-driven sentences. The model is based on an unified approach to integrate priori knowledge and learning by example. The priori knowledge, injected into the network connections, can be of different levels, while learning is mainly conceived as a refinement process, and is responsible of dealing with uncertainty. We describe a small prototype for problems of isolated word recognition.*

1. Introduction

Many researchers have recently used connectionist models for emulating intelligent tasks. Much attention has been paid to pattern recognition and particularly to speech processing. As for other pattern recognition problems, in speech processing many successful models have dealt with the detection of "low level features". Supervised learning schemes have turned out to be particularly useful for tasks that, like phoneme recognition, cannot be easily modeled by explicit rules. Many of these schemes rely upon improvements of Back-Propagation Networks. For example, Time Delay Neural Networks [11] and recurrent networks for supervised learning [5, 10, 12, 13], have led to significant increasing of performance in phoneme recognition. In spite of these results, similar models have not changed the perspective concerning problems like isolated word recognition and understanding of small protocol-driven sentences.

Several researchers have tried to use "tabula-raza neural models", like those used for phoneme recognition, for recognizing isolated words. Many of these attempts refer to digit recognition or to other small dictionaries [1, 8, 9]. Apart from such results, which seem quite promising, it is easy to realize that the neural models, used so far, do not scale up very well to large dictionaries. From a theoretical point of view, these difficulties are strictly related with the approach used. For example, Judd [7] has proven that loading the weights of a feedforward nets is NP-complete. Another face of the same problem, comes out by exploring the problem of local minima. Such investigations have been suggesting that Back-Propagation has succeeded for many "quasi-linearly-separable patterns", whereas does not seem neither reliable, nor successful for seriously non-linearly-separable problems [6].

---

* This work was partially supported by MURST 40%.

The integration of explicit knowledge and learning by example appears to be a natural way of evolving connectionist models. Our hypothesis is that for a model to be effective, this integration should be as uniform as possible. This means that explicit and learned rules should be represented in the same way by the weight connections of our networks. We investigate the possibility of this integration in the framework of recurrent nets and propose a model, called KL (a priori Knowledge and Learning by example), based on an architecture composed of two cooperating subnets. The first one is designed in order to inject the available explicit knowledge for speech tasks, whereas the second one is learned to allow management of uncertain information. A first application of this model is proposed for recognizing isolated words. The basic idea resembles that of Hidden Markov Models in that, for each word, a sort of chain is used as model. Obviously, a chain can also be used for modeling more sub-words, thus saving connections significantly. The model assumes that a lower level exists which provides phonetic information for each speech frame. These phonemes, represented by continuous values, supply KL net.

The most relevant difference with respect to tabula raza neural nets is that the lexical knowledge is explicitly represented into the connections of "K" network. This makes it possible to model each word separately. After scanning the input phonemes, the networks which implement these models provide continuous values representing a sort of probability that the analyzed speech section represents a given word. "L" network is devoted to refine the explicit lexical knowledge of "K" using a learning by example from "tabula-raza". Its connections are tuned by considering a dictionary subset composed of those words which are more likely to be confused one each other. In so doing the learning task is relieved significantly. Using the same approach, more challenging tasks, like understanding small protocol-driven sentences, can, in principle, be explored.

2. KL model

KL is a connectionist model based on an architecture composed of two cooperating blocks, N_K and N_L, devoted to explicit and learned rule representation, respectively (see Fig. 1). In terms of neuron connections, a recurrent net is assumed in which the computations are performed synchronously with the applications of input

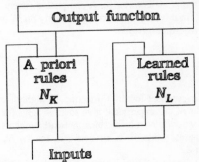

Fig. 1 *The proposed architecture which integrates a priori with learned rules.*

values. Recurrent networks of this kind seem better suited than Boltzmann machines or Hopfield nets for tasks that, like speech recognition, need to capture sequential information [5, 12]. Explicit rules, in the form of ordinary automata, are injected into net N_K's connections. The automaton is specified by means of its transition rules. The states are properly coded by dynamic neurons capable of latching information. The inputs to these neurons are responsible of state transitions which can be controlled by setting the network's weights properly. The conditions concerning state transitions are representable in the linear programming framework, and lead to a set of weights which must belong to a certain region Ω of the weights space [4].

Basically, the rules defined by the automaton can be represented in several different ways. When changing the weights of network N_K in the admissible region Ω, the explicit rules remain valid, provided that the state transitions occur in a certain number of steps. As shown in the following section, this property, which is naturally exhibited by N_K net, is very useful for speech recognition in order to avoid spurious state transitions. Another remarkable feature of network N_K, realized as an automaton, is that it is capable of dealing with information represented by continuous values. The explicit rules are provided by considering the sign of these values, but the actual network behavior is dependent on continuous values. Moreover, a sort of learning can also be exploited concerning this net, in the attempt of finding out which weights perform the explicit rules better. The basic idea is that the learning process must not destroy the explicit rules.

Learning the uncertain information is mainly accomplished by N_L. It is a full-connected recurrent net, randomly initialized, which is charged of discovering hidden rules. A supervised learning paradigm is assumed. For each speech frame in which a supervision label is placed, the network outputs are compared with target values and the learning algorithm tries to minimize the error between these values. We use a discrete version of Pearlmutter's algorithm for the entire recurrent network composed of blocks N_K and N_L, where the weights of N_K are bounded in the admissible region Ω [4]. Basically, the task of this net is that of capturing all those regularities which, though non explicit, are very important in speech processing. In so doing, learning is essentially conceived as a refinement process, and it is relieved from the problem of discovering complex deterministic rules.

Model KL is a particular recurrent network which integrates in an uniform way explicit and learned rules. As far the learning, no difference exists. We have just to consider that the weights associated with explicit rules are bounded in order not to destroy the priori knowledge. A complete different approach could be that of considering N_K as a "symbolic automaton". In this case the learning acts only on N_L nets, and N_K outputs can be considered as external inputs to the global recurrent network.

3. IWR using KL model

In the following, we propose an experiment for discriminating 10 highly-confused Italian words, only composed of vowels and nasals. The results of this experiment give some insights for word recognition in large lexicons. In order to accomplish this task, we selected a hierarchical network architecture in which a first net N_P was devoted to perform phoneme hypotheses, while 10 other nets N_W^i, fed by N_P's outputs, were used for modeling the words, as indicated in section 2.

N_P was implemented with a Local Feedback Multi-Layered Network [3]. This kind of architecture is an extension of MLN, in which some neurons exhibit dynamic behavior. Feedback connections are only allowed from dynamic neurons to themselves (self-loops). Such constraints make learning possible by means of an algorithm (BPS [5]) which is both local in space and in time, and which exhibits the same complexity as Back-Propagation. For the present application, the task of this network was to spot Italian vowels /a/, /e/, /i/, /o/, /u/,

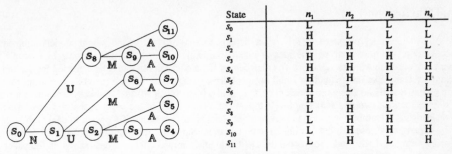

State	n_1	n_2	n_3	n_4
S_0	L	L	L	L
S_1	H	L	L	L
S_2	H	H	L	L
S_3	H	H	H	L
S_4	H	H	H	H
S_5	H	H	L	H
S_6	H	L	H	L
S_7	H	L	H	H
S_8	L	H	L	L
S_9	L	H	H	L
S_{10}	L	H	H	H
S_{11}	L	H	L	H

Fig. 2 *Automaton devoted to detect the Italian word /Numa/. Self-loops are not represented.*

and nasals /m/, /n/ in continuous speech. A detailed description of this network can be found in [2].

Each net N_w^i was devoted to detect a word of the dictionary and the highest network output criterion was used to perform word prediction. The subnet for priori rule representation had a chain-like structure. It was conceived for representing the automaton of Fig. 2. For each state, subsequent occurrences of the same phoneme do not produce state transitions. Moreover the automaton is capable of dealing with phoneme skips. It behaves like a string parser, whose final state is reached only if the right phoneme string is applied. Basically, automata of this kind solve directly the problem of insertions and deletions of phonetic symbols.

As mentioned in section 2, we are not interested in implementing exactly the automaton described in Fig. 2. We want our net to consider state transitions only after 2 or 3 speech frames in order to avoid several noisy predictions of phoneme net N_P. This feature is particularly useful to decrease the cross-talk from the other words. Moreover it should not be forgotten that nets N_w^i have to deal with analog values representing the evidence for a given phoneme.

A fully-recurrent network composed of two neurons was adopted as net N_L. The weights of subnet N_K were found by following the method described in [4], whereas the "refinement" was performed by Pearlmutter's learning procedure [10], adapted for discrete time. We investigated the effect of this refinement, particularly on N_L's neurons. As we expected from theoretical considerations, rules which were not included in N_K automaton net were automatically learned. In practice we want the learning process to develop rules which do not appear explicit or which are affected heavily by uncertainty.

Experimental results are discussed in detail in [4], and we report here just a short summary of them. A preliminary speaker independent small test based on 284 words was performed. The maximum output decision criterion was adopted. We found a recognition rate as high as 92.3%. The task is not simple, since the words considered are only composed of vowels and nasals. We notice that although the dictionary is small (only 10 words), the model proposed is likely to scale much better than others suggested in literature [1, 8, 9]. This is mainly due to subnet N_K, which only accept acoustic strings corresponding to the words that it models. It is worth mentioning that if only a learning by example approach is used for modeling each word, no guarantee at all can be provided to ensure that a given word net do not reacts to other words.

4. Conclusions

The model proposed in this paper departs to some extent to the neural models adopted in speech recognition. We have analyzed the idea of integrating explicit knowledge and learning by example for coping with large lexicon word recognition. The idea behind KL model can obviously be extended for dealing with other complex tasks, like understanding small protocol-driven languages. We are currently exploring this possibility for a simple artificial language which permits to deal with a "block world". In this system, the priori knowledge involves the syntactic and semantic levels too. A basic conclusion of the paper is that the integration of explicit knowledge and learning by example in neural networks is surely needed if we want to deal with large problems. The experimental research concerning large dictionaries, and understanding tasks are at the beginning. We have just experimented KL model for recognition of the highly-confused Italian words shown in the paper and we do not have any comparison with existing successful techniques.

References

[1] De Michelis P., Fissore L., Laface P., Micca G., and Piccolo E., "On the Use of Neural Networks for Speaker Independent Isolated Word Recognition", Proc. of IEEE-ICASSP89, Glasgow - Scotland, 1989.
[2] Frasconi P., Gori M., and Soda G., "Recurrent Networks for Continuous Speech Recognition", Computational Intelligence 90, Milan (Italy), September 1990, Elsevier.
[3] Frasconi P., Gori M., Soda G. "Local Feedback Multi Layered Networks", Neural Computation (to appear).
[4] Frasconi P., Gori M., Maggini M., and Soda G., "An Unified Approach for Integrating Explicit Knowledge and Learning by Example in Recurrent Networks", Proc. of IEEE-IJCNN91, Seattle (Washington), 1991. (to appear).
[5] Gori M., Bengio Y. and De Mori R., BPS: "A Learning Algorithm for Capturing the Dynamical Nature of Speech". Proceedings of the IEEE-IJCNN89. Washington June 18-22.
[6] Gori M., Tesi A., "On the Problem of Local Minima in Back-Propagation", IEEE Trans. PAMI (to appear).
[7] Judd S, "On the Complexity of Loading Shallow Neural Networks", Journal of Complexity, 4, 1988.
[8] Kammerer B.K. and Kupper W.A., "Design of Hierarchical Perceptron Structures and their Application to the Task of Isolated Word Recognition", Proceedings of the IEEE-IJCNN89. Washington June 18-22.
[9] Pealing S.M., Moore R. K., and Tomlinson M.J., "The Multi-Layer Perceptron as a Tool for Speech Pattern Processing Research", Proc. of the 10th Autumn Conference on Speech and Hearing, 1986.
[10] Pearlmutter B. A., "Learning State Space Trajectories in Recurrent Neural Networks", Neural Computation, vol 1, no. 2, Summer 1989.
[11] Waibel A., Hanazawa T., Hinton G., Shikano K., Lang K., "Phoneme Recognition Using Time-Delay Neural Networks", IEEE Transactions on ASSP, vol. 37, no. 3, March 1989.
[12] Watrous R.L. "Speech Recognition Using Connectionist Networks", Ph.D. Thesis, University of Pennsylvania, Philadelphia, PA 19104, November 1988.
[13] Williams R.J., Zipser D., "A Learning Algorithm for Continually Running Fully Recurrent Neural Networks". Neural Computation, vo. 1, no. 1, pp. 270-280, 1989.

Lexical Discrimination within a Multilevel Semantics Approach

Alberto Lavelli   Bernardo Magnini
IRST, Istituto per la Ricerca Scientifica e Tecnologica
I - 38050 Povo TN, Italy
e-mail: magnini@irst.it

Abstract

This paper describes a computational approach to lexical discrimination. A multilevel semantics approach is assumed in which at least two levels are relevant: the lexical level, described here, at which lexical discrimination is carried out, and the logical-interpretative level, at which the sentence interpretation is accomplished within the system domain model. Given that both the lexical and the interpretation level make reference to the same knowledge a strategy is proposed to maintain consistency among lexical discrimination, sentence interpretation and domain model knowledge.

1. Motivations

In natural language processing systems syntactic analysis usually produces several interpretations, because of the intrinsic ambiguity of natural language; in order to reduce such an ambiguity, systems try to select only the sentence readings meaningful in a given domain model (DM) using lexical discrimination: if the propositional content of a reading does not comply with certain semantic requirements, then it is "discriminated", which means that the reading under analysis is not further considered. Two fundamental problems arise in lexical discrimination: (i) to establish general principles able to separate meaningful readings in DM from non-meaningful readings; (ii) to find an efficient way to discriminate, possibly recognizing unsound readings as soon as possible.

A traditional technique to carry out semantic discrimination is to use frame languages to represent the knowledge available to the system (*Knowledge Semantics*) [Hirst 87]. This has led to use of reasoning capabilities that are peculiar to knowledge representation languages (i.e. taxonomic reasoning, inheritance); as a consequence the discrimination process takes advantage of a complex set of semantic relations. More recently, in some systems [Allgayer *et al.* 89] [Weischedel 89] hybrid representation languages have been introduced, which make it possible to separate general knowledge about the domain (TBOX) from the set of facts assumed in the domain (ABOX). This way it is possible to use the world knowledge as the model over which the sentence interpretation is carried out.

By introducing semantic modules working on more than one level (*multilevel semantics*) [Scha 83], semantic analysis is decomposed in several phases. While the advantage of this approach is that each level can be specialized in a certain analysis task, improving the system modularity, a problem arises in deciding of the right level for lexical discrimination. One of the first multilevel based systems is the BBN spoken language system [Boisen *et al.* 89]. It includes two separated analysis phases: a domain independent level (EFL), in which lexical ambiguities are kept; a domain dependent level (WML) in which semantic discrimination is carried out and where the representation becomes unambiguous. The discrimination process is carried out during the crossing between the EFL and the WML level, when domain dependent rewriting rules are called. A type checking mechanism provides acceptance only for interpretations for which a domain knowledge compatible type has been computed. While having sound theoretical foundations, the main drawback of this approach is that it postpones semantic discrimination until domain knowledge is available; in the meantime, a complete sentence representation is built for each analysis the parser produces.

Another system with a clear distinction between the domain independent and the domain dependent level is XTRA [Allgayer *et al.* 89]. However, in this case at each level the knowledge representation language SB-ONE is used. The domain independent level (FSS), is intended as an intermediate structure that incorporates linguistic knowledge, substantially invariant in respect to the particular application domain. On the contrary, the domain dependent level (CKB), is necessary to adequately model the relations of the underlying expert system. In XTRA it is necessary that each analysis produced by the parser is consistent with the FSS level: this is achieved by means of a classification of the sentence instance with the SB-ONE mechanisms (the realizer and the matcher). In this approach the discrimination process is profitably anticipated, and a powerful (even though computationally expensive) checking mechanism for consistency is provided. However, it is not clear what kind of consistency may be obtained based on the FSS linguistic knowledge. More precisely, given the fact that, at least theoretically, a domain can always exist in which a sentence can have meaning, it seems impossible to base the discrimination on a kind of knowledge that is, by definition, domain independent.

2. Semantic Architecture

This section is devoted to the presentation of the main ideas of our approach. First, it seems useful to consider lexical discrimination as an incremental process: if discrimination works in parallel with the parser, it is possible to discriminate over single syntactic phrases, checking the semantic content of each phrase. Secondly, to actually reduce the number of syntactic analyses, lexical discrimination must consider the application domain knowledge. Moreover, in the context of a multilevel architecture, it seems necessary to guarantee the consistency among the analysis phases; one way to achieve this requirement is to establish a general connection rule among the levels.

In our approach the semantic lexicon is built from the application domain. Semantic analysis is decomposed into two levels, both of them having access to the DM [Figure 1]: (a) the *lexical level*, in which the discrimination process and the resolution of certain semantic ambiguities is carried out in an incremental way during the parsing; (b) the *logical-interpretative level*, in which quantification ambiguities are resolved and the sentence interpretation is carried out.

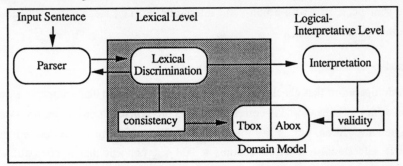

Figure 1: Sketch of the semantic process. The lexical semantics part is boxed.

After checking the syntactic requirements for a (partially recognized) phrase, semantic consistency is also checked for each sense the phrase admits within the domain model. If none of the phrase semantic interpretations succeeds, then the syntactic structure under analysis is rejected; otherwise, for all the phrase senses that are consistent in DM, a semantic interpretation is associated to the syntactic structure. Two effects are achieved: reduction of the structural attachment possibilities and selection among the word senses (i.e. lexical discrimination). Algorithms that are defined at the two levels, just as the translation rules among the levels, are domain independent. In such an approach the domain change requires that the semantic lexicon only must be rebuilt. Our approach is within the multilevel semantics, in the sense that semantic analysis consists of various phases: however, it is different from other systems in that each level has the same access to the DM information. The approach is also within the Knowledge Semantics framework, given the fact that the aim of semantic analysis is to find a sort of mapping within the facts the knowledge base contains. While in this paper the attention is over the lexical level, the logical-interpretative level is presented in detail in [Strapparava 91].

Given that the two semantic levels make reference to the same knowledge, within this architecture it becomes important to establish a strict connection between the discrimination process at the lexical level, the interpretation process at the logical-interpretative level and the knowledge the DM contains. Our approach assumes a hybrid representation language for the DM: this way the general knowledge about the domain is contained in DM_{Tbox}, while the facts the system considers are contained in DM_{Abox}.

Both lexical discrimination and interpretation refer to DM knowledge. Lexical discrimination checks the *consistency* while interpretation the *validity* of the sentence propositional content. The consistency relation is defined over the DM_{Tbox}: the propositional content of a sentence is consistent with a given DM_{Tbox} iff it is satisfiable w.r.t. the theory defined by DM_{Tbox}. The validity relation is defined over the DM_{Abox}: the propositional content of a sentence is valid within a given DM_{Abox} iff there exists a set of facts such that they represent the sentence denotation. Being defined over a particular DM_{Abox} the validity relation is more restrictive than the consistency relation. An important consequence of this distinction is that there can be consistent sentences, still with a non-valid interpretation (i.e., meaningful sentences with no referred entities in the DM_{Abox}).

3. Consistency checking

The basic operation that checks semantic consistency is a test that compares a selectional-restriction with the semantic-head corresponding to the syntactic constituent proposed to fill a given argument position. Let us call this operation *Consistency-test*, and define it such that it succeeds if selectional-restriction denotes a DM_{Tbox} concept that is compatible with the concept denoted by the semantic-head.

There exist several possibilities to check the compatibility between two concepts within a terminological hierarchy. First of all, it seems reasonable to achieve a success when semantic-head is a more specific concept than selectional-restriction (e.g. "To paint a fresco"), or when it is an instance (e.g. "Giotto paints"). The systems ABSIDY [Hirst 87] and PUNDIT [Palmer 90] implement a similar test. However, there are cases for which we expect the test to succeed, while it is semantic-head that includes selectional-restriction. This case, for instance, frequently occurs in interrogative sentences (e.g. "Which artist painted Gioacchino's Cacciata?"). Within the JANUS system [Weischedel 89] the semantic test is implemented by means of a double subsumption check that guarantees a success both when semantic-head is a descendant of selectional-restriction and when it is an ancestor. Systems that use a simple inclusion test deal with this case by placing more general selectional-restrictions (e.g. the agent of paint must be animate). However, the drawback of this method is that the conceptual structure becomes less informative as generic concepts are introduced. Although more complete, the double subsumption test does not consider the cases, sometimes relevant, in which semantic-head is a brother concept of selectional-restriction (e.g. "Has a sculptor painted a fresco?"); this case recursively extends to all the cases in which semantic-head is a brother either of a descendant or of an ancestor for a selectional-restriction (e.g. "Which object did Giotto paint?"). This case is slightly more complex than the others. In fact, while it is always true that along the ISA hierarchy there can be a non-empty intersection between two concepts, this is not true for concepts that are brothers. If an explicit disjointness is placed between two brother concepts, there cannot be a common intersection and the consistency procedure must fail; otherwise it is assumed that a common intersection can exist, and the consistency-test procedure will succeed. Knowledge representation languages that do not provide for disjointness are only able to accept the double subsumption test. If this is the case, it seems reasonable to consider brother concepts as implicitly disjoint, so that semantic test will always fail. On the contrary, KR languages with disjointness are usually provided with a specific predicate holding between two concepts when their intersection is empty (e.g. "disjoint?" in YAK [Franconi 90], "disjoint-p" in LOOM [Mac Gregor, Bates 87]). It is worth noting that this predicate includes all the subsumption cases among concepts, in which cases it is always false.

Making use of a disjointness predicate in order to define the consistency guarantees that the propositional content of a sentence is satisfiable in DM_{Tbox} (as we have assumed at the end of the previous section).

4. Implementation

The work presented here is implemented in the lexical module [Lavelli, Magnini 91] of the multimedial interactive system ALFresco [Stock 91]. Lexical level works in parallel with the parser WEDNESDAY 2 [Stock 89]; expressions of the lexical language are built during parsing applying compositional rules. The lexical representation is then converted into the logical form that is used at the logical-interpretative level. The ALFresco domain concerns Italian art history of the Fourteenth Century, and information is represented by means of the KR hybrid language YAK. The module is implemented in CommonLisp and runs on SUN4. On confirmation of the module portability, it will be used within the MAIA (Artificial Intelligence Advanced Module) IRST global project.

References

[Allgayer et al. 89] Allgayer, J., Jansen-Winkeln, R., Reddig, C., Reithinger, N. "Bidirectional Use of Knowledge in the Multi-Modal NL Access System XTRA", Proc. IJCAI-89, Detroit, Michigan, 1989.

[Boisen et al. 89] Boisen, S., Chow, Y., Ingria, R., Roukos, S., Scha, R., Stallard, D, Vilain, M. "Integration of Speech and Natural Language Final Report", Report No. 6991, BBN System and Technologies Corporation, 1989.

[Franconi 90] Franconi, E. "The YAK (Yet Another Krapfen) Manual", IRST Manual, Trento, Italy, 1990. Also as 'Progetto Finalizzato CNR - Sistemi Informatici e Calcolo Parallelo'.

[Hirst 87] Hirst, G. Semantic Interpretation and the Resolution of Ambiguity, Cambridge University Press, 1987.

[Lavelli, Magnini 91] Lavelli, A., Magnini, B. "Lexical Discrimination within the ALFresco System", IRST Technical Report, Trento, Italy, 1991.

[Mac Gregor, Bates 87] Mac Gregor, R.M., Bates, R. "The LOOM Knowledge Representation Language", Techical Report ISI/RS-87-188, USC/Information Science Institute, 1987.

[Palmer 90] Palmer, M. "Customizing Verb Definitions for Specific Semantic Domains", Machine Translation, 5(1): 5-30, 1990.

[Scha 83] Scha, R. "Logical Foundations for Question Answering", Philips Research Laboratories, M.S. 12.331, Eindhoven, The Netherlands, 1983.

[Stock 89] Stock, O. "Parsing with Flexibility, Dynamic Strategies, and Idioms in Mind", Computational Linguistics, 15(1): 1-18, 1989.

[Stock 91] Stock, O. "Natural Language and Exploration of an Information Space: The ALFresco Interactive System", Proc. IJCAI-91, Sydney, Australia, 1991.

[Strapparava 91] Strapparava, C. "From Scopings to Interpretation: The Semantic Interpretation within the ALFresco System", Proc. AIIA-91, Palermo, Italy, 1991.

[Weischedel 89] Weischedel, R. M. "A Hybrid Approach to Representation in the Janus Natural Language Processor", Proc. ACL-89, Vancouver, British Columbia, 1989.

Metalevel Representation of Analogical Inference

Stefania **Costantini**, Gaetano Aurelio **Lanzarone**
Universita' degli Studi di Milano, Dipartimento di Scienze dell'Informazione
Via Moretto da Brescia 9, I-20133, Milano, Italy

1. Introduction

Interest in analogy representation has been growing in the AI community, since analogical inference is an important capability of a reasoning agent. Several approaches have been proposed in the literature (see [Hal89], [Lei90] for comprehensive surveys). Our preference is for a general (rather than ad hoc), declarative and formal (logic–based) approach. We restate as follows a specification of analogical inference that recurs in several logical approaches [Gre88], [DaR87], [Goe89], [Rus89]. Given: a theory Th, i.e. a consistent set of logical sentences about both the target analogue T and the source analogue S, as well as other general knowledge; a single logical sentence G, called *goal*, expressing the target problem; a set An of potentially refutable analogical sentences suggesting certain similarities between S and T; try to establish the (analogical conclusion) G under the following conditions:

1: Th $\not\models$ G(T); 2: Th $\cup$ An $\models$ G(T); 3: Th $\not\models$ ¬G(T); 4: Th $\models$ G(S)

Condition 1 rules out analogical inference used only to speed up the derivation of a conclusion which could be drawn from the theory alone (e.g. [Ker89]). Condition 2 specifies purpose–directed analogy: not all analogies between S and T are searched for (like in [Win80]), but only those which are sufficient to solve G. Condition 3 requires G(T) not to be known false, in order to keep the resulting theory Th' = Th $\cup$ {G(T)} consistent. Condition 4 reinforces the use of S to provide a basis for the analogical inference, by insisting that S satisfies the same analogy formula as T. An indicates common properties between S and T, but does not specify which properties nor how they should be mapped over. The proposed approaches differ in this respect: the mapping may relate only objects [DRu87], or only relations [Gen88], or both [Ind88]. The objective of this paper is not to propose a specific model of analogy, but to show that a metalevel representation can easily accomodate several of them, provided the language has appropriate capabilities. With the aim of a declarative representation of metaknowledge, we have developed a metalogic programming language, called Reflective Prolog (RP for short), introduced in [CL89] and extensively described in [CL91]. We will discuss the advantages of a metalevel approach to analogical inference in this framework, presenting examples taken from the literature.

2. The Metalevel Framework

Main feature of Reflective Prolog is the representation of knowledge and metaknowledge at distinct but connected levels, uniformly in the same language, and processed by the same inference mechanism which assures an automatic interaction between levels. RP extends Horn clauses, which form the *object level,* with three main additional features. First, there is a *naming* mechanism, which allows syntactic entities of the language to be represented in the language itself by means of metaterms and metavariables. Metaknowledge is thus expressed in facts and rules containing metaterms and metavariables, called *metalevel clauses.* Second, there is a particular class of rules, expressed by the user and defining the distinguished predicate solve, which allow the declarative extension of the intended meaning of the other predicates. These are called *metaevaluation clauses,* and form the *metaevaluation level* of a program, while all the other (object and meta) clauses form the *base level.* Third, there is an extended resolution including *implicit reflection,* that uses the solve rules as auxiliary inference rules, to derive extensions of the ordinary deductive closure of the theory expressed at the lower–levels.

The naming mechanism provides: *quoted name constants,* which represent constant, variable and function symbols (e.g. "c","V", "fun"); *bracketed name constants,* which represent predicate symbols (e.g. <pred>); compound name terms, which represent terms and atoms; *predicate metavariables* (syntax: #<name>), to be bound to bracketed name constants only; *general metavariables* (syntax: $<name>), to be bound to any metaterm. Passing from an object to its name or vice versa is called *referencing/dereferencing.* Unification is extended to deal with metavariables and with terms/atoms of different levels. Resolution is extended to include reflection. Briefly, a goal can either be resolved at its level, or give rise to *upward reflection,* which switches from the base–level to the metaevaluation level, or else vice versa, by *downward reflection.* Upward/downward reflection automatically performs referencing/dereferencing of goals. The RP interpreter adopts a Prolog–like depth–first search strategy, considering base–level clauses first, and metaevaluation clauses only when the former fail.

As a first example of an RP program, consider the following situation. Knowing that an object named a has property p, we assert p(a). Then we want to express that object a can equivalently be named b (the two names are synonyms), and be able to derive p(b):

```
p(a).                                              /* object level */
equivalent("b","a").                               /* meta level */
solve(#P($X)):-equivalent($X,$Y),solve(#P($Y)). /* metaevaluation level */
```

The goal ?–p(b) is solved by the following derivation. Failing at the object level, it is referenced by upward reflection and the metaevaluation goal :–solve(<p>("b")) is generated. This unifies, by extended unification, with the head of the metaevaluation rule, with substitution #P/<p>, $X/"b", thus generating the goal :–equivalent("b",$Y),solve(<p>($Y)). The first subgoal unifies with the metafact with substitution $Y/"a", leaving the subgoal :–solve(<p>("a")). This is dereferenced by downward reflection, giving :–p(a), which succeeds at the object level.

3. Analogies as Equality Assumptions

Goebel's account of analogy [Goe89] is the first one that we reconsider in our framework. Goebel conjectures that analogical reasoning consists of using similarity information, which can and must be expressed as various kinds of equality assumptions. He represents these assumptions in the Theorist hypothetical reasoning model, where hypothesys schemas H are given to the system together with theory Th; the system is used to find a set An of instances of H such that Th ∪ An ⊨ G, i.e. identifies refutable hypotheses that support the desired conclusion.

To show these features, Goebel first considers the following example. Th = {p(a)}, where p(a) is source knowledge and there is neither target nor other general knowledge. The only similarity assumption is H = { ∀ x,y. x = y }. The goal G = p(b) is to establish property p for the target b. An = {a = b} provides a solution, and the conditions of the specification of analogy are satisfied: p(b) has been concluded on the basis of source knowledge p(a) and the analogical mapping a = b. This example is rendered by the previous RP program, where the metafact equivalent("b","a") is replaced by the more general equivalent($X,$Y). Now the goal ?–p(b) is solved as before, except that when the goal :–equivalent("b",$Y),solve(<p>($Y)) is generated, the first subgoal succeeds without instantiating $Y, and the second succeeds at the object level, instantiating $Y to "a". In Goebel's terms, the derivation is successful, based on the instance equivalent("b","a") of the hypothesys schema equivalent($X,$Y).

To show another kind of equality assumptions, Goebel then discusses the problem of transferring properties from source to target by using rules like "If the source is sufficiently similar to the target and has a property of interest, then ascribe that property to the target". He notices that, to enable this transfer, a representation is needed, in which "properties are cast as individuals and attributed to other individuals with a has_property relation, e.g. has_property(juliette,beautiful)". This kind of 'reification', i.e. treating properties as ordinary first–order objects, was first introduced in AI by McCarthy [McC79]. By cleanly formalizing reification, RP most naturally expresses the above "property ascription" rule:

solve(<has_property>($T,$X)):–similar($S,$T),solve(<has_property>($S,$X)).

The similarity assumption (or analogical mapping) is given e.g. by similar("cinderella","juliette") and from the known fact has_property("juliette",<beautiful>) the analogical conclusion ?–has_property("cinderella",<beautiful>) can be drawn. Goebel comments that analogical reasoning must be capable of preferring some analogues over possible others, by selecting the most relevant similarities. The following elaboration of the previous example shows how this capability is naturally rendered in our framework.

beautiful(juliette).	1
similar("cinderella","juliette",aspect).	2
similar("anna","juliette",temper).	3
concerning(<beautiful>,aspect).	4
relevant(Characteristic,#P):–concerning(#P,Characteristic).	5

```
sufficiently_similar($Target,$Source,#Property):-                              6
    similar($Target,$Source,Characteristic),relevant(Characteristic,#Property). 7
solve(#P($X)):-sufficiently_similar($X,$Y,#P),solve(#P($Y)).                   8
```

Here the third argument of relation similar specifies in which respect the given objects are similar (clause 2,3). Relation concerning relates property beautiful to aspect (4). Clause (5) states that a characteristic is relevant to a property if it is known to be related to that property. The solve rule (8) performs analogy on sufficiently similar objects, i.e. similar in a respect which is relevant to the considered property . Thus, query ?-beautiful(cinderella) is unswered positively, and ?-beautiful(anna) negatively.

4. Analogical Reasoning with Determination Rules

Davies and Russel consider [DRu87], [Rus89] reasoning by analogy as the process of inferring that a conclusion property q holds of a target object T from the fact that T shares a (set of) properties p with the source object S that has property q: from p(S) ∧ q(S), p(T) infer q(T). As the conclusion does not follow syntactically from the premises, its plausibility depends on information not provided in the premise. A determination relation: p determines q, gives a justification, expressing the assumed premise that existing similarities p between S and T determine the inferred similarities q. By stating, for example [DRu87]: nationality(P,N) determines language(P,L), knowledge of the language of at least one person of a certain nationality can be generalized by analogy to all the other people known to be of the same nationality. Determination relations provide higher-level domain knowledge about relevance. Being relations among predicates, they are best expressed in RP at the metalevel: determines(<nationality>,<language>), while the analogical inference rule is defined at the metaevaluation level:

```
    solve(#R($P,$L)):- determines(#D,#R), solve(#D($P,$N)),
                    solve(#D($PP,$N)),solve(#R($PP,$L)).
```

Suppose we have the following object-level information:

nationality(jack,uk).	male(jack).	height(jack,6).
nationality(giuseppe,italy).	male(giuseppe).	height(giuseppe,6).
language(giuseppe,italian).	nationality(jill,uk).	female(jill).
height(jill,5).	language(jill,english).	

The query ?-native_language(jack,L) is solved by the following derivation steps:

:-solve(<language>("jack",$L).	(#R/<language>, #P/"jack", L/$L)
:- determines(#D,<language>),	(#D/<nationality>)
solve(<nationality>("jack",$N),	($N/"uk")
solve(<nationality>($PP,"uk"),	($PP/"jill")
solve(<language>("jill",$L)	(by downward reflection)
:-language(jill,L)	(L = uk)

Notice that the possible source Giuseppe, more similar in the number of common properties, is ignored, and that the irrelevant facts about Jack and Jill are not examined.

464

5. Other issues on analogy and conclusive remarks

Most authors have stressed that analogies are based on abstractions represented by higher–order predicates [DaR88],[Gre88],[Ind88]. An analogy can e.g. be established between a family structure and a tree structure, so as to map concepts from one into the other. Alternatively, a common schema can be identified, as an abstraction for both. A representation in RP of analogy as such a common abstraction is shown in [CL89].

Another important issue [DaR88]) is that flexibility of representation is essential for analogical reasoning. The choice between alternative representations must usually be made "a priori", and cannot be modified from the inside of the description. In RP such different representations can coexist and be interchanged automatically, by providing appropriate metaevaluation rules, as shown in [CL91].

To summarize, we have shown that metalevel representation can accomodate several types of analogies. The metalevel view is non committal about the ontological status of analogical statements: they can be regarded as facts like in [Gre88], or as hypotheses like in [Goe89], or as additional premises like in [DRu87]. This representation can be achieved in a general logic programming language, with no need of ad hoc systems, such as those reported in [Gre88], [Goe89], [DRu87].

References

[CL89] Costantini S., Lanzarone G.A., *A Metalogic Programming Language*, in: Levi G., Martelli M. (eds.), Logic Programming, MIT Press, 1989, pp. 218–233.
[CL91] Costantini S., Lanzarone G.A., *A Metalogic Programming Approach: Language, Semantics and Applications*, submitted paper.
[DaR88] Darden L., Rada R., *Hypothesis Formation via Interrelations*, in: [Pri88].
[DRu87] Davies T.R., Russel S.J., *A Logical Approach to Reasoning by Analogy*, Procs. of Tenth IJCAI, Morgan Kaufmann, 1987, vol I, 264–270.
[Gen88] Gentner D., *Analogical Inference and Analogical Access*, in: [Pri88], 63–88
[Goe89] Goebel R., *A Sketch of Analogy as Reasoning with Equality Hypotheses*, in: [Jan89], 243–253.
[Gre88] Greiner R., *Learning by Understanding Analogies*, AI 35, 1988, 81–125.
[Hal89] Hall R.P. *Computational Approaches to Analogical Reasoning: A Comparative Analysis*, AI 39, 1989, 39–120.
[Ind88] Indurkhya B., *Constrained Semantic Transference: A Formal Theory of Metaphors*, in: [Pri88], 129–157.
[Jan89] Jantke K.P. (ed.), *Analogy and Inductive Inference*, Lecture Notes in Artificial Intelligence n. 397, 1989.
[Ker89] Kerber M., *Some Aspects of Analogy in Mathematical Reasoning*, in: [Jan89].
[Lei90] Leishman D., *An Annotated Bibliography of Works on Analogy*, Int. Journal of Intelligent Systems, vol.5, 1990, 43–81.
[McC79] McCarthy J., *First Order Theories of Individual Concepts and Propositions*, in: Machine Intelligence n.9.
[Pri88] Prieditis A. (ed.), *Analogica*, Pitman, 1988.
[Rus89] Russel S.J., *The Use of Knowledge in Analogy and Induction*, Pitman, 1989
[Win80] Winston P.H., *Learning and Reasoning by Analogy*, CACM 23 1980, 689–703.

SEMANTIC INTERPRETATION OF COPULATIVE SENTENCES

L. Ardissono, P. Terenziani
Dipartimento di Informatica - Universita' di Torino
C.so Svizzera 185 - 10149 Torino - Italy

ABSTRACT

In the paper, we propose our approach to the study of the semantics of copulative "be" in Natural Language Understanding. In particular, we analyse the way in which the meaning of sentences containing a copula depends on the generic vs specific vs attributive readings of the subject NP and of the predicate nominal NP (when the second is present). Moreover, we propose a semantic net formalism for the representation of these meanings, whose purpose is to maintain ambiguities as local as possible, and to account for an incremental interpretation process, so that the initial ambiguous representation (which features all possible meanings for the copula) may be worked on whenever new pieces of information allow further disambiguation. Finally, we describe the interpretation process, that uses information conveyed by the input sentence in order to determine the final meaning of the copula.

1. INTRODUCTION

The analysis of the semantics of copulative be is a hard problem in Natural Language Understanding, since its meaning depends substantially on the referential properties of the two arguments of the verb (the subject and the object of the predicate).

Jackendoff [7] deals with copulative be, when both the subject and the object are NPs (non predicative be) and distinguishes three main types of meaning: Identity, Ordinary Categorization and Generic Categorization. Identity occurs when both the NP referents are specific objects, and establishes their equality. Ordinary Categorization can hold between a specific object and a generic set and corresponds to the IS-A relation of Semantic Nets. Finally, Generic Categorization corresponds to the Subset relation. On the contrary, Hirst [6] distinguishes between two different relations established by non predicative copula: Intensional and Extensional Identity. In both cases there is an identification of the referents of the two NPs. However, Intensional Identity has also a definitional character (one of the concepts is expressed in function of the other, and their instances inherit the properties of both). Moreover, Hirst also considers predicative be (i.e. the case in which the predicate nominal is an adjective) stating that it attributes the property denoted by the predicate nominal to the referents of the subject NP. Whilst in these approaches only specific and generic arguments are analysed for the copula, in [5] also "attributive readings" [3] are considered, and are represented by "roles", which may assume different values in different Mental Spaces (Mental Spaces are contexts -i.e. sets of entities and relationships- built up by linguistic indicators, such as propositional attitudes).

The goal of our work is to develop a unifying approach that treats uniformly the different aspects of the meaning of the copula. The proposed representation enables us to clearly distinguish among the various meanings described above and supports an incremental interpretation process. In the paper, we show how such goals have been obtained by extending the GULL system, a NLU system for the Italian Language based on production rules (see [1], [2], [8]). The basic assumption of GULL is that a context-independent semantic representation of NL sentences can be provided and must be considered as the first step for further contextual processing. Moreover, we follow the principle of representing separately different kinds of semantic information. For instance, the propositional content of a sentence is represented in three planes: the Content Plane (CP) contains the information about the main predication and the descriptions used for the participants in the event (the arguments of the predicate); the Reference Plane (RP) contains the RASs (Referential Ambiguity Spaces) that make explicit reference ambiguities; the Semantic Plane (SP) contains the domain theory expressed as a terminological semantic net [2]. RASs contain three nodes, each one denoting one of the basic possible readings of NPs: C (the "Concept" or "generic" node), R (the "Role" or "attributive" node) and S (the "Specific" node)[1]. Beyond the three planes described above, there is the Lexical Ambiguity Plane (LAP), which contains the LASs (Lexical Ambiguity Spaces) for dealing with lexical ambiguities. In the paper, we show how such a basic formalism has been extended in order to cope with the meaning of copulative sentences. In particular, our formalism allows us to represent ambiguities locally and may be worked on as soon as new information allows further disambiguation. Finally, we briefly describe the interpretation process of the copula.

2. MEANINGS OF THE COPULA

The copula may assume different meanings, depending on whether the predicate nominal is an adjective (predicative copula) or a noun phrase. However, a further level of distinction may be

---

[1] A precise characterization of the meaning of these nodes in terms of parameters such as the context, the world and the time of utterance may be found in [1].Actually, in [1], eight different meanings for NPs are distinguished. The eight readings proposed there are a further specialization of the three basic meanings considered here (the correspondences among the eight readings and the generic, specific and role readings are described in [1]). In this paper, we do not adopt such a further specialization for the sake of clearness, since it is not strictly required for coping with the meaning of the copula. In [1] the distributive/collective ambiguity is also considered, and it is treated by introducing a suitable Ambiguity Space in the CP.

considered by analysing the referential properties of the subject and of the predicate nominal (in case of non predicative copula).

• **PREDICATIVE COPULA**: we identify two different kinds of predication for the copula, PREDICATION and PREDICATION*, depending on whether the subject NP assumes a specific, generic or role reading.

- **PREDICATION (PRED)** holds for specific subject NPs (e.g."Quella ragazza e' bella" -That girl is nice -). In such a case, the property specified by the nominal predicate is attributed to the individual denoted by the subject NP (or to the group of individuals, if the NP is plural). In case of plural subject NP, the property may be attributed to each individual in the set (distributive reading, e.g. in "Questi ragazzi sono (ciascuno) ricchi" -These boys are (each one) rich-), or to the set itself (collective reading, e.g. in "In questa corsa, gli italiani sono numerosi" - In such a race, Italians are numerous-).

- **PREDICATION* (PRED*)** holds for generic and role subject NPs. While the PRED relation attributes a property to a specific individual (or set of individuals) in a specific world, PRED* attributes the property to the referents of the subject NP in different "possible worlds" [4] (intuitively, the relation PRED* iterates the PRED in different possible worlds). In case of generic subject, (e.g. "I triangoli sono convessi" -Triangles are convex-), the property is attributed to the class (collective reading) or to the members of the class (distributive reading) denoted by the subject NP, in each possible world. In case of role (attributive) subject (e.g. "L'assassino (chiunque esso sia) e' pazzo" -The murderer (whoever s/he is) is insane-), the property is attributed to the fillers of the role denoted by the subject NP in each possible world.

• **NON PREDICATIVE COPULA**: in this case six different meanings of the copula may be distinguished, depending on the referential properties of the subject and the object NPs: EQUAL, EQUAL*, IS-A, IS-A*, SUBSET, SUBSET*

- **EQUAL (EQ)** only holds when both the subject and the predicate nominal NPs have a specific reading, (e.g. "La ragazza bionda e' la studentessa che ho incontrato ieri" -The blonde girl is the student I met yesterday-). In such a case, the identity of two individuals is stated.

- **EQUAL* (EQ*)** holds when the subject and predicate nominal are both definite generic or both roles and it establishes equality in different "possible worlds". In particular, in case of generic subjects and objects, EQ* states the equality of the denoted concepts, in each possible world (e.g. "Il triangolo e' il poligono a tre lati" -The triangle is the polygon with three sides-). In case of roles, it identifies the fillers of the roles in each possible world (e.g. "Il vincitore (chiunque esso sia) sara' il miglior ballerino (chiunque esso sia)" -The winner (whoever he is) will be the best dancer (whoever he is)-). In an analogous way, while **IS-A** holds for specific (singular) subjects and generic (singular) objects (e.g. "Fido e' un cane" -Fido is a dog-) and establishes a membership relation in a given world, **IS-A*** holds for role (singular) subjects and generic (singular) objects (e.g. "L'assassino (chiunque esso sia) e' un uomo dai capelli grigi" -The murderer (whoever he is) is a grey-haired man-) and it states the membership of the role filler to the extension of the generic concept, in different possible worlds. Finally, **SUBSET (SS)** and **SUBSET* (SS*)** establish a subset relation in a given world and in different possible worlds, respectively.

The eight meanings above may be represented with the introduction of a suitable LAS in the LAP, which internally embodies lexical ambiguities. Fig.1 shows the basic ambiguous representation of the copula. Node N1 represents the copula in the CP and is connected to LAS1 in LAP. Each node in LAS1 corresponds to a different possible meaning of the verb and is linked to the representation of this meaning (situated in the SP), via a node in the RP. All the nodes in LAS1 are marked as active, in order to represent the fact that, in principle, all the interpretations are possible.

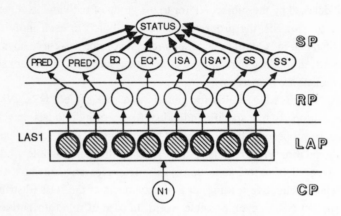

Fig.1 Basic representation of the copula. All the nodes in LAS1 are bold, in order to represent the fact that they are active. Note that the PRED, PRED*, ... , SS* concepts are specializations of the general STATUS concept.

3. PROCESSING SENTENCES CONTAINING A COPULA

As shown in section 2, the meaning of copulative be depends on the reading (generic/role/specific) of the subject NP and of the predicate nominal . Therefore, the rules for the interpretation of the copula are invoked when both the subject NP and the object of the predicate have been analysed and their representation has been built, as well as the basic ambiguous one for the verb (see Fig.1). At this point, the referential ambiguities of the arguments of the copula may have already been solved, using disambiguation rules [1] and, possibly, considering the information conveyed by previous sentences. So, the disambiguation rules for the copula can operate on the LAS of the copula, and disable all the meanings which may be excluded.

A first level of rules deals with the distinction between predicative and not predicative be: in case of predicative be, all the nodes in the LAS corresponding to the copula are disabled, except the ones corresponding to the PRED and PRED* meanings; otherwise, only the PRED and PRED* nodes in the LAS are disabled.

A second level of rules further specifies the meaning of the copula, by considering the (specific vs generic vs role) readings of the subject NP and (when present) the object NP. If the readings of the subject and the object NPs have been unambiguously determined by the previous analysis, a set of rules is activated in order to select the corresponding meaning of the copula, according to the analysis proposed in section 2. On the contrary, if the kind of reference of one or both the NPs is still ambiguous, more complex rules are applied which, depending on the still admissible kinds of reference of the NPs and, sometimes, on syntactic information (e.g. the fact that the NPs are singular or plural, definite or indefinite, etc.), restrict the number of possible interpretations for the copula (for example, a rule disables the SS and SS* meanings, in case the subject or the object NP is singular and does not admit a generic reading). More than one meaning may be still available for the copula after the execution of such rules, so that further processing considering contextual information may be required in order to disambiguate.

CONCLUSIONS

In the paper, we have briefly presented a formalism for representing the different meanings of copulative be, depending on the referential properties of its subject and (when present) object NPs. In particular, a unifying approach has been proposed, in which generic, specific and attributive readings of NPs are considered at the same time.

The distinctive feature of the proposed approach is that the representation maintains the ambiguity locally, until the information needed for the disambiguation is made available.

We are currently extending our approach for analysing copulative sentences containing some optional cases, such as the Prepositional Phrase "in the movie" in the sentence:

"In the movie, Cleopatra is Liz Taylor".

In such cases, the copula may still assume each one of the eight meanings described in section 2, but the predication it establishes may connect elements of different spaces (in our example, between the individual Cleopatra, in the space of the movie, and the individual Liz Taylor, in the speaker's space), as predicted in [5].

REFERENCES

[1] L. Ardissono, L. Lesmo, P. Pogliano, P. Terenziani: "Representation of Determiners in Natural Language". To appear in Proc. IJCAI 91, Sidney, 1991.

[2] B. Di Eugenio, L. Lesmo: "Representation and Interpretation of Determiners in Natural Language". Proc. IJCAI, Milano (1987), 648-653.

[3] K. S. Donnellan: "Reference and Definite Description". Philosophical Review, 75 (1966), 281-304.

[4] D. R. Dowty, R. E. Wall, S. Peters: **"Introduction to Montague semantics"**. D. Reidel Publ. Co. (1981).

[5] G. Fauconnier: **"Mental Spaces"**. MIT Press (1985).

[6] G. Hirst:**"Semantic interpretation and the resolution of ambiguity"**. Cambridge Univ. Press (1987), 61-66.

[7] R. Jackendoff: **"Semantics and cognition"**. MIT Press (1983).

[8] P. Terenziani, L. Lesmo. "Un sistema a regole per l'interpretazione semantica del linguaggio naturale". Proc. 1st Congresso della Associazione Italiana per l'Intelligenza Artificiale, Trento (1989), 40-49 (in Italian).

TYPICALITY FOR PLAUSIBLE REASONING

Silvana Badaloni
Dipartimento di Elettronica e Informatica
Via Gradenigo 6A - I-35131 Padova
email: badaloni@pdcnr1.pd.cnr.it

Alberto Zanardo
Dipartimento di Matematica Pura ed Applicata
Via Belzoni 7 - I-35131 Padova
email: mat015@ipdunivx.bitnet

Abstract. We describe the key ideas of an approach to non-monotonic reasoning (HP-logic) involving an implicit notion of typicality. In this framework, the problem of irrelevant information is addressed and the deductive power and the reliability of the system are compared with those of the Circumscription approach to non-monotonic reasoning.

1. The notion of typicality.

A common pattern of natural language assertions which seems to give rise to the phenomenon of non-monotonicity is constituted by statements like

"generally, the elements of the set X have the property Q"   (A)

which may be interpreted as: the elements of X which do not have the property Q are to be considered as exceptional in X, or as: the majority of the elements of X has the property Q. Then, two possible rewritings of (A) could be

"the typical elements of the set X have the property Q", and   (A')
"most of the elements of the set X have the property Q"   (A")

The form (A') of (A) underlies the Circumscription approach to non-monotonic reasoning [McCarthy 80,86]. In this approach the assertion (A) is translated as

$$\forall x(P(x) \land \neg ab_p(x) \to Q(x)) \tag{1}$$

where the properties P and ab_p have respectively by extensions the set X and the set of 'abnormal', or 'exceptional', individuals. with respect to P. As a consequence of this, when dealing with assertions like (A), the language must also contain the relative 'abnormality predicate', ab_p , for every predicate P.

The necessity of enlarging the language at hand by new predicates does not occur in the approaches which, reading (A) as (A"), are usually based on probability. Sentences like (A) can be viewed as fragments of probabilistic information: it could be translated into terms of the statistical percentage of the elements of X that have the property Q.

An initial objection to the use of probabilistic approach, however, is that in general it is very difficult to insert the truth or falsity of expressions like (A) into a numerical scale. This difficulty is, indeed, removed in the ε–semantics [Pearl 89] which, on the other hand, is based on an abstraction that does not seem very close to a natural way of reasoning since it applies only to extreme probabilities.

Another difficulty connected with the probabilistic approach is illustrated by the nearly classical instance of (A) in the literature: "Generally, birds fly". If, for instance, the number of non-flying birds is exactly the same as that of birds living in Rome, then, taking only probability into account, we could assert that "Generally, birds live outside Rome" in the same way as we assert that "Generally, birds fly", but the truth of the first assertion is rather doubtful. The point is that, according to Circumscription, assertions like (A) involve a notion of typicality which is not dealt with in the probabilistic approach: all typical birds are able to fly but not all typical birds live outside Rome.

The first main aspect of the approach to plausible reasoning presented in [Badaloni and Zanardo 91], can be viewed as a trend to overcome the difficulties connected with Circumscription and probability shown above. Contrary to the probability approach, we think that assertions like (A) do involve a notion of 'typical element of X', but at the same time, differently from the Circumscription approach, we think that it is possible to capture the meaning of this notion in a formal system without involving an extensional and explicit description of the notion of a 'typical' or 'non-abnormal' element of a given set.

Our idea is that it is surely plausible to think that typical individuals in a set have a given property, even if we are not able to specify which individuals are typical. We hold that (A) can be represented by a relation Π between the predicate P and the predicate Q (or, extensionally, a relation π between the set X and the extension Y of Q), and we hold also that this relation can express high plausibility rather than probability.

The aim of the present work is to describe briefly and discuss the key-ideas underlying the approach of High Plausibility Logic presented in [Badaloni and Zanardo 91] to which we refer for the technical aspect of the work. Furthermore, a qualitative comparison with the Circumscription approach will be provided and the problem of irrelevant information will be addressed.

2. The Π determiners.

In first order logic, the sets of individuals are represented by open formulas; so, the linguistic counterpart of the relation π is a binary determiner, Πx, acting on formulas. In this way, if α and β are formulas, then $\Pi x(\alpha,\beta)$ is also a formula and the truth of $\Pi x(\alpha,\beta)$ expresses the fact that the set of individuals fulfilling $\alpha(x)$ and the set of individuals fulfilling $\beta(x)$ are in relation π. Thus, (A) is obviously expressed by $\Pi x(P(x),Q(x))$.

According to the meaning of (A), the formula $\Pi x(\alpha,\beta)$ is understood to mean that "in general, the x's fulfilling $\alpha(x)$ also fulfil $\beta(x)$" or "the set of x's fulfilling $\beta(x)$ (and $\alpha(x)$) constitutes a relevant subset of the set of x's fulfilling $\alpha(x)$" or "it is highly plausible that the individuals having the property $\alpha(x)$ also have the property $\beta(x)$". Then, the following three standard properties (usually adopted for the determiners) are assumed:

$$\pi(X,X) , \quad \pi(X,Y) \Rightarrow \pi(X,Y\cap X) , \quad \pi(X,Y) \text{ and } Y\subseteq Y' \Rightarrow \pi(X,Y') \qquad \text{P1-3}$$

The assumption of a further property called *Quantity* qualifies the determiners as the (logically) generalized quantifiers (see [van Benthem 86], 1.6). Quantity can be justified by asserting that no individual has a privileged role.

In our approach, we cannot accept the quantity property because we think that a privileged role should be given to typical individuals. Thus we will depart from the usual semantics for the generalized quantifiers in an attempt to grasp the intensional character of the notion of typicality, which we will assume as a primitive one, involved in assertion (A). In order to avoid assertions like (A) being vacuous, we must admit that some typical element of X exists; thus we substitute the quantity property with:

$$(X,Y_i) \text{ for all } i\in I \text{ and } X \neq \varnothing \Rightarrow \bigcap_{i\in I}Y_i \neq \varnothing \qquad \text{P 4}$$

3. Non-standard evaluation of the constants.

The second key idea concerns the treatment of the constants. Often uncertainty rises from the fact that knowledge about an individual denoted by a constant is not complete. Taking this fact into account, we admit that, in general, the constants have a *range of uncertainty* : we express this by evaluating them on sets of individuals instead of on single individuals. The evaluation of a constant is the set of all individuals that, at the present stage of knowledge, that constant could denote.

This fact leads to significant departures from the usual semantics for first order logic. First, the logic becomes a three-valued logic: an atomic formula of the form P(c) has the undefined truth value whenever the valuation of c is not contained either in the extension of P or in the extension of $\neg P$. Another departure is relative to the notion of identity; we adopt "possible identity" as a primitive notion: we add the symbol $\overset{\Diamond}{=}$ to the language and we write $\vartheta_1 \overset{\Diamond}{=} \vartheta_2$ to mean that "it is possible that the terms ϑ_1 and ϑ_2 denote the same individual", that is, "the evaluations of ϑ_1 and ϑ_2 are not disjoint". As for the variables, we let them range over single individuals, since we want the departure from first order logic to be minimal. Then, the open formula $x \overset{\Diamond}{=} c$ is true under any valuation assigning an element of the valuation of c to x, and hence the extension of this open formula is simply the valuation of c.

By the observations above, the formula $\forall x\, (x \overset{\Diamond}{=} c \equiv P(x)\,)$ is the formal translation of:

"everything we know about constant c is that it has property P" (B)

Consider now assertion (A) in the equivalent form:

"it is highly plausible that the individuals having property P (A''')
also have property Q"

which is expressed by $\Pi x(P(x),Q(x))$, and is true whenever the extension Y of Q covers a relevant subset of the set X, extension of P. If (B) also holds, then $\forall x(x \overset{\Diamond}{=} c \equiv P(x))$ is true and this means that the evaluation C of the constant c coincides with the extension X of the predicate P. Thus, by simple substitution of first order equivalents, it follows that $\Pi x(x \overset{\Diamond}{=} c, Q(x))$ is true, and hence this formula is a consequence of the conjunction of (A''') and (B) and it represents that:

"it is highly plausible that constant c has property Q". (C)

The deduction of (C) from (A), or (A'''), and (B) constitutes in particular our solution of the 'Tweety problem'[1]. From (T1) "generally, birds fly" and (T2) "everything we know about Tweety is that it is a bird" we infer that: (T3) "it is highly plausible that Tweety can fly", in the same way as we infer (C) from (A) and (B). Formally,

$$\Pi x(Bird(x),Fly(x)),\ \forall x(x \overset{\Diamond}{=} Tweety \equiv Bird(x)) \vdash \Pi x(x \overset{\Diamond}{=} Tweety, Fly(x)).$$

The addition of the information that (T2') "Tweety is a penguin and no penguin flies" makes false the premise (T2) used to infer (T3). In this case, the constant 'Tweety' is contained in the set of penguins and, hence, the formula $\forall x(x \overset{\Diamond}{=} Tweety \equiv Bird(x))$ is false as well as $\Pi x(x \overset{\Diamond}{=} Tweety, Fly(x))$.

To pass from (T3) to the conclusion that (T4) "Tweety can fly" we have to define the conditions under which high plausibility can be replaced by truth: when truth is not available, it is natural to use high plausibility in its place and thus make it become truth. In [Badaloni and Zanardo 91], a set of formulas (the set of *meaningful formulas*) is determined such that, for every consistent subset of it, the substitution of high plausibility by truth gives rise to a consistent set of first order formulas. Roughly speaking, a meaningful formula is a formula that does not involve negative occurrences of $\Pi x(x \overset{\Diamond}{=} c, Q(x))$; indeed, from the information that it "is not highly plausible that constant c has property Q" we cannot reasonably infer anything about whether c actually has property Q or not. In the 'Tweety example", if the set of premises which yielded (T3) is consistent, then the same holds for (T4).

So, in our approach, non-monotonicity is dealt with as follows. As shown above, the conclusion (T4) is drawn from the set L consisting of the premises (T1) and (T2). If we add the

---

[1]"Tweety flies" is deduced from the premises "Generally, birds fly" and "Tweety is a bird", whereas the additional information that "Tweety is a penguin and no penguin flies", yields the opposite conclusion.

information that "Tweety is a penguin and no penguin flies" (which actually increases our knowledge about Tweety) to the information (T1) and that "Tweety is a bird", we obtain a set L' of premises which does not contain L. The premise (T2) is not in L': the added information about Tweety makes this premise false. From set L' it is possible to conclude ¬Fly(Tweety) because the valuation of Tweety is included in the set of penguins and hence in the extension of ¬Fly. Thus, in our approach, non-monotonic patterns of reasoning are possible, while the logic itself remains monotonic.

5. Comparison with Circumscription: other properties of π.

As a further example of inference, assume that the information

"Sam is a penguin and no penguin flies"   (T5)

is available together with (T1) and (T2). In the circumscriptive approach, the new information affects the process of minimizing the predicate ab so that the conclusion that "Tweety can fly" is no longer possible. The possibility of still concluding "Tweety can fly" is generally recovered by assuming explicitly that "Tweety and Sam are different", or by adopting a strong notion of identity and holding that two names cannot denote the same individual. In our approach, since the deductions do not involve an "external process" like minimization, assumption (T5) has no consequence on the original deduction of (T4) and this seems to correspond suitably to the fact that there is no relation between (T5) and the previous information.

On the other hand, contrary to what happens with Circumscription, in our approach the deduction that "it is highly plausible that Tweety can fly" is sensitive to new information like "Tweety is not a penguin"; if new information about Tweety is added, then the premise that "everything we know about Tweety is that it is a bird" is no longer true: what is true now is that "everything we know about Tweety is that it is a bird and it is not a penguin". Given our previous deduction (T1),(T2)⊢ (T3), the possibility of still deducing (T3) depends on whether or not the capability to fly is a typical property of 'birds which are not penguins'; formally, this possibility depends on whether the formula $\Pi x(Bird(x) \wedge \neg Penguin(x) , Fly(x))$ is true or not.

Therefore, the problem is how to transfer typical properties to subsets of the first argument of π. If only properties P1-P4 are assumed, there is no way to do this: given $\pi(X,Y)$, these properties do not involve any subset of X. However, the particular case at hand suggests a very reasonable new property of the operator π: if Q is a typical property of X and this set is deprived of elements which do not have the property Q, that is, X is deprived of exceptions to Q, then Q is a typical property also for the remaining set X'. Actually, we could say that, given the hypotheses above, the fact that Q is also a typical property for the remaining set X' is an *a fortiori* conclusion. Formally, this property is expressed by:

$\pi(X,Y)$ and $Z \subseteq$ not-Y implies $\pi(X-Z,Y)$.   **P 5**

The linguistic counterpart of P5 is $\Pi x(\alpha,\beta) \wedge \forall x(\gamma \rightarrow \neg\beta) \rightarrow \Pi x(\alpha \wedge \neg\gamma,\beta)$. If added as an axiom to the theory, this formula permits us to get $\Pi x(Bird(x) \wedge \neg Penguin(x) , Fly(x))$ from $\Pi x(Bird(x),Fly(x))$ (and $\forall x(Penguin(x) \rightarrow \neg Fly(x))$).

Let's now analyze a major problem: if the added information is strictly irrelevant then conclusions must be protected in the light of this new but irrelevant information. Suppose that the added new information is that "Tweety is yellow". Again, this information does not affect the circumscriptive deduction that "Tweety can fly", substantially because Bird(x) ∧ Yellow(x) does not imply ¬Fly(x). In our approach, however, since everything we know about Tweety is that it is a yellow bird, the conclusion depends on the truth of

$\Pi x(Bird(x) \wedge Yellow(x) , Fly(x))$ (2)

If the conclusion "Tweety can fly" is still desirable, then the properties of π have to be enlarged. A possible way of doing this could be connected to some *default* principle like "if the information Yellow(x) (and Bird(x)) does not contradict Fly(x), then, under the hypothesis

Πx(Bird(x),Fly(x)), we allow the conclusion (2)". The fact that the conjunction of certain properties is not contradictory corresponds to the fact that the intersection of the extensions of those properties is non-empty. Thus, a possible refinement of the properties of the relation π could be

$$\pi(X,Y) \text{ and } X \cap Y \cap Z \neq \emptyset \text{ implies } \pi(X \cap Z,Y), \qquad \textbf{P6}$$

Note that the set of properties P1-P6 is consistent because all these properties hold if we replace $\pi(X,Y)$ by $X \subseteq Y$. The linguistic counterpart of P6 is $\Pi x(\alpha,\beta) \wedge \exists x(\alpha \wedge \beta \wedge \gamma) \rightarrow \Pi x(\alpha \wedge \gamma, \beta)$. If we assume this formula as an axiom and we prove $\exists x(Bird(x) \wedge Yellow(x) \wedge Fly(x))$, then we can also prove (2). Note that the several default approaches require only that the formula "$\forall x(Bird(x) \wedge Yellow(x) \rightarrow \neg Fly(x))$ be non-provable, whereas our approach requires that the negation of this formula be provable.

An equivalent form of P6 is $\pi(X,Y)$ and $X' \subseteq X$ and $X' \cap Y \neq \emptyset$ implies $\pi(X',Y)$; so, a possible reading of P6 is that typical properties transfer to a subset whenever some element of the subset has those properties. In this form, P6 actually looks very strong from the point of view of the original meaning of the relation π. Perhaps, the solution to the problem of transferring typical properties is to impose high plausibility conditions; for instance, a possible weakening of P6 could be

$$\pi(X,Y) \text{ and not-}\pi(Z \cap X, \text{not-}Y) \text{ implies } \pi(X \cap Z,Y). \qquad \textbf{P6*}$$

If P6* were accepted, then, in order to have (2), we should prove $\neg \Pi x(Bird(x) \wedge Yellow(x), \neg Fly(x))$; that is, we should prove that the property of being unable to fly is not a typical property of yellow birds.

The above examples show how the properties of the determiner π can influence the deductive power of HP-logic. In particular, having introduced property P6, we obtain a deductive system which, even though weaker, is comparable with the Circumscription approach. On the other hand, our approach to non-monotonicity does not involve second order logic and deductions are strictly logical without involving the models of the theory or the global notion of consistency.

Aknowledgements.

This work was supported by the Italian C.N.R. and M.U.R.S.T. We are deeply grateful to J. van Benthem, A. Cortesi, E. Pagello and Y. Shoham for their suggestions and comments.

6. References.

[Badaloni and Zanardo 91]. S. Badaloni, A. Zanardo: A High Plausibility Logic for Reasoning with Incomplete Knowledge, submitted to the *J. of Philosophical Logic* for publication, 1991.

[van Benthem 86]. J. van Benthem: *Essays in Logical Semantics*, D. Reidel Publishing Company, Dordrecht, 1986.

[Mc Carthy 80]. J. Mc Carthy: Circumscription - a form of non-monotonic reasoning, *Artificial Intelligence*, 13:1-2, 1980, pp.27-39.

[Mc Carthy 86]. J. Mc Carthy: Application of Circumscription to Formalize Common-sense Reasoning, Artificial Intelligence, 28, 1986, pp.89-116.

[Pearl 89]. J. Pearl: Probabilistic Semantics for Nonmonotonic Reasoning: a Survey, *Proc. of the 1st Int. Conf. on Principles of Knowledge Representation and Reasoning*, Toronto, Canada, 1989.

[Reiter 87]. E. Reiter: Non monotonic Reasoning, *Annual Review of Computer Science*, Vol.2, 1987, pp.147-186.

A DISTRIBUTED IMAGE–UNDERSTANDING SYSTEM

Vito Roberto
Dipartimento di Matematica e Informatica, Università di Udine
Via Zanon 6, I–33100 Udine, Italy

1. Introduction

Distributed Artificial Intelligence (DAI) systems are sets of physically-separated expert nodes, each of which specialised in the solution of a subtask in the problem domain [1,2]. Such systems have been employed with success in signal interpretation; they are particularly promising in domains where the lack of robust and detailed models, and/or the amount of data to be handled, require more flexible problem-solving strategies.
This paper presents the architecture of a DAI system designed to support the interpretation in geophysical prospection; our concern will be on the control aspects, as well as the integration of perceptual and conceptual components of the expert knowledge.

2. Issues and Motivations from the Problem Domain

The aim of geophysical interpretation is providing descriptions of an area of interest; in such descriptions geometrical structures detected in the data are given consistent geological labels. Data are often given in form of images (*seismic sections*; an example is reported in Fig. 3A), which may be supported by more detailed information (*well-logs*); such input data should be matched against a-priori geological knowledge to provide the local descriptions. The large amount of data, the uncertainty and incompleteness of models suggest the adoption of a knowledge-based approach as proposed in image-understanding systems [3].
In addition, the complexity of tasks involved in interpretation is such that the cooperation of *a team of experts* is necessary. Each expert has a partial view of the problem environment (called *stratigraphic, structural, lithologic...*), and cannot provide fully consistent descriptions; he/she uses a well defined body of concepts, objects and strategies to accomplish more specific tasks; shares with his/her colleagues selected pieces of data and knowledge, and, finally, exchanges partial results with them, thus establishing the cooperation that ultimately solves the problem.
These observations naturally led us to look at a DAI system as a good candidate to automate the interpretation.
We propose a system composed of four nodes, as sketched in Fig. 1: besides the three experts quoted above, the user is seen as an additional one. A node is given data and independent problem-solving capabilities: it is intended as an *autonomous agent,* in that self-consistent (although not complete) descriptions can be issued according to its view of the problem environment.

3. The Node : Functionalities and Structure

Several models of cooperation and teamwork have been proposed in the literature; in particular, Ref. [4] contains useful suggestions to our problem domain.

Cooperation is achieved through *internode communication*; this, in turn, is specified by suitable protocols. Control in a node is hierarchical: problem decomposition is accomplished iteratively, by *dynamically planning* actions according to the status of computation.

In addition, specific aspects of the problem domain require that, within a node, communication and control modules provide *explicit scheduling* of the task-solving actions; *integration* is needed of perceptual knowledge (i.e. that operating on input data to construct internal world representations) with the conceptual one (acting at the symbolic level to perform cognitive tasks); dialogue with the user must be supported.

Fig. 2 reports the typical architecture of a node: it refers to the scheme of the *stratigraphic* expert.

– *Front-end Processor*: is the internode communication facility; a phrase structure grammar acts as a protocol to exchange information.

– *Meta-Level Structures*: explicit coding in form of frames is provided of the problems a node can solve. The task decomposition of a problem is coded in form of *and-or graphs*. A *planner* module selects one specific plan using a graph-visiting technique; revisions are possible, according to the current status of problem solving; this, in turn, is detected by the *solver* module, via *monitor* data quality assessment.

– *Blackboard*: acts as a working memory for the task solvers (the Knowledge Sources, KSs), by maintaining several data representations at different levels of abstraction.

– *Internal Control*: *Scheduling* the KSs is done via an associative table, of a specific subtask name in a plan with the set of KS names solving it. The lowest level of control is strictly procedural, coded by *agents,* dynamically defined as procedure-data pairs and activated by the KSs.

– *Permanent Databases*: are needed to encode facts, objects, concepts and their relations (e.g. a library of seismic profiles).

4. Solving an Interpretive Problem

An interpretation is initialised by the user; all nodes evaluate their attitudes to solve the problem according to their meta-level knowledge; one of them (if any) starts its internal activity by putting the task name on the blackboard; this, in turn, activates the planner module, which selects the task node and starts the graph expansion. The task decomposition is pursued until a subtask is found with an associated set of executable KSs: then the subtask is 'solvable', and a plan exists in form of sequence of subtasks (a path in the graph); control is transferred to the scheduler for sequential activations of the KSs. Results are written on the blackboard. The plan can be further pursued by synthesizing the results accordingly, i.e. by following the path from the tip node upwards.

5. Perceptual and Conceptual Representations

In the problem domain, perception is essential to individuate the semantic primitives for interpretation.

The path to a suitable internal representation of data is composed of sequential steps. At first, an *enhancement* step is performed, by picking up the extrema grey levels: an iconic representation named *peak matrix* has been defined. *Texture analysis* is accomplished by means of *run-length detection,* acting on the peak matrices; texels are labelled according to the average orientation of their linear patterns; a relaxation labelling step is further applied in order to stabilize the attributions.

Run-lengths are converted into more continuous line patterns called *segments,* using heuristic operators. A symbolic representation (the *segment descriptor list*) acts as intermediate data structure for further inspection; it has been graphically reported in Fig. 3B.

A more detailed account on all of these processes can be found in [5].

Symbolic structures and processes are the *conceptual knowledge* in the problem domain. *Archetypes* are instantiated frame structures encoding features of the geological profiles; confidence factors encode the uncertainty in this kind of description. Fig. 4B shows the frame-like representation of the *parallel* profile, graphically sketched in Fig. 4A. A permanent database called *archetype library* is present in the stratigraphic node.

A similar frame structure (a *schema*) is designed as the data representation at the highest level of abstraction; confidence factors are included to model the uncertainties arising from data (noise, errors, gaps).

Matching archetypes with schemata is accomplished by a set of associative rules. The degree of confidence in the matching itself is obtained by an empirical combination of the confidence factors in a schema and its archetype counterpart.

6. The Prototype. Tests and Performances

A prototype named *Horizons* has been developed on a SUN 3/110 workstation; its current status includes the stratigraphic and the structural nodes, as well as several communication facilities; the definition of the user node is not yet complete.

– *The Stratigraphic Expert.* All modules in the architectural scheme were implemented in the C-language (numerical procedures and structures) and in Prolog (symbolic structures, inferences and matching). Perceptual and conceptual representations were constructed; internal problem solving includes matching, hypothesis generation, validation, revision and justification. Tests were carried out on real data.

– *The Structural Expert.* This node has not been fully tested. Its structure closely resembles that of the stratigraphic partner; all modules were implemented. Five KSs perform all knowledge processing steps, acting on input representations (the segment descriptor lists) which were developed by the stratigraphic colleague. Descriptions of the world are issued; preliminary tests were carried on simulated data.

– *Communication and Cooperation.* All nodes (user included) are equipped with a Front-end Processor. Cooperation among the three nodes was tested during the stratigraphic problem-solving. Since cooperation entails communication, an important test concerns the relative amount of time spent by a node for communication with respect to internal

478

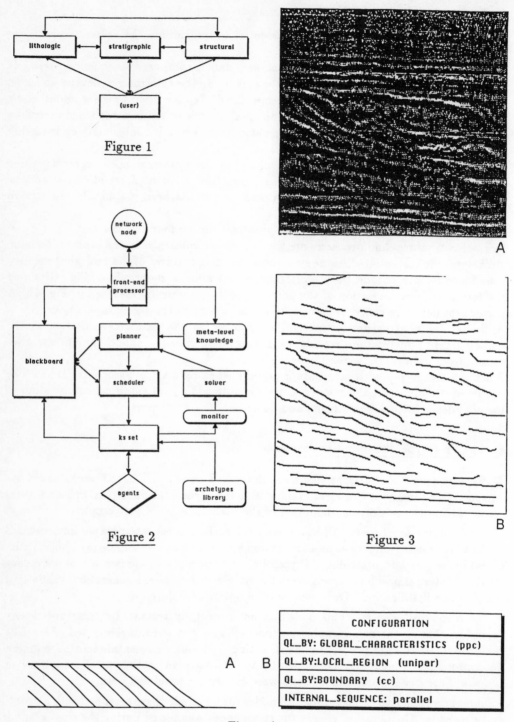

Figure 1

Figure 2

Figure 3

CONFIGURATION

QL_BY: GLOBAL_CHARACTERISTICS (ppc)

QL_BY:LOCAL_REGION (unipar)

QL_BY:BOUNDARY (cc)

INTERNAL_SEQUENCE: parallel

Figure 4

problem solving. We estimated such ratio for both nodes; in all cases it was found not to exceed 5%; we consider this test as an indication that the distribution of tasks among processing nodes is appropriate.

7. Conclusions and Perspectives

Knowledge modelling and representation in a distributed image-understanding system were the main concerns of the present paper.

– *Distribution of tasks.* At the highest level, the computation is distributed among four expert nodes (user included), cooperating in a non-hierarchical way.

– *Internal problem solving.* Iterative problem decomposition within a node has led to a hierarchical control scheme, where a plan is executed by suitable scheduling of KS actions, which, in turn, use agent calls for procedural steps.

– *Integration and data fusion.* Data and knowledge representations of different kind (numerical, symbolic) coexist in the blackboard, partitioned into appropriate abstraction levels; matching and data fusion are performed by associative rules.

Such features in our system are problem-independent; they can be applied to different domains, where signal or data interpretation is achieved by a team of experts.

As far as future perspectives are concerned, the system will undergo substantial developments. Communication and its impact on problem solving will be carefully analysed; the resolution of possible conflicts among expert nodes will be included; finally, attention will be paid to the synthesis of output descriptions in a unique, consistent view of the world.

References

[1] Chandrasekaran, B., Natural and Social System Metaphors for Distributed Problem Solving: Introduction to the Issue, *IEEE Transactions on Systems, Man and Cybernetics,* 11, (1981), pp. 1–5.

[2] Decker, K., Distributed Problem-Solving Techniques: a Survey, *IEEE Transactions on Systems, Man and Cybernetics,* 17 (1987), pp. 729–740.

[3] Draper, B. A., Collins, R. T., Brolio, J., Hanson, A. R., and Riseman, E. M., Issues in the Development of a Blackboard-based Schema System for Image Understanding, in *Blackboard Systems,* R. S. Engelmore and A. J. Morgan (Eds.), pp. 353–386 (1988).

[4] Yang, J. D., Huhns, M. N, and Stephens, L. M., An Architecture for Control and Communications in Distributed Artificial Intelligence Systems, *IEEE Transactions on Systems, Man ad Cybernetics,* 15, (1985), pp. 316–326.

[5] Roberto, V., Peron, A., and Fumis, P. L., Low-level Processing Techniques in Geophysical Image Interpretation, *Pattern Recognition Letters,* 10 (1989), pp. 111–122.

Lecture Notes in Artificial Intelligence (LNAI)

Lecture Notes in Computer Science